MATHEMATICAL FOUNDATION OF COMPUTER SCIENCE

MATHEMATICAL FOUNDATION OF COMPUTER SCIENCE

Y N Singh
Professor
Department of Computer Science & Engineering
Institute of Engineering & Technology
Lucknow, U P

Publishing Globally

NEW AGE INTERNATIONAL (P) LIMITED, PUBLISHERS
LONDON • NEW DELHI • NAIROBI
Bangalore • Chennai • Cochin • Guwahati • Hyderabad • Kolkata • Lucknow • Mumbai
Visit us at **www.newagepublishers.com**

Published by New Age International (P) Ltd., Publishers
First Edition: 2005
Reprint: 2017

GLOBAL OFFICES

- **New Delhi** — **NEW AGE INTERNATIONAL (P) LIMITED, PUBLISHERS**
7/30 A, Daryaganj, New Delhi-110002, (INDIA)
Tel.: (011) 23253771, 23253472, **Telefax:** 23267437, 43551305
E-mail: contactus@newagepublishers.com • Visit us at www.newagepublishers.com
- **London** — **NEW AGE INTERNATIONAL (UK) LTD.**
27 Old Gloucester Street, London, WC1N 3AX, UK
E-mail: info@newacademicscience.co.uk • Visit us at www.newacademicscience.co.uk
- **Nairobi** — **NEW AGE GOLDEN (EAST AFRICA) LTD.**
Ground Floor, Westlands Arcade, Chiromo Road (Next to Naivas Supermarket)
Westlands, Nairobi, KENYA, **Tel.:** 00-254-713848772, 00-254-725700286
E-mail: kenya@newagepublishers.com

BRANCHES

- **Bangalore** — 37/10, 8th Cross (Near Hanuman Temple), Azad Nagar, Chamarajpet, Bangalore- 560 018
Tel.: (080) 26756823, **Telefax:** 26756820, **E-mail: bangalore@newagepublishers.com**
- **Chennai** — 26, Damodaran Street, T. Nagar, Chennai-600 017, **Tel.:** (044) 24353401, **Telefax:** 24351463
E-mail: chennai@newagepublishers.com
- **Cochin** — CC-39/1016, Carrier Station Road, Ernakulam South, Cochin-682 016, **Tel.:** (0484) 2377303, **Telefax:** 4051304
E-mail: cochin@newagepublishers.com
- **Guwahati** — Hemsen Complex, Mohd. Shah Road, Paltan Bazar, Near Starline Hotel, Guwahati-781 008,
Tel.: (0361) 2513881, **Telefax:** 2543669, **E-mail: guwahati@newagepublishers.com**
- **Hyderabad** — 105, 1st Floor, Madhiray Kaveri Tower, 3-2-19, Azam Jahi Road, Near Kumar Theater, Nimboliadda Kachiguda, Hyderabad-500 027, **Tel.:** (040) 24652456, **Telefax:** 24652457
E-mail: hyderabad@newagepublishers.com
- **Kolkata** — RDB Chambers (Formerly Lotus Cinema) 106A, 1st Floor, S N Banerjee Road, Kolkata-700 014
Tel.: (033) 22273773, **Telefax:** 22275247, **E-mail: kolkata@newagepublishers.com**
- **Lucknow** — 16-A, Jopling Road, Lucknow-226 001, **Tel.:** (0522) 2209578, 4045297, **Telefax:** 2204098
E-mail: lucknow@newagepublishers.com
- **Mumbai** — 142C, Victor House, Ground Floor, N.M. Joshi Marg, Lower Parel, Mumbai-400 013
Tel.: (022) 24927869, **Telefax:** 24915415, **E-mail: mumbai@newagepublishers.com**
- **New Delhi** — 22, Golden House, Daryaganj, New Delhi-110 002, **Tel.:** (011) 23262368, 23262370, **Telefax:** 43551305
E-mail: sales@newagepublishers.com

ISBN: 978-81-224-1667-1
C-17-01-10089

Printed in India at Sanjeev Offset, Delhi.
Typeset at Goswami Associates, Delhi.

NEW AGE INTERNATIONAL (P) LIMITED, PUBLISHERS
7/30 A, Daryaganj, New Delhi-110002
Visit us at **www.newagepublishers.com**
(CIN: U74899DL1966PTC004618)

PREFACE

To understand the fundamentals of computer science it is essential for us to begin with study of the related mathematical topics ranging from discrete mathematics, concepts of automata theory and formal languages. It is high time to recognize the importance of discrete mathematics as it finds various applications in the field of computer science. However, it requires a full fledged study and its potential with respect to computer sciences and natural sciences have long been well recognized. To understand the principles of computer science that is evenly acknowledged as mathematical foundation of computer science, this book present a selection of topics both from discrete mathematics and from automata theory and formal languages. The objective of selection of topics was due to my aspiration to commence with most of the fundamental terminology employed in higher courses in computer science as plausible. As per the requirements of the study, the formal appearance of the discrete mathematics includes *set theory, algebraic systems, combinatorics, Boolean algebra, propositional logic, and other relevant issues*. Likewise, *abstract models of computations, models of computability, language theory concepts, and the application of language theory ideas* are the subject matter of the concepts of automata and formal languages. These topics will also assist to understand the concepts and philosophies used in advanced stages of computer learning such as computation theory and computability, artificial intelligence, switching theory and logic design, design of softwares like high speed compilers, sophisticated text processors and programming languages, assembly and rescue of information.

The texts of this book are intended primarily for use in graduate as well as post graduate courses in 'Mathematical Foundation of Computer Science', 'Discrete Mathematics' and 'Automata Theory and Formal Languages'. Although, the topics discussed in the book primarily focuses on the mathematical aspects of engineering in context of computer science, however it is also suited to the technical professionals.

MOTIVATION

The manuscript presented in this book is an outcome of the experience gained in the teaching the courses like discrete mathematics, automata theory, and mathematical foundation of computer science at Department of Computer Science & Engineering at I E T, UP Technical University, Lucknow and elsewhere for last ten years. I am hopeful that presentation of this text imitates the planning of the lectures. I always tried to avoid the mathematical-rigors, complicated concepts and formalisms and presented them in a more precise and interesting manner. Moreover, I hope during my teaching students not only learned the courses as a powerful mathematical tool but also widened their ability and understanding to perceive, devise, and attempt the mathematical problems with the application of the theory to computer science. The prolific and valuable feedback from my students motivates me to prepare this manuscript. Ultimately, I expect that this text would extend the understanding of mathematical theory of computer science with the explosion of computer science, computer application, engineering, and information technology.

FEATURE OF THE BOOK

The interesting feature of this book is its organization and structure. That consists of systematizing of the definitions, methods, and results that something resembling a theory. Simplicity, clarity, and precision of mathematical language makes theoretical topics more appealing to the readers who are of mathematical or non-mathematical background. For quick references and immediate attentions—concepts and definitions, methods and theorems, and key notes are presented through highlighted points from beginning to end. Whenever, necessary and probable a visual approach of presentation is used. The amalgamation of text and figures make mathematical rigors easier to understand. Each chapter begins with the detailed contents which are discussed inside the chapter and conclude with a summary of the material covered in the chapter. Summary provides a brief overview of all the topics covered in the chapter. To demonstrate the principles better, the applicability of the concepts discussed in each topic are illustrated by several examples followed by the practice sets or exercises.

The material of this book is divided into ***5 Units*** that are distributed among ***12 chapters.***

Unit I gives general overview of discrete objects theory its relations and functions, enumeration, recurrence relations and algebraic structures. It contains four chapters.

Chapter 1 is a discussion of *discrete objects theory its relations and functions*. We start our discussion from the theory of discrete objects which is commonly known as algebra of sets. The concepts of relations and functions are presented after a discussion of algebra of sets. This chapter is concluded with the study of natural numbers, Peano axioms and mathematical induction.

Chapter 2 discusses enumeration that includes discrete numeric functions and generating functions. This chapter covers a class of functions whose domain is the set of natural numbers and the range is the set of real numbers—better known as discrete numeric functions that are widely used in digital computations. An alternative way to represent the numeric functions efficiently and conveniently the reader will also find a discussion over generating function in the chapter.

Chapter 3 is concerned with recurrence relation and the methods of finding the solution of the recurrence relation (difference equation). A variety of common recurrences obtained from the algorithms like divide & conquer and chip & conquer is given. The chapter concludes the methods to obtain the solution of the recursive procedure codes.

Chapter 4 Latter in this unit we emphasized the algebraic structures where a thorough discussion of group theory and brief discussion of other algebraic structures like rings and fields are presented. This discussion is in fact very important in formal language theory and automata. This chapter concludes with the discussion of class of group mappings like homomorphism, isomorphism, and automorphism.

Unit II is devoted to the discussion of *propositional logic and lattices* that are presented in two chapters.

Oaf! After a successful study of mathematical–rigors, readers find an interesting and detail overview of *logic* in ***Chapter 5***. An elementary introduction to logic not only enlightens the students who are eager to know the role of logic in computer science but equally to other students of human sciences, philosophy, reasoning, and social sciences as well. A brief discussion of the theory of inference persuades the criteria to investigate the validity of an argument is included. In the chapter the stress is mainly on the natural deduction methods to investigate the validity of an argument instead a lengthy and tedious approach using truth table. Furthermore, the introduction of predicate logic and inference theory of predicate logic along with a number of solved examples conclude the chapter.

Chapter 6 deals the *Order Theory* that includes partial ordered sets (posets) and lattices. This chapter also covers a detail discussion on lattice properties and its classification along with a number of solved examples.

Unit III, IV, and **V** are concerned with automata theory and introduction to formal languages, which comprises chapters 7, 8–9, and 10–12 correspondingly. ***Chapter 7*** starts with the study of introduction to the languages and finite automata. The class of finite automata - deterministic and nondeterministic is included with the definition, representation, and the discussion of the power of them.

Chapter 8 deals the relationship between the classes of finite automata. Examples are given to explain better how one form of finite automata is converted to other form of automata with preservance of power. Of course, a brief illustration of the state minimization problem of deterministic finite automata concludes the chapter.

Chapter 9 discusses about the regular expressions. Since generalization of regular expression gives regular language which is the language of the finite automaton. So this chapter illustrates the relationship between finite automata and regular expressions and vice-versa. This chapter also introduces another form of finite automata called finite automata with output such as Melay and Moore machines, which operate on input string and returns some output string. It also included the discussion on equivalence of Melay and Moore machines.

Chapter 10 deals with regular and non-regular languages. To prove whether any language is regular or not we discuss a lemma called pumping lemma of regular language. This lemma is necessarily checking the regularity of the language. The characterizations of regular languages and decision problems of regular languages are also discussed here.

Chapter 11 begins with the study of grammars. Classification of grammars of type 0, type 1, type 2, and type 3 are discussed here. A detailed discussion of non-regular grammar such as context free grammar (type 2) and context free language its characteristics, ambiguity features are presented in this chapter. The automaton which accepts the context free language is called pushdown automata. This chapter also discusses about the pushdown automata. Reader will also find the simplification method of any grammar including normal forms of grammars. Pumping lemma for proving any language is context free language or not and a brief discussion on decision problems concludes the chapter.

Chapter 12 deals the study of an abstract machine introduced by Allen Turing called Turing machine. Turing machine is a more general model of computation in such a way that any algorithmic procedure that can be carried by human could be possible by a Turing machine. Chapter includes a brief discussion on this hypothesis usually referred as Church-Turing hypothesis which laid the theoretical foundation for the modern computer. Variations of Turing machines and its computing power concluded the study of this chapter.

In ***Appendix*** a discussion on *Boolean algebra*, where reader will find the basic theorems of Boolean algebra and its most common postulates. A preamble to Boolean function, simplification of Boolean function and its application in the logic deign of digital computers is presented at last.

ATTENTIONS

Even after immense forethoughts a book covering this variety of text it is probable to contain errors and lapses. I would appreciate you if you find any mistakes or have any constructive suggestions it will be my pleasure to look into your suggestions. You can mail your comments to

Mathematical Foundation to Computer Science—Y N Singh

Department of Computer Science & Engineering

Institute of Engineering & Technology,

UP Technical University, Lucknow-226 021

Alternatively you can use e-mail ynsingh_iet@yahoo.com to submit errors, lapses and constructive suggestions.

ACKNOWLEDGEMENTS

I owe my deep concerns to many individuals whose encouragements, guidance, and suggestions have resulted in a better manuscript:

Prof D S Chauhan	Hon' ble Vice Chancellor, UP Technical University, Lucknow
Prof V K Jain	(Ex.) Director & Head, Deptt. of CSE, HBTI, Kanpur
Prof L S Yadav	Director, IET, Lucknow
Prof S N Singh	Deptt. of Electrical Engineering, IIT, Kanpur
Prof S K Bajpai	Head, Deptt. of Computer Sc., IET, Lucknow
Prof N P Padhey	Deptt. of Computer Sc., IIT, Roorkee
Prof B N Misra	Coordinator Deptt. of Biotechnology, IET, Lucknow
Prof V K Singh	Examination Controller & Head Deptt. of Applied Science, IET, Lucknow

Additionally I thank to my colleagues' faculty members and friends. My special thanks go to the students in Mathematical foundation of computer science & automata theory classes who provided me valuable feedback and critical appraisal.

I experience a pleasure working with New Age International Press. Every one contributed immensely to the quality of the final manuscript. I specially thanks to L N Misra for his encouragement, support and assistance.

Finally I pay my gratitude to the family members Saraswati (wife), Siddhartha (son), Divyanshi & Lavantika (daughters) for their love and patience during writing this book. At this moment, I can't forget to memorize my late father B R Singh Rajput and my late teacher Dr Srikant Srivastawa who has been my hub of inspiration. I affectionately dedicate this book to all of them.

I E T, Lucknow

Y N Singh

SEMESTER SCHEDULE

Week	Unit	Topic	Reading/Assignments
1	I	Set theory review & study of Group theory	Chap 1
2	I	Ordered theory &	Chap 2
3	I	Discrete Numeric Functions	Chap 3
		Assignment 1 given out & submit up to 4th week	
4	II	Study or Recurrences	Chap 4
5	II	Boolean Algebra	Chap 5
6	II	Logic & Inference Theory	Chap 6
		Assignment 2 given out & submit up to 7th week	
7	III	Concepts of Finite Automatons	Chap 7
8	IV	Equivalence of DFA & NFA	Chap 8
		Assignment 3 given out & submit up to 9th week	
9	IV	Study of Regular Expressions	Chap 9
10	V	Regular or Non Regular languages	Chap 10
		Assignment 4 given out & submit up to 11th week	
11	V	Study of Grammar, Classification of Grammar	
12	V	Context free Grammar	

CONTENTS

11 Non-Ragular Grammars 275

12 Introduction to Turning Machine 333

Appendix—Boolean Algebra

DISCRETE THEORY, RELATIONS AND FUNCTIONS

1 Discrete Theory, Relations and Functions

1.1 INTRODUCTION

The major objective of the study of this subject is to study the theory of discrete objects and relationship among them. The term discrete objects refers a variety of items that we frequently seen and go through in our day today life such as students, books, programs, numbers, projects etc. We study some of the basic concepts dealing with different kinds of discrete objects under the theory of set algebra which we discussed next. Initially, the notation of set theory is introduced and certain operations are defined. The concepts of relations and functions are presented after a discussion of algebra of sets. We conclude this chapter with the study of natural numbers, Peano axioms and mathematical induction.

1.2 ELEMENTARY THEORY OF SETS

In this section we start our study to introduce the notation used for specifying sets. A set is the known collection of objects that are distinct in nature.

For example,

- A set of books,
- A set of alphabets,
- A set of real numbers,
- A set of Ist semester of MCA students,
- A group of students of UP Technical University, Lucknow,
- A group of meritorious students of the university,
- A collection of coins,
- A aggregation of live projects,

The words 'group', 'collection', 'aggregation', are have similar meaning of set. The set is recognizes by the uniqueness of its members. The important characteristic of the set is that its members share some common, unique, and well defined property through which the set is recognized or named. A set is represented by a symbol. We use the convention capital letter to represent a set, and lower case letters to represent the members of the set. For example X is the set of alphabets i.e. $X = \{a, b, c, ..., z\}$; the set of natural numbers $N = \{0, 1, 2, ...\}$ etc. The objects of the set are often called the *members* of the set or element of the set for example, a, b, c, ..., z are the members of the set X. It is discretionary that in the set the members occur in any order.

Let set $X = \{x, y, z\}$ then elements x, y, and z are the members of the set X, this can also be represented by $x \in X$, $y \in X$ and $z \in X$ but for the element $a \notin X$ it means that a is not the member of the set X. Since, the elements of the set are all unique so incident of repeated elements doesn't change the nature of the set.

The important aspect of the study of the sets is its representation such that how can we describe the members of the sets conveniently. For example, assume a set S contains hundred million natural numbers. We can represent this set by using the expression that describes its members conveniently by,

$$S = \{x/x \text{ is a natural number and } x \text{ is upto hundred million}\}$$

Consider another example of a set X is the students of UP Technical University studying in MCA program. It can be describe by the following expression by,

$$X = \{x/x \text{ is studying in MCA program of UP Technical University}\}$$

Here x is the member of the set X and the it's members share a unique and common property 'studying in MCA program' through which the set X is recognized or by defining x the set X is completely defined.

Alternatively, a set is well defined if it is possible to determine the members of the set by means of certain statute.

Since, there is no restriction on the size of the objects that can be in a set. It may possible that a set contains themselves one or more sets for example,

$$X = \{1, 2, \{a, b\}, \{p, r, s\}, \$\}$$

Here, sets $\{a, b\}$ and $\{p, q, r\}$ are the members of the set X i.e. $\{a, b\} \in X$ and $\{p, q, r\} \in X$ but the element $a, b \notin X$ and also $p, q, r \notin X$.

The *cardinality* of the set X is denoted by the $|X|$, which is the number of elements the set contains or it also defines the *size of the set*. $|X|$ may be finite or infinite depending upon the set finite or infinite. For example, the size of the set X shown above is 5; because it contains the first two elements 1 and 2, along with two elements that are sets $\{a, b\}$ and $\{p, q, r\}$ and one element \$. The cardinality of the empty set is $|\varnothing| = 0$. We set $|X| = \infty$ whenever set X is infinite. An infinite set has infinite number of distinct elements. An infinite set that can be put into a one-to-one correspondence with the natural numbers is ***countable infinite*** (i.e. set of integers) otherwise it is ***uncountable*** (i.e. set of reals). The sets have the same cardinality if their elements shown one-to-one correspondence. A finite set X with $|X| = n$ is called an ***n-set***. A 1-set is called a ***singleton***.

1.3 SET RULES AND SETS COMBINATIONS

In this section we shall discuss the rules that are the basic tools for enumeration and the diversity of sets combinations.

1.3.1 (S1) Rule of Equality

To discuss the concepts of equality between sets we first discuss the meaning of the *subset*. Given two finite sets X and Y if every element of X is an element of Y, then set X is a subset of Y and it is denoted by, $X \subseteq Y$. For example, set $\{a, b, c\}$ is a subset of the set $\{p, q, r, a, b, w, c\}$; but not a subset of $\{p, q, r, a, \$, c\}$. Consider, another example, a set of first year MCA students is a subset of the set of students that contains all year of MCA students.

Reader should note that,

- A set is subset to itself i.e. $X \subseteq X$ (reflexive).
- If $X \subseteq Y$ then it doesn't necessarily mean $Y \subseteq X$.

- If X $\subseteq$ Y and Y $\subseteq$ Z then certainly, X $\subseteq$ Z (transitive).
- A set with no element (empty set) is the subset of all the sets i.e. { } $\subseteq$ X (for any set X)
- $\{a, b, c\}$ is not a subset of $\{\{a, b, c\}\}$; because former set has the elements a, b, and c but the latter set has a element which is themselves a set $\{a, b, c\}$.

Hence, two sets X and Y are said to be equal if and only if (1) X is the subset of Y and also (2) Y is a subset of X. Alternatively, if X and Y are two finite sets and if there exists a bijection between them, then | X | = | Y | is called ***rule of equality***.

For example, $\{a, b, c\} = \{a, a, b, c\} = \{a, c, b\}$ [$\therefore$ $\{a, a, b, c\} = \{a, b, c\}$ and so $|\{a, b, c\}| = 3 = |\{a, c, b\}|$]. But $\{a, b, c\} \neq \{\{a, b\}, c\}$. Also $\{1\} \neq \{\{1\}\}$ because $\{1\} \in \{\{1\}\}$ but $\{1\}$ is not a subset of the set $\{\{1\}\}$.

Rule of equality of sets is reflexive, symmetric, and transitive that is describes respectively as,

- A set X is equal to itself i.e., A = A.
- For two sets X and Y if X = Y then also Y = X.
- For any sets X, Y, and Z if X = Y and Y = Z then also X = Z.

After describing the meaning of a subset we shall now define proper subset. Given two sets X and Y if X $\subseteq$ Y and X is not equal to Y then, set X is called the ***proper subset*** of Y and is denoted by X $\subset$ Y. It means, the set Y contains at least one distinct and extra element than the set X. Therefore, proper subset is not reflexive and symmetric but it is transitive i.e., if X $\subset$ Y and Y $\subset$ Z then X $\subset$ Z.

Empty Set

A set with no elements is called an ***empty set***. An empty set is also known as a null set and it is denoted by { } or $\varnothing$. For example,

- $\varnothing = \{x/x$ is an integer and $x^2 + 5 = 0\}$
- $\varnothing = \{x/x$ are living beings who never die$\}$
- $\varnothing = \{x/x$ is the MCA student of age below 15$\}$
- $\varnothing = \{ x/x$ is the set of persons of age over 200$\}$
- $\varnothing = \{x/x + 5 = 5$ and $x > 5\}$

Remember a set $\{\varnothing\}$ is not an empty set, because it contains an element $\varnothing$. Similarly the set $\{\{ \}\} \neq \{ \}$, because former set is not empty, it contains an element $\varnothing$ but latter is an empty set.

1.3.2 Study of Sets Combinations

The sets may be combined into a variety of ways so that new sets are formed. For example, there is a set of student of girls which is combined with the other set of student of boys then we get a set of student of either girls, or boys or both girls and boys. What is the set of the senior students (both girls and boys)? To study these representations 'union' and 'intersection' are the basic operations over which the sets are combined. In this section we shall discuss these sets operations in detail.

Union

Given two sets X and Y, then X ***union*** Y denoted by X $\cup$ Y is the set of all elements either (1) from the set X, or (2) from the set Y, or (3) from both the set X as well as Y.

i.e.

$$X \cup Y = \{x/x \in X \textbf{ OR } x \in Y\}$$

For example,

- $\{a,, b, c\} \cup \{1, 2\} = \{a, b, c, 1, 2\}$ and others.
- $\{a,, b, c\} \cup \{a, b, c\} = \{a, b, c\}$
- $\{a,, b, c\} \cup \{\ \}$ or $\varnothing = \{a, b, c\}$
- $\{a,, b, c\} \cup \{\{a, b\}, c\} = \{a, b, \{a, b\}\}$ or $\{\{a, b\}\}$ and others.

In general we conclude that elements of the union of the sets have at least one of the property embraces by elements of set X or set Y.

Similar to the union of two sets, if there are n-sets $X_1, X_2, \ldots\ldots\ldots X_n$ then there combination using union operator is denoted by,

$$X_1 \cup X_2 \cup \ldots\ldots\ldots X_n = (\ldots.((X_1 \cup X_2) \cup X_3) \ldots\ldots\ldots X_n) = \underset{k=1\text{to}\,n}{\cup} X_k$$

where, set X_k is also called ***indexed-set***.

Intersection

Given two sets X and Y, then ***intersection*** of X and Y denoted by $X \cap Y$ is the set that has all the common elements of both the sets X and Y, i.e.,

$$X \cap Y = \{x/x \in X \textbf{ and } x \in Y\}$$

For example,

- $\{a, b, c\} \cap \{a, b, c, d, e\} = \{a, b, c\}$

Two sets are said to be ***disjoint*** if they have no common element, i.e.,

- $\{a, b, c\} \cap \{1, 2\} = \{\ \}$ or $\varnothing$
- $\{a, b, c\} \cap \{\ \} = \{\ \}$ or $\varnothing$
- $\{\varnothing, a, b, c\} \cap \{\ \} = \{\ \}$ or $\varnothing$
- But $\{\varnothing, a, b, c\} \cap \{\{\ \}\} = \{\varnothing\}$ is not disjoint sets.

In general, the elements of the intersection of the sets embrace both the elements property of the set X as well as the elements property of the set Y.

In the similar mode we can combine the n-sets $(X_1, X_2, \ldots\ldots\ldots X_n)$ using intersection operations as,

$$X_1 \cap X_2 \cap \ldots\ldots\ldots X_n = (\ldots.((X_1 \cap X_2) \cap X_3) \ldots\ldots\ldots X_n) = \underset{k=1\text{to}\,n}{\cup} X_k$$

where, set X_k is an indexed-set.

We can also see that union and intersection operations are commutative and associative, i.e.

(*i*) $X \cup Y = Y \cup X$ and (*ii*) $X \cup (Y \cup Z) = (X \cup Y) \cup Z$

also (*i*) $X \cap Y = Y \cap X$ and (*ii*) $X \cap (Y \cap Z) = (X \cap Y) \cap Z$

Example 1.1. *Set $X = \{x / x$ is an integer s.t. $x \geq 10\}$, $Y = \{1, 2, 3, \ldots..\}$ and $Z = \{3, 5, 7, 9\}$ find $X \cup Y$, $X \cup Z$, $X \cap Y$ and $X \cap Z$.*

Sol. $X \cup Y = \{1, 2, 3, \ldots..\}$

[This set contains all elements of set X and all elements of set Y].

$X \cup Z = \{3, 5, 7, 9, 10, 11, 12, \ldots..\}$.

$X \cap Y = \{10, 11, \ldots\ldots\}$ and $X \cap Z = \varnothing$.

Difference

Given two sets X and Y, then difference of X and Y denoted by X – Y is the set taken all those elements of X that are not in Y i.e.,

$$X - Y = \{x/x \in X \textbf{ AND } x \notin Y\}$$

For example,

- $\{a, b, c, \$\} - \{a, b, c\} = \{\$\}$
- $\{a, b, c\} - \{a, b, c, \$\} = \varnothing$
- $\{\{a, b\}, c, d\} - \{a, b, c, d\} = \{\{a, b\}\}$
- $\{1, a, b\} - \{1, a\ \ b\} = \varnothing$
- $\{a, b, c\} - \{\ \} = \{a, b, c\}$

We can also define the ***symmetric difference*** of the two sets X and Y, which is denoted by X ~ Y, is the set taken all the elements of X or Y but not in both i.e.,

$$X \sim Y = \{x/x \in (X - Y) \cup x \in (Y - X)\}$$

For example,

- $\{a, b, c\} \sim \{c, d\} = \{a, b, d\}$
- $\{a, b, c\} \sim \{\ \} = \{a, b, c\}$
- $\{a, b, c\} \sim \{a, b, c\} = \varnothing$

Complement

Often all the sets are probably the subsets of a general larger set U called **universal set**. For example, if we are considering various sets made up only of integers, thus the set S of integers is an appropriate universal set. Given a universal set U, we define the complement of a set X as,

$$X' = U - X$$

For any set $X \subseteq U$, we obtain following equivalence,

- $X'' = X$ **[De Morgan's Law]**
- $X \cap X' = \varnothing$
- $X \cup X' = U$

Assume X and Y are two sets (i.e. $X, Y \subseteq U$) then De Morgan's law can be written with complements, i.e.

- $(X \cap Y)' = X' \cup Y'$
- $(X \cup Y)' = X' \cap Y'$

1.3.3 Power Set

Given a set X, then power set of X is denoted by P(X), is the set take in all the subsets of X. For a finite set X with $|X| = n$, then $|P(X)| = 2^n$ or number of elements in the power set is 2^n including the null set ∅.

For example,

- Let set $X = \{\alpha, \beta, \gamma\}$, then power set of X will be $P(X) = \{\varnothing, \{\alpha\}, \{\beta\}, \{\gamma\}, \{\alpha, \beta\}, \{\alpha, \gamma\}, \{\beta, \gamma\}$, and $\{\alpha, \beta, \gamma\}\}$
- Let set $X = \{1, 2, \varnothing\}$, then $P(X) = \{\varnothing, \{1\}, \{2\}, \{\varnothing\}, \{1, 2\}, \{1, \varnothing\}, \{2, \varnothing\}, \{1, 2, \varnothing\}\}$.
- Let $X = \varnothing$, then $P(X) = \{\varnothing\}$ or power set of empty set is not empty.
- For any set X, $\varnothing \in P(X)$ or $\varnothing \subseteq P(X)$.

(S2) Rule of Sums

Let X_k {for k = 1 to n}, is a finite family of finite pair wise disjoint sets, then

$$\left| \bigcup_{k=1 \text{to} n} X_k \right| = \sum_{k=1 \text{to} n} |X_k|$$

1.3.4 Multisets

Since, we know that the elements of the sets are all distinct, but often we see that the elements are not necessarily distinct, we may say that there are repeated occurrence of some elements in the set. Such sets may be pronounced as redundant representation of set called *multiset*. For example, {a, b, b, c, b}, {a, a, a, a}, { a, b, c}, { } etc. are all multisets.

A multiset on X is a set X together with a function $f : X \to N$, where N = {0, 1, 2, ...} giving the multiplicity of the elements of X. Multiplicity of the elements is given by the number of times the element appears in the multiset. Multiset is a set where multiplicity of its elements are all 1 and it is a null set where element multiplicity is 0.

We can denote the multiset M on X is $M = \{a^{m_a} : a \in X\}$ with $m_a = f(a)$, $a \in X$. The usual operations for sets can be carried over to multisets. For instance, if $M = \{a^{m_a} : a \in X\}$ and $N = \{a^{n_a} : a \in X\}$ then

- $M \subseteq N = \; m_a \leq n_a \quad$ for all $a \in X$,
- $M \cup N = \{a^{\max(m_a, n_a)} : a \in X]$, and
- $M \cap N = \{a^{\min(m_a, n_a)} : a \in X]$;
- $M - N = \{a^{(m_a - n_a)} : (m_a - n_a) \geq 1$ and $a \in X\}$;

[It also seen that multisets on a set X forms a lattice under inclusion ($\subseteq$)] for lattice see more in chapter 2.

1.3.5 Ordered Sets

In the sets the order of the elements are discretionary. So a set may be further defined as an unordered aggregation of objects or elements. In this section we will concentrate on the ordered set of objects. *A couple (duo) of objects is said to be ordered if it is arranged distinctly*. We can denote the ordered couple by (x, y) where component x and y referring the first and second objects of the ordered couple. Ordered couple is different from the set in the sense that ordering of the objects is important simultaneously objects need not to be distinct in the ordered pair. Because of distinct ordering of the objects $(x, y) \neq (y, x)$ while sets $\{x, y\} = \{y, x\}$.

Resemblance, to that idea of ordered couple can be extended to ordered triple, ordered quadruple, ..., and ordered n - tuples. Alternatively, an ordered triple e.g. (x, y, z) is an ordered couple $((x, y), z)$ where first component is itself is an ordered couple. Likeness to that, an ordered quadruple (w, x, y, z) has first component is an ordered triple e.g. $((w, x, y), z)$ and so $(((w, x), y), z)$. Therefore, an ordered n-tuples $(x_1, x_2.......x_n)$ has first component is an ordered $(n - 1)$ tuples e.g. $((x_1, x_2.......x_{n-1}), x_n)$.

1.3.6 Cartesian Products

Given two sets X and Y, then Cartesian product of sets X and Y denoted by X × Y, is the set of all ordered couples (x, y) such that $x \in X$ and $y \in Y$.

i.e. $$X \times Y = \{(x, y) / x \in X \text{ and } y \in Y\}$$

For example,

- For the sets X = $\{x_1, x_2\}$ and Y = $\{y_1, y_2\}$ then X × Y = $\{(x_1, y_1), (x_1, y_2), (x_2, y_1), (x_2, y_2)\}$.
- Due to distinct ordering X × Y ≠ Y × X, hence these two sets are disjoints e.g.

$$(X \times Y) \cap (Y \times X) = \varnothing.$$

- Let sets X = ∅ and Y ≠ ∅ then X × Y = ∅ and also Y × X = ∅.

(S3) Rule of Products

Let X_k {for k = 1 to n}, is a finite family of finite sets, then for the Cartesian product $\prod_{k=1 \text{to} n} X_k$,

$$\left| \prod_{k=1 \text{to} n} X_k \right| = \prod_{k=1 \text{to} n} |X_k|$$

1.4 RELATIONS

The important aspect of the any set is the relationship between its elements. The association of relationship established by sharing of some common feature proceeds comparing of related objects. For example, assume a set of students, where students are related with each other if their sir names are same. Conversely, if set is formed a class of students then we say that students are related if they belong to same class etc. Hence, we say that *a relation is a predefined alliance of objects*. The examples of relations are viz. husband and wife, brother and sister, and mathematical relation such as less than, greater than, and equal etc. The relations can be classifying on the basis of its association among the objects. For example, relations said above are all association among two objects so these relations are called binary relation. Similarly, relations of parent to their children, boss and subordinates, brothers and sisters etc. are the examples of relations among three/more objects known as tertiary relation, quadratic relations and so on. In general an n-ary relation is the relation framed among n objects. In this section we shall contemplate and study more about binary relation.

1.4.1 Binary Relation

A relation between two objects is a binary relation and it is given by a set of ordered couples. Let X and Y are two sets then a binary relation from set X to Y, denoted by *XRY* is a subset of X × Y.

For example,

- Relation of husband and wife can be described by an ordered couple (h, w) i.e.

  R = {(h, w)/h is husband of w}
- Let I^+ is positive integer, then relation R i.e.

  R = $\{(\sqrt{x}, x\}/x \in I^+\}$ defines the relation of square root of a positive integer.

Besides ordered couple representation, binary relations can also shown graphically and through tabular form. Consider sets X = $\{x_1, x_2, x_3\}$, Y = $\{y_1, y_2\}$ and let a relation R = $\{(x_1, y_1), (x_1, y_2), (x_2, y_2), (x_3, y_1)\}$. Then relation R can be shown as Fig. 1.1 (a) and (b).

Consider another example of binary relation, Let X = {MCA01, MCA11, MCA17, MCA28, MCA42} be a set of top five MCA students in a class and Y = {TCS, SAIL, HCL, OIL, WIPRO, INFOSYS} be another set of companies offering jobs through campus selections. We may describe a binary relation R_1 (shown in Fig 1.2) from X to Y such that students are called for interview by the companies.

	y_1	y_2
x_1	1	1
x_2	0	1
x_3	1	0

(*a*)

(Tabular representation of relation R) where cell entries 1's (0's) stands for presence (absence) of the ordered couple in the relation.

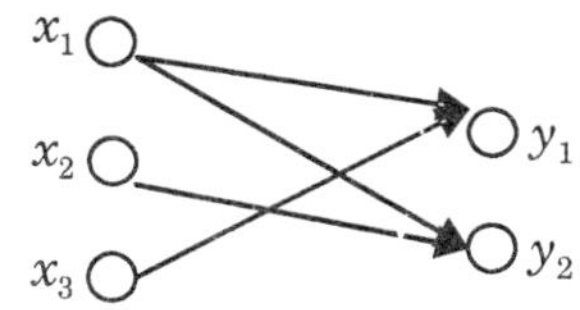

(*b*)

(Graph of relation R) where arrows shows the couple ordering in the relation.

Fig 1.1

	TCS	SAIL	HCL	OIL	WIPRO	INFOSYS
MCA 01	1	1	0	1	0	1
MCA11	0	1	1	0	1	0
MCA17	0	1	0	1	0	1
MCA28	0	0	1	0	0	1
MCA42	0	0	1	0	0	0

Fig. 1.2 Tabular representation of relation R_1.

Fig. 1.3 shows another binary relation R_2 from X to Y that describes the jobs offer by the companies to the students.

	TCS	SAIL	HCL	OIL	WIPRO	INFOSYS
MCA 01	1	1	0	0	0	0
MCA11	0	0	1	0	1	0
MCA17	0	1	0	1	0	1
MCA28	0	0	1	0	0	0
MCA42	0	0	0	0	0	0

Fig. 1.3 Tabular representation of relation R_2.

Domain Set and Range Set of Binary Relation

Let R be a binary relation, then *domain set* (domain) of relation R denoted by D(R), contains all first components of the ordered couples i.e.

$$D(R) = \{x/(x, y) \in R\}$$

Further, if $R = X \times Y$ then $D(R) \subseteq X$.

Similarly the *range set* (range) of relation R denoted by R(R), contains all second components of the ordered couples i.e.

$$R(R) = \{y/(x, y) \in R\}$$

Further, if $R = X \times Y$ then $R(R) \subseteq Y$.

For example,

- Let a relation $R = \{(x_1, y_1), (x_1, y_2), (x_2, y_2), (x_3, y_1)\}$ then its domain set and the range set will be $D(R) = \{x_1, x_2, x_3\}$ and $R(R) = \{y_1, y_2\}$ correspondingly.
- Let $R = \{(\sqrt{x}, x\}/x \in I^+\}$ where $I^+ = \{1, 2, 3, ...\}$ then

$$D(R) = \{1, \sqrt{2}, \sqrt{3}, ...\} \text{ and } R(R) = \{1, 2, 3, ...\}.$$

- Let $R = \{(x, \log_7 x\}/x \in N_0\}$ where $N_0 = \{0, 1, 2, ...\}$ then

$$D(R) = N_0 = \{0, 1, 2, ...\} \text{ and } R(R) = \{\log_7 0, \log_7 1, \log_7 2, ...\}.$$

If a relation is defined over same sets of objects then relation named as ***universal relation*** i.e. if $R_1 = X \times X$ then R_1 is a universal relation over set X. A relation defines over empty set named as ***void relation*** i.e. if $R_2 = X \times Y$ such that either $X = \varnothing$ or $Y = \varnothing$ or both $X = Y = \varnothing$ then R_2 is a void relation.

Example 1.2. *Let X = {1, 2, 3, 4, 5} and Y = {7, 11, 13} are two sets.*

(*i*) Consider a relation R i.e $R = \{(x, y)/x \in X$ and $y \in Y$ and $(y - x)$ is a perfect square$\}$ then relation R contains the following ordered couples,

$$R = \{(3, 7), (2, 11), (4, 13)\}$$

(*ii*) Consider another relation R′ i.e. $R' = \{(x, y)/x \in X$ and $y \in Y$ and $(y - x)$ is divisible by 6$\}$ then relation R' will be,

$$R' = \{(1, 7), (5, 11), (1, 13)\}$$

(*iii*) $R \cup R' = \{(1, 7), (1, 13), (2, 11), (3, 7), (4, 13), (5, 11)\}$.

(*iv*) $R \cap R' = \{\ \}$ or $\varnothing$.

Properties of Binary Relation

Here we discuss the general properties hold by a binary relation such that reflexive, symmetric, and transitive.

Let R be a binary relation defined over set X then

- Relation R is said to be *reflexive* if ordered couple $(x, x) \in R$ for $\forall x \in X$. (Conversely, relation R is *irreflexive* if $(x, x) \notin R$ for $\forall x \in X$).
- Relation R is said to be *symmetric* if, ordered couple $(x, y) \in R$ and also ordered couple $(y, x) \in R$ for $\forall x, \forall y \in X$. (Conversely, relation R is *antisymmetric* if $(x, y) \in R$ but $(y, x) \notin R$ unless $x = y$).
- Relation R is said to be *transitive* if ordered couple $(x, z) \in R$ whenever both ordered couples $(x, y) \in R$ and $(y, z) \in R$.

1.4.2 Equivalence Relation

A binary relation on any set is said an *equivalence* relation if it is reflexive, symmetric, and transitive. Further, if a relation is only reflexive and symmetric then it is called a *compatibility* relation. A table shown in Fig. 1.4 represents a compatibility relation. So, we can say that every equivalence relation is a compatibility relation, but not every compatibility relation is an equivalence relation.

	x	y	z
x	1	1	1
y	1	1	—
z	1	—	1

Fig. 1.4 Compatibility relation.

Example 1.3. *Let N = {1, 2, 3, ...} then show that relation R = {(x, y) / (x – y) is divisible by 2 for every x and y ∈ N} is an equivalence relation.*

Sol. Since,

- For any $x \in$ N, $(x - x)$ is divisible by 2 therefore, relation R is reflexive.
- For any $x, y \in$ N, if $(x - y)$ is divisible by 2 then also $(y - x)$ is divisible by 2 therefore, relation R is symmetric.
- For any x, y, and $z \in$ N, if $(x - y)$ is divisible by 2 and $(y - z)$ is divisible by 2 then also $(x - z)$ is divisible by 2; because $(x - z)$ can be written as $(x - y) + (y - z)$ and since both $(x - y)$ and $(y - z)$ is divisible by 2 then also $(x - z)$. Therefore, relation R is reflexive.

Hence, relation R is an equivalence relation.

Equivalence Class

Let R be an equivalence relation on set X, then equivalence class denoted by $[x]$ is generated by the elements $y \in$ X such that,

$$[y] = \{x/x \in X \quad \text{and} \quad (y, x) \in R\}$$

Since, set $[y]$ consists of all virtual of y in the set X. Hence, $[y] \subseteq$ X. A family of equivalence classes generated by the elements of X defines a *partition* of set X. Such partition is a unique partition. So, we may say that equivalence classes generated by any two elements are either disjoint or equal. e.g.

$$[y] \cap [z] = \varnothing \quad \text{or} \quad [y] = [z]$$

where $[y]$ and $[z]$ are equivalence classes respect to relation R.

Also, the unions of all the equivalence classes generated by the elements of set X (partitions) respect to relation R return the set X.

Example 1.4. *Consider a relation R = {(x, y) / x, y ∈ I^+ and (x – y) is divisible by 3} where I^+ is the set of positive integers. Find the set of equivalence classes generated by the elements of set I^+.*

Sol. The equivalence classes are,

- [0] = {0, 3, 6, 9, ...} (when $(x - y)$ % 3 = 0),
- [1] = {1, 4, 7, 10, ...} (when $(x - y)$ % 3 = 1), and
- [2] = {2, 5, 8, 11, ...} (when $(x - y)$ % 3 = 2)

See, unions of these equivalence classes return the set I^+, i.e.

$$I^+ = [0] \cup [1] \cup [2] = \{0, 1, 2, ...\}$$

Let x and y are two elements from the set of integers I^+, then the relation R is said to be *congruent relation* such that,

$$R = \{(x, y)/x, y \in I \text{ and } (x - y) \text{ is divisible by } m(\in I^+)\}$$

Hence, relation shown in example 1.4 is a congruent relation of modulo 3.

1.4.3 Pictorial Representation of Relations

As shown in the fig. 1.1 (*b*), a relation can also be represented pictorially by drawing its *graph* (directed graph). Consider a relation R be defined between two sets X = $\{x_1, x_2, \ldots\ldots, x_l\}$ and Y = $\{y_1, y_2, \ldots\ldots, y_m\}$ *i.e.*, x_i Ry_j , that is ordered couple $(x_i, y_j) \in$ R where $1 \le i \le l$ and $1 \le j \le m$. The elements of sets X and Y are represented by small circle called nodes. The existence of the ordered couple such as (x_i, y_j) is represented by means of an edge marked with an arrow in the direction from x_i to y_j, *i.e.*

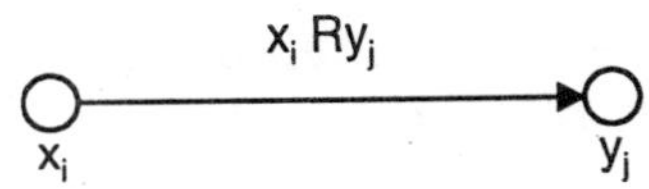

While all nodes related to the ordered couples in R are connected by proper arrows, we get a directed graph of the relation R. For the ordered couples x_i Ry_j and y_j Rx_i we draw two arcs between nodes x_i and y_j, *i.e.*

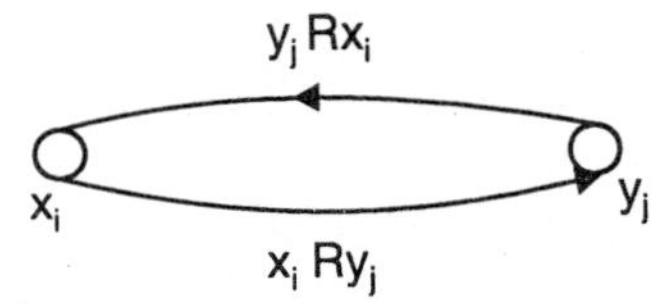

If ordered couple is like x_i Rx_i or $(x_i, x_i) \in$ R then we get self loop over the node x_i, *i.e.*

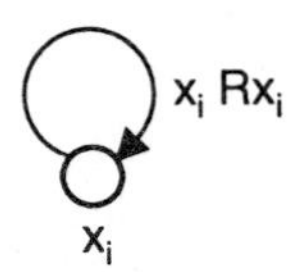

From the directed graph of a relation we can easily examine some of its properties. For example if a relation is reflexive, then we must get a self loop at each node. Conversely if a relation is irreflexive, then there is no self loop at any node. For symmetric relation if one node is connected to another, then there must be a return arc from second node to the first node. For antisymmetric relation there is no such direct return arc exist. Similarly we examine the transitivity of the relation in the directed graph.

1.4.4 Composite Relation

When a relation is formed over stages such that let R_1 be one relation defined from set X to Y, and R_2 be another relation defined from set Y to Z, then a relation R denoted by $R_1 \Diamond R_2$ is a composite relation, i.e

$$R = R_1 \Diamond R_2 = \{(x, z)/\text{for any } (x \in X, y \in Y, z \in Z) \text{ such that } (x, y) \in R_1 \text{ and } (y, z) \in R_2\}$$

Composite relation R can also represented by a diagram shown in Fig 1.5

Fig. 1.5

For example, let $R_1 = \{(p, q), (r, s), (t, u), (q, s)\}$ and $R_2 = \{(q, r), (s, v), (u, w)\}$ are two relations then,

$R_1 \Diamond R_2 = \{(p, r), (r, v), (t, w), (q, v)\}$, and

$R_2 \Diamond R_1 = \{(q, s)\}$

1.4.5 Ordering Relation (Partial Ordered Relation)

A binary relation R is said to be partial ordered relation if it is reflexive, antisymmetric, and transitive. For example,

$$R = \{(w, w), (x, x), (y, y), (z, z), (w, x), (w, y), (w, z), (x, y), (x, z)\}$$

In a partial ordered relation objects are related through superior/inferior criterion. For example,

- In the arithmetic relation 'less than or equal to' or '≤' (or 'greater than or equal to' or '≥') are partial ordered relations. Since, every number is equated to itself so it is reflexive. Also, if m and n are two numbers then ordered couple $(m, n) \in$ R if $m = n \Rightarrow n \nleq m$ so $(n, m) \notin$ R hence, relation is antisymmetric. Further, if $(m, n) \in$ R and $(n, k) \in$ R $\Rightarrow m = n$ and $n = k \Rightarrow m = k$ so $(m, k) \in$ R hence, R is transitive.

In the next chapter we shall discuss the partial ordered relations in detail.

1.5 FUNCTION

Function is a relation. Function establishes the relationship between objects. For example, in computer system input is fed to the system in form of data or objects and the system generates the output that will be the function of input. So, function is the mapping or transformation of objects from one form to other. In this section we will concentrate our discussion on function and its classifications.

We are given two sets X and Y. A relation f from X to Y is called a function or mapping i.e.

$$f : X \to Y,$$

where $f(x) = y$, $\forall x \in$ X and $\forall y \in$ Y, and the triple (X, Y, f) is called ***morphism***.

In general, sets X and Y in most instances are finite sets. Assume, $|X| = m$ and $|Y| = n$ are the cardinalities of the sets. Then we may describe f by the expression,

$$f = \begin{pmatrix} \ldots\ldots x \ldots\ldots \\ \ldots f(x) \ldots\ldots \end{pmatrix}_{(x \in X)}$$

This we call as the *standard representation* of $f : X \to Y$. Usually, the domain X and the codomain (range) Y are totally ordered in some natural way, but , obviously any ordering is possible. For example, the expressions

$$\begin{pmatrix} x_1 & x_2 & x_3 & x_4 \\ y_1 & y_1 & y_2 & y_2 \end{pmatrix}, \begin{pmatrix} x_1 & x_4 & x_3 & x_2 \\ y_1 & y_2 & y_2 & y_1 \end{pmatrix}, \begin{pmatrix} x_4 & x_3 & x_1 & x_2 \\ y_2 & y_2 & y_1 & y_1 \end{pmatrix}$$

represents the same mapping f.

1.5.1 Classification of Functions

Let (X, Y, f) be a morphism. With $f : X \to Y$ we define *image* img (f) and the *argument* arg(f), where

$$\text{img}(f) = \bigcup_{x \in X} f(x) ;$$

$\arg(f) = \biguplus_{x \in \text{img}(f)} f^{-1}(y)$; ▲ (symbol ⊎ indicates that the sets involved for union are disjoint to each other)

- The function is an ***empty function*** $f_\varnothing$, if **img** $(\mathbf{f}_\varnothing) = \varnothing$ and undefined argument.
- The function is called ***identity function*** if **img (f) = x**, where $f : X \to X$, for all $x \in X$.
- The function is called ***surjective*** if **img (f) = Y**. Such that, every element of Y is the image of one/more elements of X, i.e., $| X | \geq |Y|$. Otherwise it is not surjective.
- The function is called ***injective*** if **arg(f) = 0**, i.e., if $x_1 \neq x_2 \Rightarrow f(x_1) \neq f(x_2)$ for all $x_1, x_2 \in X$. Such that each element of X has a unique image in Y, i.e., $| X | = | Y |$.
- Functions that are both surjective and injective are called ***bijective***. It follows that number of elements of both sets be strictly equal, i.e., $| X | = | Y |$.

A function of finite set X into itself, i.e., $f : X \to X$, the classes surjective, injective, and bijective coincides. For the set of infinite size this is no longer true. For example, $f : N \to N$ where N = {0, 1, 2, ...} then $f(n) = 2n$, is injective, but not surjective.

Suppose that both sets X and Y are endowed with a partial order. Function $f : X \to Y$ is called ***monotone*** if it preserves the order relation. i.e., if $x_1 = x_2$ then $f(x_1) = f(x_2)$ for all $x_1, x_2 \in X$, and it is called ***antitone*** if $x_1 = x_2$ then $f(x_1) = f(x_2)$ for all $x_1, x_2 \in X$.

Observe that if X is totally unordered set then monotone function is an arbitrary function, regardless of the order on Y.

Example 1.5. (A). *Classify which of the following function is surjective, injective, and bijective.*

(I) Let N = {0, 1, 2, ...} and $f : N \to N$, where $f(x) = x^2 + 1$. then

Since,

at, $x = 0$; $f(0) = (0)^2 + 1 = 1$

at, $x = 1$; $f(1) = (1)^2 + 1 = 2$

at, $x = 2$; $f(2) = (2)^2 + 1 = 5$

....

So we observe that distinct elements of N are mapped into distinct elements of the image set N, hence function is *injective*.

(II) Let $f : N \to \{0, 1\}$, where $f(x) = 1$, if x is even, otherwise 0.

Since, image set contains the elements 0 and 1, and all even numbers of N are mapped to element 1 and all odd numbers are mapped to the element 0 of N. So, img (f) = {0, 1}, hence mapping or function is *surjective*.

(III) Let $f : N \to N$, where $f(x) = 1$, if x is even, otherwise 0.

Here, img (f) = {0, 1} but there are other elements in the image set N that are nor the image of any element of argument N. Hence, function is not surjective.

(IV) Let $f : P \to P$, where P = {0, 1, 2, 3, 4} and $f(x) = x$ % 5 or (x mod 5).

▲ If the function $f : X \to Y$ is surjective, then we can define ***inverse function*** f^{-1}, i.e.,

$$f^{-1}: Y \to X;$$

where, $f^{-1}(y) = x \Leftrightarrow f(x) = y$, for any $x \in X$ and $y \in Y$. The composite of function f and f^{-1} is an identity function, i.e.,

$$f \lozenge f^{-1} = \text{I (Identity function)} = f^{-1} \lozenge f$$

(see example 1.5)

We find that at $x = 0 \Rightarrow f(0) = 0 \% 5 = 0$; at $x = 1 \Rightarrow f(1) = 1 \% 5 = 1$; at $x = 2 \Rightarrow f(2) = 2 \% 5 = 2$; at $x = 3 \Rightarrow f(3) = 3 \% 5 = 3$; and $x = 4 \Rightarrow f(4) = 4 \% 5 = 4$. Since, img (f) = P and arg$(f) = 0$ (that is no element left in the argument set), therefore mapping is bijective, or function is bijective.

(B). Let X = {1< 2 < 3 < 4} and

Y = 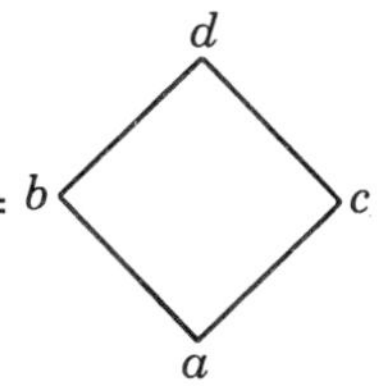

are partial ordered sets. Then classify the following function $(f : X \rightarrow Y)$ expressions,

$(i)\ f = \begin{pmatrix} 1 & 2 & 3 & 4 \\ a & b & c & d \end{pmatrix}$ $\quad$ $(ii)\ f = \begin{pmatrix} 1 & 2 & 3 & 4 \\ d & b & c & a \end{pmatrix}$

For the solution of (i) since we know that if function preserved the partial ordered relation then it is monotone, i.e., if $x_1 \leq x_2$ then $f(x_1) \leq f(x_2)$ for all $x_1, x_2 \in$ X. Since, first row of the expression consists of the elements of X, i.e. there ordering is $1 < 2 < 3 < 4$ and the second row of the expression consists of image elements of Y, i.e. there ordering is $a < b < c < d$. Thus we have,

$$1 < 2 < 3 < 4 \quad \Rightarrow \quad f(1) < f(2) < f(3) < f(4) \quad \Rightarrow \quad a < b < c < d$$

Therefore, function is monotone.

In the given function (ii) we have the ordering of the elements shown in the first row of the expression is $1 < 2 < 3 < 4$ and the ordering of their corresponding image elements is $d > b > c > a$. Thus we have,

$$1 < 2 < 3 < 4 \quad \Rightarrow \quad f(1) > f(2) > f(3) > f(4) \quad \Rightarrow \quad d > b > c > a$$

Therefore, function is antitone.

Example 1.6. *Let* $X = \{1, 2, 3\}_{<}$ *and* $Y = \{a, b, c\}_{<}$ *are partial ordered sets. Compute* $| f : X \rightarrow Y |$ *when, (1) f is arbitrary, (2) f is surjective, (3) f is injective, (4) f is bijective, (5) f is monotone, and (6) f is antitone.*

Sol. We first list the set of possible strings generated by the arbitrary function f, which is shown in Fig. 1.6.

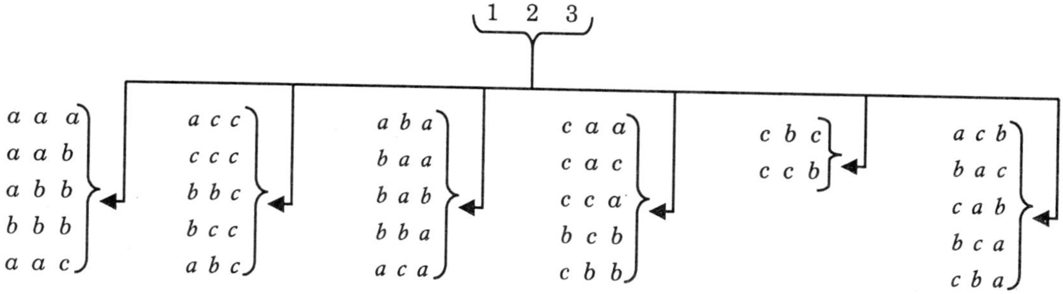

Fig. 1.6

Thus,

1. $| f : X \to Y | = 27$, when f is arbitrary.
2. For surjective mapping img $(f) = \{a, b, c\}$. So, we have the last column and '$a\ b\ c$' gives the $| f : X \to Y | = 6$.
3. Since, the last column together with '$a\ b\ c$' gives that each element of X has a unique image in Y hence, $| f : X \to Y | = 6$.
4. The last column together with '$a\ b\ c$' gives the bijective mapping, so $| f : X \to Y | = 6$.
5. The monotone mapping are those in the first two columns, so $| f : X \to Y | = 10$.
6. The antitone mapping are found in the columns three, four, fifth, and six are

$$| f : X \to Y | = 2 + 3 + 0 + 1 = 6.$$

1.5.2 Composition of Functions

Given two function $f : X \to Y$ and $g : Y \to Z$, then $g \lozenge f$ is called composite function, where, $g \lozenge f = g(f(x)) = \{(x, z)/x \in X$ and $z \in Z$ and $(y = f(x)$ and $z = g(y))$ for any $y \in Y\}$.

Therefore, the necessary condition for $g \lozenge f$ is, img $(f) \subseteq$ arg (g), Otherwise $g \lozenge f = \varnothing$. Conversely, $f \lozenge g$ may or may not exist. It exists if and only if img $(g) \subseteq$ arg (f).

Example 1.7. *Let $f : R \to R$; $f(x) = -x^2$ and $g : R_+ \to R_+$; $g(x) = \sqrt{x}$ where R is the set of real numbers and R_+ is the set of positive real numbers. Determine $f \lozenge g$ and $g \lozenge f$.*

Sol. We have mapping $f = \begin{pmatrix} \ldots\ldots -2, -1, 0, 1, 2, \ldots \\ \ldots\ldots -4, -1, 0, 1, 4, \ldots \end{pmatrix}$ and $g = \begin{pmatrix} 0, 1, 2, \ldots\ldots \\ \sqrt{0}, \sqrt{1}, \sqrt{2}\ , \ldots\ldots \end{pmatrix}$

To determine $f \lozenge g$ we must have img $(g) \subseteq$ arg (f), because $R_+ \subseteq R$.

Since, $\quad f \lozenge g = f(g(x)) = f(\sqrt{x}) = -(\sqrt{x})^2 = -x.$

Therefore, $\quad f \lozenge g = \{(x, -x)/x \in R\}$;

Similarly to determine $g \lozenge f$; since img $(f) \not\subseteq$ arg (f) because img $(f) \in R$ and arg $(g) \in R_+$ so $R \not\subseteq R_+$. Hence, $g \lozenge f$ does not exist.

Example 1.8. *Let a function $f : R \to R$, where $f(x) = x^3 - 2$ and R is the set of real numbers, find f^{-1}. Also show that $f \lozenge f^{-1} = I$.*

Sol. Given mapping is represented by the expression, i.e.

$$f = \begin{pmatrix} \ldots x \ldots \\ \ldots x^3 - 2 \ldots \end{pmatrix}_{x \in R} \quad \Rightarrow \quad f = \begin{pmatrix} \ldots -2, -1, 0, 1, 2 \ldots \\ \ldots -10, -3, -2, -1, 6 \ldots \end{pmatrix}$$

Since $f : R \to R$ is surjective, so f^{-1} exists, i.e.

$$f^{-1} : R \to R$$

Since, $f(x) = x^3 - 2 = y$ (assume); then $f^{-1}(y) = x$.

$\Rightarrow \quad x = (y + 2)1/3$

$\Rightarrow \quad y = (x + 2)1/3 \quad$ [replace x and y]

Therefore, inverse of $f(x)$ is $(x + 2)1/3$.

Let $(x + 2)1/3 = g(x)$,

So, $\quad f \lozenge f^{-1} = f \lozenge g = f(g(x))$

$= f((x + 2)1/3)$

$= ((x + 2)1/3)^3 - 2$;

$= (x + 2) - 2;$

$= x$

Therefore, $f \lozenge f^{-1} = \{(x, x)/x \in R\}$ is an identity or function.

1.5.3 Inverse Functions

If the function $f : X \rightarrow Y$ is surjective, then we can define ***inverse function*** f^{-1}, *i.e.*,

$f^{-1}: Y \rightarrow X$;

where, $f^{-1}(y) = x \Leftrightarrow f(x) = y$, for any $x \in X$ and $y \in Y$. The composite of function f and f^{-1} is an identity function, *i.e.*,

$$f \lozenge f^{-1} = I \text{ (Identity function)} = f^{-1} \lozenge f$$

Reader must note that a function $f : X \rightarrow X$ is called Identity function if,

$f = \{(x, x) / x \in X\}$

such that, $I \lozenge f = f \lozenge I = f.$

Let $f : X \rightarrow Y$ and $g : Y \rightarrow X$ are two functions then function g is equal to f^{-1} only if

$g \lozenge f = I = f \lozenge g$

Example 1.9. Show that the function $f(x) = x^{-2}$ and $g(x) = x^2$ for real x are inverse of one other.

Sol. Since,

$f \lozenge g = f(g(x)) = f(x^2) = x = I$

and $g \lozenge f = g(f(x)) = g(x^{-2}) = x = I$

hence, $f = g^{-1}$ or $g = f^{-1}$.

1.5.4 Recursively Defined Functions

Consider the function which refers a function in terms of itself. For example, the factorial function $f(n) = n!$, for n as integer, is defined as,

$$f(n) = \begin{cases} 1 & \text{for } n \le 1 \\ n \,.\, f(n-1) & \text{for } n > 1 \end{cases}$$

Above definition states that f(n) equals to 1 whenever n is less than or equal to 1. However, when n is more than 1, function $f(n)$ is defined *recursively* (function invokes itself). In loose sense the use of f on right side of equation result a circular definition for example, $f(2) = 2. f(1) = 2.1 = 2$ and $f(3) = 3.f(2) = 3*2 = 6$.

Take another example of Fibonacci number series, which is defined as,

$$f_0 = 0 ; \quad f_1 = 1 ; \quad f_n = f_{n-1} + f_{n-2} \text{ for } n > 1$$

To compute the Fibonacci numbers series, f_0 and f_1 are the base component so that computation can be initiated. $f_n = f_{n-1} + f_{n-2}$ is the recursive component that viewed as recursive equations. In the previous function definition the base component is $f(n) = 1$ for $n = 1$ and recursive component is $f(n) = n \,.\, f(n - 1)$ while for the second function, base components are $f_0 = 0$, $f_1 = 1$ and recursive component is $f_n = f_{n-1} + f_{n-2}$ for $n > 1$.

Recursive defined functions arise very naturally to express the resources used by recursive procedures. A *recurrence relation* defines a function over the natural number, say $f(n)$ in terms of its own value at one /more integers smaller than n. In others words, $f(n)$ defines inductively. As with all inductions, there are base cases to be defined separately, and the recurrence relation only applies for n larger than the base cases. *To study more about recursive functions see chapter 3 section 3.5.*

1.6 MATHEMATICAL INDUCTION AND PIANO'S AXIOMS

Induction is the mechanism for proving a statement about an infinite set of objects. In many cases induction is done over set of natural numbers *i.e.*, N = {0, 1, 2, 3.......}. However induction method is equally valid over more general sets which have following properties,

- The set is partial ordered, which means an ordered relationship is defined between some pairs of elements of the set, and
- The set contains no infinite chain of decreasing elements.

Using the principal of mathematical induction we can prove a collection of statements which can be put in one–to–one correspondence with the set of natural numbers. So in this section we shall examine the set of natural numbers and study the important properties or axioms of the set of natural numbers which leads us to formulate the principle of mathematical induction.

Let Ø the empty set. The set of natural numbers N can be generated by the starting with the empty set Ø and its successor sets Ø∪{Ø}, Ø∪{Ø}∪{Ø∪{Ø}}, Ø∪{Ø}∪{Ø∪{Ø}} ∪{Ø∪{Ø}∪{Ø∪{Ø}}}, ...These sets can be simplified to Ø, {Ø}, {Ø, {Ø}}, {Ø, {Ø}, {Ø, {Ø}}}, ...If the set Ø be rename as 0 then {Ø} = 1, {Ø, {Ø}} = {0, 1}= 2, and {Ø, {Ø}, {Ø, {Ø}}} = {0, 1, 2} = 3, ...so we obtain the set {0, 1, 2, 3, ...} where each element is the successor set of the previous element except for the element 0 which is assumed to be present in the set. Thus we conclude that the set of natural numbers N can be obtained from the following axioms,

- $0 \in N$
- If $n \in N$, then its successor, *i.e.* $n \cup \{n\} \in N$.
- If a subset $X \subseteq N$ follows the properties

  (i) $0 \in X$, and

  (ii) if $n \in X$, then $n \cup \{n\} \in X$

then, X = N.

These axioms are known as ***Peano axioms***.

Last property of the Peano axioms provides the basis of the principle of mathematical induction. This axiom can be expressed in an easy computational form as,

Assume n is the induction variable. Let P(n) be any proposition defined for all $n \in N$ and (*i*) If P(0) is true, (*ii*) If P(k) ⇒ P(k+1) or, its successor for any $k \in N$, then P(n) holds for all $n \in N$.

For example let proposition P(n) be defined as

$$\sum_{i=1}^{n} i(i+1)/2 = n(n+1)(n+2)/6$$

Now show that P(n) is true for every $n \geq 0$.

Basic Step

The proof is by induction on n, the upper limit of the sum. **The base case is** $n = 0$. We must show that P(0) is true. Proposition P(0) is 0 = 0(0 + 1) (0 + 2) /6, which is obviously true.

Induction Hypothesis

For *n* greater then 0, assume that

$$\sum_{i=1}^{k} i(i+1)/2 = k(k+1)(k+2)/6$$

holds for all $k \geq 0$ such that $k < n$.

(Induction Hypothesis with $k = n - 1$)

$$\sum_{i=1}^{n-1} i(i+1)/2 = (n-1)\,n(n+1)/6$$

Since, $$\sum_{i=1}^{n} i(i+1)/2 = \sum_{i=1}^{n-1} i(i+1)/2 + (n+1)/2$$

Therefore $$\sum_{i=1}^{n} i(i+1)/2 = (n-1)n(n+1)/6 + n(n+1)/2$$

$$= n(n+1)(n+2)/6. \quad \textbf{Proved}$$

Example 1.10. Show that for any $n \geq 4$, $n! > 2^n$.

Sol. Let P(n) is $n! > 2^n$. For $0 \leq n < 4$, P(n) is not true. For $n = 4$, P(4) is $4! < 2^4$ (*i.e.*, $24 < 16$) so it is true. Assume that P(k) is true for any $k > 4$, *i.e.*,

$$k! > 2^k$$

or, $$2 * k! > 2 * 2^k$$

since, $(k + 1) > 2$ for any $k > 4$, hence

$$(k+1) * k! > 2 * k! > 2 * 2^k$$

$$\Rightarrow \quad (k+1)! > 2^{k+1}$$

Therefore, P(k + 1) is true. Hence P(n) is true for any $n \geq 4$.

Example 1.11. Show that for every $n \geq 0$, $x^{n-1} - 1$ is divisible by $x - 1$.

Sol. Let P(n) is $x^{n-1} - 1$. We begin by checking that P(n) is true for the starting values of n, *i.e.*, for n = 0, $x^{0-1} - 1 = x^{-1} - 1 = -(x-1)/x$ which is divisible by $(x - 1)$. For n = 1, $x^{1-1} - 1 = 0$, and 0 is divisible by $(x - 1)$. Assume that P(k) is true for any $k \geq 0$, *i.e.*, $x^{k-1} - 1$ is divisible by $(x - 1)$.

Since by division,

$$(x^k - 1)/(x - 1) = x^{k-1} + (x^{k-1} - 1)/(x - 1)$$

if $(x^{k-1} - 1)$ is divisible by $(x - 1)$, then $(x^k - 1)$ is also divisible by $(x - 1)$. Therefore P(+ 1) is true. Hence P(n) is true for all $n \geq 0$.

Example 1.12. Prove that for any $n \geq 1$,

$$\sum_{i=1}^{n} i * 2^i = (n-1) * 2^{n+1} + 2$$

Sol. Let P(n): $$\sum_{i=1}^{n} i * 2^i = (n-1) * 2^{n+1} + 2$$

Here the base case is $n = 1$. For this case both sides of the equation return value 2. For n greater than 1, assume that

$$\sum_{i=1}^{k} i*2^i = (k-1)*2^{k+1} + 2$$

true for all $k \geq 1$ such that $k < n$.

Induction hypothesis with $k = n - 1$

$$\sum_{i=1}^{n-1} i*2^i = (n-2)*2^n + 2$$

Since,
$$\sum_{i=1}^{n} i*2^i = \sum_{i=1}^{n-1} i*2^i + n*2^n$$

Thus,
$$\sum_{i=1}^{n} i*2^i = \{(n-2)*2^n + 2\} + n*2^n$$

$$= (n-2+n)*2^n + 2 = (n-1)*2^{n+1} + 2.$$ **Proved.**

Example 1.13. Show that for any $n \geq 0$,

$$\sum_{i=1}^{n} 1/i(i+1) = n/(n+1)$$

Sol. Let P(n):
$$\sum_{i=1}^{n} 1/i(i+1) = n/(n+1)$$

For $n = 0$, P(0) is true. For n greater than 0, assume that

$$\sum_{i=1}^{k} 1/i(i+1) = k/(k+1)$$

holds for all $k \geq 0$ such that $k < n$.

For $k = n - 1$,

$$\sum_{i=1}^{n-1} 1/i(i+1) = (n-1)/n$$

Since,
$$\sum_{i=1}^{n} 1/i(i+1) = \sum_{i=1}^{n-1} 1/i(i+1) + 1/n(n+1)$$

$$\sum_{i=1}^{n} 1/i(i+1) = (n-1)/n + 1/n(n+1)$$

$$= (n^2 - 1 + 1)/n(n+1) = n/(n+1).$$ **Proved.**

EXERCISES

1.1 For the set X = {1, 2, 3, ∅}construct the following :

(*i*) X ∪ P(X) (*ii*) X ∩ P(X)

(*iii*) X – ∅ (*iv*) X – {∅}

(*v*) Is ∅ ∈ P(X) ?

(where P(X) is the power set of X)

1.2 Define the finite set and infinite set; countable set and uncountable set. State which set is finite or infinite, countable or uncountable?

(*i*) {.........2BC, 1BC, 1AD, 2AD, ...2004AD, ...}

(*ii*) {0, 1, 2, 3, ...}

(*iii*) {x/x is positive integer}

(*iv*) {$x/x \in \{a, b, c, ... y, z\}$}

(*v*) The set of living beings on the universe.

(*vi*) The set of lines passes through the origin.

(*vii*) $X = \{x/x^2 + 1 = 0\}$

(*viii*) $X = \{1/2, 3, 5, \sqrt{2}, 7, 9\}$.

1.3 Does every set have a proper subset?

1.4 Prove that if A is the subset of ∅ then A = ∅.

1.5 Find the power set of the set $X = \{a, \{a, b\}, \{\varnothing\}\}$.

1.6 Prove if $X \cap Y = \varnothing$ then $X \subset Y'$.

1.7 Consider the universal set U = {x/x is a integer}, and the set X = {x/x is a positive integer}, Z = {x/x is a even integer}, and Y = {x / x is a negative odd integer}, then find,

(*i*) $X \cup Y$ (*ii*) $X' \cup Y$

(*iii*) $X - Y$ (*iv*) $Z - Y'$

(*v*) $(X \cap Y) - Z'$

1.8 Define a binary relation. When a relation is said to be reflexive, symmetric, and transitive.

1.9 Distinguish between a relation and a mapping.

1.10 Let a relation $R = \{(x, y)/x, y$? R and $4x^2 + 9y^2 = 36\}$ then find the domain of R, the range of R, and the R^{-1}.

1.11 State the condition when a relation R in a set X

(*i*) not reflexive (*ii*) not symmetric

(*iii*) not antisymmetric (*iv*) not transitive.

1.12 Let R_1 and R_2 are two relations then in a set X then prove the following :

(*i*) If $R_1$and R_2 is symmetric then $R_1 \cup R_2$ is also symmetric.

(*ii*) If R_1 is reflexive then $R_1 \cap R_2$ is also reflexive.

1.13 Let a relation $R = \{(x, y)/x, y \in N$ and $(x - y)$ is divisible by 3}then Show that R is an equivalence relation.

1.14 Comment on the relation R i.e., if $R \cap R^{-1} = \varnothing$ and if $R = R^{-1}$.

1.15 Let X be the set of people and R be the relation defined between the element of the set X, i.e.

(*i*) $R = \{(x, y)/x, y \in X$ and 'x is the husband of y'}

(*ii*) $R = \{(x, y)/x, y \in R$ and 'x is poorer than y'}

(*iii*) $R = \{(x, y)/x, y \in R$ and 'x is younger than y'}

(*iv*) $R = \{(x, y)/x, y \in R$ and 'x is thirsty than y'}

Find the inverse of each of the relation.

1.16 If X = {1, 2}, Y = {a, b, c} and Z = {c, d}. Find $(A \times B) \cap (A \times C)$.

1.17 Which of the following graphs represents injective, surjective, and bijective function ?

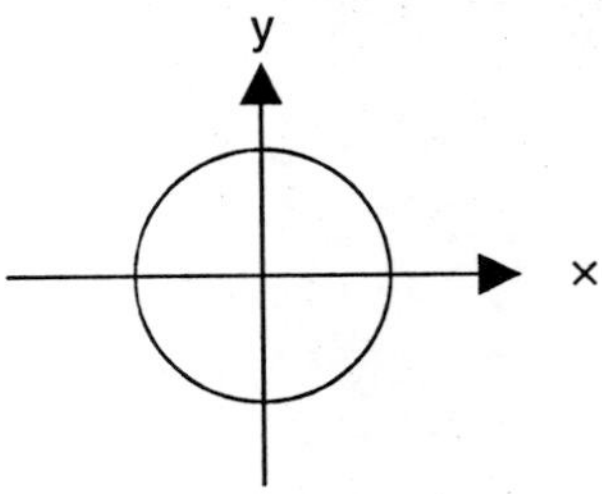

(i) Circle

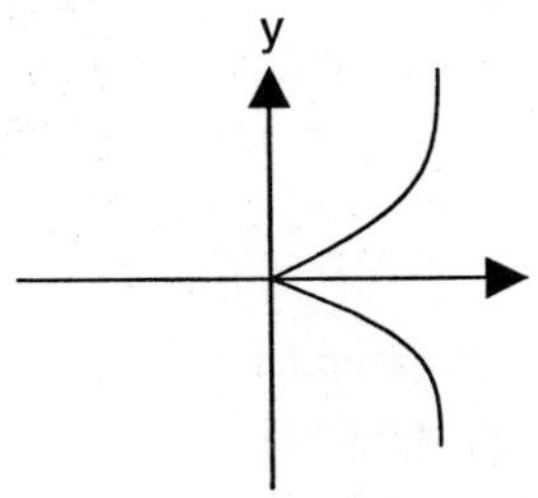

(ii) Cissoid

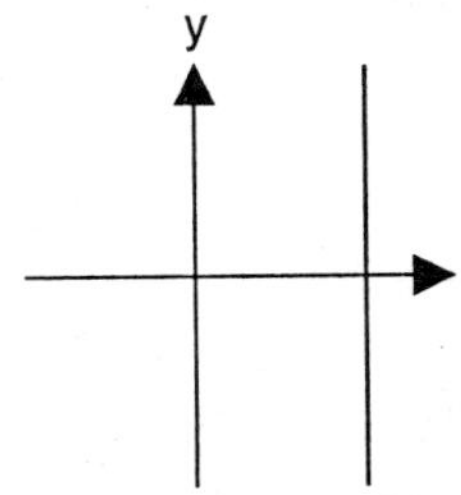

(iii) Straight line

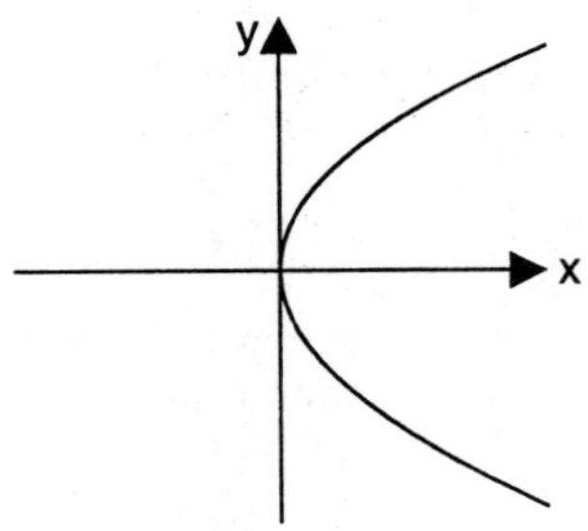

(iv) Parabola

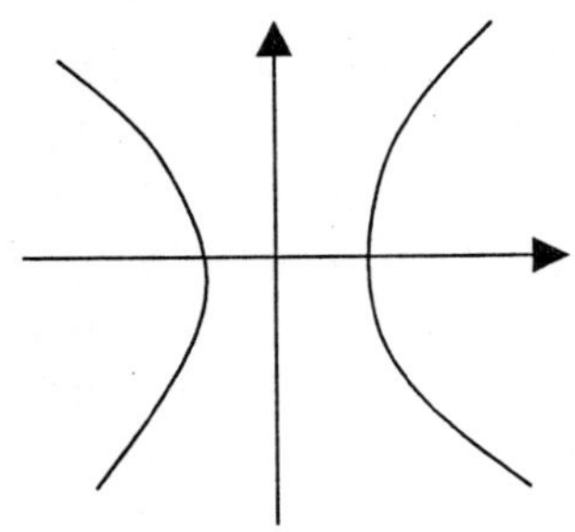

(v) Hyperbola

1.18 Let a function $f : R \to R$ be defined i.e., $f(x) = 1$ if x is rational and $f(x) = -1$ if x is irrational then find

(*i*) $f(2)$ (*ii*) $f(1/2)$

(*iii*) $f(1/3)$ (*iv*) $f(22/7)$

(*v*) $f(\sqrt{2})$ (*vi*) $f(\sqrt[4]{8})$

1.19 Let a function $f : R \to R$ be defined as

$$f(x) = \begin{cases} 1 - 2x^2 & \text{for } -2 \le x \le 4 \\ x^2 + 4 & \text{for } 5 \le x \le 7 \\ x - 3 & \text{for } 8 \le x < 12 \end{cases}$$

Find :

(*i*) $f(-3)$ (*ii*) $f(4)$

(*iii*) $f(7)$ (*iv*) $f(12)$

(*v*) $f(u - 2)$

1.20 Let f be a function such that f^{-1} exist then state properties of the function f.

1.21 Let a function $f : R \to R$ be defined as $f(x) = x^2$, then find

(*i*) $f^{-1}(-4)$ (*ii*) $f^{-1}(25)$

(*iii*) $f^{-1}(4 \le x \le 25)$ (*iv*) $f^{-1}(-\infty < x \le 0)$

1.22 Find the f^{-1} if function $f(x) = (4x^2 - 9)/(2x + 3)$ (by assuming f is surjective).

1.23 Let function f and g are surjective then show that

$$(g \circ f)^{-1} = (f^{-1} \circ g^{-1})$$

1.24 Find x and y in the following ordered pair :

(*i*) $(x + 3, y - 4) = (3, 5)$ (*ii*) $(x^{-2}, y + 3) = (y + 4, 2x - 1)$

1.25 Let X = {1, 2, 3, 4} and Y = {a, b, c}, can a injective and surjective function $f : X \to Y$ may be defined. Give reasons.

1.26 Prove that the sum of cubes of the first n natural numbers is equal to $\left\{\frac{n(n+1)}{2}\right\}^2$.

1.27 Prove that for every $n \geq 0$, $1 + \sum_{i=1}^{n} i * i! = (n+1)!$

1.28 Prove that for every $n \geq 2$ $1 + \sum_{i=1}^{n} \frac{1}{\sqrt{i}} > \sqrt{x}$

1.29 Prove by mathematical Induction for every $n \geq 0$,

$$2 + 2^2 + 2^3 + \ldots + 2^n = 2(2^n - 1)$$

1.30 Show that $n^3 + 2n$ is divisible by 3 for every $n \geq 0$.

1.31 Prove by Induction that for every $n \geq 1$, the number of subsets of $\{1, 2, \ldots, n\}$ is 2^n.

Discrete Numeric Functions And Generating Functions

2 Discrete Numeric Functions and Generating Functions

2.1 INTRODUCTION

In Chapter 1 we have studied that function is a process of transformation of objects from one form to other. Thus, function is binary relation from set of objects called *domain* to set of objects called *range* and from the domain set each object has a unique value in the range set. Present chapter discuss special purpose functions called numeric functions that are common in computation theory and digital systems. In this context numeric functions over discrete set of objects are of greater concern.

Discrete Numeric function is defined from set of natural numbers to set of real numbers. So, if f is a discrete numeric function then

$$f : \{\text{set of natural no.}\} \rightarrow \{\text{set of real no.}\}$$

Here domain set consists of natural numbers and range set consists of real number. Discrete numeric function can also be represented as,

$$f_n = f(n) \qquad \text{for } n = 0, 1, 2, \ldots\ldots$$

where n is the natural number and function f_n returns value $f(n)$ that is an expression of n.

For example, if A_n will be amount on initial deposit of Rs 100 after n years at interest rate of 5% per annum then

$$A_n = 100\,(1 + 5/100)^n \qquad \text{[using simple compound interest formula]}$$

or $$A_n = 100\,(1.05)^n \qquad [\text{ for } n = 0]$$

Now Fig. 2.1 shows the output returned for various values of n (0, 1, 2, ...).

n	0	1	2	3	4	5	......
A_n	100	105	110.25	115.76	121.55	127.63	......

Fig. 2.1

Consider another example, as we experience that due to policy decisions of the government interest rates are fluctuating. Suppose a person credited Rs 1000 on rate of interest per annum 15 %. After couple of years interest rate lifted to 18 % per annum and after 5 years interest rate down to 10 %. Then the amount in the account appeared after each changing year will be A_n, *i.e.*,

$$A_n = 1000\,(1 + 15/100)^n = 1000\,(1.15)^n \qquad \text{for} \quad 0 \le n \le 2$$

Since $1000(1.15)^2$ = Rs 1322.5, therefore

$$A_n = 1322.5 + 1322.5\,(1 + 18/100)^n \qquad \text{for} \quad 2 \le n \le 8$$

Since $1322.5 + 1322.5\ (1 + 18/100)5 = 1322.5 + 1322.5\ (1.18)5 = \text{Rs } 4348.06$

Therefore, $A_n = 4348.06 + 4348.06\ (1 + 10/100)^n$ for $8 \le n$

Below in this section we will see couple of examples that concisely represent the numeric functions. In general we use convention small letters to represent the numeric functions.

Example 2.1.

- $a_n = 3n^2 + 1$ for $n \ge 0$

  (A simple expression of numeric function for every n is defined)

- $b_n = \begin{cases} 5n & \text{for } 0 \le n \le 3 \\ 0 & \text{for } n \ge 4 \end{cases}$

  (Here two different numeric expressions are defined for different domain sets)

- $c_n = \begin{cases} n-3 & \text{for } 0 \le n \le 7 \\ n+3 & \text{for } n \ge 8 \text{ and } n \,\%\, 8 = 0 \\ n/3 & \text{for } n > 7 \text{ and } n \,\%\, 8 \ne 0 \end{cases}$

  (Here different numeric expressions are defined for different domain sets)

Example 2.2. *Consider an example of airplane, lets h_n be the altitude of the plane (in thousand of feet) at nth minute. The plane land off after 10 minutes on the ground and ascend to an altitude 10000 feet in 10 minutes at a uniform speed. Plane starts to descend uniformly after one hour of flying and after 10 minutes it lands. Thus we have different numeric functions that measure the altitude for different slices of the plane journey.*

Sol.

$$h_n = \begin{cases} 0 & \text{for } 0 \le n \le 10 & \text{[upto 10 minutes plane remain on ground]} \\ n - 10 & \text{for } 11 \le n \le 20 & \text{[Plane ascend uniformly at 1000 feet per minute so altitude is proportional to time or } (n-10)\text{]} \\ 10 & \text{for } 21 \le n \le 80 & \text{[next 1 hour plane will remain on altitude 10]} \\ 90 - n & \text{for } 81 \le n \le 90 & \text{[next 10 minutes plane returns to ground with uniform speed, after first minute of time plane will be at height 9000 feet and so on...]} \\ 0 & \text{for } n > 90 & \text{[Plane remain in ground so no altitude]} \end{cases}$$

2.2 PROPERTIES OF NUMERIC FUNCTIONS

In this section we shall discuss the behavior of numeric functions over unary and binary operations.

2.2.1 Let a_n and b_n are two numeric functions then its addition $(a_n + b_n)$ given by c_n is also a numeric function. The value of c_n at n will be the addition of values of numeric functions a_n and b_n at n. **(Addition property of numeric functions)**

For example, $a_n = \begin{cases} 0 & \text{for } 0 \le n \le 2 \\ 2^n & \text{for } n \ge 3 \end{cases}$ and $b_n = 2^n$ for $n \ge 0$

then $$c_n = a_n + b_n = \begin{cases} 0 + 2^n = 2^n & \text{for } 0 \le n \le 2 \\ 2^n + 2^n = 2^{n+1} & \text{for } n \ge 3 \end{cases}$$

Example 2.3. *Add the numeric functions*

$$a_n = \begin{cases} 0 & \text{for } 0 \le n \le 5 \\ 3^{-n} + 2 & \text{for } n \ge 6 \end{cases} \quad \text{and} \quad b_n = \begin{cases} 1 - 3^n & \text{for } 0 \le n \le 2 \\ n + 5 & \text{for } n \ge 3 \end{cases}$$

Sol. Let $a_n + b_n = c_n$, then c_n will be given as,

$$c_n = \begin{cases} 0 + 1 - 3^n = 1 - 3^n & \text{for } 0 \le n \le 2 \\ 0 + n + 5 = n + 5 & \text{for } 3 \le n \le 5 \\ 3^{-n} + 2 + n + 5 = 3^{-n} + n + 7 & \text{for } n \ge 6 \end{cases}$$

Example 2.4. *Add the numeric functions*

$$a_n = \begin{cases} 0 & \text{for } 0 \le n \le 2 \\ 2^{-n} + 5 & \text{for } n \ge 3 \end{cases} \quad \text{and} \quad b_n = \begin{cases} 3 - 2^n & \text{for } 0 \le n \le 1 \\ n + 2 & \text{for } n \ge 2 \end{cases}$$

Sol. Let $a_n + b_n = c_n$, then c_n will be given as,

$$c_n = \begin{cases} 0 + 3 - 2^n = 3 - 2^n & \text{for } 0 \le n \le 1 \\ 0 + (2 + 2) = 4 & \text{for } n = 2 \\ 2^{-n} + 5 + n + 2 = 2^{-n} + n + 7 & \text{for } n \ge 3 \end{cases}$$

Addition property of numeric function can also be applied between two/ more numeric functions. Lets we have numeric functions $a_1, a_2, \ldots\ldots a_n$ then their addition $a_1 + a_2 + \ldots\ldots + a_n$ will also a numeric function whose value at n is equal to the sum of values of all the numeric functions at n. For example,

$$a_n = \begin{cases} 1 & \text{for } n = 0 \\ 2 & \text{for } n = 1 \\ 0 & \text{for } n \ge 2 \end{cases}$$

$$b_n = \begin{cases} 0 & \text{for } 0 \le n \le 2 \\ 2^n & \text{for } n \ge 3 \end{cases} \quad \text{and} \quad c_n = \begin{cases} 1 & \text{for } n = 0 \\ 0 & \text{for } n \ge 1 \end{cases}$$

then
$$a_n + b_n + c_n = \begin{cases} 1 + 0 + 1 = 2 & \text{for } n = 0 \\ 2 + 0 + 0 = 2 & \text{for } n = 1 \\ 0 + 0 + 0 = 0 & \text{for } n = 2 \\ 0 + 2^n + 0 = 2^n & \text{for } n \ge 3 \end{cases}$$

2.2.2 Similar to additions of numeric functions, ***multiplication of numeric functions*** also returns a numeric function. Let a_n and b_n are two numeric functions then its multiplication $(a_n * b_n)$ will be a numeric function and its value at n will be the multiplication of values of numeric functions at n. (*Multiplication property of numeric functions*).

For example, the numeric functions

$$a_n = \begin{cases} 0 & \text{for } 0 \le n \le 2 \\ 2^n & \text{for } n \ge 3 \end{cases} \quad \text{and} \quad b_n = 2^n \quad \text{for } n \ge 0$$

then
$$a_n * b_n = \begin{cases} 0 * 2^n = 0 & \text{for } 0 \le n \le 2 \\ 2^n * 2^n = 2^{n+1} & \text{for } n \ge 3 \end{cases}$$

Example 2.5. *The multiplication of numeric functions given in example 3.4, will be*

$$a_n * b_n = \begin{cases} 0 * (3 - 2^n) = 0 & \text{for } 0 \le n \le 1 \\ 0 * (n + 2) = 0 & \text{for } n = 2 \\ (2^{-n} + 5) * (n + 2) & \text{for } n \ge 3 \end{cases}$$

Example 2.6. *Let a_n be a numeric function such that a_n is equal to the reminder when integer is divided by 17. Assume b be other numeric function such that b_n is equal to 0 if integer n is divisible by 3, and equal to 1 otherwise.*

(i) Let $c_n = a_n + b_n$, then for what values of n, $c_n = 0$ and $c_n = 1$.

(ii) Let $d_n = a_n * b_n$, then for what values of n, $d_n = 0$ and $d_n = 1$.

Sol. Construct the numeric functions for a and b,

Here,
$$a_n = \begin{cases} 0 & \text{for } n = 0, 17, 34, \ \ldots\ldots \ = 17k \\ 1 & \text{for } n = 18, 35, \ \ldots\ldots \ = 17k+1 \\ 2 & \text{for } n = 19, 36, \ \ldots\ldots \ = 17k+2 \\ .. & \ldots \quad \ldots \quad \ldots\ldots \quad \ldots \\ .. & \ldots \quad \ldots \quad \ldots\ldots \quad \ldots \\ 16 & \text{for } n = 33, 50, \ \ldots\ldots \ = 17k+16 \end{cases}$$
(for k = 0, 1, 2, ...)

and
$$b_n = \begin{cases} 0 & \text{for } n = 0, 3, 6, \ldots\ldots = 3k \\ 1 & \text{otherwise} \end{cases}$$

(*i*) Since $c_n = a_n + b_n$, then $c_n = 0$ only when both a_n and b_n equal to zero, at $n = 0$.

To determine other coincident points we observe that when a_n is also divisible by 3, $c_n = 0$,

i.e., $n = 17\,k * 3 = 51\,k$ (for k = 0, 1, 2, ...)

Therefore, for n = 0, 51, 102, ...; $c_n = 0$.

Likewise $c_n = 1$, if $a_n = 0$ and $b_n = 1$, or $a_n = 1$ and $b_n = 0$.

$a_n = 0$ for $n = 17\,k$ and $b_n = 1$ for n is not a multiple of 3. Therefore, $c_n = 1$ when n is divisible by 17 and not a multiple of 3.

Otherwise, $a_n = 1$ for $n = 17k + 1$ and $b_n = 0$ for n is a multiple of 3. Therefore, $c_n = 1$ when $n = 17k + 1$ and multiple of 3.

(*ii*) Since, $d_n = a_n * b_n$, and $d_n = 0$ on following conditions,

- $a_n = 0$ and $b_n = 0$, when $n = 51\,k$
- $a_n = 0$ and $b_n \neq 0$, when $n = 17\,k$ and not a multiple of 3
- $a_n \neq 0$ and $b_n = 0$, when n is not a multiple of 17 and 3

2.2.3 ***Multiplication with a scalar factor*** to numeric function returns a numeric function. For example, let a_n be a numeric function and m be any scalar (real number), then $m.a_n$ will be a numeric function whose value at n is equal to m times a_n.

For example, if numeric function $a_n = 2^n + 3$ for $n \geq 0$, then $5.a_n = 5.(2^n + 3)$ or $5.2^n + 15$ for $n \geq 0$ is a numeric function.

2.2.4 Let a_n and b_n are two numeric functions then the ***quotient*** of a_n and b_n is denoted by a_n/b_n is also a numeric function, and its value at n is equal to the quotient of a_n/b_n.

2.2.5 Let a_n be a numeric function then ***modulus*** of a_n is denoted by $|a_n|$, and defined as,

$$|a_n| = \begin{cases} -a_n & \text{if } n < 0 \\ a_n & \text{otherwise} \end{cases}$$

For example, let $a_n = (-1)^n\,(3/n^2)$ for $n \geq 0$, then

$$|a_n| = (3/n^2) \text{ for } n \geq 0$$

2.2.6 Let a_n be a numeric function and I is any integer positive, then $\mathbf{S^I\,a_n}$ is a numeric function and defined as,

$$\mathrm{S^I}\,a_n = \begin{cases} 0 & \text{for } 0 \leq n \leq \mathrm{I}-1 \\ a_{n-1} & \text{for } n \geq \mathrm{I} \end{cases}$$

Similarly we define numeric function $\mathbf{S^{-I}\, a_n}$, *i.e.*,

$$S^{-I}\, a_n = a_n + I \qquad \text{for } n \geq 0$$

For example, let $a_n = \begin{cases} 1 & \text{for } 0 \leq n \leq 10 \\ 2 & \text{for } n \geq 11 \end{cases}$

Then, $S^5\, a_n = \begin{cases} 0 & \text{for } 0 \leq n \leq 5-1(=4) \\ a_{n-5} & \text{for } n \geq 5 \end{cases}$

Now determine a_{n-5}, for $n \geq 5$, so there exists two cases,

- Since $a_n = 1$ (independent of n) for $0 \leq n \leq 10$, now replace n by $n - 5$, therefore $a_{n-5} = 1$ for $0 \leq n - 5 \leq 10$ or $5 \leq n \leq 15$.
- Similarly, $a_{n-5} = 2$ for $n - 5 \geq 11$ or $n \geq 16$.

Hence, $S^5\, a_n = \begin{cases} 0 & \text{for } 0 \leq n \leq 4 \\ 1 & \text{for } 5 \leq n \leq 15 \\ 2 & \text{for } n \geq 16 \end{cases}$

and $S^{-5}\, a_n = a_{n+5}$ for $n \geq 0$

To determine a_{n+5}, for $n \geq 0$, we obtain

$$S^{-5}\, a_n = a_{n+5} = \begin{cases} 1 & \text{for } 0 \leq n+5 \leq 10 \text{ or } 0 \leq n \leq 5 \,(\text{since } n \geq 0) \\ 2 & \text{for } n+5 \geq 11 \text{ or } n \geq 6 \end{cases}$$

Example 2.7. *Let a_n be a numeric function such that*

$$a_n = \begin{cases} 2 & \text{for } 0 \leq n \leq 3 \\ 2^{-n} + 5 & \text{for } n \geq 4 \end{cases}$$

Find $S^2\, a_n$ and $S^{-2}\, a_n$.

Sol. Using definition $S^2\, a_n$, we have

$$S^2\, a_n = \begin{cases} 0 & \text{for } 0 \leq n \leq 1 (= 2-1) \\ a_{n-2} & \text{for } n \geq 2 \end{cases}$$

Now to determine numeric function a_{n-2}, for $n \geq 2$ we have,

- For $2 \leq n \leq 3$, $a_n = 2$ (independent of n) therefore $a_{n-2} = 2$ for $2 \leq n - 2 \leq 3$ or $4 \leq n \leq 5$.
- For $n \geq 4$, $a_n = 2^{-n} + 5$, so $a_{n-2} = 2^{-(n-2)} + 5$ for $n - 2 \geq 4$ or $n \geq 6$.

Therefore,

$$S^2\, a_n = \begin{cases} 0 & \text{for } 0 \leq n \leq 1 \\ 2 & \text{for } n = 2 \\ 2 & \text{for } n = 3 \\ 2 & \text{for } 4 \leq n \leq 5 \\ 2^{-(n-2)} + 5 & \text{for } n \geq 6 \end{cases}$$

From the definition of $S^{-2}\, a_n$, we have

$$S^{-2}\, a_n = a_{n+2} \quad \text{for } n \geq 0$$

To determine the numeric function a_{n+2}, for $n \geq 0$ we have,

- Since $a_n = 2$, for $0 \leq n \leq 3$, therefore $a_{n+2} = 2$, for $0 \leq n + 2 \leq 3$ or $0 \leq n \leq 1$
- For $n \geq 4$, $a_n = 2^{-n} + 5$, therefore $a_{n+2} = 2^{-(n+2)} + 5$, for $n + 2 \geq 4$ or $n \geq 2$.

Hence, $S^{-2}\, a_n = \begin{cases} 2 & \text{for } 0 \leq n \leq 1 \\ 2^{-(n+2)} + 5 & \text{for } n \geq 2 \end{cases}$

Example 2.8. *Let a_n be a numeric function s.t.*

$$a_n = \begin{cases} 1 & \text{for } 0 \le n \le 50 \\ 3 & \text{for } n \ge 51 \end{cases}$$

Find $S^{-25} a_n$.

Sol. Using definition we have $S^{-25} a_n = a_{n+25}$ for $n \ge 0$. To determine the numeric function a_{n+25}, for $n \ge 0$, we have

- Since $a_n = 1$ for $0 \le n \le 50$, also $a_{n+25} = 1$ for $0 \le n + 25 \le 50$ or $0 \le n \le 25$.
- For $n \ge 51$, $a_n = 3$, also $a_{n+25} = 3$ for $n + 25 \ge 51$ or $n \ge 26$.

Therefore, $$S^{-25} a_n = \begin{cases} 1 & \text{for } 0 \le n \le 25 \\ 2 & \text{for } n \ge 26 \end{cases}$$

2.2.7. Let a_n be a numeric function then ***accumulated sum*** of a_n is defined by

$$\sum_k a_n \qquad \text{(for } k = 0 \text{ to } n\text{)}$$

is a numeric function. For example if a_n describes the monthly income of worker then its annual income is given by the accumulated sum (b_n) of a_n where,

$$b_n = \sum_{k=0}^{12} a_n$$

Example 2.9. *Let $a_n = P\,(1.11)^n$ for $n = 0$. Find accumulated sum of a_n for $n = m$.*

Sol. Let b_n be the accumulated sum of a_n, *i.e.*,

$$b_n = \sum_{k=0}^{m} a_n = \sum_{k=0}^{m} P(1.11)^k \quad \text{for} \quad m \ge 0$$

$$= P\,(1 + 1.11 + 1.11^2 + \ldots\ldots.. + 1.11^m)$$

$$= P\,(1.11^{m+1} - 1)/\,(1.11 - 1)$$

$$= 100\,P\,(1.11^{m+1} - 1)/11 \text{ for } m \ge 0$$

2.2.8 Let a_n be a numeric function then its ***forward difference*** is denoted by Δa_n, and defined as,

$$\Delta a_n = a_{n+1} - a_n \text{ for } n = 0$$

Likewise, ***backward difference*** is denoted by ∇a_n, and defined as,

$$\nabla a_n = \begin{cases} a_0 & \text{for } n = 0 \\ a_n - a_{n-1} & \text{for } n \ge 1 \end{cases}$$

For example, if an describes the annual income of a worker then,

- Δa_n will describe the change in income from nth year to $(n + 1)$th year, and
- ∇a_n will describe the change in income from nth year over $(n - 1)$th year.

Consider a numeric function a_n. i.e.

$$a_n = \begin{cases} 0 & \text{for } 0 \le n \le 7 \\ 1 & \text{for } n \ge 8 \end{cases}$$

then $\Delta a_n = a_{n+1} - a_n$ for $n \ge 0$

So determine a_{n+1} for $n \geq 0$,

- Since $a_n = 0$ for $0 \leq n \leq 7$, so $a_{n+1} = 0$ for $0 \leq n_{+1} \leq 7$ or $0 \leq n \leq 6$.
- Also $a_n = 1$ for $n \geq 8$, so $a_{n+1} = 1$ for $n + 1 = 8$ or $n \geq 7$.

Therefore,

$$\Delta a_n = \begin{cases} 0-0=0 & \text{for } 0 \leq n \leq 6 \\ 1-0=1 & \text{for } n=7 \\ 1-1=0 & \text{for } n \geq 8 \end{cases}$$

Now to determine ∇a_n, we first determine a_{n-1} for $n \geq 1$, since we have

- $a_n = 0$ for $0 \leq n \leq 7$, so $a_{n-1} = 0$ for $0 \leq (n-1) \leq 7$ or $1 \leq n \leq 8$, and
- $a_n = 1$ for $n \geq 8$, so $a_{n-1} = 1$ for $n - 1 \geq 8$ or $n \geq 9$

Thus, putting these values in the definition of ∇a_n we obtain,

$$\nabla a_n = \begin{cases} 0 & \text{for } 0 \leq n \leq 7 \\ 1 & \text{for } n=8 \\ 0 & \text{for } n \geq 9 \end{cases}$$

Example 2.10 *Let* $a_n = \begin{cases} 0 & \textit{for } 0 \leq n \leq 2 \\ 2^{-n} + 5 & \textit{for } n \geq 3 \end{cases}$

Determine Δa_n *and* ∇a_n.

Sol. Using definition of forward difference (Δa_n), we have

$$\Delta a_n = a_{n+1} - a_n \text{ for } n \geq 0$$

We determine Δa_{n+1} for $n \geq 0$, using

- $a_n = 0$ for $0 \leq n \leq 2$, so $a_{n+1} = 0$ for $0 \leq n + 1 \leq 2$ or $0 \leq n \leq 1$, and
- $a_n = 2^{-n} + 5$ for $n \geq 3$, so $a_{n+1} = 2^{-(n+1)} + 5$ for $n + 1 \geq 3$ or $n \geq 2$.

Therefore,

$$\Delta a_n = \begin{cases} 0-0=0 & \text{for } 0 \leq n \leq 1 \\ 2^{-3}+5-0=41/8 & \text{for } n=2 \\ 2^{-(n+1)}+5-2^{-n}-5=-2^{-(n+1)} & \text{for } n \geq 3 \end{cases}$$

Now From the definition of backward difference (∇a_n), we have

$$\nabla a_n = \begin{cases} a_0 & \text{for } n=0 \\ a_n - a_{n-1} & \text{for } n \geq 1 \end{cases}$$

So, find a_{n-1} for $n \geq 1$, from given an,

- $a_n = 0$ for $0 \leq n \leq 2$, so $a_{n-1} = 0$ also for $0 \leq n - 1 = 2$ or $1 \leq n \leq 3$, and
- $a_n = 2^{-n} + 5$ for $n \geq 3$, so $a_{n-1} = 2^{-(n-1)} + 5$ for $n - 1 \geq 3$ or $n \geq 4$.

Therefore,

$$\nabla a_n = \begin{cases} 0-0=0 & \text{for } 0 \leq n \leq 2 \\ 2^{-3}+5-0=41/8 & \text{for } n=3 \\ 2^{-n}+5-2^{-(n-1)}-5=-2^{-n} & \text{for } n \geq 4 \end{cases}$$

Example 2.11 *Show that* $S^{-1}(\nabla a_n) = \Delta a_n$.

Sol. *LHS*, since we know that $\nabla a_n = a_n - a_{n-1}$, for $n \geq 1$; and 0 for $n = 0$.

Thus,

$$S^{-1} (\nabla a_n) = S^{-1} (a_n - a_{n-1}) = S^{-1} a_n - S^{-1} a_{n-1} \text{ for } n \geq 1.$$

$\therefore$ $$S^{-1} a_n = a_{n+1} \text{ for } n \geq 1 \text{ and } S^{-1} a_{n-1} = a_{n-1+1} \text{ for } n \geq 1$$

Hence,

$$S^{-1} a_n - S^{-1} a_{n-1} = a_{n+1} - a_n \quad \text{for } n \geq 1 = \Delta a_n \ RHS$$

Example 2.12. *Let a numeric function a_n, i.e.,*

$$a_n = n^3 - 2n^2 + 3n + 2 \quad \text{for } n \geq 0$$

Then determine Δa_n, $\Delta^2 a_n$, $\Delta^3 a_n$, ..., $\Delta^n a_n$.

Sol. Remember the asked terms Δa_n, $\Delta^2 a_n$, $\Delta^3 a_n$, ..., $\Delta^n a_n$ are known as first order, second order, third order and so on the nth order forward difference.

Since, $\Delta a_n = a_{n+1} - a_n$, for $n \geq 0$, then we can determine a_{n+1} from a_n as,

$$a_n = n^3 - 2n^2 + 3n + 2 \quad \text{for } n \geq 0$$

so $$a_{n+1} = (n + 1)^3 - 2(n + 1)^2 + 3(n + 1) + 2 \quad \text{for } (n + 1) \geq 0 \text{ or } n \geq 0.$$

Therefore,

$$\Delta a_n = a_{n+1} - a_n = \{(n + 1)^3 - n^3\} - 2\{(n + 1)^2 - n^2\} + 3\{(n + 1) - n\}$$

$$\mathbf{\Delta a_n = 3n^2 - n + 2 \quad for\ n \geq 0}$$

Now find $\Delta^2 a_n = \Delta(\Delta a_n)$, let $\Delta a_n = b_n$.

So $$\Delta^2 a_n = \Delta(b_n) = b_{n+1} - b_n \quad \text{for } n \geq 0$$

Since, $b_n = 3n^2 - n + 2$, so $b_{n+1} = 3(n + 1)^2 - (n + 1) + 2$, for $n \geq 0$

Therefore, $\Delta(b_n) = b_{n+1} - b_n = 3(2n + 1) - 1 = 6n + 2$ for $n \geq 0$.

Hence, $\mathbf{\Delta^2 a_n = 6n + 2 \quad for\ n \geq 0}$

Further assume that $c_n = \Delta^2 a_n = 6n + 2$ so $c_{n+1} = 6(n + 1) + 2$ for $n \geq 0$.

Then

$$\Delta^3 a_n = \Delta(\Delta^2 a_n) = \Delta(c_n) = c_{n+1} - c_n = 6(n + 1) + 2 - 6n - 2$$

$$\mathbf{\Delta^3 a_n = 6\ for\ n \geq 0.}$$

Similarly we can determine $\mathbf{\Delta^i a_n = 0}$ **(where $\mathbf{i \geq 4}$) for $\mathbf{n \geq 0}$.**

Example 2.13. *Let a numeric function a_n be a polynomial of the form $\alpha_0 + \alpha_1 n + \alpha_2 n^2 + ... + \alpha_k n^k$. Show that $\Delta^{k+1} a_n = 0$.*

Sol. From the previous example we have seen that increase in the degree of the forward difference then the degree of the polynomial is reduced by one on successive steps, i.e., if

$$a_n = \alpha f^k(n) \text{ where } \alpha \text{ is an scalar, then}$$

$$\Delta a_n = \alpha f^{k-1}(n)$$

$$\Delta^2 a_n = \alpha f^{k-2}(n)$$

$$\cdots$$

$$\Delta^k a_n = \alpha f^0(n) = \alpha$$

Therefore if we go further and determine the forward difference of k + 1th order then we have,

$$\Delta^{k+1} a_n = \Delta(\Delta^k a_n) = \Delta(\alpha) = \alpha - \alpha = 0. \qquad [\because \ a_{n+1} = \alpha \text{ and so } a_n = \alpha]$$

Hence, proved.

Example 2.14 *Let a_n and b_n are two numeric functions such that*

$$a_n = n + 1 \text{ and } b_n = a^n \quad \text{for } n \geq 0.$$

Determine $\Delta(a_n b_n)$.

Sol. Recall the multiplication property of the numeric functions i.e., if a_n and b_n are two numeric functions then $a_n b_n$ will also be a numeric function.

So, $a_n b_n = (n + 1) . a^n$ for $n \geq 0$

$= c_n$ (let)

Now $\Delta(a_n b_n) = \Delta(c_n) = c_{n+1} - c_n$ for $n \geq 0$

$= (n + 2)\, a^{n+1} - (n + 1)\, a^n$

$= a^n (a^n - n + 2a - 1)$ for $n \geq 0$.

Example 2.14 *Let* $c_n = a_n . b_n$*, then show that* $c_n = a_{n+1} (\Delta b_n) + b_n(\Delta a_n)$.

Sol. From the definition of forward difference $\Delta c_n = c_{n+1} - c_n$ for $n \geq 0$,

where c_{n+1} will be $a_{n+1} . b_{n+1}$ so

$$\Delta c_n = a_{n+1} . b_{n+1} - a_n . b_n \quad \text{for } n \geq 0$$

$$= a_{n+1} . b_{n+1} - a_{n+1} . b_n - a_n . b_n + a_{n+1} . b_n$$

$$= a_{n+1} (b_{n+1} - b_n) + b_n (a_{n+1} - a_n)$$

$$= a_{n+1} (\Delta b_n) + b_n (\Delta a_n)$$

RHS

Example 2.15 *Let* a_n *and* b_n *are two numeric functions let* $d_n = a^n / b^n$ *is another numeric function (whose value at n is equal to the quotient of* a^n / b^n*), then show that*

$$\Delta d_n = \{b_n (\Delta a_n) - a_n(\Delta b_n)\} / b_n\, b_{n+1}.$$

Sol. From the definition of forward difference of numeric function d_n we have,

$$\Delta d_n = d_{n+1} - d_n \quad \text{for } n \geq 0$$

Since we have $d_n = a_n/b_n$, so $d_{n+1} = a^{n+1}/b^{n+1}$

Therefore, $\Delta d_n = a_{n+1}/b_{n+1} - a^n/b^n$ *LHS*

$$= \{a_{n+1}\, b_n - a_n\, b_{n+1}\}/b_n\, b_{n+1}$$

$$= \{a_{n+1}\, b_n - a_n\, b_n + a_n\, b_n - a_n\, b_{n+1}\}/b_n\, b_{n+1}$$

$$= bn\, \{a_{n+1} - a_n\} - a_n\, \{b_{n+1} - b_n\}/b_n\, b_{n+1}$$

$$= \{b_n\, (\Delta a_n) - a_n\, (\Delta b_n)\}/b_n\, b_{n+1}$$

RHS

2.2.9 Let a_n and b_n are two numeric functions then ***convolution*** of a_n and b_n, is denoted as $a_n * b_n$ is a numeric function and it is defined as,

$$a_n * b_n = a_0\, b_n + a_1\, b_{n-1} + a_2\, b_{n-2} + \ldots\ldots\ldots\ldots\ldots + a_k\, b_{k-1} + \ldots\ldots\ldots + a_{n-1}\, b_1 + a_n\, b_0$$

$$= \sum_{k=0}^{n} a_k\, b_{n-x}$$

which is a numeric function let it be c_n.

For example, let $a_n = p^n$ for $n \geq 0$

$b_n = q^n$ for $n \geq 0$

Then convolution of a_n & b_n will be given as,

$$a_n * b_n = \sum_{k=0}^{n} p^k\, q^{n-k}$$

Example 2.16 *Let* a_n *and* b_n *are two numeric functions i.e.,*

$$a_n = \begin{cases} 1 & \text{for } 0 \leq n \leq 2 \\ 0 & \text{for } n \geq 3 \end{cases} \quad \text{and} \quad b_n = \begin{cases} 1 \text{ for } 0 \leq n \leq 2 \\ 0 \text{ for } n \geq 3 \end{cases}$$

Determine $a_n * b_n$.

Sol. Using the convolution formula,

$$c_n = a_n * b_n = \sum_{k=0}^{n} a_k b_{n-k} = a_0 b_n + a_1 b_{n-1} + \ldots\ldots + a_{n-1} b_1 + a_n b_0$$

Since we have,

$$a_0 = a_1 = a_2 = 1 \quad \text{and} \quad a_3 = a_4 = \ldots\ldots = 0$$

and $$b_0 = b_1 = b_2 = 1 \quad \text{and} \quad b_3 = b_4 = \ldots\ldots = 0$$

Hence,

$$c_0 = a_0 b_0 = 1.1 = 1$$
$$c_1 = a_0 b_1 + a_1 b_0 = 1.1 + 1.1 = 2$$
$$c_2 = a_0 b_2 + a_1 b_1 + a_2 b_0 = 1.1 + 1.1 + 1.1 = 3$$
$$c_3 = a_0 b_3 + a_1 b_2 + a_2 b_1 + a_3 b_0 = 0.0 + 1.1 + 1.1 + 0.1 = 2$$
$$c_4 = a_0 b_4 + a_1 b_3 + a_2 b_2 + a_3 b_1 + a_4 b_0 = 1.0 + 1.0 + 1.1 + 0.1 + 0.1 = 1$$
$$c_5 = a_0 b_5 + a_1 b_4 + a_2 b_3 + a_3 b_2 + a_4 b_1 + a_5 b_0$$
$$= 1.0 + 1.0 + 1.0 + 0.1 + 0.1 + 0.1 = 0$$

Similarly we find that rests of the values of c for $n > 5$ are all zero.
Therefore, convolution is given as,

$$c_n = \begin{cases} 1 & \text{for } n = 0 \\ 2 & \text{for } n = 1 \\ 3 & \text{for } n = 2 \\ 2 & \text{for } n = 3 \\ 1 & \text{for } n = 4 \\ 0 & \text{otherwise} \end{cases}$$

Example 2.17 *Let* $a_n = 1$ *for* $n \geq 0$ *and*

$$b_n = \begin{cases} 1 & \text{for } n = 1 \\ 2 & \text{for } n = 3 \\ 3 & \text{for } n = 5 \\ 6 & \text{for } n = 7 \\ 0 & \text{otherwise} \end{cases}$$

Determine $a_n * b_n$.

Sol. Let, $c_n = a_n * b_n = \sum_{k=0}^{n} a_k b_{n-k}$

For $n = 0$, $c_0 = a_0.b_0 = 1.1 = 1$

For $n = 1$, $c_1 = \sum_{0}^{1} a_k b_{1-k} = a_0 b_1 + a_1 b_0 = 1.1 + 1.0 = 1$

For $n = 2$, $c_2 = \sum_{0}^{2} a_k b_{2-k} = a_0 b_2 + a_1 b_1 + a_2 b_0 = 1.0 + 1.1 + 1.0 = 1$

For $n = 3$, $c_3 = \sum_{0}^{3} a_k b_{3-k} = a_0 b_3 + a_1 b_2 + a_2 b_1 + a_3 b_0 = 1.2 + 0 + 1.1 + 0 = 3$

For $n = 4$, $c_4 = \sum_{0}^{4} a_k b_{4-k} = a_0 b_4 + a_1 b_3 + a_2 b_2 + a_3 b_1 + a_4 b_0 = 0 + 1.2 + 0 + 1.1 + 0 = 3$

For $n = 5$, $c_5 = \sum_{0}^{5} a_k b_{5-k} = a_0 b_5 + a_1 b_4 + a_2 b_3 + a_3 b_2 + a_4 b_1 + a_5 b_0 = 6$

For $n = 6$, $c_6 = \sum_{0}^{6} a_k b_{6-k} = a_0 b_6 + a_1 b_5 + a_2 b_4 + a_3 b_3 + a_4 b_2 + a_5 b_1 + a_6 b_0 = 6$

Similarly, we find $c_7, c_8, \ldots\ldots = 0$

Therefore, $$c_n = \begin{cases} 1 & \text{for } 0 \le n \le 2 \\ 3 & \text{for } 3 \le n \le 4 \\ 6 & \text{for } 5 \le n \le 6 \\ 0 & \text{for } n \ge 7 \end{cases}$$

Example 2.18 *Consider the numeric functions $a_n = 2^n$, for all n and $b_n = 0$, for $0 \le n \le 2$ and 2^n, for $n \ge 3$. Determine the convolution $a_n * b_n$.*

Sol. Let $c_n = a_n * b_n$. Since we have the values for a_n and b_n for different values for n i.e.,

$a_0 = 2, a_1 = 2, a_2 = 4, a_3 = 8, \ldots\ldots\ldots\ldots\ldots\ldots\ldots\ldots$

and $b_0 = 0, b_1 = 0, b_2 = 0, b_3 = 2^3, b_4 = 2^4, \ldots\ldots\ldots\ldots$

Hence, $c_0 = a_0 b_0 = 2.0 = 0$

$c_1 = a_0 b_1 + a_1 b_0 = 2.0 + 1.0 = 0$

$c_2 = a_0 b_2 + a_1 b_1 + a_2 b_0 = 4.0 + 2.0 + 1.0 = 0$

$c_3 = a_0 b_3 + a_1 b_2 + a_2 b_1 + a_3 b_0 = 0 + 1.2^3 = 1.2^3$

$c_4 = a_0 b_4 + a_1 b_3 + a_2 b_2 + a_3 b_1 + a_4 b_0 = 2.2^3 + 1.2^4 = 2.2^4$

$c_5 = a_0 b_5 + a_1 b_4 + a_2 b_3 + a_3 b_2 + a_4 b_1 + a_5 b_0$

$= 4.2^3 + 2.2^4 + 1.2^5 + 3.2^5 = 3.2^5$

Or, in general $c_n = (n - 2)\, 2^n$

Therefore, the convolution is given as,

$$c_n = \begin{cases} 0 & \text{for } 0 \le n \le 2 \\ (n-2)2^n & \text{for } n \ge 3 \end{cases}$$

Example 2.19 *Let a_n, b_n and c_n are the numeric functions, i.e., $a_n * b_n = c_n$, where*

$$a_n = \begin{cases} 1 & \text{for } n = 0 \\ 0 & \text{for } n \ge 2 \end{cases} \quad \text{and} \quad c_n = \begin{cases} 1 & \text{for } n = 0 \\ 0 & \text{for } n \ge 1 \end{cases}$$

Determine b_n.

Sol. Since we have $c_n = a_n * b_n = \sum_{k=0}^{n} a_k b_{n-k}$

Therefore,

For $n = 0$, $c_0 = a_0.b_0 \Rightarrow 1 = 1.b_0 \Rightarrow b_0 = 1$

For $n = 1$, $c_1 = \sum_{0}^{1} a_k b_{1-k} = a_0 b_1 + a_1 b_0 \Rightarrow 1.\, b_1 + 2.\, b_0 = 0$. Using $b_0 = 0, b_1 = (-2)^1$.

For $n = 2$, $c_2 = \sum_{0}^{2} a_k b_{2-k} = a_0 b_2 + a_1 b_1 + a_2 b_0$

$\Rightarrow 1.\, b_2 + 2.\, b_1 + 0.\, b_0 = 0$. So $b_2 = -2\, b_1 \Rightarrow b_2 = (-2)^2$.

For $n = 3$, $c_3 = \sum_{0}^{3} a_k b_{3-k} = a_0 b_3 + a_1 b_2 + a_2 b_1 + a_3 b_0$

$\Rightarrow$ $1. b_3 + 2. b_2 + 0. b_1 + 0 = 0$. So $b_3 = -2b_2 = (-2)^3$.

In general, we obtain $b_n = (-2)^n$ for $n \geq 0$.

Example 2.20 *Let a_n, b_n and c_n are the numeric functions, where*

$$a_n = \begin{cases} 1 & for\ n = 0 \\ 3 & for\ n = 1 \\ 2 & for\ 2 \leq n \leq 5 \\ 0 & for\ n \geq 6 \end{cases}, \quad b_n = \begin{cases} 0 & for\ 0 \leq n \leq 10 \\ 1 & for\ n \geq 11 \end{cases} \quad and \quad c_n = \begin{cases} 2 & for\ 0 \leq n \leq 9 \\ 3 & for\ n \geq 10 \end{cases}$$

Determine $c_n * (a_n * b_n)$.

Sol. Let $a_n * b_n = c'_n = \sum_{k=0}^{n} a_k b_{n-k}$

Since,

- $b_n = 0$ for $0 \leq n \leq 10$, therefore $c'_n = 0$ for $0 \leq n \leq 10$, and
- $b_n = 1$ for $n \geq 11$, therefore

$$c'_n = \sum_{k=0}^{11} a_k b_{11-k} = a_0 b_{11} + 0 = 1.1 = 1$$

So we have $c'_n = \begin{cases} 0 & \text{for } 0 \leq n \leq 10, \text{ and} \\ 1 & \text{for } n \geq 11 \end{cases}$

and given $c_n = \begin{cases} 2 & \text{for } 0 \leq n \leq 9, \text{ and} \\ 3 & \text{for } n \geq 10 \end{cases}$

Now we find the convolution of c_n with c'_n and let, $c_n * (c'_n) = d_n$ i.e.,

$$d_n = c_n * c'_n = \sum_{k=0}^{n} c_k c'_{n-k}$$

- For $0 \leq n \leq 10$, $d_n = 0$ [$\therefore$ $c'_n = 0$ for $0 \leq n \leq 10$]
- For $n \geq 11$, d_n can be determine as follows,

$$d_{11} = \sum_{0}^{11} c_k c'_{11-k} = c_0 c'_{11} + 0 = 1.2$$

$$d_{12} = \sum_{0}^{12} c_k c'_{12-k} = c_0 c'_{12} + c_1 c'_{11} + 0 = 2.1 + 2.1 = 2.2$$

$$d_{11} = \sum_{0}^{13} c_k c'_{13-k} = c_0 c'_{13} + c_1 c'_{12} + c_2 c'_{11} + 0 = 3.2$$

Similarly we can determine d_{20} upto $n = 20$, i.e. $d_{20} = 10.2$

And for $n = 21$,

$$d_{21} = \sum_{0}^{21} c_k c'_{21-k} = (c_0 + c_1 + \ldots.. + c_9) + c_{10}$$

[$\therefore$ c'_{21} to $c'_{11} = 1$ and rest are 0]

$$= (10.2) + 1.3$$

$$d_{22} = \sum_{0}^{22} c_k\, c'_{22-k} = (c_0 + c_1 + \ldots.. + c_9) + c_{10} + c_{11}$$

$$= (10.2) + 3.1 + 3.1 = (10.2) + 2.3$$

In general we can summarize the numeric function d_n as,

$$d_n = \begin{cases} 0 & \text{for } 0 \le n \le 10 \\ (n-10).2 & \text{for } 11 \le n \le 20 \\ 10.2 + (n-20).3 & \text{for } n \ge 21 \end{cases}$$

2.3 ASYMPTOTIC BEHAVIOR (PERFORMANCE) OF NUMERIC FUNCTIONS

Let a_n and b_n are two numeric functions i.e.,

$a_n = C_1 n^2 + C_2 n$ and

$b_n = C_3 n$ where C_1, C_2, and C_3 are constants

corresponding to the time taken by the two sorting algorithms to sort n numbers. Then we compare the performance between two algorithms. Algorithm b_n will be faster if n is sufficiently large. For small value of n, either algorithm would be faster depending on constant C_1, C_2, and C_3. If $C_1 = 1$, $C_2 = 2$ and $C_3 = 100$ then $C_1 n^2 + C_2 n \le C_3 n$ for $n \le 98$ and $C_1 n^2 + C_2 n > C_3 n$ for $n \ge 99$. If $C_1 = 1$, $C_2 = 2$ and $C_3 = 1000$ then $C_1 n^2 + C_2 n \le C_3 n$ for $n \le 998$. Here our point of interest is to see the behavior of the numeric functions a_n and b_n with large value of n. We observe that no matter what the constants are there will be a limit of n beyond that the numeric function b_n is faster then a_n. This limiting value of n is called *threshold point*. If threshold point is zero, then b_n is always faster or at least as fast than a_n. In fact exact threshold point can't be determined analytically. To handling this situation we introduce asymptotic notations that create a meaningful observation over inexactness statements.

The asymptotic notation describes the behavior of the numeric functions that is, how the function propagates for large values of n.

Fig. 2.2 shows some of the commonly used asymptotic functions that typically contain a single term in n with a multiplicative constant of one.

Asymptotic Function	**Name**
1	Constant
$\log n$	Logarithmic
N	Linear
$n \log n$	$n \log n$
n^2	Quadratic
n^3	Cubic
2^n	Exponential
$n!$	Factorial
$1/n$	Inverse

Fig 2.2

To illustrate more, let numeric function, $a_n = 7$, for $n \geq 0$ then its behavior remain constant for increase in n. If $a_n = 3 \log n$, for $n \geq 0$ then behavior of numeric function is of logarithmic nature for increase in n. For $a_n = 5\, n^3$, for $n \geq 0$ then its behavior is cubic. For $a_n = 7.2^n$, for $n \geq 0$ then numeric function grows exponentially for increase in n. And for $a_n = 2^5/n$, for $n \geq 0$ then function is diminishing for increase in n and finally approach to zero for large n.

Continue to the previous discussion of comparing the behavior of numeric functions, a_n asymptotically dominates b_n, if and only if there exist positive constants C and C_0, i.e.

$$| b_n | \leq C \,| a_n | \qquad \text{for} \qquad n \geq C_0$$

(Ignore the sign of numeric functions)

a_n asymptotically dominates b_n signifies that a_n grows faster then b_n for n beyond (the threshold point) the absolute value of b_n lies under a fixed proportion of absolute a_n. For example, let $a_n = n^2$, for $n \geq 0$ and $b_n = n^2 + 5n$, for $n \geq 0$ then a_n asymptotically dominates b_n for $C = 2$ and $C_0 = 5$, i.e.

$$| n^2 + 5n | \geq 2 \,| n^2 | \qquad \text{for} \qquad n \geq 5$$

Consider another example let numeric functions are,

$$a_n = 2^n, \qquad \text{for } n \geq 0 \qquad \text{and}$$
$$b_n = 2^n + n^2 \qquad \text{for } n \geq 0$$

Then a_n asymptotically dominates b_n for $C = 2$ and $C_0 = 4$, i.e.,

$$| 2^n + n^2 | \leq 2 \,| 2^n | \qquad \text{for } n \geq 4$$

Alternatively we may say that b_n doesn't asymptotically dominates a_n, for any constants C and C_0, although there exists a constant n_0 i.e.,

$$n_0 \geq C_0 \qquad \text{and} \qquad | a_{n0} | > C \,| b_{n0} |$$

Latter in this section we will see the asymptotic dominance of numeric functions with numeric function obtain after applying unary and binary operations.

(Assume a_n and b_n are numeric functions)

- $a_n \leq C \,| a_n |$ for $n \geq C_0$ (C and C_0 are positive constants)
- if $| b_n | \leq C \,| a_n |$ for $n \geq C_0$ then for any scalar k, $| k\, b_n | \leq C \,| a_n |$ for $n \geq C_0$
- if $| b_n | \leq C \,| a_n |$ for $n \geq C_0$ then $| S^I b_n | \leq C \,| S^I a_n |$ for $n \geq C_0$
- if $| b_n | \leq C_1 | a_n |$ for $n \geq C_{01}$ and $| c_n | \leq C_2 | a_n |$ for $n \geq C_{02}$ then for any scalar k and m,

$$| k\, b_n + m\, c_n | \leq C_3 \,| a_n | \text{ for } n \geq C_{03}$$

(where C_1, C_2, C_3, C_{01}, C_{02}, C_{03} are positive constants and a_n, b_n and c_n are numeric functions)

- if $| b_n | \leq C_1 | a_n |$ for $n \geq C_{01}$ then also $| a_n | \leq C_2 | b_n |$ for $n \geq C_{02}$.

(where C_1, C_2, C_{01}, C_{02} are positive constants)

For example,

$$a_n = n^2 + n + 1 \qquad \text{and} \qquad b_n = 10^{-3} n^2 - n^{1/3} - 11 \quad \text{for } n \geq 0$$

- Conversely, if $| b_n | \not\leq C_1 | a_n |$ for $n \geq C_{01}$ then also $| a_n | \not\leq C_2 | b_n |$ for $n \geq C_{02}$.

(where C_1, C_2, C_{01}, C_{02} are positive constants)

For example,

$$a_n = \begin{cases} 1 & \text{for } n\ 0, 2, 4, \ldots\ldots \text{(even)} \\ 0 & \text{for } n = 1, 3, 5, \ldots\ldots \text{(odd)} \end{cases}$$

and
$$b_n = \begin{cases} 0 & \text{for } n = 0, 2, 4, \ldots\ldots \text{(even)} \\ 1 & \text{for } n = 1, 3, 5, \ldots\ldots \text{(odd)} \end{cases}$$

Then it is worthless to talk about asymptotic dominance among a_n and b_n.

- It is also possible that, if $| c_n | \leq C_1 | a_n |$ for $n \geq C_{01}$ and $| c_n | \leq C_2 | b_n |$ for $n \geq C_{02}$, then $| b_n | \not\leq C_3 | a_n |$ for $n \geq C_{03}$ and $| a_n | \not\leq C_4 | b_n |$ for $n \geq C_{04}$

(where $C_1, C_2, C_3, C_4, C_{01}, C_{02}, C_{03}, C_{04}$ are positive constants)

For example,

$$a_n = \begin{cases} 1 & \text{for } n = 3I \text{ or } 3I + 1 \quad (I \geq 0) \\ 0 & \text{for } n = 3I + 2 \quad (I \geq 0) \end{cases}$$

and
$$b_n = \begin{cases} 1 & \text{for } n = 3I \text{ or } 3I + 2 \quad (I \geq 0) \\ 0 & \text{for } n = 3I + 1 \quad (I \geq 0) \end{cases}$$

and
$$c_n = \begin{cases} 1 & \text{for } n = 3I \quad (I \geq 0) \\ 0 & \text{otherwise} \end{cases}$$

Then we see that both an and bn asymptotically dominates c_n, i.e.,

$$| c_n | \leq 1. | a_n | \quad \text{for } n \geq 0 \qquad (a_n \text{ asymptotically dominates } c_n)$$

(for C = 1, C_0 = 3I or 3I + 1 or otherwise $C_0 \geq 0$, we have $1 \leq 1.\ 1$ or $0 \leq 1.\ 0$)

Similarly, $| c_n | \leq 1. | b_n |$ for $n \geq 0$

(b_n asymptotically dominates c_n for C = 1 and $C_0 \geq 0$)

Further we will see that a_n doesn't asymptotically dominates b_n. So, for any choice of C & C_0 there exists a constant n_0 i.e.

$$n_0 \geq C_0 \qquad \text{and} \qquad | b_{n0} | = C. | a_{n0} |$$

Since C0 is zero so $n_0 \geq 0$, therefore $| b_{n0} | \geq | a_{n0} |$. Likewise we would also see that b_n doesn't asymptotically dominates a_n.

2.3.1 Big–Oh (O) Notation

Big–Oh notation is the upper bound; it bounds the value of the numeric function from above. Let a_n be a numeric function then Big–Oh of a_n denoted as $O(a_n)$ is the set of all numeric functions b_n that are asymptotically dominated by a_n, i.e.,

$$b_n = O(a_n) \quad \Rightarrow \quad | b_n | \leq C | a_n | \quad \text{for } n \geq C_0$$

where C and C_0 are positive constants. Here symbol '=' is read as 'is' not as 'equal'. So the definition states that numeric function b_n is at most C times the numeric function a_n except possibly when n is smaller than C_0. Thus numeric function a_n asymptotically dominant (an upper bound) on b_n for all suitably large values of n i.e. $n \geq C_0$. $O(a_n)$ is also read as 'order of' a_n.

For example,

- Let $a_n = 3n + 2$; since $3n + 3 \leq 4n$ for $n \geq 3$, therefore $a_n = O(n)$.
- Let $a_n = 100n + 3$; since $100n + 3 \leq 100n + n$ for $n \geq C_0 = 3$, therefore $a_n = O(n)$.

Hence these numeric functions are bounded from above by a linear function for suitably large n.

Consider other numeric functions,

- Let $a_n = 10n^2 + 2n + 2$; since $10n^2 + 2n + 2 \leq 10n^2 + 3n$ for $n \geq 2$. For $n \geq 3$, $3n \geq n^2$. Hence for $n \geq C_0 = 3$, $a_n \leq 10n^2 + n^2 = 11n^2$. Therefore $a_n = O(n^2)$.
- Let $a_n = 3.\ 2^n + n^2$; since for $n \geq 4$, $n^2 \leq 2^n$. So, $3.\ 2^n + n^2 \leq 4.\ 2^n$ for $n \geq 4$, therefore $a_n = O(2^n)$.
- Let $a_n = 7$, then $a_n = O(1)$. Because $a_n = 7 \leq 7.\ 1$, by setting $C = 7$ and $C_0 = 0$.

It is also observed that for $a_n = 3n + 2 = O(n^2)$, because of $3n + 2 \leq 3n^2$ for $n \geq 2$. So, n^2 is the upper bound (loose bound) for a_n. For $a_n = 10n^2 + 2n + 2 = O(n^4)$, because of $10n^2 + 2n + 2 \leq 10n^4$ for $n \geq 2$. Again, n^4 is not a tight upper bound for a_n. Similarly, for $a_n = 3.\ 2^n + n^2 = O(n^2\ 2^n)$ is a loose bound comparison to $O(n\ 2^n)$ and further $O(2^n)$ is a tight bound for a_n.

It can also observe that $a_n = 3n + 2 \neq \mathbf{O}(1)$, because there is no $C > 0$ and C_0, i.e. $3n + 3 < C$ for $n \geq C_0$. Similarly, $a_n = 10n^2 + 2n + 2 \neq \mathbf{O}(n)$ and $a_n = 3.\ 2^n + n^2 \neq O(2^n)$.

Consider another example of numeric functions that are given as,

$$a_n = 3n + 2\ ;\ b_n = n^2 + 1\ ;\ \text{and } c_n = 9\ ;$$

Then we formulate asymptotic relationship between the numeric functions that are summaries as follows,

- $a_n = O(b_n)$, because for $C = 1$ and $C_0 = 4$, $|\ a_n\ | \leq 1.\ |\ b_n\ |$ for $n \geq 4$. Thus, b_n asymptotically dominates a_n.
- $c_n = O(1)$, because for $C = 9$ and $C_0 = 0$, $|\ c_n\ | \leq C.\ |\ 1\ |$ or $9 \leq 9.1$ for $n \geq 0$.
- $c_n = O(a_n)$, because for $C = 1$ and $C_0 = 3$, $|\ c_n\ | \leq C.\ |\ a_n\ |$ or $9 \leq 1.(3n + 2)$ for $n \geq 3$. Thus, a_n asymptotically dominates c_n.

Also the order of the above numeric functions is given in the Fig 2.3 where column 1 of the order shows the tight bound and rest of the column (2, 3, ..) shows loose bound for the corresponding numeric functions.

Numeric Function	**Order**		
$a_n = 3n + 2$	$O(n)$	$O(n^2)$	$O(n^3)$, ...
$b_n = n^2 + 1$	$O(n^2)$	$O(n^3)$	$O(n^4)$, ...
$c_n = 9$	$O(1)$	—	—
	1	2	3

Fig. 2.3

Hence we reach to the following conclusions,

- a_n is $O(b_n)$.
- b_n is not $O(a_n)$ and nor $O(c_n)$.
- c_n is $O(1)$, but c_n is not $O(a_n)$, nor $O(b_n)$.

Reader must also note that when a numeric function b_n is $O(n \log n)$, it means that b_n is asymptotically dominated by the numeric function $n \log n$, let it be a_n. Thus, b_n is $O(a_n)$, that is b_n doesn't grow faster than a_n, but it grow much slower than a_n. However, if b_n is $O(2^n)$ then it is rightly says that b_n grows much slower than 2^n.

The features of asymptotic dominance of numeric function in terms of 'Big–Oh' notation is further states as follows, (let a_n, b_n and c_n are numeric functions)

- a_n is $O(|a_n|)$.
- If b_n is $O(a_n)$ then also $k.b_n$ is $O(a_n)$, for any scalar k.
- If b_n is $O(a_n)$ then also $S^I.b_n$ is $O(S^I a_n)$, where I is any integer.
- If b_n is $O(a_n)$ and c_n is $O(a_n)$ then also $k.b_n + m\, c_n$ is $O(a_n)$, for any scalars k and m.
- If c_n is $O(b_n)$ and b_n is $O(a_n)$ then c_n is $O(a_n)$.
- It is possible that if a_n is $O(b_n)$ then also b_n is $O(a_n)$. For example, the numeric functions, $a_n = 3n^2$ and $b_n = 2n^2 + 1$, then a_n is $O(b_n)$ and b_n is $O(a_n)$.
- It is possible that if $a_n \neq O(b_n)$ then also $b_n \neq O(a_n)$. For example, the numeric functions, $a_n = n^2 + 1$ and $b_n = 3 \log n$, then $a_n \neq O(b_n)$ and also $b_n \neq O(a_n)$.
- It is possible that both c_n is $O(a_n)$ and c_n is $O(b_n)$ but $a_n \neq O(b_n)$ and also $b_n \neq O(a_n)$.

Example 2.21 *Let a_n be a numeric function such that*

$a_n = a_m n^m + a_{m-1} n^{m-1} + a_{m-2} n^{m-2} + \dots\dots\dots\dots + a_1 n + a_0$ and $a_m > 0$, then show that $a_n = O(n^m)$.

Sol. Since,
$$a_n \le \sum_{k=0}^{m} |a_k| n^k$$
$$\le n^m \sum_{0}^{m} |a_k| n^{k-m}$$
$$\le n^m \sum_{0}^{m} |a_k| \quad \text{for } n \ge 1$$

Therefore, $a_n = O(n^m)$, or a_n is $O(n^m)$.

Example 2.22 *Let $a_n = 3n^3 + 2n^2 + n$, then show asymptotic behaviors of a_n.*

Sol. For given numeric function $a_n = 3n^3 + 2n^2 + n$, it is clear that,

- a_n is $O(n^3)$ for $n \ge 3$, because $3n^3 + 2n^2 + n \le 3n^3 + n^3$ or $2n^2 + n \le n^3$ for $n \ge 3$.
- Also, a_n is $3n^3 + O(n^2)$ for $n \ge 2$, because $2n^2 + n \le 3n^2$ for $n \ge 2$.
- And also, a_n is $3n^3 + 2n^2 + O(n)$ for $n \ge 0$, because $n \le 1.n$ for $n \ge 0$.

Hence, we summarize the behavior of the numeric function a_n as,
$$\{3n^3 + 2n^2\} + O(n) < \{3n^3\} + O(n^2) < O(n^3).$$

Example 2.23 *Let* $$a_n = \sum_{k=0}^{n} k^2$$

(i) Show $a_n = O(n^3)$.

(ii) Show $a_n = (n^3/3) + O(n^2)$.

Sol. (*i*) We have,
$$a_n = \sum_{k=0}^{n} k^2 = 0^2 + 1^2 + 2^2 + \dots\dots + n^2$$
$$= n(n+1)(2n+1)/6$$
or
$$a_n = 1/3\, n^3 + 1/2\, n^2 + 1/6 n$$
Since $1/3\, n^3 + 1/2\, n^2 + 1/6\, n \le 2/3\, n^3$ for $n \ge 2$

Therefore, $|a_n| \le 2/3\, |n^3|$ for $n \ge 2$, hence $a_n = O(n^3)$.

(*ii*) Since, $a_n = 1/3\, n^3 + 1/2\, n^2 + 1/6\, n$

so $1/3\, n^3 + \{1/2\, n^2 + 1/6\, n\} \le 1/3\, n^3 + \{1/2\, n^2 + 1/2\, n^2\}$ for $n \ge 0$
$$\le \{1/3\}\, n^3 + n^2$$

or $$a_n \le \{1/3\}\, n^3 + O(n^2)$$

Hence, a_n is $\{1/3\}\, n^3 + O(n^2)$.

Example 2.23 *Simplify the expression*

$$\{\log n + O(1/k)\}\{k + O(\sqrt{k})\} \quad \text{for any constant } k.$$

Sol. Let
$$\begin{aligned}
a_n &= \{\log n + O(1/k)\}\{k + O(\sqrt{k})\} \\
&= \{k.\log n + k.O(1/k) + \log n.\ O(\sqrt{k}) + O(1/k).\ O(\sqrt{k})\} \\
&= \{k.\log n + O(1) + \log n.\ O(\sqrt{k}) + O(1/\sqrt{k})\} \\
&= \{k + O(\sqrt{k})\}.\log n + \{O(1) + O(1/\sqrt{k})\} \\
&= C_1 \log n + C_2 \quad \text{(where } C_1 \text{ and } C_2 \text{ are constants)}
\end{aligned}$$

Therefore, $a_n \approx \log n$.

Example 2.24 *Let $a_n = \log_e n$, show that $a_n = O(n^e)$ for $e > 0$.*

Sol. Since, $\log_e n \le n^e$ for $n \ge e$

Therefore, $|\, a_n \,| \le 1.\ |\, n^e \,|$ for $n \ge e$, hence a_n is asymptotically denoted by n^e.

Consequently, $a_n = O(n^e)$.

Example 2.25 *Given a numeric function a_n, let*

$$b_n = \begin{cases} a_n + a_{n/2} + a_{n/4} + \ldots\ldots + a_{n/2}\ i & \text{for } n = 2^i \\ 0 & \text{for } n \ne 2^i \end{cases}$$

if $a_n = O(\sqrt{n})$, then show that $b_n = O(\sqrt{n}\ \log n)$.

Sol. For $n = 2^i$ given numeric function

$$b_n = a_n + a_{n/2} + a_{n/4} + \ldots\ldots\ldots + a_n/2^i$$

since $a_n = O(\sqrt{n})$, therefore we have

$$\begin{aligned}
b_n &= O(\sqrt{n}) + O(\sqrt{n}/2) + O(\sqrt{n}/4) + \ldots\ldots\ldots + O(\sqrt{n}/2^i) \\
&= O(\sqrt{n}).\ 1 + O(\sqrt{n}).\ 1/\sqrt{2} + O(\sqrt{n}).\ 1/\sqrt{4} + \ldots\ldots\ldots + O(\sqrt{n}).\ 1/\sqrt{2}^{\,i} \\
&= O(\sqrt{n}).\ \{1 + 1/\sqrt{2} + 1/\sqrt{4} + \ldots\ldots\ldots + 1/\sqrt{2}^{\,i}\} \\
&= O(\sqrt{n}).\ \{1 + (1/\sqrt{2})^1 + (1/\sqrt{2})^2 + \ldots\ldots\ldots + (1/\sqrt{2})^i\}
\end{aligned}$$

Find the sum and since $n = 2^i$, so put $i = \log_2 n$ we get the required result, i.e.

$$b_n = O(\sqrt{n}\ \log n)$$

Similar to the 'Big–Oh' notation other notations like Omega (Ω) and Theta (θ) are also commonly used.

2.3.2 Omega (Ω) Notation

Omega notation is the lower bound; it bounds the value of numeric function from below. Let a_n be a numeric function then Omega of a_n denoted as $\Omega(a_n)$ is the set of all numeric functions b_n that grows at least as fast as a_n, i.e.,

$$b_n = \Omega(a_n)$$

It define as, $|\, b_n \,| \ge C\ |\, a_n \,|$ for $n \ge C_0$, where C and C_0 are constant.

Alternatively, we can say that numeric function b_n is at least C times the numeric function a_n except possibly when n is smaller than C_0. Thus, a_n is lower bound on the value of b_n for all suitably large n, i.e. $n \ge C_0$.

For example,

- Let $a_n = 3n + 2$, then $3n + 2 > 3n$ for $n \geq 0$, therefore $a_n = \Omega(n)$.
- Let $a_n = 100n + 3$, then $100n + 3 > 100n$ for $n \geq 0$, therefore $a_n = \Omega(n)$.

Hence, above numeric functions are bounded from below by a linear function.

Consider other numeric functions,

- Let $a_n = 10n^2 + 2n + 2$; since $10n^2 + 2n + 2 > 10n^2$ for $n \geq 0$, therefore $a_n = \Omega(n^2)$.
- Let $a_n = 3.\ 2^n + n^2$; since $3.\ 2^n + n^2 > 3.\ 2^n$ for $n \geq 0$, therefore $a_n = \Omega(2^n)$.

It is also observe that $3n + 1 = \Omega(1)$; $10n^2 + 2n + 2 = \Omega(n)$; $10n^2 + 2n + 2 = \Omega(1)$; $3.\ 2^n + n^2 = \Omega(n^{100})$; $3.\ 2^n + n^2 = \Omega(n^2)$; $3.\ 2^n + n^2 = \Omega(n)$; and also $3.\ 2^n + n^2 = \Omega(1)$;

But $3n + 2 \neq \Omega(n^2)$; We can prove this result by method of contradiction. Assume, $3n + 2 = \Omega(n^2)$ then there exist positive constants C and C_0 such that $3n + 2 \geq C.\ n^2$ for all $n \geq C_0$. Therefore, $C.n^2/(3n + 2) \leq 1$ for all $n \geq C_0$. This equality can't be true because, $C.n^2/(3n + 2)$ grows faster and reaches to infinity for larger value of n. Therefore, $C.n^2/(3n + 2) \not\leq 1$. Hence, $3n + 2 \neq \Omega(n^2)$.

2.3.3 Theta (θ) Notation

Theta notation is the average bound; it bounds the value of numeric function both from above and below. Let a_n be a numeric function then theta of a_n denoted by $\theta(a_n)$ is the set of all numeric functions b_n such that there exist positive constants C_1, C_2, and C_0, i.e.,

$$C_1.\ |\ a_n\ | \leq |\ b_n\ | \leq C_2.\ |\ a_n\ | \quad \text{for } n \geq C_0$$

That can be written as, $b_n = \theta(a_n)$

It means, numeric function b_n lies between C_1 times the numeric function a_n and C_2 times the numeric function a_n except possibly when n is smaller then C_0. Thus, a_n is both a lower bound and an upper bound on the value of a_n for all suitably large n, i.e. $n \geq C_0$. In other words, b_n grows similar as a_n. From the definition, it is also concluded that a_n is both $\Omega(b_n)$ and $O(b_n)$.

For example,

- Let $a_n = 3n + 2$; since $3n + 2 > 3n$ for $n \geq 0$ and $3n + 2 \leq 4n$ for $n \geq 3$. Combining these inequalities we have $3n \leq 3n + 2 \leq 4n$ for $n \geq 3$. Hence, $a_n = \Omega(n)$ and $a_n = O(n)$. Therefore $a_n = \theta(n)$.
- Let $a_n = 10n^2 + 2n + 2$; since $10n^2 \leq 10n^2 + 2n + 2 \leq 11n^2$ for $n \geq 2$. Therefore $a_n = \theta(n^2)$.
- Let $a_n = 3.\ 2^n + n^2$; since $3.\ 2^n \leq 3.\ 2^n + n^2 \leq 4.\ 2^n$ for $n \geq 4$. Therefore $a_n = \theta(2^n)$.

Consider another numeric function $a_n = 3 \log_2 n + 5$; since $\log_2 n < 3 \log_2 n + 5 \leq 4 \log_2 n$ for $n \geq 32$. Therefore $a_n = \theta(\log_2 n)$.

Previously we showed that $3n + 3 \neq O(1)$, therefore $3n + 3 \neq \theta(1)$. Also we have shown that $3n + 2 \neq \Omega(n^2)$ so $3n + 2 \neq \theta(n^2)$. Since, $10n^2 + 2n + 2 \neq O(n)$ therefore $10n^2 + 2n + 2 \neq \theta(n)$ and also $10n^2 + 2n + 2 \neq \theta(1)$.

Example 2.26 *Let numeric functions $a_n = 3^n$ and $b_n = 2^n$ for $n \geq 0$, then show that*

(i) Does a_n asymptotically dominates b_n.

*(ii) Does a_n*b_n asymptotically dominates b_n.*

*(iii) Does a_n*b_n asymptotically dominates a_n.*

Sol. (*i*) Numeric function a_n asymptotically dominates b_n if there exists positive constants C and C_0 i.e.,

$$| b_n | \leq C | a_n | \qquad \text{for} \quad n \geq C_0$$

So we have the equality

$$| 2^n | \leq C. | 3^n | \qquad \text{for} \quad n \geq C_0$$

That is true for C = 1 and $C_0 = 0$, i.e. $2^n \leq 1.\ 3^n$ for $n \geq 0$. Hence a_n asymptotically dominates b_n. (But its reverse is not true)

(*ii*) Determine $a_n{*}b_n$ i.e.,

$$a_n{*}b_n = \sum_{k=0}^{n} a_k\, b_{n-k}$$

$$= \sum_{k=0}^{n} 3^k\, 2^{n-k}$$

Since, $\sum_{k=0}^{n} | 2^k | \leq \sum_{k=0}^{n} | 3^k\, 2^{n-k} |$ for $n \geq 0$

So, $a_n{*}b_n$ asymptotically dominates b_n.

(*iii*) Similarly we can show that $a_n{*}b_n$ asymptotically dominates a_n.

2.4 GENERATING FUNCTIONS

Before going to start the exact discussion on generating functions let us begin our tour from the origin of generating functions. Assume a series $a_0 + a_1 + a_2 + \ldots\ldots + a_n$ in which, from and after a certain term is equal to the sum of a fixed number of preceding terms multiplied respectively by certain constant is called *recurring series*. For example in the series $1 + 2z + 3z^2 + 4z^3 + 5z^4 + \ldots$, where each term after the second is equal to the sum of the two preceding terms multiplied respectively by the constants $2z$ and $-z^2$. These quantities being constants because they are remain same for all values of n. Thus,

$$5z^4 = (2z).\ 4z^3 + (-z^2).\ 3z^2$$

Therefore we assume that

$$a_4 = 2z.\ a_3 - z^2.\ a_2$$

In general when n is greater then 1, each term is represented by its two immediately preceded terms through the equation,

$$a_n = 2z.\ a_{n-1} - z^2.\ a_{n-2}$$

or

$$a_n - 2z.\ a_{n-1} + z^2.\ a_{n-2} = 0 \tag{2.1}$$

Equation 2.1 is called *scale of relation* in which coefficients a_n, a_{n-1}, and a_{n-2} are taken with their proper signs. Thus the series $1 + 2z + 3z^2 + 4z^3 + 5z^4 + \ldots\ldots$ has scale of relation $1 - 2z + z^2$. Consequently, if the scale of relation of a recurring series is given, then we could find any term of the series, from sufficient number of known preceding terms.

For example, let

$$1 - pz - qz^2 - wz^3 \tag{2.2}$$

is the *scale of relation* of the series $a_0 + a_1 z + a_2 z^2 + \ldots\ldots + a_n z^n$ (2.3)

Then we have, $a_n z^n \geq p_z.\ a_{n-1} z^{n-1} + qz^2.\ a_{n-2} z^{n-2} + wz^3.\ a_{n-3} z^{n-3}$;

or

$$a_n = p.\ a_{n-1} + q.\ a_{n-2} + w.\ a_{n-3}; \tag{2.4}$$

Thus, any coefficient can be found when coefficients of the three preceding terms are known.

Let us take a series shown in (2.3) and extended up to infinite terms, i.e.,

$$a_0 + a_1 z + a_2 z^2 + \ldots\ldots + a_n z^n + \ldots\ldots\ldots \tag{2.5}$$

and assume the scale of relation is $1 - pz - qz^2$. So we have

$$a_n - p\,a_{n-1} - q\,a_{n-2} = 0$$

$$\begin{aligned}
\text{Assume,}\quad A(z) &= a_0 + a_1 z + a_2 z^2 + \ldots\ldots\ \ldots\ldots + a_{n-1} z^{n-1} \\
-pz.A(z) &= -pa_0 z - pa_1 z^2 - \ldots\ldots\ldots\ldots - p_{an-2} z^{n-1} - p\,a_{n-1} z^n \\
-qz^2.A(z) &= -qa_0 z^2 - \ldots\ldots\ldots\ldots - qa_{n-3} z^{n-1} - q\,a_{n-2} z^n - qa_{n-1} z^{n+1}
\end{aligned}$$

$$(1 - pz - qz^2)\,A(z) = a_0 + (a_1 - pa_0)\,z + \ldots\ldots\ldots - (pa_{n-1} + qa_{n-2})\,z^n - qa_{n-1}.z^{n+1}$$

For the coefficient of every other power of z is zero in consequence of the relation

$$a_n - p\,a_{n-1} - q\,a_{n-2} = 0$$

i.e., $A(z) = [a_0 + (a_1 - pa_0)\,z]/(1 - pz - qz^2)$

$$-\ [(pa_{n-1} + qa_{n-2})\,z^n - qa_{n-1}\,z^{n+1}]/(1 - pz - qz^2) \tag{2.6}$$

For large value of n series (2.5) is infinite and so second fraction of the equation (2.6) decreases indefinitely. Thus we have the sum

$$A(z) = [a_0 + (a_1 - pa_0)\,z]/(1 - pz - qz^2) \tag{2.7}$$

If we develop this fraction in ascending powers of z, we shall obtain as many terms of the original series as we please. Therefore, the expression (2.7) is called ***generating function*** of the infinite series (2.5).

As we mention in the previous section that for a numeric function a_n we uses $a_0, a_1, a_2, \ldots, a_n, \ldots$..to denote its values at 0, 1, 2, ..., n, ... Here we introduce an alternative way to represent numeric functions, such as for a numeric function $(a_0, a_1, a_2, \ldots, a_n, \ldots..)$ we define an infinite series,

$$a_0 + a_1 z + a_2 z^2 + \ldots\ldots + a_n z^n + \ldots\ldots\ldots$$

Here z is a formal variable and powers of z is used as generator in the infinite series such that the coefficient of z^n returns the value of the numeric function at n. For a numeric function a_n we write $A(z)$ to denote its generating function and so the above infinite series can be written in closed form as shown in equation (2.7), i.e.,

$$A(z) = [a_0 + (a_1 - pa_0)z]/(1 - pz - qz^2)$$

(where $(1 - pz - qz^2)$ is the scale of relation)

For example, the numeric function $(5^0, 5^1, 5^2, \ldots, 5^n, \ldots..)$ we define an infinite series,

$$5^0 + 5^1 z + 5^2 z^2 + \ldots\ldots + 5^n z^n + \ldots\ldots\ldots$$

Therefore we obtain the summation of infinite series $A(z) = 1/(1 - 5z)$. $A(z)$ is the generating function that represent the numeric function in a compact way. Hence for a numeric function we can easily obtain its generating function and vise - versa. In fact an alternate way to representing numeric function leads to efficiency and easiness in some context that we wish to carry out.

Consider a numeric function $a_n = 1$ for $n \geq 0$, then its generating function $A(z) = 1/(1 - z)$. Similarly the generating function of the numeric function $b_n = k^n$ for $n \geq 0$ will be $B(z) = 1/(1 - kz)$. It is quite often that generating function can be expressed as a group of equivalent partial fractions and the general term of series may be easily found where the coefficient of z^n represent the corresponding numeric function. Thus, suppose generating function can be decomposed into partial fractions,

$$P/(1 - \alpha z) + Q/(1 + \beta z) + R/(1 - \gamma z)$$

Then coefficient of the z^n in the general term is

$$\{P.\ \alpha^n + (-1)^n\ B.\ \beta^n + (n+1)\ R.\ \gamma^n\} \quad \text{for } n \geq 0$$

that will be equivalent to numeric function.

Example 2.27 *Find the numeric function for the generating function*

$$A(z) = (1 - 8z) / (1 - z - 6z^2)$$

Sol. Since A(z) can be expressed in partial fraction i.e.,

$$A(z) = 2/(1 + 2z) - 1/(1 - 3z)$$

Then obtain the coefficient of z^n in the general term and it will come out to be

$$(-1)^n\ 2^{n+1} - 3^n \quad \text{for } n \geq 0$$

That is the required numeric function of A(z). Alternatively, we say $a_n = (-1)^n\ 2^{n+1} - 3^n$ for $n \geq 0$.

Example 2.28 *Find the generating function and the numeric function for the series*

$$1 + 6 + 24 + 84 + \ldots\ldots\ldots\ldots.$$

Sol. The given series is transformed into another infinite series by introducing a formal parameter z and using power of z as generator in it, i.e.

$$1 + 6z + 24z^2 + 84z^3 + \ldots\ldots\ldots\ldots. \tag{2.8}$$

The scale of relation of the above series is $(1 - 5z + 6z^2)$. To explain the method of determining the scale of relation, let's assume $(1 - pz - qz^2)$ is the scale of relation for the series (2.8). Therefore to obtain p and q we have the equations,

$$24 - 6p - q = 0 \quad \text{and} \quad 84 - 24p - 6q = 0$$

whence, $p = 5$, and $q = -6$, So the scale of relation is $(1 - 5z + 6z^2)$.

Hence, using equation (2.7) we obtain the generating function

$$A(z) = (1 + z)/(1 - 5z + 6z^2).$$

Since A(z) can be written as,

$$A(z) = 4/(1 - 3z) - 3/(1 - 2z)$$

Now obtain the coefficient of z^n in the general term of A(z) that will return the numeric function a_n i.e.

$$a_n = 4.3^n - 3.2^n \quad \text{for } n \geq 0$$

Example 2.29 *Find numeric function for generating function*

$$A(z) = 2 / (1 - 4z^2)$$

Sol. Since A(z) can be written as

$$A(z) = 1/(1 - 2z) + 1/(1 + 2z)$$

Thus we obtain the numeric function a_n as,

$$a_n = 2^n + (-1)^n\ .\ 2^n \quad \text{for } n \geq 0$$

or

$$a_n = \begin{cases} 0 & \text{if } n \text{ is odd} \\ 2^{n+1} & \text{if } n \text{ is even} \end{cases}$$

Now we shall discuss the common features of generating function corresponding to the features of numeric functions. Let a_n, b_n, and c_n are numeric function and A(z), B(z), and C(z) are their corresponding generating functions then,

- If $c_n = a_n + b_n$ then corresponding generating function C(z) = A(z) + B(z). For example, Let $a_n = 2^n$ and $b_n = 3^n$ for $n \geq 0$ then $c_n = 2^n + 3^n$ for $n \geq 0$. So $C(z) = 1/(1 - 2z) + 1/(1 - 3z) = (2 + 3z - 6z^2)/(1 - 2z)$.
- If $b_n = ka_n$, where k is any arbitrary constant then corresponding generating function is $B(z) = kA(z)$. For example let $a_n = 5.2^n$ for $n \geq 0$ then $A(z) = 5/(1 - 2z)$ is the numeric function.

- If $b_n = k^n a_n$, where k is any arbitrary constant then corresponding generating function is $B(z) = A(kz) = 1/(1 - kz)$. Since numeric function b_n is expressed in infinite series as

$$a_0 + k.a_1 z + k^2 a_2 z^2 + \dots\dots\dots + k^n a_n z^n + \dots\dots$$
$$= a_0 + a_1(kz) + a_2(kz)^2 + \dots\dots\dots + a_n (kz)^n + \dots\dots$$

Therefore, generating function $B(z) = A(kz) = 1/(1 - kz)$.

- Since $A(z)$ is the generating function of function a_n so generating function of $S^I a_n$ will be $z^I A(z)$, for any positive integer I. For example, let generating function $B(z) = z^8/(1 - 3z)$ then it can be written as,

$$B(z) = z^8. 1/(1 - 3z) \equiv z^I A(z)$$

Then its corresponding numeric function will be $S^8 a_n$ where a_n is the numeric function for the function $1/(1 - 3z)$ that is equal to 3^n.

Therefore, we obtain numeric function $S^8 3^n$, i.e.,

$$S^8 3^n = \begin{cases} 0 & \text{for } 0 \le n \le 7 \\ 3^{n-8} & \text{for } n \ge 8 \end{cases}$$

- Likewise, generating function for the numeric function S^{-I} an for any integer I, will be

$$z^{-I} [A(z) - a_0 - a_1 z - a_2 z^2 - \dots\dots - a_{I-1} z^{I-1}]$$

Since $\quad A(z) = a_0 + a_1 z + a_2 z^2 + \dots\dots + a_{I-1} z^{I-1} + a_I z^I \dots\dots + a_n z^n + \dots$

or, $\quad A(z) - a_0 - a_1 z - a_2 z^2 - \dots\dots - a_{I-1} z^{I-1} = a_I z^I + a_{I+1} z^{I+1} + \dots + a_n z^n + \dots$

Multiplied both side by z^{-I}, hence we obtain

$$z^{-I} [A(z) - a_0 - a_1 z - a_2 z^2 - \dots\dots - a_{I-1} z^{I-1}] = a_I + a_{I+1} z + \dots + a_n z^{n-I} + \dots$$
$$= a_{n+I} z^n \quad \text{for } n \ge 0$$

That is equivalent to $S^{-I} a_n$.

For example, let $a_n = 3^{n+5}$ for $n \ge 0$ which is equivalent to numeric function $S^{-5}.3^n$ and its corresponding generating function can be computed by using the expression,

$$A(z) = z^{-I} [A(z) - a_0 - a_1 z - a_2 z^2 - \dots\dots - a_{I-1} z^{I-1}]$$

i.e., $\quad A(z) = z^{-5} [1/(1 - 3z) - 3^0 - 3^1 z - 3^2 z^2 - 3^3 z^3 - 3^4 z^4]$

$$= z^{-5} [3^5.z^5/(1 - 3z)] = 3^5/(1 - 3z).$$

Example 2.30 *Find the generating function for the numeric function a_n such that*

$$a_n = \begin{cases} 0 & \text{for } 0 \le n \le 5 \\ 1 & \text{for } n = 6 \\ 2 & \text{for } n = 7 \\ 3 & \text{for } n = 8 \\ 4 & \text{for } n = 9 \\ 0 & \text{for } n \ge 10 \end{cases}$$

Sol. Let $A(z)$ is the generating function for a_n where,

$$A(z) = a_0 + a_1 z + a_2 z^2 + \dots\dots + a_n z^n + \dots$$

Since values of a_0 to a_5 and a_{10} onwards are equal to zero. So

$$A(z) = a_6 z^6 + a_7 z^7 + a_8 z^8 + a_9 z^9 + a_{10} z^{10}$$
$$= 1.z^6 + 2.z^7 + 3.z^8 + 4.z^9 + 0.z^{10}$$
$$= z^6.(1 + 2z + 3z^2 + 4z^3)$$

Note that Generating function to the convolution of numeric functions i.e. $c_n = a_n * b_n$ will be A(z) . B(z). Since

$$c_n = a_n * b_n = a_0 b_n + a_1 b_{n-1} + \ldots\ldots\ldots\ldots\ldots + a_{n-1} b_1 + a_n b_0$$

which is the coefficient of z^n in the product of series

$$(a_0 + a_1 z + a_2 z^2 + \ldots\ldots + a_n z^n + \ldots) \,.\, (b_0 + b_1 z + b_2 z^2 + \ldots + a_n z^n + \ldots)$$

And it's generating function is equal to the product of the generating functions of both A(z) and B(z), i.e.

$$C(z) = A(z) \,.\, B(z)$$

Example 2.31 *Let $a_n = 3^n$ and $b_n = 5^n$ for $n \geq 0$, then determine the generating function for the convolution of numeric functions a_n and b_n.*

Sol. Since generating function corresponding to numeric function a_n and b_n are A(z) = 1/(1 – 3z) and 1/(1 – 5z) respectively. Let $c_n = a_n * b_n$ then its generating function is given by C(z) = A(z) . B(z). Therefore

$$C(z) = 1/(1 - 3z) \,.\, 1/(1 - 5z)$$

Alternatively, C(z) can be written as using partial fraction

$$C(z) = -\,3/2(1 - 3z) + 5/2(1 - 5z)$$

Therefore its numeric function will be,

$$c_n = -\,3/2.\, 3^n + 5/2 \,.\, 5^n \qquad \text{or} \qquad c_n = (-\,1/2).\, 3^{n+1} + (1/2)\,.5^{n+1} \quad \text{for } n \geq 0$$

- If $c_n = \sum_{I=0}^{n} a_I$ then its generating is C(z) = A(z) . 1/(1 – z) where A(z) is the generating function for function a_I for I = 0 to n. To prove this fact we recall that if the convolution of numeric function a_n and b_n is c_n, then

$$c_n = \sum_{I=0}^{n} a_I \,.\, b_{n-I}$$

And its generating function is given as C(z) = A(z) . B(z)

Assume $b_{n-I} = 1$ then

$$c_n = \sum_{I=0}^{n} a_I \,.\, 1$$

Since generating function for function $b_{n-I} = 1$ for $n \geq 0$ or (1, 1, 1, ... 1, ...) is B(z) = 1/(1 – z). Therefore,

$$C(z) = A(z) \,.\, 1/(1 - z)$$

where A(z) is the generating function of the numeric function $\sum_{I=0}^{n} a_I$

Example 2.32 *Determine the generating function for the numeric function (1, 2, 3, ..., n, ...).*

Sol. Since $1/(1 - z) = 1 + z + z^2 + z^3 \ldots\ldots\ldots\ldots + z^n + z^{n+1} + \ldots$

Differentiate both side w.r.t.z, i.e.,

$$1/(1 - z)^2 = 1 + 2z + 3z^2 + \ldots\ldots\ldots\ldots + nz^{n-1} + (n + 1)z^n + \ldots$$

Thus, we obtain the generating function $1/(1 - z)^2$ for the numeric function (1, 2, 3, ..., n, ...).

Conversely, for generating function $1/(1 - z)^2$, the coefficient of z^n (general term) will be,

$$= (-\,1)^n\, (-\,2)\, (-\,2 - 1) \ldots\ldots (-\,2 - n + 1)/n!$$

$= 2\ .3\ ....\ (n + 1)/n!$

$= (n + 1)$

Therefore we obtain the numeric function $a_n = n + 1$ for $n \geq 0$ for it values $(1, 2, ..., n, ..)$

Example 2.33 *Determine the generating function for the numeric function* $(0^2, 1^2, 2^2, ..., n^2, ...)$.

Sol. Since $1/(1 - z) = 1 + z + z^2 + z^3 .... + z^n + ...$

Differentiate both sides w.r.t.z, i.e.,

$$1/(1 - z)^2 = 1 + 2z + 3z^2 + ... + nz^{n-1} + ...$$

Multiply both sides by z so we obtain

$$z.1/(1 - z)^2 = 1.z + 2z^2 + 3z^3 + ... + nz^n + ...$$

Differentiate again w.r.t.z and multiply both sides with z, i.e.,

$$z.(1 + z)/(1 - z)^3 = 0^2 + 1^2.z + 2^2.z^2 + 3^2.z^3 + ... + n^2.z^n + ...$$

Thus, we obtain the generating function $z.(1 + z)/(1 - z)^3$ for the numeric function $(0^2, 1^2, 2^2, ..., n^2, ...)$.

Conversely, the coefficient of z_n in $z.(1 + z)/(1 - z)^3$ is n^2†, therefore $a_n = n^2$ for $n \geq 0$.

Example 2.34 *Find generating functions of the following discrete numeric functions*

(i) $1, 2/3, 3/9, 4/27, ...(n + 1)/3^n, ...$

(ii) $0.5^0, 1.5^1, 2.5^2, ..., n.5^n, ...$

Sol. (*i*) Let A(z) is the generating function of the series $(1, 2/3, 3/9, 4/27, ... (n + 1)/3^n, ...)$, i.e.,

$$A(z) = 1 + z.2/3 + z^2.3/9 + z^3.4/27 + ... + z^n.(n + 1)/3^n + ...$$

or

$$A(z) = 1 + 2.(z/3) + 3.(z/3)^2 + 4.(z/3)^3 + ... + (n + 1).(z/3)^n + ...$$

Since, $1/(1 - z)^2 = 1 + 2z + 3z^2 + ... + (n + 1)z^n + ...$

Replace z by $z/3$ so above equation becomes

$$1/(1 - z/3)^2 = 1 + 2.(z/3) + 3.(z/3)^2 + ... + (n + 1).(z/3)^n + ...$$

Therefore, $1/(1 - z/3)$ is the required generating function.

(*ii*) Let B(z) is the generating function of the series $(0.5^0, 1.5^1, 2.5^2, ..., n.5^n, ...)$, i.e.,

$$B(z) = 0.5^0 + 1.5^1 z + 2.5^2 z^2 + ... + n.5^n z^n + ...$$

Since, $1/(1 - z) = 1 + z + z^2 + z^3 .... + z^n + ...$

Replace z by $5z$ thus we obtain the equation

$$1/(1 - 5z) = 1 + 5z + (5z)^2 + (5z)^3 .... + (5z)^n + ...$$

---

† Since general term of $1/(1 - z)^3$, is given as

$$= (-1)^n.\ z^n\ .(-3).\ (-4).\ ....(-3 - n + 1)/n!$$

Thus, the coefficient of z^n in $1/(1 - z)^3$ is

$$= (3).\ (4).\ ....\ (2 + n)/n!$$

$$= (n + 2)\ (n + 1)/1.\ 2$$

Therefore the coefficient of z^n in the expansion of $z.(1 + z)1/(1 - z)^3$ is

$$= n\ .(n + 1)/2 + (n - 1)\ .n/2$$

$$= n\ .2n/2$$

$$= n^2$$

Differentiate w.r.t z

$$1.5/(1-5z)^2 = 0 + 5.1 + 2.5^2z + 3.5^3z^2 + \ldots\ldots\ldots + n.5^n z^{n-1} + \ldots\ldots\ldots\ldots\ldots\ldots$$

or
$$5/(1-5z)^2 = 0.5^0 + 1.5^1 + 2.5^2z + 3.5^3z^2 + \ldots\ldots\ldots + n.5^n z^{n-1} + \ldots\ldots\ldots\ldots$$

Multiply both sides with z, so we have

$$5z/(1-5z)^2 = 0.5^0 z + 1.5z + 2.5^2z^2 + 3.5^3z^3 + \ldots\ldots\ldots + n.5^n z^n + \ldots\ldots\ldots\ldots$$

or
$$5z/(1-5z)^2 = 0.5^0 + 1.5z + 2.5^2z^2 + 3.5^3z^3 + \ldots\ldots\ldots + n.5^n z^n + \ldots\ldots\ldots\ldots\ldots$$

Therefore, $5z/(1-5z)^2$ is the generating function for $(0.5^0, 1.5^1, 2.5^2, \ldots\ldots, n.5^n, \ldots\ldots\ldots\ldots)$.

Example 2.35 *Determine generating function and discrete numeric function of series*

$$-3/2 + 2 + 0 + 8 + \ldots\ldots$$

Sol. Let scale of relation of the given series be $1 - pz - qz^2$. Obtain p and q from the equations,

$$0 - 2p + 3/2q = 0 \quad \text{and} \quad 8 - 0 - 2q = 0$$

So we obtain $q = 4$ and $p = 3$. Whence, scale of relation is $1 - 3z - 4z^2$.

Hence, the generating function A(z) for series, $-3/2 + 2.z + 0.z^2 + 8.z^3 + \ldots\ldots$ is

$$= [-3/2 + (2 + 3.3/2)z]/(1 - 3z - 4z^2) \qquad \text{(using equation (2.7))}$$

$$= (-3/2 + 13/2z)/(1 - 3z - 4z^2)$$

So, $\quad A(z) = (-3/2 + 13/2z)/(1 - 3z - 4z^2)$

Since A(z) can be written as (using partial fraction)

$$= (8/5)/(1+z) - (31/10)/(1-4z)$$

So numeric function will be the coefficient of z_n that will be,

$$a_n = (8/5).(-1)^n.1 - (31/10).4^n$$

or
$$a_n = (-1)^n.(8/5) - (31/10).4^n \quad \text{for } n \geq 0.$$

2.5 APPLICATION OF GENERATING FUNCTION TO SOLVE COMBINATORIAL PROBLEMS

The important application of generating function representation of numeric function is the solving of combinatorial problems. Consider the numeric function a_n, i.e.,

$$a_n = \binom{m}{n} \text{ for a fixed value of } n$$

Since,
$$a_n = \begin{cases} \binom{m}{n} = 1 & \text{for } n = 0 \\ \binom{m}{n} = 0 & \text{for } n > m \end{cases}$$

we recall following definitions that are frequently used in solving of combinatorial problems,

- The expression $n(n-1) \ldots. 2.1$ is called n – factorial, and denoted by $n!$, with the convention $0! = 1$.
- $\binom{m}{n}$ is called binomial coefficient, i.e., (number of n – subsets of an m – set)

$$\binom{m}{n} = m!/n!\,(m-n)!$$

- Binomial coefficients $\binom{m}{n}$ have no combinatorial meaning for negative values of m.

But we formally extend its previous definition to negative arguments by using the definition of lower factorials, i.e.,

$$\binom{-m}{n} = (-m)(-m-1)\ldots(-m-n-1)/n!$$
$$= (-1)^n m(m+1)\ldots(m+n-1)/n!$$

The expressions $m(m+1)\ldots(m+n-1)$ are called rising factorials of length n and its value is 1 for $n = 0$.

Since different values derived from numeric function $a_n = \binom{m}{n}$ are,

$$\left\{\binom{m}{0}, \binom{m}{1}, \binom{m}{2}, \ldots\ldots\ldots\ldots \binom{m}{n}, \ldots\ldots\ldots\ldots\right\}$$

Let us assume that A(z) is the generating function of a_n, i.e.,

$$A(z) = \binom{m}{0} + \binom{m}{1}z + \binom{m}{2}z^2 + \ldots\ldots + \binom{m}{n}z^n + \ldots\binom{m}{m}z^m + \ldots$$
$$= (1+z)^m$$
$$= \sum_{k=0}^{m}\binom{m}{k}z^k$$

If we put $z = 1$, i.e.,

$$A(z) = \binom{m}{0} + \binom{m}{1} + \binom{m}{2} + \ldots\ldots\ldots\ldots + \binom{m}{n} + \ldots\binom{m}{m} + \ldots$$
$$= \sum_{k=0}^{m}\binom{m}{k} = 2^m,$$

and for $z = -1$, we have

$$A(z) = \binom{m}{0} - \binom{m}{1} + \binom{m}{2} - \ldots\ldots\ldots\ldots + (-1)^n\binom{m}{n} + \ldots + (-1)^m\binom{m}{m} + \ldots$$
$$= \sum_{k=0}^{m}(-1)^k\binom{m}{k} = 0 \quad (\text{for } m \geq 1)$$

EXERCISES

2.1 Let a_n be an numeric function such that a_n is equal to the reminder when the integer n is divided by 17. Let b_n be a another numeric function such that is equal to 0 if the integer n is divisible by 3, and is equal to 1 otherwise,

- Let $c_n = a_n + b_{n,}$, then for what values of n, $c_n = 0$ and $c_n = 1$.
- Let $d_n = a_n * b_{n,}$, then for what values of n, $d_n = 0$ and $d_n = 1$.

2.2 Find the generating function for the following discrete numeric functions :

(*i*) 1, 1, 2, 2, 3, 3, 4, 4, ...

(*ii*) 1, 2/3, 3/9, 4/27, ...

(*iii*) 1, $1^* 3^0$, $1^* 3^1$, $1^* 3^2$, $1^* 3^3$, ...

(*iv*) 3, $(3+3)^{-3}$, $(3+3^2)^{-5}$, $(3+3^3)^{-5}$, ...

2.3 Determine generating function and discrete numeric function of the following series :

(*i*) 2 + 5 + 13 + 35 +.......................

(ii) – 1 + 6 + 30 + ...

(iii) 1 + 6 + 24 + 84 + ...

(iv) 2 + 7 + 25 + 19 + ...

2.4 Determine the generating function of the numeric function a_n where

$$a_n = \begin{cases} 5^n & \text{for } n \text{ is even} \\ -5^n & \text{for } n \text{ is odd} \end{cases}$$

2.5 Determine the discrete numeric functions corresponding to the following generating functions

(i) $A(z) = (1 + 3z)/(1 + 11z + 28z^2)$

(ii) $A(z) = (2z + 1)/(z^2 + 1)(z - 1)$

(iii) $A(z) = (1 - z + 2z^2)/(1 - z)^3$

(iv) $A(z) = (7 + z)/(1 + z)(1 + z^2)$

(v) $A(z) = (2 + z)^n + (2 - z)^{-n}$

2.6 Determine the asymptotic order of the following numeric functions

(i) $a_n = 8n + C$ where $C > 1024$

(ii) $a_n = 3n^3 + 2n^2 + 1$

(iii) $a_n = 2^n n^3 + n$

(iv) $a_n = n!$

(v) $a_n = 3n^3 + 2n^2 + 1$

(vi) $a_n = n \log n + n^2$

(vii) $a_n = n^{2n} + 5*2^n$

(viii) $a_n = n^{1.5} + n \log n$

(ix) $a_n = n^{1.001} + n \log n$

(x) $a_n = \sum_{k=0}^{n} k^2$

(xi) $a_n = \sum_{k=0}^{n} k^3$

2.7 In how many ways can $3n$ men can be selected form $2n$ men of white hairs, $2n$ men of curly hairs, and $2n$ men of silky hairs.

2.8 Let a_n denote the number of ways to seat 7 students in a row of n chairs so that no two students will occupy adjacent seats. Determine the generating function of the discrete numeric function.

2.9 Determine the numeric function and the generating function of the following series :

(i) $\binom{n}{0}^2 + \binom{n}{1}^2 + \binom{n}{2}^2 + \ldots\ldots\ldots\ldots + \binom{n}{k}^2 + \ldots\ldots\ldots\ldots + \binom{n}{n}^2$

(ii) $\binom{n}{0} + 2\binom{n}{1} + 2^2\binom{n}{2} + \ldots\ldots\ldots\ldots + 2^k\binom{n}{k} + \ldots\ldots\ldots\ldots + 2^n\binom{n}{n}$

(iii) $\binom{n}{0} + \ldots\ldots\ldots\ldots + \binom{2n-k}{n-k} + \ldots\ldots\ldots\ldots + \binom{2n-1}{n-1} + \binom{2n}{n}$

(iv) $2\binom{n}{0} + 2^2/2\binom{n}{1} + 2^3/3\binom{n}{2} + \ldots\ldots\ldots\ldots + 2^{n+1}/n+1\binom{n}{n}$

(v) $\binom{n}{0}^2 - \binom{n}{1}^2 + \binom{n}{2}^2 - \ldots\ldots\ldots\ldots + (-1)^k\binom{n}{k}^2 + \ldots\ldots\ldots\ldots + (-1)^n\binom{n}{n}^2$

2.10 Determine the time complexity of the following programs :

(i)
```
//a function which return the summation of n numbers placed in
the array A[0, n - 1]
    int Sum1(int A[ ], int n)
    {
        int sum = 0;
        for (int I = 0; I < n ; I ++ )
            sum = sum + A[I];
        return sum;
    }
```

(*ii*)
```
//function of summation of n numbers using recursion
   int Sum2(int A[ ], int n)
   {
      if(n > 0)
      return Sum2(A,n - 1) + A[n-1];
      return 0;
   }
```

(*iii*)
```
// a function that adds two matrices A[0,n-1][0,m-1]
and B[0,n-1][0,m-1] and result stored in the same size matrix C.
Void Add(int **A, int **B, int **C, int n, int m)
   {
      for (int I = 0; I < n; I ++)
         for (int J = 0; J < m; J ++)
            C[I][J] = A[I][J]+B[I][J]
   }
```

(*iv*)
```
//a function that multiplies two matrices A[0,n-1] [0,n-1]
and B[0,n-1][0,n-1] and result stored in the same size matrix C.
Void Multiply(int **A, int **B, int **C, int n)
   {
      for (int I = 0; I < n; I ++)
         for (int J = 0; J < n; J ++)
         {
            int sum = 0;
            for (int K = 0; K < n; K ++)
               sum = sum + A[I][K]+B[K][J]
            C[I][J] = sum;
         }
   }
```

(*v*) //a function to evaluate the polynomial of degree n i.e.,

$$p(x) = \sum_{i=0}^{n} a_i \; x^n$$

```
int Poly1(int a[],int n, const &x)
   {
      int T = 1, val = a[0];
      for (int I = 1; I = n; I++)
      {
         T = T * x;
         val = val + T * a[I];
      }
     return val;
   }
```

(*vi*)

```
// a function for polynomial evaluation using Horner's rule
int Poly2(int a[],int n, const &x)
   {
         int val = a[n];
         for (int I = 1; I = n; I++)
            val = val * x + a[n - I];
      return val;
   }
```

Recurrence Relations With Constant Coefficients

3 Recurrence Relations with Constant Coefficients

3.1 INTRODUCTION

In mathematics, we often refer a function in terms of itself. For example, the factorial function $f(n) = n!$, for n as integer, is defined as,

$$f(n) = \begin{cases} 1 & \text{for } n \le 1 \\ n.f(n-1) & \text{for } n > 1 \end{cases} \qquad (3.1)$$

Above definition states that $f(n)$ equals to 1 whenever n is less than or equal to 1. However, when n is more than 1, function $f(n)$ is defined *recursively* (function invokes itself). In loose sense the use of f on right side of equation (3.1) result a circular definition for example, $f(2) = 2.\,f(1) = 2.1 = 2$ and $f(3) = 3\ .\ f(2) = 3*2 = 6$.

Take another example of Fibonacci number series, which is defined as,

$$f_0 = 0\ ; \qquad f_1 = 1\ ; \qquad f_n = f_{n-1} + f_{n-2} \quad \text{for } n > 1 \qquad (3.2)$$

To compute the Fibonacci numbers series, f_0 and f_1 are the base component so that computation can be initiated. $f_n = f_{n-1} + f_{n-2}$ is the recursive component that viewed as recursive equations. In equation (3.1) the base component is $f(n) = 1$ for $n = 1$ and recursive component is $f(n) = n\ .\ f(n-1)$.

Recurrence equations arise very naturally to express the resources used by recursive procedures. A *recurrence relation* defines a function over the natural number, say $f(n)$ in terms of its own value at one/more integers smaller than n. In others words, $f(n)$ defines inductively. As with all inductions, there are base cases to be defined separately, and the recurrence relation only applies for n larger than the base cases.

For discrete numeric functions ($a_0, a_1, a_2, \ldots\ldots, a_n, \ldots\ldots$), an equation relating a_n for any n to one/more of a_i's ($i < n$) is the recurrence relation of the numeric functions. A recurrence relation is also called a *difference equation*.

For example, let a numeric function $a_n = (2^0, 2^1, 2^2, \ldots\ldots, 2^n, \ldots\ldots)$, then the function expression of $a_n = 2^n$ for $n \ge 0$. Same numeric function can be specified by another way. Since the value of a_n is twice the value of a_{n-1} for all n, so once we know the value of a_{n-1} we can compute a_n. The value of a_{n-1} is twice of a_{n-2} which is again twice of a_{n-3} and so on. Thus we reach to a_0 whose value is known to be 1. Hence we write the relation

$$a_n = 2\ .\ a_{n-1} \qquad \text{for } n \ge 0 \qquad (3.3)$$

provided that $a_0 = 1$ is the recurrence relation that specify the numeric function a_n.

It is also clear that by recurrence relation, we can carry out step-by-step computation to determine a_n from $a_{n-1}, a_{n-2}, \ldots\ldots$, to determine a_{n+1} from $a_n, a_{n-1}, \ldots\ldots\ldots$ and so on using base conditions. We thus conclude that a numeric function can be described by a recurrence relation together with the base conditions. *The numeric function is also referred to as the solution of the recurrence relation.*

In section 3.2 we will discuss a simple class of recurrence relations known as *linear recurrence relation with constant coefficients* (LRRCC). Section 3.3 illustrates method for solving of linear recurrence relation with constant coefficients. In this section we will discuss the homogeneous solution and the particular solution of the differential equation along with an alternate method discuss in section 3.4 where we will find out the solution through generating function. We will also see that for a given set of base conditions the solution to a LRRCC is unique. Common recurrences obtain from algorithms will be discussed in Section 3.5. We describe several categories of recurrence equations obtain using algorithm paradigm such as divide-and-conquer and chip-and-conquer and also the solution of these recurrences.

3.2 RECURRENCE RELATION FOR DISCRETE NUMERIC FUNCTIONS (Linear Recurrence Relation with Constant Coefficients LRRCC)

A class of recurrence relation of the general form

$$A_0 a_n + A_1 a_{n-1} + A_2 a_{n-2} + \ldots\ldots + A_k a_{n-k} = f(n) \qquad (3.4)$$

where A_i's are constant (some may be zero) is known as linear recurrence relation with constant coefficients (LRRCC) for some constant $k \geq 1$.

For example, the Fibonacci recurrence equation (3.2) corresponds to $k = 2$ and $f(n) = 0$ with base conditions $a_0 = 0$ and $a_1 = 1$.

In the recurrence relation of equation (3.4) if coefficients A_0 and A_k are not zero then it is kth order recurrence relation. For example, the recurrence relation $3\,a_n + a_{n-1} = n$ is a first order LRRCC.

Consider another example,

$$a_n - 2a_{n-1} + 3a_{n-2} = n^2 + 1 \qquad (3.5)$$

and

$$a_n + a_{n-2} + 5a_{n-4} = 2n$$

are second-order and fourth-order LRRCC respectively. Also, the recurrence relation viz. $a^2_n + 3\,a_{n-1} = 5$ is not a LRRCC.

Let us take the recurrence relation in (3.5), with base conditions $a_3 = 1$ and $a_4 = 2$. We can compute a_5 as,

$$a_5 = 2\,a_4 - 3\,a_3 + (5^2 + 1)$$
$$= 2\,.2\ - 3\,.\,1 + \ 26 = 27$$

we then compute a_6 accordingly as,

$$a_6 = 2\,a_5 - 3\,a_4 + (6^2 + 1)$$
$$= 2.27 - 3\,.2 + \ 37 = \ 85$$

Similarly we determine a_7, a_8, ……and so on. We can also compute a_2 as,

$$a_2 = (1/3)\,(\,a_4 - 2\,a_3 - (4^2 + 1))$$
$$= (1/3)\,(\,2 - 2\,.1 - 17) \quad = -\,17/3$$

and so $a_1 = 7/9$ and $a_0 = -\,110/27$. This way, we can completely specifiy the *discrete numeric function* a_n.

FACT

In general, for the kth order LRRCC

1. If, k consecutive values of a numeric function are known then numeric function return unique solution.

2. if, k^{th} order LRRCC has fewer than k values of numeric function then numeric function does not return unique solution. For example, the recurrence relation,

$$a_n + a_{n-1} + a_{n-2} = 4 \tag{3.6}$$

and base condition $a_0 = 2$, then we can determine many numeric functions (shown below) that will satisfy both the recurrence relation and the base condition.

$$2, 0, 2, 2, 0, 2, 2, 0, \ldots\ldots$$
$$2, 2, 0, 2, 2, 0, 2, 2, \ldots\ldots$$
$$2, 5, -3, 2, 5, -3, 2, \ldots\ldots$$

3. More than k values of numeric functions might be impossible for the existence of a numeric function that satisfies the recurrence relation and the given base condition/s. For example, the recurrence relation in (3.6), if we have the base conditions $a_0 = 2$, $a_1 = 2$ and $a_2 = 2$ then a_0, a_1 and a_2 doesn't satisfy the recurrence relation simultaneously. Therefore, no numeric function simultaneously satisfies the recurrence relation and the base condition both.

3.3 FINDING THE SOLUTION OF LRRCC

The discrete numeric function which is the solution of a linear difference equation is the sum of two discrete numeric functions–the homogeneous solution and the particular solution. Consider the linear recurrence relation with constant coefficients (LRRCC) equation (3.4)

$$A_0\, a_n + A_1\, a_{n-1} + A_2\, a_{n-2} + \ldots\ldots + A_k\, a_{n-k} = f(n)\,;$$

Then, the solution $a_{(h)} = (a_{0(h)}, a_{1(h)}, a_{2(h)}, \ldots\ldots, a_{n(h)}, \ldots)$ that satisfies the difference equation (3.7) is called *homogeneous solution* where subscript h denotes the homogenous solution values.

$$A_0\, a_{n(h)} + A_1\, a_{n-1(h)} + A_2\, a_{n-2(h)} + \ldots\ldots + A_k\, a_{n-k(h)} = 0\,; \tag{3.7}$$

Simultaneously, a solution $\mathbf{a}_{(\mathbf{p})} = (a_{0(p)}, a_{1(p)}, a_{2(p)}, \ldots\ldots, a_{n(p)}, \ldots)$ that satisfies the equation,

$$A_0\, a_{n(p)} + A_1\, a_{n-1(p)} + A_2\, a_{n-2(p)} + \ldots\ldots + A_k\, a_{n-k(p)} = f(n)\,; \tag{3.8}$$

is called *particular solution* where subscript p denotes the particular solution values.

Thus we have,

$$A_0\,(a_{n(h)} + a_{n(p)}) + A_1\,(a_{n-1(h)} + a_{n-1(p)}) + A_2\,(a_{n-2(h)} + a_{n-2(p)}) \ldots + A_k\,(a_{n-k(h)} + a_{n-k(p)}) = f(n); \tag{3.9}$$

Clearly, the difference equation (3.4) has the *complete solution* $\mathbf{a} = \mathbf{a}_{(\mathbf{h})} + \mathbf{a}_{(\mathbf{p})}$ which is the summation of the homogeneous solution and the particular solution.

3.3.1 Method of Finding Homogenous Solution

Let
$$A_0\, a_n + A_1\, a_{n-1} + A_2\, a_{n-2} + \ldots\ldots + A_k\, a_{n-k} = 0\,; \tag{3.10}$$
is the *homogenous equation*,

Step 1

Find the characteristic equation for the above recurrence relation. Therefore substitute $A\alpha^n$ for a_n in equation (3.10). Thus we have

$$A_0\,(A\alpha^n) + A_1\,(A\alpha^{n-1}) + A_2\,(A\alpha^{n-2}) + \ldots\ldots + A_k\,(A\alpha^{n-k}) = 0\,;$$

or
$$A_0\,\alpha^n + A_1\,\alpha^{n-1} + A_2\,\alpha^{n-2} + \ldots\ldots + A_k\,\alpha^{n-k} = 0\,;$$

After simplification we obtain the equation

$$A_0\,\alpha^k + A_1\,\alpha^{k-1} + A_2\,\alpha^{k-2} + \ldots\ldots + A_k = 0\,; \tag{3.11}$$

So equation (3.11) is called *characteristic equation.*

If α_1 is one of the roots of this equation then $A\alpha_1^n$ is a homogenous solution to the difference equation.

Step 2

Solve the characteristic equation and find out the roots to satisfy the homogenous equation. A characteristic equation of kth degree has k characteristic roots. The roots are of following nature,

Case 1. Let all roots are distinct s.t. $\alpha_1, \alpha_2, \ldots\ldots \alpha_k$ then homogenous solution is given as,

$$a_{n(h)} = C_1\,\alpha_1^n + C_2\,\alpha_2^n + \ldots\ldots + C_k\,\alpha_k^n \qquad (3.12)$$

where C_i's $(1 \le i \le k)$ are the constants to be determined (see example 3.1)

Case 2. Suppose some roots of the characteristic equation are multiple roots. Let α_1 be a root of multiplicity m then homogenous solution is given as,

$$a_{n(h)} = (C_1\,n^{m-1} + C_2\,n^{m-2} + \ldots\ldots + C_{m-1}\,n + C_m)\,\alpha_1^n \qquad (3.13)$$

(see example 3.2)

Case 3. If some roots of the characteristic equation are multiple roots and remaining are distinct (combination of above cases 1 and 2), *i.e.*, $\alpha_1 = \alpha_2 = \alpha_3$; $\alpha_4 \ne \alpha_5 \ne \ldots\ldots \ne a_k$ then homogenous solution is

$$a_{n(h)} = (C_1\,n^2 + C_2\,n + C_3)\,\alpha_1^3 \;+\; C_4\,\alpha_4^n \;+ C_5\,\alpha_5^n \ldots\ldots + C_k\,\alpha_k^n \qquad (3.14)$$

(see example 3.3)

Step 3

Determine the constants C_i's $(1 \le i \le k)$ using base conditions.

Example 3.1. *Consider the Fibonacci number series recurrence equation (3.2), this recurrence can be equivalently specifies as,*

$$a_n = a_{n-1} + a_{n-2} \qquad \textit{(with base conditions are } a_0 = 0 \textit{ and } a_1 = 1)$$

So, the homogenous equation is $a_n - a_{n-1} - a_{n-2} = 0$ and its corresponding characteristic equation is obtain by substituting α^2 for a_n, *i.e.*,

$$\alpha^2 - \alpha - 1 = 0$$

Hence we obtain two distinct roots $(1+\sqrt{5})/2$ and $(1-\sqrt{5})/2$

Therefore, the homogenous solution

$$a_n = C_1\,((1+\sqrt{5})/2)^n + C_2\,((1-\sqrt{5})/2)^n\ ;$$

Coefficient C_1 and C_2 are determined by using base conditions such that put $a_0 = 0$ and $a_1 = 1$ in the homogenous solution.

Thus, we obtain $C_1 = 1/5$ and $C_2 = -1/5$;

Therefore, the homogenous solution is

$$a_n = 1/5\,((1+\sqrt{5})/2)^n - 1/5\,((1-\sqrt{5})/2)^n\ ;$$

Example 3.2. *Consider another recurrence of multiple roots*

$$a_n - 9a_{n-2} + 4a_{n-3} + 12a_{n-4} = 0.$$

Thus, we have the characteristic equation is

$$\alpha^4 - 9\alpha^2 + 4\alpha + 12 = 0\ ; \qquad \textit{(here } k = 4 \textit{ and so substitute } \alpha^4 \textit{ for } a_n)$$

After solving we obtain multiple roots – 3, – 3, – 3 and – 3. Therefore, the homogenous solution is

$$a_n = (C_1 n^{4-1} + C_2 n^{4-2} + C_3 n^{4-3} + C_4 n^{4-4}) (-3)^4 ;$$

or, $$a_n = (C_1 n^3 + C_2 n^2 + C_3 n + C_4) (-3)^4 ;$$

Example 3.3. *Consider the recurrence*

$$a_n - 11\, a_{n-1} + 44\, a_{n-2} - 76\, a_{n-3} + 48\, a_{n-4} = 0$$

Thus, corresponding characteristic equation is

$$\alpha^4 - 11\,\alpha^3 + 44\,\alpha^2 - 76\,\alpha + 48 = 0 \quad \text{(here } k = 4 \text{ and so substitute } \alpha^4 \text{ for } a_n)$$

Hence we obtain the roots 2, 2, 3 and 4. Therefore, the homogenous solution is

$$a_n = (C_1 n + C_2) (2)^2 + C_3(3)^n + C_4(4)^n.$$

3.3.2 Method of Finding Particular Solution

The particular solution of the linear difference equation with constant coefficients (or LRRCC) shown in equation (3.4) is determined by method of inspection. In other words, there is no general method known for finding out the particular solution of the linear difference equation with constant coefficients. By inspection, we shall go through following steps,

Step 1

Let the linear difference equation with constant coefficients equation (3.4) is

$$A_0\, a_n + A_1\, a_{n-1} + A_2\, a_{n-2} + \ldots\ldots + A_k\, a_{n-k} = f(n)$$

Assume that general form of particular solution is decided according to $f(n)$

Case 1. If $f(n)$ is a polynomial of degree t of n, *i.e.*,

$$f(n) = F_1 n^t + F_2 n^{t-1} + \ldots\ldots + F_t n + F_{t+1}$$

(where F_i's are the coefficients of the polynomial) then, corresponding particular solution will be of the form

$$P_1 n^t + P_2 n^{t-1} + \ldots\ldots + P_t n + P_{t+1} \tag{3.15}$$

where P_i's are the constants to be determined.

Case 2. If $f(n)$ is a constant, then particular solution is also a constant, let it be P.

Case 3. If $f(n)$ is of form β^n where β is not the characteristic root, then corresponding particular solution is of the form

$$P\beta^n \tag{3.16}$$

Case 3.1. Further, if $f(n)$ is a polynomial of degree t of n followed by β^n *i.e.*

$$(F_1 n^t + F_2 n^{t-1} + \ldots\ldots + F_t n + F_{t+1})\, \beta^n$$

then corresponding particular solution is of the form

$$(P_1 n^t + P_2 n^{t-1} + \ldots\ldots + P_t n + P_{t+1})\, \beta^n \tag{3.17}$$

where P_i's are the constants to be determined

Case 4. If $f(n)$ is a polynomial of degree t of n followed by β^n, where β is a characteristic root of multiplicity $(m - 1)$ *i.e.*

$$(F_1 n^t + F_2 n^{t-1} + \ldots\ldots + F_t n + F_{t+1})\, \beta^n$$

then corresponding particular solution is of the form

$$n^{m-1}(P_1 n^t + P_2 n^{t-1} + \ldots\ldots + P_t n + P_{t+1})\, \beta^n \tag{3.18}$$

where P_i's are the constants to be determined.

Step 2

Substitute general form of the particular solution into difference equation (3.4) to obtain the constant/s P_i's.

Step 3

Put values of constant/s P_i's into the general form of particular solution we get the required particular solution.

Example 3.4. *Determine the particular solution for the following difference equations :*

(a) $a_n + 5\,a_{n-1} + 6\,a_{n-2} = 3\,n^2 - 2n + 1$; (b) $a_n + 5\,a_{n-1} + 6\,a_{n-2} = 1$;

(c) $a_n + 5\,a_{n-1} + 6\,a_{n-2} = 3\,.\,2^n$; (d) $a_n + a_{n-1} = 2\,n\,.3^n$;

(e) $a_n - 2\,a_{n-1} = 3\,.\,2^n$; (f) $a_n - 2\,a_{n-1} + a_{n-2} = (n+1).\,2^n$;

(g) $a_n = a_{n-1} + 5$; (h) $a_n - 2\,a_{n-1} + a_{n-2} = 7$;

(i) $a_n - 5\,a_{n-1} + 6\,a_{n-2} = 3^n + n$.

Sol.

(a) Comparing the given recurrence $a_n + 5a_{n-1} + 6a_{n-2} = 3n^2 - 2n + 1$ with the difference equation (3.4) we find $f(n) = 3\,n^2 - 2n + 1$; which is a polynomial of degree 2, thus we assume the particular solution will be of the form

$$P_1 n^2 + P_2 n + P_3 \qquad \text{[From equation (3.15)]}$$

Substitute above expression into given recurrence/difference equation, we obtain

$$(P_1n^2 + P_2n + P_3) - 5\,(P_1(n-1)^2 + P_2\,(n-1) + P_3) + 6\,(P_1\,(n-2)^2 + P_2\,(n-2) + P_3) = 3n^2 - 2n + 1;$$

which is simplifies to

$$12P_1\,n^2 - (34P_1 - 12P_2)n + (29P_1 - 17P_2 + 12P_3) = 3n^2 - 2n + 1 ; \qquad (3.19)$$

Coefficients P_1, P_2 and P_3 are determine by comparing the coefficients of n^2, n and n_0 in the equation (3.19). Thus, we obtain the equations,

$$12\,P_1 = 3;$$
$$34\,P_1 - 12\,P_2 = 2;$$
$$29\,P_1 - 17\,P_2 + 12\,P_3 = 1;$$

which yields $P_1 = 1/4$, $P_2 = 13/24$, and $P_3 = 71/288$;

Therefore, the particular solution is

$$a_{n(p)} = 1/4\,n^2 + 13/24\,n + 71/288;$$

(b) For the difference equation $a_n + 5\,a_{n-1} + 6\,a_{n-2} = 1$; we find $f(n) = 1$, which is a constant. So particular solution will also a constant P. Substituting P into the difference equation we obtain,

$$P + 5\,P + 6\,P = 1\,;$$

so $$P = 1/12\,;$$

Hence, particular solution is

$$a_{n(p)} = 1/12;$$

(c) Consider difference equation

$$a_n + 5\,a_{n-1} + 6\,a_{n-2} = 3\,.\,2^n$$

Here, $f(n) = 3.2^n$, that is of form β^n (where $\beta = 2$ and not a characteristic root). So, we assume the general form of the particular solution is like expression (3.16), *i.e.*

$$P\,\beta^n \quad \text{or} \quad P\,2^n$$

Substituting P. 2^n into the difference equation we obtain,

$$P\, 2^n + 5\, P\, 2^{n-1} + 6P\, 2^{n-2} = 3.\, 2^n\ ;$$

It simplifies to $5P\, 2^n = 3.\, 2^n$; so $P = 3/5$;

Hence, particular solution is

$$a_{n(p)} = 3/5\ .\ 2^n;$$

(*d*) Consider the difference equation

$$a_n + a_{n-1} = 2\, n\, .3^n;$$

Here, $f(n) = 2.\ n.\ 3^n$; where n is a polynomial of degree 1 followed by 3^n and 3 is not a characteristic root then the particular solution is of the form of expression (3.17), *i.e.*

$$(P_1 n + P_2)\ .\ 3^n$$

Substituting $(P_1 n + P_2)\ .\ 3^n$ into the difference equation, we obtain

$$(P_1 n + P_2)\ .\ 3^n + (P_1(n-1) + P_2)\ .\ 3^{n-1} = 2.n.3^n;$$

Then after simplification we obtain

$$P_1 = 3/2 \text{ and } P_2 = 3/8;$$

Hence, the particular solution is

$$a_{n(p)} = (3/2n + 3/8).3^n;$$

(*e*) Consider the difference equation $a_n - 2\, a_{n-1} = 3.2^n$; Here $f(n)$ is 3.2^n which is of the form β^n, where $\beta = 2$. Since 2 is a characteristic root of multiplicity 1 therefore general form of the particular solution is like expression (3.18) *i.e.*

$$P.n.2^n\ ;$$

Substituting $P.n.2^n$ into the difference equation, we obtain

$$P.n.2^n - 2P.(n-1).2^{n-1} = 3.2^{n'};$$

that yields $P = 6$.

Hence, the particular solution is

$$a_{n(p)} = 6.n.2^n.$$

(*f*) Consider difference equation $a_n - 2\, a_{n-1} + a_{n-2} = (n+1).\ 2^n$ where, $f(n) = (n+1).2^n$ which is a polynomial of degree 1 followed by 2^n. Since 2 is a characteristic root of multiplicity 2 so the general form of the particular solution will be like expression (3.18) *i.e.*

$$n^2\, (P_1 n + P_2).2^n;$$

Substituting above expression into the difference equation we obtain,

$$n^2\, (P_1 n + P_2).2^n - 2(n-1)^2\, (P_1\, (n-1) + P_2).2^{n-1} + (n-2)^2\, (P_1(n-2) + P_2).2^{n-2} = (n+1).2n\ ;$$

After simplifing and comparing the coefficients of 2^n and the constant term we get the values of P_1 & P_2

Hence, particular solution will be

$$a_{n(p)} = n^2\, (P_1 n + P_2).2^n\ ;$$

(*g*) Consider the difference equation $a_n - a_{n-1} = 5$; Since, 1 is the characteristic root of the difference equation, so we can write $f(n) = 5.1^n$. Thus the form of particular solution is

$$P.\ n.\ 1^n \text{ or } P\, n\ ;$$

Since expression $P.n$ satisfies the difference equation so we obtain,

$$P.\ n. - P.(n-1) = 5\ ; \quad \text{or} \quad P = 5\ ;$$

Hence, Particular solution is

$$a_{n(p)} = 5.\ n$$

***NOTE** Here f(n) is a constant and accordingly if we assume the general form of the particular solution to be P, then we obtain nonexistence form of the equation P – P = 5. Therefore the correct way to assume the form of f(n) is 5.1^n.*

(*h*) Consider the difference equation $a_n - 2\,a_{n-1} + a_{n-2} = 7$; Since 1 is the characteristic root of multiplicity 2 of the difference equation. So, $f(n)$ can be written as 7.1^n. Thus the particular solution is of the form

$$n^2.P.1^n \quad \text{or} \quad n^2.P\,;$$

Substitute $n^2.P$ into the difference equation and simplify it, thus we obtain

$$P = 7/2$$

Hence, the particular solution is

$$a_{n(p)} = n^2.7/2$$

(*i*) For the difference equation $a_n - 5\,a_{n-1} + 6\,a_{n-2} = 3^n + n$; since 2 and 3 are its characteristic roots. Here, $f(n) = 3^n + n$. So, the form of $f(n)$ is the combination of β^n (where $\beta = 3$) and a polynomial of degree 1. Thus, corresponding form of particular solution is the combination of $P_1.n.3^n$ and $(P_2.n + P_3)$ respectively.

or $$P_1.n.3^n + (P_2.n + P_3)\,;$$

Substitute particular solution into the difference equation and after simplification we obtain

$$P_1 = -3, \qquad P_2 = 1/3 \qquad \text{and } P_3 = 7/9;$$

Hence, the particular solution is

$$a_{n(p)} = (-3).n.3^n + (1/3).n + 7/9\,;$$

Now we summarize that section 3.3 discussed the method of finding the solution of LRRCC in terms of the homogeneous solution and the particular solution. The complete solution of the LRRCC is the combination of both homogenous solution and the particular solution which is a discrete numeric function. In the homogenous solution the unknown coefficients can be determined using base condition/s. For a *k*th order difference equation the *k*-unknown coefficients $C_1, C_2, \ldots\ldots C_k$ in the homogenous solution can be determined by using base conditions $a_{n0}, a_{n1}, \ldots\ldots\ldots a_{nk-1}$ (where $a_{nj} = a_{nj-1+1}$ for $0 < j \le n_{k-1}$).

Let complete solution is of the form

$$a_n = a_{n(h)} + a_{n(p)}$$

i.e. $$a_n = \sum_{i=1}^{k} C_i \alpha_i^{\,n} + P(n) \qquad (3.20)$$

Substituting the values of base conditions in equation (3.20), we obtain *k* linear equations, *i.e.*

$$a_{n0} = \sum_{i=1}^{k} C_i \alpha_i^{\,n0} + P(n_0)\,;$$

$$a_{n1} = \sum_{i=1}^{k} C_i \alpha_i^{\,n1} + P(n_1)\,;$$

$$\vdots$$

$$a_{nk-1} = \sum_{i=1}^{k} C_i \alpha_i^{\,nk-1} + P(n_{k-1})\,;$$

In general $$\sum_{j=0}^{k-1} a_{nj} = \sum_{j=0}^{k-1} \sum_{i=0}^{k} C_i \alpha_1{}^j + P(j) \tag{3.21}$$

Thus, equation (3.21) yields the coefficients C_i's (for i = 1 to k).

Example 3.5. *Solve the difference equation $a_n - 5\,a_{n-1} + 6\,a_{n-2} = 3^n + n$ for base conditions a_0 = 0 and a_1 = 1.*

Sol. For the homogenous solution $a_{n(h)}$, the characteristic equation is

$$\alpha^2 - 5\alpha + 6 = 0\ ;$$

So, characteristic roots are 2 and 3.

Thus $$a_{n(h)} = C_1.2^n + C_2.3^n\ ;$$

Find out the particular solution $a_{n(p)}$(see example 3.4 (i)) that is,

$$a_{n(p)} = (-\,3).n.3^n + (1/3).n + 7/9;$$

Therefore, the complete solution is,

$$a_n = a_{n(h)} + a_{n(p)}$$

$$a_n = C_1.2^n + C_2.3^n + (-\,3).n.3^n + (1/3).n + 7/9\ ; \tag{3.22}$$

using base conditions we have the linear equations

$$C_1 + C_2 = -\,7/9 \quad \text{and} \quad 2C_1 + 3C_2 = 80/9\ ;$$

that yields $$C_1 = -\,101/9 \quad \text{and} \quad C_2 = 94/9$$

Putting these values of C_1 and C_2 in the equation (3.22) we obtain complete solution

$$a_n = (-\,101/9)\ 2^n + (94/9)\ 3^n - 3^{n+1}\ n\ + (1/3).n + 7/9\ ;$$

FACT

It should be noted that for a kth order LRRCC, uniqueness of the complete solution is depend on the uniqueness of the homogenous solution. That is, the unique solution obtains after solving k linear equations using base conditions that consist of k-consecutive values. Consequently, the unknown coefficients can be determined uniquely by the value of the numeric functions at k-consecutive points.

The non-uniqueness of the homogenous solution occurs under following conditions:

1. If number of linear equations is less than k this condition arises when given base conditions are fewer than k.

2. If base conditions are more than k.

3. If k values of base conditions are non-consecutive.

4. If kth order recurrence relation is non-linear.

3.4 ALTERNATE METHOD (Finding Solution of LRRCC by Generating Function)

In the last section we have seen that, more often we can determine the numeric function from the generating function conveniently. To find out the solution of LRRCC, previously we solve the difference equation and then determine the numeric function. An alternate method is that we firstly determine the generating function for the difference equation and then find the corresponding numeric function. The procedure is pictorially shown in Fig. 3.1.

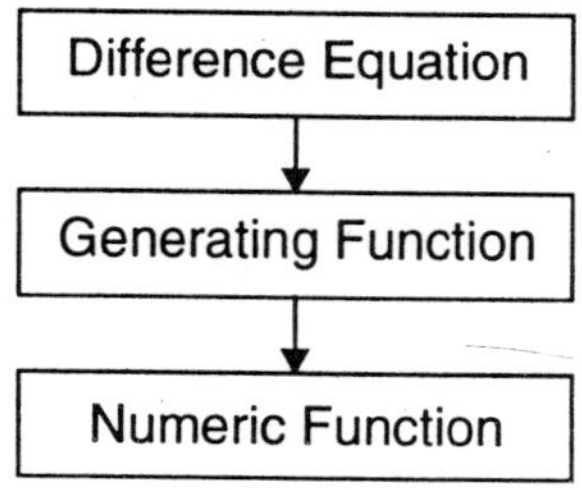

Fig. 3.1 Procedure to solve LRRCC (Alternate Method).

Let LRRCC be of equation (3.4), i.e.,

$$A_0 a_n + A_1 a_{n-1} + A_2 a_{n-2} + \ldots\ldots + A_k a_{n-k} = f(n)$$

(for $n - k \geq 0$ or $n \geq k$ because $n - k$ should not be negative)

Multiplying equation (3.4) by z^n and summing for $k \leq n \leq \infty$.

Thus, we have

$$\sum_{n=k}^{\infty} z^n (A_0 a_n + A_1 a_{n-1} + A_2 a_{n-2} + \ldots\ldots + A_k a_{n-k}) = \sum_{n=k}^{\infty} f(n)$$

or

$$\sum_{n=k}^{\infty} [A_0 (a_n z^n) + A_1 (a_{n-1} z^n) + A_2 (a_{n-2} z^n) + \ldots\ldots + A_k (a_{n-k} z^n)) = \sum_{n=k}^{\infty} f(n) z^n ;$$

We know that, the numeric function $\mathbf{a} = (a_0, a_1, a_2, \ldots\ldots a_n, \ldots\ldots)$ can be expressed by the generating function $A(z)$,where

$$A(z) = a_0 + a_1 z + a_2 z^2 + \ldots\ldots + a_n z^n + \ldots\ldots ;$$

or

$$a_n z^n = A(z) - a_0 - a_1 z - a_2 z^2 + \ldots\ldots a_{k-1} z^{k-1} ;$$

Thus,

$$\sum_{n=k}^{\infty} A_0 (a_n z^n) = A_0 [A(z) - a_0 - a_1 z - a_2 z^2 + \ldots\ldots - a_{k-1} z^{k-1}] ;$$

similarly

$$\sum_{n=k}^{\infty} A_1 (a_{n-1} z^n) = A_1 z [A(z) - a_0 - a_1 z - a_2 z^2 + \ldots\ldots - a_{k-2} z^{k-2}] ;$$

and so on..... ....

$$\sum_{n=k}^{\infty} A_k (a_{n-k} z^n) = A_k z^k [A(z) - a_0 - a_1 z - a_2 z^2 + \ldots\ldots - a_{n-k-1} z^{n-k-1}] ;$$

Add and solve above equations for $A(z)$, so we obtain

$$A(z) = 1/(A_0 + A_1 z + \ldots\ldots + A_k z^k) [\sum_{n=k}^{\infty} f(n) z^n + A_0 (a_0 + a_1 z + \ldots\ldots + a_{k-1} z^{k-1})$$
$$+ A_1 z (a_0 + a_1 z + \ldots\ldots + a_{k-2} z^{k-2}) + A_2 z^2 (a_0 + a_1 z + \ldots\ldots + a_{k-2} z^{k-2}) + \ldots\ldots$$
$$+ A_k z^k (a_0 + a_1 z + \ldots\ldots + a_{n-k-1} z^{n-k-1})] ; \quad (3.23)$$

Example 3.6. *Solve the difference equation $a_n + 5 a_{n-1} + 6 a_{n-2} = 5$ given in example 4.4 (b) for $n \geq 2$ (using alternate method) and base conditions $a_0 = 1$ and $a_1 = 2$.*

Sol. We first determine the generating function $A(z)$ for the difference equation. Since difference equation is valid for $n \geq 2$, so multiply the difference equation to z^n and take sum from $n = 2$ to ∞. Thus we obtain,

$$\sum_{n=2}^{\infty} a_n z^n + 5.\sum_{n=2}^{\infty} a_{n-1} z^n + 6\sum_{n=2}^{\infty} a_{n-2} z^n = \sum_{n=2}^{\infty} z^n \qquad (3.24)$$

Since, $\sum_{n=2}^{\infty} a_n z^n = A(z) - a_0 - a_1 \quad \Rightarrow \quad A(z) - 1 - 2z$

$$\sum_{n=2}^{\infty} a_{n-1} z^n = z(A(z) - a_0) \quad \Rightarrow \quad z(A(z) - 1)$$

$$\sum_{n=2}^{\infty} a_{n-2} z^n = z^2 .A(z) \quad \Rightarrow \quad z^2.A(z)$$

and $\sum_{n=2}^{\infty} z^n = z^2 + z^3 + z^4 \ldots\ldots \infty \quad \Rightarrow \quad 1/(1-z) - 1 - z = z^2/(1-z)$;

putting these values in equation (3.24) and simplified for A(z),

$$A(z) - 1 - 2z + 5z\,(A(z) - 1) + 6\,z^2\,A(z) = z^2/(1 - z)\ ;$$

Thus, $A(z) = (1 + 6z - 6z^2)/(1 + 5z + 6z^2)\,(1 - z)$;

Equivalent to, $A(z) = (1/12)/(1 - z) + (14/3)/(1+2z) + (-\,15/4)/(1+3z)$;

Therefore corresponding numeric equation a^n is,

$$a_n = (1/12)\,.1^n + (14/3)\,(-\,2)^n - (15/4)\,(-\,3)^n\ ;$$

3.5 COMMON RECURRENCES FROM ALGORITHMS

The purpose of this section is the study of the recurrence equation obtained from the procedure codes, and describes some commonly occurring patterns from algorithms. Simultaneously, you will also find the methods to solve some of the typical recurrence equations obtain by this way in the next section.

We can describe several categories of recurrence equations that occurs frequently and can be solved (to some degree) by standard methods. In all cases sub problems refers to a smaller instance of the main problem and that to be solved by recursive call.

Divide-and-Conquer

Divide-and-Conquer strategy is like modularization approach of the software design. A large problem instance is divided into two/more smaller instance problems. Solve smaller instance problems using divide-and-conquer strategy recursively. Finally, combine the solutions of the smaller instance problems to get the solution of the original problem.

We can apply divide-and-conquer strategy to the sorting problems. Sorting problem is the problem where we must sort n elements into non decreasing order. The divide-and-conquer paradigm suggests sorting algorithms with the following general structure :

If n is one, terminate; otherwise partition the set of elements into two/more subsets; sort each; combine the sorted subsets into a single sorted set. Let one set gets a fraction n/k of the elements and other set gets the rest $(n - n/k)$. Now both slices are to be separately sorted by recursive application of divide-and-conquer scheme. Then it merges the sorted fractions. The procedure is shown in Fig. 3.2.

Algorithm (divide-and-conquer sort)

```
Input:    Array S of n elements; k is global;
Output:   Sorted array S of same elements;
void  Sort (int S, int n)
    {
            if (n = k) {
                        I = n/k;
                        J = n - I;
    //Assume array A consists of first I elements of S.
    //Assume array B consists of rest J elements of S.
    Sort (A, I);
    Sort (B, J);
    Merge(A, B, S, I, J);     //   merge the sorted array A & B into S
                        }
    return;
    }
```

Fig. 3.2

Let T(n) be the worst case time of the divide-and-conquer sort algorithm then we obtain the following recurrence for T

$$T(n) = \begin{cases} a & \text{for } n < k \\ T(n/k) + T(n - n/k) + f(n) & \text{for } n \geq k \end{cases} \qquad (3.25)$$

where a and b are constants and $f(n)$ is the nonrecursive cost function that required to split the problems into subproblems and/or to merge the solutions of the subproblems into a solution of the original problem. T(n/k) and T($n - n/k$) are the division time that depends upon the size of the input.

Merge Sort

A procedure merge sort partition the set of elements into two halves (more balanced) and sorts each halves separately (recursively). Then it merges the sorted halves partitions into almost equal halves, which requires

$$n/k \approx n - n/k$$

that is only possible when $k = 2$. Substituting $k = 2$ in (3.25) the recurrence for T(n), we obtain the recurrence relation for merge sort,

$$T(n) = \begin{cases} a & \text{for } n < k \\ T(n/2) + T(n/2) + f(n) & \text{for } n \geq k \end{cases}$$

The presence of floor and selling operators makes this recurrence difficult to interpret. To overcome this difficulty we assume that n is a power of 2

then $$(\lfloor n/2 \rfloor) = (\lceil n/2 \rceil)$$

Thus, recurrence equation will be

$$T(n) = \begin{cases} a & \text{for } n = 1 \\ 2T(n/2) + f(n) & \text{for } n > 1 \end{cases}$$

The generation of the recurrence equation (3.26) can be visualized in Fig. 3.3 called recursion tree. Recursion tree provides a tool for analyzing the cost (time/ other factors) of the recurrence equation.

From the recursion tree shown in Fig. 3.3, we observe that size as a function of node depth is given $n/2, n/4, n/8, \ldots\ldots n/2^d$ for depth 1, 2, 3, ... d (respectively). Thus, the base case occur about at $d = \log(n)$. Since, sum of each row is n (total for the tree), therefore, *recursion tree evaluation* obtains the value T(n) is about $n \log(n)$.

Latter, in this section we will see that the solution of this recurrence obtains using fundamental methods is $\theta(n \log n)$.

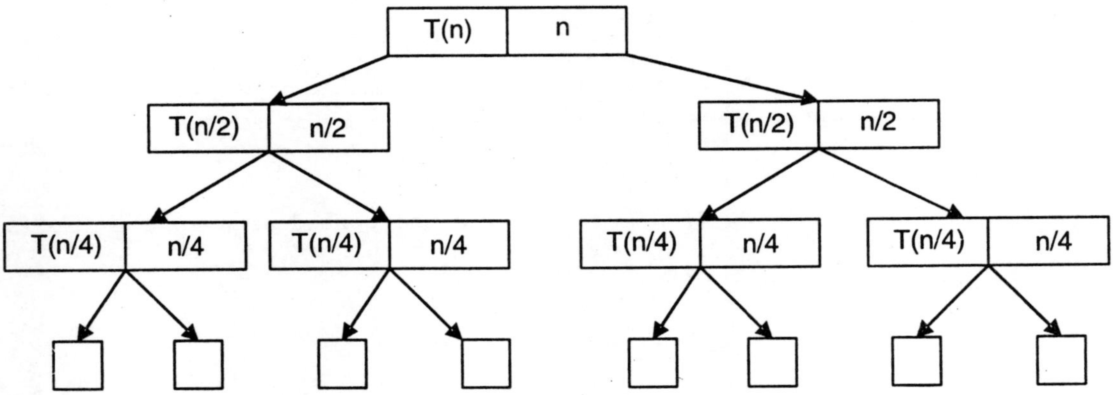

Fig. 3.3 Recursion tree.

Chip-and-Conquer

Let the main problem of size n can be 'chipped-down' to subproblems of size s and $(n\text{-}s)$ $(s > 0)$, with nonrecursive cost $f(n)$ (to split out the problem into subproblems and/or to combine the solution of subproblems into a solution to main problem).

Then the recurrence equation is,

$$T(n) = T(s) + T(n - s) + f(n) \quad \text{for} \quad s > 0 \tag{3.27}$$

Quick Sort

Quick sort strategy is to rearrange the elements to be sorted such that all small elements come first to large elements in the array. Then quick sort sorts the two subranges of small and large keys recursively with the result that entire array is sorted. Quick sort algorithm is shown in Fig. 3.4.

Algorithm (Quick Sort)

```
Input:    Array S of n elements;
Output:   Sorted array S of same elements;

Select an element from array S[0:n-1]for middle;
Partition the remaining elements into two segment left and right, s.t.
All elements in left have lesser than that of middle and
All elements in right have larger than middle.
Sort left with quick sort recursively.
Sort right with quick sort recursively.
Result is left followed by middle followed by right.
```

Fig. 3.4

Let T(n) be the time needed to sort an n-element array. When $n \le 1$, T(n) = a, for some constant a. Assume $n > 1$, let s be the size of the left slice then size of the right slice will be ($n - s - 1$) because pivot element is in middle. So the average time to sort the left slice is T(s) and the right slice is T($n - s - 1$) and the partitioning time $f(n)$.

Since $0 \le s \le (n - 1)$, thus we obtain following recurrence

$$T(n) \le \sum_{s=0}^{n-1} (1/n)\,[T(s) + T(n-s-1)] + f(n)$$

That can be simplified to

$$T(n) = \sum_{s=0}^{n-1} (2/n)\,T(s) + f(n)\,;$$

This recurrence is more complicated because value of T(n) depends on all earlier values. We can attempt some cleverness approach to solve this recurrence. We assume a case in which quick sort works well such that on each time partition will split the set into two equal halves (of size $n/2$). So we have more simplified recurrence equation,

$$T(n) = 2\,T(n/2) + f(n) \tag{3.28}$$

Therefore, T(n) is $\theta(n \log n)$. [see example 3.9 (2)]

3.6 METHOD FOR SOLVING RECURRENCES

Since recurrences of the form of (3.26) or (3.28) arises frequently in analyzing recursive divide-&-conquer algorithms. We shall discuss the methods of finding of the solution of recurrences in general. This section presents three methods for solving the recurrences which return the solution in asymptomatic 'θ' or 'O' bounds. Theorem 3.1 illustrates ***Iteration method*** that converts the recurrence into the summation of the terms then relies on techniques for bounding summations to solve the recurrence. ***Master method*** (theorem 3.2) requires the memorization of the cases that provides bounds for the recurrence of the form T(n) = a T(n/b) + $f(n)$ (where $a \ge 1, b \ge 1$) illustrated in theorem 3.2. At the end theorem 3.3 illustrates ***Substitution method*** that guesses the bounds, corresponding to that it memorizes the appropriate bounds.

3.6.1 Iteration Method

Theorem 3.1. Let a, b and c are nonnegative constants then solution to the recurrence

$$T(n) = \begin{cases} a & \text{for } n = 1 \\ aT(n/b) + f(n) & \text{for } n > 1 \end{cases}$$

where n is a power of b is

$$T(n) = \begin{cases} O(n) & \text{for } a < b \\ O(n \log n) & \text{for } a = b \\ O(n^{\log_b a}) & \text{for } a > b \end{cases} \tag{3.29}$$

Proof. Since n is a power of b, *i.e.* $n = b^k$ then

$$T(n) = n \sum_{k=0}^{\log_b n} x^k\,;\text{(where } x = a/b) \tag{3.30}$$

Now analyze the equation (3.30) so we have following statements,

1. if $a < b \Rightarrow x < 1$; then summation converge, therefore $T(n) = O(n)$.

2. if $a = b \Rightarrow x = 1$; then each term of the sum is unity, since there are $O(\log n)$ terms therefore, $T(n) = O(n \log n)$.

3. if $a > b \Rightarrow x > 1$; then sum terms grows exponentially and there summation is

$$n(x^{1+\log n} - 1)/(x - 1) = O(a^{\log_b n}) \text{ or equally } O(n^{\log_b a}).$$

The theorem states that dividing a problem into two subproblems of equal size results an $O(n \log n)$ time. If number of subproblems are 3, 4 or 8 then algorithm time would be $n^{\log_2 3}$, $n^{\log_2 4} = n^2$, $n^{\log_2 8} = n^3$ respectively and so on. Dividing the problems into four subproblems of size $n/4$ (case 2 when $a = b$) results an $O(n \log n)$ and 9 and 16 subproblems give $O(n^{\log_4 8})$ and $O(n^{\log_4 16}) = O(n^2)$.

3.6.2 Master Theorem

Theorem 3.2. The solution of the recurrence equation

$$T(n) = a\,T(n/b) + f(n)$$

(where $a \geq 1$, $b > 1$ are constants) is given as,

$$T(n) = \begin{cases} \theta(n^{\log_b a}) & \text{if } f(n) = O(n^{\log_b a - \epsilon}) \\ \theta(n^{\log_b a} \log n) & \text{if } f(n) = \theta(n^{\log_b a}) \\ \theta(f(n)) & \text{if } f(n) = \Omega(n^{\log_b a + \epsilon}) \text{ or} \\ & \quad f(n) = O(n^{\log_b a + \delta}) \end{cases} \tag{3.31}$$

for some constant $\epsilon > 0$ and some $\delta \geq \epsilon$.

By careful observation of the results obtain using master theorem we find that the solution of the recurrence is based on the dominance of the function $n^{\log_b a}$ and $f(n)$. As in case 1, function $n^{\log_b a}$ is dominant, so $T(n) = \theta(n^{\log_b a})$. In case 3, function $f(n)$ is dominant, so $T(n) = \theta(f(n))$. And as in case 2, two functions are same, so we multiply by a logarithmic factor, and we obtain the solution $T(n) = \theta(n^{\log_b a} \log n)$.

3.6.3 Substitution Method

Theorem 3.3. The solution of the recurrence

$$T(n) = \begin{cases} a & \text{for } n = 1 \\ aT(n/b) + f(n) & \text{for } n > 1 \end{cases}$$

is given as

$$T(n) = n^{\log_b a}\,[T(1) + g(n)] \tag{3.32}$$

where

$$g(n) = \sum_{j=1}^{i} h(b^j) \quad \text{and} \quad h(n) = f(n)/n^{\log_b a}$$

We obtain $h(n)$ from the recurrence equation. Then find corresponding value of $g(n)$ from the table shown in Fig. 3.4. Entries of the table allows to obtain bounds of $T(n)$ for many recurrences we run-into using divide-and-conquer.

$h(n)$		$g(n)$
$O(n^k)$	for $k < 0$	$O(1)$
$\theta((\log n)^k)$	for $k \geq 0$	$\theta((\log n)^{k+1})/(k+1)$
$\Omega(n^k)$	for $k > 0$	$\theta(h(n))$

Fig. 3.4

Example 3.9. *Solve the following recurrence*

1. $T(n) = 8\ T(n/2) + n^2$ *for* $n = 2$ *and* n *is a power of* 2
2. $T(n) = 2\ T(n/2) + n$ *for* $n = 2$ *and* n *is a power of* 2
3. $T(n) = 64\ T(n/4) + n^6$ *for* $n = 4$ *and* n *is a power of* 4
4. $T(n) = 2\ T(n/2) + cn \log n$ *for* $n = 2$ *and* n *is a power of* 2

In each case assume $T(1) =$ *constant.*

Sol. We can solve above recurrences by any of the method discussed above. We attempt the solution of the recurences using both methods, first by master theorem and later by substitution method.

Master Theorem

1. For the recurrence $T(n) = 8\ T(n/2) + n^2$; we have $a = 3$, $b = 8$ and $f(n) = n^2$. Determine $n^{\log_b a} = n^{\log_2 \theta} = \theta(n^3)$. Since $f(n) = O(n^{\log_2 \theta - \epsilon})$, where $\epsilon = 1$ (case 1 of theorem 3.2) that return the solution $T(n) = \theta(n^{\log_2 \theta}) = \theta(n^3)$.
2. For the recurrence $T(n) = 2\ T(n/2) + n$; we have $a = 2$, $b = 2$ and $f(n) = n$, thus $n^{\log_b a} = n^{\log_2 2} = n$. Since $f(n) = \theta(n^{\log_2 2}) = \theta(n)$ (apply case 2 of theorem 3.2). Therefore, the solution of the recurrence is $T(n) = \theta(n^{\log_2 2} \log n) = \theta(n \log n)$.
3. In the recurrence $T(n) = 64\ T(n/4) + n^6$; we have $a = 64$, $b = 4$, and $f(n) = n^6$ and so $n^{\log_b a} = n^{\log_4 64} = n^3$. Since $f(n) = \Omega(n^{\log_4 64 + \epsilon})$, where $\epsilon = 3$ (case 3 of the theorem 3.2). Hence, the solution $T(n) = \theta(f(n)) = \theta(n^6)$.
4. Recurrence $T(n) = 2\ T(n/2) + cn \log n$; can not solved through master theorem. Since, $f(n) = cn \log n$ is asymptotically dominant than $n^{\log_b a} = n$, but not polynomially dominant. So, no case will determine the solution of this recurrence.

Substitution Method

1. In the recurrence $T(n) = 8\ T(n/2) + n^2$; $a = 8, b = 2$ and $f(n) = n^2$. Thus, $n^{\log_b a} = n^3$ and $h(n) = f(n)/n^{\log_b a} = n^2/n^3 = n^{-1} = O(n^k)$ where $k = -1 < 0$. Therefore, $g(n) = O(1)$.(from the table Fig. 3.4). Hence the solution is
$$T(n) = n^3\ [T(1) + O(1)] = \theta(n^3).$$
2. Recurrence $T(n) = 2\ T(n/2) + n$; we obtain $n^{\log_b a} = n^{\log_2 2} = n$ and $h(n) = n/n = 1 = \theta((\log n)^0)$. From Fig. 3.4 we obtain corresponding $g(n) = \theta(\log n)$, hence, solution is
$$T(n) = n[T(1) + \theta(\log n)] = \theta(n \log n).$$
3. For the recurrence $T(n) = 64\ T(n/4) + n^6$; we obtain $h(n) = n^6/n^{\log_4 64} = n^3 = \Omega(n^k)$ where $k = 3 > 0$. From the table we find corresponding $g(n) = \theta(h(n)) = \theta(n^3)$. Hence the solution
$$T(n) = n^{\log_4 64}\ [T(1) + \theta(n^3)] = \theta(n^6).$$
4. Unsolved recurrence $T(n) = 2\ T(n/2) + cn \log n$; can be solved using substitution method. We obtain $h(n) = cn \log n/n^{\log_2 2} = c \log n = c\ \theta((\log n)^1)$. The corresponding $g(n)$ will be $c\theta((\log n)^2/2)$. Hence the solution
$$T(n) = n\ [T(1) + c\ \theta((\log n)^2/2)] = \theta(n \log^2 n).$$

3.7 MATRIX MULTIPLICATION

Let A and B are two $n \times n$ matrices and there product is another $n \times n$ matrix C, *i.e.*,

$$C(I, K) = \sum_{j=1}^{n} A(I, J)^* B(J, K) ; \quad (3.33)$$

(where $1 \le I \le n$ and $1 \le K \le n$)

From the equation (3.33), computation of each C(I,K) requires n multiplications and $(n-1)$ additions. Thus, computation of all terms of matrix C required a total of $n^2.n + n^2.(n-1)$ operations. Therefore the complexity of such straight forward matrix multiplication method is of order $\theta(n^3)$.

Let us assume n is a power of two viz. $n = 1, 2, 4, 8,$....... If $n = 1$ then we have single element matrices A and B to multiply and we obtain matrix C of single element. Otherwise ($n > 1$), we can divide the matrix A, B and C into 4 submatrices of each size $n/2 \times n/2$ (since n is a power of 2) say A_i's, B_i's and C_i's; for $1 \le i \le 4$.

$$\begin{pmatrix} A_1 & A_2 \\ A_3 & A_4 \end{pmatrix} * \begin{pmatrix} B_1 & B_2 \\ B_3 & B_4 \end{pmatrix} = \begin{pmatrix} C_1 & C_2 \\ C_3 & C_4 \end{pmatrix}$$

where
$$C_1 = A_1B_1 + A_2B_2$$
$$C_2 = A_1B_2 + A_2B_4$$
$$C_3 = A_3B_1 + A_4B_3$$
$$C_4 = A_3B_2 + A_4B_4$$

The computations of all C_i's (for $i = 1$ to 4) required 8 multiplications and 4 additions of $n/2 \times n/2$ matrices using divide-&-conquer paradigm.

Now we discuss a better scheme for matrix multiplication known as Stressman's method that involves 7 multiplications and 18 additions/subtractions operations of $n/2 \times n/2$ matrices. The seven smaller products are matrices M, N, O, P, Q, R and S where,

$$M = A_1*(B_2 - B_4)$$
$$N = A_4*(B_3 - B_1)$$
$$O = B_1*(A_3 + A_4)$$
$$P = B_4*(A_1 + A_2)$$
$$Q = (A_3 - A_1) * (B_2 - B_4)$$
$$R = (A_2 - A_4) * (B_3 + B_4)$$

and
$$S = (A_1 + A_4) *(B_1 +B_4)$$

along with 6 additions and 4 subtractions of $n/2 \times n/2$ matrices. The matrices C_i's will be computed from above seven matrices as,

$$C_1 = N + R + S - P$$
$$C_2 = M + P$$
$$C_3 = N + O$$
$$C_4 = M + Q + S - O$$

That requires another 6 additions and 2 subtractions of $n/2 \times n/2$ matrices. Therefore Stressman's method requires a total of 7 multiplications and 18 addition/subtraction operations of $n/2 \times n/2$ matrices. If we compare these two methods of matrix multiplication we conclude that for $n = 8$ Stressman's method is more efficient. In general, let $T(n)$ denotes the time required by the Stressman's divide-and-conquer method, thus the recurrence is,

$$T(n) = \begin{cases} \theta(1) & \text{for } n \le 1 \\ 7T(n/2) + 18n^2 & \text{for } n > 1 \end{cases}$$

Solve this recurrence using theorem 3.3 (Method of substitution). Since, we have $a = 7$, $b = 2$ and $f(n) = 18n^2$. That gives $h(n) = f(n)/n^{\log_b a} = 18n^2/n^{\log_2 7} = 18n^{2-\log_2 7}$.

Since, $2 - \log_2 7 < 0$ therefore $g(n) = O(1)$ (from the table shown in Fig. 3.4).

Hence, the solution $T(n) = n^{\log_2 7}[\theta(1) + O(1)] = \theta(n^{\log_2 7})$ (assume $\theta(1)$ is constant).

$$= \theta(n^{\simeq 2.81})$$

Therefore, the time complexity of the matrix multiplication problem is $\theta(n^{2.81})$.

EXERCISES

3.1 Solve the recurrence $a_n + 3a_{n-1} + 2a_{n-2} = f(n)$, where

$$f(n) = \begin{cases} 1 & \text{for } n = 2 \\ 0 & \text{otherwise} \end{cases}$$

and the base conditions $a_0 = a_1 = 0$.

3.2 Solve the following recurrence relations :

(i) $a_n + a_{n-1} + a_{n-2} = 0$, where $a_0 = 0$ and $a_1 = 2$.

(ii) $a_n - a_{n-1} - a_{n-2} = 0$, where $a_0 = 0$ and $a_1 = 1$.

(iii) $a_n + 6a_{n-1} + 9a_{n-2} = 5^n$, where $a_0 = 0$ and $a_1 = 2$.

(iv) $a_n + 3a_{n-1} + 2a_{n-2} = f(n)$, where $f(n) = 6$ for $n = 2$ and 0 otherwise with base conditions $a_0 = 0$ and $a_1 = 0$.

(v) $a_n + 5a_{n-1} + 6a_{n-2} = f(n)$, where $f(n) = 0$ for $n = 0, 1, 5$ and 6 otherwise with $a_0 = 0$ and $a_1 = 2$.

(vi) $a_n - 4a_{n-1} + 4a_{n-2} = 2^n$, where $a_0 = 0$ and $a_1 = 0$.

3.3 Solve the following difference equations :

(i) $a_n^2 - 2a_{n-1}^2 = 1$, where $a_0 = 2$.

(ii) $na_n + na_{n-1} - a_{n-1} = 2^n$, where $a_0 = 273$.

(iii) $a_n^2 - 2a_{n-1} = 0$, where $a_0 = 4$.

(iv) $a_n - na_{n-1} = n!$, for $n \ge 1$ and $a_0 = 2$.

(v) $a_n = \sqrt{a_{n-1}} + \sqrt{a_{n-2}} + \sqrt{a_{n-3}} + \sqrt{\ldots\ldots}$, where $a_0 = 4$.

3.4 Find the asymptotic order of the solutions for the following recurrence equations :

(i) $T(n) = T(n/2) + c\,n \log n$

(ii) $T(n) = a\,T(n/2) + c\,n^c$

(iii) $T(n) = 3T(n/2) + c\,n$

(iv) $T(n) = 9T(n/2) + n^2\,2^n$

assume $T(1) = 1$, the recurrence is for $n > 1$ and c is some positive constant.

3.5 Let a problem of input size n is subdivided into $\sqrt{n}$ subproblems of size about $\sqrt{n}$.

Show that the solution of the recurrence

$$T(n^2/2^r) = nT(n) + bn^2 \qquad \text{(where } r \text{ is an integer, } r \ge 1)$$

is $O(n(\log n)^r \log \log n)$.

3.6 Equation (3.2) defined the Fibonacci sequence as $f_n = f_{n-1} + f_{n-2}$ for $n > 1$, $f_0 = 0$ and $f_1 = 1$. Prove the correct statement between the following :

(i) for $n \ge 1$, $f_n \le 100\,(3/2)^n$

(ii) for $n \ge 1$, $f_n \ge .01\,(3/2)^n$

3.7 Show that the solution of the Fibonacci recurrence i.e., $f_n = f_{n-1} + f_{n-2}$ for $n > 1$, $f_0 = 0$ and $f_1 = 1$ is $\theta(\varnothing^n)$, where $\varnothing = \frac{1}{2}(1 + \sqrt{5})$.

3.8 Solve the following recurrences, given T(1) = 1.

(*i*) $T(n) = 3T(n/8) + n^2 2^n \log n$, $n \geq 8$ and n is power of 8.

(*ii*) $T(n) = 27T(n/3) + 11n^3$, $n \geq 3$ and n is power of 3.

(*iii*) $T(n) = 128T(n/2) + 2^n/n$, $n \geq 2$ and n is power of 2.

(*iv*) $T(n) = 128T(n/2) + \log^3 n$, $n \geq 2$ and n is power of 2.

3.9 Use Strassen's algorithm to compute the product $\begin{pmatrix} 1 & 3 \\ 5 & 7 \end{pmatrix}\begin{pmatrix} 2 & 4 \\ 6 & 8 \end{pmatrix}$.

ALGEBRAIC STRUCTURE

4 Algebraic Structure

4.1 INTRODUCTION

In the context of algebra a system consisting of a set and one or more n-ary operations on the set is called an algebraic system. Let X be a finite and nonempty set then algebraic system is denoted by (X, $\boxdot$, $\circledast$, ….), where $\boxdot$, $\circledast$, ….are the operations on X. Since, the operations over the set represent a structure between the elements; therefore an algebraic system is also known as *algebraic structure*. Groups, rings, fields, vector spaces, etc. are the examples of the algebraic systems.

As we said a set with number of operations over the set describes an algebraic system. Here we restrict our study of algebraic systems to those operations that are only unary or binary in nature. For example, consider the set of natural number N with usual addition operation +. Hence, (N, +) represent an algebraic system. Clearly, (N, +, $\star$) is an algebraic system with two usual operations, addition and multiplication, + and $\star$. It is possible to consider that more than one set together with different operations describe similar algebraic systems if operations are of same degree. Conversely, two different algebraic systems (X, $\boxdot$, $\circledast$) and (Y, $\blacktriangle$, $\bullet$) are of same type if, the operations $\boxdot$ and $\blacktriangle$, and operations $\circledast$ and $\bullet$ are of same degree.

Since, every systems posses their own property that is obviously, the property holds by any of its operations, so we now listed some common properties of an algebraic system (X, $\circledast$) where $\circledast$ is a binary operation on X, are as follows,

I. *Closure.* Operator $\circledast$ is said to be closed, if, $x \circledast y \in$ X and unique for $\forall(x$ and $y) \in$ X.

II. *Commutative.* Operator $\circledast$ is commutative over set X, if, $x \circledast y = y \circledast x$, for $\forall(x$ and $y) \in$ X

III. *Associative.* Operator $\circledast$ is associative over set X, i.e. if x, y and $z \in$ X , then we have,

$$x \circledast (y \circledast z) = (x \circledast y) \circledast z$$

IV. *Existence of an unique Identity Element.* There exists an identity element ę for $\forall x \in$ X with respect to operation $\circledast$, i.e.,

$$\underset{\textit{right identity}}{x \circledast ę} = \underset{\textit{left identity}}{ę \circledast x} = x$$

For example, 0 is the identity element for algebraic system (I, +), where I is the set of integers and '+' is the usual addition operation of integers, i.e., $x + 0 = 0 + x = x$, for $\forall x \in$ I. Therefore, 0 is called *additive identity*. (Reader self verify that 1 will be *multiplicative identity*).

V. *Existence of Inverse Elements.* There exists an inverse element $y \in$ X for every $x \in$ X with respect to operation $\circledast$, i.e.,

$$x \circledast y = ę = y \circledast x$$

For example, the additive inverse define the subtraction i.e., $x + (-x) = ę$. Similarly, the multiplication inverse defines division i.e., $x \star (1/x) = ę$.

Assume an algebraic system consists of two operators (X, $\boxdot$, $\circledast$), then

VI. *Distributive Property.* Since $\boxdot$ and $\circledast$ are two binary operations on set X, and if x, y and $z \in$ X then operator $\boxdot$ is said to be distributive over $\circledast$ whenever,

$$x \boxdot (y \circledast z) = (x \boxdot y) \circledast (x \boxdot z)$$

and also operator $\circledast$ is distributive over $\boxdot$ whenever,

$$x \circledast (y \boxdot z) = (x \circledast y) \boxdot (x \circledast z)$$

For example *field* is an algebraic system. A field is defined by a set of elements, binary operations + and $\star$, a set of properties 1 to 5, and combination of both operations fulfilling property 6. A field of real numbers is a common example consists of set of real numbers (R), with binary operations + and $\star$ denoted by (R, +, $\star$). It is the basis for ordinary algebra.

Example 4.1. *Let X = {1, 2, 3, 4} and (X, X, f) is a morphism, where function f is represented by the expression,*

$$f = \begin{pmatrix} 1 & 2 & 3 & 4 \\ 2 & 3 & 4 & 1 \end{pmatrix}$$

Prove that (F, ◊) is an algebraic system, where F is the set of unique composite functions of f.

Sol. From the composite functions,

$$f \lozenge f = f^2;\ f^2 \lozenge f = f^3;\ f^3 \lozenge f = f^4; \text{ and so on.}$$

Determine $f^2, f^3, f^4, \ldots$ so we obtain

$$f \lozenge f = f^2 = \begin{pmatrix} 1 & 2 & 3 \\ 3 & 4 & 1 \end{pmatrix}, f^2 \lozenge f = f^3 = \begin{pmatrix} 1 & 2 & 3 \\ 4 & 1 & 2 \end{pmatrix}, f^3 \lozenge f = f^4 = \begin{pmatrix} 1 & 2 & 3 \\ 1 & 2 & 3 \end{pmatrix}$$

Since, f^4 is an identity function or mapping, i.e, $f^4 = \{(x, x)/x \in X\} = f^0$ (assume) and all others composite of functions are repeated in the set F = $\{f, f^2, f^3, f^0\}$ or $\{f^0, f^1, f^2, f^3\}$. Since operation ◊ is closed, commutative and associative together with the existence of an identity functions, which results (F, ◊) is an algebraic system.

4.2 GROUPS

Let X be an nonempty set and $\circledast$ be an binary operation on X, then algebraic system (X, $\circledast$) is called a group, if operation $\circledast$ satisfies the following postulates,

1. $\circledast$ is closed,

2. $\circledast$ is associative,

3. Existence of an identity element, and

4. Existence of the unique inverse.

(Postulates 1 – 4 are called group axioms)

For example, algebraic system (X, $\circledast$), where X = {+, –} and binary operation $\circledast$ is defined in the table show in Fig. 4.1.

$\circledast$	+	–
+	+	–
–	–	+

Fig. 4.1 Operation table

Since,

Operation ⊛ is associative and closed, because of, + ⊛ + = + ∈ X and similarly it is true for others in the table.

Operation ⊛ is also associative, because of,

+ ⊛ (– ⊛ +) = + ⊛ – = – ; which is same to (+ ⊛ –) ⊛ + = – ⊛ + = – ; and similarly true for others in the table.

There exists an identity element for each element of X i.e.,

+ ⊛ + = + ⊛ + = + and – ⊛ + = + ⊛ – = –

(For both operations + and – identity element is +)

For every element of X there exists a unique inverse, i.e.

– ⊛ – = + (identity element) and + ⊛ + = + (identity element)

Therefore, algebraic system (X, ⊛) is a group.

In a group (X, ⊛) the cardinality of the set X i.e. | X | gives the order of the group. If | X | is finite and consists of n elements, then group is said to be a finite group of order n, conversely if | X | = ∞, then group is an infinite group.

N H Abel (in early 19's) had make something their own and the group called ***Abelian group***, i.e., a group (X, ⊛) is said to be abelian if the binary operation is *commutative* as well. For example, system (I, +), where I is the set of all integers and operation + is addition of integers is an abelian group.

If an algebraic system (X, ⊛) follows only restrictions **1 and 2** such that, binary operation ⊛ is closed and associative then (X. ⊛) is called a ***semigroup***. For example, algebraic system (I^+, +) is a semigroup, where I^+ is the set of positive integers and operation + is usual addition operations; because addition operation is closed and associative on I^+. Similarly, system (I^+, ×) is also a semigroup, where operation × is usual multiplication operation.

Consider another example, Let N be the set of natural numbers, i.e. N = {0, 1, 2, ...} and + is an addition operation then algebraic system (N, +) and (N, ×) are semigroup in addition to that there exists an identity element 0 and 1 with respect to operations + and × respectively. Such semigroups are called monoids. A semigroup there may or may not have an identity element.

An algebraic system (X, ⊛) is called ***monoid***, if operation ⊛ satisfies the following postulates **1, 2, and 3** i.e.,

1. ⊛ is closed,

2. ⊛ is associative, and

3. Existence of an identity element,

For example, let Σ = {a, b, c} and Σ* = {ε, a, b, c, a b, b c, c a, ...} is the set of all possible strings form over the alphabets Σ then algebraic system (Σ*, .) is monoid, where . is a binary concatenation operation, i.e., for any two strings x, y ∈ Σ*, $x.y$ yields the string xy.

Since,

1. For any x any $y \in \Sigma^*$, $x \,.\, y \Rightarrow xy \in \Sigma^*$; hence operation . is closed.

2. For any x, y, and $z \in \Sigma^*$, $(x \,.\, y) \,.\, z = x \,.\, (y \,.\, z) \Rightarrow x\,y\,z \in \Sigma^*$; so operation . is associative.

3. Set Σ* contains an identity element ε called null string i.e. | ε | = 0, then for any $x \in \Sigma^*$,

$$x \,.\, \varepsilon = \varepsilon \,.\, x = x$$

Therefore, algebraic system (Σ^*, .) is a monoid. If we replace the set Σ^* by Σ^+, where $\Sigma^+ = \Sigma^* - \{\varepsilon\}$, where set Σ^+ contains all possible strings formed over the alphabet Σ except null string (ε) then algebraic system (Σ^+, .) is not a monoid due to non existence of an identity element with respect to operation concatenation but a semigroup.

Operation Table

The properties hold by an algebraic system can be easily observed from the operation table. Let (X, $\circledast$) is an algebraic system, where $\circledast$ is a binary operation on X, then operation table presented an arrangement of values resulted after performing the binary operation $\circledast$ over the elements of set X. For example, the algebraic structure (X, $\oplus$) is a monoid, where $\oplus$ is a binary operation defined over set X = {0, 1, 2, 3}, i.e.

$$a \oplus b = a + b, \text{ if } a + b \leq 3, \text{ otherwise } a + b - 4$$

Construct the transition table for algebraic system (X, $\circledast$)

$\oplus$	**0**	**1**	**2**	**3**
0	0	1	2	3
1	1	2	3	0
2	2	3	0	1
3	3	0	1	2

Fig. 4.2 Operation table.

From the operation table shown in Fig. 4.2 we derive following conclusions,

- Since each element in table belongs to set X, hence operation $\oplus$ is closed.
- Operation is associative.
- Values of the first column are similar to the corresponding element of the set when operated on $\oplus$ over element 0, hence 0 is a unique identity element.

Therefore, algebraic system (X, $\oplus$) is a monoid. Further, we see that algebraic system (X, $\oplus$) is also a group.

- Since there is an occurrence of the identity element 0 in each row in the operation table which shows the existence of the inverse element for every element of X, i.e.,

$$0 \oplus 0 = 0; \; 1 \oplus 3 = 0; \; 2 \oplus 2 = 0; \;\; 3 \oplus 1 = 0.$$

- Also corresponding rows and column are same in the table; hence operation $\oplus$ holds commutative property.

Therefore, algebraic system (X, $\oplus$) is an Abelian group.

Example 4.2. *Let X = {p, q, r} and binary operation $\otimes$ defines in the operation table shown in Fig. 4.3 then algebraic system (X, $\otimes$) is a semi group but not monoid.*

Sol.

$\oplus$	**p**	**q**	**r**
p	*p*	*p*	*p*
q	*q*	*q*	*q*
r	*r*	*r*	*r*

Fig. 4.3 Operation table.

- Operation $\otimes$ is closed, since all elements in the table belong to set X.
- Operation is associative.

Hence, (X, ⊗) is a semigroup. Further,

- Algebraic structure (X, ⊗) not posses a unique identity element for all elements of X. Here elements identity elements are $\{p, q, r\}$.
- Since corresponding rows and columns are not same hence operation ⊗ is not commutative.

Therefore, (X, ⊗) is not monoid and also not a group.

Example 4.3. *Let X = {1, – 1, i, – i} and the binary operation ⋆ is define in the operation table (Fig. 4.4). Prove that algebraic system (X, ⋆) is a group.*

Sol.

⋆	**1**	**– 1**	**i**	**– i**
1	1	– 1	i	$-i$
– 1	– 1	1	$-i$	i
i	i	$-i$	– 1	1
– i	$-i$	i	1	– 1

Fig. 4.4 Operation table.

(Ready self verify that operation table holds all restrictions required by a group)

Modulo Operation

Now we define two special operations called additional modulo and multiplication modulo over the set X, where

- *Additional Modulo n* if $a, b \in$ X then a addition b modulo n is defined as,

$$(a +_n b) = (a + b) \textbf{ mod } n = r \text{ (where } r > 0)$$

For example, let $a = 11$ and $b = 6$ then its addition modulo 5 is given by $(11 +_5 6) = (11 + 6)$ mod $5 = 2$ (> 0). Consider another set of values such that $a = -15$ and $b = 5$, then

$$(-11 +_5 5) = (-11 + 5) \textbf{ mod } 5 = (-6) \textbf{ mod } 5 = [(-5 * 2) + 4] \textbf{ mod } 5 = 4\ (> 0).$$

Let $a = -10$ and $b = -7$ then

$$(-10 +_5 7) = (-10 + (-7)) \textbf{ mod } 5 = (-17) \textbf{ mod } 5 = [(-5 * 4) + 3] \textbf{ mod } 5 = 3\ (> 0).$$

- *Multiplication Modulo n* if $a, b \in$ X then a multiplication b modulo n is defined as,

$$(a *_n b) = (a * b) \textbf{ mod } n = r \text{ (where } r > 0)$$

Example 4.4. *Let (X, ×) be a group, where × is the multiplication operation on X, then for any $x, y \in X$ prove that,*

1. $(x^{-1})^{-1} = x$, *and*
2. $(x \times y)^{-1} = y^{-1} \times x^{-1}$ *or* $(x \times y) = (y^{-1} \times x^{-1})^{-1}$;

Sol.

1. Recall the definition of the group, such that for every element x ∈ X there exists an unique inverse say $x' \in$ X i.e.,

$$x \times x' = e \text{ (identity element)} = x' \times x;$$

From the symmetricity,

$$x' = x^{-1} \qquad \text{or} \qquad x'^{-1} = x$$

Replace value of x' by x^{-1} in so, we get

$$(\mathbf{x^{-1}})^{-1} = \mathbf{x}$$ **(Proved)**

2. From the result of equality (1), for any $x \in$ X, we have the inverse element x^{-1}, where $x \times x^{-1} = ę$; and also $y \times y^{-1} = ę$ for any $y \in$ X. Since, operation × is closed so $x \times y \in$ X,

Let $u = x \times y$ and $w = y^{-1} \times x^{-1}$, then

$$u \times w = (x \times y) \times (y^{-1} \times x^{-1})$$
$$= x \times (y \times y^{-1}) \times x^{-1} \quad \text{(by Associativity)}$$
$$= x \times ę \times x^{-1} \quad (\text{since } y \times y^{-1} = ę)$$
$$= x \times x^{-1}$$
$$= ę \quad \text{(identity element)}$$

Thus we have,

$$(x \times y) \times (y^{-1} \times x^{-1}) = ę = (y^{-1} \times x^{-1}) \times (x \times y) \text{ also.}$$

$\Rightarrow$ $(x \times y) = (y^{-1} \times x^{-1})^{-1}$, and due to symmetricity

$$(x \times y)^{-1} = (y^{-1} \times x^{-1}).$$ **(Proved)**

Example 4.5. *Let W = {1, ω, ω²}, where ω is cube root of unity i.e.* $\omega^3 = 1$ *and* $1 + \omega + \omega^2 = 0$, *then show that algebraic system (W, ×) is a group.*

Sol. Since,

1. Operation × is closed for W, i.e.
$1 \times \omega = \omega \in$ W; $\omega \times \omega^2 = \omega^3 = 1 \in$ W; $1 \times \omega^2 = \omega^2 \in$ W; and others.
2. Operation × is associative over W, viz.
$\omega^2 \times (1 \times \omega) = (\omega^2 \times 1) \times \omega = \omega^3$; and others.
3. Existence of an identity element i.e.,
$\omega \times ę = x = x \times ę$ for any $x \in$ W
if $x = \omega$ then $ę = 1$, i.e. $1 \times \omega = \omega \times 1 = \omega$;
if $x = \omega^2$ then $ę = 1$, i.e. $1 \times \omega^2 = \omega^2 \times 1 = \omega^2$;
4. Existence of unique inverse element for every element of W, i.e.,
$x \times y = y \times x = ę$ where $x, y \in$ W and y is inverse of x.
if $x = 1$ then $y = 1$, so $1 \times 1 = ę$;
if $x = \omega$ then $y = \omega^2$, so $\omega \times \omega^2 = \omega^3 = 1 = ę$;
if $x = \omega^2$ then $y = \omega$, so $\omega^2 \times \omega = \omega^3 = 1 = ę$;

Therefore, Algebraic system (W, ×) is a group.

4.3 SEMI SUBGROUP

Let algebraic system (X, ⊛) is a semi group and let Y ⊆ X, then (Y, ⊛) is said to be a semi subgroup if, (Y, ⊗) is itself a semigroup, i.e.

$$(Y, \otimes) \subseteq (X, \otimes)$$

For example, (I^+, +) is semigroup, where binary operation + is defines over set of positive integers I^+. Now consider two subsets of I^+ i.e., (1) positive integers that are all even (J) and (2) positive integers that are all odd (K). Thus,

$$J \subseteq I^+ \quad \text{and} \quad K \subseteq I^+$$

Now test whether (J, +) is a semigroup or (K, +) is a semigroup. Former, is a semigroup because operation + is closed and associative over J but latter is not a semigroup due to violation of closure property by operation + over K (since addition of two positive odd integers must be an even positive integer that is not in the set K). Therefore, (J, +) is a sub semigroup of $(I^+, +)$, or

$$(J, +) \subseteq (I^+, +)$$

4.4 COMPLEXES

Let $(X, \oplus)$ be a group, and $Y \subseteq X$ then Y is called the complex of group $(X, \oplus)$. For example, consider $X = \{1, -1, i, -i\}$ and operation is usual multiplication '×' then (X, ×) is a group. Now $\{1, -1\}$, $\{1, i\}$, $\{1, -i\}$, $\{-1, i\}$, $\{-1, -i\}$, and $\{i, -i\}$ are subsets of X are called complexes of the group (X, ×). Out of these complexes some complexes may form a group or may not form a group under bounding operation '×'.

4.5 PRODUCT SEMIGROUPS

Let $(X, \oplus)$, and $(Y, \otimes)$ are two semigroups, define $Z = X \times Y$ such that the elements of Z are ordered pair (x, y) where $x \in X$ and $y \in Y$. Then (Z, #) is also a semigroup by assuming $(a, b) \in Z$ and $(c, d) \in Z$ i.e., $(a, b) \# (c, d) = (a \oplus c, b \otimes d)$. Hence, (Z, #) is called a product semigroup.

Consider an example, algebraic system $(R^+, \times)$ where × is usual multiplication operation defines over the set of positive real numbers R^+ forms a semigroup. Similarly $(I, +_4)$ where $+_4$ is addition modulo 4 operation define over set of Integers forms a semigroup. Let S is the direct product, i.e., $S = R^+ \times I$, then check whether (S, #) is a semigroup or not. Assume ordered pairs $(a, b) \in S$ and $(c, d) \in S$, where elements a, c belongs to R^+, and elements b, d belongs to I then

$$(a, b) \# (c, d) = (a \times c, b +_4 d)$$

Since operation × is closed in R^+ and operation $+_4$ is closed in I, hence operation # is closed. Also, since operation × and $+_4$ are associative hence # also holds associativity. Therefore, direct product is a semigroup.

4.6 PERMUTATION GROUPS

Let X be a group and $p : X \to X$ is a mapping to be permutation of X if p is bijective (one-one and onto). Such groups are called permutation groups. Let $X = \{a, b, c, \ldots\}$ be a set and let p denotes a permutation of the elements of X; i.e., $p : X \to X$ is a bijective, then

$$p = \begin{pmatrix} a & b & c\ldots\ldots \\ p(a) & p(b) & p(c)\ldots\ldots \end{pmatrix}$$

is called permutation group, where image of the element of X is entered below the element. For example, let $X = \{1, 2, 3\}$ and suppose $p(1) = 2, p(2) = 3, p(3) = 1$ then we may represent p as,

$$p = \begin{pmatrix} 1 & 2 & 3 \\ 2 & 3 & 1 \end{pmatrix} \text{ or } \begin{pmatrix} 1 & 3 & 2 \\ 2 & 1 & 3 \end{pmatrix} \text{ or } \begin{pmatrix} 3 & 1 & 2 \\ 1 & 2 & 3 \end{pmatrix}$$

and so on. In general, a group of n-elements can have a total of n ! permutations that is called order of *permutation* and the *degree of permutation* is the number of the elements of the set X. In the said example, the degree of permutation is 3 and the order of permutation is 6.

Let $p_1, p_2, \ldots\ldots p_{n!}$ are all possible permutations of a set of n elements then it is called symmetric set of permutations. In the previous example $\{p_1, p_2, \ldots p_6\}$ are the symmetric set of permutations that are shown below.

$$p_1 = \begin{pmatrix} 1 & 2 & 3 \\ 2 & 3 & 1 \end{pmatrix}, p_2 = \begin{pmatrix} 1 & 3 & 2 \\ 2 & 1 & 3 \end{pmatrix}, p_3 = \begin{pmatrix} 3 & 1 & 2 \\ 1 & 2 & 3 \end{pmatrix}$$

and $$p_4 = \begin{pmatrix} 3 & 2 & 1 \\ 1 & 3 & 2 \end{pmatrix}, p_5 = \begin{pmatrix} 2 & 1 & 3 \\ 3 & 2 & 1 \end{pmatrix}, p_6 = \begin{pmatrix} 2 & 3 & 1 \\ 3 & 1 & 2 \end{pmatrix}$$

Let p be the permutation where,

$$p = \begin{pmatrix} a_1 & a_2 & a_3 \\ b_1 & b_2 & b_3 \end{pmatrix}$$

then, inverse of permutation is denoted by p^{-1} and is defined as,

$$p^{-1} = \begin{pmatrix} b_1 & b_2 & b_3 \\ a_1 & a_2 & a_3 \end{pmatrix}$$

Similarly, a permutation is said to be an identity *permutation* if image of every element of set X is same to the corresponding element, i.e., if X = $\{a, b, c\}$ then $p(a) = a$, $p(b) = b$, and $p(c) = c$, then permutation p where,

$$p = \begin{pmatrix} a & b & c \\ a & b & c \end{pmatrix}$$ is called an identity permutation.

4.7 ORDER OF A GROUP

Let (X, ⊛) be a group, then order of the X is denoted by O(X) is the number of elements in group X. For example if group X consisting of m elements then O(X) = m. If X is infinite then O(X) = ∞.

Let $x \in$ X then *order of an element x*, denoted as O(x) is n if $a^n = e$ (identity element). For example, consider X = $\{1, -1, i, -i\}$ is a group under usual multiplication operation × i.e. (X, ×).

Then order of the group is, i.e., O(X) = 4. The order of its elements is determined as follows :

- O(1) = 1 [∵ $1^1 = 1$ (identity element)]
- O(– 1) = 2 [∵ $(-1)^2 = 1$ (identity element)]
- O(i) = 4 [∵ $(i)^4 = 1$ (identity element)]
- O($-i$) = 4 [∵ $(-i)^4 = 1$ (identity element)]

Example 4.6. *Let X = {1, ω, ω²} where ω is cube root of unity, is a group (X, +). Determine the order of the group X and order of its elements.*

Sol. Since, set X contains three elements hence, O(X) = 3. The order of the elements is determined as follows :

From the operation table shown in Fig. 4.5 the group (X, ×) has an identity element 1

Therefore,

- O(1) = 1 [∵ 11 = 1 (identity element)]
- O(ω) = 3 [∵ $(\omega)^3 = 1$ (identity element)]
- O(ω²) = 3 [∵ $(\omega^2)^3 = 1$ (identity element)]

×	1	ω	$ω^2$
1	1	ω	$ω^2$
ω	ω	$ω^2$	1
$ω^2$	$ω^2$	1	ω

Fig 4.5 Operation Table.

4.8 SUBGROUPS

Let algebraic system (X, ⊛) is a group, where X be a nonempty set and ⊛ be a binary operation on X. A subset Y of X such that (Y, ⊛) is said to be a subgroup of X if (Y, ⊛) is also a group together following conditions are satisfie,

1. ⊛ is closed,
2. ⊛ is associative,
3. Existence of an identity element $e \in$ Y, where e is the identity element of (X, ⊛), and
4. Existence of unique an inverse for (X, ⊛) and also for (Y, ⊛).

We can use the following notation for a subgroup,

Y < X, where (Y, ⊛) is the subgroup of (X. ⊛).

For example, algebraic system (I, +), where I is the set of integers and operation + is usual addition operations of integers, is a group. Also, $I^+ \subseteq I$ (where I^+ is the set of all positive integers) and since, $(I^+, +)$ is a group and satisfy all the restrictions 1 – 4 therefore, $(I^+, +)$ is a subgroup.

We further define, if Y and Z are two subsets of a group X, then

- $YZ = (yz/y \in Y, z \in Z\}$ and
- $Y^{-1} = \{y^{-1}/y \in Y\}$; inverse of Y is also the subset of group X.
- We define, Y^k (for $k = 0, 1, 2, ...$) i.e.

$Y^1 = Y$; $Y^2 = YY$; ....; similarly $Y^{k+1} = Y^k Y$; and $Y^0 = \{e\}$

where,

$$Y^2 = \{y_1y_2/y_1, y_2 \in Y\}, \text{ and so on.}$$

The subset Y^{-k} is defined as $(Y^{-1})^k$.

In particular, we write, for $x \in X$,

$$Y x = \{yx/y \in Y\} \quad \text{or,}$$
$$x Y = \{xy/y \in Y\}$$

If Y ≠ Ø, then we can see that

$$\mathbf{YX = XY = X; \quad X^{-1} = X; \quad Xe = eX = e;}$$

Example 4.7. *Let Y is a subgroup of X, i.e. Y < X if and only if $YY^{-1} \subset Y$.*

Sol. $YY^{-1} \subset Y \Rightarrow$ if $a, b \in Y$ then $ab^{-1} \in Y$.

Necessity is obvious.

For Sufficiency,

if $a \in Y \Rightarrow aa^{-1} \in YY^{-1} \subset Y$;

$\Rightarrow aa^{-1} \in Y$, i.e. $e \in Y$.

So, $\quad a^{-1} \in Y\,Y^{-1} \subset Y$, thus $a^{-1} \in Y$.

Similarly, if $a, b \in Y \Rightarrow b^{-1} \in Y$ and $ab^{-1} \in Y$;

So, $\quad (ab^{-1})^{-1} \in YY^{-1} \subset Y$, i.e. $a, b \in Y$

Thus, $a \in Y \Rightarrow a^{-1} \in Y$ and $a, b \in Y \Rightarrow a\,b \in Y$, hence Y becomes a subgroup.

Example 4.8. *Let Y and Z are two subgroups of X, then product of YZ is a subgroup of X if and only of YZ = ZY.*

Sol. ***Necessary Condition***. Since, Y, Z, and YZ are subgroups of X, i.e.

$$Y < X, \quad Z < X, \quad \text{and} \quad YZ < X$$

Therefore, $\quad Y^{-1} = Y,\; Z^{-1} = Z, \quad (YZ)^{-1} = YZ,$

But $\quad (YZ)^{-1} = Z^{-1}Y^{-1}, = ZY$

Thus, $\quad ZY = YZ$

(Sufficient condition) To claim YZ < X, from given Y < X, Z < X, and YZ = ZY

Since, we have $\quad Y^2 = Y = Y^{-1}$ and $Z^2 = Z = Z^{-1}$

Assume $\quad S = YZ$

Then, $\quad S^2 = (YZ)\,(YZ) = Y\,(ZY)\,Z = Y\,(YZ)\,Z$ (Commutivity)

$= (YY)\,(ZZ)$

$= Y^2\,Z^2$

$= YZ$ $\quad (\therefore \quad Y^2\,Z^2 = YZ)$

$= S$

also, $\quad S^{-1} = (YZ)^{-1} = Z^{-1}\,Y^{-1}$

$= ZY$

$= YZ$ $\quad (\therefore \quad ZY = YZ)$

$= S$

So, we have $S^2 = S = S^{-1}$, therefore S is a subgroup of X, or YZ < X.

4.9 CYCLIC GROUPS

A group (X, x) is said to be cyclic group if $\forall x \in X$, there exists a, fixed element g such that, $g^n = x$ for some integer n, where g is called generator of the cycle. Alternatively, a group X is said to be cyclic with generator g if every element of X is in g^*, where g^* is of the form,

$$g^0 = e;\, g^1 = g;\, g^2 = g \times g;\, \ldots\ldots\ldots\ldots;\, g^n = g \times g \times g \,\ldots\ldots\ldots \times g \text{ } (n \text{ times})$$

(where $n \in I$)

- Consider an example of group $(X, \times)$, where $X = \{1, -1, i, -i\}$. Since every element of X is generated from one of the element 'i' of the set, i.e.,

$$i^4 = \mathbf{1};\, i^2 = -\mathbf{1};\, i^3 = \mathbf{i};\, i^4 = -\mathbf{i}.$$

Since each element can be expressed in some power of i so i is one of the generator of the cyclic group, hence,

$$g = [i]$$

Similarly, other element '$-i$' also generates all the elements of the set X, hence other generator, i.e., $g = [-i]$, where -i is the inverse element of i.

Hence, we can say that if a is the generator of the cyclic group X then a^{-1} is also a generator of X.

Therefore, $g = [i]$ or $[-i]$ are two generators of the cyclic group X.

- Consider another example of group (X, ×), i.e. X = {1, ω, ω^2}, where ω is cube root of unity. Then group is cyclic with the generator g = [ω] because, the elements of X are expressed in ω^3, ω, ω^2 respectively for 1, ω, and ω^2. Further, the inverse element of ω i.e., ω^2 is also the generator. Therefore, g = [ω] and [ω^2].

Example 4.9. *Show that group (I, +) is a cyclic group. Find its generator (where I is the set of integers)*

Sol. Since, the set I = {......– 2, – 1, 0, 1, 2, ...}. The elements of I can be generated from on of the element '1' i.e., $n = 1 + 1 + \ldots\ldots + 1$ (n times) = $n.\,g$. Since + is closed operation on generator g, so we can write as, $g + g + \ldots\ldots + g$ (n times) = $n.\,g$, where,

$(1)^0 = 0$ (identity element),

$(1)^1 = 1$, (1 itself)

$(1)^2 = 1 + 1 = 2$,

$(1)^3 = 1 + 1 + 1 = 3$, and so on.

Similarly,

$(1)^{-1} = [(1)^1]^{-1} = [1]^{-1} = -1$,

$(1)^{-2} = [(1)^2]^{-1} = [2]^{-1} = -2$, and so on.

Therefore, g = [1] and also [– 1].

Example 4.10. *Show that group X = ({1, 2, 3, 4, 5, 6}, $\times_7$) is a cyclic group, where $\times_7$ is a multiplication modulo 7 operator.*

Sol. Since the elements of the group X are generated from the element 3 and 5, and there generations are shown below.

$(3)^0 = 1$ (identity element),

$(3)^1 = 3$, (generator itself)

$(3)^2 = 3 \times_7 3 = 2$,

$(3)^3 = 3 \times_7 3 \times_7 3 = 6$,

$(3)^4 = 3 \times_7 3 \times_7 3 \times_7 3 = 4$,

$(3)^5 = 3 \times_7 3 \times_7 3 \times_7 3 \times_7 3 = 5$

Also, $(5)^0 = 1$ (identity element),

$(5)^1 = 5$, (generator itself)

$(5)^2 = 5 \times_7 5 = 4$,

$(5)^3 = 5 \times_7 5 \times_7 5 = 6$,

$(5)^4 = 5 \times_7 5 \times_7 5 \times_7 5 = 2$,

$(5)^5 = 5 \times_7 5 \times_7 5 \times_7 5 \times_7 5 = 3$

Therefore, g = [3] and [5].

(here 5 is the inverse element of 3)

Facts

- We can denote the cyclic group X generated by g as,

$$X = \langle g \rangle$$

- A cyclic group $X = \langle g \rangle$ of order m can be define as, i.e., it consists of the powers,

$$X = \langle g \rangle = \{g^0, g, g^2, \ldots\ldots, g^{m-1}\}, \text{ where } g^m = e;$$

- Every subgroup of a cyclic group is cyclic.
- If a is the generator of the cyclic group X then inverse element of a is also the generator of X.

4.10 COSETS

For a group (X, ⊛) let (Y, ⊛) is a subgroup of X (i.e. Y ⊆ X), then we define the cosets of Y for any arbitrary $x \in$ X are,

(Left coset) $x \circledast Y = \{x \circledast y / y \in Y\}$, and

(Right coset) $Y \circledast x = \{y \circledast x / y \in Y\}$

Left cosets and right cosets may or may not be equal. They are equal only for commutative groups, otherwise they are unequal.

For example, let I be the additive group of integers, i.e. (I, +) now take a subset of I is J where J = 3I, so J = {......, – 6, – 3, 0, 3, 6, ...} [J ⊆ I]

Thus cosets of J in I generated by element 0, 1, 2 (∴ 0, 1, 2 ∈ I) are correspondingly given as,

$$\begin{aligned}
0 + J &= \{ ......, -6, -3, 0, 3, 6, ...\}, \\
1 + J &= \{......, -5, -2, 1, 4, 7, ...\}, \\
2 + J &= \{......, -4, -1, 2, 5, 8, ...\}, \\
3 + J &= \{......, -6, -3, 0, 3, 6, ...\} = 0 + J \\
4 + J &= \{......, -5, -2, 1, 4, 7, ...\} = 1 + J \\
5 + J &= \{......, -4, -1, 2, 5, 8, ...\} = 2 + J \\
6 + J &= \{......, -6, -3, 0, 3, 6, ...\} = 0 + J
\end{aligned}$$

and so on, hence cosets,

$$\begin{aligned}
0 + J = 3 + J = 6 + J = ... &= \{ ......, -6, -3, 0, 3, 6, ...\} \\
1 + J = 4 + J = 7 + J = ... &= \{......, -5, -2, 1, 4, 7, ...\} \\
2 + J = 5 + J = 8 + J = ... &= \{......, -4, -1, 2, 5, 8, ...\}
\end{aligned}$$

From these cosets we can easily find the entire set I, i.e.,

$$I = (0 + J) \cup (1 + J) \cup (2 + J)$$

Therefore, cosets are the way of partitioning the entire set into smaller sets.

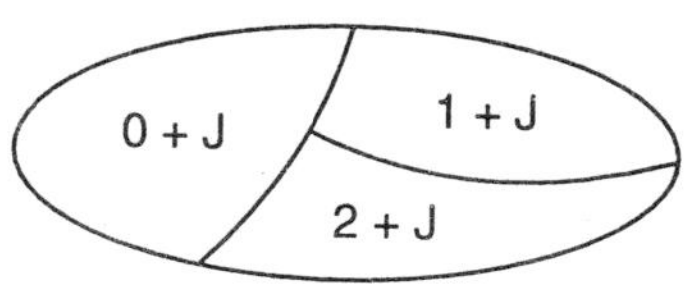

I

Fact

Let X is a group and Y is its subgroup then, number of distinct cosets of Y is called the ***index*** of Y in X and is denoted by [X:Y], i.e.

$$[X : Y] = O(X)/O(Y) \qquad \text{(index formula)}$$

Immediate consequence of the above discussed index formula resulted a theorem known as Lagrange theorem.

Lagrange Theorem

If Y is the subgroup of finite group X, then order of Y and index of Y in X divides the order of the group X.

i.e., O(Y) is divisor of O(X), and [X: Y] is divisors of O(X).

Hints

Let order of group X is n, i.e., O(X) = n. Consider any element g in X. Let g be order m, then

$$Y = \langle g \rangle = \{g^0, g^1, g^2, ..., g^{m-1}\}, \text{ where } g^0 = e \text{ and } g^m = e$$

Whence, the subgroup of X in particular the cyclic group generated by n, i.e.,

$$m = O(g) = O(Y) = O(\langle g \rangle)$$

that concludes the theorem.

Hence, from the theorem we obtain that, if X is finite group and $g \in X$ then O(X) is divisors of O(g).

Example 4.11. *If X be a finite group of order n, then for every $x \in X$, $x^n = e$.*

Sol. Since, O(X) = n. let m = O(g), and from the conclusion of the previous theorem,

$$O(g)/O(X) = m/n,$$

Putting $n = m \cdot k$, since $m = O(g)$, and we have, $g^m = e$

So, $g^n = g^{m.k} = (g^m)^k = e$

Thus $g^n = e$, for all $g \in X$.

Hence, g satisfies the equation $x^n = e$.

Example 4.12. *If X = < g > is a cyclic group of order m, then show that*

$$O(g^k) = m/gcd(k, m), \quad \text{where } gcd(k, m) = \text{greatest common divisor of } k \text{ and } m.$$

Sol. Let Y = $< g^k >$, then $O(g^k)$ = O(Y)

Putting, $j = gcd(k, m)$

Claim, $Y = < g^k > = < g^j >$

Since, for j/k and j/m we can write $k = j \cdot k'$ and $m = j \cdot m'$

So, $g^k = g^{jk'} = (g^j)^{\cdot k'} \in < g^j >$

Thus, $< g^k > \subset < g^j >$

In order to prove the reverse inclusion, we use the fact that *gcd* of two numbers can be expressed into the linear combination of these two numbers, i.e.

$$j = pk + qm \qquad \text{(where } p \text{ and } q \text{ are integers)}$$

so we have $g^j = g^{pk+qm} = g^{pk} \cdot g^{qm} = g^{pk} \cdot e^q = g^{pk}$ (since $g^m = e$)

so, $g^j = (g^p)^k \in < g^k >$

Therefore, $< g^j > \subset < g^k >$

Hence, claim is proved. It resulted,

$$Y = \{e, g^j, g^{2j}, \ldots\ldots g^{jm'}\}, m = j \cdot m' \Rightarrow m' = m/j$$

$$\Rightarrow \quad O(Y) = m' = m/j = m/gcd(k, m)$$

4.11 GROUP MAPPING

Suppose there are algebraic systems of the same types, defined on X and Y, e.g., groups, rings, etc. A mapping $f : X \circledast Y$ which preserves all operations is called homomorphism.

Let (X, ⊛) and (Y, □) are two groups, then a mapping $f : X \rightarrow Y$ such that for any x_1, $x_2 \in X$

$$f(x_1 \circledast x_2) = f(x_1) \,\square\, f(x_2)$$

is called a group homomorphism from (X, ⊛) to (Y, □).

- If group homomorphism f is surjective then, f is called epimorphism.
- If group homomorphism f is injective then, f is called monomorphism.
- If group homomorphism f is bijective then, f is called isomorphism.

We can also have, if Y = X, then a mapping

$$g : X \rightarrow X$$

is called an automorphism of X if it is also isomorphism, otherwise it is called endomorphism of X.

Now we discuss the properties of a group homomorphism, that are,

(*i*) Preservance of identities

(*ii*) Protection of inverses

(*iii*) Shield of subgroups

Now we shall prove above facts,

(*i*) Let e_x and e_y are the identities of the groups X and Y correspondingly, then $f(e_x) = e_y$. To prove this fact, assume $x \in$ X then its image $f(x) \in$ Y, so

$$f(x) \,.\, e_y = f(x) \qquad \text{(since } e_y \text{ is the identity element of Y)}$$
$$= f(x \,.\, e_x) \qquad \text{(since } e_x \text{ is the identity element of X)}$$
$$= f(x) \,.\, f(e_x)$$
$$f(x) \,.\, e_y = f(x) \,.\, f(e_y)$$
$$\Rightarrow \quad e_y = f(e_y)$$

(*ii*) To prove the fact that for any $x \in$ X, $f(x^{-1}) = [f(x)]^{-1}$, assume $x \in$ X thus $x^{-1} \in$ X therefore

$$f(x \circledast x^{-1}) = f(e_x) \qquad (\because \; x \circledast x^{-1} = e_x)$$
$$= e_y \qquad (\because \; f(e_x) = e_y)$$
$$\Rightarrow \quad f(x) \boxdot f(x^{-1}) = e_y$$

Conversely,

$$f(x^{-1} \circledast x) = f(e_x) \qquad (\because \; x^{-1} \circledast x = e_x)$$
$$\Rightarrow \quad = e_y \qquad (\because \; f(e_x) = e_y)$$
$$\Rightarrow \quad f(x^{-1}) \boxdot f(x) = e_y$$

That implies, $\quad f(x^{-1}) = [f(x)]^{-1}$

(*iii*) Assume, (S, $\circledast$) is the subgroup of (X, $\circledast$) with identity element e_x i.e., $e_x \in$ S. Since, $f(e_x) = e_y$ i.e. $e_y \in f$(S). Now, for any $x \in$ S, $x^{-1} \in$ S, and $f(x) \in f$(S) and also $f(x^{-1}) \in f$(S) $\Rightarrow$ $[f(x)]^{-1} \in f$(S). Further for $x_1, x_2 \in$ S, $x_1 \circledast x_2 \in$ S and so for $f(x_1), f(x_2) \in f$(S), and $f(x_1 \circledast x_2) = f(x_1) \boxdot f(x_2) \in f$(S). Hence, ($f$(S), $\boxdot$) is a subgroup of (Y, $\boxdot$) due to every element of f(S) must be written as f(x_2) for some $x_2 \in$ S.

Example 4.13 *Consider two groups (R, ×) and (R⁺, ×) where R is the set of reals and R⁺ is the set of positive reals and there is a mapping f : R → R⁺, i.e., f(x) = eˣ for all x ∈ R. Then prove that R and R⁺ is not isomorphism to each other.*

Sol. From the definition of group isomorphism if f is bijective (one – one and onto) and $f(x \times y) = f(x) \times f(y)$ then group R and R+ is isomorphism to each other.

- Assume x_1 and $x_2 \in$ R, then $f(x_1) = e^{x1}$ and $f(x_2) = e^{x2}$. If $f(x_1) = f(x_2)$ then $e^{x1} = e^{x2}$, it means, $x_1 = x_2$. Hence, f is *one – one*. Also, since $f(x) = e^x = y$ ($\in$ R⁺) $\Rightarrow$ $\log y = x$ or, $f(\log y) = e^{\log y} = y$. It means, for every element y of set R⁺ has a preimage $\log y$, which is real, hence it is in R. Thus, f is also *onto*.

Therefore, f is *surjective*.

- To prove second condition, let $x, y \in$ R, so $f(x \times y) = e^{xy} = (e^x)^y$, and $f(x) \times f(y) = e^x \times e^y = e^{x+y}$. So, $f(x + y) = f(x) \times f(y)$.

Hence, we conclude that groups (R, ×) and (R⁺, ×) are not isomorphism to each other.

Reader must note that if we change the first group as (R, +), then R and R+ are isomorphism to each other. Because, clearly mapping $f : R \to R^+$ is surjective. Let $x, y \in R$, so $f(x + y) = e^{x+y} = e^x e^y$, and $f(x) \times f(y) = e^x \times e^y = e^{x+y}$. So, $f(x + y) = f(x) \times f(y)$. Therefore, groups (R, +) and (R^+, ×) are isomorphism to each other.

4.12 RINGS

In the previous sections we have discussed the algebraic systems that are defined with one binary operation only. In this section we will discuss different algebraic systems viz. rings, fields, etc. that are defined with the composition of two binary operations additions and multiplication denoted respectively by + and •.

Ring

Let X be an nonempty set and + and • are two binary addition and multiplication operations on X, then algebraic system (X, +, •) is called a ring, if it holds following properties :

1. (X, +) is a Abelian group,

[Closure, Associative, identity and Inverse law for addition and Commutative]

2. (X, •) is a semigroup, and

[Closure and Associative law for multiplication]

3. The operation • is distributive over the operation +, i.e., for any x, y and $z \in X$

$x \bullet (y + z) = (x \bullet y) + (x \bullet z)$ **[Left Distributive law]**

or, $(y + z) \bullet x = (y \bullet x) + (z \bullet x)$ **[Right Distributive law]**

Property **1** assert that algebraic structure (X, +) is a abelian or commutative group, whose natural element will be denoted by 0, i.e.,

$$0 = x + (-x) \text{ for all } x \in X, \quad \text{and} \quad x + 0 = x \text{ for all } x \in X.$$

So, (X, +) is marked as the additive group of the ring.

In addition to the properties **1, 2, and 3** if commutative law holds for multiplication also, i.e.,

$$x \bullet y = y \bullet x \quad \text{for all } x, y \in X$$

then (X, +, •) is called a **commutative ring**.

Further if (X, •) has an identity element 1. It means, once semigroup becomes monoid, then ring (X, +, •) is called a ***ring with unity***.

Assume X is the set of real numbers (R) or set of integers (I) then, algebraic system (R, +, •) and (I, +, •) are the examples of *rings*. Since, (I, +) is a Abelian group, (I, •) is a semigroup and operation • is distributive over operation + in the set I. Hence, (I, +, •) is a ring. Further, algebraic structure (I, •) has an identity element 1 so (I, •) is also a monoid. Therefore, (I, +, •) is a ring with unity. It is also a commutative ring, because operation multiplication (•) holds commutativity over I.

Example 4.14. *Let set X = 2I where I is the set of integers, i.e., X = {….-4, -2, 0, 2, 4, …..}, then (X, +, .) is not a ring with unity, but it is a commutative ring.*

Sol. Since X is the set of even integers. We first check whether algebraic system (I, +, •) is a ring. Since, (X, +) is a Abelian group, (X, •) is a semigroup, and operation • is distributive over + hence, (X, +, •) is a ring.

Now check whether (X, •) is a monoid or not. If (X, •) is a monoid then it should have an identity element 1. It means, for all $x \in X$, there exists an unique y, i.e., $x \bullet y = x$ then y is called an identity element. Since $y = 1 \notin X$ or for no y, $x \bullet y = x$. So it has not an identity element 1. Therefore, (X, +, •) is a ring without unity.

Further, (X, •) is commutative, i.e., for all $x, y \in X$, $x \bullet y = y \bullet x$, hence a commutative ring.

Example 4.15. *Let Y = {0, 1, 2, 3, 4, 5}, then algebraic system (Y, $+_6$, $\times_6$) is a ring, a ring without unity, and a commutative ring.*

Sol. Construct the operation table for both the operation addition modulo 6 ($+_6$) and multiplication modulo 6 ($\times_6$).

$+_6$	0	1	2	3	4	5
0	0	1	2	3	4	5
1	1	2	3	4	5	0
2	2	3	4	5	0	1
3	3	4	5	0	1	2
4	4	5	0	1	2	3
5	5	0	1	2	3	4

$\times_6$	0	1	2	3	4	5
0	0	0	0	0	0	0
1	0	1	2	3	4	5
2	0	2	4	0	2	4
3	0	3	0	3	0	3
4	0	4	2	0	4	2
5	0	5	4	3	2	1

Fig. 4.6 Operation Table.

From the operation table shown in Fig. 4.6 (Y, $+_6$) is Abelian, because,

- Each element in the table belongs to set Y hence operation $+_6$ is closed.
- $+_6$ is associative.
- Element 0 is an identity element. (Shown in bold at first column).
- Occurrence of 0 (identity) in each row of table $+_6$ implies existence of the inverse element for each element of Y.
- Entries of corresponding rows and columns are same hence $+_6$ is commutative.

Also (Y, $\times_6$) is a semigroup, because,

- $\times_6$ is closed.
- Since, $2 \times_6 (3 \times_6 4) = 0 \times_6 2 = 0$. Also, $(2 \times_6 3) = 0$, $(2 \times_6 4) = 2$ so $(0 \times_6 2) = 0$. So this is true for all elements of Y, hence, operation ×6 is associative.

Distributive law holds, i.e. $\times_6$ is distributive over $+_6$, i.e., let $a, b, c \in Y$ then

$$a \times_6 (b +_6 c) = (a \times_6 b) +_6 (a \times_6 c)$$

where, $(b +_6 c)$ returns least nonnegative number when $(b + c)$ is divisible by 6. So, LHS returns least nonnegative number when $a \times (b + c)$ is divisible by 6, that is RHS.

Since (Y, $\times_6$) does not posses an identity element 1 hence, algebraic structure (Y, $+_6$, $\times_6$) is not a ring with unity. Although it is a commutative ring, due to the correspondence between rows and columns of operation table for $\times_6$.

Using definition of the ring we obtain following results,

- From the property of the additive group (X, +) of the ring, there is an existence of zero – element of X i.e.

$$x + 0 = x \qquad \text{for all } x \in X$$

- There exists precisely one element $-x$, i.e.

$$x + (-x) = 0 \qquad \text{for all } x \in X, \quad \text{or}$$

instead of $y + (-x)$ we simply write $y - x$ for any $x, y \in X$.

- For a natural number n (1, 2, 3......) we put

$$n \bullet x = x + x + \ldots\ldots + x \ (n \text{ times})$$

- For a negative number n' ($-1, -2, \ldots\ldots$) we put

$$n' \bullet x = (-n) \bullet x = n \bullet (-x) = (-x) + (-x) + \ldots\ldots + (-x) \ (n \text{ times})$$

- For the number 0, we put, for any $x \in X$

$$0 \bullet x = x \qquad \text{(the zero – element of X)}$$

- Let I is the set of all integers ($0, \pm 1, \pm 2, \ldots\ldots, \pm n, \ldots\ldots$) then for all $p, q \in I$ and $x, y \in X$, we have

$$(p + q) \bullet x = p \bullet x + q \bullet x \ ; \qquad p \bullet (q \bullet x) = (p\, q)\, x \ ;$$

and $\quad q(x + y) = q\,x + q\,y$

- Therefore, it is easy to verify that,

$$x \bullet (-y) = -(x\,y) \ ; \ (-x) \bullet y = -(x\,y) \ ; \ (-x)(-y) = x \bullet y \ ;$$

also, $\quad x \bullet (y - z) = x \bullet y - x \bullet z \ ; \ (y - z) \bullet x = y \bullet x - z \bullet x$

also, $\quad x \bullet (y_1 + y_2 + \ldots\ldots + y_n) = x\,y_1 + x\,y_2 + \ldots\ldots + x\,y_n$

also, $\quad (y_1 + y_2 + \ldots\ldots + y_n) \bullet x = y_1\,x + y_2\,x + \ldots\ldots + y_n\,x$

further we have,

$$x^p \bullet x^q = x^{p+q} = x^q \bullet x^p \ ;$$

also, $\quad (x^p)^q = x^{pq} \ ;$

- If (X, +, •) is a commutative ring, i.e., $x \bullet y = y \bullet x$ for all $x, y \in X$ then

$$(x \bullet y)^p = x^p \bullet y^p \ ;$$

Ring with zero divisors

Let (X, +, •) be a ring. If $x, y \in X$ such that $x \bullet y = 0$ (Additive identity) for $x \neq 0$ and $y \neq 0$, then ring is zero divisor ring and the element x is called zero divisor of ring.

Consider the ring (Y, $+_6$, $\times_6$) that was discussed in previous example, this is a zero divisor ring. Because, searching of two elements $x, y \in Y$ i.e., $x \times_6 y$ should be zero provided $x \neq 0$ and $y \neq 0$. If we take two elements 2 and 3 from set Y then $(2 \times_6 3) = 0$ (additive identity), another pair of elements is 4 and 3 i.e., $(4 \times_6 3) = 0$.

Ring without zero divisor

Let (X, +, •) be a ring. If $x, y \in X$ such that $x \,.\, y = 0$ (Additive identity) for either $x = 0$ or $y = 0$, then (X, +, •) is a ring without zero divisor.

For example, (I, +, •) is a ring without zero divisor. Because, for any pair of elements $x, y \in I$, $x \in y = 0$ only when either element $x = 0$ or $y = 0$, or both are zero.

Integral Domain

A ring (X, +, •) is called an ***integral domain*** if,

- It is a commutative ring,
- It is a ring with unity, and
- It is a ring without zero divisors.

For example, ring (I, +, •) is an integral domain but ring (2I, +, •) is not an integral domain because it is not the ring with unity.

Also from the previous example ring (Y, $+_6$, $\times_6$) is not an integral domain because, (Y, $+_6$, $\times_6$) is not a ring with unity. Although this a commutative ring and not a ring with zero divisors.

Invertible element

Let (X, +, •) be ring and an element $x \in X$, then x is said to be invertible element if there exists an element $y \in X$ i.e., $x \cdot y = 1$ (multiplicative identity).

For example, consider a ring (I, +, •) of integers. Take an element 2 from I, now find an element y in I, i.e., $2 . y = 1$. It is only possible when $y = ½ \notin$ I. Hence, element 2 is not invertible in this ring. Consider another element $1 \in I$, then $1 \cdot y = 1 \cdot y = 1 \Rightarrow$ I so 1 is invertible. Similarly, – 1 is also invertible. Therefore, [– 1, 1] is the set of invertible elements for the ring (I, +, •).

Consider another example of ring of reals i.e., (R, +, •). In the set R all elements are invertible because, let $a \in R$ then there exists an element $b \in R$ i.e., $a \cdot b = 1 \Rightarrow b = 1/a \in R$.

Boolean ring

A ring (X, +, •) is called a Boolean ring if, for all $x \in X$, we have $x^2 = x$ (Law of Idempotent]. Form the definition of Boolean ring if every element is idempotent then following conditions hold,

(*i*) $x + x = 0$ for all $x \in X$

(*ii*) $x + y = 0 \Rightarrow x = y$ for $x, y \in X$

(*iii*) Ring X is commutative

(*iv*) Ring X with more than two elements contains divisors of zero.

Proof

(*i*) Since, $x^2 = x \Rightarrow (x + x)^2 = x + x$ [by replacing x by $(x + x)$]

$LHS \Rightarrow (x + x)(x + x)$

$\Rightarrow x(x + x) + x(x + x)$ [Distributive law]

$\Rightarrow x^2 + x^2 + x^2 + x^2$

$\Rightarrow x + x + x + x = x + x$ [$\because$ $x^2 = x$]

Hence by cancellation $\Rightarrow$ $\mathbf{x + x = 0}$

[Such that every element of X is additive inverse to its own $(-x = x)$]

(*ii*) Since, $x + y = 0 \Rightarrow x + y = x + x$ [$\because$ $x + x = 0$ from condition (*i*)]

$\Rightarrow y = x$ [left cancellation law]

(*iii*) Let $x, y \in X$ so we have

$$x + y = (x + y)^2 = (x + y)(x + y)$$

$\Rightarrow x(x + y) + y(x + y)$ [Distributive law]

$\Rightarrow x^2 + x\,y + y\,x + y^2$

So, $x + y = x + x\,y + y\,x + y$ [$\because$ $x^2 = x$ & $y^2 = y$]

By cancellation, we obtain

$$x\,y + y\,x = 0$$

$\Rightarrow x\,y = -y\,x = y\,x$ [$\because$ $-y = y$ self inverse]

$\Rightarrow \mathbf{x\,y = y\,x}$

Therefore, ring is a commutative ring.

(*iv*) If ring X contains more than two elements then there exist distinct elements 0, x and y. Since $x + y \neq 0$, if $x + y = 0$ then $x = y$ which contradicts the facts that x and y are distinct.

Now consider, $x \cdot y$, if $x \cdot y = 0$ then x and y are zero divisors.

Conversely, if $x \cdot y \neq 0$ then $x\,y\,(x + y) = x\,y\,x + x\,y^2$ [Distributive law]

$\Rightarrow \quad x\,x\,y + x\,y^2$ [$\therefore\ x\,y = y\,x$]

$\Rightarrow \quad x\,y + x\,y$ [$\therefore\ x^2 = x\ \&\ y^2 = y$]

$\Rightarrow \quad 0$ [from (*ii*)]

Therefore, $x\,y$ and $x + y$ are zero divisors.

Example 4.16. *Show that a Boolean ring with more than two elements has zero divisors.*

Sol. Let a ring B in which every element is idempotent ($\therefore\ x^2 = x$ for any $x \in$ B) is called a Boolean ring. A Boolean ring is commutative and also $x + x = 0$ for any $x \in$ B.

Let B contain more than two distinct elements these are 0, a, and b. Consider $a + b$ and $a\,b$

$$a + b \neq 0 \quad \text{for} \quad a + b = 0 \quad \Rightarrow \quad a = b$$

If $a\,b = 0$, then a and b are zero divisors and if $a\,b \neq 0$, then $a\,b\,(a + b) = a\,b\,a + a\,b^2$

$$\Rightarrow \quad a(b\,a) + a\,b$$

$$\Rightarrow \quad a(a\,b) + a\,b$$

$$\Rightarrow \quad a^2\,b + a\,b$$

$$\Rightarrow \quad a\,b + a\,b = 0$$

Hence $a\,b$ and $a + b$ are zero divisors.

4.13 FIELDS

An algebraic system (X, +, •), where + and • are two usual binary addition and multiplication operations, is called a *field* if,

1. (X, +, •) is a commutative ring with unity and
2. Every nonzero element of X is invertible.

For example, let X is the set of real numbers (R) then (R, +, •) is a field. Consider another examples, assume X is the set of all complex numbers (C) or set of rational numbers (Q) then algebraic structure (C, +, •) and (Q, +, •) are fields. But, if X = I or set of integers then algebraic structure (I, +, •) of integers is not a field, because (I, +, •) is a commutative ring and a ring with unity but, not every nonzero element of I is invertible.

Example 4.17. *Show that algebraic system (Y, $+_5$, $\times_5$) is a field, where Y = {0, 1, 2, 3, 4} and the operations $+_5$ and $+_5$ are addition modulo 5 and multiplication modulo 5 respectively.*

Sol. Since, algebraic system (Y, $+_5$, $\times_5$) is a ring. Now we will show that this is a commutative ring with unity and every nonzero element of Y is invertible. To prove that we construct the operation table for the operation $\times_5$ that is shown below (Fig. 4.7)

$\times_5$	0	1	2	3	4
0	0	0	0	0	0
1	0	1	2	3	4
2	0	2	4	1	3
3	0	3	1	4	2
4	0	4	3	2	1

Fig. 4.7 Operation table for X_5

Form the operation table our observations is follows,

- It has an identity element 1, so it is a ring with unity.
- Rows are similar to the corresponding columns, i.e. row 1 = column 1, row 2 = column 2, and others. Hence, ring is commutative.
- Every nonzero element of Y is invertible, i.e.

Let 1^{-1} is y so, $1 \times_5 y = 1$(identity) $\Rightarrow y = 1$, so $1^{-1} = 1$.

Similarly, 2^{-1} will be 3 [$\therefore$ $2 \times_5 3 = 1$], 3^{-1} will be 2 [$\therefore$ $3 \times_5 2 = 1$], 4^{-1} will be 4 [$\therefore$ $4 \times_5 4 = 1$]. Therefore, $(Y, +_5, \times_5)$ is a field.

This ring is an integral domain because it is a commutative ring with unity. Also it is a ring without zero divisors, due to entries of the first column of the operation table which shows that for all $x \in Y$, $x \times_5 y = 0$ when $y = 0$ and whatever the x is.

Example 4.18. *Show that the algebraic system $(Y, +_6, \times_6)$ is not a field where $Y = \{0, 1, 2, 3, 4, 5\}$.*

Sol. Since we have already saw that algebraic system $(Y, +_6, \times_6)$ is a ring (example 1.30). To show that $(Y, +_6, \times_6)$ is a field then it should be a commutative ring with unity followed that every nonzero element of Y is invertible. Observe the operation table for $\times_6$.

$\times_6$	0	1	2	3	4	5
0	0	0	0	0	0	0
1	0	1	2	3	4	5
2	0	2	4	0	2	4
3	0	3	0	3	0	3
4	0	4	2	0	4	2
5	0	5	4	3	2	1

- Operation table posses an identity element 1 hence it is a ring with unity.
- Row1 = column 1, row 2 = column2, and so on hence ring is commutative.
- Every nonzero element is not invertible, for example 2, 3, and 4 are not invertible. It means for no $y \in Y$, we have $2 \times_6 y = 1$, $3 \times_6 y = 1$, and $4 \times_6 y = 1$.

Therefore, $(Y, +_6, \times_6)$ is not a field.

Skew Field

Let $(X, +, \bullet)$ be a field then it is called a skew field if it a ring with unity and where every nonzero element has multiplicative inverse. Hence, if a skew field is commutative then it becomes a field.

For example, let M be a set of matrices i.e.,

$$M = \begin{pmatrix} u + i\,v & w + i\,x \\ -w + i\,x & u - i\,v \end{pmatrix}$$

where u, v, w, and $x \in R$ and the binary operations are usual addition (+) and multiplication $(\bullet)$ then $(M, +, \bullet)$ is a ring. It is a ring with unity, where unity matrix of M is,

$$M_I = \begin{pmatrix} 1 & 0 \\ 0 & 1 \end{pmatrix} = \begin{pmatrix} 1 + 0i & 0 + i0 \\ -0 + 0i & 1 - i0 \end{pmatrix}$$

and every nonzero element has a multiplicative inverse, since M^{-1} exists if M is singular matrix or $|M| \neq 0$. Since, $|M| = u^2 + v^2 + w^2 + x^2 \neq 0$. Therefore, $(M, +, \bullet)$ is a skew field.

Example 4.19. *Test the following statements are **true** or **false**.*

1. If x is an element of ring and $m, n \in$ N, then $(a^m)^n = a^{mn}$. **[True]**
2. Every subgroup of an abelian group is not necessarily abelian. **[False]**
3. The relation of isomorphism in the set of all groups is not an equivalence relation. **[False]**
4. If $\circledast$ is a binary operation on any set X, then $x \circledast x = x$ for all $x \in$ X. **[False]**
5. If $\circledast$ is any commutative binary operation on any set X, then
   $x \circledast (y \circledast z) = (y \circledast z) \circledast x$ for all x, y, and $z \in$ X. **[True]**
6. If $\circledast$ is associative then $x \circledast (y \circledast z) = (y \circledast z) \circledast x$ for all x, y, and z Î X. **[False]**

Example 4.20. *Test the following statements are **true** or **false**.*

1. Every binary operation defined over a set of one element is both commutative and associative. **[True]**
2. A binary operation defined over a set X assigns at least one element of X to each ordered pair of elements of X. **[False]**
3. A binary operation defined over a set X assigns exactly one element of X to each ordered pair of elements of X. **[True]**

Example 4.21. *Prove that a group G is abelian, if for a, b $\in$ G*

(*i*) $a^2 = e$ (*ii*) $(a\,b)^2 = a^2\,b^2$

(*iii*) $b^{-1}\,a^{-1}\,b\,a = e$

Sol.

(*i*) Since, $a^2 = e \Rightarrow a^{-1} = a$

Further since $a^{-1} = a$ and $b^{-1} = b$ then $a\,b = a^{-1}\,b^{-1} = (b\,a)^{-1} = b\,a$ (because $(b\,a)^{-1} = b\,a$).

Hence G is abelian.

(*ii*) Since $(a\,b)^2 = a^2\,b^2 \Rightarrow a\,b\,a\,b = a\,a\,b\,b$

$\Rightarrow b\,a = a\,b$ [by cancellation law]

Hence G is abelian.

(*iii*) Given, $b^{-1}\,a^{-1}\,b\,a = e$

Since $a\,b$ can be written as $a\,b\,e$ or

$a\,b = a\,b\,e = a\,b\,b^{-1}\,a^{-1}\,b\,a$ [replace e by $b^{-1}\,a^{-1}\,b\,a$]

$\Rightarrow a(b\,b^{-1})\,(a^{-1}\,b\,a)$ [$\because$ $b\,b^{-1} = e$]

$\Rightarrow (a\,a^{-1})\,b\,a$

$\Rightarrow b\,a$ [$\because$ $a\,a^{-1} = e$]

Hence G is abelian.

Example 4.22. *Examine whether the set of rational number (1 + 2p) / (1 + 2q), where p and q are integers, forms a group under multiplication.*

Sol. Assume two rational numbers are $(1 + 2p)/(1 + 2q)$ and $(1 + 2P)/(1 + 2Q)$, where p, q, P, and Q are integers. So we find, $[(1 + 2p)/(1 + 2q)] \bullet [(1 + 2P)/(1 + 2Q)] = (1 + 2p + 2P + 2pP)/(1 + 2q + 2Q + 2qQ)$ that returns again a rational number. Therefore set is closed under multiplication. Associative property is also satisfied that can also verified. For identity,

$$1 = (1 + 2 \bullet 0)/(1 + 2 \bullet 0)$$

and the inverse of $(1 + 2p)/(1 + 2q)$ is $(1 + 2q)/(1 + 2p)$.

Hence set of rational numbers of the form $(1 + 2p)/(1 + 2q)$ forms an abelian group under multiplication.

EXERCISES

4.1 Let X = {0, 1, 2, 3, 4} then show that,

(*i*) Algebraic structure (X, $+_5$) is an Abelian group and

(*ii*) Algebraic structure (X, $*_5$) is also an Abelian group.

where binary operations '$+_5$' and '$*_5$' are addition modulo 5 and multiplication modulo 5 respectively.

4.2 Is the algebraic structure (X, $*_5$) forms an finite Abelian group where the set X = {1, 2, 3, 4, 5, 6}. Determine the order of the group.

4.3 Define homomorphism on a semigroup. Explain when a homomorphism becomes an isomorphism.

4.4 Define a cyclic group. Show that following groups are cyclic,

(*i*) Algebraic structure ({1, – 1, *i*, – *i*}, *) where $\sqrt{i} = -1$.

(*ii*) Algebraic structure Σ where ω is cube root of unity.

4.5 Show that group (C, *7) is a cyclic group, where set C = {1, 2, 3, 4, 5, 6}.

4.6 Define the order of an element in a group. Find the order of each element in the following multiplicative group,

(*i*) ({1, – 1, *i*, – *i*}, *) (*ii*) ({1, ω, ω^2}, *).

4.7 Let (R^+, ⊗) is an algebraic structure where operation ⊗ is define as, $a \otimes b = ab/2$ for all $a, b \in R^+$, then (R^+, ⊗) is an Abelian group.

4.8 Consider $M = \begin{pmatrix} A & A \\ A & A \end{pmatrix}_{2\times 2}$

Define a set of matrices, where A is nonzero real number. Then prove Algebraic structure (M, *) where * is ordinary multiplication operation is a group.

4.9 Prove that nth root of unity forms a group under ordinary multiplication. Show also it is an Abelian group.

4.10 Find all the subgroups of X generated by the permutations

$$\begin{pmatrix} 1 & 2 & 3 & 4 \\ 2 & 3 & 1 & 4 \end{pmatrix} \quad \text{and} \quad \begin{pmatrix} a & b & c & d \\ 3 & 2 & 4 & 9 \end{pmatrix}$$

(*i*) (*ii*)

4.11 Let (X, *) be a group and $y \in X$. Let $f : X \to X$ be given by $f(x) = y * x * y^{-1}$ for all $x \in X$ then show that f is an isomorphism of X into X.

4.12 If an Abelian group has subgroups of orders *m* and *n*, then show that it has a subgroup whose order is the least common multiple of *m* and *n*.

4.13 Define the left coset and the right coset. If (I, +) is a additive group of integers and the set H = {...... – 6, – 3, 0, 3, 6, ...} then show that

$$I = (H + 0) \cup (H + 1) \cup (H + 2).$$

4.14 Define a ring with unity. Is the set of even integers i.e., J = 2I = {...... – 4, – 2, 0, 2, 4, ...} is a ring with unity under the binary operation addition and multiplication. Is the ring (J, +, •) is commutative also.

4.15 What do you understand by zero divisors of a ring? Give an example of ring with zero divisors and without zero divisors.

4.16 Define a field. Prove that ({0, 1, 2, 3, 4}, $+_5$, $*_5$) is a finite field.

4.17 What is a skew field? Is every skew field is a field. If not, give an example.

PROPOSITIONAL LOGIC

5 Propositional Logic

5.1 INTRODUCTION TO LOGIC

Study of logic is greatly concerned for the verification of reasoning. From a given set of statements the validity of the conclusion drawn from the set of statements would be verified by the rules provided by the logic. The domain of rules consists of proof of theorems, mathematical proofs, conclusion of the scientific theories based on certain hypothesis and the theories of universal laws. Logic is independent of any language or associated set of arguments. Hence, the rules that encoded the logic are independent to any language so called *rules of inference*.

Human has feature of sense of mind. Logic provides the shape to the sense of mind. Consequently, logic is the outcome of sense of mind. Rules of inference provide the computational tool through which we can check the validity of the argument framed over any language. (Fig. 5.1) Logic is a system for formalizing natural language statement so that we can reason more accurately.

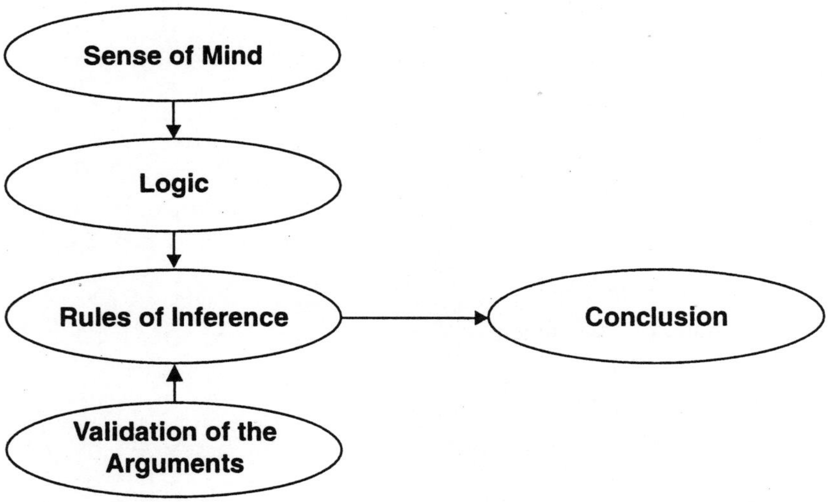

Fig. 5.1

In this chapter we start our discussion from the beginning that, how we provide the shape to the logic. In other words, how we represent the rules of inference. A formal language will be used for this purpose. In a formal language, syntax is well defined and the statements have not inherited any ambiguous meaning. It is easy to write and manipulate. These features of the formal language are the prime necessities for the logic representation. Logic is manuscripted in symbolic form (object language). Arguments are prepared in natural language (English/Hindi) but their representation (symbolic logic) need object language and so they are ready for validation checking computation.

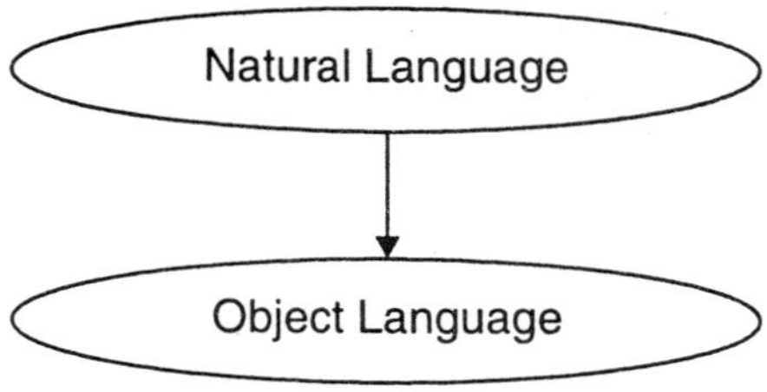

Fig. 5.2

Section 5.2 starts with discussion of statements and symbolization of statements.

5.2 SYMBOLIZATION OF STATEMENTS

A statement is a declarative sentence. It assigns one and only one of the two possible truth values *true* or *false*. A statement is of two types. A statement is said to be *atomic statement* if it can not be decomposable further into simple statement/s. Atomic statements are denoted by distinct symbols like,

A, B, C, ...X, Y, Z.
$a, b, c,$ ....$x, y, z.$
A1, A2, ...
B1, B2,.........................
Etc...

These symbols are called *propositional variables*. Second type of statements are *compound statements*. If a statement is formed over composition of several statements through connectives like conjunction, disjunction, negation and implication etc. then it is a compound statement. In other words statements are closed under *connectives*. In the latter section, we shall discuss the connectives in more detail. The compound statement is denoted by the string of symbols, connectives and parenthesis. Parenthesis is used to restrict the scope of the connective over symbols. The compound statement also assigns one and only one of the two possible truth values *true* or *false*. That will be the out come of the truth value attain from all the statements of the compound statement.

Therefore, set of statements both atomic and composite, formed language called object language so that we can symbolize the statements.

Example 5.1. *Illustrates the meaning of the statement.*

1. *India is a developing country.*
2. *L K Adwani is the leader of USA.*
3. *Henry Nikolas will be the richest person after 10 years.*
4. *False never encumbered truth.*
5. *It will rain today.*
6. *Leave the room*
7. *Bring my coat and tie.*

The sentences 1, 2, 3, 4 and 5 are statements that have assigned the truth value either *true/false* on there context. For example sentence 5 is a statement and has assign value *true* if it will rain today and *false* if there will no rain today. The sentences 6 and 7 are command sentences so they are not considered as statement as per the definition above.

Since, we admit only two possible truth values for a statement therefore our logic is sometimes called a *dual-value logic*.

As we mention above, throughout the text we shall use capital letters A, B, ...X, Y, Z to represent the statements in symbolic logic.

For example,

Statement (1): Delhi is capital.

Symbolic logic: D

Here the statement definition 'Delhi is capital' is represented by the symbol'D'. Consequently symbol 'D' corresponds to the statement 'Delhi is capital'. That is, the truth value of the statement (2) is the truth value of the symbol'D'.

Statement (2): Hockey is our national game.

Symbolic Logic: H

The statement (2) is represented by the symbolic logic 'H' that is, the truth value of 'H' is the truth value of the statement (2).

Since, compound statements are formed by use of operator's conjunction, disjunction, negation and implication. These operators are equivalent to our everyday language connectives such that 'and', 'or', 'not' and 'if-then' respectively.

Conjunction (AND/∧)

Let A and B are two statements, then conjunction of A and B is denoted as A ∧ B (read as "A and B") and the truth value of the statement A ∧ B is *true* if, truth values of both the statements A & B are *true*. Otherwise, it is *false*.

These conditions of the conjunction are specified in the truth table shown in Fig. 5.3.

A	B	A ∧ B
F	F	F
F	T	F
T	F	F
T	T	T

Fig. 5.3 (Truth table for conjunction)

Conjunction may have more than two statements and by definition it returns *true* only if all the statements are *true*. Consider the example,

Statement (1) : Passengers are waiting (symbolic logic) P

Statement (2) : Train comes late. (symbolic logic) T

Using conjunction connective we obtain the compound statement,

'Passengers are waiting "and" train comes late'

Given statement can be equally written in symbolic logic as, P ∧ T

Take another example,

Statement (1) : Stuart is an efficient driver (symbolic logic) K

Statement (2) : India is playing with winning spirit (symbolic logic) S

Then the compound statement will be 'Stuart is an efficient driver "and" India is playing with winning spirit'. We can also refer the compound statement in symbolic logic as, $K \wedge S$. In fact, the combination of statements (1) and (2) are appear unusual but logically they are represented correctly.

It must also be clear that, the meaning of the connective 'and' (in natural language) is similar to the meaning of logical 'AND'. Since conjunction is a binary operation s.t. truth values of $K \wedge S$ and of $S \wedge K$ are same (from the previous example). Then, the word 'and' of natural language must have the similar meaning.

Consider another example,

'I reach the station late "and" train left'.

Here conjunction 'and' is used in *true* sense of 'then' because one statement performs action followed by another statement action. So, the *true* sense of the compound statement is,

'I reach the station late "then" train left'.

So, readers are given advice to clearly understand the meaning of connective 'and'.

Disjunction (OR/$\vee$)

Let A and B are two statements then disjunction of A and B is denoted as $A \vee B$ (read as "A Or B") and the truth value of the statement $A \vee B$ is *true* if the truth value of the statement A or B or both are *true*. Otherwise it is *false*.

These conditions of the conjunction are specified in the truth table shown in Fig. 5.4.

Disjunction may have more than two statements and by definition it returns truth value *true* if truth value of any of the statement is *true*.

A	B	$A \vee B$
F	F	F
F	T	T
T	F	T
T	T	T

Fig. 5.4 (Truth table for disjunction)

However the meaning of disjunction is logical 'OR' that is similar to the meaning of connective "or" of natural language. In the next example we see the meaning of disjunction is 'inclusive-OR' (not 'exclusive-OR).

For example, consider a composite statement-

'Nicolas failed in university exam "or" he tells a lie'.

Here the connective "or" is used as its appropriate meaning. That is, either 'Nicolas failed in university exam' or 'he tells a lie' or both situation occurs 'Nicolas failed in university exam' and also 'he tells a lie'. Equivalently, we represent above statement by symbolic logic $N \vee T$. (where symbol 'N' stands for Nicolas failed in university exam; and symbol 'T' stands for he tells a lie)

Consider another example,

'I will take the meal "or" I will go'.

Here sense of connective "or" is exclusive-OR. The statement means either 'I will take the meal' or 'I will go' but both situations are not simultaneously occurs.

Negation (~)

Connective Negation is used with unary statement mode. The negation of the statement inverts its logic sense. That is similar to the introducing "not" at the appropriate place in the statement so that its meaning is reverse or negate.

Let A be an statement then negation of A is denoted as ~ A (read as "negation of A" or "not A") and the truth value of ~ A is reverse to the truth value of A. Fig. 5.5 defines the meaning of negation.

A	~ A
F	T
T	F

Fig. 5.5 (Truth table for negation)

For example, the statement,

'River Ganges is now profane'. 'G' (symbolic representation)

Then negation of statement means 'River Ganges is sacred' or 'River Ganges is not profane now'. That is denoted by symbolic logic ~ G.

Implication (→)

Let A and B are two statements then the statement A → B (read as "A implies B" or "if A then B") is an implication statement (conditional statement) and the truth value of A → B is *false* only when truth value of B is *false*; Otherwise it is *true*. Truth values of implication are specified in the truth table shown in fig 5.6.

A	B	A → B
F	F	T
F	T	T
T	F	F
T	T	T

Fig. 5.6 (Truth table for Implication)

In the implicative statement (A → B), statement A is known as *antecedent* or *predecessor* and statement B is known as *consequent* or *resultant*.

Example 5.2. *Consider the following statements and their symbolic representation,*

It rains	:	*R*
Picnic is cancelled	:	*P*
Be wet	:	*W*
Stay at home	:	*S*

Write the statement in symbolic form.

(i) If it rains but I stay home. I won't be wet.

Given statement is equivalent to,

⇒ (If it rains but I stay home) "then" (I won't be wet).

⇒ (If it rains "and" I stay home) "then" (I won't be wet).

⇒ $(R \wedge S) \to (\sim W)$

so $\mathbf{(R \wedge S) \to \sim W}$ will be its symbolic representation.

(ii) I'll be wet if it rains.

Then the equivalent statement is

⇒ If wet then rains (is a meaningless sentence)

So the meaningful sentence is,

⇒ (If it rains) "then" (I will be wet).

⇒ $\mathbf{R \to W}$ will be its symbolic representation.

(iii) If it rains and the picnic is not cancelled or I don't stay home then I'll be wet.

Given statement is equivalent to,

⇒ ((If it rains "and" the picnic is not cancelled) "or" (I don't stay home)) "then" (I'll be wet)

⇒ $\mathbf{((R \wedge \sim P) \vee \sim S) \to W}$

(iv) Whether or not the picnic is cancelled, I'm staying home if it rains.

Above statement is equivalent to.

⇒ (Picnic is cancelled "or" picnic is not cancelled), (I'm staying home if it rain).

⇒ (If it rain "and" (picnic is cancelled "or" picnic is not cancelled)) "then" (I'm staying home).

Now it is easier to symbolize the sentence.

⇒ $\mathbf{(R \wedge (P \vee \sim P)) \to S.}$

(v) Either, it doesn't rain or I'm staying home.

⇒ $\mathbf{\sim R \vee S}$

(vi) Picnic is cancelled or not, I will not stay at home so I'll be wet.

Above statement is equivalent to,

⇒ (Picnic is cancelled "or" picnic is not cancelled) "but" (I will not stay home) "so" (I'll be wet).

⇒ (If (picnic is cancelled "or" picnic is not cancelled) "and" (I will not stay home)) "then" (I'll be wet).

⇒ $\mathbf{((P \vee \sim P) \wedge \sim S) \to W}$

5.3. EQUIVALENCE OF FORMULA

Assume A and B are two statement formulas (symbolic logic) then formula A is equivalent to formula B if and only if the truth values of formula A is same to the truth values of formula B for all possible interpretations.

Equivalence of formula A and formula B is denoted as $A \Leftrightarrow B$ (read as "A is equivalent to B").

Now we discuss a theorem that shows the equivalence of formulas. And, also purposely we state the theorem here. As we see that basic connectors are conjunction ($\wedge$), disjunction ($\vee$)

and negation (~). Other connectors like implication (→), equivalence (⇔) that are also used to form a compound statement they are all represented using basic connectors (∧, ∨, ~).

Theorem 6.1

(i) $(A \rightarrow B) \Leftrightarrow (\sim A \vee B)$ *(ii)* $(A \Leftrightarrow B) \Leftrightarrow (A \wedge B) \vee (\sim A \wedge \sim B)$

(iii) $(A \oplus B) \Leftrightarrow (A \wedge \sim B) \vee (\sim A \wedge B)$ *(iv)* $(A \leftrightarrow B) \Leftrightarrow (A \rightarrow B) \wedge (B \rightarrow A)$

(v) $(A \wedge B) \Leftrightarrow \sim (\sim A \vee \sim B)$ *(vi)* $(A \vee B) \Leftrightarrow \sim (\sim A \wedge \sim B)$

The equivalence of illustrated formulas (*i*) — (*vi*) can be proved by the truth table.

(for the *truth table* see section 5.4.5)

For example, verify the equivalence between the LHS and RHS of the Implication formula shown in (*i*). Construct the truth table and compare the truth values of both the formulas shown in column 3 and 5. We observe that for all possible interpretations of propositional variables A and B truth values of both the formulas are same.

A	B	**(A → B)**	~ A	**(~ A ∨ B)**	
F	F	T	T	T	
F	T	T	T	T	
T	F	F	F	F	
T	T	T	F	T	
1	2	3	4	5	⟵ Column number

Fig. 5.7

Similarly verify other equivalence formulas.

(*ii*) $\mathbf{(A \Leftrightarrow B) \Leftrightarrow (A \wedge B) \vee (\sim A \wedge \sim B)}$

(Equivalence formula)

A	B	(A ⇔ B)	(A ∧ B)	(~ A ∧ ~ B)	(A ∧ B) ∨ (~ A ∧~ B)
F	F	T	F	T	T
F	T	F	F	F	F
T	F	F	F	F	F
T	T	T	T	F	T

Fig. 5.8

(*iii*) $\mathbf{(A \oplus B) \Leftrightarrow (A \wedge \sim B) \vee (\sim A \wedge B)}$

(Exclusive-OR formula)

A	B	(A⊕B)	(A ∧ ~ B)	(~ A ∧ B)	(A ∧ ~ B) ∨ (~ A ∧ B)
F	F	F	F	F	F
F	T	T	F	T	T
T	F	T	T	F	T
T	T	F	F	F	F

Fig. 5.9

(*iv*) Here, the LHS formula **(A ↔ B),** which read as "A if and only if B" is called a *biconditional* formula. The formula **(A ↔ B)** return the truth value *true* if truth values of A and B are identical (that is either both *true* or both *false*).

A	B	(A ↔ B)	(A → B)	(B → A)	(A → B) ∧ (B → A)	
F	F	T	T	T	T	
F	T	F	T	F	F	
T	F	F	F	T	F	
T	T	T	T	T	T	
1	2	3	4	5	6	← Column number

Fig. 5.10

Truth table shown in Fig. 5.10 proves the equivalence formula *i.e.*

$$(\mathbf{A} \leftrightarrow \mathbf{B}) \Leftrightarrow (\mathbf{A} \rightarrow \mathbf{B}) \wedge (\mathbf{B} \rightarrow \mathbf{A})$$

Similarly verify the equivalence formula listed (*v*) and (*vi*).

5.4. PROPOSITIONAL LOGIC

Continuation to the previous section 5.2 symbolization of the statements, we now define the term propositional logic. Propositional logic has following character,

- It contains Atomic or Simple Statements called propositional variables.
  viz. (A, B, C, ...) or (*a*, *b*, *c*, ...) or (A1, A2, A3, ...) or (B1, B2, ...) etc.
- It contains Operator Symbols or Connectors.
  viz. ∧, ∨, ~, →
- It contains Parenthesis.
  i.e (, and)
- Nothing else is allowed.

Thus statements are represented by the propositional logic called *statement formula*. A statement formula is an expression consisting of propositional variables, connectors and the parenthesis. The scope of propositional variable/s is/are controlled by the parenthesis.

Let X is a set containing all statements and Y is another set consists of truth values (*true* or *false*). Let we define the relation *f* i.e.,

$$f : X \otimes X \rightarrow Y$$

where, ⊗ is a boolean operator viz. ∧, ∨, ..., then relation f illustrates the mapping of compound statements that are formed over set X using operator ⊗ to set Y that is either *true* (T) or *false* (F). Assume statements A & B are in X then,

$$f(A, B) \rightarrow \{T, F\}$$

or, $$\otimes (A, B) \rightarrow \{T, F\}$$

Now the question arises, how many different boolean operators are possible for ⊗. Since, we are talking about *dual-logic paradigm* so each statement has two values T or F. For two statements total numbers of possible different boolean operators are $2^{2^2} = 2^4 = 16$. These are shown in Fig. 5.11.

A	**B**	$\otimes_1$	$\otimes_2$	$\otimes_3$	$\otimes_4$	$\otimes_5$	$\otimes_6$	$\otimes_7$	$\otimes_8$	$\otimes_9$	$\otimes_{10}$	$\otimes_{11}$	$\otimes_{12}$	$\otimes_{13}$	$\otimes_{14}$	$\otimes_{15}$	$\otimes_{16}$
F	F	F	F	F	F	T	F	F	F	T	T	T	F	T	T	T	T
F	T	F	F	F	T	F	T	F	T	F	T	F	T	F	T	T	T
T	F	F	F	T	F	F	F	T	T	T	F	F	T	T	F	T	T
T	T	F	T	F	F	F	T	T	F	F	F	T	T	T	T	F	T

Fig. 5.11

In general if set X has n statements then there are as many as 2^{2^n} different combinations or formulas can be seen.

5.4.1 Well Formed Formula (wff)

That valid statement that has following characteristic is called well formed formula.

- Every atomic statement is a *wff*.
- If A is a *wff* then ~ A is also *wff*.
- If A and B are *wff* then (A ⊗ B) is also *wff* . (where operator ⊗ : ~, ∧, ∨, →)
  For example statement formula A ∧ B is not a *wff* while (A ∧ B) is a *wff*.
- Nothing else is a *wff*.

Example 5.3

(i) (A ∧ B) → C is not a wff (due to missing of parenthesis), while ((A ∧ B) → C) is a wff.

(ii) (A ∧) is not a wff, because A ∧ is not a wff.

(iii) ~ A ∨ B is not a wff, while (~ A ∨ B) is a wff.

5.4.2 Immediate Subformula

Let A & B are wff, then

(*i*) if A is a atomic statement then it has no immediate subformula.

(*ii*) the formula ~ A has A as its only immediate subformula *i.e.* ~ (A ∧ B) has (A ∧ B) is immediate subformula.

(*iii*) the formula (A ⊗ B) (where ⊗ : ~, ∧, ∨) has A and B as its immediate subformula. For example,

((A ∨ B) ∧ ~ C) has (A ∨ B) and ~ C are immediate subformula.

5.4.3. Subformula

(*i*) all immediate subformula of A are also subformula of A.

(*ii*) A is a subformula of itself.

(*iii*) if A is a subformula of B and B is a subformula of C then, A is also subformula of C. For example,

Formula ((A ∨ B) ∧ ~ C) has (A ∨ B) and ~ C are immediate subformula.

Further, subformulas are:

((A ∨ B) ∧ ~ C) → ((A ∨ B) ∧ ~ C)

→ (A ∨ B), ~ C

→ A, B and C

5.4.4. Formation Tree of a Formula

Let A be a formula, then

(*i*) put A at the root of the tree.

(*ii*) If a node in the tree has formula B as its label, then put all immediate subformula of B as the son of this node.

Example 5.4. *Fig. 5.12 shows the formation tree of the formula* $((A \vee B) \wedge \sim C)$.

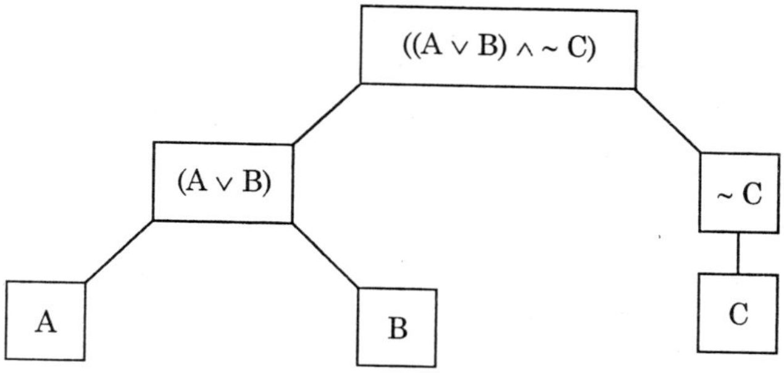

Fig. 5.12

Example 5.6. *Construct the formation tree of the formula* $((P \vee (\sim Q \wedge (R \rightarrow S))) \rightarrow \sim Q)$.

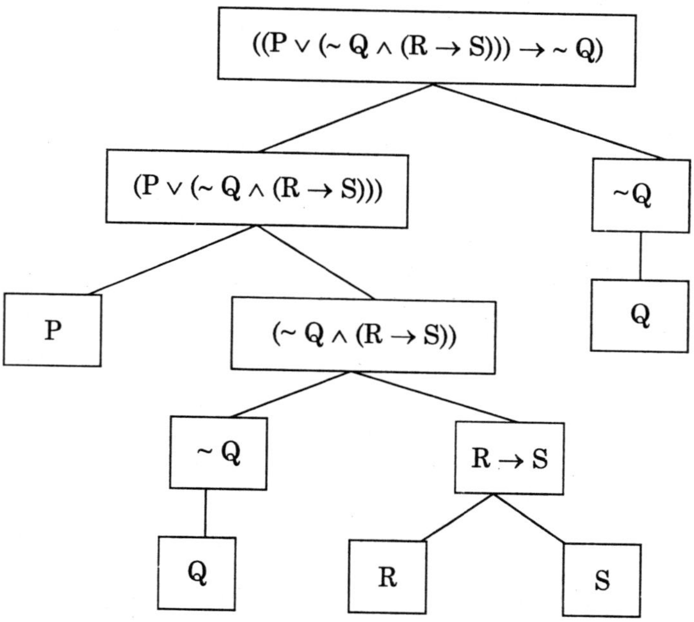

Fig. 5.13

All formula appearing at node/leaf in the formation tree are subformula of formula as root and every formula appearing at parent node will be the immediate subformula to their children.

Formation tree provide convenient way to determine the truth value of the formula over particular set of truth values of its propositional variables.

Consider the formation tree shown in Fig. 5.13. Determine the truth value of the formula for the truth values of propositional variables (P, Q, R, S) are (T, F, F, T) respectively.

Putting truth values to corresponding variables shown at leaf and obtains the truth value of its immediate subformula in that path and moves one level up in the tree. Continue, this process until we reach to root node with truth value. Here we find the truth value of the formula (at root) is T (Fig. 5.14).

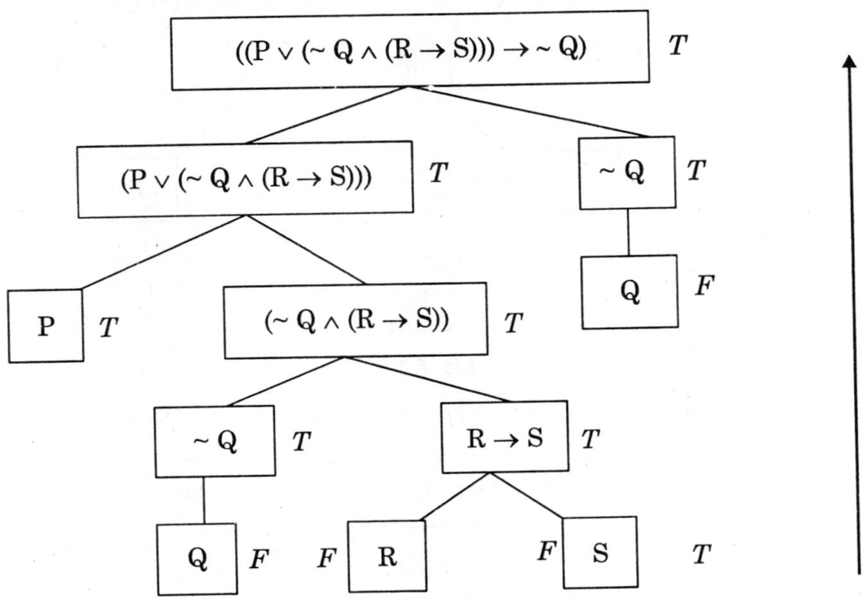

Fig. 5.14

5.4.5. Truth Table

A *wff* may consist of several propositional variables. In the dual-logic paradigm the propositional variables have only possible truth value T or F. To determine the truth values of *wff* for all possible combinations of the truth values of the propositional variables-a table is prepared-called *truth table.*

Assume a formula contains two propositional variables then there are 2^2 possible combinations of truth values are to be considered in the truth table. In general, if a formula contains n distinct propositional variables then, possible combination of truth values are 2^n or total number of possible different ***interpretation*** are 2^n.

The process of arbitrarily assignments of truth value (T/F) to the propositional variables is called ***atomic valuation***. Thus, we get the truth values of the formula called ***valuation***. It can't assign the truth values arbitrary.

There is another term frequently used in propositional logic that is ***boolean valuation***. Boolean valuation is a valuation under some restrictions.

Lets '*v*' be a boolean valuation, then

- If the formula X gets value T under '*v*' then '*v*' must assign F to ~ X. Conversely, if formula X gets value F under '*v*' then ~ X must get value T under '*v*'.
- The formula (X ∧ Y) can get value T under '*v*' if and only if both X and Y get value T under '*v*'.

- The formula (X ∨Y) can get value F under '*v*' if and only if both X and Y get value F under '*v*'.
- The formula (X → Y) can get value F under '*v*' if and only if X get the value T and Y get value F under '*v*'.

Boolean valuation provides the truth value to the formula over connectives: ~, ∧, ∨, →.

For a formula, construction of truth table is a two step method.

Step 1. Prepare all possible combinations of truth values for propositional variables (that gives the total number of rows in the truth table). Number of variables gives the initial number of columns.

Step 2. Obtain the truth values of each connective and put these truth values in a new column.

Entries of the final column show the truth values of the formula.

Example 5.7. *Construct the truth value for (P ∧ ~ Q)*

Step 1. Since, formula (P ∧ ~ Q) has two variables (2 columns), so there are four possible combinations of truth values for P and Q (4 rows).

Step 2. Add column 3 (for connective negation) to determine truth values of ~ Q, add column 4 (for connective conjunction) to determine truth values of (P ∧ ~ Q).

Since there are no more connectives left, hence we get the truth table shown in Fig. 5.15 and the truth values of the formula (P ∧ ~ Q) are shown in column 4.

P	Q	~ Q	P ∧ ~ Q
F	F	T	F
F	T	F	F
T	F	T	T
T	T	F	F
1	2	3	4

Fig. 5.15

Example 5.8. *Construct the truth table for the formula,*

((P → Q) ∧ (~ P ∨ Q)) ∨ (~ (P → Q) ∧ (~ P ∨ Q)) : *(let it be X)*

P	Q	(P → Q)	~P	(~P ∨ Q)	~(P → Q)	~(~P ∨ Q)	(P → Q) ∧ (~P ∨ Q)	~(P → Q) ∧ ~(~P ∨ Q)	X
F	F	T	T	T	F	F	T	F	T
F	T	T	T	T	F	F	T	F	T
T	F	F	F	F	T	T	F	T	T
T	T	T	F	T	F	F	T	F	T
1	2	3	4	5	6	7	8	9	10

Fig. 5.16

5.5. TAUTOLOGY

A formula which is *true* (T) under all possible interpretation is called a ***tautology***. Conversely, a formula which is *false* (F) under all possible interpretation is called a ***contradiction***. Hence, negation of contradiction is a tautology.

As we know entries in the last column of the truth table shows the truth value to the formula. If this column has all entries *true* (T) then the formula is a tautology. Consequently, the truth value of the tautology is *true* (T) always.

For example, the formula (A ∨ ~ A) is a tautology. Because truth value entries in the truth table at last column are all T. (Fig. 5.17)

A	**~ A**	**(A ∨ ~ A)**
F	T	T
T	F	T

Fig. 5.17

Example 5.9. *Show the formula* $((P \rightarrow Q) \wedge (\sim P \vee Q)) \vee (\sim (P \rightarrow Q) \wedge (\sim P \vee Q))$ *is a tautology.*

Truth values of the formula are shown in truth table (Fig. 5.16). From the truth table we observe that truth values shown at column 10 are all T. Therefore, formula is a tautology.

5.6. THEORY OF INFERENCE

The objective of the study of logic is to determine the criterion so that validity of an argument is determined. The criterion is nothing but the computational procedure based on rules of inference and the theory associated such rules is known as inference theory. It is concerned with the inferring a conclusion from set of given premises. The computation process of conclusion from a set of premises by using rules of inference is called *formal proof* or *deduction*.

Assume that there are k statements $S_1, S_2, S_3, \ldots\ldots\ldots S_k$. These statements are facts/ premises/ hypothesis. Let these statements draw a conclusion C.

That is,

(i)	S_1
(ii)	S_2
(iii)	S_3
....	....
(k)	S_k
∴	C

For example, premises	*(i)*	S_1	:	If it rains I will not go to Institute.
and	*(ii)*	S_2	:	It is raining.
Conclusion,	Therefore, I will not go to Institute. : C			

Corresponding to above, symbolic logic of two premises & conclusion are shown below,

(*i*) $R \rightarrow C$ where, R : it rains
(*ii*) R C : I will not go to Institute

$\therefore$ C

From given set of premises and the conclusion, we can justify that argument is valid or invalid by formal proof. An argument is a ***valid argument*** if truth values of all premises is *true* (T) and truth value of conclusion must also be *true* (T). Consequently, if particular set of premises derived the conclusion then it is a ***valid conclusion***.

If truth value of all premises is *true* (T) but truth value of the conclusion is *false* (F) then argument is ***invalid argument***. Consequently, if we find any one interpretation which makes the premises *true* (T) but conclusion is *false* (F) then argument is an invalid argument. Similarly, if set of premises not derived the conclusion correctly then it is an ***invalid conclusion***.

To investigate the validity of an argument we take the preveious example, *i.e.*,

(*i*) $R \rightarrow C$
(*ii*) R

$\therefore$ C

R	C	$R \rightarrow C$	
F	F*	T	←
F	T	T	
T	F*	F	←
T	T	T	

Fig. 5.18

Form the table shown in Fig. 5.18 we find conclusion (C) is F when,

(*i*) R is F and $R \rightarrow C$ is T; or
(*ii*) R is T and $R \rightarrow C$ is F

Thus, we find no interpretation so that argument is invalid. Hence, we have a valid conclusion and the argument is a valid argument.

Validity of an argument is also justified by assuming that particular set of premises and the conclusion construct a formula (say X). Rule for constructing the formula X is as follows,

Let premises are $S_1, S_2, S_3, \ldots\ldots\ldots S_k$ that derives the conclusion C then formula X will be,

$$X: \ ((\ldots\ldots\ldots((S_1 \wedge S_2) \wedge S_3)\ldots\ldots\ldots \wedge S_k) \rightarrow C)$$

Here formula X is an *implication formula* that will be obtained by putting the conjunction of all premises as the *antecedent* part and the conclusion as the *consequent* part.

It means we have the only conclusion,

$$\therefore \quad ((\ldots\ldots\ldots((S_1 \wedge S_2) \wedge S_3)\ldots\ldots\ldots \wedge S_k) \rightarrow C)$$

- If antecedent part is T and also consequent part is T i.e.,

  $\Rightarrow \quad T \rightarrow T \ \Rightarrow \ T$

  Hence, argument is a valid argument.
- If antecedent part is F and consequent part is T i.e.,

  $\Rightarrow \quad F \rightarrow T \ \Rightarrow \ T$

  Again, argument is a valid argument.
- If antecedent part is T and consequent part is F i.e.,

  $\Rightarrow \quad T \rightarrow F \ \Rightarrow \ F$

Hence, argument is invalid.

Thus, we conclude that formula X must be tautology for valid argument.

In the next sections we will discuss several methods to test the validity of an argument. A simple and straight forward method is truth table method discussed in section 5.6.1. That method is based on construction of truth table. Truth table method is efficient when numbers of propositional variables are less. This method is tedious if number of variables are more. Natural deduction method is general and an efficient approach to prove the validity of the argument that will illustrated in section 5.6.2.

5.6.1 Validity by Truth Table

Assuming a set S of premises (S_1, S_2, S_3,.........S_k) derives the conclusion C then we say that conclusion C logically follows from S if and only if,

$$S \rightarrow C$$

Or, $$((.........((S_1 \wedge S_2) \wedge S_3)..........\wedge S_k) \rightarrow C)$$

So we have the only conclusion i.e.,

$$((.........((S_1 \wedge S_2) \wedge S_3)..........\wedge S_k) \rightarrow C)$$

Thus, we obtain a formula $((.........((S_1 \wedge S_2) \wedge S_3)..........\wedge S_k) \rightarrow C)$ let it be X. Now test the tautology for X. If X is a tautology then argument is valid; Otherwise argument is invalid. By use of truth table we test the tautology of the formula.

For example, given set of premises and conclusion,

(*i*) $R \rightarrow C$
(*ii*) R

∴ C

---

we obtain the formula,

$$((R \rightarrow C) \wedge R) \rightarrow C) : \text{(say) } X$$

Construct the truth table for X (Fig. 5.19).

R	**C**	**$R \rightarrow C$**	**$(R \rightarrow C) \wedge R$**	**$((R \rightarrow C) \wedge R) \rightarrow C : X$**
F	F	T	T	T
F	T	T	F	T
T	F	F	F	T
T	T	T	F	T

Fig. 5.19 (Truth table for X)

Since, truth values of the formula X are all T therefore, X is a tautology. Hence argument is valid.

Example 5.10. *Show that argument is invalid.*

(*i*) $R \rightarrow C$
(*ii*) C

∴ R

Sol. From the given premises & conclusion, we obtain the formula,

$$((R \rightarrow C) \wedge C) \rightarrow R) : \text{(say) } X$$

Now construct the truth table for X, we observe that formula X is not a tautology. Therefore, argument is invalid. (Fig. 5.20)

R	**C**	**R** $\rightarrow$ C	**(R** $\rightarrow$ **C)** $\wedge$ **C**	**((R** $\rightarrow$ **C)** $\wedge$ **C)** $\rightarrow$ **R : X**
F	F	T	F	T
F	***T***	***T***	***T***	***F***
T	F	F	F	T
T	T	T	T	T

Fig. 5.20 Truth table for X.

You will also see that argument is invalid for,

(*i*)	R $\rightarrow$ C	: **T**
(*ii*)	C	: **T**
$\therefore$	R	: **F**

Example 5.11. *Demonstrate that following argument is invalid.*

(*i*)	$((A \rightarrow B) \wedge C) \rightarrow D$
(*ii*)	$A \vee C$
(*iii*)	$(B \vee D) \rightarrow (E \wedge F)$
(*iv*)	$(E \wedge F) \rightarrow G$
(*v*)	$(G \wedge A) \rightarrow H$
$\therefore$	H

Sol. An argument is invalid if and only if, *true* (T) truth values of all premises must derive the *false* (F) conclusion.

We assume that H is *false* (F),

- if H is F then (G $\wedge$ A) must be F $\Rightarrow$ either G is F or A is F : from premise (*v*)
- if G is F then (E $\wedge$ F) must be F $\Rightarrow$ either E is F or F is F : from premise (*iv*)
- if E is F then (B $\vee$ D) must be F $\Rightarrow$ B is F and D must be F : from premise (*iii*)
- Since D is F, so antecedent part of premise (*i*) must be F $\Rightarrow$ either C is F or A is F (since B is F and (A $\rightarrow$ B) is F so A is F).

Above discussed situation will be seen in Fig. 5.21.

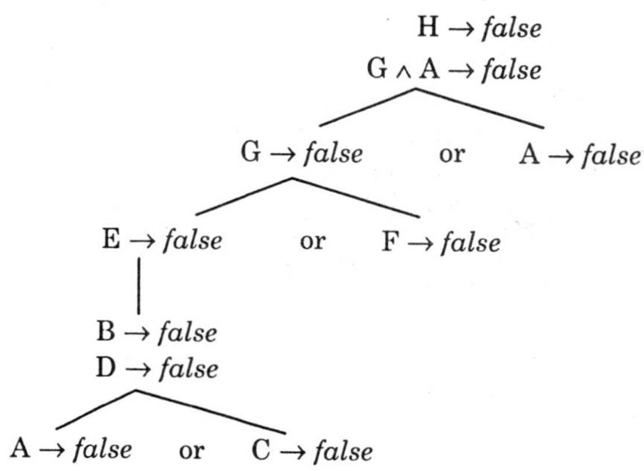

Fig. 5.21

Thus, for following truthvalues, argument is invalid,

A : T
B : F
C : ......(T/F)
D : F
E : F
F : ....(T/F)
G : F
H : F

Example 5.12. *For what (truth) values of V, H and O following argument is invalid.*

$$
\begin{array}{ll}
(i) & V \rightarrow O \\
(ii) & H \rightarrow O \\
\hline
\therefore & V \rightarrow H \\
\hline
\end{array}
$$

Sol. Form the truth table shown in Fig 5.22 for the given argument; we find one such condition s.t. V → H is T and H → O is also T and conclusion V → H is F, so the argument is invalid. We also observe from the truth table shown in Fig. 5.22 that the conclusion is F and premises are both T when V is T, H is T and O is T.

V	H	O	V → O	H → O	V → H
F	F	F	T	T	T
F	F	T	T	T	T
F	T	F	T	F	T
F	T	T	T	T	T
T	F	F	F	T	F
T	***F***	***T***	***T***	***T***	***F***
T	T	F	F	F	T
T	T	T	T	T	T

Fig. 5.22

Example 5.13. *Justify the validity of the argument.*

"If prices fall then sell will increase; if sell will increase then Stephen makes whole money. But Stephen does not make whole money; therefore prices are not fall."

Sol. Represent the statement into the symbolic form,

$$
\begin{array}{ll}
(i) & P \rightarrow S \\
(ii) & S \rightarrow J \\
(iii) & \sim J \\
\hline
\therefore & \sim P \\
\hline
\end{array}
$$

(by assuming) { prices falls : P; sell will increase : S; John makes whole money : J }

From the given premises & conclusion we obtain the formula i.e.,

$$(((P \rightarrow S) \wedge (S \rightarrow J) \wedge \sim J) \rightarrow \sim P) : \text{(say) } X$$

and construct the truth table for X. From Fig. 5.23 we find that formula X is a tautology, therefore argument is a valid argument. Hence, given statement is a valid statement.

S	P	J	P → S	S → J	~ J	S_1 (let) (P → S) ∧ (S → J)	S_2 (let) S1 ∧ ~ J	~ P	S2 → ~ P
F	F	F	T	T	T	T	T	T	*T*
F	F	T	T	T	F	T	F	T	*T*
F	T	F	T	F	T	F	F	F	*T*
F	T	T	T	T	F	T	F	F	*T*
T	F	F	F	T	T	F	F	T	*T*
T	F	T	T	T	F	T	F	T	*T*
T	T	F	F	F	T	F	F	F	*T*
T	T	T	T	T	F	T	F	F	*T*

Fig. 5.23

As we observe that when number of propositional variables appeared in the formula are increases then construction of truth table will become lengthy and tedious. To, overcome this difficulty, we must go through some other possible methods where truth table is no more needed.

5.6.2 Natural Deduction Method

Deduction is the derivation process to investigate the validity of an argument. When a conclusion is derived from a set of premises by using rules of inference then, such a process of derivation is called a *deduction* or *formal proof.*

Natural deduction method is based on the rules of Inference that are shown in Fig 5.24.

The process of derivation can be describe by following two steps,

Step 1. From given set of premises, we derive new premises by using rules of inference.

Step 2. The process of derivation will continues until we reaches the required premise that is the conclusion (every rule used at each stage in the process of derivation, will be acknowledged at that stage).

I. Rules of Inference

Here we discuss 9 rules of inference, by truth table we can verify that the arguments followed by these rules are valid arguments. (Assume P, Q, R and S are propositional variables)

Rule 1. **Modes Ponens (MP)**	**Rule 2.** **Modes Tollens (MT)**
(*i*) P → Q (*ii*) P ∴ Q	(*i*) P → Q (*ii*) ~ Q ∴ ~ P

Rule 3. Hypothetical Syllogism (HP)

(*i*) $P \rightarrow Q$

(*ii*) $Q \rightarrow R$

$\therefore P \rightarrow R$

Rule 4. Disjunctive Syllogism (DS)

(*i*) $P \vee Q$

(*ii*) $\sim P$

$\therefore Q$

Rule 5. Constructive Dilemma (CD)

(*i*) $(P \rightarrow Q) \wedge (R \rightarrow S)$

(*ii*) $P \vee R$

$\therefore Q \vee R$

Rule 6. Destructive Dilemma (DD)

(*i*) $(P \rightarrow Q) \wedge (R \rightarrow S)$

(*ii*) $\sim Q \vee \sim S$

$\therefore \sim P \vee \sim R$

Rule 7. Simplification (Simp)

(*i*) $P \wedge Q$

$\therefore P$

Rule 8. Conjunction (Conj)

(*i*) P

(*ii*) Q

$\therefore P \wedge Q$

Rule 9. Addition (Add)

(*i*) P

$\therefore P \vee Q$

Fig. 5.24

While derivation the rule will be acknowledge by its abbreviated name that was shown in brackets.

Note. *Reader must note that by applying rules of inference we extend the list of premises and further all these premises including the new premises are equally participated in derivation process.*

Example 5.14. *Show that $B \rightarrow E$ is a valid conclusion drawn from the premises*

$$A \vee (B \rightarrow D),\ \sim C \rightarrow (D \rightarrow E),\ A \rightarrow C \text{ and } \sim C.$$

Sol. First, we list the premises,

1. $A \vee (B \rightarrow D)$

2. $\sim C \rightarrow (D \rightarrow E)$

3. $A \rightarrow C$

4. $\sim C$ $\quad / \therefore B \rightarrow E$

(Apply rules of inference and obtain new premises until we reach to conclusion)

5. $D \rightarrow E$ **2 & 4, MP**

6. $\sim A$ **3 & 4, MT**

7. $B \rightarrow D$ **1 & 6, DS**

8. $B \rightarrow E$ **7 & 5, HS**

Since we reach to conclusion therefore, derivation process stops. Hence, premises 1-4 derive the valid conclusion.

Example 5.15. *Show conclusion E follows logically from given premises:*

$$A \to B, B \to C, C \to D, \sim D \text{ and } A \vee E.$$

Sol. Given premises are,

1.	$A \to B$	
2.	$B \to C$	
3.	$C \to D$	
4.	$\sim D$	
5.	$A \vee E$	$/ \therefore \; E$

(Apply rules of inference and obtain new premises until we reach to conclusion)

6.	$A \to C$	**1 & 2, HS**
7.	$A \to D$	**6 & 3, HS**
8.	$\sim A$	**7 & 4, MT**
9.	E	**5 & 8, DS**

Thus we reach to conclusion; hence conclusion logically follows from given premises.

In fact, there are possibly several different deductions (derivation sequences) to reach the conclusion. For this particular example, there is another possible deduction shown below.

We have 1 – 5 premises, (Apply rules of inference and obtain new premises until we reach to conclusion)

6.	$\sim C$	**3 & 4, MT**
7.	$\sim B$	**2 & 6, MT**
8.	$\sim A$	**1 & 7, MT**
9.	E	**5 & 8, DS**

Example 5.16. *Show premises $A \to B$, $C \to D$, $\sim B \to \sim D$, $\sim\sim A$, and $(E \wedge F) \to C$ will derive the conclusion $\sim (E \wedge F)$.*

Sol. List the premises,

1.	$A \to B$	
2.	$C \to D$	
3.	$\sim B \to \sim D$	
4.	$\sim\sim A$	
5.	$(E \wedge F) \to C$	$/ \therefore \; \sim (E \wedge F)$

(Apply rules of inference and obtain new premises until we reach to conclusion)

6.	$(A \to B) \wedge (C \to D)$	**1 & 2, Conj**
7.	$\sim A \vee \sim C$	**6 & 3, DD**
8.	$\sim C$	**7 & 4, DS**
9.	$\sim (E \wedge F)$	**5 & 8, MT**

Since, we get the conclusion hence deduction process stop. Therefore conclusion is valid.

Example 5.17. *Show*

1. $A \wedge B$ $\qquad / \therefore \; B$

Sol. Deduction using rules of inference could not solve this problem. (From the list of rules of inference no rule will applicable here). In other words the 9 rules of inference are not sufficient to solve the problem. Hence, we have another 10 rules. These rules are called rules of replacement that are listed in Fig. 5.25.

II. Rules of Replacement

Rule 1. De Morgan's (DeM) (*i*) $\sim(P \vee Q) \Leftrightarrow \sim P \wedge \sim Q$, (*ii*) $\sim(P \wedge Q) \Leftrightarrow \sim P \vee \sim Q$	**Rule 2. Commutation (Comm)** (*i*) $(P \vee Q) \Leftrightarrow Q \vee P$ (*ii*) $(P \wedge Q) \Leftrightarrow Q \wedge P$
Rule 3. Association (Assoc) (*i*) $(P \vee Q) \vee R \Leftrightarrow P \vee (Q \vee R)$ (*ii*) $(P \wedge Q) \wedge R \Leftrightarrow P \wedge (Q \wedge R)$	**Rule 4. Distribution (Dist)** (*i*) $P \wedge (Q \vee R) \Leftrightarrow (P \wedge Q) \vee (P \wedge R)$ (*ii*) $P \vee (Q \wedge R) \Leftrightarrow (P \vee Q) \wedge (P \vee R)$
Rule 5. Double Negation (DN) $\sim\sim P \Leftrightarrow P$	**Rule 6. Transportation (Trans)** $P \rightarrow Q \Leftrightarrow \sim Q \rightarrow \sim P$
Rule 7. Material Implication (Imp) $P \rightarrow Q \Leftrightarrow \sim P \vee Q$	**Rule 8. Explanation (Exp)** $(P \wedge Q) \rightarrow R \Leftrightarrow P \rightarrow (Q \rightarrow R)$
Rule 9. Tautology (Taut) (*i*) $P \Leftrightarrow P \wedge P$ (*ii*) $P \Leftrightarrow P \vee P$	**Rule 10. Equivalence (Equiv)** $(P \rightarrow Q) \wedge (Q \rightarrow P) \Leftrightarrow (P \wedge Q) \vee (\sim P \wedge \sim Q)$

Fig. 5.25

The major difference between rules of inference and the rules of replacement is that, rules are inference applies over full line but rules of replacement apply on part of line also.

Now attempt the problem of example 5.17 and solve.

1. $A \wedge B$ $/\therefore B$

(Apply rules of inference and rules of replacement whenever required and obtain new premises until we reach to conclusion)

2.	$B \wedge A$	**1, Comm**
3.	B	**2, Simp**

Thus, we obtain the required conclusion, hence deduction stop.

Example 5.18. *Verify the argument*

1. $(A \vee B) \rightarrow (C \wedge D)$

2. $\sim C$ $/\therefore \sim B$

(Apply rules of inference and rules of replacement whenever required and obtain new premises until we reach to conclusion)

3.	$\sim C \vee \sim D$	**2, Add**
4.	$\sim(C \wedge D)$	**3, DeM**
5.	$\sim(A \vee B)$	**1 & 4, MT**
6.	$\sim A \wedge \sim B$	**5, DeM**
7.	$\sim B \wedge \sim A$	**6, Comm**
8.	$\sim B$	**7, Simp**

Example 5.18.

1.	$J \vee (\sim K \vee J)$	
2.	$K \vee (\sim J \wedge K)$	$/ \therefore \ (J \wedge K) \vee (\sim J \wedge \sim K)$
		(Apply rules of inference and rules of replacement whenever necessary and obtain new premises until we reach to conclusion)
3.	$(J \vee \sim K) \vee J$	**1, Assoc**
4.	$J \vee (\sim K \vee J)$	**3, Assoc**
5.	$J \vee (J \vee \sim K)$	**4, Comm**
6.	$(J \vee J) \vee \sim K$	**5, Assoc**
7.	$J \vee \sim K$	**6, Taut**
8.	$(K \vee \sim J) \wedge (K \vee K)$	**2, Dist**
9.	$(K \vee \sim J) \wedge K$	**8, Taut**
10.	$(K \vee \sim J)$	**9, Simp**
11.	$\sim J \vee K$	**10, Assoc**
12.	$J \rightarrow K$	**11, Imp**
13.	$\sim K \vee J$	**7, Comm**
14.	$K \rightarrow J$	**13, Imp**
15.	$(J \rightarrow K) \wedge (K \rightarrow J)$	**12, & 14, Conj**
16.	$(J \wedge K) \vee (\sim J \wedge \sim K)$	**15, Equiv**

Thus given premises derived the valid conclusion. Hence argument is valid.

III. Rule of Conditional Proof (CP)

We shall now introduce another rule of inference known as conditional proof, which is only applicable if the conclusion is an implicative statement.

Assume the argument,

1. X_1
2. X_2
....
....
....
***k*.** X_k

$\therefore \quad A \rightarrow B$

So, we obtain the formula $(\ldots\ldots(X_1 \wedge X_2) \wedge \ldots\ldots\wedge X_k) \rightarrow (A \rightarrow B)$

Assume $(\ldots\ldots(X_1 \wedge X_2) \wedge \ldots\ldots\wedge X_k) \ : \ P$

Thus, we have $P \rightarrow (A \rightarrow B)$

$\Leftrightarrow \quad (P \wedge A) \rightarrow B$ by rule **Exp** **...(A)**

We observe that, if antecedent part of conclusion goes to the set of premises then we will have the consequent part as conclusion.

That is,

1.	X_1
2.	X_2
....	
....	
....	
***k*.**	X_k
***k*+1.**	A
∴	B

So we construct the formula, $((\ ......(X_1 \wedge X_2)\ ....\wedge X_k) \wedge A) \rightarrow B$

Assume $(\ ......(X_1 \wedge X_2)\ ....\wedge X_k) : P$

Thus we have, $(P \wedge A) \rightarrow B$ **...(B)**

We will see that expression (A) and expression (B) are similar.

Hence we conclude that ***rule CP*** *is applied when conclusion is of the form A → B. In such a case, A is taken as an additional premise and B is derived from set of premises including A.*

Example 5.19. *Show that A → B derives the conclusion A → (A → B).*

Sol. Here, we observe that the conclusion is of implication form. Hence, we can apply rule of conditional proof, so the antecedent part of conclusion will be added to the list of premise, therefore we have,

1.	$A \rightarrow B$	$/\therefore A \rightarrow (A \wedge B)$	
2.	A	$/\therefore A \wedge B$	**CP**
			(Apply rules of inference and rules of replacement whenever necessary and obtain new premises until we reach to conclusion)
3.	B		**1 & 2, Imp**
4.	$A \wedge B$		**2 & 3, Conj**

Since, we obtain the conclusion, therefore argument 2, is valid hence previous argument is valid.

Example 5.20. *Show that (A ∨ B) → ((C ∨ D) → E)* $/\therefore$ *A → ((C ∧ D) → E).*

Sol. Since conclusion is of implication form, hence we proceed with conditional proof. That is, instead of deriving $A \rightarrow ((C \wedge D) \rightarrow E)$, we shall include A as an additional premise and derive the conclusion $(C \wedge D) \rightarrow E$. That is also an implication conclusion, so apply again Conditional proof s.t. $(C \wedge D)$ as an additional premise and E will be the final conclusion.

s.t.

1.	$(A \vee B) \rightarrow ((C \vee D) \rightarrow E)$	$/\therefore A \rightarrow ((C \wedge D) \rightarrow E)$	
2.	A	$/\therefore (C \wedge D) \rightarrow E$	**CP**
3.	$C \wedge D$	$/\therefore E$	**CP**
4.	$A \vee B$	**2, Add**	
5.	$(C \vee D) \rightarrow E$	**1 & 4, MP**	
6.	C	**3, Simp**	
7.	$C \vee D$	**6, Add**	
8.	E	**5 & 7, MP**	

Since we find the conclusion; therefore conclusion is valid at stage 3. Thus, conclusion is valid at stage 2 at hence old conclusion must be valid.

IV. Rule of Indirect Proof

Example 5.21. *Show that*

1. $A \quad /\therefore \quad B \vee \sim B$

Sol. In order to show that a conclusion follows logically from the premise/s, we assume that the conclusion is *false*. Take negation of the conclusion as the additional premise and start deduction. If we obtain a contradiction (s.t. $R \wedge \sim R$ where, R is any formula) then, the negation of conclusion is *true* doesn't hold simultaneously with the premises being *true*. Thus negation of conclusion is *false*. Therefore, conclusion is *true* whenever premises are *true*. Hence conclusion follows logically from the premises. Such procedure of deduction is known as ***Rule of Indirect Proof (IP)*** or ***Method of Contradiction*** or *Reductio Ad Absurdum*.

Therefore,

1.	A	$/\therefore \quad B \vee \sim B$
2.	$\sim (B \vee \sim B)$	**IP**
3.	$\sim B \wedge \sim \sim B$	**2, Dem**

Since, we get a contradiction, so deduction process stops. Therefore, the assumption negation of conclusion is wrong. Hence, conclusion must be *true*.

Example 5.22. *Show* $\sim (H \vee J)$ *follows logically from* $(H \to I) \wedge (J \to K)$, $(I \vee K) \to L$ *and* $\sim L$.

Sol.

1.	$(H \to I) \wedge (J \to K)$	
2.	$(I \vee K) \to L$	
3.	$\sim L$	$/\therefore \sim (H \vee J)$
4.	$\sim (I \vee K)$	**2 & 3, MT**
5.	$\sim I \wedge \sim K$	**4, Dem**
6.	$\sim I$	**5, Simp**
7.	$\sim K \wedge \sim I$	**5, Comm**
8.	$\sim K$	**7, Simp**
9.	$H \to I$	**1, Simp**
10.	$\sim H$	**9 & 6, MT**
11.	$(J \to K) \wedge (H \to I)$	**1, Comm**
12.	$J \to K$	**11, Simp**
13.	$\sim J$	**12 & 8, MT**
14.	$\sim H \wedge \sim J$	**13 & 10, Conj**
15.	$\sim (H \vee J)$	**14, DeM**

There is alternate method to reach the conclusion using Indirect Proof

Since we have 1 – 3 premises; so

4.	$\sim \sim ((H \vee J)$	**Indirect Proof (IP)**
5.	$H \vee J$	**4, DeM**
6.	$I \vee K$	**1 & 5, CD**
7.	L	**2 & 6, MP**
8.	$L \wedge \sim L$	**7 & 3, Conj**

We obtain a contradiction therefore, our assumption is wrong at stage 4. Hence conclusion must be *true*.

It will be seen that method of indirect proof may cut short the steps of deduction. Therefore, we conveniently proved the conclusion is valid. Deduction through method of contradiction also shows the inconsistency of premises. Alternatively, a set of given premises P_1, P_2, ...P_n is inconsistence if formal proof obtain a contradiction (at any stage) i.e.,

1. P_1
2. P_2

....

....

....

n. P_n

$n + 1$. $(P_1 \wedge P_2 \wedge \ldots\ldots\ldots\ldots \wedge P_n)$

....

....

m. $R \wedge \sim R$

We obtain a contradiction $R \wedge \sim R$ (where R is any formula), that is necessary and sufficient to imply that $(P_1 \wedge P_2 \wedge \ldots\ldots\ldots\ldots \wedge P_n)$ be a contradiction.

Example 5.23. *Prove that following statements are inconsistent.*

1. *If Nelson drives fast then he reaches the Institute in time.*
2. *If Nelson drives fast then he is not lazy.*
3. *If Nelson reaches the Institute then he is lazy.*
4. *Nelson drives fast.*

Sol. Write the statement in symbolic logic,

Assume, D : Nelson drives fast

I : Nelson reaches the Institute in time

L : Nelson is very lazy

So the premises are,

1.	$D \rightarrow I$	
2.	$D \rightarrow L$	
3.	$I \rightarrow \sim L$	
4.	D	
5.	L	**2 & 4 MP**
6.	I	**1 & 4 MP**
7.	$\sim L$	**3 & 6 MP**
8.	$L \wedge \sim L$	**5 & 7 Conj**

Since, we obtain a contradiction hence premises are inconsistent. Therefore statements are inconsistent.

Example 5.24. *Prove following statements are inconsistent.*

1. *Stephen loves Joyce since graduation and Matrye is not happy but their parents are happy.*
2. *If Stephen marries with Joyce, his collegiate Shalezi and Matrye will be happy.*
3. *Stephen marries with Joyce if Joyce loves Stephen.*

Sol.

Assume, S : Stephen loves Joyce
M : Matrye is happy
P : parents are happy
L : Shalezi will be happy
J : Stephen marries with Joyce

Then, symbolic representations of the statements are,

1.	$S \wedge (\sim M \wedge P)$	
2.	$J \rightarrow (L \wedge M)$	
3.	$S \rightarrow J$	
4.	$S \rightarrow (L \wedge M)$	**3 & 2, HS**
5.	$\sim S \vee (L \wedge M)$	**4, Imp**
6.	$(\sim S \vee L) \wedge (\sim S \vee M)$	**5, Dist**
7.	$(\sim S \vee M) \wedge (\sim S \vee L)$	**6, Comm**
8.	$(\sim S \vee M)$	**7, Simp**
9.	$\sim (S \wedge \sim M)$	**8, DeM**
10.	$(S \wedge \sim M) \wedge P$	**1, Assoc**
11.	$(S \wedge \sim M)$	**10, Simp**
12.	$(S \wedge \sim M) \wedge \sim (S \wedge \sim M)$	**11 & 9, Add**

Since we obtain a contradiction therefore given statements are inconsistent.

Example 5.25. *Prove that the formula $B \vee (B \rightarrow C)$ is a tautology.*

Sol. Apply method of contradiction and assume that negation of formula is *true*. Thus,
We have

$/\therefore \quad B \vee (B \rightarrow C)$

1.	$\sim (B \vee (B \rightarrow C))$	**IP (Indirect proof)**
2.	$\sim B \wedge \sim (B \rightarrow C)$	**1, DeM**
3.	$\sim B$	**2, Simp**
4.	$\sim (B \rightarrow C) \wedge \sim B$	**2, Comm**
5.	$\sim (B \rightarrow C)$	**4, Simp**
6.	$\sim (\sim B \vee C)$	**5, Imp**
7.	$\sim \sim B \wedge \sim C$	**6, DeM**
8.	$\sim \sim B$	**7, Simp**
9.	$\sim \sim B \wedge \sim B$	**9 & 3, Conj/Add**

Since, we get a contradiction hence deduction process stops. Hence the assumption negation of conclusion is *false*. Therefore, Formula is *true* or tautology.

Example 5.26. *Prove that*

$$/\therefore \quad ((A \rightarrow B) \wedge (B \rightarrow C)) \rightarrow (A \rightarrow C) \text{ is a tautology.}$$

Sol. Since formula is of implication form, hence we use method of conditional proof. So we shall include antecedent part as an additional premise and $(A \rightarrow C)$ is the only conclusion. Still we have the conclusion is of implicative type so apply again method of conditional proof.

Thus we have,

$/\therefore \quad ((A \rightarrow B) \wedge (B \rightarrow C)) \rightarrow (A \rightarrow C)$

1.	$((A \rightarrow B) \wedge (B \rightarrow C))$	$/\therefore \quad (A \rightarrow C)$	**CP**
2.	A	$/\therefore \quad C$	**CP**

Assume that the negation of formula is *true* and apply method of contradiction.

Therefore,

3.	$\sim C$	**IP**
4.	$A \rightarrow B$	**1, Simp**
5.	B	**4 & 2, MP**
6.	$(B \rightarrow C) \wedge (A \rightarrow B)$	**1, Comm**
7.	$(B \rightarrow C)$	**6, Simp**
8.	C	**7 & 5, MP**
9.	$C \wedge \sim C$	**8 & 3 Conj**

Since we obtain a contradiction therefore our assumption must be wrong. Hence, formula must be tautology.

So far our discussion to prove the validity of an argument using natural deduction method we have complete our study with,

- 9-Inference Rules
- 10-Replacement Rules
- 1-Conditional Proof Method
- 1-Indirect Proof Method

This set of rules is called '***Complete***'. For any valid argument the *complete* must be follow. Consequently, *complete* must be the basis for the valid argument.

5.6.3 Analytical Tableaux Method (ATM)

In section 5.6.2 we discussed the solution to the problem for validity is provided by the truth table method. The method of natural deduction just discussed determines whether argument is valid in finite number of steps. On the other hand, if the argument is invalid, then it is very difficult to decide, after a finite number of steps. Also, Deduction a lot depends upon the practice, familiarity and ingenuity of the person to make the right decision at each step. To overcome these problems we shall now describe another method namely ***analytical tableaux method*** which is based on the formation tree of the formula, that do allow one to determine after a sequence of steps, whether an argument is valid or invalid.

Analytical tableaux method is based on the formation tree of the formula. There are two categories of the formulas. One category of formula is called **α-formula** and other category is ***β-formula.*** Fig 5.26 shows the list of α-formulas, where α_1 or α_1 and α_2 are its extended formula/s; similarly other column shows the ß-formulas and β_1 or β_2 are its extended formulas.

α-formula	β-formula
$\dfrac{\sim\sim X : \alpha}{X : \alpha_1}$	$\dfrac{(X \lor Y) : \beta}{\beta_1 : X \mid Y : \beta_2}$
$\dfrac{(X \land Y) : \alpha}{\begin{matrix} X : \alpha_1 \\ Y : \alpha_2 \end{matrix}}$	$\dfrac{\sim (X \land Y) : \beta}{\beta_1 : \sim X \mid \sim Y : \beta_2}$
$\dfrac{\sim (X \lor Y) : \alpha}{\begin{matrix} \sim X : \alpha_1 \\ \sim Y : \alpha_2 \end{matrix}}$	$\dfrac{(X \to Y) : \beta}{\beta_1 : \sim X \mid Y : \beta_2}$
$\dfrac{\sim (X \to Y) : \alpha}{\begin{matrix} X : \alpha_1 \\ \sim Y : \alpha_2 \end{matrix}}$	The literals like, X or ~ X not occurred in either α or β-formula.

Fig. 5.26

Let X be any well formed formula (wff) then tábleaux for formula X will be defined as follows,

The tableaux is a tree, where each node of the tree is labeled by some formula the tableaux has following characteristics.

I. Formula X will be at the label of root.

II. If a path in tableaux contains an α-formula then we may extend this path by putting either α_1-formula or α_2-formula as the son of the leaf (usually we put both formula α_1 and α_2 one after other).

III. If a path in the tableaux contains a β-formula then we may extend this path by putting formula β_1 as the left child of the leaf of this path and formula β_2 as the right child of the leaf of this path.

Suppose T is a tableaux (formation tree) for the formula X shown in Fig. 5.27. The path in the tableaux contains one or more α and/or β-formula/s. If the path contains a α-formula then this path will extended beyond leaf with additional α_1 and α_2-formula. Either, if the path contains a β-formula then this path will extend to β_1 and β_2-formula as left and right child respectively beyond leaf. Thus, we obtain the tableaux T_1 that is an immediate extension of Tree T. Reader must note that in the tableaux T_1-Rule II or Rule III may be applied only once.

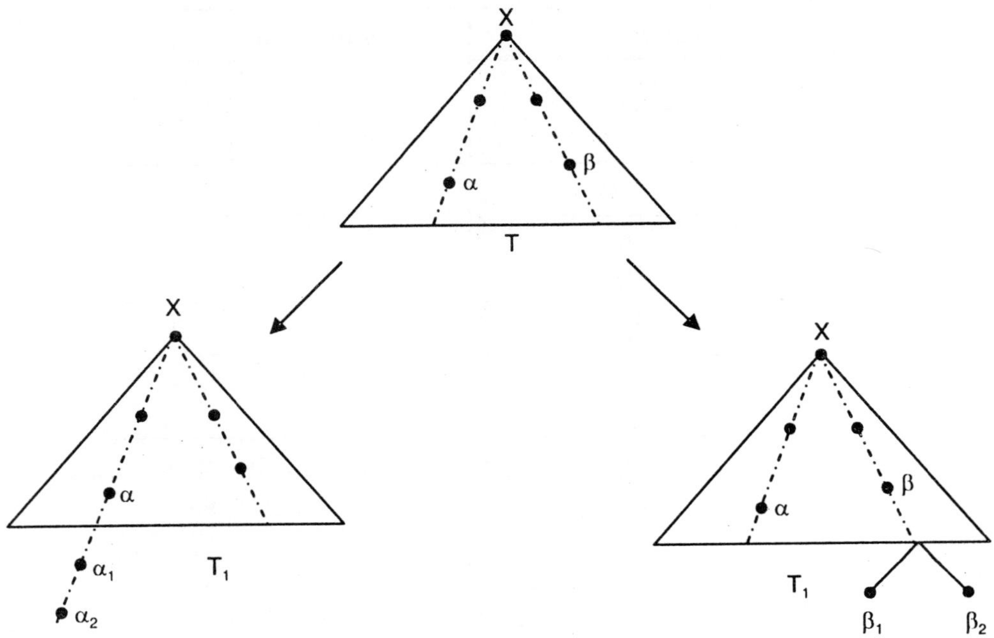

Fig. 5.27

Now we shall define few terms of the tableaux on the basis of that we shall take the decision about the validity of the formula.

Closed Path

If a path in the tableaux contains a formula R and ~ R then path is a closed path (where R is a formula). A closed path is never extended. We will designate the closed path by putting sign × under this path.

Closed Tableaux

If all paths in the tableaux are closed then tableaux is closed.

Open Path

A path that is not closed is an open path.

True Path

For a path if, there exists an interpretation '*v*' which makes all formulas of this path *true* then path is a *true* path.

Complete Path

A path for which all its formulas are expended is a complete path.

True Tableaux under Interpretation '*v*'

If tableaux contain at least one *true* path under interpretation '*v*' then tableaux is a *true* tableaux under '*v*'.

(where interpretation means, a particular combination of the truth value of the propositional variables of the formula)

For example, consider the formula X: $(((P \to Q) \wedge P) \to Q)$

Then tableaux of X will be,

$(((P \to Q) \wedge P) \to Q)$ (β)

(β_1) $\sim ((P \to Q) \wedge P)$ | Q (β_2)

(β_{11}) $\sim ((P \to Q)$ | $\sim P$ (β_{12})

P (α_{111})

$\sim Q$ (α_{112})

Consider the same formula with negation of it then X will be $\sim (((P \to Q) \wedge P) \to Q)$. For this formula we obtain different tableaux that is shown below.

$\sim (((P \to Q) \wedge P) \to Q)$ (α)

$((P \to Q) \wedge P)$ (α_1)

$\sim Q$ (α_2)

$(P \to Q)$ (α_{11})

P (α_{12})

(β_{111}) $\sim P$ | Q (β_{112})

Theorem 5.1. *If T_1 is an "immediate extension" of T_2 then T_1 is true under all those interpretation for which T_2 is true.*

Proof. Fig. 5.28 shows tableaux T_1 is the immediate extension of tableaux T_2. Assume that θ and θ_1 are the paths of tableaux T_2. Also assume tableaux T_2 is true under interpretation 'v'. It follows that, there exist at least one true path in tableaux T_2 under 'v'. Let this true path be θ.

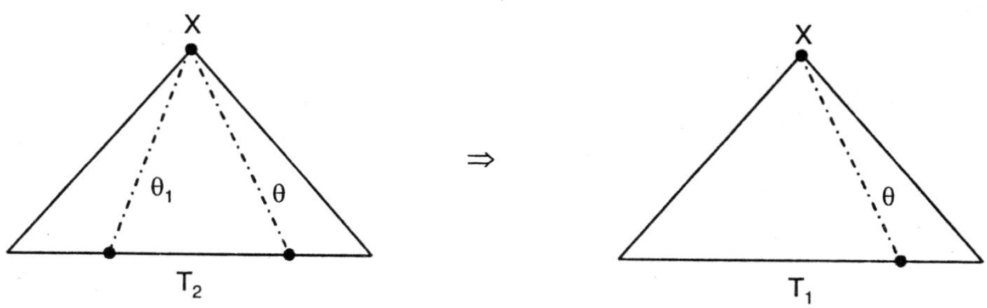

Fig. 5.28

Now, extend the path of T_1 by assuming that it contains a β-formula or a α-formula.

These possibilities are shown below in Fig. 5.29.

Or,

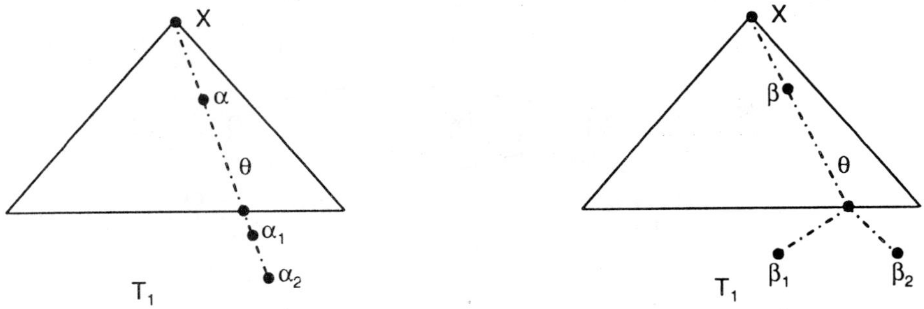

Fig. 5.29

Thus if $\quad v(\alpha) = \text{true};$

then $\quad (v(\alpha_1) = \text{true}) \wedge (v(\alpha_2) = \text{true});$

else if $\quad v(\beta) = \text{true};$

then $\quad (v(\beta_1) = \text{true}) \vee (v(\beta_2) = \text{true});$

Hence, T_1 is true.

That concludes the result.

Theorem 5.2. *If formula at the root of the tableaux is true then tableaux is true.*

Proof. The statement pronounced by the theorem is an implicative type.

i.e., if (...............) then (...............);

that is, if (formula at the root of the tableaux is *true*) *then* (tableaux is *true*) under 'v';

The statement is equivalently to its symbolic view,

if (P) *then* (Q); where antecedent part is P and consequent is Q

$\Rightarrow \quad P \rightarrow Q$

$\Leftrightarrow \quad \sim Q \rightarrow \sim P$ (using transportation rule)

$\Rightarrow$ if (~Q) then (~ P);

$\Rightarrow$ if (tableaux is not true) *then* (formula at root is not *true*) under 'v';

Since, a tableaux is not *true*, only when there is no *true* path in the tableaux; It follows that tableaux is closed.

We already know that a formula which is *false* under all possible interpretations is called as 'contradiction'. Therefore we say that,

if (X is a 'contradiction') *then* (~ X will be tautology);

$\Leftrightarrow$ if (X is a tautology) then (~ X is a contradiction);

So, if tableaux is closed then formula at the root is a contradiction.

Example 5.26. *Show*

1. $A \rightarrow B$
2. $A \qquad /\therefore \; B$

Sol. From the given argument we can determine the formula say X,

where, $X : ((A \rightarrow B) \wedge A) \rightarrow B)$

Put negation of X so we have, $\sim (((A \rightarrow B) \wedge A) \rightarrow B)$

Now construct the tableaux for this formula

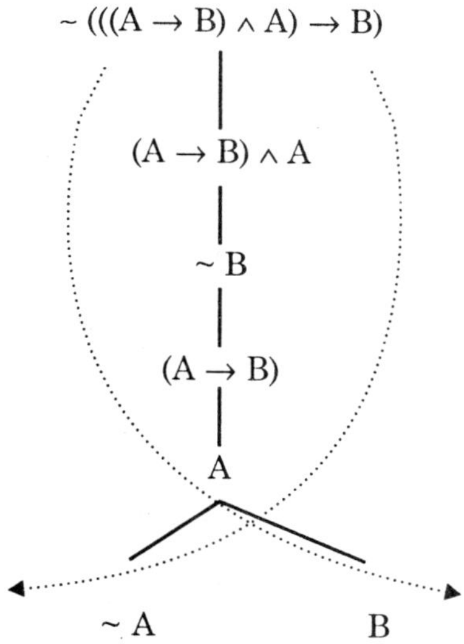

Moving according to this path we get a contradiction (A & ~ A) ×

× moving according to this path we get a contradiction (B & ~ B)

So, both paths in the tableaux are closed, therefore tableaux is closed. It follows the formula (~ X) labeled at the root is a contradiction. Therefore, X is a tautology and so argument is a valid argument.

Example 5.27. *Show that*

1. $M \to J$
2. $J \to \sim H$
3. $\sim H \to \sim T$
4. $\sim T \to M$
5. $M \to \sim H$ $\quad\quad /\therefore \;\; \sim T$

Sol. Assume premises 1, 2, 3, 4, 5 are denoted by X_1, X_2, X_3, X_4, X_5 respectively. So the argument has the formula (say X), where

$$X: \;\; (((((X_1 \wedge X_2) \wedge X_3) \wedge X_4) \wedge X_5) \to \sim T);$$

So, $\;\; \sim X : \sim (((((X_1 \wedge X_2) \wedge X_3) \wedge X_4) \wedge X_5) \to \sim T);$

Fig. 5.30 shows the tableaux for ~ X. In which we find one open and complete (since all formulas in this path are expended) path so tableaux is not closed. It implies that formula at root ~ X is not a contradiction or X is a contradiction. Therefore, X is not a tautology and so argument is invalid.

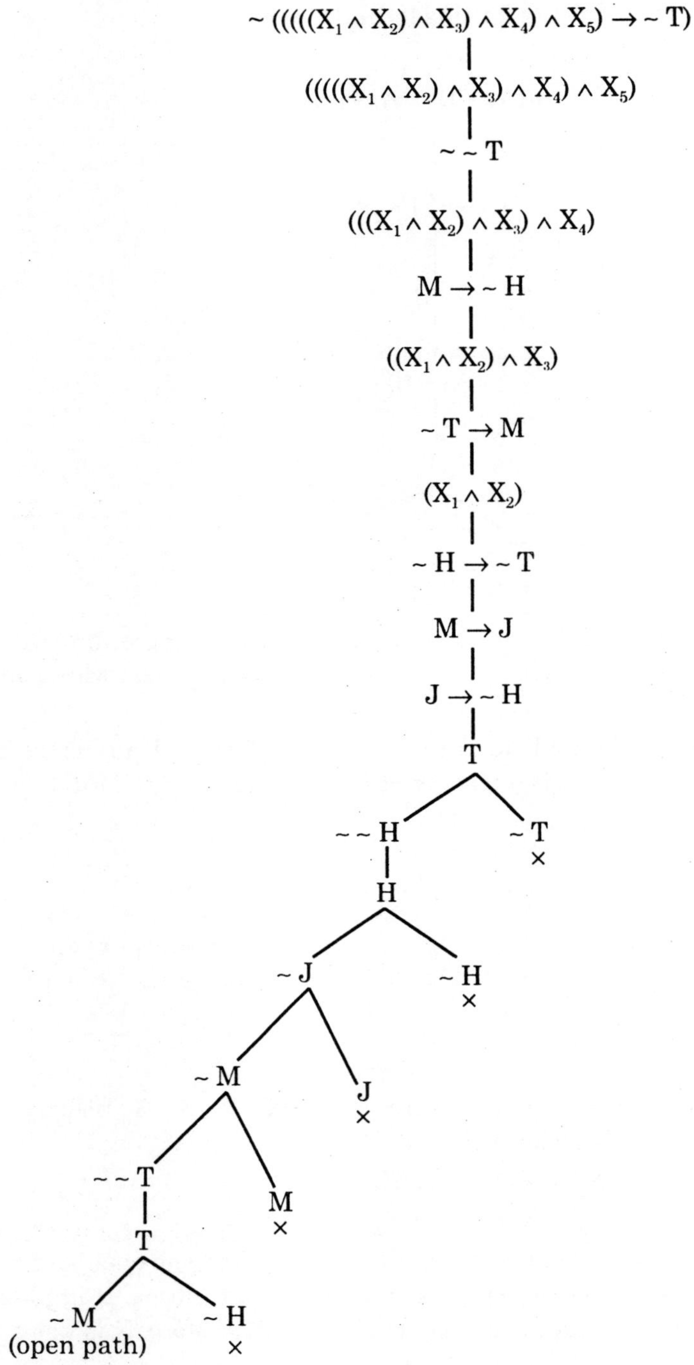

Fig. 5.30

In this example, we will also determine the interpretation for which the argument is invalid. Since we know that an argument is invalid when *true* premise/s derives a *false* conclusion.

That is,

1. X_1 : True
2. X_2 : True
3. X_3 : True
4. X_4 : True
5. X_5 : True /∴ ~ T : False

Therefore argument is invalid for following interpretation,

T : True
M : False (since T is true; so ~ T → M will be True only when M is false)
H : True (since T is true; so ~ H → ~ T will be true only when H is true)
J : false (since H is true; so J → ~ H will be true only when J is false)

Example 5.28. *Prove formula (P ∨ ~ P) is a tautology.*

Sol. We will see that by assuming negation of the formula we find a contradiction, which concludes that X will be tautology.

Using ATM, expand the tableaux by assuming ~ (P ∨ ~ P) will be labeled at root.

~ (P ∨ ~ P)
|
~ P
|
~ ~ P
|
P
×

So, we find a closed path, therefore tableaux is closed. Hence formula is a tautology.

5.7 PREDICATE LOGIC

So far our discussion of symbolic logic and inference theory are concern statements and the propositional variables are the basic units which are silent about the analysis of the statements. In order to investigate the property in common between the constitute statements; the concept of a predicate is introduced. The predicate is the property of the statement and the logic based upon the analysis of the predicate of the statement is called *predicate logic*. Consider an argument,

1.	All human are mortal	:	A
2.	John is a human	:	J
/∴	John is mortal	:	M

If we express these statements by symbols, then the symbols do not expose any common feature of these statements. Therefore, particular to this symbolic representation inference theory doesn't derive the conclusion from these statements. But in course, conclusion appears unthinkingly *true*. The reason for such deficiency is the fact that the statement "All human are mortal" can't be analyzed to say anything about an individual or person. If the statement is slices from its property "are mortal" to the part "All human" then it might be possible to consider any particular human.

5.7.1 Symbolization of Statements Using Predicate

Since, predicate is used to describe the feature of the statement, therefore a statement could be written symbolically in terms of the predicate symbol followed by the name to which, predicate is applied.

To symbolize the predicate and the name of the object we shall use following convention,

- A predicate is symbolize by a capital letter (A, B, C, ...Z).
- The name of the individual or object by small letter ($a, b, c, \ldots\ldots z$).

For example, consider the statement

"Rhodes is a good boy"

where the predicate is "good boy" and denoted symbolically by the predicate symbol G and the name of the individual "Rhodes" by r. Then the statement can be written as G(r) and read as "r is G".

Similarly the statement "Stephen is a good boy" can be translated as G(s) where s stands for the name "Stephen" and the predicate symbol G is used for "good boy".

To translate the statement "Stephen is not a good boy" that is the negation of the previous statement which can be written as ~ G(s). In the similar sense it is possible that name of the individual or objects may varies for the same predicate. In general, any statement of the type "r is S" can be denoted as S(r) where r is the object and S is the predicate.

As we said earlier that every predicate describes something about one/more objects. Let we define a set D called domain set of universe (never be empty). From the set D we may take a set of objects of interests that might be infinite. Let's consider the statement,

G(r) : where r is a good boy

then, $G \subseteq D$

That can be described as, $G = \{r \in D \,/\, r \text{ is a good boy}\}$

Since such type of predicate requiring single object is called *one- place predicate*.

When the number of names of the object associated with a predicate are two to form a statement then predicate is *two-place predicate*. In *true* sense, the statement expressed by two place predicate there exist a binary relation between the associated names. For example the statement,

G(x, y) : (where x is greater than y) is a two-place predicate

then, $G \subseteq D \times D$; where G consists of sets of pairs

where, set $G = \{(x, y) \in D \,/\, x > y\}$. For example if D is the set of positive integers (I^+) then $G = \{(2, 1), (3, 1), (3, 2), \ldots\ldots..\}$.

Similarly, we can define a three-place predicate, for example the statement

P(x, y, z) : (where y and z are the parents of x)

then, $P \subseteq D \times D \times D$ s.t. $(a, b, c) \in P$

In general, a predicate with n objects is called *n-place predicate*.

then, $P \subseteq D \times D \times D \ldots\ldots\ldots\ldots \times D$, n times

s.t. $(t_1, t_2, t_3, \ldots\ldots\ldots\ldots\ldots\ldots\ldots t_n) \in P$

The truth values of the statement can also be determined on the basis of domain set D. Assume set D is defined as,

$$D = \{1, 2, 3, 4\}$$

In order to determine the truth value of (one-place predicate) statement E(x) : where x is a even number will be *true*, because

$$E = \{2, 4\}.$$

The truth value for the statement M(x): where x is greater than 5, will be *false* because set M find no element from given domain set D.

The truth value for 2-place predicate statement G (x, y) : where $x > y$ will also be *true* where, set G = {(2, 1), (3, 1) (4, 1), (3, 2), (4, 2), (4, 3)}.

If G(x, y) *i.e.* x is greater or equal to y then its truth value also be *true* where, set G contains all above elements including (1, 1), (2, 2), (3, 3) and (4, 4).

5.7.2 Variables and Quantifiers

Consider the statement discussed earlier,

"Rhodes is a good boy" : G (r), where G be the predicate "good boy" and r is the name "Rhodes"

Consider another statement,

"Stephen is a good boy" : G(s), where predicate G "good boy" is same with different name "Stephen" symbolizes by s.

Consider one more similar statement,

"George is a good boy" : G(g) with same predicate G and different name "George" symbolizes by g.

These statements G(r), G(s), G(g) and possibly several other statements shared the property in common that is predicate G "good boy" but subject is varies from one statement to the other statement. If we write G(x) in general that states "x is G" or "x is a good boy" then the statements G(r), G(s), G(g) and infinite many statements of same property can be obtained by replacing x by the corresponding name. So, the role of x is a substitute called *variable* and G(x) is a simple (atomic) statement function.

G(x)

Predicate Symbol ——↑↑—— Variable

We can obtain the statement from statement function G(x), when variable x is replaced by the name of the object.

A compound statement function can be obtain from combining one/more atomic statement function using connectives *viz*, $\wedge$, $\vee$, ~, $\rightarrow$ etc. for example,

G(x) $\wedge$ M(x); G(x) $\vee$ M(x); ~ G(x); G(x) $\rightarrow$ M(x); *etc.*

The idea of statement function of two/more variables is straightforward.

Quantifier

Consider the statement,

"Everyone is good boy"

The translation of the statement can be written by G(x) s.t. "x is a good boy". To symbolize the expression "every x" or "all x" or "for any x" we use the symbol "($\forall x$)" that is called ***universal quantifier***. So, given statement can be expressed by an equivalent statement expression,

($\forall x$) G(x) : read as "for all x, x is G" (where G stands for good boy)

This expression is also called a predicate expression or predicate formula.

In true sense symbol "∀" quantifies the variable x therefore, it is called quantifier.

Let's take another statement

"Some boys are good"

To translate the statement we required to symbolize the expression like "there exists some x" or "few x" or "for some x". For that we use the symbol "$(\exists x)$" and this symbol is called ***existential quantifier***. Thus, the statement symbolize equivalently by the expression

$(\exists x)$ G(x) : read as "there exists some x such that x is good boy"

It must also be noted that, quantifier symbols ("∀" or "∃") always be placed before the statement function to which it states.

To make things more clear we illustrated few examples to symbolize the statements using quantifiers.

Example 5.29

1. "There are white Tigers"

We use the statement functions

T(x) : *i.e.*, "x is Tiger"

and W(x) : *i.e.*, "x is white"

Then, $(T(x) \wedge W(x))$: translated as "x is white Tiger". To translate the statement "There are white Tigers" which is equivalent to the statement "There exists some white Tigers" or "There are few white Tigers" we can write,

$$\mathbf{(\exists x)\ (T(x) \wedge W(x))}$$

Reader should not worry about the unique predicate expression for a statement. Possibly, a statement can be translated into several different predicate expressions. Like if G(x) s.t. "x is white Tiger" then predicate expression $(\exists x)$ G(x) is also a correct translation of the above statement.

2. All human are mortal"

Assume, M(x) : *i.e.*,"x is mortal"

H(x) : *i.e.*,"x is human"

So, the sense of the statement "if human then mortal" can be translated using symbol

$$(H(x) \to M(x)).$$

To symbolize "for all x", quantify the variable x by introducing "$(\forall x)$" and put before the statement expression s.t.

$$\mathbf{(\forall x)\ (H(x) \to M(x))}$$

(Expression is read as "for all x, if x is human then x is mortal" ? "All human are mortal")

3. "John is human"

Simply translated by H(j), where H be the predicate "human" and j is the name "John".

4. "For every number there is a number greater than it"

The statement can be equivalently expressed by,

"For all x, if x is a number then there must exist another number (say y) such that y is greater than x".

Assume, G(x, y) : *i.e.*, "y is greater than x"

N(x) : ,, "x is a number"

N(y) : ,, "y is a number"

Then we translate the statement straightforward by,

$$(\forall \mathbf{x})\ [\mathbf{N(x)} \rightarrow ((\exists \mathbf{y})\ \mathbf{N(y)} \wedge \mathbf{G}(x, y))]$$

5. *"Gentleman prefers honesty to deceit.*

Let, G(x) :"x is gentleman"

H(x) : "x is honest"

D(x) : "x is deceit"

And P(x, y, z) : "x prefers y over z"

Then, using the universal quantifiers the predicate expression of the statement will be,

$$(\forall \mathbf{z})\ (\forall \mathbf{y})\ (\forall \mathbf{x})\ [(\mathbf{G}(x) \wedge \mathbf{H}(x) \wedge \mathbf{D}(x)) \rightarrow \mathbf{P}(x, y, z)$$

6. *"There are no Holy Ganges in Purva"*

Using the symbol expressions,

H(x) : "x is Holy"

G(x) : "x is Ganges"

P(x) : "x is Purva"

Then the statement can be expressed by equivalent expressions like as,

$\sim (\exists x)\ [\mathbf{H(x)} \wedge \mathbf{G}(x) \wedge \mathbf{P}(x)]$; (there exists some x for that x is holy and x is ganges and x is purva is not true)

or, $(\forall x)\ [(\mathbf{P}(x) \wedge \mathbf{G}(x)) \rightarrow \sim \mathbf{H}(x)]$; (for all x, if x is purva and x is ganges then x is not holy)

or, $(\forall x)\ [(\mathbf{H}(x) \wedge \mathbf{G}(x)) \rightarrow \sim \mathbf{P}(x)]$; (for all x, if x is holy and x is ganges then x is not purva)

or, $(\forall x)\ [(\mathbf{H}(x) \wedge \mathbf{P}(x)) \rightarrow \sim \mathbf{G}(x)]$; (for all x, if x is holy and x is purva then x is not ganges)

or, $(\forall x)\ [\sim \mathbf{H}(x) \vee \sim \mathbf{G}(x)) \vee \sim \mathbf{P}(x)]$; (for all x, x is not holy or x is not ganges or x is not purva)

In order to determine the truth values of the statements involving universal and/or existential quantifier/s, one may be able to persuade the truth values of the statement functions. Since statement functions don't have the truth values, and when the name of the individuals is substituted in place of variables then the statement have a truth value. Of course, we can determine the truth value of the statement on the basis of the domain set D.

For example, D = {1, 2, 3, 4}

- Then, truth value of the predicate expression

$(\forall x)\ (\exists y)\ [E(y) \wedge G(y, x)]$: where E(y) stands "y is a even number" and G(y, x) stands "$y \geq x$"

will be true; because for all numbers of the set D, we can find at least a number greater than or equal to that number.

- Truth value of the predicate expression

$(\forall x)\ (\exists y)\ [\sim E(y) \wedge G(y, x)]$: where ~ E(y) stands "y is not a even number" and G(x, y) stands "$y \geq x$"

will be false; because for the number 4 there is no odd number in the set which is greater than or equal to it.

- Similarly, the truth value of the expression

$(\forall x)\ (\exists y)\ [E(y) \wedge G(y, x)]$: where $E(y)$ stands "y is a even number" and $G(x, y)$ stands "$y > x$"

will also be false.

- If set D = {1, 2, 3, ...}

Then the truth value of the predicate expression

$(\forall x)\ G(x, y)$: where $G(x, y)$ stands for "$y = x$"

will be true, because every number is successor to their predecessor. The same expression will have the truth value false if the set D = {1, 2, 3, 4}.

Therefore we shall conclude that the governing factors to determine the truth value of the predicate expression are the domain set and the predicate.

5.7.3 Free and Bound Variables

The occurrence of free variables and bound variables are true for every object. The variable occurring just after the quantifier symbol is a *bound variable* and the variable lying in the scope of the quantifier is bounded by that quantifier.

Consider the predicate expression,

$$(\forall x)\ (P(x) \vee Q(x))$$

bounded by x

Here the variable x in P as well as in Q is a bound variable due to the variable lies in the scope of the quantifier. Consider another expression,

$$(\forall x)\ P(x) \vee Q(x)$$

bounded by x — x is not bounded

Here, the variable x in P is a bound variable that is lying in the scope of the universal quantifier but x in Q is not a bound variable.

Any variable which is not bound is a *free variable*. A predicate formula may have both free and bound variables.

In order to determine the scope of the quantifier involving in the predicate formula is the smallest formula that follows the quantifier.

i.e.

- $(\forall x)\ ((P(x) \wedge Q(y)) \rightarrow R(z)$

  scope of the quantifier

- $(\forall x)\ ((P(x) \vee Q(y)) \rightarrow R(z)$

  scope of the quantifier

Conversely, the variables lies in the scope of the quantifier "$\forall$" or "$\exists$" are bound variables. *i.e.*,

- $(\forall x)\ ((P(x) \wedge Q(y)) \rightarrow R(z)$

  x is bounded y is free z is free

- $(\forall y)\ (G(x, y) \wedge Q(y))$

  x is free

  y is bounded

A statement could not have any free variable. For example,

- "Everything is P" : $(\forall x)\ P(x)$
- "Everything is P or Q" : $(\forall x)\ (P(x) \vee Q(x))$
- "For every number x there must exist another even number y s.t. $y > x$":

  x is bounded

$(\forall x)\ (\exists y)\ [E(y) \wedge G(y, x)]$; where E($y$) stands "$y$ is a even number" and G(x, y) stands "$y > x$"

y is bounded

Example 5.30. *Consider the predicate expression*

$$(\forall z)\ [\ (\forall x)\ [Q(x, y) \rightarrow (\exists y)\ \{P(x, y,z) \wedge \sim Q(y, z)\}]]$$

determine the free and bound variables.

Sol.

y is free

$$(\forall z)\ [(\forall x)\ [Q(x, y) \rightarrow (\exists y)\ \{P(x, y, z) \wedge \sim Q(y, z)\}]]$$

Here dashed lines shows the boundness of the variables.

- Variable z in P and in Q is bounded due to lying in the scope of the quantifier *i.e.*, "$(\forall z)$"
- Variable x in Q and in P is bounded due to lying in the scope of quantifier *i.e.*, "$(\forall x)$" but another variable y of same Q is free.
- Variable y in P and in Q is bounded due to lying in the scope of quantifier *i.e.*, "$(\exists y)$".

A statement can be expressed by a predicate formula. A predicate formula is a *valid predicate formula (VPF)* if and only if the truth value of the formula is true for all possible interpretations. The possible interpretations for a predicate formula may be infinite. On the other hand, if the predicate formula gets the truth value true for at least one interpretation then formula is a *satisfiable predicate formula (SPF)*. Thus, a VPF is also a SPF. Conversely, a VPF be a tautology. For example, *e.g.*

- $(\forall x)\ P(x) \vee (\exists x) \sim P(x)$; is a valid predicate formula (VPF) and so a tautology. To discuss the fact, let domain set D = $\{a, b, c\}$ and arbitrary set P = $\{a, c\}$; also assume $P(a)$, $P(b)$ and $P(c)$ are all true then the formula

  $A \Leftrightarrow (\forall x)\ P(x)$ is false (F)

  and $B \Leftrightarrow (\exists x) \sim P(x)$ is true (T) [the in universe there exists at least one item for which $\sim P(x)$ is true]

  Therefore, $F \vee T \Rightarrow T$; Hence formula is a tautology.
- $(\exists x)\ P(x) \vee \sim (\exists x)\ P(x)$; is a valid predicate formula and also tautology due to the fact that $A \vee \sim A$ is a tautology [where A is $(\exists x)\ P(x)$].

5.8. INFERENCE THEORY OF PREDICATE LOGIC

Continuation to the section 5.6 where we were discussed the inference theory of symbolic logic in this section we shall cover-up the inference theory of predicate logic or predicate calculus. The importance fact to discuss inference theory is to check the validity of an argument that symbolizes by using predicate logic. Since, we know from the inference theory of symbolic logic that natural method of deduction is an important tool to justify the validity of an argument. We can extend the deduction approach used earlier as in case of natural method of deduction for the predicate logic also. As like the previous study for the validity of an argument we have successfully applied method of deduction using following set of rules,

- 9-Rules if Inferences
- 10-Rules of Replacement
- 1-Rule of Conditional Proof
- 1-Rule of Indirect proof

To check the validity of the predicate formula we required few more rules, now we discuss those additional rules.

Rule I. Universal Instantiation (UI)

Let $(\forall x)$ A be any predicate formula (premise), then it can conclude to a specific predicate expression A(*y*) where variable *x* is replaced by *y* such that we can drop the quantifier in the derivation. For example,

1. :
   :
   :

k. $(\forall x)$ A
   :

n. A_x^y

Or,

$$\frac{(\forall x)\ A}{/\therefore\ A_y^x}$$

where, A_y^x : in the predicate formula A whenever *x* occurs, replace *x* with *y* where *y* is any variable/constant.

This rule is called *universal instantiation* and is denoted by *UI* in the inference theory. Therefore, according to rule UI, whenever universal quantifier exists it will drop with introducing other variable say j in place of x.

For example, consider the argument:

"All human are mortal. John is human. Therefore, John is mortal".

The argument can be translated into predicate premises and conclusion *e.g.*

1.	$(\forall x)\,(H(x) \rightarrow M(x))$		
2.	$H(j)$	$/\therefore$	$M(j)$
3.	$H(j) \rightarrow M(j)$		**1, UI**
4.	$M(j)$		**3 & 2, MP**

Hence, argument is valid.

Rule II. Universal Generalization (UG)

$$\begin{array}{ll} & \vdots \\ n. & A \\ & \vdots \\ \hline /\therefore & (\forall x)\, A_x^{\,y} \\ \hline \end{array}$$

Let A be any predicate formula then it can conclude to $(\forall x)\, A_x^{\,y}$ *i.e.*, whenever y occurring put x provided following restriction,

- y is an arbitrary selected variable.
- A is not in the scope of any assumption, it contains free y.

e.g.,

$$\begin{array}{ll} & \vdots \\ & \vdots \\ \rightarrow & (\ \ldots\ldots\ldots) \quad \text{free occurrence of } y \\ & \vdots \\ & \vdots \\ n. & A \\ \hline n+m. & (\forall x)\, A_x^{\,y} \\ \hline \end{array}$$

since it violate second restriction, hence wrong.

Above rule is called *universal generalization* and is denoted as *UG*. UG will permit to add the universal quantifier in the conclusion and variable x is replaced by an arbitrary selected variable y.

Consider an argument,

I. "No mortal are perfect. All human are mortal. Therefore, no human are perfect".

(where we symbolize $M(x)$: "x is mortal"; $P(x)$: "x is perfect"; $H(x)$: "x is human")

Thus, we express the corresponding predicate premises and conclusion as,

1.	$(\forall x)\,(M(x) \rightarrow \sim P(x))$		
2.	$(\forall x)\,(H(x) \rightarrow M(x))$	$/\therefore$	$(\forall x)\,(H(x) \rightarrow \sim P(x))$
3.	$M(y) \rightarrow \sim P(y)$		**1, UI**
4.	$H(y) \rightarrow M(y)$		**2, UI**
5.	$H(y) \rightarrow \sim P(y)$		**4 & 3, HS**
6.	$(\forall x)\,(H(x) \rightarrow \sim P(x))$		**5, UG**

Hence argument is valid.

Consider another argument,

II. "India is democratic. Therefore, anything is democratic".

Thus, the corresponding predicate argument is,

1. $D(i)$ $/\therefore\ (\forall x)D(x)$

---

2. $(\forall x)\ D(x)$ **1, UG** ×

Although, it proved valid but it violates the first restriction, hence argument is invalid.

III. "Not everything is edible, therefore nothing is edible".

Thus we have the predicate expressions,

1. $\sim (\forall x)\ E(x)$ or, $(\exists x) \sim E(x)$ $/\therefore\ (\forall x) \sim E(x)$

→ **2.** $E(y)$ Assume the predicate formula
3. $(\forall x)\ E(x)$ **2, UG ×** (violates the second restriction)

---

4. $E(y) \rightarrow (\forall x)\ E(x)$ **2 & 3, CP (Conditional Proof)**
5. $\sim E(y)$ **4 & 1, MT**
6. $(\forall x) \sim E(x)$ **5, UG**

It seems that argument is valid but at step 3 it violates the restriction second, hence argument is invalid.

Rule III. Existential Generalization (EG)

Let A by any predicate formula then it can conclude to $(\exists x)\ A_x^{\ y}$. The rule existential generalization denoted as EG will permit us that when A be any premise found at any step of deduction, then add A with existential quantifier in the conclusion and whenever y occurs put x; where$y$ is a variable/ constant; without imposing any other additional restrictions. This rule is called existential generalization or EG.

e.g.,

:
:
A
:

$/\therefore\ (\exists x)\ A_x^{\ y}$ [whenever y (variable/constant) occurrs put x]

Rule IV. Existential Instantiation (EI)

According to rule existential instantiation or EI, from the predicate formula $(\exists x)$ A, we can conclude $A_k^{\ x}$, such that variable x is replaced by a new constant k with restriction that k doesn't appeared in any of the previous derivation step.

e.g.,

:
:
$(\exists x)$ A

$/\therefore\ A_k^{\ x}$

For example, consider an argument,

I. "All dogs are barking. Some animals are dogs. Therefore, some animals are barking".

Then corresponding predicate expressions are,

1. $(\forall x)\ (D(x) \to B(x))$

2. $(\exists x)\ (A(x) \wedge D(x))$ $/ \therefore (\exists x)\ (A(x) \wedge B(x))$

---

3. $A(k) \wedge D(k)$	**2, EI**
4. $D(k) \to B(k)$	**1, UI**
5. $D(k) \wedge A(k)$	**3, Comm**
6. $D(k)$	**5, Simp**
7. $B(k)$	**4 & 6, MP**
8. $A(k)$	**3, Simp**
9. $A(k) \wedge B(k)$	**8 & 7, Conj**
10. $(\exists x)\ A(x) \wedge B(x)$	**9, EG**

It concludes that argument is valid.

II. "Some cats are animals. Some dogs are animals. Therefore, some cats are dogs".

The statement can be translated into corresponding predicate premises and conclusion,

1. $(\exists x)\ (C(x) \wedge D(x))$

2. $(\exists x)\ (D(x) \wedge A(x))$ $/ \therefore (\exists x)\ (C(x) \wedge D(x))$

---

3. $C(k) \wedge A(k)$	**1, EI**	
4. $D(k) \wedge A(k)$	**2, EI** ×	[wrong, because k is used earlier so, this violates the restriction of rule EI]
5. $D(k)$	**4, Simp**	
6. $C(k)$	**3, Simp**	
7. $C(k) \wedge D(k)$	**6 & 5, Simp**	
8. $(\exists x)\ (C(x) \wedge D(x))$	**7, EG**	

It proves valid, but truly given argument is invalid due to violation of Rule IV.

Therefore, now we have following set of rules -

- 9-Rules of Inferences
- 10-Rules of Replacement
- 1-Generalized Conditional Proof (CP/IP)
- Rules of UG, UI, EG and EI

These set of rules are essentially followed by a valid argument.

Some equivalence predicate formulas

(i) $\sim (\forall x)\ P(x) \Leftrightarrow (\exists x) \sim P(x)$

(ii) $\sim (\exists x)\ P(x) \Leftrightarrow (\forall x) \sim P(x)$

(iii) $(\forall x)\ P(x) \Leftrightarrow \sim (\exists x) \sim P(x)$

(iv) $(\forall x)\ (\exists y)\ [P(x) \vee Q(y)] \Leftrightarrow (\exists y)\ (\forall x)\ [P(x) \vee Q(y)$

(v) $(\exists y)\ [P(x) \vee Q(y)] \Leftrightarrow [P(x) \vee (\exists y)\ Q(y)]$

(vi) $(\forall x)\ [P(x) \vee Q(y)] \Leftrightarrow [\ (\forall x)\ P(x) \vee Q(y)]$

We can prove above equivalence formulas. For example, to prove the (*iii*) equivalence formula,we will prove that both of the following formulas be valid,

I. $(\forall x)\ P(x) \rightarrow \sim (\exists x) \sim P(x)$ and,

II. $\sim (\exists x) \sim P(x) \rightarrow (\forall x)\ P(x)$

$/ \therefore\ (\forall x)\ P(x) \Leftrightarrow \sim (\exists x) \sim P(x)$

Proof.

1. $(\exists x) \sim P(x)$	Premise (Assumed)
2. $\sim P(y)$	,, (Assumed)
3. $(\forall x)\ P(x)$	,, (Assumed)
4. $F(y)$	**3, UI**
5. $(\forall x)\ P(x) \rightarrow P(y)$	**3 - 4, CP**
6. $\sim (\forall x)\ P(x)$	**2 & 5, MT**
7. $\sim (\forall x)\ P(x)$	**1, 2 - 6, EI**
8. $(\exists x) \sim P(x) \rightarrow \sim (\forall x)\ P(x)$	**1 - 7, CP**
9. $\sim(\sim (\forall x)\ P(x)) \rightarrow \sim ((\exists x) \sim P(x))$	**8, Trans**
10. $(\forall x)\ P(x) \rightarrow \sim (\exists x)\ \sim P(x)$	**9, Dem**

Hence equivalence formula is valid.

Alternatively, above equivalence can also be proved as follows,

$/ \therefore\ \sim (\exists x) \sim P(x) \rightarrow (\forall x)\ P(x)$

Proof,

1. $\sim (\exists x) \sim P(x)$	Premise (assumed)
2. $\sim P(y)$	,, ,,
3. $(\exists x) \sim P(x)$	**2, EG**
4. $\sim P(y) \rightarrow (\exists x) \sim P(x)$	**2 - 3, CP**
5. $\sim \sim\ P(y)$	**1 & 4, MT**
6. $P(y)$	**5, Dem**
7. $(\forall x)\ P(x)$	**6, UG**
8. $\sim (\exists x) \sim P(x) \rightarrow (\forall x)\ P(x)$	**1 - 7, CP**

Hence, equivalence formula is valid.

EXERCISES

5.1 Let A be "It is cloudy" and let B be "It is raining". Give a simple verbal sentence which describes each of the following statements :

(*i*) $\sim A$

(*ii*) $A \rightarrow \sim B$

(*iii*) $\sim \sim B$

(*iv*) $\sim A \wedge \sim B$

(*v*) $(A \wedge \sim B) \rightarrow B$

(*vi*) $B \leftrightarrow A$

(*vii*) $A \leftrightarrow \sim B$

(*viii*) $(A \rightarrow B) \leftrightarrow A$.

5.2 Let R be "He is richer" and let C be "He has a car". Write each of the following statements in the symbolic form using R and C.

(*i*) He is richer and has a car.

(*ii*) He is richer but not has a car.

(*iii*) It is not true that he is poorer and has a car.

(*iv*) He is neither richer nor has a car.

(*v*) It is true that he is poorer and not has a car.

(*vi*) He is richer so he has a car therefore he is not poor.

5.3 Construct the truth tables of the following prepositions,

(*i*) $\sim (P \to \sim Q)$ (*ii*) $\sim (P \wedge Q) \vee \sim (Q \leftrightarrow P)$

(*iii*) $(P \to Q) \leftrightarrow (\sim P \vee Q)$ (*iv*) $(P \wedge (Q \to P)) \to Q$.

5.4 Find the truth values of the following propositions under the given truth values of P and Q as *True* and R and S as *False*.

(*i*) $(P \to Q) \vee \sim (P \leftrightarrow \sim Q)$ (*ii*) $(P \vee (Q \to (R \vee \sim P))) (Q \vee \sim S)$

(*iii*) $(P \to ((\sim Q \wedge R) \wedge \sim (Q \vee (\sim P \leftrightarrow Q)))$.

5.5 Show the following equivalence,

(*i*) $(P \to Q) \to R \Leftrightarrow (\sim P \vee Q) \to R \Leftrightarrow (P \wedge Q) \to R$

(*ii*) $P \to (Q \vee R) \Leftrightarrow (P \to Q) \vee (P \to R)$

(*iii*) $\sim (P \wedge Q) \Leftrightarrow P \wedge \sim Q$

(*iv*) $(P \vee Q) \wedge (\sim P \wedge (\sim P \wedge Q)) \Leftrightarrow (\sim P \wedge Q)$

(*v*) $P \wedge (Q \leftrightarrow R) \Leftrightarrow P \wedge ((Q \to R) \wedge (R \to Q))$

(*vi*) $P \to (Q \vee R) \Leftrightarrow (P \wedge \sim Q) \to R$

(*vii*) $(P \to R) \wedge (Q \to R) \Leftrightarrow (P \vee Q) \to R$.

5.6 Show that following formulas are tautology :

(*i*) $(((R \to C) \wedge R) \to C)$ (*ii*) $(P \wedge Q) \to P$

(*iii*) $B \vee (B \to C)$ (*iv*) $((A \to B) \wedge (B \to C)) \to (A \to C)$

(*v*) $(P \to (P \vee Q))$ (*vi*) $(A \to B) \vee (A \to \sim B)$

(*vii*) $(A \to (B \wedge C)) \to (((B \to (D \wedge E)) \to (A \to D))$.

5.7 Determine the truth values of the following composite statements :

(*i*) If $2 < 5$, then $2 + 3 \neq 5$.

(*ii*) It is true that $6 + 6 = 6$ and $3 + 3 = 6$.

(*iii*) If Delhi is the capital of India then Washington is the capital of US.

(*iv*) If $1 + 1 \neq 2$, then it is not true that $3 + 3 = 8$ if and only if $2 + 2 = 4$.

5.8 From the given premises show the validity of the following arguments, which drives the conclusion shown on right.

(*i*) $P \to Q, Q \to R$ $/\therefore P \to R$

(*ii*) $(A \to B) C, A \wedge D, B \wedge T$ $/\therefore C$

(*iii*) $(P \to Q) \wedge (P \to R), \sim (Q \wedge R), S \vee P$ $/\therefore S$

(*iv*) $A \to B, (A \to (A \wedge B)) \to C$ $/\therefore C$

(*v*) $Q \vee (R \to S), (R \to (R \wedge S)) \to (T \vee U), (T \to Q) \wedge (U \to V)$ $/\therefore (Q \vee V)$

(*vi*) $(E \vee F) \to G, H \to (I \wedge G),$ $/\therefore (E \to G) \wedge (H \to I)$

(*vii*) $M \to J, J \to \sim H, \sim H \to \sim T, \sim T \to M, M \to \sim H$ $/\therefore \sim T$

(*ix*) $(H \to J) \wedge (J \to K), (I \vee K) \to L, \sim L$ $/\therefore \sim (H \vee J)$

(*x*) $(H \to J) \wedge (J \to K), (H \vee J), (H \to \sim K) \wedge (J \to \sim I), (I \wedge \sim K) \to L, K \to (I \vee M)$

$/\therefore L \vee M$

5.9 For the given premises determine a suitable conclusion so that the argument is valid,

(*i*) $P \rightarrow \sim Q, \sim P \rightarrow R$ (*ii*) $P \rightarrow \sim Q, R \rightarrow P, Q$

(*iii*) $P, P \wedge R, P \rightarrow Q, Q \rightarrow S$ (*iv*) $P \rightarrow (R \wedge S), \sim (R \wedge S), \sim P \rightarrow S$

5.10 Prove argument is valid

1. $(H \rightarrow J) \vee (J \rightarrow K)$ 2. $(I \wedge K) \rightarrow L$

3. $\sim L$ $/\therefore \sim (H \vee J)$

5.11 Prove formula $(P \rightarrow (P \vee Q)$ is a tautology.

5.12 Determine the interpretation for which argument is invalid

1. $J \rightarrow (K \rightarrow L)$ 2. $K \rightarrow (\sim L \rightarrow M)$

3. $(L \vee M) \rightarrow N$ $\therefore \sim (J \rightarrow N)$

5.13 Prove argument is valid

1. $Q \vee (R \rightarrow S)$ 2. $(R \rightarrow (R \wedge S)) \rightarrow (T \vee U)$

3. $(T \rightarrow Q) \wedge (U \rightarrow V)$ $\therefore Q \vee V$

5.14 (*i*) No academician is wealthy. Some scientists are wealthy.

$/\therefore$ (*a*) some scientists are academicians.

(*b*) Some academician is not scientists.

(*ii*) All artists are interesting people. Some philosophers are mathematicians. Some agents are salesmen. Only uninteresting people are salesmen.

$/\therefore$ (*a*) some philosophers are not salesmen.

(*b*) Salesmen are not mathematicians.

(*c*) Some agents are not philosophers.

(*d*) Artists are salesmen but they are not interesting people.

5.15 Let {1, 2, 3, 4, 5} be the universal set, determine the truth value of each of the statements,

(*i*) $(\exists x)(\forall y), x^2 < y + 1$ (*ii*) $(\forall x)(\exists y), x^2 + y^2 = 25$

(*iii*) $(\exists x)(\forall y)(\exists z), x^2 > y + z$ (*iv*) $(\exists x)(\exists y)(\exists z), x^2 + y^2 = 2z^2$

5.16 Negate the following statements :

(*i*) $(\exists x)\, P(x) \rightarrow (\forall y)\, Q(y)$ (*ii*) $(\exists x)\, P(x) \wedge (\forall y)\, Q(y)$

(*iii*) $\sim (\exists x)\, P(x) \vee (\forall y) \sim Q(y)$ (*iv*) $(\forall x)(\exists y)\, [P(x) \vee Q(y)]$

(*v*) $\sim (\exists x) \sim P(x) \rightarrow (\forall x)\, P(x)$ (*vi*) $(\forall x)\, [P(x) \vee Q(y)]$

5.17 Show that following are valid formulas :

(*i*) $(\exists y)[(\exists x)F(x) \rightarrow F(y)]$ (*ii*) $(\exists y)[P(y) \rightarrow (\forall x)P(x)]$

(*iii*) $(\exists x)H(x) \vee \sim (\exists x)\, H(x)$ (*iv*) $(\forall x)F(x) \vee (\forall x)G(x)(x)] \rightarrow (\forall x)\, [F(x) \vee G(x)]$

5.18 Show that from given premises drives the conclusion shown on right.

(*i*) $(\forall x)[H(x) \rightarrow M(x)]$ $/\therefore (\exists x)[H(x) \wedge M(x)]$

(*ii*) $(\forall x)[H(x) \rightarrow M(x)], (\exists y)H(y)$ $/\therefore (\exists x)[H(x) \wedge M(x)]$

(*iii*) $(\exists x)[H(x) \wedge M(x)] \rightarrow (\exists y)[P(y) \wedge Q(y)], (\exists y)[P(y) \wedge \sim Q(y)]$ $/\therefore (\forall x)[H(x) \rightarrow \sim M(x)]$

5.19 Symbolizes and prove the validity of the following arguments :

(*i*) No mortal are perfect. All human are mortal. Therefore no human are perfect.

(*ii*) Himalaya is large. Therefore every thing is large.

(*iii*) All human are mortal. Jorge is human. Therefore Jorge is mortal.

(*iv*) Not every thing is edible. Therefore nothing is edible.

(*v*) All cats are animals. Some dogs are animals. Therefore some cats are dogs.

LATTICE THEORY

6 Lattice Theory

6.1 INTRODUCTION

In this chapter we shall first discuss what is meant by a partial ordered set and how partial ordered set is represented through a directed graph which is commonly known as Hasse diagram by giving suitable examples. The role of partial ordered is significant while we study the algebraic systems. In section 6.3 we will discuss the properties of partial ordered set. Section 6.4 covers the important concept of partial ordered set that has additional characteristics called lattices. In latter sections we will discuss the properties of lattices and the classifications of the lattices where we study some special type of lattices like sublattices, distributed lattices, complemented lattices, product of lattices and the lattice homomorphism.

6.2 PARTIAL ORDERED SET

Let us start our discussion with partial ordered relation. If a binary relation R defined over set X is (1) reflexive, (2) antisymmetric, and (3) transitive then relation R is a partial ordered relation. Conventionally, partial ordered relation is denoted by symbol "≤" (the symbol "≤" doesn't mean of 'less than or equal to'), i.e.,

- A binary relation R over set X is ***reflexive*** *iff*, $\forall\, x \in$ X, i.e., $(x, x) \in$ R.
- A binary relation R over set X is ***antisymmetric*** *iff*, $\forall\, x, y \in$ X, whenever $(x, y) \in$ R and $(y, x) \in$ R, then $x = y$.
- A binary relation R over set X is ***transitive*** *iff*, $\forall\, x, y$, and $z \in$ X whenever, $(x, y) \in$ R and $(y, z) \in$ R then $(x, z) \in$ R.

Since, symbol "≤" is a partial ordered relation defined over set X, so the ordered pair (X, ≤) is called a *partial ordered set*. Partial ordered set is also known as *poset*. The partial ordered set (X, ≤) will be called *linearly ordered set* if, $\forall\, x$ and $y \in$ X, we have $x \le y$ or $y \le x$. A linearly ordered set is a special case of partial ordered set and it is also called a *chain*.

If (X, ≤) is partial ordered set defined by relation R, then (X, ≥) will also be a partial ordered set, and it is defined for inverse of relation R. Hence, poset (X, ≥) is dual of poset (X, ≤). Some of the examples of posets are given below.

1. The relation "less than or equal to" defined over set of real numbers (R) is a partial ordered relation i.e., (R, ≤).
2. The relation "greater than or equal to" defined over set of real numbers is a partial ordered relation i.e., (R, ≥).

3. Similarly the relation "less than" or relation "greater than" are also partial ordered relation over set of real numbers i.e., (R, $<$) or (R, $>$).
4. The relation "$\subseteq$" (inclusion) defined over power set of X is a partial ordered relation i.e., (P(X), $\subseteq$). Let X = $\{a, b\}$; then power set of X is P(X) = $\{\emptyset, \{a\}, \{b\}, \{a, b\}\}$. Since, every element of P(X) is subset of itself so relation "$\subseteq$" over P(X) is reflexive. It is also antisymmetric and transitive i.e. for the element $\emptyset \subseteq \{b\}$ and $\{b\} \subseteq \{a, b\}$ then, $\emptyset \subseteq \{a, b\}$ and similarly true for all elements of P(X).
5. The relation "perfect division" or "integral multiple" defined over set of positive integer (I^+) are partial ordered relation. For example let X = $\{2, 3, 4, 6\} \in I^+$; then partial ordered relation '$\leq$' is "perfect division" (i.e., for any x and $y \in$ X the relation "x divides y") over X will be given as,

$$\text{'}\leq\text{'} = \{(2, 2), (3, 3), (4, 4), (6, 6), (2, 4), (2, 6), (3, 6)\}$$

Similarly, partial ordered relation "integer multiple" (i.e., for any x and $y \in$ X, and any integer k; $y = x\,k$; 'y is an integer multiple of x') will be given as,

$$\geq = \{(2, 2), (3, 3), (4, 4), (6, 6), (4, 2), (6, 2), (6, 3)\}$$

Here, we used partial ordered relation symbol '$\geq$' because; last poset is dual of previous poset.

Comparability and Noncomparability

Let (X, $\leq$) be a poset, then elements x and $y \in$ X are said to be comparable if $x = y$ or $y = x$. If x and y are not related i.e., $x \nleq y$ or $y \nleq x$ then they are called noncomparable. For example, the elements of power set of X say P(X) are noncomparable with respect to partial ordered relation "$\subseteq$".

6.3 REPRESENTATION OF A POSET (HASSE DIAGRAM)

A poset (X, $\leq$) is represented by a diagram called Hasse diagram. *Hasse diagram is a directed graph, where ordered between the elements are preserved.* Since, it is a directed graph which consists of vertices and edges where, all elements of X are in set of vertices that are represented by a circle or dot and the connections between vertices (elements of X) called edges that will be drawn as follows,

- For the element $x, y \in$ X if $x > y$ and there is no element $z \in$ X i.e., $x \geq z \geq y$ then circle for y is putted below the circle for x and are connected by a direct edge.
- Otherwise, if $x > y$ and there exist at least an element $z \in$ X i.e., $x \geq z \geq y$ then they are not connected by a direct edge, however they are connected by other elements of set X.

Example 6.1. *Consider set X = {2, 3, 4, 6, 8, 24} and the partial ordered relation '$\leq$' be i.e.,*

$$x \leq y \Rightarrow \text{"}x \text{ divides } y\text{" (perfect division)}$$

then, poset (X, $\leq$) will be given as,

$$\leq = \{(2, 2), (2, 4), (2, 6), (2, 8), (2, 24), (3, 3), (3, 6), (3, 24), (4, 4), (4, 8), (4, 24), (6, 6), (6, 24), (8, 8), (8, 24)\}$$

Since, relation is understood to be reflexive, so we can leave the pairs of similar elements. Since, relation is understood to be transitive, so we can leave the pairs that come in sequence of pairs i.e. it need not to write the pair (2, 24), if the sequence of pairs (2, 6) and (6, 24) are there.

Thus, a simplified poset will be,

$$\leq = \{(2, 4), (2, 6), (3, 6), (4, 8), (6, 24), (8, 24)\}$$

and there graphical representation is shown below in Fig. 6.1.

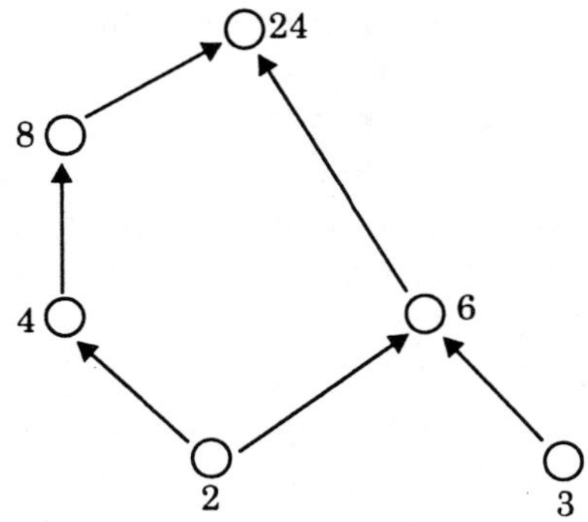

Fig. 6.1

To simplify further, since all arrows pointed in one direction (upward) so, we can omit the arrows. Such a graphical representation of a partial ordered relation in which all arrow heads are understood (to be pointed upward) is called Hasse diagram of the relation shown in Fig. 6.2.

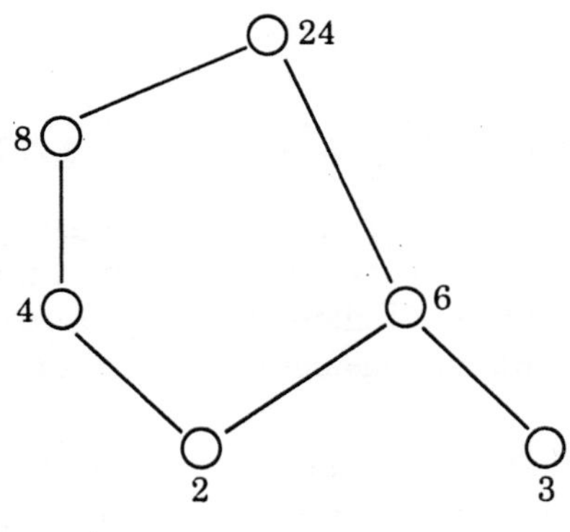

Fig. 6.2 Hasse diagram.

Example 6.2. *Let set X = {α, β, γ} then draw the Hasse diagram for the poset (P(X), ⊆).*

Sol. The P(x) is the power set of X. So we have,

$$P(X) = \{\emptyset, \{\alpha\}, \{\beta\}, \{\gamma\}, \{\alpha, \beta\}, \{\beta, \gamma\}, \{\alpha, \gamma\}, \{\alpha, \beta, \gamma\}\}$$

Therefore, the vertices in the Hasse diagram will corresponds to all elements of P(X) and the edges are constructed according to the partial ordered relation inclusion (⊆) which are given as,

$$\subseteq = \{(\emptyset, \{\alpha\}), (\emptyset, \{\beta\}), (\emptyset, \{\gamma\}), (\{\alpha\}, \{\alpha, \beta\}), (\{\alpha\}, \{\alpha, \gamma\}), (\{\beta\}, \{\alpha, \beta\}), (\{\beta\}, \{\beta, \gamma\}), (\{\gamma\}, \{\alpha, \gamma\}), (\{\gamma\}, \{\beta, \gamma\}), (\{\alpha, \beta\}, \{\alpha, \beta, ?\}), (\{\beta, \gamma\}, \{\alpha, \beta, \gamma\}), (\{\alpha, \gamma\}, \{\alpha, \beta, \gamma\})\}.$$

Thus, the Hasse diagram is shown in Fig. 6.3.

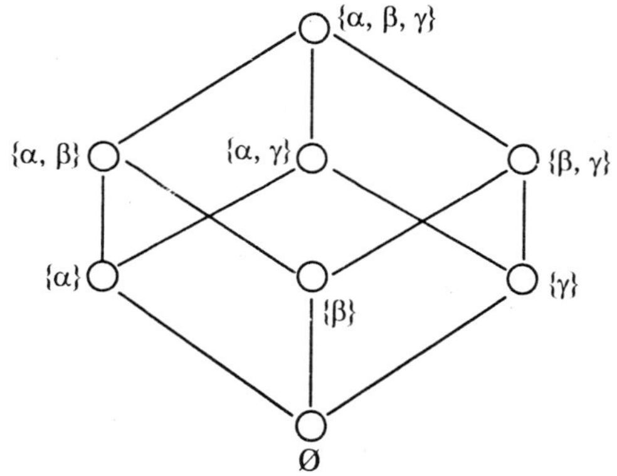

Or,

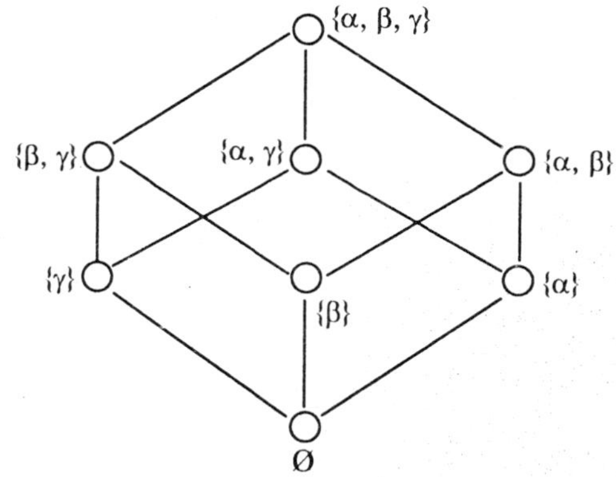

Fig. 6.3 Hasse diagrams.

Note. *For a given poset, Hasse diagram is not unique (e.g. in Fig. 6.3 the vertices order may different on the same level). Conversely, Hasse diagram may be same for different poset. For example, the Hasse diagram for the poset (X, ≤) i.e., for the set X = {1, 2, 3, 4, 6, 8, 12, 24} and the relation ≤ be such that $x = y$ if x divides y; will be same as shown in Fig. 6.3.*

The Hasse diagram of linearly ordered set (X, ≤) consisting of circles one above other is called a ***chain***. For example, if we define the partial ordered relation ≤ is "less than or equal to" over the set X = {1, 2, 3, 4, 5}; then Hasse diagram for poset (X, ≤) is shown in Fig. 6.4.

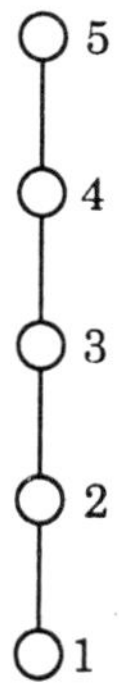

Fig. 6.4

We obtain the same Hasse diagram as above for the poset (X, ≤) where the relation ≤ is "divisibility" i.e., ∀ $x, y \in$ X we have $x = y \Leftrightarrow$ 'x divides y'; over the set X = {1, 2, 4, 8, 16}.

Example 6.3. *Draw the Hasse diagram for the poset (S, ≤), where set S = {1, 2, 3, 4, 6, 8, 9, 12, 18, 24} and the relation "≤" is "divisibility".*

Sol. The vertices of the Hasse diagram will corresponds to the elements of X and the edges will be formed as,

$$\leq = \{\{1, 2\}, \{1, 3\}, \{2, 4\}, \{2, 6\}, \{3, 6\}, \{3, 9\}, \{4, 8\}, \{4, 12\}, \{6, 12\}, \{6, 18\}, \{8, 24\}, \{9, 18\}, \{12, 24\}\}$$

that represent the poset.

Hence the Fig. 6.5 shows the Hasse diagram for poset (S, ≤)

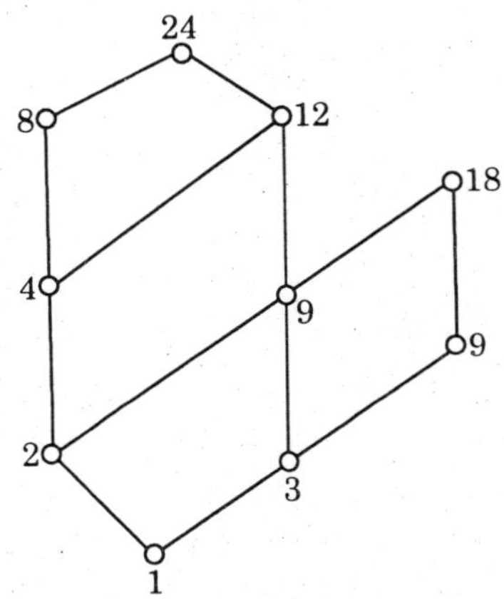

Fig. 6.5

Example 6.4 *1. Draw the Hasse diagram for factors of 6 under relation divisibility.*
2. Draw the Hasse diagram for factors of 8 under relation divisibility.

Sol. 1. Let D_6 is the set that contains possible elements that are factors of 6, i.e., D_6 = {1, 2, 3, 6} then poset will be {{1, 2}, {1, 3}, {2, 6}, {3, 6} whose Hasse diagram is shown in Fig. 6.6.

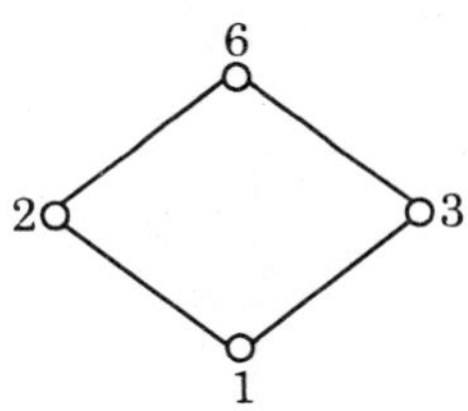

Fig. 6.6

2. Similarly for D_8 = {1, 2, 4, 8} under the relation divisibility the poset will be {1, 2}, {2, 4}, {4, 8}. Hence, its Hasse diagram will be a chain that is shown in Fig. 6.7. Here all elements are comparable to each other such poset is called ***toset.*** Remember, all tosets must be posets but all posets are not necessarily tosets.

Fig. 6.7

Upper Bound

Let (X, ≤) be a poset and $Y \subseteq X$, then an element $x \in X$ be the upper bound for Y if and only if, $\forall y \in Y$ s.t. $y \le x$.

Lower Bound

Let (X, ≤) be a poset and Y ⊆ X, then an element $x \in$ X be the lower bound for Y if and only if, $\forall y \in$ Y s.t. $y \geq x$.

Least Upper Bound (LUB)

Let (X, ≤) be a poset and Y ⊆ X, then an element $x \in$ X be a least upper bound for Y if and only if, x is an upper bound for Y and $x \leq z$ for all upper bounds z for Y.

Greatest Lower Bound (GLB)

Let (X, ≤) be a poset and Y ⊆ X, then an element $x \in$ X be a greatest lower bound for Y if and only if, x is an lower bound for Y and $z \geq x$ for all lower bounds z for Y.

Reader must note that for every subset of poset has a unique LUB and a unique GLB if exists. For example, the GLB and LUB for the poset whose Hasse diagram shown in Fig. 6.3 will be Ø and {α, β, γ} respectively.

Well ordered set

A poset (X, ≤) is called well ordered set if every nonempty subset of X has a least element. This definition of well ordered set follows that poset is totally ordered. Conversely, a totally ordered set need not to be always well ordered.

Meet and Join of elements

Let (X, ≤) be a poset and x_1 and x_2 are elements ∈ X, then greatest lower bound (GLB) of x_1 and x_2 is called meet of elements x_1 and x_2 where meet of x_1 and x_2 is represented by $(x_1 \wedge x_2)$ i.e.,

$$(x_1 \wedge x_2) = \text{GLB}\ (x_1, x_2)$$

Similarly, the join of x_1 and x_2 is the least upper bound (LUB) of x_1 and x_2 where join of x_1 and x_2 is represented by $(x_1 \vee x_2)$ i.e.,

$$(x_1 \vee x_2) = \text{LUB}\ (x_1, x_2)$$

6.4 LATTICES

The purpose of the study of the previous sections was to understand the concept of ordered relations. Partial ordered relations plays a significant role in the study of algebraic systems that we shall discuss in the latter sections. Lattice is the partial ordered set that possesses additional characteristics. The feature of lattice as an algebraic system is also significant. The importance of lattice theory associated with Boolean algebra is not only to understand the theoretical aspects and design of computers but many other fields of engineering and sciences.

Definition

A poset (X, ≤) is called a lattice if every pair of elements has a unique LUB and a unique GLB. Let x_1 and x_2 are two elements ∈ X, then for a poset (X ≤) we have,

$$\text{GLB}(x_1, x_2) = x_1 \wedge x_2 \qquad \text{and} \qquad \text{LUB}(x_1, x_2) = x_1 \vee x_2;$$

- Where the symbols ∧ and ∨ are binary operations 'AND' and 'OR' respectively over X.
- In certain cases, symbols ∧ and ∨ are also used as the abstraction of '∩' and '∪' respectively.

For example, assume P(X) is the power set for a known set X then over the relation 'inclusion' poset (P(X), ⊆) is a lattice. To show it assume set X = {α, β}; so P(X) = {Ø, {α}, {β}, {α, β}}. Then, poset (P(X), ⊆) in which each pair have a unique LUB & a unique GLB e.g. for the pair ({α, β}, {β}) meet and join will be,

$$\text{GLB}(\{\alpha, \beta\}, \{\beta\}) = \{\alpha, \beta\} \wedge \{\beta\} \Rightarrow \{\alpha, \beta\} \cap \{\beta\} = \{\beta\}$$

$$\text{LUB}(\{\alpha, \beta\}, \{\beta\}) = \{\alpha, \beta\} \vee \{\beta\} \Rightarrow \{\alpha, \beta\} \cup \{\beta\} = \{\alpha, \beta\}$$

(Reader can also verify these results from the Hasse diagram shown in Fig. 6.3)

Similarly we can determine the LUB & GLB for every pair of the poset (P(X), ⊆) that are listed in table shown in Fig. 6.5.

GLB	**Ø**	**{α}**	**{β}**	**{α, β}**
Ø	Ø	Ø	Ø	Ø
{α}	Ø	{α}	Ø	{α}
{β}	Ø	Ø	{β}	{β}
{α, β}	Ø	{α}	{β}	{α, β}

LUB	**Ø**	**{α}**	**{β}**	**{α, β}**
Ø	Ø	{α}	{β}	{α, β}
{α}	{α}	{α}	{α, β}	{α, β}
{β}	{β}	{α, β}	{β}	{α, β}
{α, β}	{α, β}	{α, β}	{α, β}	{α, β}

Fig. 6.5

Example 6.5. Consider the poset (I^+, ≤) where I^+ is the set of positive integers and the partial ordered relation ≤ is defined as i.e. if x and $y \in I^+$ then $x \leq y$ means 'x divides y'. Then poset (I^+, ≤) is a lattice. Because,

$$\text{GLB}(x, y) = x \wedge y = lcm(x, y) \qquad [lcm\text{: least common divisor}]$$

and

$$\text{LUB}(x, y) = x \vee y = gcd(x, y) \qquad [gcd\text{: greatest common divisor}]$$

Example 6.6. Let R be the set of real numbers in [0, 1] and the relation '≤' be defined as 'less than or equal to' over the set R, then poset (R, ≤) is a lattice. Assume r_1 and r_2 are the elements ∈ R s.t. $0 \leq r_1, r_2 \leq 1$ then meet and join are given by,

$$\text{GLB}(r_1, r_2) = r_1 \wedge r_2 = \text{Min}(r_1, r_2)$$

and

$$\text{LUB}(r_1, r_2) = r_1 \vee r_2 = \text{Max}(r_1, r_2)$$

In the next section we will discuss the theorems that shows the relationship between the partial ordered relation '≤' and the binary operations GLB & LUB in a lattice (X, ≤).

Theorem 6.4.1. *Let (X, ≤) be a lattice, then for any x, y ∈ X,*

(i) $x \leq y \Leftrightarrow GLB(x, y) = x$

and, *(ii)* $x \leq y \Leftrightarrow LUB(x, y) = y$

Proof. (Immediately follows from the definition of GLB and LUB)

Assume $x \leq y$, since we know that $x \leq x \Rightarrow x \leq \text{GLB}(x, y)$.

From the definition of GLB(x, y), we have GLB$(x, y) \leq x$.

Hence, $x \leq y \Rightarrow \text{GLB}(x, y) = x$.

Further assume, GLB$(x, y) = x$; but it is possible only if $x \leq y$.

So $\text{GLB}(x, y) = x \Rightarrow x \leq y$. It proved the equivalence (*i*).

To prove the equivalence (*ii*) $x \leq y \Leftrightarrow \text{LUB}(x, y) = y$; we proceed similarly.

Alternatively, since GLB$(x, y) = x$. so we have,

$$\text{LUB}(y, \text{GLB}(x, y)) = \text{LUB}(y, x) = \text{LUB}(x, y)$$

But $\text{LUB}(y, \text{GLB}(x, y)) = y$

Therefore, $\text{LUB}(x, y) = y$ follows from $\text{GLB}(x, y) = x$.

Similarly we can show that GLB$(x, y) = x$ follows from LUB$(x, y) = y$, that proved the equivalence.

Theorem 6.4.2. *Let (X, ≤) be a lattice, then for any x, y and z ∈ X*

$$y \leq z \quad \Rightarrow \begin{cases} GLB(x, y) \leq GLB(x, z) & (i) \\ LUB(x, y) \leq LUB(x, z) & (ii) \end{cases}$$

Proof. From the result of the previous theorem $y \leq z \Leftrightarrow \text{GLB}(y, z) = y$;

To prove GLB$(x, y) \leq$ GLB(x, z), we shall prove

$$\text{GLB}(\text{GLB}(x, y), \text{GLB}(x, z)) = \text{GLB}(x, y);$$

Since, $\text{GLB}(\text{GLB}(x, y), \text{GLB}(x, z)) = \text{GLB}(x, \text{GLB}(y, z));$

$= \text{GLB}(x, y)$ proved.

Similarly prove the (*ii*) equality.

Theorem 6.4.3. *Let (X, ≤) be a lattice, then for any x, y and z ∈ X*

(*i*) $x \leq y \wedge x \leq z \Rightarrow x \leq GLB(y, z)$

(*ii*) $x \leq y \wedge x \leq z \Rightarrow x \leq LUB(y, z)$

Proof. (*i*) Inequality can be proved from the definition of GLB and from the fact that both y and z are comparable.

(*ii*) Inequality is obvious from the definition of LUB.

Since we know that poset (X, ≤) is dual to the poset (X, ≥). So, if A ⊆ X then LUB of A w.r.t. poset (X, ≤) is same as GLB for A w.r.t. poset (X, ≤) and vice-versa. Thus, if the relation interchanges from '≤' to '≥' then GLB and LUB are interchanged. Hence, we say that operation GLB and LUB are duals to each other like as the relation '≤' and '≥'. Therefore, lattice (X, ≤) and (X, ≥) are duals to each other. So, above theorem can be restated as,

(*i*) $x \geq y \wedge x \geq z \Rightarrow x \geq \text{LUB}(y, z)$

(*ii*) $x \geq y \wedge x \geq z \Rightarrow x \geq \text{GLB}(y, z)$

Theorem 6.4.4. *Let (X, ≤) be a lattice, then for any x, y and z ∈ X*

(*a*) $LUB(x, GLB(y, z)) = GLB(LUB(x, y), LUB(x, z));$

(*b*) $GLB(x, LUB(y, z)) = LUB(GLB(x, y), GLB(x, z));$

(These are called distributive properties of a lattice)

Proof. (*a*) Since, $x \leq \text{LUB}(x, y)$ and $x \leq \text{LUB}(x, z)$;

Then, from (*i*) equality of theorem 6.4.3

$$x \leq \text{GLB}(y, z) \Rightarrow x \leq \text{GLB}(\text{LUB}(x, y), \text{LUB}(x, z)); \quad (iii)$$

Further, $\text{GLB}(y, z) \leq y \leq \text{LUB}(x, y);$

and $\text{GLB}(y, z) \leq z \leq \text{LUB}(x, z);$

Again using equality (*i*) we obtain,

$$GLB(y, z) \le GLB\ (LUB(x, y), LUB(x, z)); \qquad (iv)$$

Hence from (*iii*), (*iv*) and (*i*)′ we get the required result that's,

$$LUB(x, GLB(y, z)) \le GLB\ (LUB(x, y), LUB(x, z)); \quad \text{Proved.}$$

Similarly we can derive the equality (*b*).

Theorem 6.4.5. *Let (X, ≤) be a lattice, then for any x, y and z ∈ X*

$$x \le z \iff LUB(x, GLB(y, z)) \le GLB\ (LUB(x, y), z).$$

Proof. Since, $x \le z \iff LUB(x, z) = z$ from (*ii*) inequality of theorem 6.4.1. Put z in place of $LUB(x, z)$ in the inequality (*a*) of theorem 6.4.4

Thus we have, $LUB(x, GLB(y, z)) \le GLB\ (LUB(x, y), z);$

$$\iff \quad x \le z.$$

(This inequality is also called *modular* inequality).

Example 6.7. *In a lattice (X, ≤), for any x, y and z ∈ X, if x ≤ y ≤ z then*

(i) $LUB(x, y) = GLB(y, z)$; *and*

(ii) $LUB(GLB(x, y), GLB(y, z)) = y = GLB(LUB(x, y), LUB(x, z))$;

Sol. (*i*) Since we know that if $x \le y \iff LUB(x, y) = y$; and also if $y = z \iff GLB(y, z) = y$ (see theorem 6.4.1), therefore

$$x \le y \le z \iff LUB(x, y) = y = GLB(y, z);$$

(*ii*) Similarly, $GLB(x, y) = x$ if $x \le y$; and $GLB(y, z) = y$ if $y \le z$.

So, put these values of x and y in (*i*), thus we have

$$LUB(GLB(x, y), GLB(y, z)) = y \qquad (\therefore \quad LUB(x, y) = y)$$

LHS

Further since, $LUB(x, y) = y$ (if $x \le y$) and also $LUB(x, z) = z$ (if $x \le z$).

From (*i*) $GLB(y, z) = y$;

Put the values of y and z in this equation we obtain,

$$GLB\ (LUB(x, y), LUB(x, z)) = y$$

RHS

Hence, *LHS = RHS;* Proved.

6.4.1 Properties of Lattices

Let (X, ≤) be a lattice, than for any x, y and $z \in X$ we have,

(*i*) $GLB(x, x) = x$; and $LUB(x, x) = x$; **[Rule of Idempotent]**

(*ii*) $GLB(x, y) = GLB(y, x)$; and $LUB(x, y) = LUB(y, x)$ **[Rule of Commutation]**

(*iii*) $GLB(GLB(x, y), z) = GLB(x, GLB(y, z))$; and

$LUB\ (LUB(x, y), z) = LUB(x, LUB(y, z))$ **[Rule of Association]**

(*iv*) $GLB(x, LUB(x, y)) = x$; and $LUB(x, GLB(x, y)) = x$ **[Rule of Absorption]**

We can prove above identities by using the definition of binary operation GLB and LUB.

(*i*) Since, we know that,

$$x \le x \iff GLB(x, x) = x \qquad \text{(from theorem 6.4.1)}$$

and also

$$x \le x \iff LUB(x, x) = x \qquad \text{(from theorem 6.4.1)}$$

Similarly we can prove the other identities (*ii*) and (*iii*). To prove identity (*iv*) we recall the definition of LUB that for any $x \in X$, $x \le x$ and $x \le LUB(x, y)$.

Therefore, $x \leq \text{GLB}(x, \text{LUB}(x, y))$;

Conversely, from the definition of GLB, we have $\text{GLB}(x, \text{LUB}(x, y) \leq x$.

Hence, $\text{GLB}(x, \text{LUB}(x, y) = x$. Proved.

Similarly, $\text{LUB}(x, \text{GLB}(x, y)) = x$.

6.4.2 Lattices and Algebraic Systems

Let (X, ≤) be a lattice, then we can define an algebraic system (X, GLB, LUB) where GLB and LUB are two binary operations on X that satisfies (1) commutative, (2) associative, and (3) rule of absorption i.e. for any $x, y \in X$

$$\text{GLB}(x, y) = x \wedge \mathbf{y};$$

and

$$\text{LUB}(x, y) = x \vee y.$$

6.4.3 Classes of Lattices

In this section we will study the classes of lattices that posses additional properties. To define lattice as an algebraic system, that can anticipate introducing the verity of lattices in a natural way.

6.4.3.1 Distributive Lattice

A lattice (X, GLB, LUB) is said to be distributive lattice if the binary operations GLB and LUB holds distributive property i.e. for any x, y and $z \in X$,

$$\text{GLB}(x, \text{LUB}(y, z)) = \text{LUB}(\text{GLB}(x, y), \text{GLB}(x, z))$$

and

$$\text{LUB}(x, \text{GLB}(y, z)) = \text{GLB}(\text{LUB}(x, y), \text{LUB}(x, z))$$

- A lattice is a distributive lattice if distributive equality must be satisfied by all the elements of the lattice.
- Not all lattices are distributive.
- Every chain is a distributive lattice.

For example, lattice shown below in Fig. 6.6 is a distributive lattice. Because if we take the elements {α}, {α, β} and {γ}) then

$$\text{GLB}(x\ \text{LUB}(y, z)) = \text{GLB}(\{a\}, \text{LUB}(\{a, b\}, \{\gamma\}))$$
$$= \text{GLB}(\{\alpha\}, \{\alpha, \beta, \gamma\}) = \{\alpha\} \quad \text{LHS}$$

Since $\text{GLB}(\{\alpha\}, \{\alpha, \beta\}) = \{\alpha\}$ and $\text{GLB}(\{\alpha\}, \{\gamma\}) = \emptyset$

Thus, $\text{LUB}(\text{GLB}(\{\alpha\}, \{\alpha, \beta\}), \text{GLB}(\{\alpha\}, \{\gamma\})) = \text{GLB}(\{\alpha\}, \emptyset) = \{\alpha\}$ RHS.

Similarly it is true for all the elements. Hence, it is an example of distributive lattice.

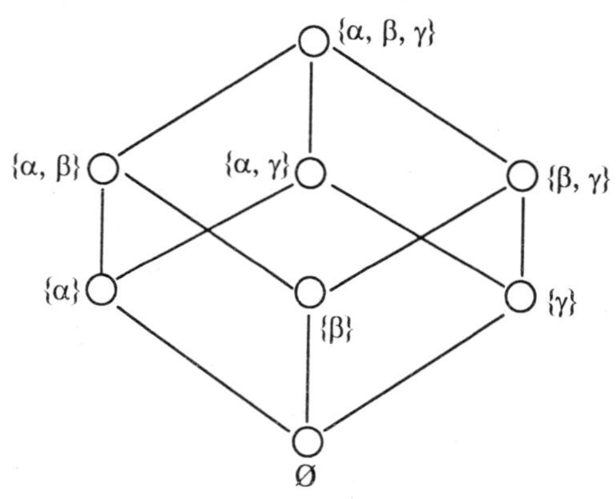

Fig. 6.6

Example 6.8. *Show that lattice of Fig. 6.7 is not a distributive lattice.*

Sol. Since, we can see that all elements of the lattice doesn't satisfies the distributive equalities. For example, between the elements y, z and r

$$\text{GLB}(y, \text{LUB}(z, r))$$
$$= \text{GLB}(y, x) = y; \quad \text{RHS}$$

and $$\text{LUB}(\text{GLB}(y, z), \text{GLB}(y, r) = \text{LUB}(s, s) = s; \quad \text{LHS}$$

Therefore RHS ≠ LHS, hence shown lattice is not a distributive lattice.

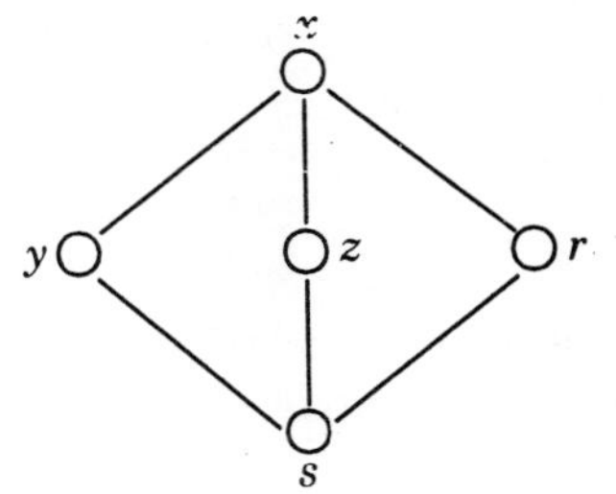

Fig. 6.7

Remember that lattices similar to the lattice of Fig. 6.7 are called 'diamond lattices' and they are not distributive lattices.

Example 6.9. *We can further see that lattice shown in the Fig. 6.8 is not a distributive lattice.*

Sol. A lattice is distributive if all of its elements follow distributive property so let we verify the distributive property between the elements n, l and m.

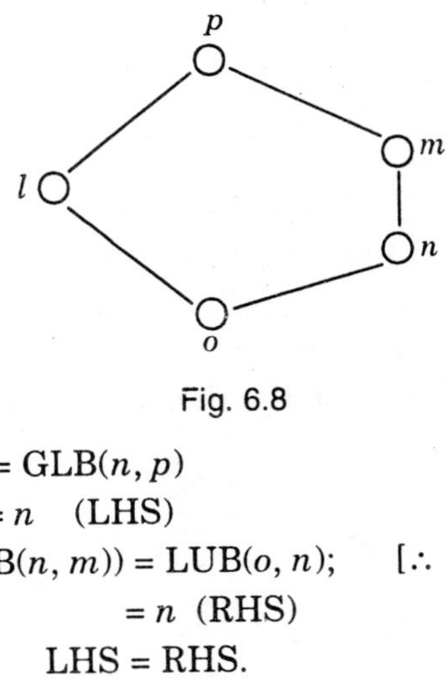

Fig. 6.8

$$\text{GLB}(n, \text{LUB}(l, m)) = \text{GLB}(n, p) \qquad [\because \text{LUB}(l, m) = p]$$
$$= n \quad (\text{LHS})$$

also $$\text{LUB}(\text{GLB}(n, l), \text{GLB}(n, m)) = \text{LUB}(o, n); \qquad [\because \text{GLB}(n, l) = o \text{ and } \text{GLB}(n, m) = n]$$
$$= n \quad (\text{RHS})$$

so $$\text{LHS} = \text{RHS}.$$

But $$\text{GLB}(m, \text{LUB}(l, n)) = \text{GLB}(m, p) \qquad [\because \text{LUB}(l, n) = p]$$
$$= m \quad (\text{LHS})$$

also $$\text{LUB}(\text{GLB}(m, l), \text{GLB}(m, n)) = \text{LUB}(o, n); \qquad [\because \text{GLB}(m, l) = o \text{ and } \text{GLB}(m, n) = n]$$
$$= n \quad (\text{RHS})$$

Thus, LHS ≠ RHS hence distributive property doesn't hold by the lattice so lattice is not distributive.

Example 6.10. *Consider the poset (X, ≤) where X = {1, 2, 3, 5, 30} and the partial ordered relation ≤ is defined as i.e. if x and y ∈ X then x ≤ y means 'x divides y'. Then show that poset (I^+, ≤) is a lattice.*

Sol. Since $\quad \text{GLB}(x, y) = x \wedge y = lcm(x, y)$

and $\quad \text{LUB}(x, y) = x \vee y = gcd(x, y)$

Now we can construct the operation table I and table II for GLB and LUB respectively and the Hasse diagram is shown in Fig. 6.9.

Table I

LUB	1	2	3	5	30
1	1	2	3	5	30
2	2	2	30	30	30
3	3	30	3	30	30
5	5	30	30	5	30
30	30	30	30	30	30

Table II

GLB	1	2	3	5	30
1	1	1	1	1	1
2	1	2	1	1	2
3	1	1	3	1	3
5	1	1	1	5	5
30	1	2	3	5	30

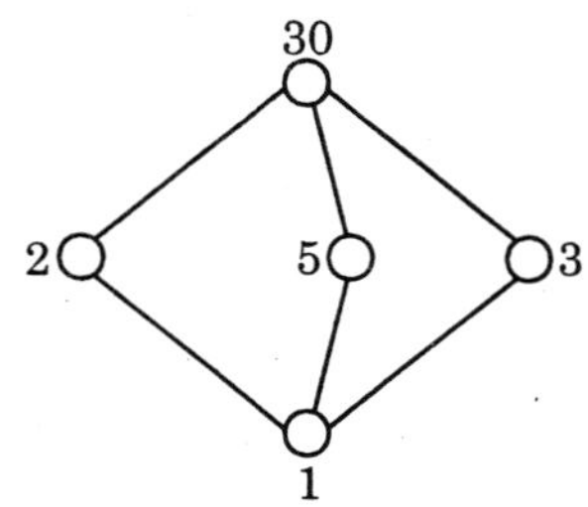

Fig. 6.9 Hasse diagram.

Test for distributive lattice, i.e.,

GLB(x, LUB(y, z)) = LUB(GLB(x, y), GLB(x, z))

Assume $x = 2$, $y = 3$ and $z = 5$, then

RHS: GLB(2, LUB(3, 5)) = GLB(2, 30) = 2

LHS: LUB(GLB(2, 3), GLB(2, 5)) = LUB(1, 1) = 1

Since *RHS* ≠ *LHS*, hence lattice is not a distributive lattice.

6.4.3.2 Bounded Lattice

A lattice (X, GLB, LUB) is said to be bounded if there exist a greatest element 'I' and a least element 'O' in the lattice, i.e.,

(*i*) O ≤ x ≤ I $\quad$ [for any x ∈ X]

(*ii*) LUB(x, O) = x $\quad$ and $\quad$ GLB(x, O) = O

(*iii*) LUB(x, I) = I $\quad$ and $\quad$ GLB(x, I) = x

(Element I and O are also known as universal upper and universal lower bound)

For example, lattice (P(X), ⊆) is a bounded lattice where I is the set X itself and O is Ø. Consider another example, a Hasse diagram shown in Fig. 6.10 is a bounded lattice. Because its greatest element (I) is '*a*' and least element (O) is '*f*'.

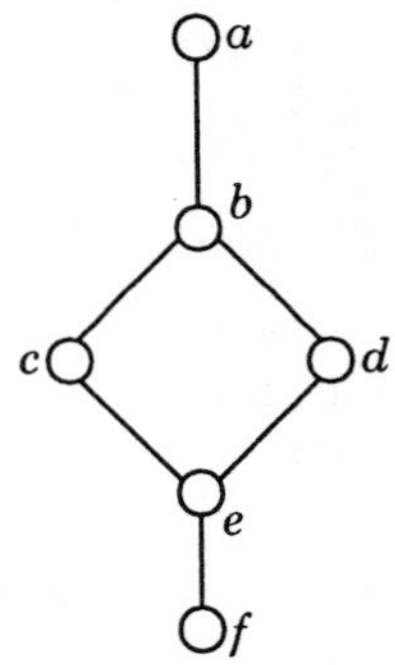

Fig. 6.10

Let $x = c$ then $\quad LUB(c, f) = c \quad$ and $\quad GLB(c, f) = f$

and $\quad LUB(c, a) = a \quad$ and $\quad GLB(c, a) = c$

Similarly, these conditions holds for any $x \in X$, hence lattice is bounded.

Example 6.12. *Lattice discussed in the example 6.7 is also a bounded lattice.*

Example 6.13. *Show that lattice (X, GLB, LUB) is a bounded lattice, where poset (X = {1, 2, 5, 15, 30}, /) (here partial ordered relation is a 'division' operation).*

Sol. Reader self verify that the Hasse diagram for the given poset is same as the Hasse diagram shown in Fig. 6.10. Since diagram is bounded whose greatest element is 30 and the least element is 1 and the rest of the conditions are also satisfied therefore lattice is a bounded lattice.

6.4.3.3 Complement Lattice

A lattice (X, GLB, LUB) is said to be complemented lattice if, every element in the lattice has a complement. Or,

A bounded lattice with greatest element 1 and least element 0, then for the elements x, $y \in X$ element y is said to be complement of x iff,

$$GLB(x, y) = 0; \quad \text{and} \quad LUB(x, y) = 1;$$

- In a complement lattice complements are always unique.
- Since operation GLB and LUB are commutative, so if y is complement of x then, x is also complement of y also 0 is the unique complement of 1 and vice-versa.
- In the lattice *it is possible that* an element has more than one complement and on the other hand it is also possible that an element has no complement.

For example consider the poset $(P(X), \subseteq)$ where $X = \{\alpha, \beta, \gamma\}$ and so the lattice (P(X), GLB, LUB) where operation GLB and LUB are $\cap$ and $\cup$ respectively is bounded with greatest element $\{\alpha, \beta, \gamma\}$ and least element Ø. (Fig. 6.11)

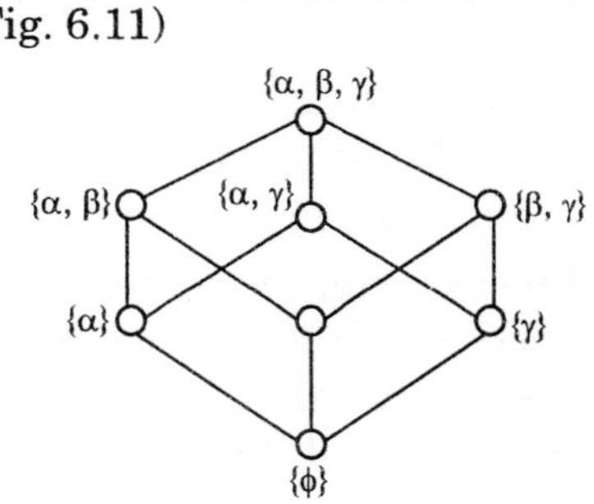

Fig. 6.11

Then we can find the complement of the elements that are listed in the table shown in Fig. 6.12.

No.	Element	Complement	Verification
1	Ø	{α, β, γ}	∴ GLB(Ø,{α, β, γ}) = {α, β, γ}; LUB(Ø,{α, β, γ}) = Ø
2	{α}	{β, γ}	∴ GLB({α}, {β, γ}) = {α, β, γ}; LUB({α}, {β, γ}) = Ø
3	{β}	{α, γ}	∴ GLB({β},{α, γ}) = {α, β, γ}; LUB({β}, {α, γ}) = Ø
4	{γ}	{α, β}	∴ GLB({γ},{α, β}) = {α, β, γ}; LUB({γ}, {α, β}) = Ø
5	{α, β}	{γ}	∴ GLB({α, γ}, {γ}) = {α, β, γ}; LUB({α, β}, {γ}) = Ø
6	{β, γ}	{α}	∴ GLB({β, γ}, {α}) = {α, β, γ}; LUB({β, γ}, {α}) = Ø
7	{α, γ}	{β}	∴ GLB({α, γ}, {β}) = {α, β, γ}; LUB({α, γ}, {β}) = Ø
8	{α, β, γ}	Ø	∴ GLB({α, β, γ}, Ø) = {α, β, γ}; LUB({α, β, γ}, Ø) = Ø

Fig. 6.12

Example 6.14. *Lattices shown in Fig. 6.13 (a), (b) and (c) are complemented lattices.*

Sol.

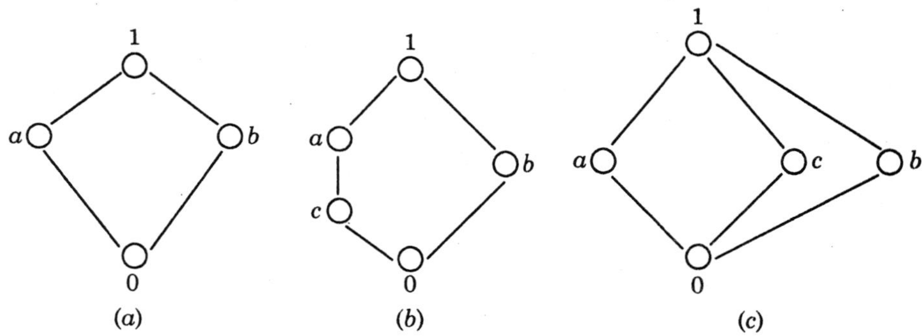

Fig. 6.13

For the lattice (a) GLB$(a, b) = 0$ and LUB$(x, y) = 1$. So, the complement a is b and vise versa. Hence, a complement lattice.

For the lattice (b) GLB$(a, b) = 0$ and GLB$(c, b) = 0$ and LUB$(a, b) = 1$ and LUB$(c, b) = 1$; so both a and c are complement of b. Hence, a complement lattice.

In the lattice (c) GLB$(a, c) = 0$ and LUB$(a, c) = 1$; GLB$(a, b) = 0$ and LUB$(a, b) = 1$. So, complement of a are b and c. Similarly complement of c are a and b also a and c are complement of b. Hence lattice is a complement lattice.

Example 6.15. *For example lattice (P(X), ⊆) is a complemented lattice. Let us discuss the existence of complement for each elements of the lattice. Since the GLB and LUB operations on P(X) are ∩ and ∪ respectively and so the universal upper bound in the lattice is set X itself (corresponds to symbol 1) and the universal lower bound in the lattice is Ø (corresponds to symbol 0). So, in the lattice (P(X), ⊆) complement of any subset Y of X is the difference of X and Y (i.e. X – Y).*

Example 6.16. *Let (X, ≤) be a distributive lattice, then for any elements x, y ∈ X if, y is complement of x then y is unique.*

Sol. We assume that element x has complement z other than x. So, we have,

$$\text{LUB}(x, y) = 1 \quad \text{and} \quad \text{GLB}(x, y) = 0;$$

and

$$\text{LUB}(x, z) = 1 \quad \text{and} \quad \text{GLB}(x, z) = 0;$$

Further we write, $\quad z = \text{GLB}(z, 1)$

$\Rightarrow$ GLB(z, LUB(x, y))

$\Rightarrow$ LUB(GLB(z, x), GLB(z, y)) (distributive property)

$\Rightarrow$ LUB(0, GLB(z, y))

$\Rightarrow$ LUB(GLB(x, y), GLB(z, y))

$\Rightarrow$ GLB(LUB(x, z), y) (distributive property)

$\Rightarrow$ GLB(1, y)

$\Rightarrow$ y

Hence, complement of x is unique.

6.4.3.4 Sub Lattices

Let (X, ≤) be a lattice and if Y ⊆ X then lattice (Y, ≤) is a sublattice of (X, ≤) if and only if Y is closed under the binary operations GLB and LUB.

[In the true sense algebraic structure (Y, GLB, LUB) is a sublattice of (X, GLB, LUB). For a lattice (X, ≤) let $x, y \in X$ s.t. $x \le y$ then, the closed interval $[x, y]$ which contains the entire elements z s.t. $x \le z \le y$ will be a sublattice of X]

Example 6.17. *Consider the lattice (I^+, ≤) where I^+ is the set of positive integers and the relation '≤' is "division" in I^+ s.t. for any a, b ∈ I^+; a ≤ b ⇒ 'a divides b'. Let A_k be the set of all divisors of k, for example set A_6 = {1, 2, 3, 6}; which is a subset of I^+. Then lattice (A_k, ≤) is a sublattice of (I^+, ≤).*

Example 6.18. *Let (X, ≤) be a lattice shown in Fig. 6.14, assume X = {$x_1, x_2, x_3, x_4, x_5, x_6$}. Let subsets of X are X_1 = {x_1, x_2, x_4, x_6}, X_2 = {x_3, x_4} and X_3 = {x_4, x_5} then lattice (X_1, ≤) is a sublattice of (X, ≤) but not lattice (X_2, ≤) and lattice (X_3, ≤).*

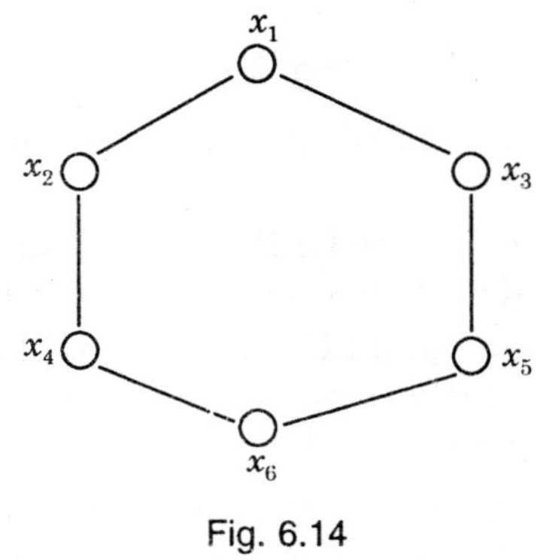

Fig. 6.14

Since,

- For the lattice (X_1, ≤); GLB(x_1, x_2) = $x_4 \in X_1$; GLB(x_2, x_4) = $x_6 \in X_1$; LUB(x_1, x_2) = $x_1 \in X_1$; LUB(x_2, x_4) = $x_1 \in X_1$ and others, we find that subset X_1 is closed under operations GLB and LUB so a sublattice.
- For the lattice (X_2, ≤); GLB(x_3, x_4) = $x_6 \notin X_2$; LUB(x_3, x_4) = $x_1 \notin X_2$; so subset X_2 is not closed under operations GLB and LUB therefore, (X_2, ≤) is not a sublattice of (X, ≤).

- Also, GLB(x_5, x_4) = $x_6 \notin X_3$; so subset X_3 is not closed under operations GLB and LUB therefore (X_3, ≤) is not a sublattice of (X, ≤).

6.4.4 Product of Lattices

Let (X, GLB_1, LUB_1) and (Y, GLB_2, LUB_2) are two lattices, then the algebraic system (X × Y, GLB, LUB) in which the binary operations GLB and LUB for any $(x_1, y_1), (x_2, y_2) \in X \times Y$ are such that

$$\text{GLB}((x_1, y_1), (x_2, y_2)) = (\text{GLB}_1(x_1, y_1), \text{GLB}_2(x_2, y_2));$$

and

$$\text{LUB}((x_1, y_1), (x_2, y_2)) = (\text{LUB}_1(x_1, y_1), \text{LUB}_2(x_2, y_2));$$

is defined as the direct product of lattices (X, GLB_1, LUB_1) and (Y, GLB_2, LUB_2).

- The operations GLB, LUB on X × Y are (1) commutative, (2) associative and (3) hold absorption law because these operations are defined over operations GLB_1, LUB_1 and GLB_2, LUB_2. Hence direct product (X × Y, GLB, LUB) is itself a lattice. In the similar sense we can extend the direct product of more than two lattices and so obtain large lattices from smaller ones. The order of lattice obtain by the direct product is same to the product of the orders of the lattices occurring in the direct product.

6.4.5 Lattice Homomorphism

Let (X, GLB_1, LUB_1) and (Y, GLB_2, LUB_2) are two lattices, then a mapping $f: X \to Y$ i.e. for any $x_1, x_2 \in X$,

$$f(\text{GLB}_1(x_1, x_2)) = \text{GLB}_2(f(x_1), f(x_2));$$

and

$$f(\text{LUB}_1(x_1, x_2)) = \text{LUB}_2(f(x_1), f(x_2));$$

is called *lattice homomorphism* from lattice (X, GLB1, LUB1) to lattice (Y, GLB2, LUB2).

- From the definition of lattice homomorphism we find that both the operations of GLB and LUB should be preserved.
- A lattice homomorphism $f: X \to Y$ is called a *lattice isomorphism* if, f is one-one onto or bijective.
- A lattice homomorphism s.t. $f: X \to X$ is called a *lattice endomorphism*. Here, image set of f will be sublattice of X.
- And if, $f: X \to X$ is a lattice isomorphism then f is called *lattice automorphism*.

EXERCISES

6.1 Draw the Hasse diagram of lattices (A_k, ≤) for k = 6, 10, 12, 24; where A_k be the set of all divisors of k such that for any $a, b \in A_k$; $a \le b \Rightarrow$ 'a divides b'. Also find the sublattices of the lattice (A_{12}, ≤) and (A_{24}, ≤).

6.2 Let X = {α, β, γ, δ} then draw the Hasse diagram for poset (P(X), ⊆).

6.3 Draw the Hasse diagram of (X, ⊆) where set X = {X_1, X_2, X_3, X_4} and the sets are given as,

$$X_1 = \{\alpha, \beta, \gamma, \delta\};\quad X_2 = \{\alpha, \beta, \gamma\};\quad X_3 = \{\alpha, \beta\};\quad X_4 = \{\alpha\};$$

6.4 In a lattice show that LUB(x, y) = GLB(y, z) if $x \le y \le z$.

6.5 Show that lattice (X, ≤) is distributive *iff* for any x, y and $z \in X$,

$$\text{GLB}(\text{LUB}(x, y), z) = \text{LUB}(x, \text{GLB}(y, z))$$

6.6 For a distributive lattice (X, ≤) show that if,

$$\text{GLB}(\alpha, x) = \text{GLB}(a, y) \quad\text{and}\quad \text{LUB}(\alpha, x) = \text{LUB}(\alpha, y)$$

for some α, then $x = y$.

6.7 Prove that every chain is a distributive lattice.

6.8 Prove De Morgan's laws holds in a distributive, complemented lattice s.t.

$$\text{GLB}(x, y)' = \text{LUB}(x', y') \text{ and } \text{LUB}(x, y)' = \text{GLB}(x', y')$$

6.9 Show that in a distributive, complemented lattice

$$x \leq y \Leftrightarrow \text{GLB}(x, y') = 0 \Leftrightarrow \text{LUB}(x', y) = 1 \Leftrightarrow y' \leq x'$$

6.10 Let X = {0, 1} and the lattices (X, ≤) and (X^2, ≤) are shown in Fig. 6.15 show that diagram of lattice (X^n, ≤) is an n-cube.

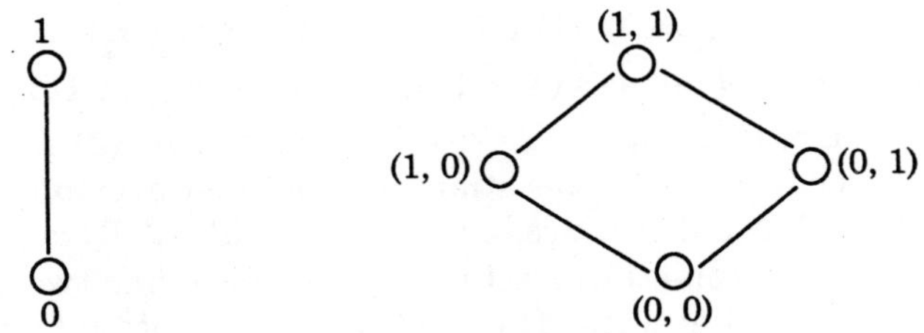

Fig. 6.15

6.11 Show that there are only five distinct Hasse diagrams possible for the partial ordered sets having three elements.

INTRODUCTION TO LANGUAGES AND FINITE AUTOMATA

7 Introduction to Languages and Finite Automata

7.1 BASIC CONCEPTS OF AUTOMATA THEORY

Before begin to the study of automata theory we shall first introduce the basic concepts and definitions used thereon. These concepts include the understanding of the terms 'alphabet', 'string', 'language', etc.

7.1.1 Alphabets

An alphabet is an atomic, finite and nonempty set of symbols. We use the convention Σ for an alphabet. For example,

- $\Sigma = \{a, b, ..., z\}$, set of all lower case letters.
- $\Sigma = \{0, 1\}$, set of binary symbols.
- $\Sigma = \{0, 1, 2, ..., 9\}$, set of numeric symbols.
- $\Sigma = \{ 0, 1, 2, ...9, a, b, ..., z\}$, set of alphanumeric symbols.

7.1.2 Strings

A string is the finite ordering of symbols chosen from some alphabet Σ. For example, *abc*, *acb*, *bca*, *abca*, are some of the strings from the alphabet $\Sigma = \{a, b, c\}$. Note that a, b, and c are also the strings from the alphabet $\{a, b, c\}$. When we write a, b, and c as the elements of Σ then these refers as symbols not strings. The strings can be usually classified by their *length*, that is, the number of occurrences of the symbols in the string. The standard denotation for the length of the string x is $|x|$. For example, $| abc | = 3$ and $| a | = 1$.

A string of zero occurrences of symbols is called *empty string* or *null string*. We denote it by $\in$ (read as "epsilon") such that $| \in | = 0$. Thus, $\in$ is a string chosen from any alphabet Σ whatsoever.

7.1.3 Power of Σ

For any alphabet Σ, the power of Σ *i.e.*, Σ^k where k is any positive integer expresses the set of all strings of length k formed over Σ. For example, let $\Sigma = \{0, 1\}$ then

- $\Sigma^0 = \{\in\}$
- $\Sigma^1 = \{0, 1\}$
- $\Sigma^2 = \{00, 01, 10, 11\}$
- ....
- $\Sigma^k = \{00......0, 0........1, 1.......0, 1........1, ...\}$, each string is of length k.

The set of all possible strings over Σ is denoted by Σ^*, where operator * is called as ***Kleeny-closure*** operator and the meaning of Σ^* is given by,

$$\Sigma^* = \Sigma^0 \cup \Sigma^1 \cup \Sigma^2 \cup \ldots\ldots\ldots\ldots\ldots$$

For example, if $\Sigma = \{0, 1\}$, then using the previous definitions of $\Sigma^0, \Sigma^1, \Sigma^2, \ldots.$ we have,

$$\Sigma^* = \{\in\} \cup \{0, 1\} \cup \{00, 01, 10, 11\} \cup \{000, 001, 010, 011, 011, \ldots\} \cup \ldots.$$
$$= \{\in, 0, 1, 00, 01, 10, 11, 000, 001, 010, 011, 011, \ldots\ldots\ldots\ldots\ldots\}$$

(this set contains infinite many strings)

From the set Σ^*, if we exclude the empty string ($\in$) then we have a set of nonempty strings over alphabet Σ. That we denoted by Σ^+ (where + is called ***Positive-closure*** operator). Therefore,

$$\Sigma^+ = \Sigma^* - \{\in\} \qquad [\therefore\ \Sigma^1 \cup \Sigma^2 \cup \ldots\ldots\ldots\ldots\ldots]$$

Conversely, we say $\quad \Sigma^* = \Sigma^+ \cup \{\in\}$

7.1.4 Languages

A language is the set of strings chosen from Σ^*, for any alphabet Σ. If L is the language over Σ then $L \subseteq \Sigma^*$. Hence, language L may contains infinite many strings. Since languages are set of strings, thus new languages can be constructed using set operations *viz.*, union, intersections, difference, and complement. For example, the complement of the language L over alphabet Σ is given by

$$L' = \Sigma^* - L,$$

where Σ^* contains all possible set of strings formed over Σ that we take the universal set. Hence, set L′ contains all those strings of Σ^* that are not in the set L.

A new language can also be constructed using *concatenation* operation over strings. Let x and y are two strings then concatenation of x and y is the string xy, that is '*string x followed by string y*'. For example, let x is the string of n symbols *i.e.*, $a_1a_2\,a_3\ldots\ldots..a_n$ and y is the string of m symbols *i.e.*, $b_1\,b_2\,\ldots\ldots..b_m$, then xy is the string of $(n + m)$ symbols *i.e.*, $a_1a_2\,a_3\ldots\ldots..a_n\,b_1\,b_2\,\ldots\ldots..b_m$. Note that concatenation is not commutative, such that $xy \neq yx$ until $x \neq y$. On the other side concatenation is associative, such that for any strings x, y, and z, $(xy)z = x(yz)$. This allows us to concatenate the strings without restricting the order in which various concatenation operations are to be performed.

We can also apply the concatenation operation over set of strings called languages. For example, let languages are $L_1 \subseteq \Sigma^*$ and $L_2 \subseteq \Sigma^*$, then there concatenation is $L_1\,L_2$, *i.e.*,

$$L_1\,L_2 = \{xy/x \in L_1 \text{ and } y \in L_2\}$$

Consider an example, Let $L_1 = \{\in\}$ and $L_2 = \{00, 01, 10, 11\}$, then

$$L_1\,L_2 = \{\in\}\,\{00, 01, 10, 11\} = \{\in 00, \in 01, \in 10, \in 11\}$$
$$= \{00, 01, 10, 11\} \qquad [\because\ \in x = x, \text{ for any string } x]$$

- Remember, concatenation of two null strings or language containing null strings only is a null string, *i.e.*,

$$\in . \in = \in$$

- If language set L_1 is empty *i.e.*, $L_1 = \{\,\}$ or $\varnothing$, then concatenation of $L_1\,L_2$ will remain empty for any language L_2. For example, let $L_2 = \{ab, bc, abc\}$, then

$$L_1\,L_2 = \varnothing\,\{ab, bc, abc\} = \{\,\} \text{ or } \varnothing$$

- If both, $L_1 = \varnothing$ and $L_2 = \varnothing$, then $L_1\,L_2 = \varnothing$.

Strings, by definition, are finite but the language contains infinite number of strings. So the important constraint of these languages is to specify them in the ways that are finite. For example, let $\Sigma = \{a\}$, then $\Sigma^* = L = \{\in, a, aa, aaa, \ldots\ldots\ldots$(infinite many strings)$\}$. The infinite strings of the language L can be equivalently represented in a finite way as, $L = \{a\}^*$. Consider another illustration, where language $L = \{0, 1\}^* \cup \{a\}\{b\}^*$. Then the language can be constructed, either by concatenating an arbitrary number of strings, each is either 0 or 1, or by concatenating the string a with an arbitrary number of copies of the string b. Similarly a language $L = \{0\,x\,0 \,/\, x \in \{a, b\}^*\}$ that contains the strings x and add 0 to each end where x is an arbitrary string formed using a and b.

- Since, we have

$$L^0 = \{\in\},$$
$$L^1 = L,$$
$$L^2 = L\,L = L^1\,L,$$
$$L^3 = L^2\,L,$$
$$\ldots\ldots\ldots$$
$$\ldots\ldots\ldots$$
$$L^k = L^{k-1}\,L,$$
$$\ldots\ldots\ldots$$

Then $$L^* = L^0 \cup L^1 \cup L^2 \cup \ldots\ldots\ldots \cup L^k \cup \ldots\ldots$$

Or, $$L^* = \bigcup_{k=1}^{\infty} L^k$$

Similarly we denote L^+ by,

$$L^+ = \bigcup_{k=1}^{\infty} L^k = L\,L^* \text{ or } L^*\,L$$

7.2 DETERMINISTIC FINITE STATE AUTOMATA (DFSA)/ DETERMINISTIC FINITE STATE MACHINE (DFSM)/ DETERMINISTIC FINITE AUTOMATA (DFA)

Deterministic Finite State Automata refers that abstract view of machine whose transition is one and only one after reading the sequence of inputs from each state. The abstract view of DFSA is shown in Fig. 7.1.

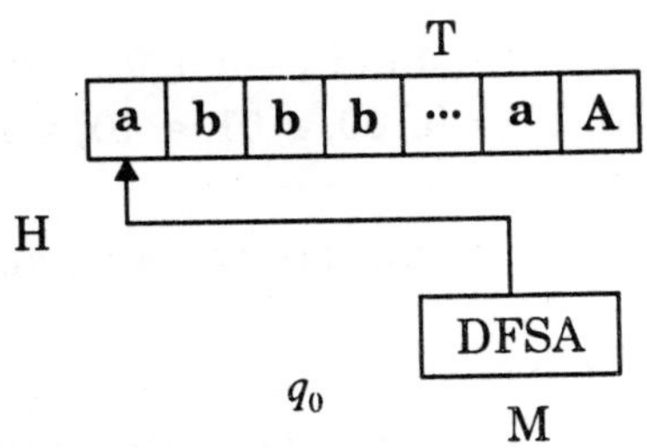

Fig. 7.1

M is the machine DFSA, has a tape T of finite length. Cells of the tape contain input symbols of a string. Machine has a tape head H, the property of the head H is read only and its movement is restricted only in forward/ right direction. Once it moves forward it never returns back or left. Suppose Automata M initially (time t = 0/no time) on state q_0. Tape head reads currently pointing symbol a, and automata goes to next state q_1. Now the tape head pointed to the symbol b. Now automata reads the symbol b and goes to next state q_2 (Fig. 7.2). In this way automaton scans all the entries of the tape cells and reaches to the last cell. We assume that, after time t automaton M reaches to final state (q_f) after scanning the whole tape and it stops (never moves).

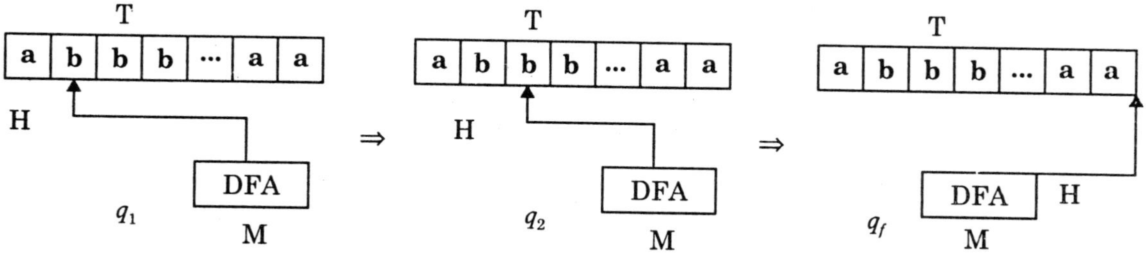

Fig. 7.2

So, after scanning the whole tape entries that contains the string, automaton M goes in the state, which is final state, it means the string is accepted by the machine M otherwise string is rejected by M (it means automata M not reaches to its end state while scanning the whole string). These possible outcomes of a DFA are shown in Fig. 7.3.

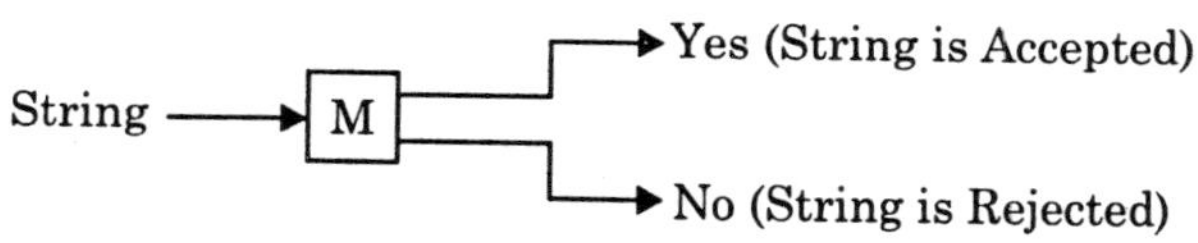

Fig. 7.3

7.2.1 Definition

A deterministic finite state automata (DFA) has:

- A finite set of states **Q**
- A finite set of input symbols Σ
- A transition function δ†, which defines the next transition (move) over an input symbol
- A start state q_0, where $q_0 \in$ Q (any one of the state in the set Q is a start state).
- A set of accepting state (final state) **F**. One or more state/s may acts as final state/s, which is certainly a subset of Q or F ⊆ Q.

So, a DFA M is defined by above discussed 5-tuples as:

$$\mathbf{M = (Q, \Sigma, \delta, q_0, F)}$$

†The Transition function δ is truly a mapping of a state (∈ Q) with an input symbol (∈ Σ) and returns to a state (∈ Q) or,

$$\delta: Q \times \Sigma \rightarrow Q$$

For example, if q is a state (∈ Q) and a symbol a (∈ Σ) that returns state p(∈ Q), then transition function δ is,

$$\delta(q, a) \rightarrow p$$

Or, automata M is in state q and after reading an input symbol a M moves on next state p. State p may be same as q means automata remains in its state on consuming the input symbol, i.e.,

$$\delta(q, a) \rightarrow q$$

7.2.2 Representation of a DFA

Obviously, A Deterministic Finite State Automata has a finite set of states and the transition between states are defined to a set of states over a set of input symbols, which returns a set of states. We can represent the DFA either through states diagram and through transition table.

7.2.2.1 In state diagram, we use following convention;

- A state is shown by a circle, suppose p is a state then it is represented as,

- The transition between states shown by an arc between them which is loaded by input symbol with direction mark by an arrow, for example
  $\delta(q, a) = p$ is represented as,

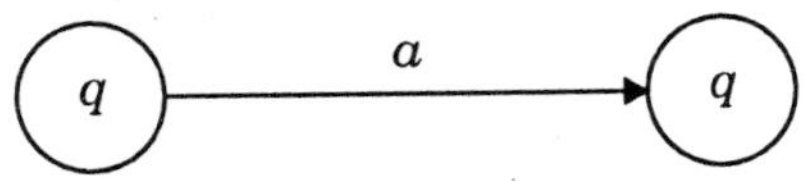

where p and q are states and the arc loaded with input symbol a shows the transition from state q to state p.

- Start (initial) state is marked by an start arrow, for example if state q is the start state then it is represented as,

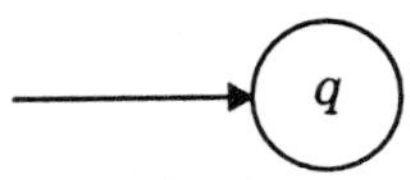

- Final/Accepting state is marked by double circle, for example if state p is the final/ accepting state then it is represented as,

Example 7.1. *A DFA* $M = (Q, \Sigma, \delta, q_0, F)$ *has* $Q = \{q_0, q_1\}$, $\Sigma = \{a, b\}$, $F = \{q_1\}$ *and* q_0 *is the initial state and the transition function* δ *is defined as:*

$$\delta(q_0, a) = q_1; \quad \delta(q_0, b) = q_0; \quad \delta(q_1, a) = q_0; \quad \delta(q_1, b) = q_1;$$

The transition diagram of above DFA M is shown below (Fig. 7.4)

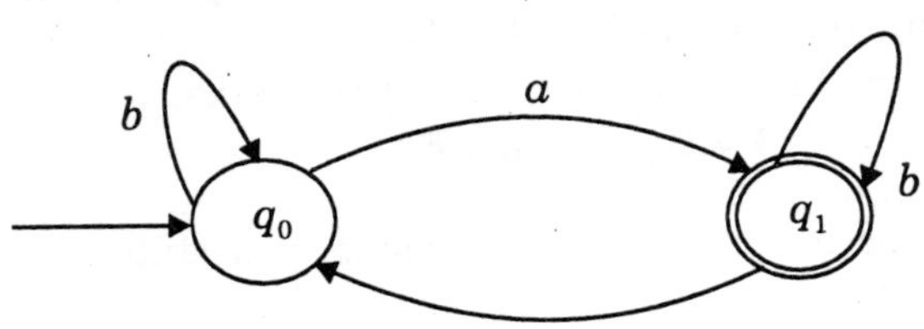

Fig. 7.4

Note: *From DFA we see that there is exactly one and only one transition (exit arc) from each state on each input symbol so the automaton M is 'Deterministic' (DFA). Conversely, if the finite automata have more than one transition/s (exit arc) from a state on single/same symbol then automata is 'Nondeterministic' (NFA).*

Example 7.2. *A Deterministic Finite Automata $M = (Q, \Sigma, \delta, q_0, F)$ has set of states $Q = \{q_0, q_1\}$, set of input symbols $\Sigma = \{a, b\}$, initial state $= \{q_0\}$ and the set of final state F contain a single state q_0 i.e., $F = \{q_0\}$ where $F \subseteq Q$ and the transition function δ is defined as:*

$$\delta(q_0, a) = q_1; \quad \delta(q_0, b) = q_0; \quad \delta(q_1, a) = q_0; \quad \delta(q_1, b) = q_1;$$

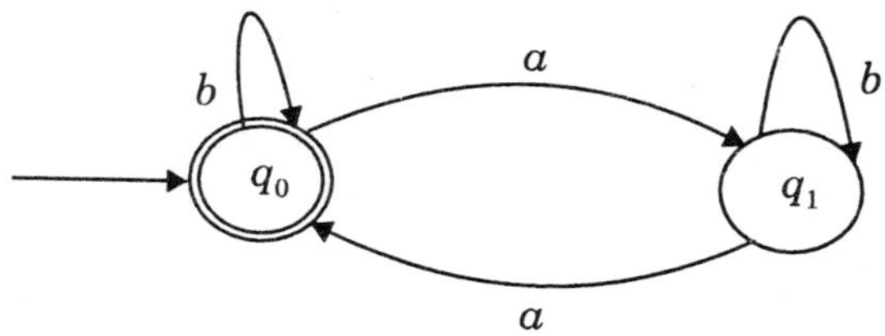

Fig. 7.5

The transition diagram of M is shown in Fig. 7.5. Here q_0 is the initial state marked by arrow and it is also a final state marked by double circle. From given transition function δ of M, following conclusions will be drawn:

- Initial state is the final state; it means that there is no transition or the transition on no input symbol which is impossible. For this purpose we assume a special string called epsilon ($\in$) *i.e.*,$\delta(q_0, \in) = q_0$: state remains unchanged.
  Hence, *string $\in$ is accepted by M.*

or, • Any string containing one/more symbols of ***b*** is also accepted *i.e.*, {*b*, *bb*, *bbb*...}

or, • If string contains a symbol ***a*** then it must contain another symbol a, so that automaton M returns to its final states q_0, *i.e.*, accepting strings are {*aa*, *aaaa*, *aaaaaa*, ...}.

or, • if starting symbol is zero/one/more *b* then accepting strings are:
{*aa*, *aaaa*, *aaaaaa*, ...} or {*baa*, *baaaa*, *baaaaaa*, ...} or
{*bbaa*, *bbaaaa*, *bbaaaaaa*, ...} or { ....}
or { *bb*.....*baa*, *bb*....*baaaa*, *bb*....*aaaaaaa*, ...}

or, • if any number of symbols *b* lies in between of *a i.e.*, the accepting strings are:
{*aba*, *abba*, ..., *abababa*, *abbabbabba*, ...,*abababababa*, *abbabbabbabbabba*, ..., *abb*...*babb*..*babb*..*ba*.........*ba* }

So, we conclude that any string containing even number of *a's* is accepted by M. Hence, following set of strings is accepted by given DFA M

{$\in$, *b*, *bb*, *bbb*, ..., *aa*, *aaaa*, ..., *aba*, *abba*, ..., *abababa*...........}

Example 7.3. *Design a DFA that accepts the string of odd number of $a^{'s}$ and $b^{'s}$ (both).*

Sol. Let DFA $M = (Q, \Sigma, \delta, q_0, F)$, where $\Sigma = \{a, b\}$, A finite set of states Q is assumed as $\{q_0, q_1, q_2, \ldots\ldots q_i\}$, where q_0 is the initial state, and one/more state(s) assumed $\in$ F those are final state(s).

1. If string containing Ist symbol is *a* (arrow 1) then next state onward there must be odd number of $b^{'s}$ (1, 3, 5...) with even numbers of $a^{'s}$ (2, 4, 6......) such that all $a^{'s}$ are odd. (Fig. 7.6)

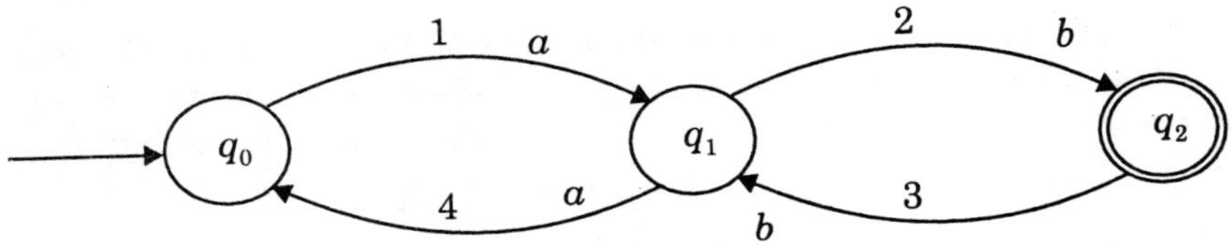

Fig. 7.6

2. If there is a string containing symbol a followed by one b (arrow 2) then it reaches to q_2 which is an accepted state. It is also true for a's, $3a$'s, 5a's ....followed by b's, $3b$'s, 5b's, ... (Fig. 7.6)

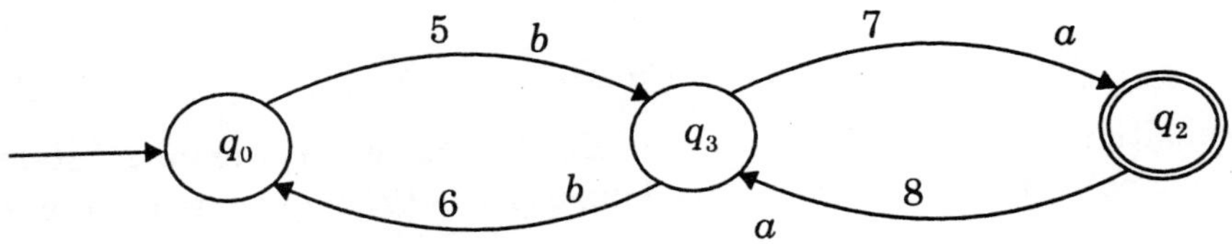

Fig. 7.7

3. If string contains First symbol b (arrow 5) then next state (q_3) onwards there must be remaining symbols in the string is odd numbers of a's (1,3,5...) with even no. of b's (2, 4, 6) s.t. all a's in the string become odd, (Fig. 7.7).
4. If there is a string containing First symbol b (arrow 5) followed by one a then (arrow 7) it must reach to an accepted state (true for odd no. of a's and b's) (Fig. 7.7).
5. Combining Fig. 7.6 and Fig. 7.7 we get the final DFA that is shown in Fig. 7.8. So the DFA M for the above language is represented as,

   $M = (\{q_0, q_1, q_2, q_3\}, \{a, b\}, \delta, q_0, \{q_1\})$

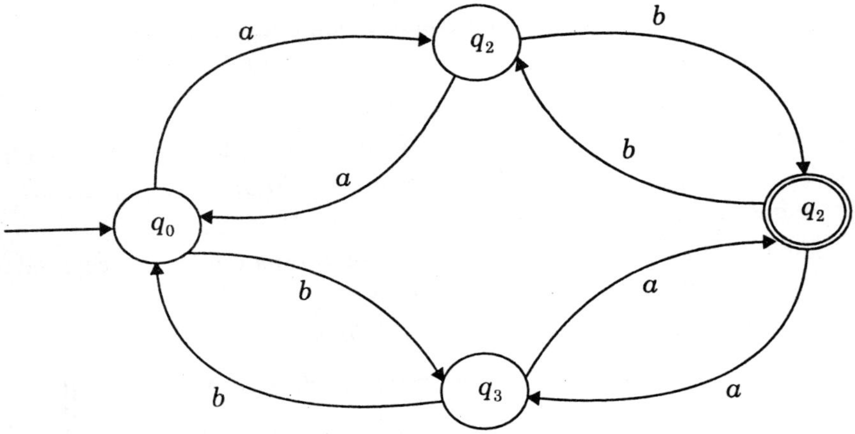

Fig 7.8

7.2.2.2 Transition Table

In spite of complex transition diagram for many DFA's there is a simpler representation of transition functions by a table. In the table entries, rows contain all the states of the set Q and columns contain all the input symbols of set S.

For example, following transition function

$$\delta(q, a) = p\ ;$$

has the transition diagram

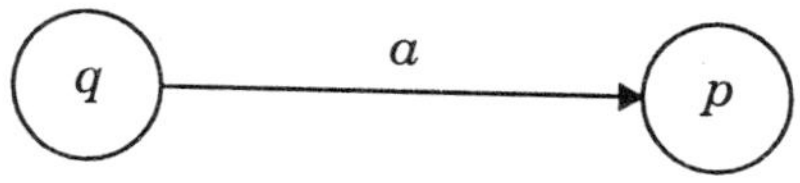

then its transition table is

State	Input symbol
	a
q	p

It shows automata is in state q and after reading (consuming) symbol a its state changes to q.

Note. *In the transition table the initial state is marked by an arrow and the final state is marked by circle. For example, the DFA shown in fig 7.8 can be represented using transition table that is shown below in Fig. 7.9.*

State	Input symbol	
	a	**a**
→ q_0	q_1	q_3
q_1	q_0	q_2
● q_2	q_3	q_1
q_3	q_2	q_1

Fig. 7.9

Example 7.4. *Construct a DFA that accepts the string having the alphabet pattern 011.*

Sol. We construct the DFA over set of alphabets $\Sigma = \{0, 1\}$ by assuming q_0 is the initial state then,

I. From the state q_0 onwards there must be a consumption of string 011 (which is necessary a substring or substring containing pattern found in all acceptable string).

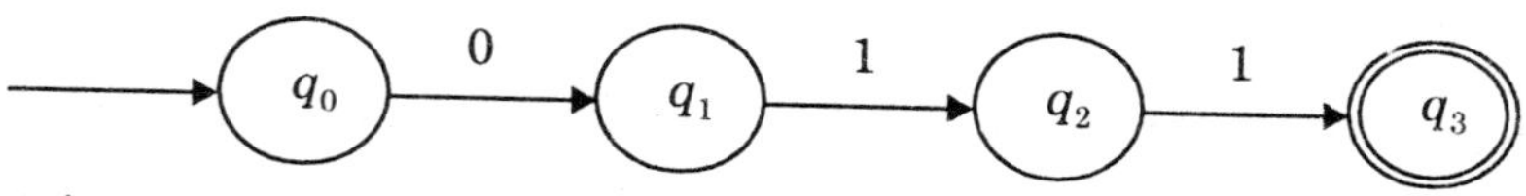

II. Any string starting with symbol 0 followed by any number of 0's before the pattern 011 is accepted s.t. {011, 0011, 00011, ...}. So there must be a repetitive transition arc in the state q_1 on symbol 0.

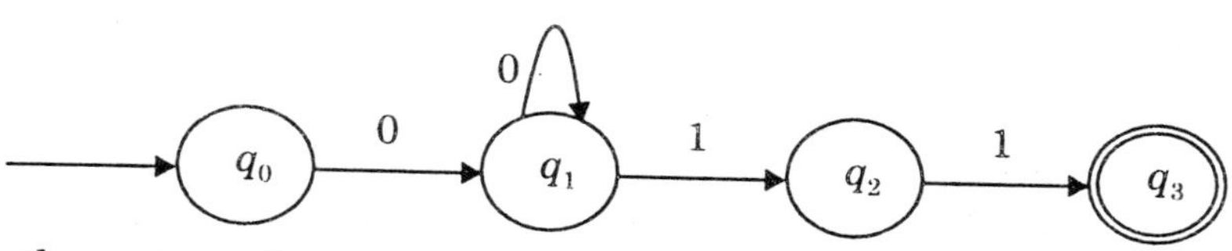

(from the state q_1 the last symbol seen was 0)

III. Similarly, any string starting with symbol 1 and followed by any number of 1's before the pattern 011 is accepted s.t. {1011, 11011, 111011,......}. So there must be repetitions of symbol 1 on state q_0.

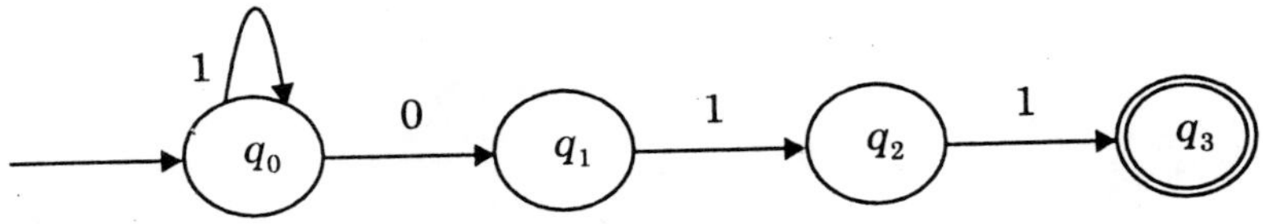

IV. Combining II and III we get the following DFA.

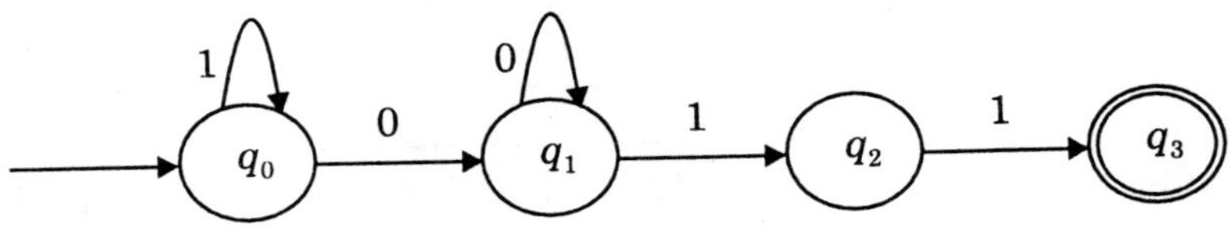

V. If the string containing 01 followed by pattern 011, then from the sate q_2 there is an arc return to state q_1 on input symbol 0, so the automata reach to its accepted state q_3 after reading the pattern 011.

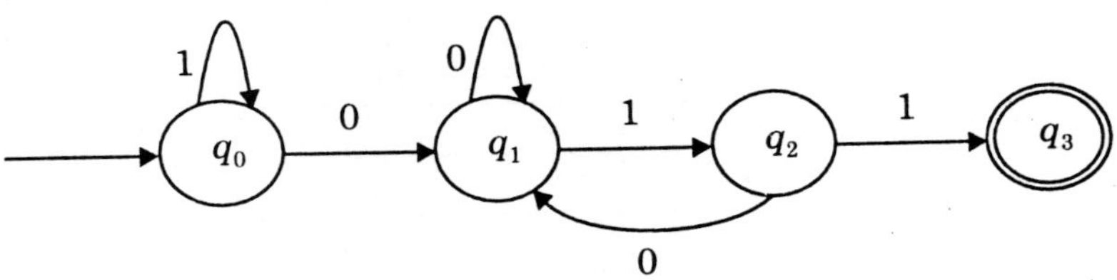

(from the state q_2 last two symbol seen were 01)

VI. After the pattern 011 the string might contain any number of 0's or/and 1's, for that there is a repetitive arc on state q_3 over symbol 0 or 1. (Fig. 7.10)

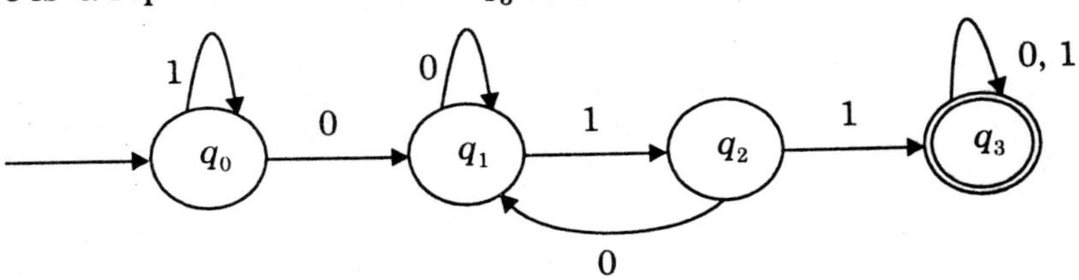

Fig. 7.10

In this automaton we observed that there is *one and only one exit on each symbol from each state.* Due to this fact automaton is 'Deterministic'.

Finally, the DFA M = $(\{q_0, q_1, q_2, q_3\}, \{0, 1\}, \delta, q_0, \{q_3\})$; where δ's are shown in the transition table:

State	Input symbol	
	0	1
→ q_0	q_1	q_0
q_1	q_1	q_2
q_2	q_1	q_3
● q_3	q_3	q_3

Fig. 7.11

Example 7.5. *Give a DFA that accepts the language over alphabet a and the string contains zero / multiples of 4 a's. Or,*

Construct the DFA that accepts the strings of the set {∈, aaaa, aaaaaaaa, ...}.

Sol. Let M be a DFA and $\{q_0\}$ is the initial state.

I. If first symbol is null string (∈) then initial state (q_0) is the final state also so state diagram will be,

II. From the state q_0 onwards there is a consumption of 4-consecutive a's followed by none/ more such sets of a's, *i.e.*,

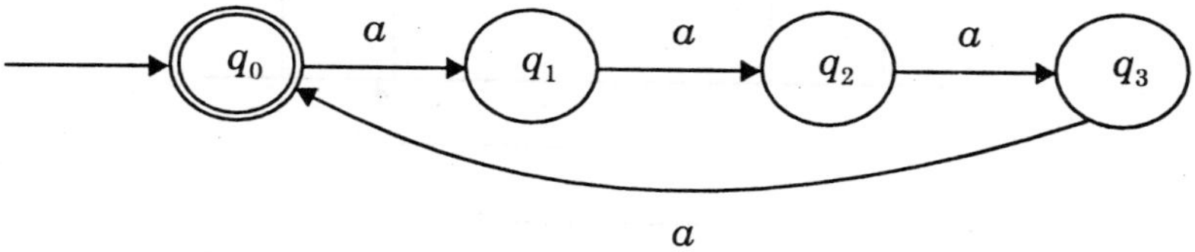

Fig. 7.12

So the final DFA M is $(\{q_0, q_1, q_2, q_3\}, \{a\}, \delta, q_0, \{q_0\})$ shown in Fig. 7.12; and the transition function δ is shown in the transition table in Fig. 7.13.

State	Input symbol
	a
→●q_0	q_1
q_1	q_2
q_2	q_0
q_3	q_0

Fig. 7.13

7.2.3 δ-head

Instead of defining the behavior of transition function over a single symbol (alphabet), which is a mapping of a state with a input symbol and returns a state *i.e.*, δ: Q × S → Q, it is also required to know the behavior of the transition function over an arbitrary string (s. t. automata not only read a single symbol but a sequence of symbols or string)) such characteristics include in the definition of δ-head.

7.2.3.1 Definition

Assume, if a string is defined over set of alphabet Σ then set of possible string is in Σ*, then δ-head is defined as:

$$\hat{\delta} : \mathbf{Q} \times \Sigma^* \rightarrow \mathbf{Q}$$

or we say that δ-head is the transition function that map a state(∈ Q) with a string (∈ Σ*) and returns a state (∈ Q).

Let automata M is in state q, after reading the string x (tape cells entries contains the string x) automaton reaches to state p. This situation is shown in Fig. 7.14 (a) and (b).

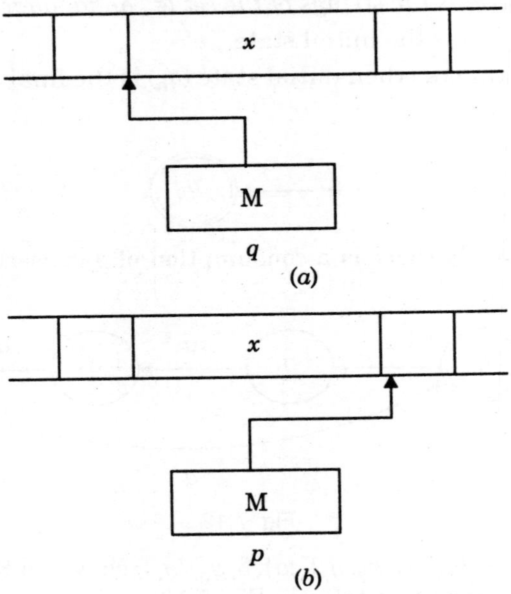

Fig. 7.14

So, the behavior of δ-head over string x is given as,

$$\hat{\delta}(q, x) = p;$$

where x is a string might be of single alphabet.

7.2.3.2 Properties of δ-head

From any state q,

I. If input string is a null string (∈) then automaton state remains unchanged *i.e.*,

$$\hat{\delta}(q, \in) = q, \ \forall q \in Q$$

If the string is of single symbol string or of length one then δ-head and δ are same *i.e.*, assume string $x = a$ then,

$$\hat{\delta}(q, x) = \delta(q, a) = p;$$

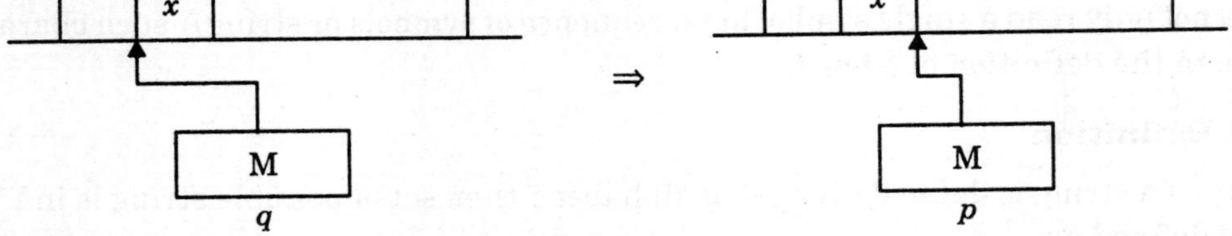

II. If string is not of single symbol string then assume string x is formed by a alphabet a and substring y, *i.e.*, $x = ay$, then

$$\hat{\delta}(q, a\,y) = \hat{\delta}(\delta(q, a), y);$$

For example if x = 1011 then a = 1 and remaining string y = 011.

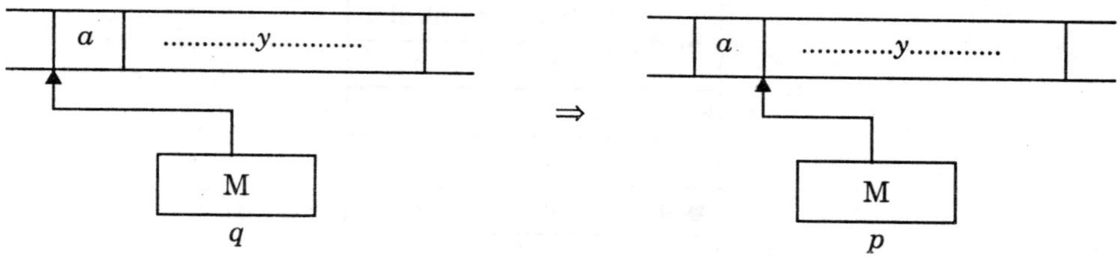

Here $\delta(q, a) = p$ and assume that after reading the remaining substring y automata reaches to state r then $\hat{\delta}(q, x) = r$

$\Rightarrow$

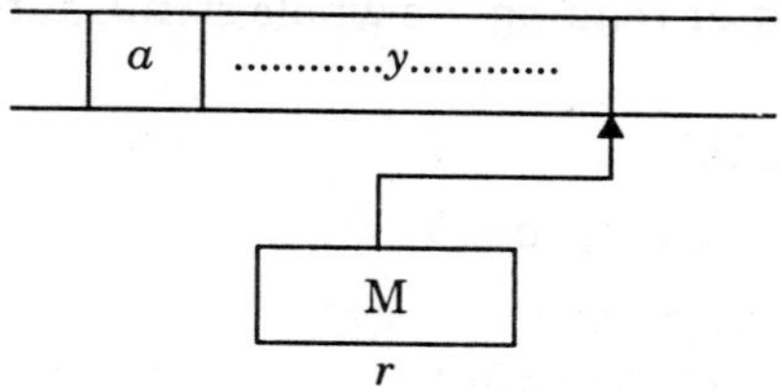

(In this way automaton complete the transitions over input string x)

Example 7.9. *A DFA* $M = (\{q_0, q_1\}, \{a\}, \delta, q_0, \{q_1\})$ *has following transition characteristics:*

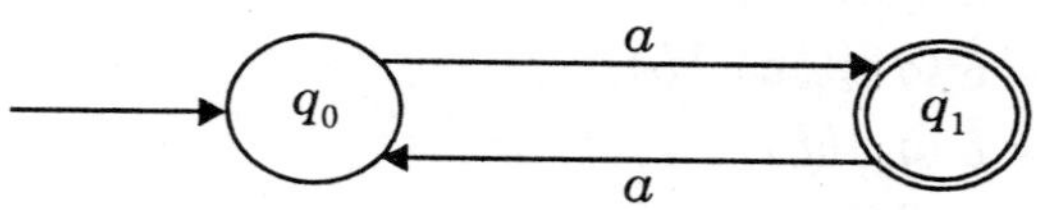

Check behavior of the DFA over string aaa.

Sol. Assume autometer is in initial state $\{q_0\}$. Now check the behaviour of DFA M over the string aaa, i.e.

$$
\begin{aligned}
\hat{\delta}(q_0, aaa) &= \hat{\delta}(\delta(q_0, a), aa) && \text{[Using II property of } \delta\text{-head]}\\
&= \hat{\delta}(q_1, aa) && [\therefore\ \delta(q_0, a) = q_1]\\
&= \hat{\delta}(\delta(q_1, a), a) && \text{[Using II property of } \delta\text{-head]}\\
&= \hat{\delta}(q_0, a) && [\therefore\ \delta(q_1, a) = q_0]\\
&= \hat{\delta}(q_0, a\,.\in) && [\therefore\ a\,.\in\, = a]\\
&= \hat{\delta}(\delta(q_0, a) && \text{[Using II property of } \delta\text{-head]}\\
&= \hat{\delta}(q_1, \in) && [\therefore\ \delta(q_0, a) = q_1]\\
&= \{q_1\} && \text{[Using Ist property of } \delta\text{-head]}
\end{aligned}
$$

Since state (q_1) is an accepted state, therefore string aaa is accepted by DFA M.

Example 7.10. *Construct the DFA accepting the set of string having both odd number of $a^{'s}$ and $b^{'s}$.*

Sol. The following DFA M accepts odd no. of $a^{'s}$ and $b^{'s}$

where, $M = (\{q_0, q_1, q_2, q_3\}, \{a, b\}, \delta, q_0, \{q_2\})$ and transition function shown in the transition table (TT) Fig. 7.15.

State	Input symbol	
	a	b
→ q_0	q_1	q_3
q_1	q_0	q_2
● q_2	q_3	q_1
q_3	q_2	q_1

Fig. 7.15

Now we define the moves of DFA over the string $abaabb$ (odd number of a's and b's both) which must be acceptable or after reading the whole string automata reaches to the final state $\{q_2\}$.

So, compute $\hat{\delta}(q_0, abaabb)$:

I. $\hat{\delta}(q_0, \text{abaabb}) = \hat{\delta}(\delta(q_0, a), baabb)$

$= \hat{\delta}(q_1, baabb)$ [$\therefore$ $\delta(q_0, a) = q_1$]

II. $\hat{\delta}(q_1, baabb) = \hat{\delta}(\delta(q_1, b), aabb)$

$= \hat{\delta}(q_2, aabb)$ [$\therefore$ $\delta(q_1, b) = q_2$]

III. $\hat{\delta}(q_2, aabb) = \hat{\delta}(\delta(q_2, a), abb)$

$= \hat{\delta}(q_3, abb)$ [$\therefore$ $\delta(q_2, a) = q_3$]

IV. $\hat{\delta}(q_3, abb) = \hat{\delta}(\delta(q_3, a), bb)$

$= \hat{\delta}(q_2, bb)$ [$\therefore$ $\delta(q_3, a) = q_2$]

V. $\hat{\delta}(q_2, bb) = \hat{\delta}(\delta(q_2, b), b)$

$= \hat{\delta}(q_1, b)$ [$\therefore$ $\delta(q_2, b) = q_1$]

VI. $\hat{\delta}(q_1, b) = \hat{\delta}(q_1, b.\in) = \delta\hat{}(\delta(q_1, b), \in)$

$= \hat{\delta}(q_2, \in)$ [$\therefore$ $\delta(q_1, b) = q_2$]

VII. $\hat{\delta}(q_2, \in) = \delta(q, \in)$ [using Ist property of δ-head)

$= \{q_2\}$

where $\{q_2\}$ is the accepted state of DFA M.

7.2.4 Language of a DFA

After knowing the behavior of the automata over an arbitrary string and finally over the set of string we can easily define the language of a DFA. Let automata M be a DFA then language accepted by M is L_M where,

$$L_M = \{x / x \in \Sigma^* \text{ and } \hat{\delta}(q_0, x) \in F\}$$

Alternatively, we say that any arbitrary string x from the set Σ^* will be the language of DFA M if from initial state after reading the complete string x it reaches to final state. Now we see that if Σ is the set of alphabet then set of all possible string formed over Σ is Σ^*. In the set Σ^* there exists two possible class of languages, *i.e.*,

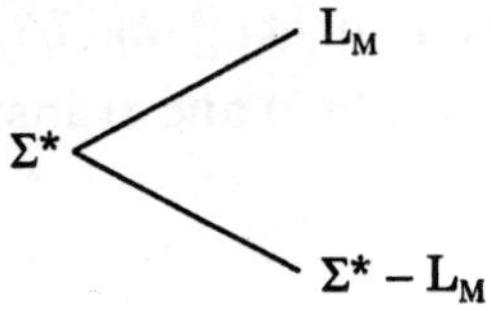

where L_M contains those set of strings that are accepted by automaton M, and remaining string ($\Sigma^* - L_M$) are those that are discarded or rejected by M. Hence, L_M and Σ^*- L_M are two disjoint sets which never meet with reference to a particular automaton M, i.e.,

$$L_M \cap (\Sigma^* - L_M) = \Phi$$

Note. *Set L_M contains infinitely many strings or a language of a DFA contains infinite number of strings but an automaton has a finite amount of space that is only available space to allocate to finite or infinitely long strings. Hence, there is a mechanism used to describe a infinitely long string into a finite number of symbols (detail discussion is out of scope of the topic) but for brief discussion see the topic languages under section basic concepts of automata in the beginning of this chapter.*

7.3 NON DETERMINISTIC FINITE STATE AUTOMATA (NDFSA)/ NON DETERMINISTIC FINITE STATE MACHINE (NDFSM)/ NON DETERMINISTIC FINITE AUTOMATA (NDFA)/NFA

In the previous section we have discussed deterministic finite state automata (DFA) whose state transitions are deterministic which means that there is one and only one exit arc from each state on an input symbol. So we can say that DFA gives somewhat *static* view of the finite automata. Now we will discuss a *dynamic/flexible* view of the finite automata whose state transitions are not of deterministic nature (non-deterministic), which means that there is the possibility of multiple transitions on some input symbols from a single state. So, the automata of such category are known as nondeterministic finite state automata (NDFSA/NDFSM/NDFA/ NFA). The feature of dynamism introduced in the finite automata provides more power to the finite automata. The abstract view of the NFA shown in Fig. 7.16 is similar to the DFA.

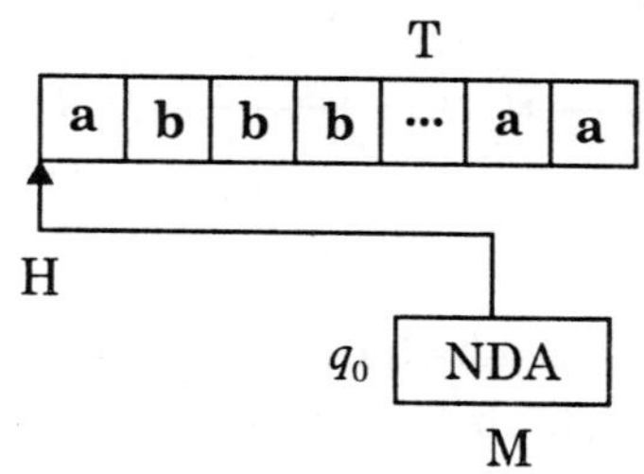

Fig. 7.16

7.3.1 Definition

We can define a nondeterministic finite automaton (NFA) with following tuples,

- Q, a finite set of states,
- Σ, a finite set of input symbols,
- q_0, an initial state, where $q_0 \in Q$
- **F**, a set of final state/s, where F is the subset of state Q *i.e.*, ($F \subseteq Q$),
- δ, a transition function which defines the next state reachable from current state over an input symbol. It reaches to either no state or single state or two/more states.
    - No state transition means, there is no actual transition define from a state on that symbol or there is no exit arc from that state on that symbol.
    - Single state transition means, there is a single transition define from a state on that symbol or there is a single exit arc from that state.

- More state transitions means, there is the possibility of two/more transitions from a state on that single symbol or there are 2/more transitions arc exit from that state.

So a NFA can be defined by these five tuples by,

$$N = (Q, \Sigma, \delta, q_0, F)$$

where transition function (δ) is the mapping of a state with an input symbol to power set of Q, it means that function returns a state that will be in the power set of state Q.

$$\delta: Q \times S \rightarrow P(Q)$$

Note. *Transition function returns the state / s that is in power set of Q, so set of final state* F is also the subset of power set of Q. *Power set includes all subset of Q including* Φ *(no state element).* Φ *defines no state transition on any symbol.*

Why δ returns the state that is in power set, the reason is due to dynamic nature of automata NFA. The transition arc on single symbol fall on either in one state(q_i) / two state (q_i, q_j) / more states(q_i,........ q_l) or possibly no state transition (Φ). These possibilities of set of states are included only in the power set of Q.

7.3.2 Representation

The representation of a NFA is similar to a DFA representation that is, we can represent the NFA either through a state diagram or through transition table (TT). I personally feel that state diagram representation provides a comprehensive view of the automata at a moment. So I always prefer state diagram over transition table representation. In the Fig. 7.17 we construct a NFA that accepts all the strings which contains the substring 011 or a pattern of symbols 011.

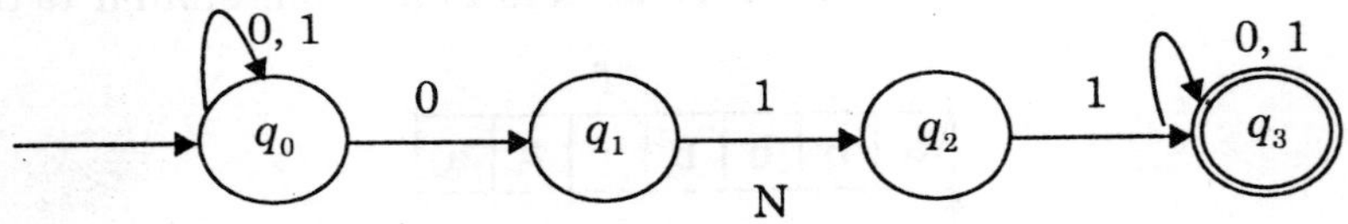

Fig. 7.17

Above NFA N can be represented by following tuples,

$$N = (\{q_0, q_1, q_2, q_3\}, \{0, 1\}, \delta, q_0, \{q_3\})$$

And transition functions δ are define as follows,

- $\delta(q_0, 0) = \{q_0\}$ and $\delta(q_0, 0) = \{q_1\}$;
  So, $\delta(q_0, 0) = \{q_0, q_1\}$ [∴ There are two exit arcs from a state q_0 on symbol 0]
- $\delta(q_0, 1) = \{q_0\}$;
- $\delta(q_1, 0) = \Phi$; [∴ no transition is defined on input symbol 0 from state q_1]
- $\delta(q_1, 1) = \{q_2\}$;
- $\delta(q_2, 0) = \Phi$;
- $\delta(q_2, 1) = \{q_3\}$;
- $\delta(q_3, 0) = \{q_3\}$;
- $\delta(q_3, 1) = \{q_3\}$;

7.3.3 δ-head

Like δ-head of DFA, δ-head of NFA defines the behavior of the transition function over an arbitrary string. Assume that if the string is defined over alphabet Σ, then set of all possible strings are Σ*. The δ-head is defined as,

$$\hat{\delta} : Q \times \Sigma^* \rightarrow P(Q)$$

Thus, δ-head is the transition function which is a mapping of a state (∈ Q) and a string of input symbols (∈ Σ*) to power set of Q or P(Q).

7.3.4 Properties of δ-head

Let NFA N is in current state q and its tape contains a string x shown in Fig. 7.18 then, behavior of δ-head over string x is determine as follows:

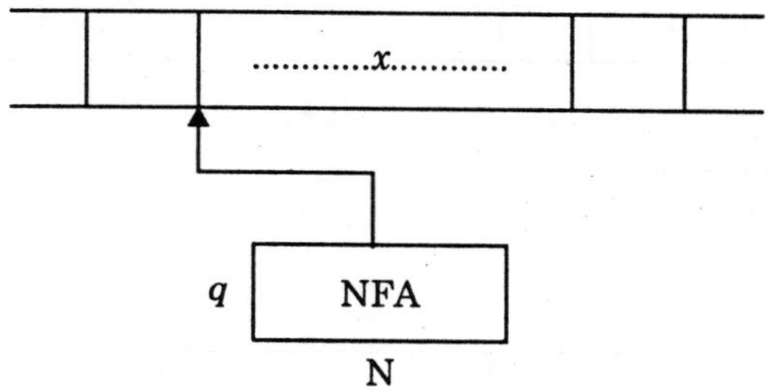

Fig. 7.18

I. If x is a null string (∈) then,

$$\hat{\delta}(q, \in) = \{q\};$$

such that if input symbol is a null string then state remains unchanged.

II. If string x is composed of two/more symbols, then decompose string x into substring y and a single symbol a such that, $x = y\,a$ then,

$$\hat{\delta}(q, x) = \hat{\delta}(q, y\,a);$$
$$= \delta(\hat{\delta}(q, y), a) \quad \text{(using definition of } \delta \text{ and } \hat{\delta}\text{)}$$

Further, assume that $\hat{\delta}(q, y) = \{p_1, p_2, p_3, \ldots\ldots, p_i\}$, that is, from the state q NFA might be reaches to these possible states after consuming the string y, that is shown in Fig. 7.19.

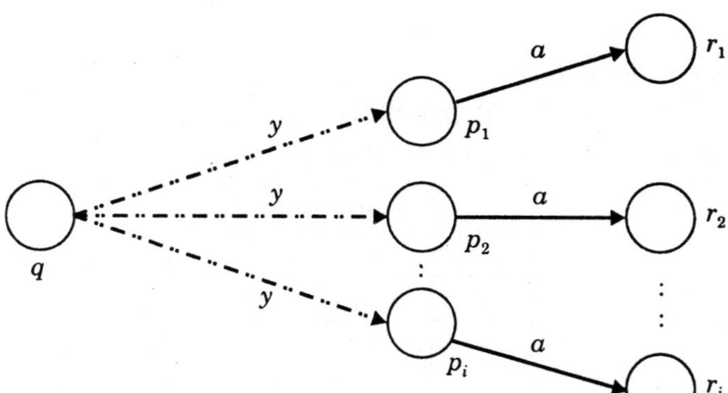

Fig. 7.19

Thus, $\delta(\hat{\delta}(q, y), a) = \delta(\{p_1, p_2, p_3, \ldots\ldots, p_i\}, a);$

$$= \delta(p_1, a) \cup \delta(p_2, a) \cup \delta(p_3, a) \cup \ldots\ldots\ldots\ldots \cup \delta(p_i, a)$$

$$= \bigcup_{k=1}^{i} \delta(p_k, a)$$

$$= \{ r_1, r_2, r_3, \ldots\ldots\ldots\ldots, r_j \}^{\ddagger}$$

Abstract view of the automata during scanning the string $x = y\ a$ is shown below in Fig. 7.20.

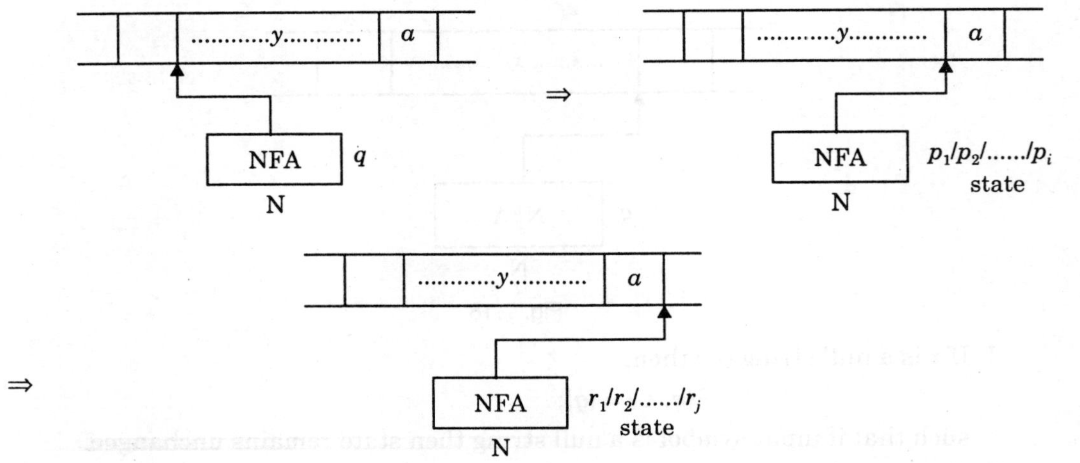

Fig. 7.20

Example7.11. *Fig. 7.21 shows a NFA N (similar to the automaton discussed in previous example), then check its nature of acceptance over the string 101101.*

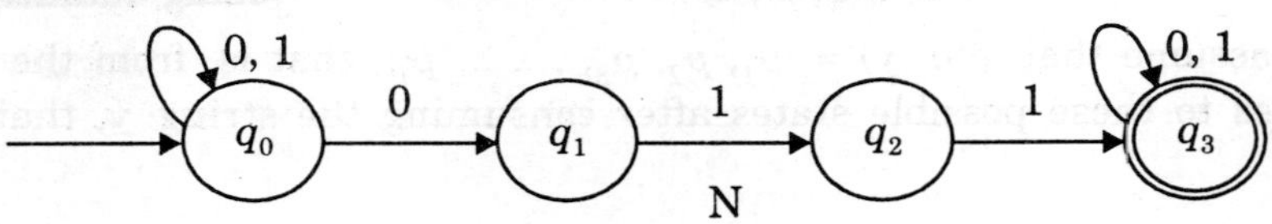

Fig. 7.21

Sol. Above NFA N can be defined as,

$$N = (\{q_0, q_1, q_2, q_3\}, \{0, 1\}, \delta, q_0, \{q_3\});$$

where δ's are shown in the following transition table (TT),

State	Input symbol	
	0	1
→ q_0	$\{q_0, q_1\}$	$\{q_0\}$
q_1	Φ	$\{q_2\}$
q_2	Φ	$\{q_3\}$
● q_3	$\{q_3\}$	$\{q_3\}$

‡ *Case I, $j = i$, when all the state have single transition on each symbol of the set Σ then, † it returns to exactly similar number of state that is equal to I or $\{ r_1, r_2, r_3, \ldots\ldots\ldots\ldots, r_j \}$.*

Case II, $j = 0$, when there is no transition arc over symbol a from state p_k ($\forall k = 1$ to i).

Case III, $j < i$ or $j > i$, depending upon the nature of transition from state p_k on input symbol a.

Above cases exists only because of dynamic nature of NFA.

Then we check the behavior of N over the string 101101, from the starting state q_0.

I. $\hat{\delta}(q_0, 101101) = \hat{\delta}(\delta(q_0, 1), 01101);$

[from TT check transition response of state q_0 on symbol 1]

$= \hat{\delta}(q_0, 01101);$ $[\because \ \delta(q_0, 1) = \{q_0\}]$

II. $\hat{\delta}(q_0, 01101) = \hat{\delta}(\delta(q_0, 0), 1101);$

$= \hat{\delta}(\{q_0, q_1\}, 1101);$ $[\because \ \delta(q_0, 0) = \{q_0, q_1\}]$

III. $\hat{\delta}(\{q_0, q_1\}, 1101\} = \hat{\delta}(q_0, 1101) \cup \hat{\delta}(q_1, 1101);$ [check each one separately]

IV(A1). $\delta\hat{}(q_0, 1101) = \hat{\delta}(\delta(q_0, 1), 101);$

$= \hat{\delta}(q_0, 101\}$ $[\because \ \delta(q_0, 1) = q_0]$

IV(A2). $\hat{\delta}(q_0, 101) = \hat{\delta}(\delta(q_0, 1), 01);$

$= \delta\hat{}(q_0, 01)$ $[\because \ \delta(q_0, 1) = q_0]$

IV(A3). $\hat{\delta}(q_0, 01) = \hat{\delta}(\delta(q_0, 0), 1);$

$= \hat{\delta}(\{q_0, q_1\}, 1);$ $[\because \ \delta(q_0, 0) = \{q_0, q_1\}]$

IV(A4). $\hat{\delta}(\{q_0, q_1\}, 1) = \hat{\delta}(\{q_0, q_1\}, 1.\in);$

[in case of $\hat{\delta}$ when symbol is alone, to make it string , it will multiply with the null string ($\in$)]

$= \hat{\delta}(q_0, 1.\in) \cup \hat{\delta}(q_1, 1.\in);$

$= \hat{\delta}(\delta(q_0, 1), \in) \cup \hat{\delta}(\delta(q_1, 1), \in);$

$= \hat{\delta}(q_0, \in) \cup \hat{\delta}(q_2, \in);$ *[see transitions of state in TT]*

$= \{q_0\} \cup \{q_2\};$ *[by applying Ist the property of $\hat{\delta}$*

$= \{\mathbf{q_0, q_2}\};$ *i.e., $\hat{\delta}(q_0, \in) = q_0$ and $\hat{\delta}(q_2, \in) = q_2$]*

So we find none state is an acceptable state.

IV(B1). $\hat{\delta}(q_1, 1101) = \hat{\delta}(\delta(q_1, 1), 101);$

$= \hat{\delta}(q_2, 101);$ *[from the TT $\delta(q_1, 1) = q_2$]*

IV(B2). $\hat{\delta}(q_2, 101) = \hat{\delta}(\delta(q_2, 1), 01\};$

$= \hat{\delta}(q_3, 01);$ *[from the TT $\delta(q_2, 1) = q_3$]*

IV(B3). $\hat{\delta}(q_3, 01) = \hat{\delta}(\delta(q_3, 0), 1);$

$= \hat{\delta}(q_3, 1);$ *[from TT $\delta(q_3, 1) = q_3$]*

IV(B4). $\hat{\delta}(q_3, 1 = \hat{\delta}(q_3, 1.\in);$ [see IV(A) explanation]

$= \hat{\delta}(\delta(q_3, 1), \in);$

$= \hat{\delta}(q_3, \in);$ *[from TT $\delta(q_3, 1) = q_3$]*

$= \{\mathbf{q_3}\};$ An acceptable state

Hence, NFA N will move over the string 101101 according to following paths,

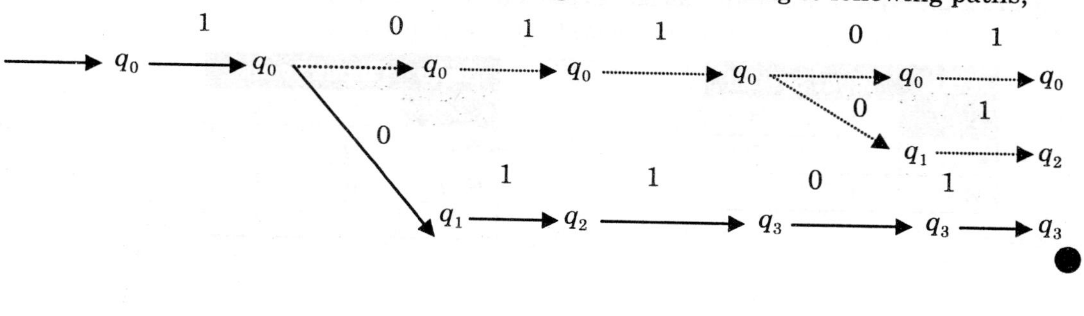

Therefore, the only acceptable path from starting state q_0 is shown by dark line. Along to this path NFA N reaches to the acceptable state q_3 at the end of the string 101101.

7.3.5 Language of an NFA

After determine the behavior of the NFA over an arbitrary string, we can easily define the language of a NFA. Let N be a NFA *i.e.*, N = (Q, Σ, δ, q_0, F), then language accepted by NFA is L_N, where,

$$L_N = \{x/x \in \Sigma^* \text{ and } \hat{\delta}(q_0, x) \in P(Q) \text{ s.t. } \hat{\delta}(q_0, x) \cap F \neq \Phi\}$$

It means, language L_N contains an arbitrary string x, chosen from the set of possible strings Σ* such that NFA N, after reading the string x (from the initial state q_0) reaches to the state that is in power set of Q, such that its relation with set F is not disjoint. That is, at least one state is common between set F and P(Q).

Example 7.12. *From the NFA given in example 7.11, test the string 10101 whch is not in the language of N.*

Sol. Assign string 10101 to x, if x is a language of N (where $x \in \Sigma^*$, *i.e.*, Σ = {0, 1}), then after reading the string x, NFA N reaches to its final state, *i.e.* any state that belongs to the power set of Q which contains the final state $\{q_3\}$. Now we can construct the moves of NFA over the string x = 10101, that is shown in Fig. 7.22.

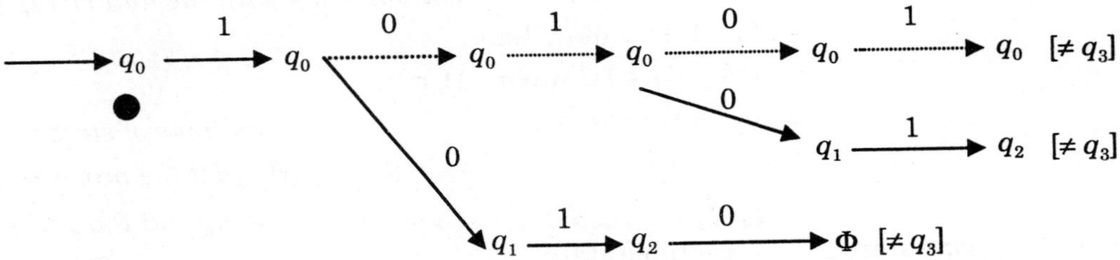

Fig. 7.22

Since, $\delta^\wedge(q_0, 10101) = \Phi$ or $\{q_0\}$ or $\{q_2\}$, so none of the set contains state $\{q_3\}$. Hence, $\delta^\wedge(q_0, 10101) \cap \{q_3\} = \Phi$. It conclude that string 10101 is not accepted by NFA N.

EXERCISES

7.1 Construct the DFA, which accept the following languages over {0, 1} :
- (*i*) The set of all strings with two consecutive 0's.
- (*ii*) The set of all strings ending with 101.
- (*iii*) The set of all strings that begin with 0 and ending with 01.
- (*iv*) The set of all strings in which no 0 is followed immediately by 1.

7.2 Construct the NFA to accept the languages given in the example 7.1.

7.3 Describe the language accepted by the following finite automatons.

(*i*)

State	Input Symbol	
	\$	#
→ A	A	B
● B	B	A

(*ii*)

State	Input Symbol	
	\$	#
→● P	Q	P
● Q	R	P
R	R	R

(*iii*)

State	Input Symbol	
	0	1
→ P	P	Q
Q	PQ	Q
● PQ	P	Q

7.4 Construct the finite automata for the language L_n (for $n \geq 1$), i.e.,
$L_n = \{x \in \{0, 1\}^* / |x| = n$ and the nth symbol from the right in x is 1$\}$

7.5 Let x be a string in $\{0, 1\}^*$ of length n. describe the finite automata that accepts the string x and no other strings. Also determine how many states are required.

7.6 Describe the language for each of the finite automatons shown in Fig. 7.23

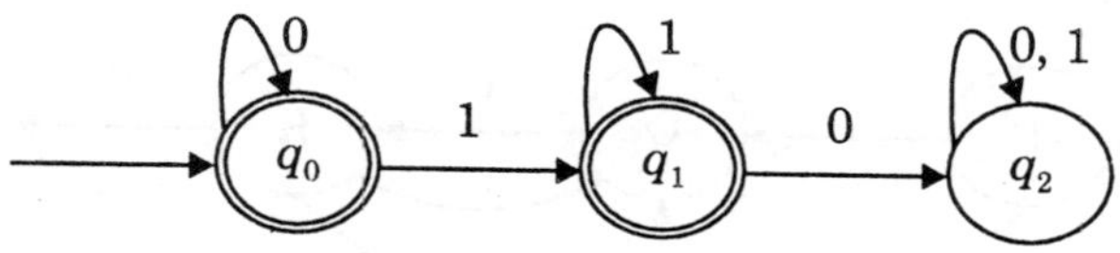

(*a*)

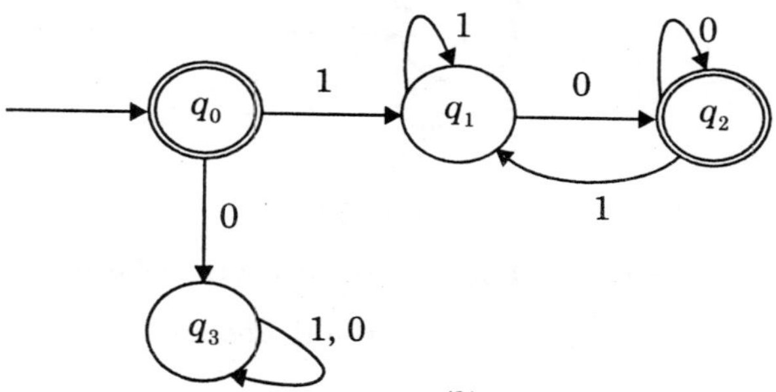

(*b*)

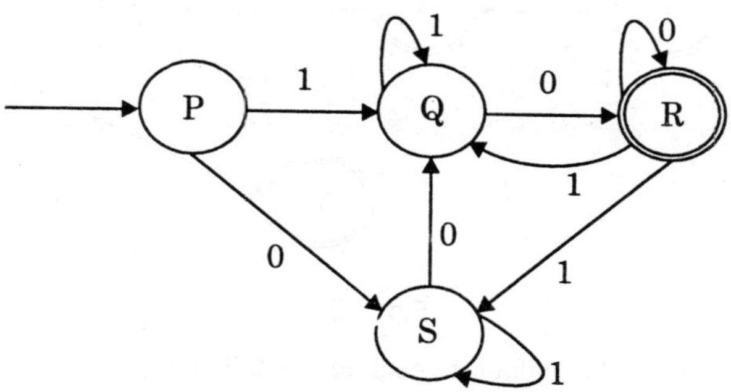

(*c*)

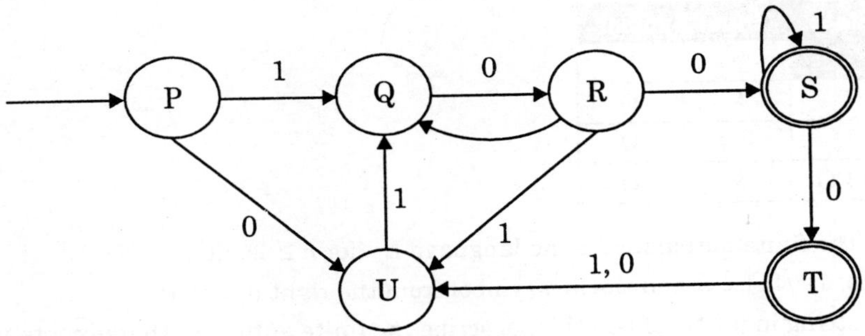

(*d*)

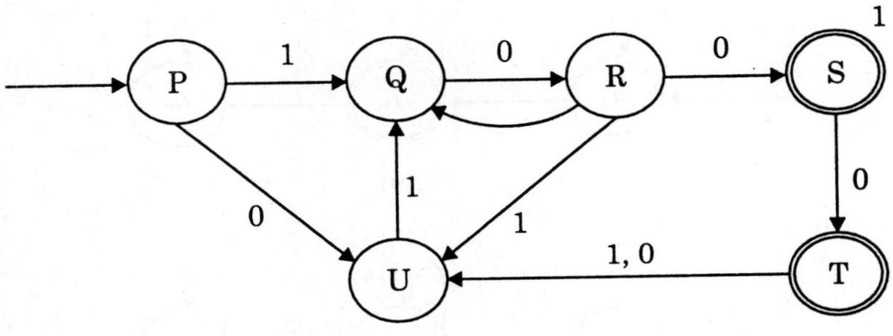

(*e*)

Fig. 7.23

7.7 In the given NFA shown in Fig. 7.24 determine each of the following :

(*i*) $\hat{\delta}$(I, *ab*) (*ii*) $\hat{\delta}$ (I, *abaab*)

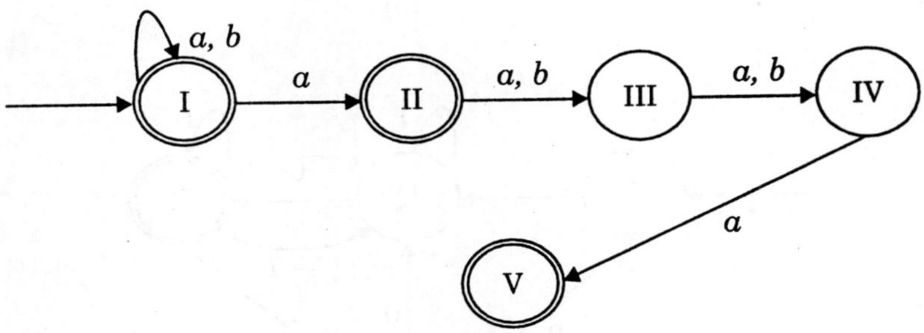

Fig. 7.24

7.8 An NFA pictured in Fig. 7.25, calculate each of the following :

(*i*) $\hat{\delta}$(S, 0000) (*ii*) $\hat{\delta}$ (S, 11111)

(*iii*) $\hat{\delta}$(S, 101010) (*iv*) $\hat{\delta}$(S, 111000).

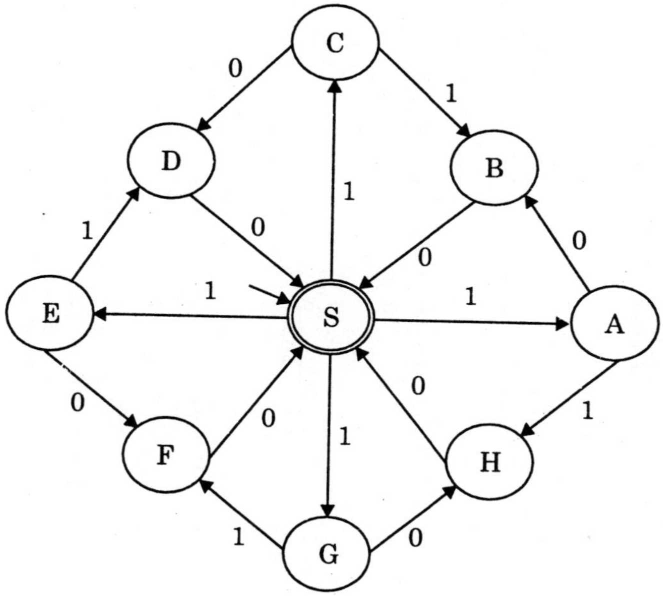

Fig. 7.25

EQUIVALENCE OF NFA AND DFA

8 Equivalence of NFA and DFA

8.1 RELATIONSHIP BETWEEN NFA AND DFA

Now we will discuss the relationship between finite automatons DFA & NFA and simultaneously study how one form of finite automata is converted into another form of finite automata. We know that the nondeterministic finite state automaton (NFA) provides flexibility in transitions of state/s over the input symbol. But, a deterministic finite state automaton (DFA) provides the fixed or static view of transitions of states over input symbol. Hence, for the same language it is comparatively easy to construct a NFA rather than a DFA, because *DFA is the limiting case of NFA, and each DFA must be the consisting part of a NFA.*

In this section we will present the quantitative view of the relationship between a NFA and a DFA by proving the following theorem.

Theorem 8.1. *If there is an NFA accepting the language L then, there exist a DFA for the same language L.*

Proof. Let N be a NFA which is defined over following tuples: Q_N, Σ, δ_N, q_{0N}, F_N (where the subscript$_N$ stands for automaton NFA), *i.e.*,

$$N = (Q_N, \Sigma, \Sigma_N, q_{0N}, F_N)$$

Since L is the language of a NFA N where L is given as,

$$L_N = \{x/x \in \Sigma^* \quad \text{and} \quad \delta^\wedge(q_0, x) \cap F \neq \Phi\}$$

Now define a DFA M on following set of tuples, Q_D, δ_D, q_{0D}, F_D and same set of input alphabet Σ, so

$$M = (Q_D, \Sigma, \delta_D, q_{0D}, F_D); \qquad \text{[where subscript}_D\text{ stands for automaton DFA]}$$

Now, establish the correspondence between the tuples of both automatons, *i.e.*,

- **Q_D with Q_N:** The set Q_D contains the states that are in power set of Q_N. Thus, $Q_D \subseteq P(Q_N)$. Alternatively, states of the DFA have been selected from the set of possible states that contains a total number of states 2^{Q_N}.
- **q_{0N} with q_{0D}:** Assume both machine accelerate from same starting state hence, $\{q_{0D}\} = \{q_{0N}\}$, Let it be $\{q_0\}$
- Suppose x is the input string so compare the moves $\hat{\delta}_D(q_0, x)$ with $\hat{\delta}_N(q_0, x)$:

1. If string x is a null string ($\in$) then,

$$\hat{\delta}_N(q_0, \in) = q_0; \quad \text{and} \quad \hat{\delta}_D(q_0, \in) = q_0; \qquad \text{[using Ist property of } \delta\text{-head]}$$

Hence, both automatons return to same state.

2. For rest of the cases of x we shall prove by using method of induction. Suppose, string $x = a_1.a_2.a_3..........a_n \,.\, a$ $\qquad [\therefore \; |x| = (n+1)]$

Now we shall prove that the theorem is true for string length $(n + 1)$, hence through induction it is true for string length n also and finally theorem is true for any length of the string.

For that, break the string x into a symbol 'a' and the substring 'y', *i.e.*,

$$x = y.a, \text{ where } y = a_1.a_2.a_3 \ldots\ldots\ldots\, a_n \quad \text{and} \quad |y| = n$$

then,

$$\hat{\delta}_N(q_0, x) = \delta_N(\hat{\delta}_N(q_0, y), a);$$

$$= \delta_N(\{p_1, p_2, p_3 \ldots\ldots\ldots\, p_i\}, a); \qquad [\text{Assume } \hat{\delta}_N(q_0, y) = \{p_1, p_2, p_3, \ldots p_i\}]$$

$$= \bigcup_{k=1}^{i} (p_k, a) \qquad \ldots(1)$$

Now from DFA,

$$\delta_D(\{p_1, p_2, p_3 \ldots\ldots\ldots\, p_i\}, a) = \bigcup_{k=1}^{i} \delta_D\,(p_{k,a}) \qquad \ldots(2)$$

and

$$\{p_1, p_2, p_3 \ldots\ldots\ldots\, p_i\} \leftarrow \hat{\delta}_D(q_0, y);$$

Thus,

$$\hat{\delta}_D(q_0, x) = \delta_D(\hat{\delta}_D(q_0, y), a);$$

$$= \hat{\delta}_D(\{p_1, p_2, p_3 \ldots\ldots\ldots p_i\}, a);$$

$$\hat{\delta}_D(q_0, x) = \bigcup_{k=1}^{i} \delta_N\,(p_k, a) \qquad \ldots(3)$$

Compare the equations (1) and (3), we obtain,

$$\hat{\delta}_N(q_0, x) = \hat{\delta}_D(q_0, x);$$

Which contains at least one state is in F_N, *i.e.*, $F_N \subseteq F_D \subseteq Q$. Hence, theorem is true for string length $(n + 1)$. Therefore, theorem is true for string length n also and finally theorem is true for any length of the string.

Thus, proof of the theorem ends with the conclusion that language of a NFA can also be the language of some DFA. So, *if nondeterminism behavior from a NFA is removed then it behaves like a DFA.*

8.2 METHOD OF CONVERSION FROM NFA TO DFA

Consider an example of NFA N where N is given as,

$$N = (\{q_0, q_1, q_2, q_3\}, \{0, 1\}, \delta, q_0, \{q_3\})$$

where δ's are shown in the following transition table (TT) (Fig. 8.1).

States	Input symbols	
	0	1
→ $\{q_0\}$	$\{q_0, q_1\}$	$\{q_0\}$
$\{q_1\}$	Φ	$\{q_2\}$
$\{q_2\}$	$\{q_3\}$	Φ
● $\{q_3\}$	$\{q_3\}$	$\{q_3\}$

Fig. 8.1 TT_{NFA}.

Then construct an equivalent DFA D *i.e.*, $D = (Q_D, \Sigma, \delta_D, q_0, F_D)$ for the given NFA.

I. Since, $Q_D \subseteq P(Q)$ or power set of Q where $Q = \{q_0, q_1, q_2, q_3\}$, hence

$$P(Q) = [\Phi, \{q_0\}, \{q_1\},\{q_2\},\{q_3\},\{q_0, q_1\},\{q_0, q_2\},\{q_0, q_3\},\{q_1, q_2\}, \{q_1, q_3\},\{q_2, q_3\}, \{q_0, q_1, q_2\}, \{q_0, q_2, q_3\}, \{q_1, q_2, q_3\}, \{q_0, q_1, q_3\},\{q_0, q_1, q_2, q_3\}]$$

From the set of P(Q) we will select the states for Q_D that are used for the construction of an equivalent DFA. It is possible that some of the states in the P(Q) might not be accessible from starting state of DFA directly or indirectly, so leave those states. Remember that club of the states shown inside the braces represents a single state. Transition from this club of state over input symbols must be same the transitions from each states in the club over same input symbol. For example, state $\{q_0, q_1, q_2, q_3\}$ is a single state and the transitions from this state satisfies all transitions of each state q_0, q_1, q_2, q_3 over $\Sigma = \{0,1\}$.

II. Both automatons start from same state, hence start state of DFA, *i.e.*, $\{q_0\} = \{q_0\}$ of NFA.

III. From NFA we know the final set of states is F_N. Certainly, the final set of states of DFA is F_D ($\subseteq Q_D$) that should contains at least one state in common with F_N *i.e.*,

$$F_D \cap F_N \neq \Phi$$

III. Now compute transition functions δ_D for DFA over input alphabet Σ for set of states Q_D.

- Transition from the state Φ that is truly no state, over symbol 0 and 1 are nothing, so return state will be Φ.
- Next state in the set Q_D is $\{q_0\}$, so

$$\delta_D(q_0, 0) = \{q_0, q_1\} \text{ and } \delta_D(q_0, 1) = \{q_0\};$$

- Transition from states $\{q_1\}$, $\{q_2\}$, $\{q_3\}$ over symbol 0 and 1 are same as shown in TT *i.e.*,

$$\delta_D(q_1, 0) = \Phi \text{ and } \delta_D(q_1, 1) = \{q_2\};$$
$$\delta_D(q_2, 0) = \{q_3\} \text{ and } \delta_D(q_2, 1) = \Phi$$
$$\delta_D(q_3, 0) = \{q_3\} \text{ and } \delta_D(q_0, 1) = \{q_3\};$$

- Transitions from the state $\{q_0, q_1\}$ is obtain as,

$$\delta_D(\{q_0, q_1\}, 0) = \delta_N(q_0, 0) \cup \delta_N(q_1, 0)$$
$$= \{q_0, q_1\} \cup \Phi = \{q_0, q_1\};$$

and
$$\delta_D(\{q_0, q_1\}, 1) = \delta_N(q_0, 1) \cup \delta_N(q_1, 1)$$
$$= \{q_0\} \cup \{q_2\} = \{q_0, q_2\};$$

- Similarly, transitions from all other states of the set P(Q) over input alphabets is determine.
- For the final state $\{q_0, q_1, q_2, q_3\}$ δ_D will be,

$$\delta_D(\{q_0, q_1, q_2, q_3\}, 0) = \delta_N(q_0, 0) \cup \delta_N(q_1, 0) \cup \delta_N(q_2, 0) \cup \delta_N(q_3, 0)$$
$$= \{q_0, q_1\} \cup \Phi \cup \{q_3\} \cup \{q_3\}$$
$$= \{q_0, q_1, q_3\};$$

and
$$\delta_D(\{q_0, q_1, q_2, q_3\}, 1) = \delta_N(q_0, 1) \cup \delta_N(q_1, 1) \cup \delta_N(q_2, 1) \cup \delta_N(q_3, 1)$$
$$= \{q_0\} \cup \{q_2\} \cup \Phi \cup \{q_3\}$$
$$= \{q_0, q_2, q_3\};$$

Hence, we obtain the following transition Table (TT) for all possible states of DFA.

States	Input Symbols	
	0	1
Φ	Φ	Φ
→ $\{q_0\}$	$\{q_0, q_1\}$	$\{q_0\}$
$\{q_1\}$	Φ	$\{q_2\}$
$\{q_2\}$	$\{q_3\}$	Φ
● $\{q_3\}$	$\{q_3\}$	$\{q_3\}$
$\{q_0, q_1\}$	$\{q_0, q_1\}$	$\{q_0, q_2\}$
$\{q_0, q_2\}$	$\{q_0, q_1, q_3\}$	$\{q_0\}$
● $\{q_0, q_3\}$	$\{q_0, q_1, q_3\}$	$\{q_0, q_3\}$
$\{q_1, q_2\}$	$\{q_3\}$	$\{q_2\}$
● $\{q_1, q_3\}$	$\{q_3\}$	$\{q_2, q_3\}$
● $\{q_2, q_3\}$	$\{q_3\}$	$\{q_3\}$
$\{q_0, q_1, q_2\}$	$\{q_0, q_1, q_3\}$	$\{q_0, q_2, q_3\}$
● $\{q_0, q_2, q_3\}$	$\{q_0, q_1, q_3\}$	$\{q_0, q_3\}$
● $\{q_1, q_2, q_3\}$	$\{q_3\}$	$\{q_2, q_3\}$
● $\{q_0, q_1, q_3\}$	$\{q_0, q_1, q_3\}$	$\{q_0, q_2, q_3\}$
● $\{q_0, q_1, q_2, q_3\}$	$\{q_0, q_1, q_3\}$	$\{q_0, q_2, q_3\}$

Fig. 8.2. TT_{DFA}.

Note that all those states that contain $\{q_3\}$ as a state are considered as final states, these states we marked with small circle along with the starting state $\{q_0\}$ which is marked with an arrow.

Now, follow the procedure to construct the actual DFA from the TT_{DFA} entries.

```
begin
        from starting state
        repeat
            find new reachable state
        until (while not found new reachable state)
end.
```

Applying the procedure we obtain a chain of reachable states from the starting state.

- From initial state $\{q_0\}$, only reachable state are $\{q_0, q_1\}$ and $\{q_0\}$ over input symbol 0 and 1 respectively. These are new reachable states so find next transitions from these states.
- From state $\{q_0, q_1\}$ reachable states are $\{q_0, q_1\}$ and $\{q_0, q_2\}$ on symbol 0 and 1. Since state $\{q_0,q_1\}$ repeat itself so find next transitions from new reachable state $\{q_0,q_2\}$.

- From state $\{q_0, q_2\}$ next reachable states are $\{q_0, q_1, q_3\}$ and $\{q_0\}$ on symbol 0 and 1. Among them $\{q_0, q_1, q_3\}$ state is the new reachable state hence find transitions from state $\{q_0, q_1, q_3\}$ only.
- From state $\{q_0, q_1, q_3\}$ next reachable states are $\{q_0, q_1, q_3\}$ and $\{q_0, q_2, q_3\}$ on symbol 0 and 1. From them $\{q_0, q_2, q_3\}$ is the new reachable state.
- From state $\{q_0, q_2, q_3\}$ next reachable states are $\{q_0, q_1, q_3\}$ and $\{q_0, q_3\}$ on symbol 0 and 1, where $\{q_0, q_3\}$ is only the new reachable state.
- From state $\{q_0, q_3\}$ next reachable states are repeated states $\{q_0, q_1, q_3\}$ and $\{q_0, q_3\}$. Hence, procedure stops.

Hence, we obtain a DFA M which is shown in Fig. 8.3.

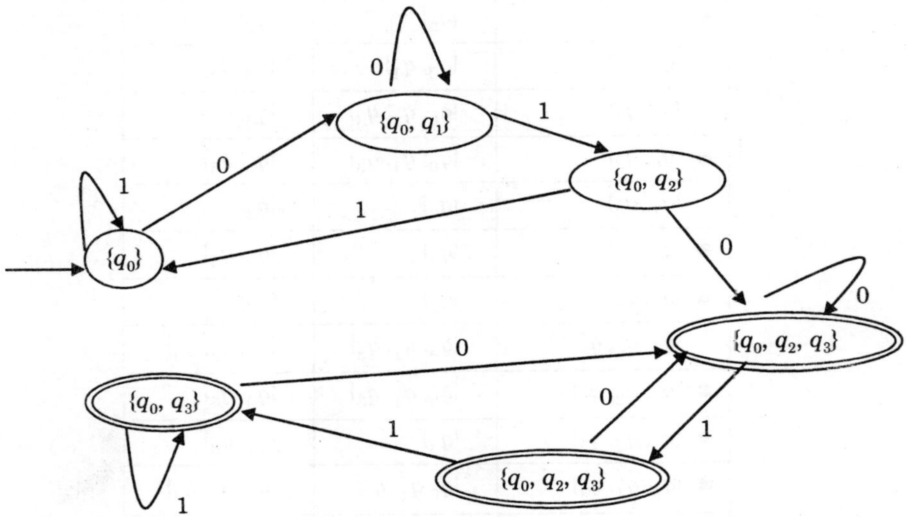

Fig. 8.3 M.

From DFA state diagram we find that there is one and only one transition defined from each state over each input symbol hence, finite automaton is deterministic finite automaton.

Example 8.1. *Construct a DFA from given NFA $N = (\{q_0, q_1, q_2, q_3\}, \{0, 1\}, \delta, \{q_0\}, \{q_1, q_3\})$, where transition functions δ are shown in the state diagram in Fig. 8.4.*

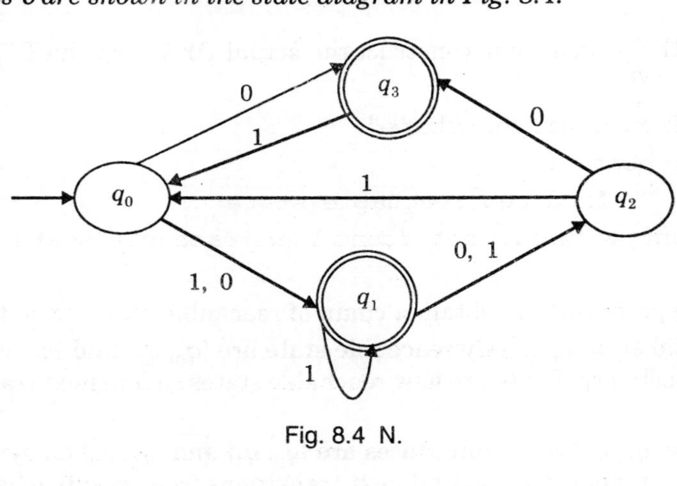

Fig. 8.4 N.

Sol. Let DFA be M, where M = $\{Q_D, \Sigma, \delta_D, \{q_{0D}\}, F_D\}$. Now determine the tuples of M from known tuples of N, as

States	Input Symbols	
	0	1
Φ	Φ	Φ
→ $\{q_0\}$	$\{q_1, q_3\}$	$\{q_1\}$
● $\{q_1\}$	$\{q_2\}$	$\{q_1, q_2\}$
$\{q_2\}$	$\{q_3\}$	$\{q_0\}$
● $\{q_3\}$	Φ	$\{q_3\}$
● $\{q_0, q_1\}$	$\{q_0, q_3, q_2\}$	$\{q_1, q_2\}$
$\{q_0, q_2\}$	$\{q_0, q_3\}$	$\{q_0, q_2\}$
● $\{q_0, q_3\}$	$\{q_1, q_3\}$	$\{q_0, q_1\}$
● $\{q_1, q_2\}$	$\{q_2, q_3\}$	$\{q_0, q_1, q_2\}$
● $\{q_1, q_3\}$	$\{q_2\}$	$\{q_0, q_1, q_2\}$
● $\{q_2, q_3\}$	$\{q_3\}$	$\{q_0\}$
● $\{q_0, q_1, q_2\}$	$\{q_1, q_2, q_3\}$	$\{q_1, q_2\}$
● $\{q_0, q_2, q_3\}$	$\{q_1, q_3\}$	$\{q_0, q_1, q_2\}$
● $\{q_1, q_2, q_3\}$	$\{q_2, q_3\}$	$\{q_0, q_1, q_2\}$
● $\{q_0, q_1, q_3\}$	$\{q_2, q_3\}$	$\{q_0, q_1, q_2\}$
● $\{q_0, q_1, q_2, q_3\}$	$\{q_1, q_2, q_3\}$	$\{q_0, q_1, q_2\}$

Fig. 8.5 TT.

- Now, $Q_D \subseteq P(Q_{NFA})$ or power set of states of NFA. Since $Q_{NFA} = \{q_0, q_1, q_2, q_3\}$ hence selection for Q_D from the set that contains 16 states including state Φ that are shown in first column of TT (Fig. 8.4).
- Set of input symbol $\Sigma = \{0, 1\}$.
- Initial state of NFA is also the initial state of DFA, *i.e.*, $\{q_{0D}\} = \{q_0\}$.
- $F_D \subseteq Q_D$ *i.e.*, $F_D \cap F_N \neq \Phi$.
- Now compute the transition functions δ_D over input symbols 0 and 1.
  Since, all those states that contain either $\{q_1\}$ or $\{q_3\}$ are considered as final state/s of DFA. So, mark those states with small circle. Now scan the TT from starting state $\{q_0\}$.
- Only reachable states from initial state are $\{q_1, q_3\}$ and $\{q_1\}$ over the input symbols 0 and 1. Hence, find the next transitions from these states only.
- From state $\{q_1, q_3\}$ the reachable states are $\{q_2\}$ and $\{q_0, q_1, q_2\}$ and from state $\{q_1\}$ the only new reachable state is $\{q_1, q_2\}$.

- Reachable states from $\{q_2\}$ are : $\{\mathbf{q_3}\}$ and $\{q_0\}$ that was earlier visited.
- Reachable states from $\{q_0,q_1,q_2\}$: $\{\mathbf{q_1, q_2, q_3}\}$ and $\{\mathbf{q_1, q_2}\}$
- Reachable states from $\{q_1,q_2\}$: $\{\mathbf{q_2, q_3}\}$ and $\{q_0,q_1,q_2\}$ a repeated state.

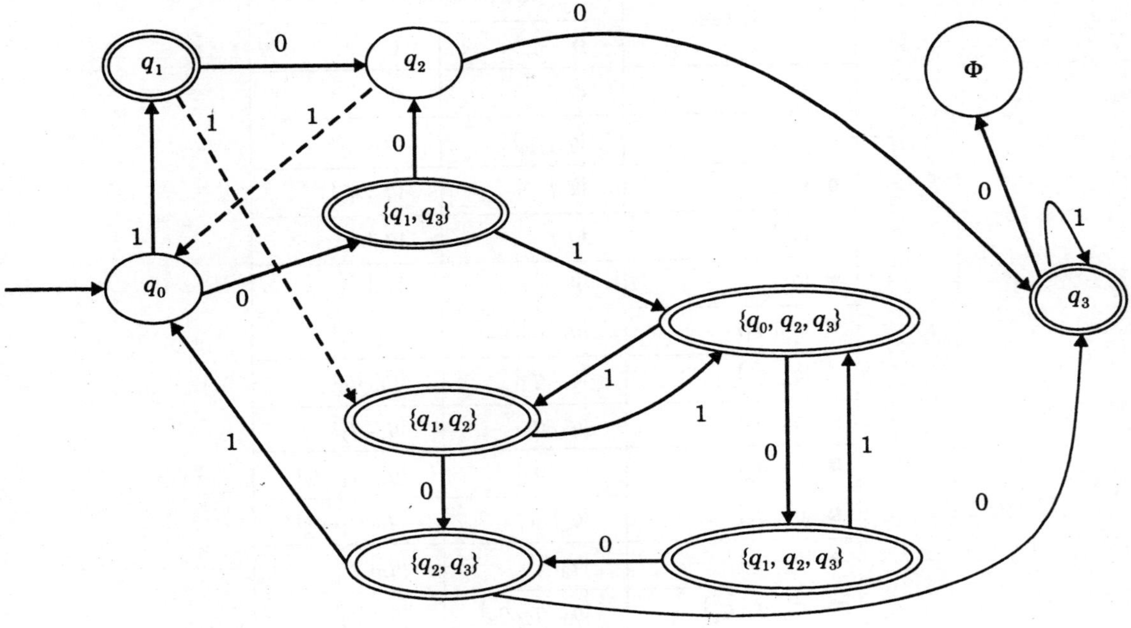

Fig. 8.6. M

For next state transitions take only new reachable state.

- Reachable states from $\{q_3\}$ are : **Φ** and $\{q_3\}$ which is a repeated state.
- Reachable states from $\{q_1, q_2, q_3\}$: $\{q_2, q_3\}$ a repeated state **and** $\{\mathbf{q_0, q_1, q_2}\}$
- Reachable states from $\{q_2, q_3\}$: $\{q_3\}$ and $\{q_0\}$ both are repeated state.
- Reachable states from $\{q_0, q_1, q_2\}$ are: $\{q_1, q_2,q_3\}$ and $\{q_1,q_2\}$ both are repeated state.
- Further, no new reachable state found hence process stop.

Thus, Fig. 8.6 shows the state diagram of final DFA.

8.3. FINITE AUTOMATA WITH ∈ MOVES

We have seen so far that a finite automaton of either deterministic or nondeterministic which changes their state transitions only over known input symbols. Experience shows that there might be a need of state transitions over no input symbol. It means, there are few states in the finite automaton such that it skips between these states without consumption of any input symbol. For this purpose, we introduce a new symbol epsilon (∈) that has a dimension and of zero length, which is also called a *null string.*

Now we will discuss the nature of finite automata specifically, over null string (∈). Since automata changes their state/s over null string so these transitions occurs over no symbol. In other words, ***automata skip between states spontaneously***. For example, automata is in state $\{q\}$ and its state changes to $\{q\}$ over symbol ∈.

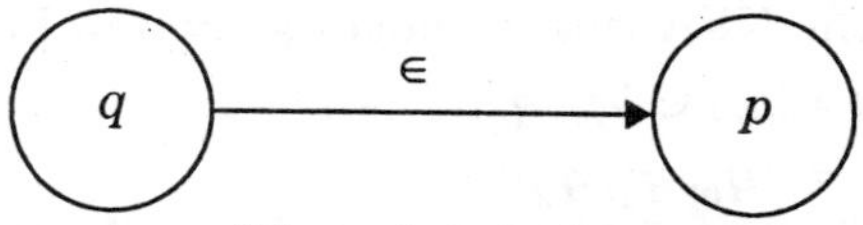

So it shows a spontaneous transition of state from state q to state p known as $\in$-transition. This characteristic provides additional flexibility to the finite automaton. Hence, a finite automaton with $\in$ moves is more powerful than either from Nondeterministic or deterministic finite automata.

8.3.1 Non Deterministic Finite Automata (NFA) with $\in$ moves

A non deterministic finite automaton with $\in$-moves is an extension of NFA. When some of the transitions in the NFA are $\in$-transitions such that, there are few transition/s of NFA are defined over null string then NFA is called NFA with $\in$-moves. It provides additional flexibility to the NFA so that automaton skips between states spontaneously. Let $N_\in$ be an NFA with-$\in$ moves, whose tuples definition is given as,

$$N_\in = (Q, \Sigma, \delta_\in, \{q_0\}, F)$$

where Q, Σ, $\{q_0\}$ and F holds similar meaning as an NFA and the transition function δ is defined as follows,

$$\delta_\in : Q \times (\Sigma \cup \{\in\}) \to P(Q)$$

where, $\delta_\in$ is the partial mapping of a state with an input symbol including $\in$ that returns to the state that are in the power set of Q. As we said earlier, the transitions over $\in$ are also known as $\in$- *transitions*.

For example, a NFA with $\in$-moves is shown in Fig. 8.7 where set of states $Q = \{q_1, q_2, q_3\}$ and set of alphabet $\Sigma = \{0, 1, 2\}$. The transition functions are shown in the TT Fig. 8.8.

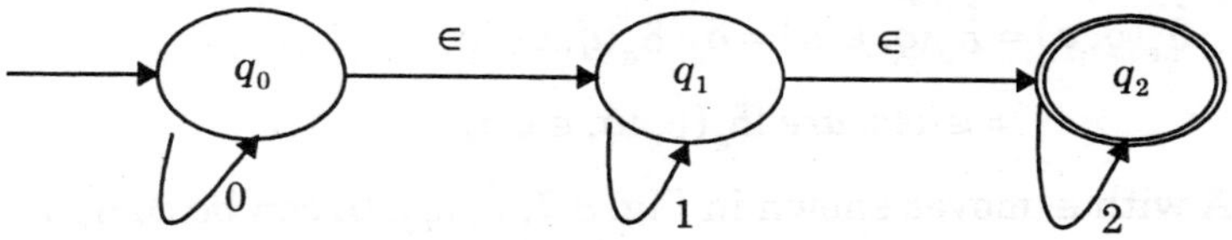

Fig. 8.7 NFA with $\in$-moves.

States	Input symbols			
	$\in$	0	1	2
→ q_0	q_1	q_0	Φ	Φ
q_1	q_2	Φ	q_1	Φ
● q_2	Φ	Φ	Φ	q_2

Fig 8.8 ($TT_{NFA\text{-}\in\ moves}$)

8.3.2 $\delta_\in$-head

As we discussed previously that transition function $\delta_\in$ gives the behavior of a 'NFA with $\in$-moves' over a single symbol including a null string ($\in$). Whereas, $\delta_\in$-head shows the nature of NFA with $\in$-moves over a string. We will now discuss the role of $\delta_\in$-head over various possible strings, *i.e.*,

- If string is a null string ($\in$) then,

  $\delta_\in^\wedge(q, \in) = \{q\} \cup$ {Set of all those states that can be reached from state q directly or indirectly along any path whose transition/s are $\in$-transition/s}

which is also called as $\in$-*closure* (q);

For example, consider the NFA with $\in$-moves shown in Fig. 8.7 so we can find,

$$\in\text{-}closure\ (q_0) = \{q_0\} \cup \{q_1, q_2\}$$
$$= \{\mathbf{q_0, q_1, q_2}\};$$

Similarly, $\in\text{-}closure\ (q_1) = \{q_1\} \cup \{q_2\}$
$$= \{\mathbf{q_1, q_2}\};$$

and, $\in\text{-}closure\ (q_2) = \{q_2\} \cup \Phi$
$$= \{\mathbf{q_2}\};$$

- Assume a string x *i.e.*, $x \neq \in$, then further assume that string x is form by a substring 'y' and a symbol 'a', *i.e.*, $x = y \,.\, a$, then

$$\hat{\delta}_{\in}(q, x) = \hat{\delta}_{\in}(q, y \,.\, a) = \delta_{\in}(\hat{\delta}_{\in}(q, y), a);$$

or, $$\hat{\delta}_{\in}(q, x) = \in\text{-}closure\ [\delta_{\in}(\hat{\delta}_{\in}(q, y), a)]^{\dagger}; \quad ...(1)$$

Thus, in general if P is the set of states, then

$$\in\text{-}closure\ \mathbf{(P)} = \bigcup_{\forall q \in P} \in\textbf{-closure (q)} \quad ...(2)$$

If string contains a single symbol 'a', then

$$\delta_{\in}\ (P, a) = \bigcup_{\forall q \in p} \delta_{\in}(q, a);$$

Similarly for a string x,

$$\delta_{\in}(P, x) = \bigcup_{\forall q \in P} \hat{\delta}_{\in}(q, x);$$

If string contains a single symbol 'a' then,

$$\hat{\delta}_{\in}(q, a) = \hat{\delta}_{\in}(q, \in .a) = \delta_{\in}(\hat{\delta}_{\in}(q, \in), a)$$
$$= \in\text{-}closure\ [\delta_{\in}(\hat{\delta}_{\in}(q, \in), a]; \quad ...(3)$$

For the NFA with $\in$-moves shown in Fig. 8.7, $\hat{\delta}_{\in}(q_0, 0)$ can be computed as follows,

$$\delta_{\in}{}^{\wedge}(q_0, 0) = \delta_{\in}{}^{\wedge}(q_0, \in .0)$$
$$= \delta_{\in}(\delta_{\in}{}^{\wedge}(q_0, \in), 0)$$
$$= \in\text{-}closure\ [\delta_{\in}(\{q_0, q_1, q_2\}, 0)]$$
$$= \in\text{-}closure\ [\delta_{\in}(q_0, 0) \cup \delta_{\in}\ (q_1, 0) \cup \delta_{\in}(q_2, 0)]$$
$$= \in\text{-}closure\ [\{q_0\} \cup \Phi \cup \Phi]$$
$$= \in\text{-}closure\ [\{q_0\}]$$
$$= \{\mathbf{q_0, q_1, q_2}\}; \quad \text{[computed previously]}$$

Note. *If we compare the result obtained by* $\delta_{\in}$ *and* $\hat{\delta}_{\in}$ *on same symbol we find that,* $\delta_{\in}(q_0, 0) = \{q_0\}$ *and* $\hat{\delta}_{\in}(q_0, 0) = \{q_0, q_1, q_2\}$ *so both are different. Hence, we conclude that,* $\delta_{\in}(q_0, 0) \neq \hat{\delta}_{\in}(q_0, 0)$.

---

† Assume that, $\hat{\delta}_{\in}(q, y) = \{p_1, p_2, ...p_k\}$ ∪ paths that may end with one or more $\in$-transition/s from p_i (for $i = 1$ to k)

let, $$\bigcup_{\forall i = 1}^{k} \delta_{\in}\ (p_i, a) = \{r_1, r_2, ...r_m\} \cup \text{ \{those states that can reach from } r_j \text{ by } \in\text{-transition\}}$$

then, $$\hat{\delta}_{\in}\ (q, x) = \bigcup_{\forall j = 1}^{m} \in -closure\ (r_j)$$

Hence, $$\hat{\delta}_{\in}(q, x) = \in\text{-closure } [\delta_{\in}\ (\hat{\delta}_{\in}(q, y), a]$$

Similarly we can compute $\hat{\delta}(q_0, 1)$ as,

$$\begin{aligned}\hat{\delta}_\in(q_0, 1) &= \hat{\delta}_\in(q_0, \in . 1)\\ &= \delta_\in(\hat{\delta}_\in(q_0, \in), 1)\\ &= \in\text{-}closure\ [\delta_\in(\{q_0, q_1, q_2\}, 1)]\\ &= \in\text{-}closure\ [\delta_\in(q_0, 1) \cup \delta_\in(q_1, 1) \cup \delta_\in(q_2, 1)]\\ &= \in\text{-}closure\ [\Phi \cup \{q_1\} \cup \Phi]\\ &= \in\text{-}closure\ [\{q_1\}]\\ &= \{\mathbf{q_1}, \mathbf{q_2}\}; \qquad \text{[computed as previously]}\end{aligned}$$

8.3.3 Language of NFA with ∈-moves

In the previous section we have defined so far the nature of an NFA with ∈-moves over an arbitrary string. Collection of all those strings over which 'NFA with ∈-moves' reaches to its final state will be in its language set. Let $L_{N\in}$ denotes the language of 'NFA with ∈-moves', where $L_{N\in}$ is defined as,

$$L_{N_\in} = \{x/x \in \Sigma^* \quad \text{and} \quad \hat{\delta}_\in(q_0, x) \cap F \neq \Phi\}$$

Alternatively for an string x, which is formed over alphabet Σ will be in the language such that while accepting the string x automaton is in the ∈-closure of state/s returned by $\hat{\delta}_\in$ whose intersection with the set of final states F will not be empty. Alternatively, $\hat{\delta}_\in$-head over x returns at least one accepting state that is in final set of state F.

8.3.4 Method of Conversion from NFA with ∈-moves to NFA

Theorem 8.2. *If $N_\in$ be a NFA with ∈-moves, then there exists a NFA N (without ∈-moves) i.e.,*

$L_{N\in} = L_N$ (where $L_{N\in}$ is the language of $N_\in$ and L_N is the language of N)

Proof. Alternatively theorem states that, language of an NFA with ∈-moves is also the language of an NFA without ∈-moves. To prove this statement let $N_\in$ is defined as,

$$N_\in = (Q_\in, \Sigma, \delta_\in, \{q_0\}_\in, F_\in).$$

So, our objective is to construct an equivalent NFA N = (Q, Σ, δ, $\{q_0\}$, F) from the known $N_\in$ such that,

- $Q = Q_\in$, both automatons operate on same set of states.
- $\{q_0\} = \{q_0\}_\in$, both automatons start operational on same state.
- $F = F_\in$, set of all final state/s of NFA with ∈-moves must also be the final state/s of NFA †.
- Both automatons operate on same set of alphabets that is Σ.
- Now we find the relationship between transition function $\delta_\in$ and δ over Σ.

Consider the same $N_\in$ that is shown in Fig. 8.7, here $Q_\in = \{q_0, q_1, q_2\}$, Σ = {0, 1, 2}, $F_\in = \{q_2\}$ and δ is given as follows:

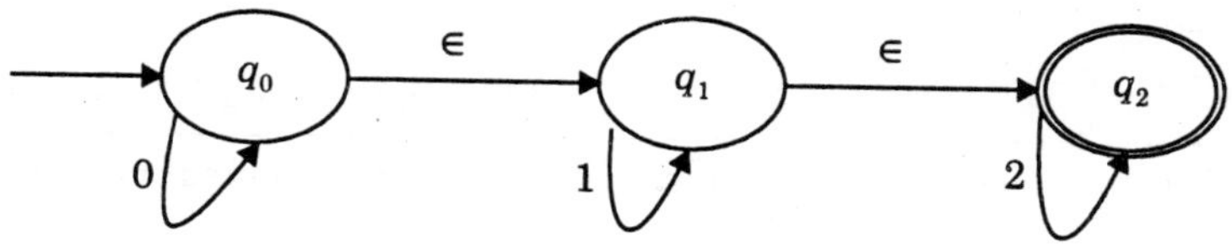

† *F contains FU $\{q_0\}$ if ∈-closure (q_0) return a state from set $F_\in$ otherwise $F = F_\in$.*

The definition of transition functions δ for NFA (over each symbol of Σ) cover all the definition of transition functions $\delta_\in$ for NFA with $\in$-moves including $\in$-transition/s. Since, $\in$-transition/s can not be the part of δ for NFA; hence all $\in$-transition/s arcs can be replaced by either of the symbol of Σ. This is because, the flexibility of spontaneous skip between $\in$-transition states over no symbol ($\in$)†. For example,

$$\begin{aligned}
\hat{\delta}_\in(q_0, 0) &= \hat{\delta}_\in(q_0, 0.\in) \\
&= \delta_\in(\delta_\in{}^\wedge(q_0, \in), 1) \\
&= \in\textit{-closure } [\delta_\in{}^\wedge(\{q_0, q_1, q_2\}, 0)]; \qquad \text{[applies } \in\text{-closure pop.]} \\
&= \in\textit{-closure } [\delta_\in(q_0 -, 0) \cup \delta_\in(q_1, 0) \cup \delta_\in(q_2, 0)] \\
&= \in\textit{-closure } [\{q_0\} \cup \Phi \cup \Phi] \\
&= \in\textit{-closure } [\{q_0\}] \qquad \text{[computed previously]} \\
&= \{\boldsymbol{q_0, q_1, q_2}\};
\end{aligned}$$

Hence, we say that on symbol 0 the state of the automaton will be either $\{\boldsymbol{q_0}\}$ or $\{\boldsymbol{q_1}\}$ or $\{\boldsymbol{q_2}\}$. That is the requirement of the NFA. So, transition function δ for NFA is given as,

$$\delta(q_0, 0) = \hat{\delta}_\in(q_0, 0).$$

In general for any input symbol $a \in \Sigma$, we have

$$\boldsymbol{\delta(q_0, a) = \hat{\delta}_\in(q_0, a)}$$

It states that the behavior of both automatons $N_\in$ and N are same on same input symbol. Hence, It concludes that in general if $L_{N\in}$ is the language of a $N_\in$ then language of a NFA N is also L_N *i.e.*,

$$L_N = L_{N\in}$$

Hence, $\delta(q_0, 0) = \hat{\delta}_\in(q_0, 0) = \{q_0, q_1, q_2\}$;

Similarly $\delta(q_0, 1) = \hat{\delta}_\in(q_0, 1) = \{q_1, q_2\}$;

$\delta(q_0, 2) = \hat{\delta}_\in(q_0, 2) = \{q_2\}$; and so on.

Therefore, the TT for NFA will be looks like, (Fig. 8.9)

State	Input symbol		
	0	0	2
→ q_0	$\{q_0, q_1, q_2\}$	$\{q_1, q_2\}$	$\{q_2\}$
q_1	Φ	$\{q_1, q_2\}$	$\{q_2\}$
● q_2	Φ	Φ	$\{q_2\}$

Fig. 8.9 TT_{NFA}.

† *It explains how to remove* $\in$*-transition/s from 'NFA with* $\in$*-moves' so that it converts to NFA (without* $\in$*-moves).*

And the transition diagram for NFA is shown in Fig. 8.10.

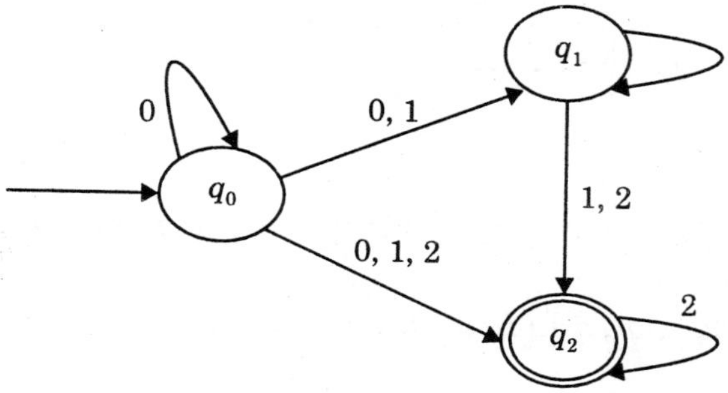

Fig. 8.10

8.3.5 Equivalence of 'NFA with ∈-moves' to DFA

We have seen that automaton 'NFA with ∈-moves' is an extension of an NFA (in terms of flexibility). Since, in the previous section, theorem 8.2 we have proved the equivalence between NFA with ∈-moves and NFA and the theorem 8.1 proves the equivalence between NFA and DFA. Therefore, it concludes that, there exists an equivalence between NFA with ∈-moves and the DFA a static nature of finite automata. This equivalence is shown in Fig. 8.11.

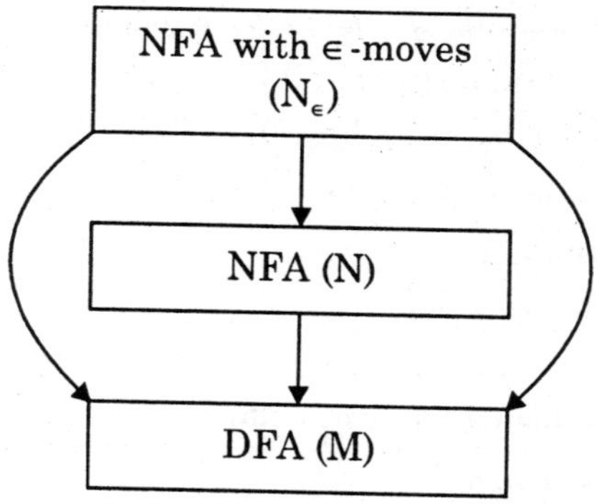

Fig. 8.11

Let $N_\in = (Q_\in, \Sigma, \delta_\in, \{q_0\}_\in, F_\in)$, then construct an equivalent DFA M where M is defined as,

$$M = (Q, \Sigma, \delta, \{q_0\}, F).$$

Now the relationship between corresponding tuples are as follows,

- $Q \subseteq P(Q_\in)$.
- Both automatons operate on same set of alphabet Σ.
- Starting state of DFA which is $\{q_0\} = \in\text{-closure}\{q_0\}_\in$. So, starting state of DFA will be the set of state containing state $\{q_0\}_\in$.
- Set of final state $F \subseteq Q$, *i.e.* $F \cap F_\in \neq \Phi$.
- Now we compute the transition functions δ for DFA over input symbol a (for $\forall\, a \in \Sigma$) as,

$$\text{Let } R = \{q_1, q_2, \ldots\ldots\ldots\ldots q_i\} \quad \text{and} \quad \bigcup_{\forall j=1}^{i} \delta(q_j, a) = \{p_1, p_2, \ldots\ldots p_k\}$$

Then, $\delta(R, a) = \cup \in\text{-closure}(\{p_1, p_2, \ldots\ldots\ldots p_k\})$

Let us solve one example so that method will become more clear.

Example 8.2. *Construct a DFA from given NFA (as shown in Fig. 8.7)*

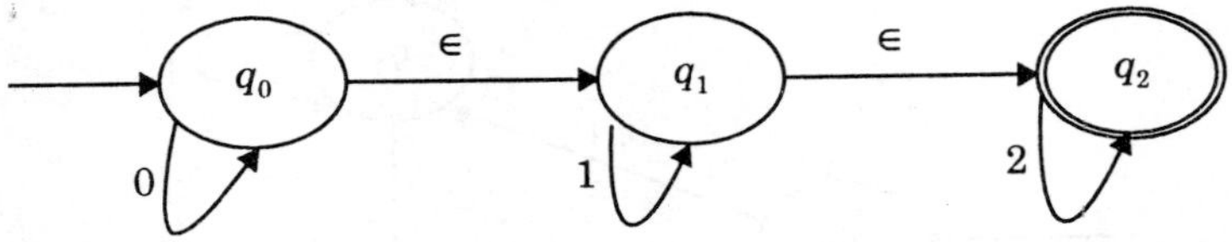

Sol. For the given NFA with ∈-moves we assume that equivalent DFA M = (Q, Σ, δ, $\{q_0\}$, F) whose tuples are determine as,

- $Q \subseteq [\Phi, \{q_0\}, \{q_1\},\{q_2\},\{q_0, q_1\},\{q_0, q_2\},\{q_1, q_2\}, \{q_0, q_1, q_2\}]$ which is a power set of $Q_\in$.
- $\Sigma = \{0, 1, 2\}$.
- Starting state of DFA is $\{q_0\}$ where, $\{q_0\}$ = ∈-closure $(q_0) = \{q_0, q_1, q_2\}$.
- All states of the set Q that contains $\{q_2\}$ as one of the state are considered as final state/s.
- The transition functions of DFA are determine as follows,

Since starting state is $\{q_0, q_1, q_2\}$ hence,

$\delta(\{q_0, q_1, q_2\}, 0) = \delta(\delta^\wedge(\{q_0, q_1, q_2\}, \in), 0)$

= ∈-closure $[\delta_\in(\delta_\in{}^\wedge(q_0, \in) \cup \delta^\wedge(q_1, \in)\delta^\wedge(q_2, \in)), 0\}]$

= ∈-closure $[\delta((\{q_0, q_1, q_2\} \cup \{q_1, q_2\} \cup \{q_2\}), 0)]$ [using ∈-closure property]

= ∈-closure $[\delta(\{q_0, q_1, q_2\}, 0)]$

= ∈-closure $[\delta(q_0, 0) \cup \delta(q_1, 0) \cup \delta(q_2, 0)]$

= ∈-closure $[q_0 \cup \Phi \cup \Phi]$ [from state diagram]

= ∈-closure$[q_0]$

= $\{\boldsymbol{q_0, q_1, q_2}\} \equiv$ A (let) [A repeated state]

and $\delta(\{q_0, q_1, q_2\}, 1)$ = ∈-closure $[\delta(q_0, 1) \cup \delta(q_1, 1) \cup \delta(q_2, 1)]$

= ∈-closure $[\Phi \cup q_1 \cup \Phi]$

= ∈-closure $[q_1]$

= $\{\boldsymbol{q_1, q_2}\} \equiv$ B (let)

$\delta(\{q_0, q_1, q_2\}, 2)$ = ∈-closure $[\delta(q_0, 2) \cup \delta(q_1, 2) \cup \delta(q_2, 2)]$

= ∈-closure $[\Phi \cup \Phi \cup q_2]$

= ∈-closure $[q_2]$

= $\{\boldsymbol{q_2}\} \equiv$ C (let)

Now compute transitions from new state $\{q_1, q_2\}$ and $\{q_2\}$ as,

$\delta(\{q_1, q_2\}, 0) = \delta(\delta^\wedge(\{q_1, q_2\}, \in), 0)$

= ∈-closure $[\delta(\delta^\wedge(q_1, \in) \cup \delta^\wedge(q_2, \in)), 0\}]$

= ∈-closure $[\delta((\{q_1, q_2\} \cup \{q_2\}), 0)]$

= ∈-closure $[\delta(\{q_1, q_2\}, 0)]$

= ∈-closure $[\delta(q_1, 0) \cup \delta(q_2, 0)]$

= ∈-closure $[\Phi \cup \Phi]$

= Φ

$$\delta(\{q_1, q_2\}, 1) = \in\text{-closure } [\delta(\{q_1, q_2\}, 1)]$$
$$= \in\text{-closure } [\delta(q_1, 1) \cup \delta(q_2, 1)]$$
$$= \in\text{-closure } [q_1 \cup \Phi]$$
$$= \in\text{-closure } [q_1]$$
$$= \{\mathbf{q_1, q_2}\} \equiv \text{B}$$ [A repeated state]

$$\delta(\{q_1, q_2\}, 2) = \in\text{-closure } [\delta(\{q_1, q_2\}, 2)]$$
$$= \in\text{-closure } [\delta(q_1, 2) \cup \delta(q_2, 2)]$$
$$= \in\text{-closure } [\Phi \cup q_2]$$
$$= \in\text{-closure } [q_2]$$
$$= \{\mathbf{q_2}\} \equiv \text{C}$$ [A repeated state]

Now compute transitions from the state $\{q_2\}$.

$$\delta(q_2, 0) = \delta(\hat{\delta}(q_2, \in), 0)$$
$$= \in\text{-closure } [\delta(\{q_2\}, 0)]$$
$$= \in\text{-closure } [\Phi]$$
$$= \Phi;$$

$$\delta(q_2, 1) = \delta(\delta\text{^}(q_2, \in), 1)$$
$$= \in\text{-closure } [\delta(\{q_2\}, 1)]$$
$$= \in\text{-closure}[\Phi]$$
$$= \mathbf{\Phi;}$$

$$\delta(q_2, 2) = \delta(\delta\text{^}(q_2, \in), 2)$$
$$= \in\text{-closure } [\delta(\{q_2\}, 2)]$$
$$= \in\text{-closure } [q_2]$$
$$= \{\mathbf{q_2}\} \equiv \text{C}$$ [A repeated state]

Further we haven't got any new state so procedure stops and we obtain the transition diagram of DFA that is shown in Fig. 8.12.

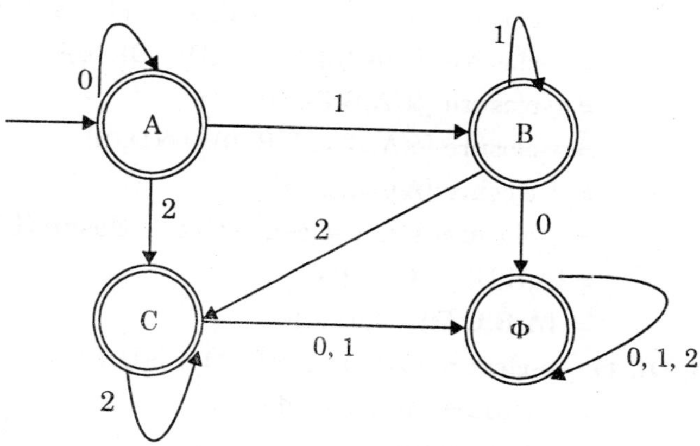

Fig. 8.12 DFA M.

Example 8.3. *Construct an equivalent DFA for given NFA with ∈-moves (Fig. 8.13).*

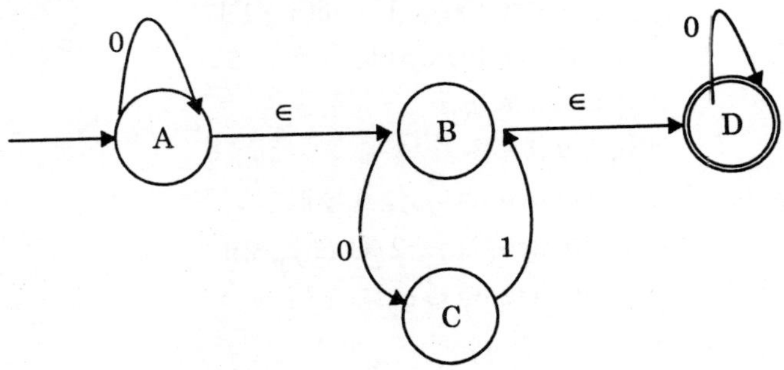

Fig. 8.13

Sol. Let equivalent DFA M = (Q, Σ, δ, $\{q_0\}$, F). So the tuples of M are obtain according as,

- Q ⊆ [Φ, {A}, {B}, {C}, {D}, {AB}, {AC}, AD}, {BC}, {BD}, {CD}, {ABC}, {ABD}, {BCD}, {ACD}, {ABCD}] which is a power set of $Q_{\in}$.
- Σ = {0, 1}.
- Starting state of DFA is the ∈-closure (A) which is equal to {A, B, D}.
- All states of the set Q that contain {D} as one of the state are considered as final states of DFA.
- Transition functions of DFA are as follows:

Find the ∈-closure of all the states, *i.e.*, {A}, {B}, {C}, and {D}, i.e.,

∈-closure (A) = {A, B, D};

∈-closure (B) = {B, D};

∈-closure (C) = {C};

∈-closure (D) = {D};

Since, Starting state is {A, B, D}; so find δ over Σ from this state onwards,

$$
\begin{aligned}
\delta(\{\mathbf{A, B, D}\}, \mathbf{0}) &= \delta(\{A, B, D\}, \in .0)) \\
&= \in\text{-closure } [\delta(\hat{\delta}(A, \in) \cup \hat{\delta}(B, \in) \cup \hat{\delta}(D, \in)),\ 0\}] \\
&= \in\text{-closure } [\delta(\ \{A,B,D\} \cup\ \{B,D\}\ \ \{D\}),\ 0)] \\
&= \in\text{-closure } [\delta(\{A,B,D\}, 0)\ ] \\
&= \in\text{-closure } [\delta(A, 0) \cup \delta(B, 0) \cup \delta(D,0)] \\
&= \in\text{-closure } [A \cup C \cup D] \\
&= \in\text{-closure}(A) \cup \in\text{-closure}(C) \in \in\text{-closure}(D) \\
&= \{A,B,D\} \cup \{C\} \cup \{D\} \\
&= \mathbf{\{A,B,C,D\}};\ \textit{new state} \\
\delta(\{\mathbf{A, B, D}\}, \mathbf{1}) &= \in\text{-closure } [\delta(A, 1) \cup \delta(B, 1) \cup \delta(D,1)] \\
&= \in\text{-closure } [\Phi \cup \Phi \cup\ \Phi] \\
&= \in\text{-closure } (\Phi) \\
&= \Phi;
\end{aligned}
$$

$\delta(\{\mathbf{A, B, C, D}\}, \mathbf{0})$ = ∈-closure [δ({A,B,C,D}, 0)]
= ∈-closure [δ(A, 0) ∪ δ(B, 0) ∪ δ(C, 0) ∪ δ(D, 0)]
= ∈-closure [A ∪ C ∪ Φ ∪ D]
= ∈-closure (A) ∪ ∈-closure(C) ∪ ∈-closure (D)
= {A, B, D} ∪ {C} ∪ {D}
= **{A, B, C, D}**; *a repeated state*

$\delta(\{\mathbf{A, B, C, D}\}, \mathbf{1})$ = ∈-closure[δ({A,B,C,D}, 1)]
= ∈-closure [δ(A, 1) ∪ δ(B, 1) ∪ δ(C, 1) ∪ δ(D, 1)]
= ∈-closure [Φ ∪ Φ ∪ B ∪ Φ]
= ∈-closure (B)
= **{B, D}**; *a new state*

$\delta((\mathbf{B, D}), \mathbf{0})$ = ∈-closure [δ({B, D}, 0)]
= ∈-closure [δ(B, 0) ∪ δ(D, 0)]
= ∈-closure [C ∪ D]
= ∈-closure (C) ∈-closure (D)
= **{C, D}**; *a new state*

$\delta((\mathbf{B, D}), \mathbf{1})$ = ∈-closure [δ({B, D}, 1)]
= ∈-closure [δ(B, 1) ∪ δ(D, 1)]
= ∈-closure [Φ ∪ Φ]
= ∈-closure (Φ)
= Φ;

$\delta((\mathbf{C, D}), \mathbf{0})$ = ∈-closure [δ({C, D}, 0)]
= ∈-closure [δ(C, 0) ∪ δ(D, 0)]
= ∈-closure [Φ ∪ D]
= ∈-closure (D)
= **{D}**; *a new state*

$\delta((\mathbf{C, D}), \mathbf{1}$ = ∈-closure [δ{C, D}, 1)]
= ∈-closure [δ(C, 1) ∪ δ(D, 1)]
= ∈-closure [B ∪ Φ]
= ∈-closure (B)
= **{B,D}**; *repeated state*

$\delta(\mathbf{D}, \mathbf{0})$ = ∈-closure [δ(D, 0)]
= ∈-closure [D]
= **{D}**; *a new state*

$\delta(\mathbf{D}, \mathbf{1})$ = ∈-closure [δ(D, 1)]
= ∈-closure [Φ]
= Φ;

Further there is no new state generated so we stop the process and finally we obtain the DFA shown in Fig. 8.14.

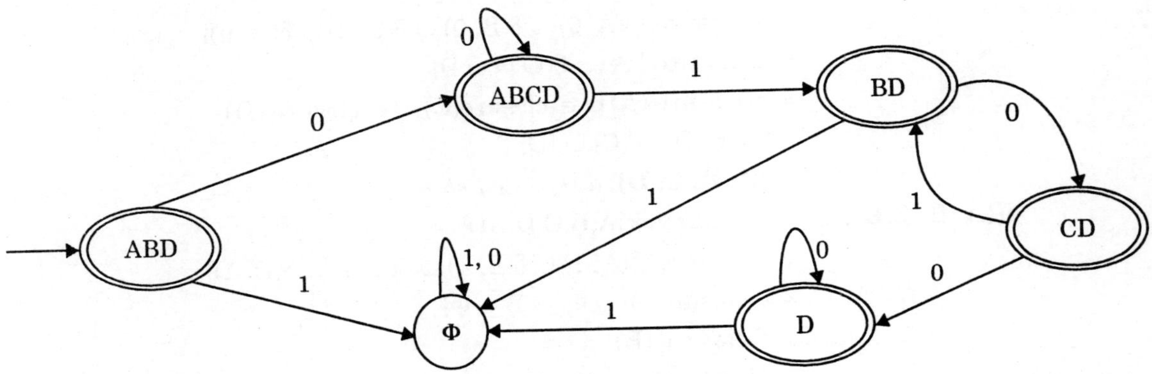

Fig. 8.14

***Note.** The nature of the state Φ is such that, when automan reaches to this state then it will disappear or it never returns back.*

EXERCISES

8.1 Construct the equivalent NFA from the shown transition tables (Fig. 8.15) given for NFA with ∈-moves.

(*i*)

State	0	∈	1
→ q_0	Φ	$\{q_1\}$	$\{q_2\}$
q_1	$\{q_1, q_2\}$	$\{q_3\}$	$\{q_2\}$
● q_2	$\{q_0, q_1\}$	Φ	Φ
q_3	Φ	Φ	$\{q_3\}$

(*a*)

(*ii*)

State	0	∈	1
→ q_0	Φ	$\{q_1\}$	Φ
q_1	$\{q_1, q_2\}$	$\{q_3\}$	$\{q_3\}$
q_2	$\{q_0, q_1\}$	Φ	$\{q_1\}$
● q_3	Φ	Φ	Φ
q_4	$\{q_3\}$	Φ	$\{q_4\}$

(*b*)

(*iii*)

State	0	∈	1
→ q_0	$\{q_0\}$	$\{q_1\}$	$\{q_0\}$
q_1	$\{q_2\}$	$\{q_2\}$	$\{q_3\}$
q_2	$\{q_{2ss}\}$	$\{q_3\}$	$\{q_1\}$
● q_3	Φ	Φ	Φ

(*c*)

Fig 8.15

8.2 Construct the equivalent DFA's from the given NFA's whose transition tables are shown in Fig. 8.16.

(*i*)

State	0	1	2
→ q_0	$\{q_0, q_1\}$	Φ	$\{q_1\}$
q_1	$\{q_1\}$	$\{q_1, q_2\}$	Φ
● q_2	$\{q_0, q_1\}$	Φ	$\{q_2\}$

(*a*)

(*ii*)

State	0	1	2
→ q_0	$\{q_0, q_1\}$	Φ	$\{q_3\}$
q_1	$\{q_1, q_2\}$	$\{q_3\}$	Φ
● q_2	$\{q_0, q_1, q_3\}$	Φ	$\{q_2\}$
● q_3	Φ	Φ	$\{q_1\}$

(*b*)

(*iii*)

State	0	1
→ q_0	Φ	$\{q_1\}$
q_1	$\{q_1, q_2\}$	$\{q_2\}$
q_2	$\{q_0, q_1\}$	$\{q_3\}$
● q_3	Φ	$\{q_3\}$

(*c*)

Fig 8.16

8.3 Construct the equivalent DFA for all the given NFA's with ∈ moves in exercise 8.1.

Regular Expressions

9 Regular Expressions

9.1 INTRODUCTION TO REGULAR EXPRESSIONS

In the previous chapter we have studied that the power of a finite automaton is given by the language it accepts, that contains finite or infinite many strings. So, Is there any convenient way to express these set of strings. In this chapter we shall focus our attention to the description of a language by an algebraic expression called as ***regular expression.*** The operations used in the formation of regular expressions are union, concatenation, and Kleeny closure. The language generated by a regular expression is called ***regular language.*** Regular expressions are capable to defining all and only the regular languages. The significance of the symbols used to represent the regular expression is different than the symbol used to specify the strings. So, we use bold symbols in representing the regular expressions while for the string we uses the symbols as usual.

Regular language is the language depicted (expressed) by the regular expression.

9.2 DEFINITION OF REGULAR EXPRESSION

Assume the set of alphabets S = $\{a_1, a_2, a_3, \ldots\ldots\ldots a_n\}$, and **r** be a regular expression defined over Σ and let the language generated by the regular expression **r** be L(**r**), then the basis regular expressions are,

1. $\mathbf{a_i}$ is the regular expression corresponding to the symbol $a_i \in \Sigma$ for $\forall\, i = 1$ to n. The language generated by regular expression $\mathbf{a_i}$ will be $L(\mathbf{a_i})$ i.e.,

   $$L(\mathbf{a_i}) = \{a_i\}, \text{ for } \forall\, i = 1 \text{ to } n.$$

2. ∈ is a regular expression corresponding to the null string (∈), and the language generated by the regular expression ∈ will be L(∈) i.e.,

   $$L(\in) = \{\in\}.$$

3. **Φ** is the regular expression corresponding to the nonexistence of any input symbol and the language generated by the regular expression Φ will be L(Φ) i.e.,

   $$L(\mathbf{\Phi}) = \Phi;$$

Above definition of regular expression can be extended further by defining its behavior over set of operators union (+), concatenation (.), and Kleeny closure (*) i.e.,

4. If $\mathbf{r_1}$ and $\mathbf{r_2}$ are two regular expressions, and their languages are $L(\mathbf{r_1})$ and $L(\mathbf{r_2})$ respectively, then $(\mathbf{r_1} + \mathbf{r_2})$ will also be a regular expression and it generates the

language $L(\mathbf{r_1}) \cup L(\mathbf{r_2})$. This property of regular expression is known as *'addition property of regular expressions'*.†

5. If $\mathbf{r_1}$ and $\mathbf{r_2}$ are two regular expressions, and their languages are $L(\mathbf{r_1})$ and $L(\mathbf{r_2})$ respectively, then $(\mathbf{r_1} \cdot \mathbf{r_2})$ will also be a regular expression and it generates the language $L(\mathbf{r_1}) . L(\mathbf{r_2})$. This property of regular expression is known as 'concatenation *property of regular expressions'*.‡

6. If $\mathbf{r}$ be a regular expression, and its language is $L(\mathbf{r})$, then $\mathbf{r}^*$ will also be a regular expression and it denotes the language $L(\mathbf{r}^*)$ or $L(\mathbf{r})^*$. This property of regular expression is called *'Kleeny closure property of regular expression'* where, $L(\mathbf{r}^*)$ is Kleeny closure of language L, i.e.,

   Let $L(\mathbf{r}^*) = L^*$,

   then
   $$L^* = \bigcup_{\forall i \geq 0} L^i$$
   $$= L^0 \cup L^1 \cup L^2 \cup \ldots\ldots\ldots\ldots \cup L^i \cup L^{i+1} \cup \ldots\ldots\ldots\ldots\ldots\infty$$

   where $L^0 = \{\in\}$ [language contains null string]
   $$L^1 = L . L^0 = L . \{\in\} = L;$$
   $$L^2 = L . L^1;$$
   $$L^3 = L . L^2;$$
   $$\ldots\ldots\ldots\ldots\ldots\ldots$$
   $$\ldots\ldots\ldots\ldots\ldots\ldots$$
   $$L^i = L . L^{i-1};$$
   $$\ldots\ldots\ldots\ldots\ldots\ldots$$

   For example, if $\mathbf{a}$ is the regular expression then its language will be given by $L(\mathbf{a})$ where, $L(\mathbf{a}) = \{a\}$ then,
   $$L(\mathbf{a})^* = \{\in, a, aa, aaa, \ldots\ldots\ldots\ldots\infty\}.$$

7. Nothing else is regular expression.

In the definition of regular expression we have discussed the nature of regular expression over following operators i.e.,

- + (addition) or ∪ (union),
- (Concatenation), and
- * (Kleeny closure)

So for the study of regular expressions over these operators and the language generated by these composite regular expressions, the precedence of operators is important, i.e., *, . , + is the sequence of precedence from higher to lower.

Example 9.1. *Now we discuss various regular expressions formed over $\Sigma = \{0, 1\}$ and see the importance of operators precedence while we enumerate the language from the composite regular expression.*

---

† For example let $L_1 = \{00, 10\}$ and $L_2 = \{0, 1, 00\}$ then addition of two languages is,
$$L_1 \cup L_2 = \{0, 1, 00, 10\},$$
If $L_1' = \{\in, 00, 10\}$ then its addition with language L_2 will be,
$$L_1' \cup L_2 = \{\in, 0, 1, 00, 10\}$$
‡ The concatenation of L_1 and L_2 is given as,
$$L_1 . L_2 = \{000, 001, 0000, 100, 101, 1000\} \text{ and,}$$
Concatenation with L_1' is,
$$L_1' . L_2 = \{0, 1, 00, 000, 001, 0000, 100, 101, 10000\}.$$

(*a*) **(0 + 1)** is a regular expression, which generates the language {0, 1}. Because, L(0) = {0} and L(**1**) = {1} and the addition of language i.e.,

$$L(\mathbf{0 + 1}) = L(\mathbf{0}) \cup L(\mathbf{1}) = \{0, 1\}; \text{ (which is either 0 or 1)}$$

(*b*) **(0 . 1*)** is a regular expression, which generates the language {0, 01, 011, 0111,....}. Here, we assume regular expression $\mathbf{r_1} = \mathbf{0}$ and $\mathbf{r_2} = \mathbf{1}^*$ so $L(\mathbf{r_1}) = \{0\}$ and $L(\mathbf{r_2}) = \{\epsilon, 1, 11, 111, ...\infty\}$. Therefore, the language generated by concatenation of regular expressions $\mathbf{r_1} . \mathbf{r_2}$ will be $L(\mathbf{r_1} . \mathbf{r_2})$ i.e.,

$$L(\mathbf{r_1} . \mathbf{r_2}) = L(\mathbf{r_1}) . L(\mathbf{r_2}) = \{0, 01, 011, 0111, ...\infty\}$$

(*c*) **(0 + 1*)** is a regular expression, that generates the language which is the union of set of all strings formed by regular expressions **0** or **1*** i.e., L(**0**) ∪ L(**1***),

where, L(**0**) = {0} and L(**1***) = {∈, 1, 11, 111,........} hence,

$$L(\mathbf{0}) \cup L(\mathbf{1^*}) = \{\epsilon, 0, 1, 11, 111, ...\}.$$

(*d*) **(0 + 1)*** is a regular expression, so its language is the set of all strings formed using symbol 0 or 1. Here we assume regular expression **r** = **(0 + 1)** then L(**r**) = {0, 1}.

Therefore, $L(\mathbf{r})^* = L^* = L^0 \cup L^1 \cup L^2 \cup L^3$ .... where $L^0 = \{\epsilon\}$; $L^1 = L . L^0 = \epsilon . \{0, 1\} = \{0, 1\}$; $L^2 = L . L^1 = \{0, 1\} . \{0, 1\} = \{00, 01, 10, 11\}$; $L^3 = L . L^2 = \{0, 1\} . \{00, 01, 10, 11\} = \{000, 001, 010, 011, 100, 101, 110, 111\}$; .....and so on.

Hence, $L^* = \{\epsilon, 0, 1, 00, 01, 10, 11, 000, ...\}$ or set of all possible strings formed over symbols 0's & 1's including the null string.

(*e*) **(0*. 1 . 1 . 0*)** is a regular expression and its language will be L(**0* . 1 . 1 . 0***). Since, L(**0***) = {∈, 0, 00, 000,...}; L(**1**) = {1}; again L(**1**) = {1}; and L(0*) = {∈, 0, 00, 000, ...} therefore,

L(**0* . 1 . 1 . 0***) = {∈, 0, 00,...}.{1}.{1}.{∈, 0, 00, ...}

= {11 *(when first and last RE† produces ∈), 011, 0011, ...(when first RE produces multiple 0's and last RE produces ∈), 110, 1100, ...(when first RE produces ∈ and last RE produces multiple 0's)*, 0110, 01100, ..., 00110, 001100, ...∞}.

Hence, language contains all strings of 0's having two consecutive 1's.

(*f*) For the regular expression **(0 + 1)* . 1 . 0 . 1 . (0 + 1)*** the language will be the set of all strings formed over 0's and 1's consisting of pattern 101. Since the presence of RE first and last produces all the strings of 0's and 1's including ∈ but the essential part of all the strings must be the presence of the substring 101 which is produced by the concatenation of RE 2nd, 3rd and 4th.

Note that if the regular expression is constructed for the language consisting of the string *x*, then its regular expression will be denoted by **x**.

In the previous example we saw how regular languages are to be generated from the given regular expressions. In the next example we will see how the regular expressions are constructed from given regular languages

Example 9.2. *Consider regular languages are defined over {0, 1} then write regular expressions for following regular languages.*

1. ***The set of all strings containing at least one 0.***

   Since, we have seen previously that, regular expression **(0 + 1)*** generates set of all strings over {0, 1}. For the occurrence of at least one zero in the set of all possible strings, regular expression **(0 + 1)*** will be concatenate with another regular expression **0**. Therefore, regular expression will be,

† RE stands for regular expression

$$(0 + 1)^* . 0 \text{ or } 0 . (0 + 1)^* \Rightarrow (0 + 1)^* . 0 . (0 + 1)^*$$

where, $L[(0 + 1)^* . 0 . (0 + 1)^*] = \{0, 00, 01, 000, \ldots\ldots\ldots\}$;

2. ***The set of all strings containing at least one 0 or at least one 1.***

Since the regular expression **(0 + 1)** generates the language either 0 or 1. So, if **(0 + 1)** is concatenated with another regular expression **(0 + 1)*** then resulting regular expression i.e.,

$(0 + 1) . (0 + 1)^*$ or $(0 + 1)^* . (0 + 1) \Rightarrow (0 + 1)^* . (0 + 1) . (0 + 1)^*$ will generates the language $L[(0 + 1)^* . (0 + 1) . (0 + 1)^*]$ where,

$L((0 + 1)^* (0 + 1) (0 + 1)^*) = \{0, 00, 01, \ldots\ldots, 1, 10, 11, \ldots\ldots\}$;

3. ***The set of all strings containing at least one 0 and at least one 1.***

From 1 we see that regular expression $(0 + 1)^* . 0 . (0 + 1)^*$ produces the language that consists of all strings of 0's and 1's with confirmation of at least a single 0. If this regular expression concatenate with **1** then resulting regular expression i.e.,

$$(0 + 1)^* . 0 . 1 . (0 + 1)^* \text{ or } (0 + 1)^* . 1 . 0 . (0 + 1)^*$$

$$\Rightarrow \quad (0 + 1)^* . (1 . 0 + 0 . 1) . (0 + 1)^*$$

will generates the language which confirms the presence of at least one 0 and at least one 1. Hence, the language is L = {01, 10, 001, 100, 010, 101, 011, 110, ...}

4. ***The set of all strings of even length.***

Since, the strings of minimum length which is even are {00, 01, 10, 11} thus the corresponding regular expression will be **(0 0 + 0 1 + 1 0 + 1 1)**. The next string of higher even length can be obtained from the concatenation of strings of minimum length 2 with zero /more times, i.e.,

$$(0 0 + 0 1 + 1 0 + 1 1)^* . (0 0 + 0 1 + 1 0 + 1 1)$$

$$\Rightarrow \quad (0 0 + 0 1 + 1 0 + 1 1)^+$$

Alternatively, **(0 0 + 0 1 + 1 0 + 1 1)** can also be written as $[(0 + 1) . (0 + 1)]$, hence $(0 0 + 0 1 + 1 0 + 1 1)^+$ can be written as $[(0 + 1) . (0 + 1)]^+$

5. ***The set of all strings of length ≤ 5.***

First we form the regular expression that generates the language consists of all strings of length 5 i.e.,

$$(0 + 1) . (0 + 1) . (0 + 1) . (0 + 1) . (0 + 1)$$

We can reduce the length of the strings below five by introducing the null string in each of the regular expression. Thus the resulting regular expression will be given as, $(0 + 1 + \epsilon) . (0 + 1 + \epsilon) . (0 + 1 + \epsilon) . (0 + 1 + \epsilon) . (0 + 1 + \epsilon)$

6. ***The set of all strings which ends with 1 and doesn't contain the substring 00.***

The minimum length strings satisfy this condition are {1, 01, 11, 101, 011, ...}. For the 1st and 2nd string of the language set the regular expression will be **(1 + 0 1)**. Kleeny closure of this regular expression i.e., $(1 + 0 1)^*$ produces all string formed over {1, 01} i.e., {∈, 1, 01, 101, 011, ...}. Since, ∈ is not in the language, hence to drop the possibility of string ∈ we take the positive closure† of regular expression i.e.,

$$(1 + 0 1)^+ \text{ or } (1 + 0 1)^* . (1 + 0 1)$$

which generates the language {1, 01, 11, 101, ...}.

---

† *Positive closure property of regular expression says that if **r** is the regular expression then r^+ will also be the regular expression, where r^+ is defined as,*

$$r^+ = r^* . r \quad \text{or} \quad r . r^*$$

9.3 EQUIVALENCE OF REGULAR EXPRESSION AND FINITE AUTOMATA

Every language which is accepted by either deterministic finite automaton (DFA) or nondeterministic finite automaton (NFA) with or without ∈-moves is known as regular language. It means that there exists a set of regular expressions that generates the strings of this class of language. So, if a language is regular then certainly it can be expressed by regular expression/s and conversely this language must be the out come from some finite automaton (Fig. 9.1).

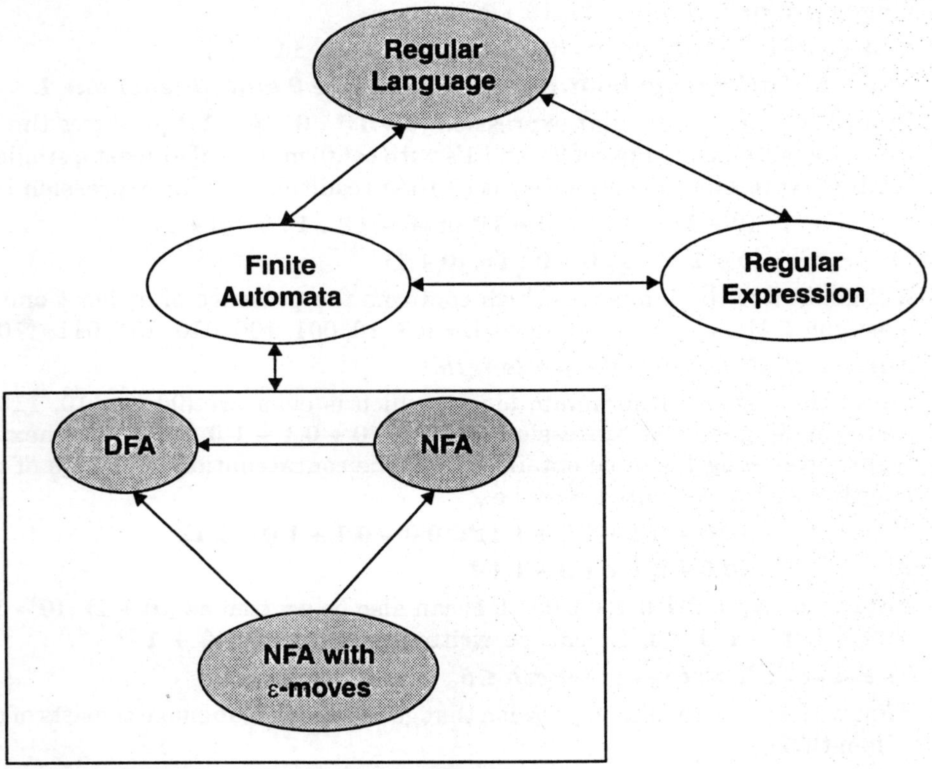

Fig. 9.1

Alternatively we may say that,

I. A regular expression can be expressed in some form of finite automata either DFA/NFA/NFA with ∈-moves (i.e., from Regular Expression to Finite Automata).

II. The acceptance power (language) of finite Automata can be expressed by regular expression (i.e., from Finite automata to Regular Expression).

Now we study in detail about the points I and II such that the method of construction of finite automaton from given regular expression and conversely the determination of regular expression from finite automaton. What we have discuss so far it can be easily verified by study of the following theorems.

9.3.1 Construction of NFA with ∈-moves from Regular Expression

Theorem 9.1. *If* ***r*** *be a regular expression and its language is L(****r****) then there exists a NFA with ∈-moves* $N_\in$ *i.e.,* $L(N_\in) = L(r)$.

(Provided that $N_\in$ has only one final state and there is no outgoing arc from the final state)

Proof. We shall prove the theorem in this way that if **r** be a regular expression and its language is L(**r**) then its all possible strings we can construct an equivalent NFA with ∈-moves which accepts same set of strings. The proof of the theorem is preceded by method of induction. First we construct the $N_\in$ for the basis regular expressions i.e. regular expressions without any operator.

- If **r** = $\mathbf{a_i}$ then L(**r**) = $\{a_i / a_i \in \Sigma$ for $\forall\ i = 1$ to $n\}$, then equivalent automaton $N_\in$ that accepts L(**r**) will be,

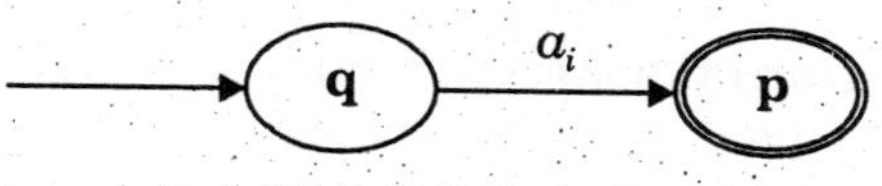

(By assuming that automaton $N_\in$ initially is in state **q** and after reading symbol a_i it reaches to state **p** and then stop)

- If **r** = ∈ then L(**r**) = {∈} then automaton $N_\in$ that accepts ∈ or null string will be,

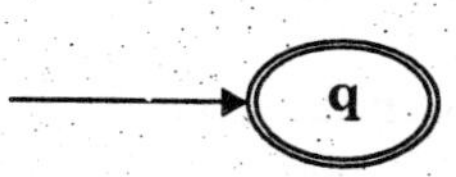

Or,

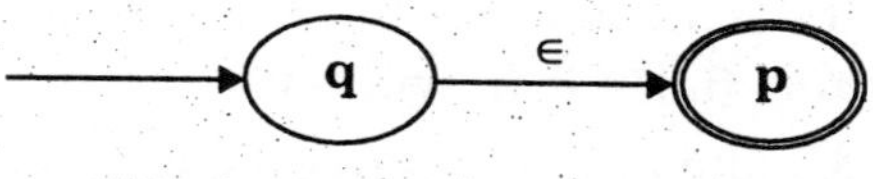

(Initially $N_\in$ is in state **q** and after reading ∈ automaton think a meaningless symbol so it remains in state **q** alternatively its state changes to **p** and then stop)

- If **r** = Φ then L(**r**) = Φ. The automaton $N_\in$ that accepts language Φ will be,

(Initially $N_\in$ is in state **q** and there is no way (set of language consists nothing) to reach to final state **p**).

Thus we have seen that we can construct the equivalent NFA with ∈ moves for the basis regular expressions. Further, we will see that $N_\in$ can also be constructed for the composite of regular expressions, which are form over operators union, concatenation and Kleeny closure. Assume that regular expression **r** is form using these *n* operators. By Induction hypothesis we assume that theorem is true if **r** has ≤ $(n - 1)$ operators (for $n \geq 1$). Let **r** has exactly *n* operators then construct an equivalent $N_\in$ for regular expression **r**. Here we will show that theorem is true for composite of two regular expressions obtained using union, concatenation, and closure operations.

Let $\mathbf{r_1}$ and $\mathbf{r_2}$ be two regular expressions then following are the possible regular expressions,

1. if **r** = ($\mathbf{r_1}$ + $\mathbf{r_2}$) then its language is L(**r**) = L($\mathbf{r_1}$) ∈ L($\mathbf{r_2}$)
2. if **r** = ($\mathbf{r_1}$. $\mathbf{r_2}$) then its language is L(**r**) = L($\mathbf{r_1}$) . L($\mathbf{r_2}$)
3. if **r** = $\mathbf{r_1}$* then its language is L(**r**) = L($\mathbf{r_1}$*)

Assume that corresponding to regular expression $\mathbf{r_1}$ $N_{\in 1}$ be the equivalent automaton accepting L($\mathbf{r_1}$) then it looks like as,

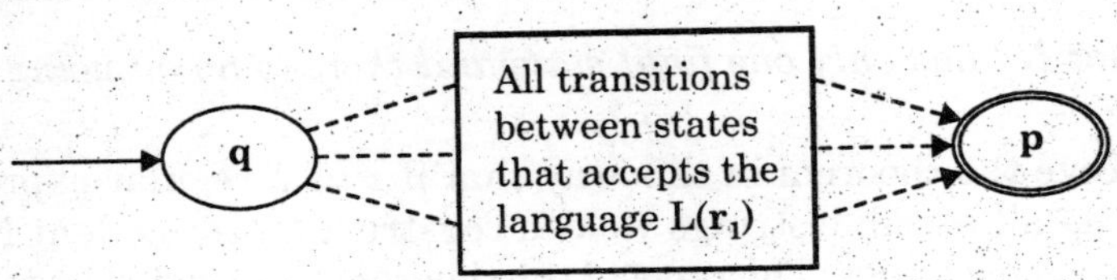

Or,

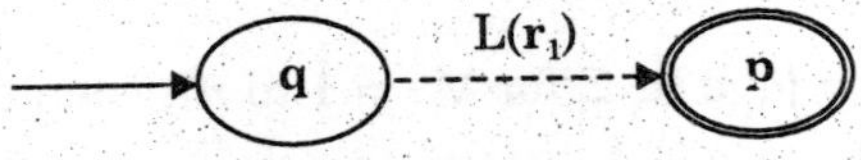

A similar structure for automata $N_{\in 2}$ for the language $L(\mathbf{r_2})$ can also be drawn.

Case 1 (Union operation) Construct the automaton $N_\in$ for the language $L(\mathbf{r})$, where

$$L(\mathbf{r}) = L(\mathbf{r_1} + \mathbf{r_2}) = L(\mathbf{r_1}) \cup L(\mathbf{r_2})$$

i.e.,
$$L(N_\in) = L(N_{\in 1}) \cup L(N_{\in 2})$$

Let $N_{\in 1}$ and $N_{\in 2}$ are define as,

$N_{\in 1} = (Q_1, \Sigma_1, \delta_{\in 1}, q_1, \{p_1\})$ and $N_{\in 2} = (Q_2, \Sigma_2, \delta_{\in 2}, q_2, \{p_2\})$ then automata $N_\in$ will be

$$N_\in = (Q_1 \cup Q_2 \cup q \cup p, \Sigma_1 \cup \Sigma_2, \delta_\in, q, \{p\}) \text{ where,}$$

- State q will be a new starting state, i.e., $\delta_\in(q, \in) = \{q_1, q_2\}$.
- States will be a new final state, i.e., $\delta_\in(p_1, \in) = \delta_\in(p_2, \in) = \{p\}$.
- Definitions of transition function $\delta_\in$ will cover,

$$\delta_\in = \delta_{\in 1} \cup \delta_{\in 2} \text{ and } \delta_\in(q, \in) = \{q_1, q_2\} \text{ and } \delta_\in(p_1, \in) = \delta_\in(p_2, \in) = \{p\}.$$

So, automaton $N_\in$ accepts the language which is accepted by automaton $N_{\in 1}$ or the language which is accepted by automaton $N_{\in 2}$. It follows that for automaton $N_\in$ if there is a path, labeled by some string x from state q to p if and only if, either there is a path labeled by string x in $N_{\in 1}$ from q_1 to p_1 or there is a path labeled by string x in $N_{\in 2}$ from q_2 to p_2.

Therefore, $L(N_\in) = L(N_{\in 1}) \cup L(N_{\in 2})$.

(To implement this definition we precede from a new start state q. The initial states of both automatons (q_1 and q_2) are connected through $\in$ transitions from the new state q. Similarly, old final states (p_1 and p_2) will converge to a new final state p through $\in$-transitions provided that the acceptance power of $N_{\in 1}$ and $N_{\in 2}$ remains unchanged. So, we get the automaton $N_\in$ which is shown in Fig. 9.2.

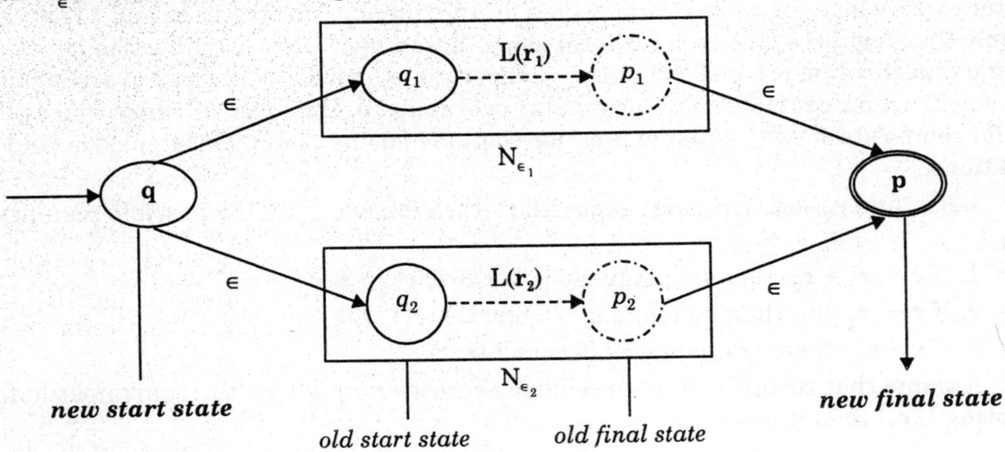

Fig. 9.2. ($N_\in$).

Case 2 (Concatenation operation) Construct the automaton N_ϵ for the language L(**r**) where,

$$L(\mathbf{r}) = L(\mathbf{r_1} . \mathbf{r_2}) = L(\mathbf{r_1}) . L(\mathbf{r_2})$$

i.e., $$L(N_\epsilon) = L(N_{\epsilon 1}) . L(N_{\epsilon 2})$$

where automaton $N_{\epsilon 1}$ and $N_{\epsilon 2}$ were defined earlier, hence automaton N_ϵ will be i.e.,

$$N_\epsilon = (Q_1 \cup Q_2, \Sigma_1 \cup \Sigma_2, \delta_\epsilon, q_1, \{p_2\}) \text{ where,}$$

Starting state will be the starting state of $N_{\epsilon 1}$ i.e. $\{q_1\}$.

Final state will be the final state of $N_{\epsilon 2}$ i.e. $\{p_2\}$.

Definitions of δ_ϵ will cover,

$$\delta_\epsilon(p_1, \epsilon) = \{q_2\} \text{ and } \delta_\epsilon = \delta_{\epsilon 1} . \delta_{\epsilon 2}$$

Hence, the automaton N_ϵ accepts the language which is accepted by automaton $N_{\epsilon 1}$ followed by the language accepted by $N_{\epsilon 2}$. It follows that, a path labeled by string x for automaton N_ϵ will traverse from q_1 to p_2 which is equivalent to the path in $N_{\epsilon 1}$ labeled by some string x' from q_1 to p_1 followed by the path in $N_{\epsilon 2}$ labeled by some other string x'' from q_2 to p_2. Thus,

$$L(N_\epsilon) = \{x' . x'' / x' \in L(N_{\epsilon 1}) \text{ and } x' \in L(N_{\epsilon 2})\}$$

(To implement it, we assume that start state of automaton $N_{\epsilon 1}$ will be the start state of N_ϵ then it passes all the transitions of $N_{\epsilon 1}$ labeled by L($\mathbf{r_1}$) and reaches to its final state p_1. The operator. is implemented by connecting state p_1 to the start state of $N_{\epsilon 2}$ which is q_2 through ϵ-transition, then pass all transitions of $N_{\epsilon 2}$ labeled by L($\mathbf{r_2}$) and finally terminate on its final state p_2. (Fig. 9.3)

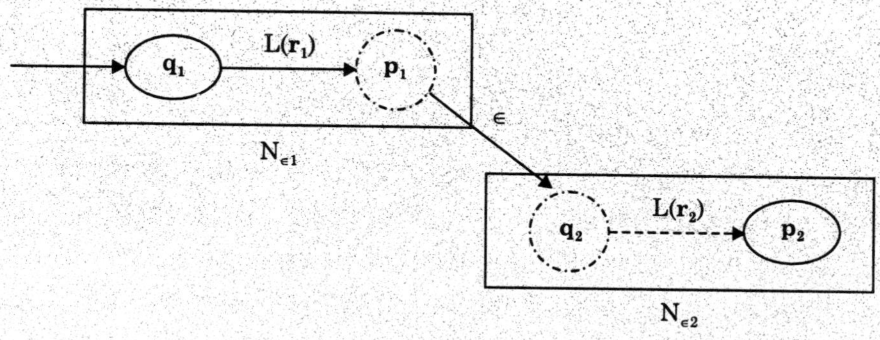

Fig. 9.3. (N_ϵ).

Case 3 (kleeny Closure) Now construct the automaton N_ϵ for the language L(**r**) where,

$$L(\mathbf{r}) = L(\mathbf{r_1}^*)$$

i.e., $$L(N_\epsilon) = L(N_{\epsilon 1})^*$$

Let $N_{\epsilon 1}$ be defined as,

$$N_{\epsilon 1} = (Q_1, \Sigma_1, \delta_{\epsilon 1}, q_1, \{p_1\})$$

then automaton N_ϵ will be given as,

$$N_\epsilon = (Q', \Sigma_1, \delta_\epsilon, q, \{p\}) \text{ where,}$$

- $Q' = Q_1 \cup \{q\} \cup \{p\}$
- Where, q will be a new starting state and p will be a new final state,

- and δ_ϵ will be defined as,

  $\delta_\epsilon(q, \epsilon) = \{q_1\}$ or $\delta_\epsilon(q, \epsilon) = \{p\}$ and,

  $\delta_\epsilon(p_1, \epsilon) = \{p\}$ or $\delta_\epsilon(p_1, \epsilon) = \{q_1\}$.

Hence, the path in automaton N_ϵ from starting state q to p follows either, through

- ϵ-transition from q to p for automaton N_ϵ, Or
- ϵ-transition from q to q_1 in automaton N_ϵ, followed by a path from q_1 to p_1 in $N_{\epsilon 1}$ followed by ϵ-transition from p_1 to p.

So, if x is the string labeled from q to p for automaton N_ϵ iff, $x = x_1.x_2.x_3 \ldots\ldots x_i$ (for $\forall\, i = 0$ i.e., if $i = 0$ then $x = \epsilon$), for $\forall\, x_i \in L(N_{\epsilon 1})$ hence,

$$L(N_\epsilon) = L(N_{\epsilon 1}).$$

Hence, from the known automaton $N_{\epsilon 1}$ that accepts the language $L(\mathbf{r_1})$ we can construct the automaton N_ϵ that accepts the language $L(\mathbf{r_1}^*)$. For N_ϵ the nature of accepting strings will be,

1. ϵ, or
2. finite repetition of the string of $L(\mathbf{r_1})$,

So, both these possibilities must be incorporated when we construct the N_ϵ such that, for 1, start state is connected to the final state by ϵ-transition and for 2, the final state of automata $N_{\epsilon 1}$ is connected to its start state through ϵ-transition that will allow the one or more repetition of the strings of $L(\mathbf{r_1})$. (Fig. 9.4)

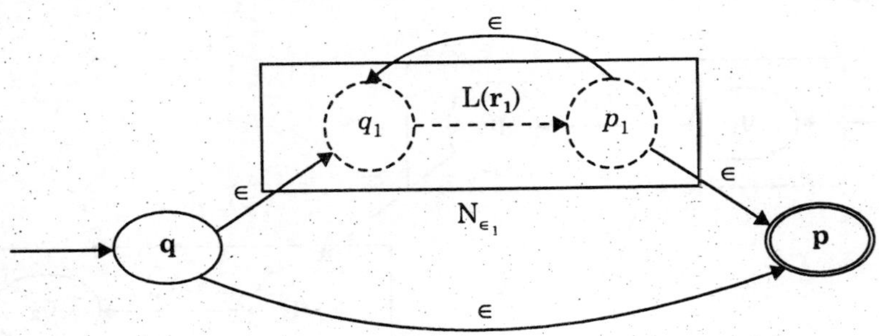

Fig. 9.4. (N_ϵ).

Hence, we see that the theorem is true for regular expressions using single operator. Through method of induction we can also show that theorem is true for regular expressions having n operators. Therefore, we conclude that theorem is true for regular expressions form over any number of operators. So, we constructed NFA with ϵ-moves for all possible forms of regular expressions, hence theorem verification is over.

Using the statement of the above theorem we can conclude followings,

- *A regular expression converges to NFA with ϵ-moves,*
- *Since we know that, NFA with ϵ-moves converges to NFA (without ϵ-moves) and*
- *Finally, NFA converges to DFA*

Therefore, DFA converges to Regular Expression. There relationship is pictured in Fig. 9.5.

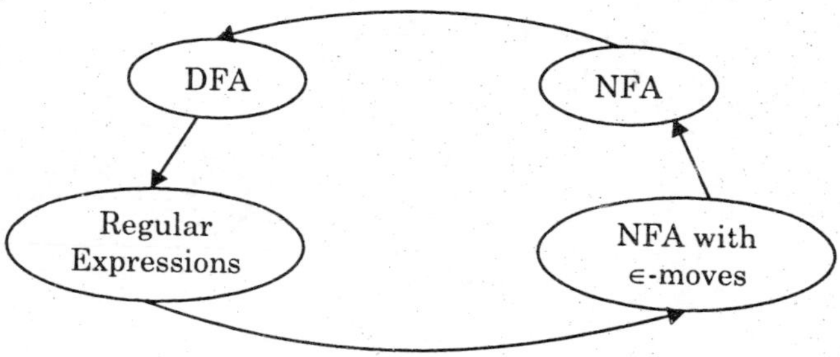

Fig. 9.5

Example 9.3. *Construct the NFA with ∈-moves for regular expression*

$$(a + b) . a . b^* . (a + b)^*.$$

Sol. Assume $\mathbf{r} = (\mathbf{a} + \mathbf{b}) . \mathbf{a} . \mathbf{b}^* . (\mathbf{a} + \mathbf{b})^*$, where **r** is formed by the concatenation of four regular expressions i.e., $\mathbf{r} = \mathbf{r_1} . \mathbf{r_2} . \mathbf{r_3} . \mathbf{r_4}$ where $\mathbf{r_1} = (\mathbf{a} + \mathbf{b})$; $\mathbf{r_2} = \mathbf{a}$; $\mathbf{r_3} = \mathbf{b}^*$ and $\mathbf{r_4} = (\mathbf{a} + \mathbf{b})^*$. Now we construct the NFA with ∈ moves for **r** using theorem 9.1 in the following steps,

Step 1. Construction of the automaton for $\mathbf{r_1} = (\mathbf{a} + \mathbf{b})$ is the addition of two automatons accepting the union of language {**a**} and {**b**} i.e., (Let it be $N_\in'$)

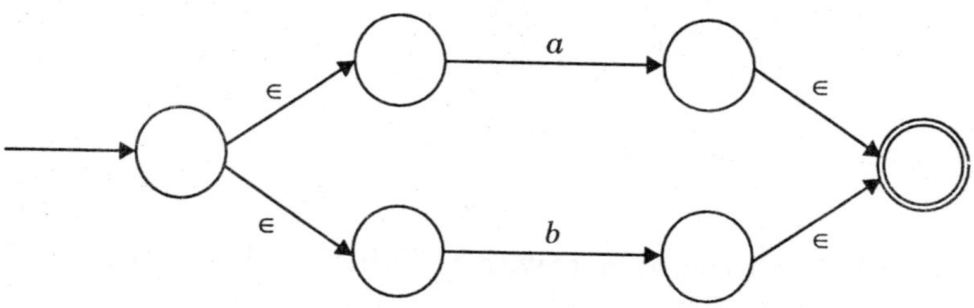

$N_\in'$

Step 2. Now regular expression $\mathbf{r_1}$ is concatenated with regular expression $\mathbf{r_2} = \mathbf{a}$ so, automaton $N_\in''$ will be constructed, i.e., $L(N_\in'') = L(N_\in') . L(\mathbf{a})$, thus $N_\in''$ will be obtain as,

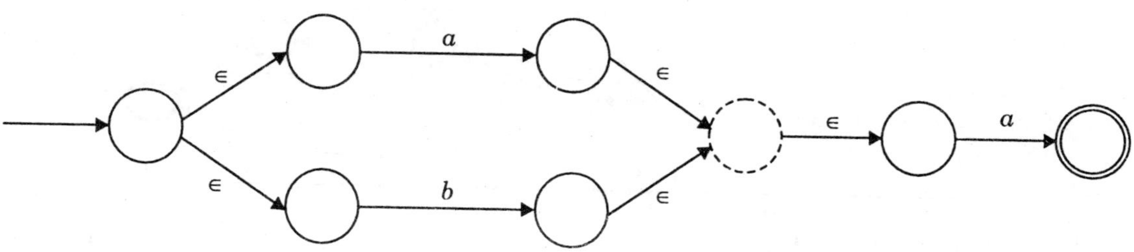

$N_\in''$

Step 3. Next, regular expression $\mathbf{r_1} . \mathbf{r_2}$ is concatenated with $\mathbf{r_3} = \mathbf{b}^*$, so again concatenation construction of $L(N_\in'')$ with automaton that accept $L(\mathbf{r_3})$. Thus we obtain $N_\in'''$.

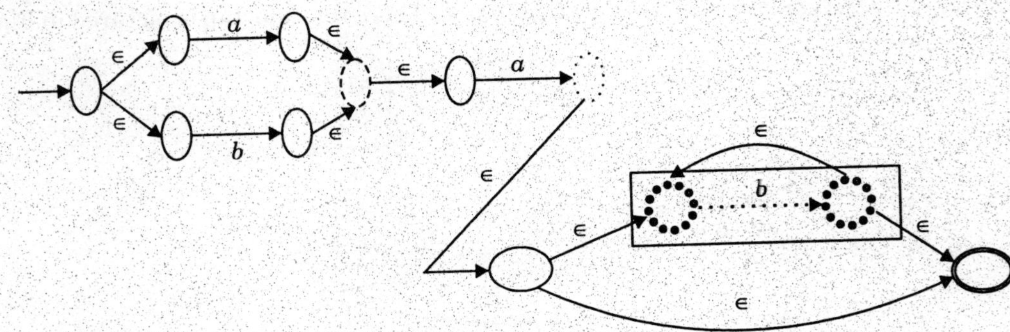

$N_{\in}'''$

Step 4. Do the concatenation construction with the previous automaton $N_{\in}'''$ to the newly constructed automaton $N_{\in}''''$ (for regular expression $\mathbf{r_4} = \mathbf{(a + b)^*}$) so we obtain the final NFA with $\in$ moves $N_{\in}$.

Since $N_{\in}''''$ will be,

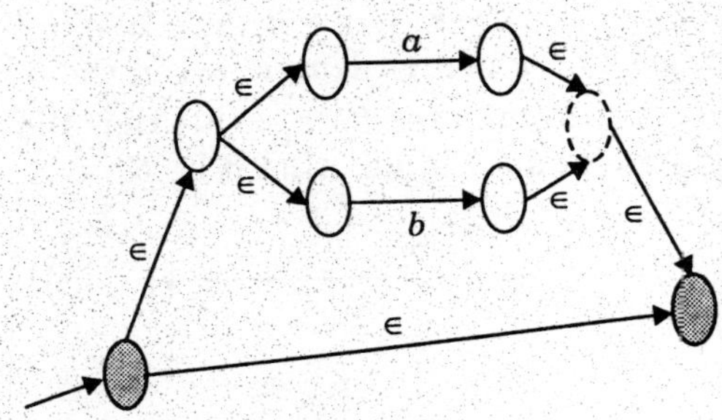

$N_{\in}''''$

Now automata $N_{\in}'''$ will concatenate with $N_{\in}''''$ that resulted $N_{\in}$ which is shown in Fig. 9.6.

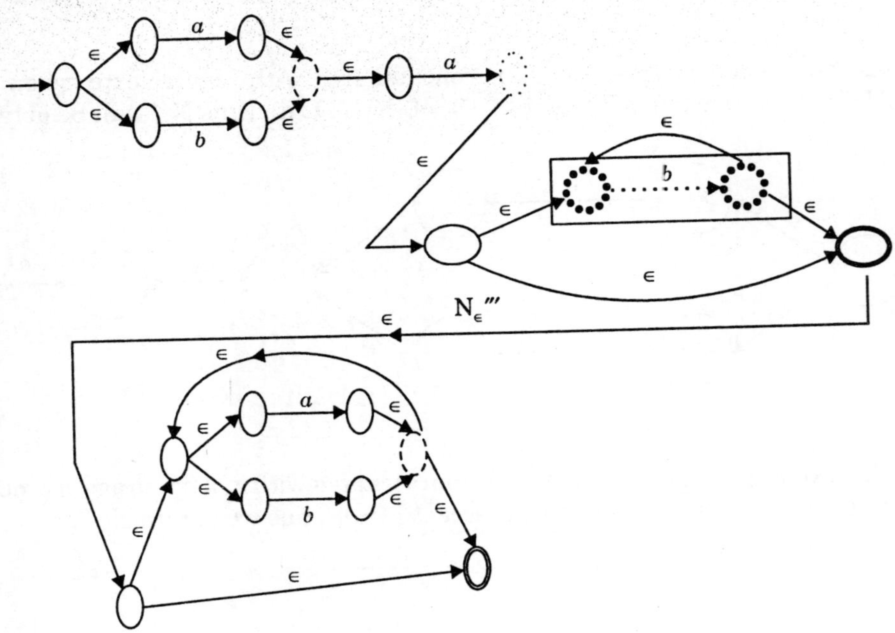

Fig. 9.6 $N_{\in}$.

9.3.2 Construction of DFA from Regular Expression

Any regular expression can be expressed by an equivalent finite automaton. Since theorem 9.1 suggests the construction of NFA with ∈-moves from regular expression. NFA with ∈-moves is an extension of NFA hence NFA is constructed from them. Since, NFA is an ease of DFA therefore from regular expression we can construct an equivalent DFA. So, this process of construction such that, from regular expression to NFA with ∈-moves, from NFA with ∈-moves to NFA, and then from NFA to a DFA is lengthy and tedious. To over comes this difficulty we can alternatively constructed a DFA from known regular expression.

Example 9.4. *Consider a regular expression* $\mathbf{r} = (0\,0 + 0\,0\,1)^*.1$ *then construct a DFA accepts the language L(r).*

Sol. Concentrate on regular expression $\mathbf{r} = (0\,0 + 0\,0\,1)^*.\,1$ we will find that its language L(**r**) can be subdivided like as,

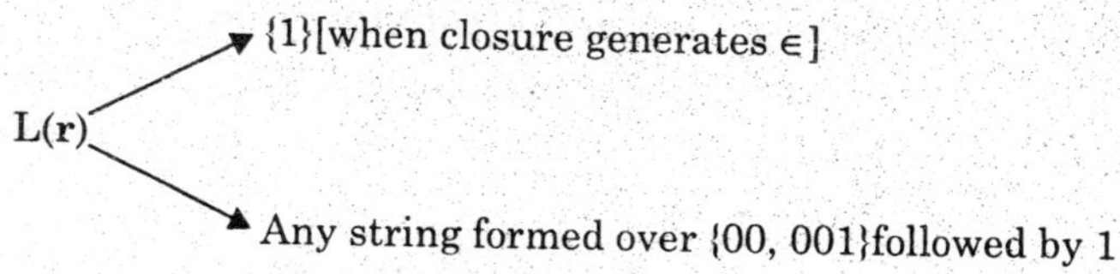

Assume A be the staring state of DFA, so from state A on symbol 1 automaton reaches to accepting state B and on symbol 0 it reaches to a new state C.

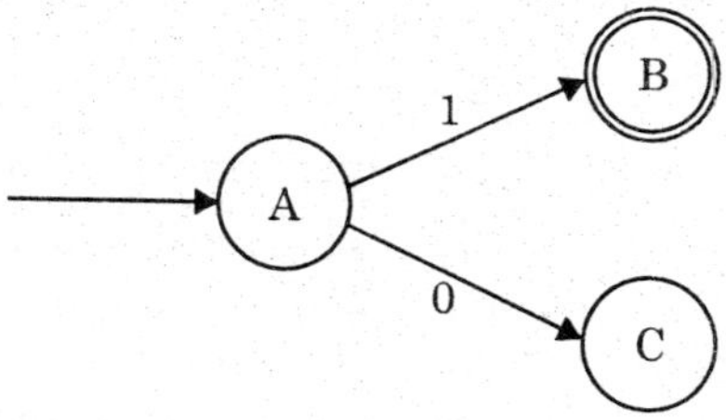

For the acceptance of the string 001 we extend the state diagram as follows :

After state C return symbol is 0, therefore, from state C automaton reaches to the final state E (return symbols on state E is 001) as shown below :

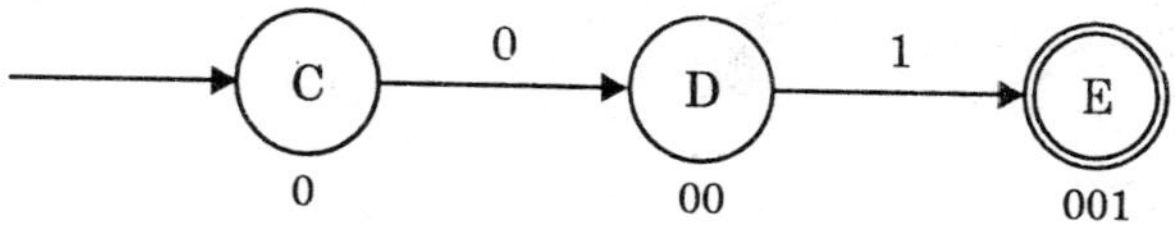

Thus, automaton look like,

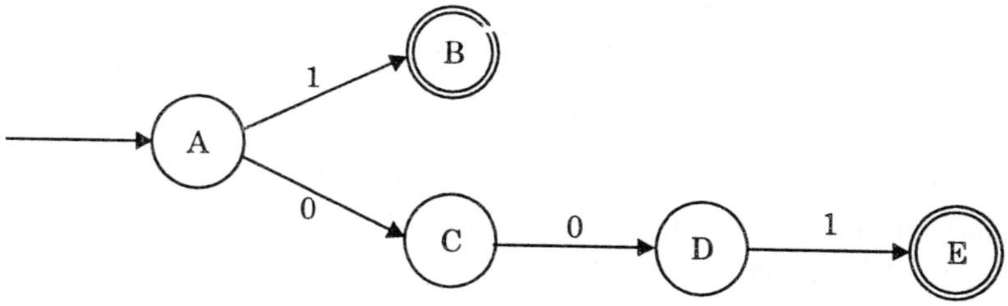

(For the acceptance of the string 0011)

Since, at state E return string is 001, then for next symbol 1 automaton reaches to final state. Hence state E connected to B by transition arc over symbol 1.

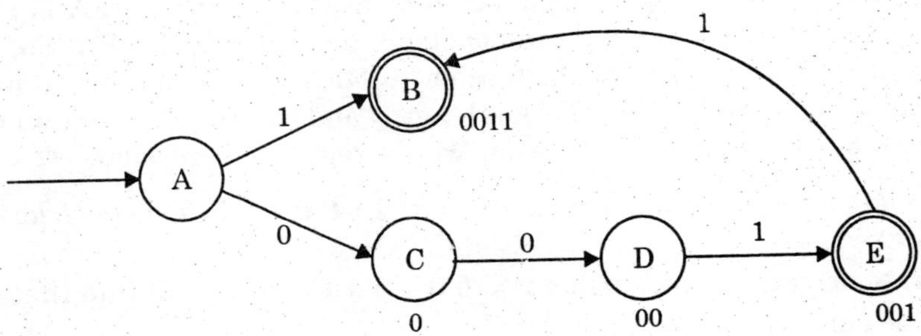

(Acceptance of the string formed over {00,001} followed by 1)

For repetitions of substring 00 one/more times, clearly an arc from state D comes back to C on symbol 0 such that return symbols at D are multiple of 00.

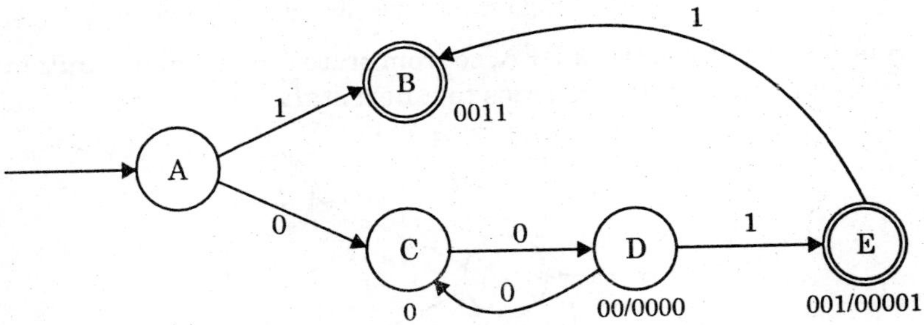

(For repetition of 001 one / more times)

From state E (return symbols 001) an arc connected to C on symbol 0.

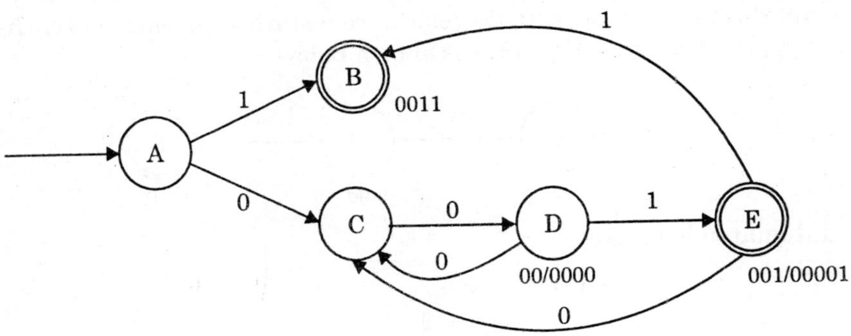

Therefore, from the starting state A over symbol 1, automaton reaches to B and halt. There is no further possibility of acceptance of symbols {0, 1} from B onwards hence; we show the transition on these symbols from B goes to state Φ. Further, no string starting with symbol 0 followed any symbol 1 is in language so it reaches to state Φ. Therefore we obtain the required DFA shown in Fig. 9.7.

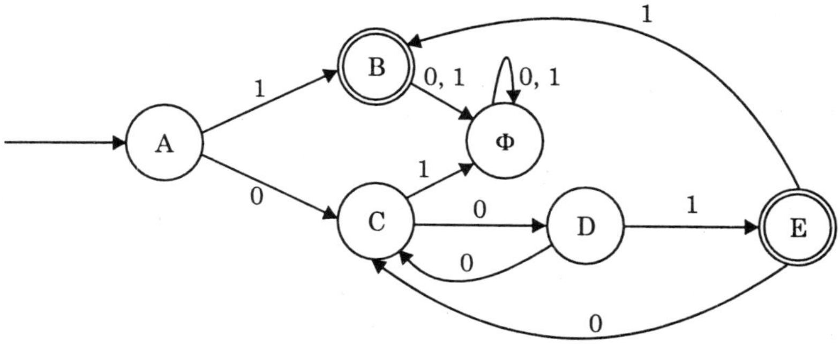

Fig. 9.7

Since automaton shown in Fig. 9.7 fulfills the deterministic requirement of the finite automaton such that from every state there is one and only one exit on each symbol hence it is a DFA.

Example 9.5. *Construct a DFA for the regular expression* ***1 (1 + 1 0)* + 1 0 (0 + 0 1)****.

Sol. Let M be an equivalent DFA for regular expression $\mathbf{r} = \mathbf{1\ (1 + 1\ 0)^* + 1\ 0\ (\ 0 + 0\ 1)^*}$ i.e., L(M) = L(**r**). Since, the regular expression **r** is formed by addition of regular expressions $\mathbf{r_1}$ and $\mathbf{r_2}$ where $\mathbf{r_1} = \mathbf{1\ (1 + 1\ 0)^*}$ and $\mathbf{r_2} = \mathbf{1\ 0\ (\ 0 + 0\ 1)^*}$ i.e., $\mathbf{r} = \mathbf{r_1} + \mathbf{r_2}$ and their language is $L(\mathbf{r_1})$ = {1 or 1 followed by any string formed over (1, 10)} or $L(\mathbf{r_2})$ = {10 or 10 followed by any string formed over (0, 01)}.

So, $$L(\mathbf{r}) = L(\mathbf{r_1}) \cup L(\mathbf{r_2})$$

Assume M_1 and M_2 are two DFA corresponding to the languages $L(\mathbf{r_1})$ and $L(\mathbf{r_2})$ hence,

$$L(M) = L(M_1) \cup L(M_2).$$

(Construction of DFA M_1)

Assume A is the start state of DFA then over symbol 1, M_1 reach to accepted state B. Since, next to state B all strings of {1, 10} should be accepted. So, from state B over symbol 1 M_1 reaches to another accepted state C, otherwise the string 1 followed by 0 is accepted by adding an repetetion arc from state C to state B over symbol 0. All repetition of symbol 1's are absorbed at state C itself. Since, there is no possibility of exit arc over symbol 0 from state A as well as state B hence these arcs terminates to state Ø. (Fig. 9.8)

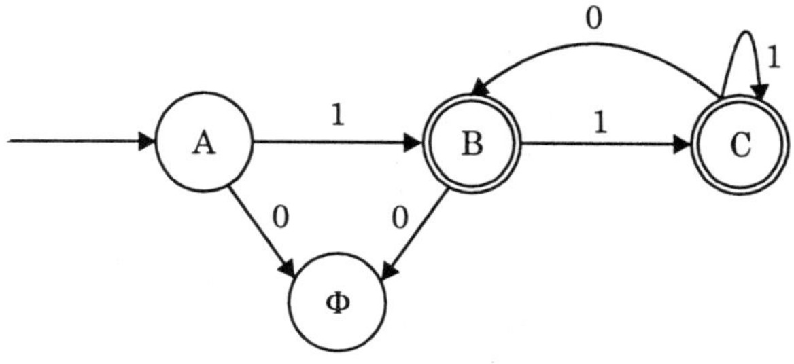

Fig. 9.8. (M_1).

(Construction of DFA M_2)

From starting state A string 10 is accepted (through P), so state Q will be accepted state. Next to state Q all strings of {0, 01} should be accepted. So, from state Q an arc reaches to another accepted state R over the symbol 0 and from R a returning arc over 1 reaches to accepted state Q. An repetitions of symbols 0 are absorbed at state R itself. Transitions of 0 from A, 1 from P and 1 from Q must terminate to state Ø. Thus we get the automaton M_2. (Fig. 9.9)

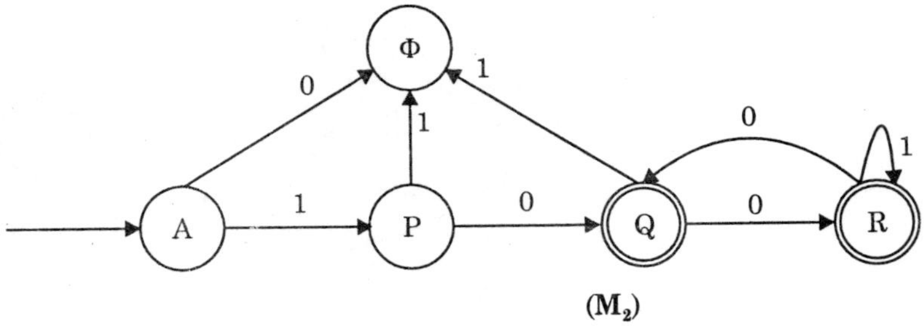

Fig. 9.9

The automaton M_1 and M_2 can be combined together so we obtain final automaton M which is shown in Fig. 9.10.

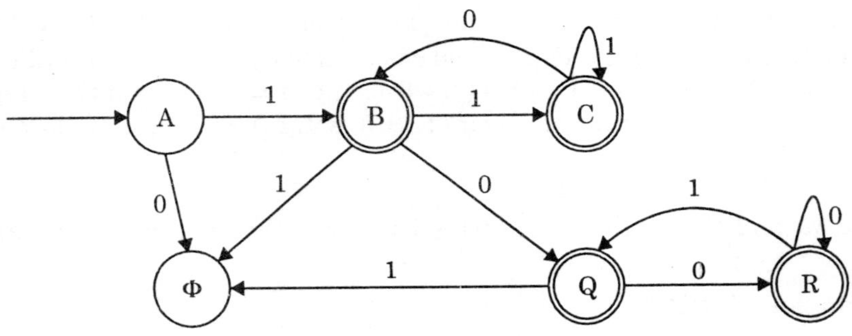

Fig. 9.10 **M.**

(For a single regular expression (regular language) there might exists more than one DFA)

9.4 FINITE AUTOMATA TO REGULAR EXPRESSION

(9.4.1 construction of DFA from regular expression)

Theorem 9.2. *Let M be a DFA then there exists a regular expression **r** i.e., L(M) = L(**r**).*

Proof. Theorem states that a finite automaton DFA can be equivalently expressed in some form of regular expression. It means, that both DFA and regular expression concur on same set of strings called regular language. The proof of the theorem illustrates how a regular expression can be constructed from a given DFA. Let M be a DFA that can be expressed as,

$M = (Q, \Sigma, \delta, q_1, F)$ [where q_1 is the start state and F is the set of final states]

Assume set Q contains n states i.e., $\{q_1, q_2, \ldots\ldots\ldots\ldots q_n\}$. Now we introduce a new term ${}_i\mathbf{R}_j^K$, which contains set of strings. Assume, string x is derived from expression ${}_i\mathbf{R}_j^K$. Then, expression ${}_i\mathbf{R}_j^K$ is defined as,

$${}_i\mathbf{R}_j^K = \{x \in \Sigma^* / \delta\hat{}(q_i, x) = q_j, \text{ i.e., } \forall q_m < q_k \text{ (for } i < \forall m < j) \text{ and}$$
$$(q_i \text{ and/or } q_j) \geq q_k, \text{ where } q_m \text{ is the intermediate state between } q_i \text{ and } q_j\}$$

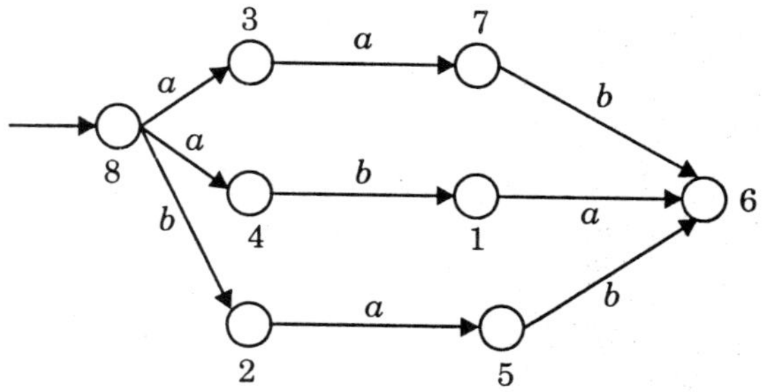

Fig. 9.11

For example, consider a state diagram shown in Fig. 9.11 then,

$${}_8\mathbf{R}_6{}^7 = \{aba, bab\}, \text{ but } aab \notin {}_8\mathbf{R}_6{}^7$$

Expression ${}_i\mathbf{R}_j{}^K$ can be obtained by using methods of induction i.e.,
Initially there is no intermediate state between q_i to q_j, so $k = 0$.
(For $k = 0$)

- ${}_i\mathbf{R}_j{}^0 = \{a_l \in \Sigma \,/\, \delta(q_i, a_l) = q_j\}$ if, $i \neq j$ and state is connected by single arc†.
- If, $i = j$ then,
  ${}_i\mathbf{R}_i{}^0 = \{a_l \in \Sigma \,/\, \delta(q_i, a_l) = q_i\} \cup \{\in\}$.‡
- If there is no symbol between q_i and q_j then,
  ${}_i\mathbf{R}_j{}^0 = \mathbf{\Phi}$ i.e., $\delta(q_i, \Phi) = \Phi$, [there is no path between them]

So, for the base cases of regular expression ${}_i\mathbf{R}_j{}^K$ can be constructed.

Apply induction hypothesis (for general k) and determine the expression ${}_i\mathbf{R}_j{}^K$ for the path from state q_i to state q_j i.e., for all intermediate states q_m, where $\forall q_m < q_k$ and $(q_i, q_j) = q_k$.

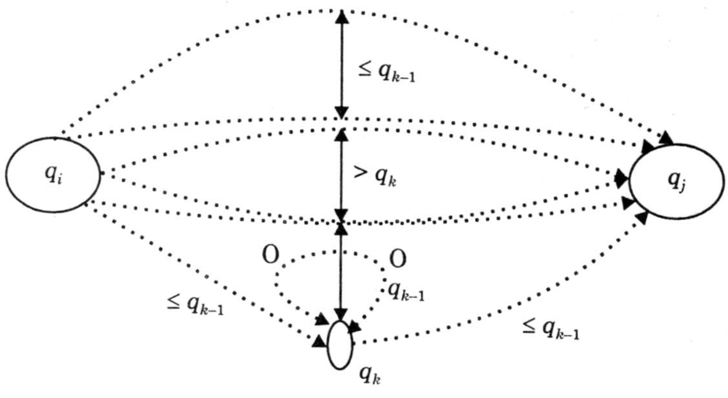

Fig. 9.12

† If there are m multiple paths from state $i \to j$ over symbols $a_1, a_2, \ldots\ldots, a_m$ then, regular expression will be $\boldsymbol{a_1 + a_2 + \ldots\ldots\ a_m}$.

‡ If there is no symbol (start state is the final state) then regular expression is $\in$.

If $a_1, a_2, \ldots\ldots, a_m$ are m multiple symbols i.e. transition on these symbols return back to same state then regular expression will be $\boldsymbol{a_1 + a_2 + \ldots\ldots\ a_m}$

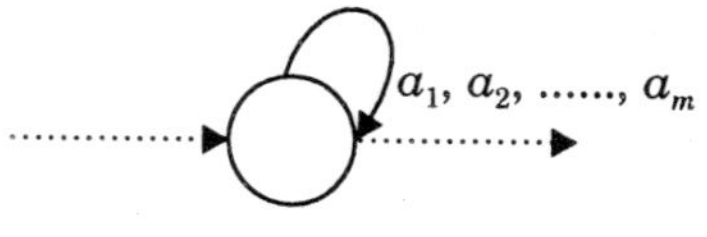

Consideration of paths are shown in Fig. 9.12, where following possibilities of paths exist,

1. There are few paths where, intermediate states are always $< k$, or states of upto $(k-1)$ will be consider hence the expression for this path will be ${}_i\mathbf{R}_j^{\mathbf{K-1}}$.
2. There are few paths where, intermediate states are always $> k$, so skip those paths.
3. A path from q_i to q_j can be divided into q_i to q_k and then q_k to q_j, i.e., In the path q_i to q_k where all intermediate sates are $\leq (k-1)$ so, expression is ${}_i\mathbf{R}_k^{\mathbf{K-1}}$, followed by
   - The path where on state k, few transitions are return back to state k itself by passing through all intermediate states $\leq (k-1)$ so, expression is $({}_k\mathbf{R}_k^{\mathbf{K-1}})^*$, followed by,
   - The path q_k to q_j where all-intermediate states $\leq (k-1)$ so, expression is ${}_k\mathbf{R}_j^{\mathbf{K-1}}$.

Thus, the combination of above possibilities we obtain the following expression,

$${}_i\mathbf{R}_j^{\mathbf{K}} = {}_i\mathbf{R}_j^{\mathbf{K-1}} \cup {}_i\mathbf{R}_k^{\mathbf{K-1}} \cdot ({}_k\mathbf{R}_k^{\mathbf{K-1}})^* \cdot {}_k\mathbf{R}_j^{\mathbf{K-1}}.$$

or,
$${}_i\mathbf{R}_j^{\mathbf{K}} = {}_i\mathbf{R}_j^{\mathbf{K-1}} + {}_i\mathbf{R}_k^{\mathbf{K-1}} \cdot ({}_k\mathbf{R}_k^{\mathbf{K-1}})^* \cdot {}_k\mathbf{R}_j^{\mathbf{K-1}}.$$

Therefore, we could also find the expression for any $k = n$ i.e., ${}_i\mathbf{R}_j^{\mathbf{n}}$.

Since, expression **R** expresses the language of DFA M so each **R** is associated with the regular expression i.e.,

$${}_i\mathbf{r}_j^{\mathbf{K}} = {}_i\mathbf{r}_j^{\mathbf{K-1}} + {}_i\mathbf{r}_k^{\mathbf{K-1}} \cdot ({}_k\mathbf{r}_k^{\mathbf{K-1}})^* \cdot {}_k\mathbf{r}_j^{\mathbf{K-1}}.$$

Assume DFA M starts from state 1 and set of final states are $\{f_1, f_2, \ldots\ldots f_p\}$ then,

$$\mathrm{L(M)} = \{{}_1\mathbf{R}_{\mathbf{f1}}^{\mathbf{n}} \cup {}_1\mathbf{R}_{\mathbf{f2}}^{\mathbf{n}} \ldots\ldots\ldots\ldots \cup {}_1\mathbf{R}_{\mathbf{fp}}^{\mathbf{n}}\}$$

So the language set contains the union of the languages consists of each path from state 1 to each state of F (final state).

Then regular expression $\mathbf{r} = {}_1\mathbf{r}_{\mathbf{f1}}^{\mathbf{n}} + {}_1\mathbf{r}_{\mathbf{f2}}^{\mathbf{n}} + \ldots\ldots + {}_1\mathbf{r}_{\mathbf{fp}}^{\mathbf{n}}$

Hence, the proof of the theorem is ended.

General rules for simplification of regular expressions

- $(\in + r)^* = r^*$

  $\therefore \quad L[(\in + r)^*] = \in + L(\in + r) + L(\in + r)\, L(\in + r) + \ldots\ldots$
  $= \in + L(r) + L(r)L(r) + \ldots\ldots$
  $= L(r)^*$

- $(\in + r)^*\, r = r^*.r = r^+$
- $(\in + r).r^* = r^* + r\,r^* = r^*$

  $\therefore \quad L(r\,r^*) = L(r)\,.L(r^*) = L(r).\, \{\in + L(r) + L(r).L(r) + \ldots\ldots\}$
  $= L(r) + L(r).\, L(r) + \ldots\ldots$

  and $\quad L(r^*) = \in + L(r) + L(r).\, L(r) + \ldots\ldots$

  so $L(rr^*) + L(r) = \in + L(r) + L(r).\, L(r) + \ldots\ldots$
  $= L(r^*)$

- $\Phi + r = \Phi$
- $\Phi\, r = \Phi$
- $(r^*)^* = r$

Example 9.6. *Construct the regular expression for the DFA shown in Fig. 9.13.*

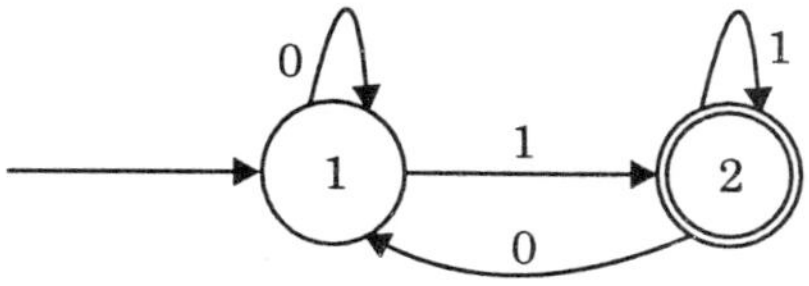

Fig. 9.13

Sol. We construct the regular expression using the theorem 9.2. So for the base case i.e. construct the expression from state 1 to the state j (where $j = 1$ and 2), and assume that there is no intermediate state ($k = 0$) between 1 and j. Hence, expression ${}_1\mathbf{R}_j{}^0$ is computed and shown in Fig. 9.14.

State Transition from	Language		Regular Expression
$1 \to 1$	${}_1\mathbf{R}_1{}^0$	Choices in between either no symbol or symbol 0	$\mathbf{0 + \in}$
$1 \to 2$	${}_1\mathbf{R}_2{}^0$	A single arc labeled by symbol 1	**1**
$2 \to 1$	${}_2\mathbf{R}_1{}^0$	A single arc labeled by symbol 0	**0**
$2 \to 2$	${}_2\mathbf{R}_2{}^0$	Choice in between either no symbol ($\in$) or symbol 1	$\mathbf{1 + \in}$

Fig. 9.14

- Now we construct the expression for inductive part (for $k = 1$), i.e., ${}_1\mathbf{R}_j{}^1$ (for $j = 1, 2$) By using the rule ${}_i\mathbf{R}_j{}^K = {}_i\mathbf{R}_j{}^{K-1} + {}_i\mathbf{R}_k{}^{K-1} \cdot ({}_k\mathbf{R}_k{}^{K-1})^* \cdot {}_k\mathbf{R}_j{}^{K-1}$.
- ${}_1\mathbf{R}_1{}^1 = {}_1\mathbf{R}_1{}^0 + {}_1\mathbf{R}_1{}^0\ ({}_1\mathbf{R}_1{}^0)^*\ {}_1\mathbf{R}_1{}^0$

  [Put the value of ${}_1\mathbf{R}_1{}^0$ from table (for $j = 1, j - 1$ returns 0 but 0 is no such state so state remains 1]

  $$= \mathbf{(0 + \in) + (0 + \in)(0 + \in)^*(0 + \in) = (0 + \in) + (0 + \in)0^*(0 + \in)}$$
  $$= \mathbf{0 + \in + 0^* = 0^*}$$
- ${}_1\mathbf{R}_2{}^1 = {}_1\mathbf{R}_2{}^0 + {}_1\mathbf{R}_1{}^0\ ({}_1\mathbf{R}_1{}^0)^*\ {}_1\mathbf{R}_2{}^0$

  $= \mathbf{1 + (0 + \in)(0 + \in)^*. 1 = 0^*\ 1}$
- ${}_2\mathbf{R}_1{}^1 = {}_2\mathbf{R}_1{}^0 + {}_2\mathbf{R}_1{}^0\ ({}_1\mathbf{R}_1{}^0)^*\ {}_1\mathbf{R}_1{}^0$

  $= \mathbf{0 + 0 . (0 + \in)^*\ (0 + \in) = 0 + 0.\ 0^* = 0.\ 0^*}$
- ${}_2\mathbf{R}_2{}^1 = {}_2\mathbf{R}_2{}^0 + {}_2\mathbf{R}_1{}^0\ ({}_1\mathbf{R}_1{}^0)^*\ {}_1\mathbf{R}_2{}^0$

  $= \mathbf{(1 + \in) + 0(0 + \in)^*\ 1 = (1 + \in) + 0\ \ 0^*\ 1}$

Hence we obtain the expression ${}_1\mathbf{R}_j{}^1$ (for $j = 1, 2$). Fig. 9.15.

State Transition from	Language		Regular Expression
1 → 1	${}_1R_1{}^1$	Choice in between either no symbol or finite number of 0's	**0***
1 → 2	${}_1R_2{}^1$	A single arc labeled by symbol 1 or Finite number of 0's followed by 1	**0* 1**
2 → 1	${}_2R_1{}^1$	A single arc labeled by symbol 0 or followed by one/more transition/s on 0's	**0. 0***
2 → 2	${}_2R_2{}^1$	Choice in between either symbol 1 or no symbol or through state 1	**1 + ∈ + 0 0*1**

Fig. 9.15

Now we construct the expression for k = 2, i.e., $1^{R}j^{2}$ (for j = 1, 2).

- ${}_1R_1{}^2 = {}_1R_1{}^1 + {}_1R_2{}^1 ({}_2R_2{}^1)^* {}_2R_1{}^1$
  $= 0^* + 0^*1 (1 + \in + 0\ 0^*1)^*\ 0\ 0^*$
- ${}_1R_2{}^2 = {}_1R_2{}^1 + {}_1R_2{}^1 ({}_2R_2{}^1)^* {}_2R_2{}^1$
  $= 0^*1 + (0^*1) [1 + \in + 0\ 0\ ^*1]^* [1 + \in + 0\ 0\ ^*1]$
  $= 0^*1 [1 + \in + 0\ 0\ ^*1]^*$
- ${}_2R_1{}^2 = {}_2R_1{}^1 + {}_2R_2{}^1 ({}_2R_2{}^1)^* {}_2R_1{}^1$
  $= 0.\ 0^* + [1 + \in + 0\ 0^*1] [1 + \in + 0\ 0^*1\ ]^* .\ 0\ 0^*$
  $= [1 + \in + 0\ 0^*1\ ]^* .\ 0\ 0^*$
- ${}_2R_2{}^2 = {}_2R_2{}^1 + {}_2R_2{}^1 ({}_2R_2{}^1)^* {}_2R_2{}^1$
  $= [1 + \in + 0\ 0^*1\ ]^+$

Hence the table for expression ${}_1R_j{}^2$ (for j = 1, 2) is shown in Fig. 9.16.

State Transition from	Language	Regular Expression
1 → 1	${}_1R_1{}^2$	**0* + 0* 1 (1 + ∈ + 0 0*1)* 0 0***
1 → 2	${}_1R_2{}^2$	**0* 1 [1 + ∈ + 0 0 *1] ***
2 → 1	${}_2R_1{}^2$	**[1 + ∈ + 0 0*1]* . 0 0***
2 → 2	${}_2R_2{}^2$	**[1 + ∈ + 0 0*1]⁺**

Fig. 9.16

Now the final regular expression for the DFA shown in Fig. 9.13 will be constructed by taking the unions of all the expression whose state 1 is the starting state and state 2 is the final state, i.e. ${}_1R_2{}^2$.

Where, ${}_1R_2{}^2 = 0^*1 [1 + \in + 0\ 0\ ^*1]^*$

Therefore the regular expression is **0*1 [1 + ∈ + 00*1]*.**

9.5 CONSTRUCTION OF REGULAR EXPRESSION FROM DFA (By Eliminating States)

From a given DFA a regular expression can be constructed directly through step-by-step eliminations of states from the state diagram. A state can be eliminated equivalently by the regular expression which is constructed in the following sequence, i.e.,

- Find the regular expression for all incoming arcs to that state,
- Find the regular expression for all repetition arcs that returns to that state itself, and
- Find the regular expression for all outgoing arcs from that state.

Consider an example of a DFA shown in Fig. 9.17.

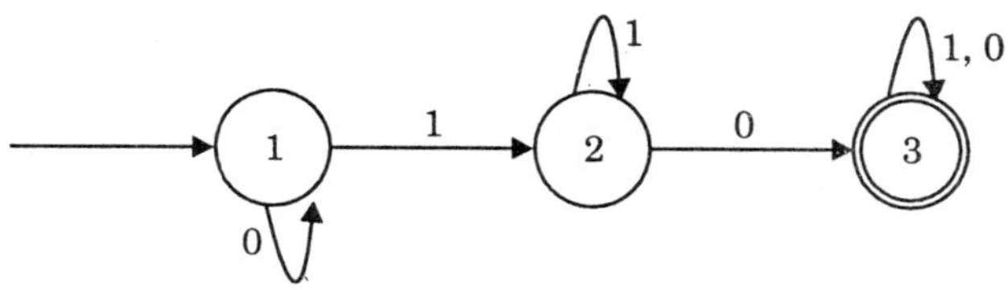

Fig. 9.17

(Let us eliminate state 2)

Regular expression for the incoming arc (from state 1 on symbol 1) is **1**. Regular expression for the repetition arc (on state 2 itself on symbol 1) is **1*** and then the regular expression for outgoing arc (from state 2 to state 3) is **0**. Hence, the transition arc from state 1 to state 3 after eliminating state 2 will be labeled by regular expression **1 . 1* . 0** which is shown in Fig. 9.18.

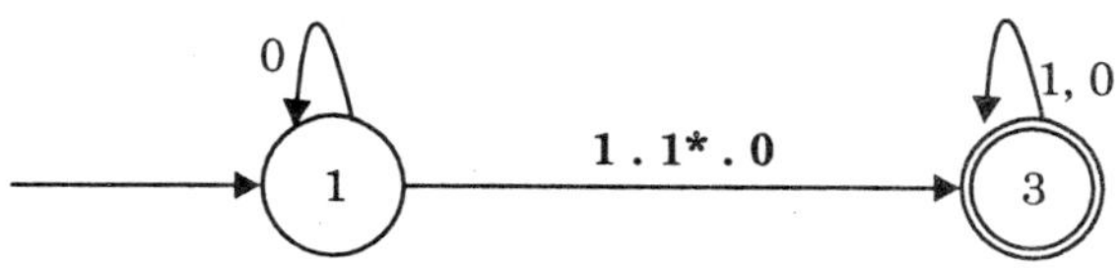

Fig. 9.18

(Now eliminate state 1)

State has an repetition arc labeled by symbol 0 so, the regular expression is **0***, followed by an outgoing arc, which is labeled by regular expression **1 . 1* . 0**. So, elimination of state 1 will result the regular expression **0*. (1 . 1* . 0)**. (Fig. 9.19)

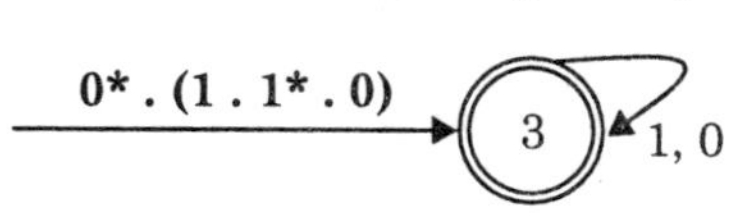

Fig. 9.19

Now the incoming arc labeled by the regular expression **0*. (1 . 1* . 0)** reaches to state 3, which is the accepting state and regular expression for the repetition arc over symbol 0 or 1 is **(1 + 0)***. Thus we obtain the final regular expression i.e.,

Example 9.7. *Convert the following DFA to regular expression.*

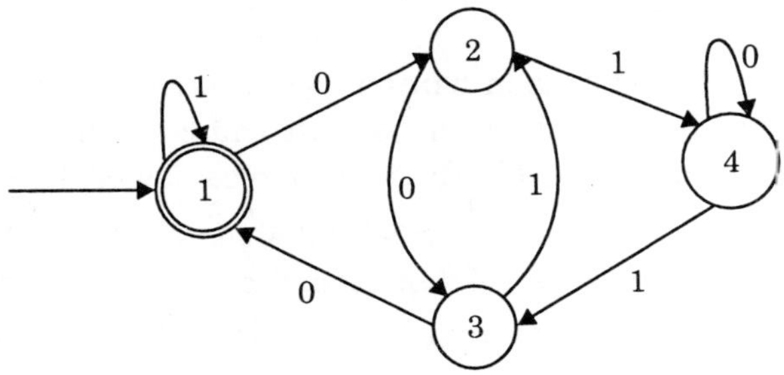

Fig. 9.20

DFA shown in Fig. 9.20 has state 1 is the starting state as well as the final state. So, let us select the state 4 is eliminated first.

- The regular expression for the incoming arc (from state 2 to 4 on symbol 1) is **1**,
- The regular expression for an repetitive arc (state 4 to itself on symbol 0) **0***,
- The regular expression for an outgoing arc (from state 4 to1 on symbol 1) is **1**.

Hence, the equivalent regular expression after eliminating the state 4 will be **1.0***. **1**. So a new arc shown in Fig. 9.21 will be labeled by this regular expression (let it be r) from state 2 to state 3. Thus, we obtain a now DFA i.e.,

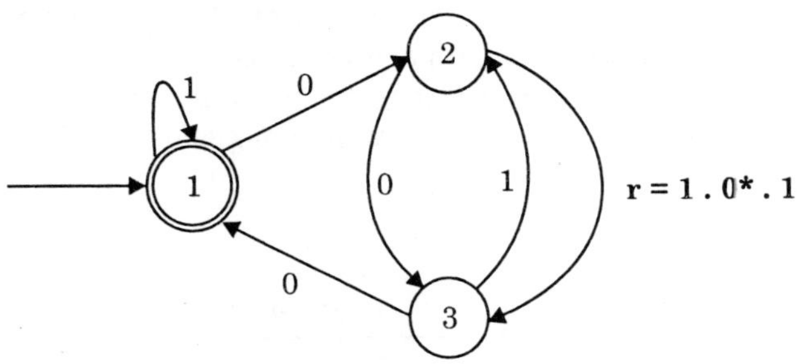

Fig. 9.21

(Now eliminate state 3)

Observe the incoming and the outgoing arcs of state 3, corresponding to them we find the equivalent regular expressions i.e.,

- The regular expression for the incoming arc from state 2 to 3 which is labeled by **r** and then the regular expression for the out going arc from state 3 to 1 on symbol 0 is **0**. So, through this path regular expression will be, **r . 0**.
- The regular expression for the incoming arc from state 2 to 3 labeled by **r** and then from the regular expression for the path from state 3 to 2 to 3 on symbol 1 followed by 0, is **1. 0** with possibility of zero/more times repetition of this path hence regular expression will be **(1. 0)***and then the regular expression for the outgoing arc from state 3 to 1 is **0**. Hence, through this path regular expression will be **r . (1. 0)* 0**

The possibilities of both discussed cases can be equivalently represented by the regular expression **r . (1. 0)* 0.**

- The regular expression for the incoming arc from state 2 to 3 on symbol 0 is **0** and the regular expression for the outgoing arc from state 3 to 1 on symbol 0 is again **0**. So, we obtain the regular expression **0.0.**

- The regular expression for the incoming arc from state 2 to 3 on symbol 0 is **0** and the regular expression for the outgoing arc from state 3 to 1 on symbol 0 is again **0**. The regular expression for the path $3 \rightarrow 2 \rightarrow 3$ is **1. 0** and also with the possibility of zero/more repetitions of this path will have the regular expression (**1. 0**)* followed by the regular expression **0** for an out going arc from state 3 to 1. Hence, the regular expression will be **0 .(1. 0)* 0.**

Now these two regular expressions can be equivalently expressed by the regular expression **0.(1. 0)* 0**. So we have the remaining states of DFA which is looking as,

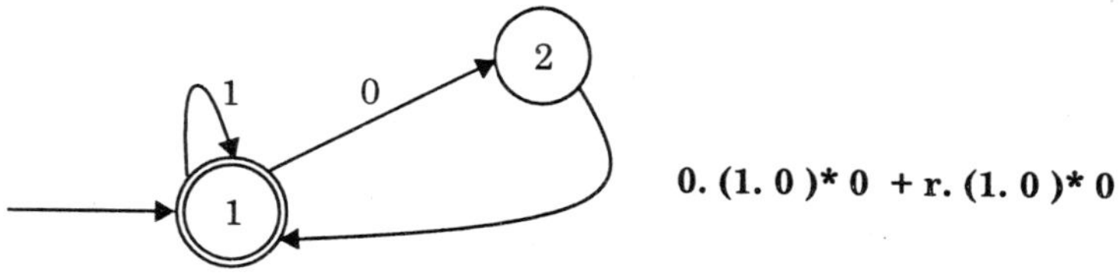

(Now eliminate the state 2)

After elimination of state 2 we obtain the equivalent regular expression **0 [0. (1. 0)* 0 + r. (1. 0)* 0]**. And finally DFA has remaining state 1, shown below.

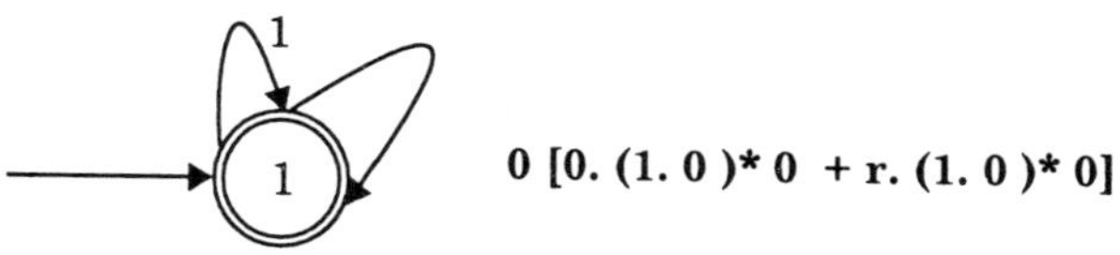

- The regular expression for repetition arc on state 1 over symbol 1 is **1***, and
- The regular expression for another repetition arc on state 1 is 0 **[0. (1. 0)*. 0 + r. (1. 0)* 0]**. Therefore the final regular expression is union of them i.e.,

1* + 0 .[0. (1. 0)* 0 + r. (1. 0)* 0]

Substitute the value of **r** thus we obtain the final regular expression

1* + 0 .[0. (1. 0)* 0 + 1. 0* 1 (1. 0)* 0]

9.6 FINITE AUTOMATONS WITH OUTPUT

In the previous chapter of finite automata we have discussed in detail the deterministic and nondeterministic nature of finite automata. The behaviors of these automatons are defined by the nature of the input strings accepted by them. That is, after processing the input string automaton generates the output in the form of decisions i.e., either *accepted* if automaton reaches to its final state/s or *rejected* if automaton never reaches to its final state/s. (Fig. 9.22) So, the nature of language which is accepted by the finite automaton designates the power of such finite automaton.

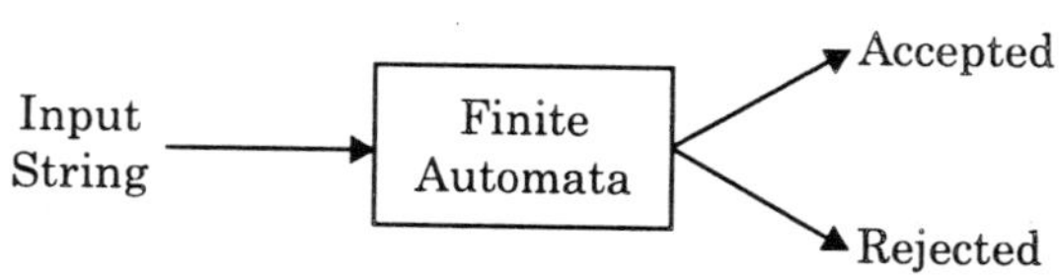

Fig. 9.22

This section introduces other forms of finite automatons, which operates on input string and returned the output in some form of string, instead of decisions. This types of finite automatons are called as *Finite Automatons with Output*. So, the behavior of finite automatons with output are captured by the nature of the output string it generates. Eventually, the significance of final state is meaningless†. Fig 9.23 shows the abstract view of a finite automata with output. Let automaton M be a finite automata with output, that operates on some input string ($\in \Sigma^*$), where Σ is the set of input symbols and it returns the output string ($\in \Delta$), where Δ is the set of output symbols.

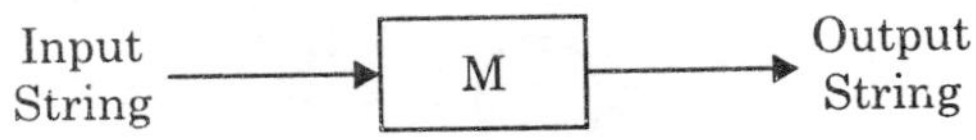

Fig. 9.23

So, the automaton M behaves as a Transducer. Let us represented it by T_M where,

$$T_M : \Sigma^* \rightarrow \Delta^*$$

Assume x be a input string i.e., $x \in \Sigma^*$ then,

$$T_M(x) = w \quad \{\text{where } w \in \Delta^*\}$$

Let x be a input string and it can break into a sub string y and a symbol a, i.e.,

$$x = y \, . \, a$$

and similarly assume w is the output string i.e., $w = y' \, . \, a'$

where, $T_M(x) = T_M(y \, . \, a) = w = y' \, . \, a'$

Assume, automata M is in starting state r_0, *and after consuming input string y it reaches to state* r_j *with return string y' as output and on next symbol a it reaches to state* r_{j+1} *with return symbol a' as output and it stops because whole string x is now consumed by M, no matter what state* r_{j+1} *is. It may be any state including starting state* r_0.

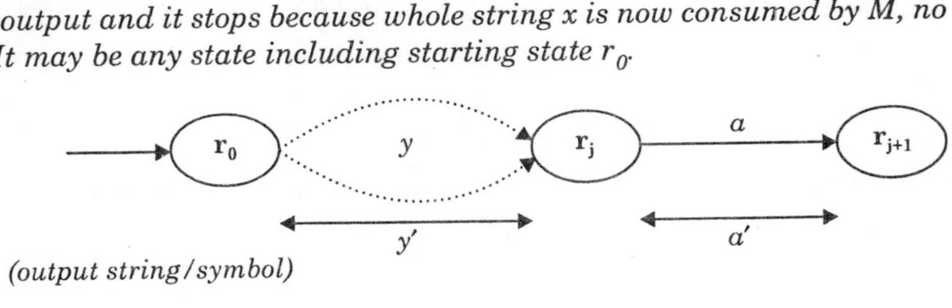

Fig. 9.24

So, the concept of final state does'nt arises here. On which state automaton stops that is depend upon the input string i.e., after reading the last symbol of the input string it will stop.

There are two types of Automatons exist under this category,

1. Melay Automaton (Machine)
2. Moore Automaton (Machine)

9.6.1 Melay Automaton

In the Melay automaton output is given over the transition arc. Assume a portion of DFA M is in Fig. 9.25, where M = ({A, B, C}, {a, b}, δ, A, Φ}, here set of final state is Φ because it is useless to talk about the final state in case of Finite automan with output.

† *Finite Automatons with output has no final state/s, because from the strating state automaton generates the output in some form of symbols on each transitions betweeen the states. Automaton can stop, any of the state ($\in$ Q) depending upon the nature of the input string.*

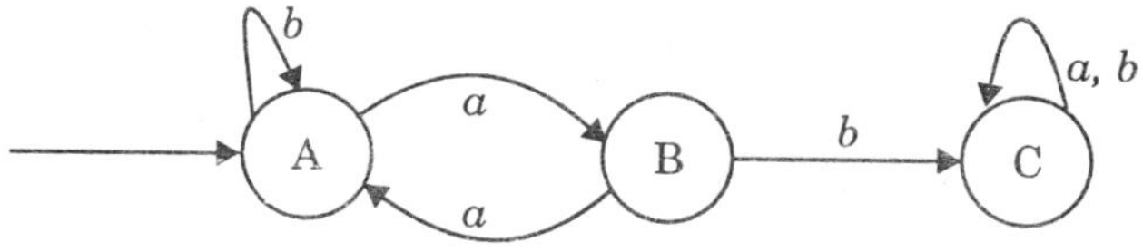

M

Fig. 9.25

Now if we put another symbol on each transition arc provided that it is associated with the output information corresponding to that input symbol then the automaton M becomes M′ shown in Fig. 9.26.

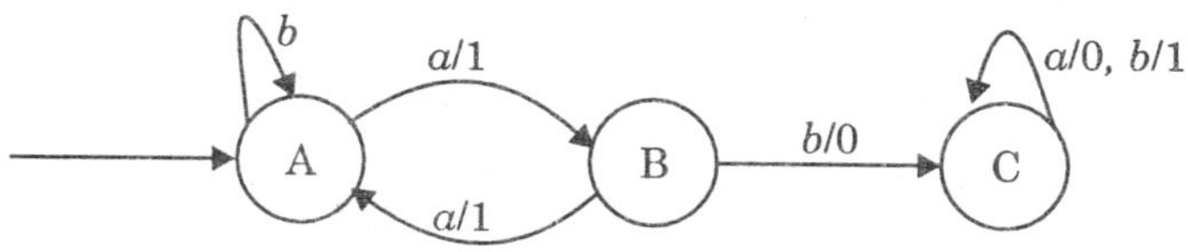

M′

Fig. 9.26

where, we assume that output symbols are in set $\Delta = \{0, 1\}$. For example, if input string is '*abba*' then automaton M′ generate an equivalent output string 1010 in the following manner,

- From starting state A, M′ reads the first symbol '*a*' and return corresponding output symbol 1 and reach to state B.
- Next input symbol is *b*, from state B, M′ reads symbol *b* and return corresponding output symbol 0 and reach to state C.
- From state C, processed the remaining symbols *a* and *b* and return corresponding symbols 0 and 1 respectively.

Hence, the input string '*abba*' returns the string 1010 as output. Therefore, this type of automaton M′ is known as *Melay automaton* & *Melay Machine*.

9.6.1.1 Definition

A Melay Machine is defined by following set of tuples,

1. A finite set of states **Q**,
2. A finite set of input symbols Σ,
3. A finite set of output symbols Δ,
4. Transition function δ,
5. Output function λ, and
6. A starting state $\mathbf{q_0}$, where $q_0 \in Q$

So, a Melay automaton $\mathbf{M_e}$ is defined using these 6 tuples as,

$$\mathbf{M_e = (Q, \Sigma, \Delta, \delta, \lambda, q_0)}$$

where the transition function δ is defined as,

$$\delta : Q \times \Sigma \rightarrow Q$$

which is the partial mapping of a state ($\in$ Q) with an input symbol ($\in \Sigma$) which returns a state ($\in$ Q). The output function λ is defined as,

$$\lambda : Q \times \Sigma \rightarrow \Delta$$

which is again the partial mapping of a state ($\in$ Q) with an input symbol ($\in \Sigma$) and return an output symbol ($\in \Delta$).

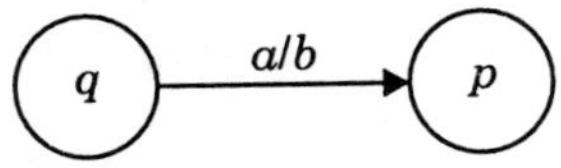

Fig. 9.27

For example, the transition diagram shown in Fig. 9.27 of Melay case,

$\lambda(q, a) = b;$ [returns a output symbol]

and $\delta(q, a) = p;$ [returns a state]

Thus, the purpose of the output function (λ) is to map the input string to output string.

9.6.1.2 Representation

The representation of the Melay machine is similar to the DFA representation such that the states are represented by the small circles and the directed edges indicating transitions between the states. Each edge is labeled with a compound symbol I/O where the edge to travel is determined by the input symbol I, while traveling with the edge the output symbol O is printed. For example, Fig. 9.28 shows a Melay machine $M_e = (\{q_0, q_1, q_2, q_3\}, \{a, b\}, \{0, 1\}, \delta, \lambda, q_0)$.

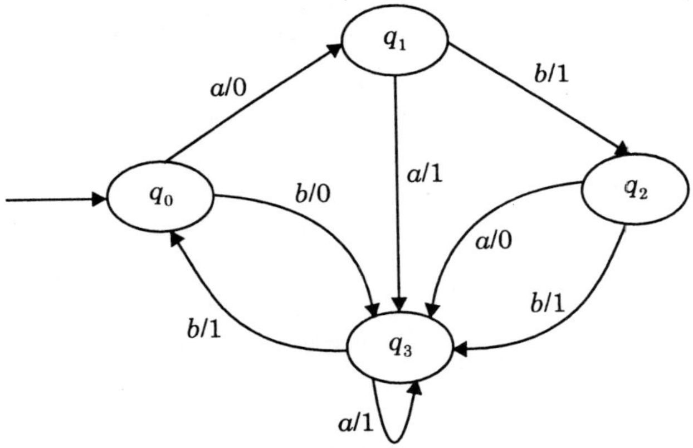

Fig. 9.28. (M_e)

So, on input strings '*abbab*' and '*aaabb*' we obtain the output strings '01111' and '01110' respectively.

FACT

- *In a Melay machine the length of the output string is same as the length of input string, i.e., if machine M_e generates the output string w on processing the input string x then $|w| = |x|$.*
- *Due to the absence of final state in the machine the language of the Melay machine doesn't define by accepting or rejecting the input strings.*

Example 9.8

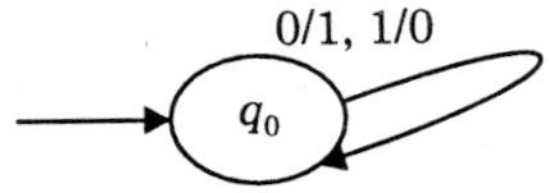

Fig. 9.29 M_e.

The Melay machine shown in Fig. 9.29 is the *1's complement machine* where $M_e = (\{q_0\}, \{0, 1\}, \{0, 1\}, \delta, \lambda, q_0\}$ and δ and λ are defined as,

$$\delta(q_0, 0) = q_0; \qquad \delta(q_0, 1) = q_0;$$

and

$$\lambda(q_0, 0) = 1; \qquad \lambda(q_0, 1) = 0;$$

For example if the input string is 1010110 then M_e generates corresponding output string 0101001 (1's complement of the string 1010110).

Example 9.9.

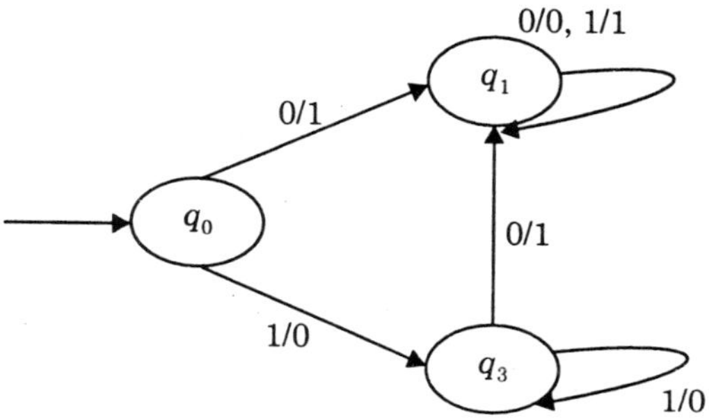

Fig. 9.30 M_e.

Melay shown in Fig. 9.30 is an incremental machine. For example, if the input string is 1000 the return string will be 1001, if input string is 0000 then we get the output string 0001, provided that the symbol read from the input string is from right to left.

Input string	1 0 0 0 ,	0 0 0 0	1 0 1 0 1 1
	←	←	←
Output string	1 0 0 1	0 0 0 1	1 0 1 1 0 0

Example 9.10. *Construct the Melay machine that accepts the string x and returns string 3 times of x, where string x is formed over $\Sigma = \{0, 1\}$.*

Sol. Consider any string of 0's and 1's i.e., $x = 0101$ then output will be 3 times the number represented by binary digits 0101, that will be 1111 i.e.,

Input string	0 1 0 1	or,	0 0 0 1 1 1
	←		←
Output string	1 1 1 1		0 1 0 1 0 1

Procedure to calculate3x

$3x$ can be calculated from x by simple three times addition of x like as,

$$\begin{array}{r} x \\ +\ x \\ x \\ \hline 3x \\ \hline \end{array}$$

For example, if $x = 000111$ calculation for $3x$ by step-by-step three times binary addition will be given as,

00	01	10	10	01	00	← Position of Input Carry
0	0	0	1	1	1	← Input string
0	0	0	1	1	1	
0	0	0	1	1	1	
0	0	0	1	0	1	← Output string
			←			Move in this direction

Now assume that these carry positions represent three different states such that initially automaton is in state C_{00}, on symbol 1 automaton reaches to state C_{01} and return the symbol 1. For next input symbol 1, return output symbol is 0 and automaton reach to state C_{10}. This state remains unchanged, if next input symbol will be 1 and return symbol is 1. At this state (digit position) if input symbol is 0 then, return symbol will be 0 and next state will be C_{01}. At this state if input symbol is 0 then automaton reach to state C_{00} and produce output symbol 1. State C_{00} remains same for input symbol 0 and it outputted the symbol 0. Thus we obtain the Melay machine shown in Fig. 9.31.

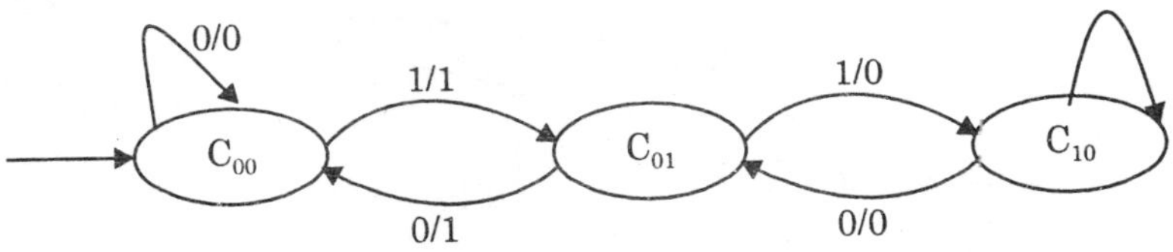

Fig. 9.31

We can verify the correctness of the above Melay machine over any input string of 0's and 1's, i.e., for example $x = (001011)_2$ or $(11)_{10}$, then machine should generate the output string $3x$ that is $(100001)_2$ or $(33)_{10}$.

01 10 01 10 01 00 ← Position of Input Carry

| 0 0 0 1 1 1 | ←— Input symbols

0 0 1 0 1 1

0 0 1 0 1 1

←— Symbols processed in this direction

| 1 0 0 0 0 1 | ←— Output symbols

Hence Melay machine works correctly and returns the 3 times of the input string. The moves between states over input symbols and the generation of the output symbols are shown in table shown in Fig. 9.32.

Current State	**Input Symbol**	**Output Symbol**	**Carry Generated**	**State Transition**
C_{00} (No Carry)	1	1	01	$C_{00} \rightarrow C_{01}$
C_{01}	1	0	10	$C_{01} \rightarrow C_{10}$
C_{10}	0	0	01	$C_{10} \rightarrow C_{01}$
C_{01}	1	0	10	$C_{01} \rightarrow C_{10}$
C_{10}	0	0	01	$C_{10} \rightarrow C_{01}$
C_{01}	0	1	00	C_{01} ® C_{00}

Fig. 9.32

9.6.2 Moore Automaton

As we seen that, in the case of Melay machine (finite automata with output), the transition arc between the states is labelled with a compound symbol such that the output is generated corresponding to input symbol. In case of Moore machine output is represented by the state itself. The names of the states are such, that it represents the output symbols. So, in case of Moore machine, the output is associated with the states. Therefore, for a given input the sequence of transitions between states is responsible for generating the output. For example, a finite automata shown in Fig. 9.33 whose start state is A, and states A, B and C are represented equivalently by the symbol 0, 0 and 1 respectively.

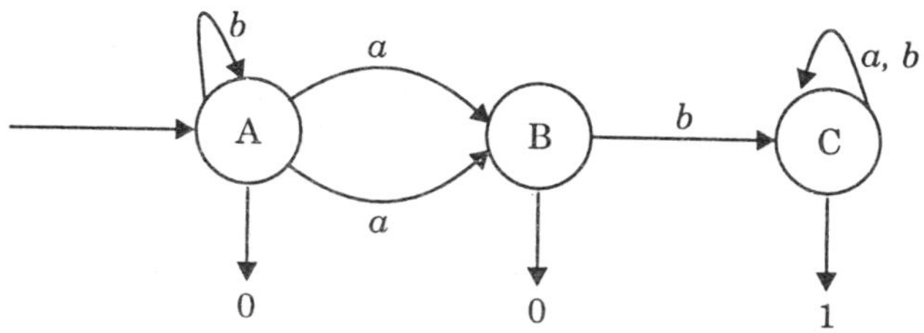

Fig. 9.33

Then for the input string '*abba*' the output string will be determine as follows,

From the start state A, following sequence of states is obtained after processing the complete string '*abba*',

$$\begin{array}{ccccccccccc} & a & & b & & b & & a & & \leftarrow & \text{Input string} \\ A & \longrightarrow & B & \longrightarrow & C & \longrightarrow & C & \longrightarrow & C & & \\ 0 & & 0 & & 1 & & 1 & & 1 & \leftarrow & \text{Output string} \end{array}$$

Corresponding to that sequence of states we obtain the output string 00111.

9.6.2.1 Definition

A Moore machine is defined as following set of tuples,

1. A finite set of states **Q**,
2. A finite set of input Symbols Σ,
3. A finite set of output Symbols Δ,
4. Transition function δ,
5. Output function λ,
6. Starting state r_0 where $r_0 \in$ Q.

Let M_o is a Moore machine, then it can be defined using above tuples as,

$$\mathbf{M_o = (Q, \Sigma, \Delta, \delta, \lambda, r_0)}$$

where, transition function δ is defined as,

$$\delta : Q \times \Sigma \rightarrow Q$$

which is the partial mapping of a state ($\in$ Q)with an input symbol ($\in \Sigma$) that return a state ($\in$ Q). Similarly the output function λ, is defined as,

$$\lambda : Q \rightarrow \Delta$$

which is the direct mapping between the state and the output symbol.

For example, consider a Moore machine M_o shown in Fig. 9.34.

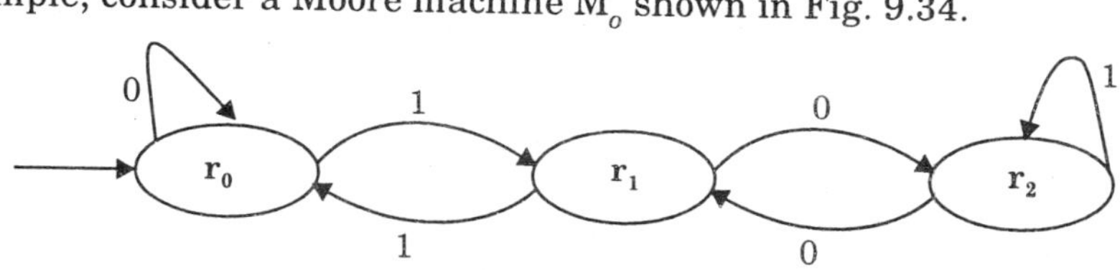

Fig. 9.34 M_o.

Assume that states r_0, r_1 and r_2 are represented by symbol 0, 1 and 2 respectively, then

$$\lambda(r_0) = 0; \quad \lambda(r_1) = 1; \quad \text{and} \quad \lambda(r_2) = 2;$$

FACT

- *In the Moore machine, the first symbol in the output string always specified the start state.*
- *In the Moore machine the output string has not the same length as the input string. If we compare the length of input string with length of output string, then we found that length of output string is one more than length of input string. So, if x is the input string and w is its output string then,*

$$|x| + 1 = |w|;$$

Since, it is assume that machine always starts from initial state. So, corresponding to the start state an additional output symbol always comes in the list of output string. While, in case of Melay machine length of the output string is no greater than the input string.
- *The language of a Moore machine doesn't define on the basis of accepted word. Since, every traceable input string generates some output string and there is no such thing as final state. The process is terminated when the last symbol of input string is read and the last output symbol is printed.*

Note. *Moore and Melay machines are Deterministic Finite State Automatons. Hence, from each state of above machines, there is exactly one and only one exit transition arc on each input symbol.*

Example 9.11. *Consider the Moore machine shown in Fig. 9.34, determine the output for the input string 10111.*

Sol. From the start state r_0, we obtain following sequence of states after reading the input string 10111,

$$\begin{array}{ccccccccccc} & 1 & & 0 & & 1 & & 1 & & 1 & \leftarrow \text{Input string} \\ r_0 & \rightarrow & r_1 & \rightarrow & r_2 & \rightarrow & r_2 & \rightarrow & r_2 & \rightarrow & r_2 \\ 0 & & 1 & & 2 & & 2 & & 2 & & 2 \leftarrow \text{Output string} \end{array}$$

Hence, the output string is 012222. If we carefully observe the nature of return string then we will find that it is the reminder of 3. See the table shown in Fig. 9.35.

For the input string 010111

Input Symbol	Equivalent Value	Operation (Value mod 3)	Output (Reminder of 3)
0	0	0 mod 3	0
1	$(01)_2$	1 mod 3	1
0	$(010)_2$	2 mod 3	2
1	$(0101)_2$	5 mod 3	2
1	$(01011)_2$	11 mod 3	2
1	$(010111)_2$	23 mod 3	2*

Fig. 9.35

From starting state r_0, if input number is 0 then it returns the number $0((0)_2 \bmod 3 = 0)$

Otherwise, if input number is 1 then output will be 1 (state r_1 number) or $((1)_2 \bmod 3 = 1)$. From state r_1, if input number is 0, so total input number received at this state is 10 then machine returns output number 2 (corresponding to state r_2) or $((10)_2 \bmod 3 = 2)$. At state r_2, received input numbers is 10 then,

- For input string 10 followed by one/more 1 (equivalent number will be either $(101, 1011, 10111\ldots)_2$ or number $(5, 11, 23, \ldots)_{10}$) the output is 2 (corresponding to state r_2) or $((101, 1011, \ldots)_2 \bmod 3 = 2)$.
- For input string 10 followed by number 0 then return number is 1 (state r_1) or $((100)_2 \bmod 3 = 2)$.
- For input string 10 followed by 1* followed by number 0 (equivalent number will be $(1010, 10110, 101110,\ldots..)_2$ or $(10, 22, 46, ..)_{10}$) the return number is 1 (state r_1) which is again reminder of 3.

At state r_1 possible strings are received,

- 100, or
- 101* 0, i.e., strings are {1010, 10110, 101110,.....}

For state transition $r_1 \to r_0$ means that above strings followed by number 1 so that the final input strings are $(1001$ or $10101, 101101, 1011101, \ldots\ldots.)_2$ or $(9, 21, 45\ldots)_{10}$, in such case reminder will be zero.

9.7 EQUIVALENCE OF MELAY & MOORE AUTOMATONS

When we study the finite automata with output such that a Melay machine and a Moore machine a general question arises, does both machines are equivalent. Alternatively, we say if M_e is the Melay machine and M_o is the Moore machine then,

$$\text{Does } M_e \equiv M_o \,?$$

In other words, we may check the equivalence of above machines with respect to the string generated by them at the output. Let x is the input string, then assume the output of machines M_e and M_o are w and w' that can be define as,

$$T_{Me}(x) = w \quad \text{and} \quad T_{Mo}(x) = w'$$

Since, $|\, w \,| \neq |\, w' \,|$, it means

$$T_{Me}(x) \not\equiv T_{Mo}(x) \quad (\text{for } \forall x)$$

Therefore, Melay machine is not equivalent to Moore machine.

Since these machines are lying in the class finite automaton with output therefore it is possible to make both these machine equivalent, i.e.,

- Equivalence of a Melay machine to a Moore machine, and
- Equivalence of a Moore machine to a Melay machine.

To make Melay machine equivalent to Moore machine i.e.,

$$M_o = M_e$$

We must introduce an additional symbol b corresponding to the start state (r_0) of the Moore machine i.e.,

$$\lambda_e(r_0) = b \text{ then } \quad b.\,T_{Me}(x) \;=\; T_{Mo}(x) \qquad (\forall x)$$

(The Meaning is that start state is the pending state by own)

Eventually, we get the same length of output string from both the machines.

9.7.1 Equivalent Machine Construction (From Moore machine-to-Melay Machine)

Let M_o be a Moore machine i.e.,

$$M_o = (Q_o, \Sigma_o, \Delta_o, \delta_o, \lambda_o, r_0)$$

then an equivalent Melay machine M_e can be constructed from M_o i.e.,

$$M_e = (Q_e, \Sigma_e, \Delta_e, \delta_e, \lambda_e, r_0)$$

(where all symbols as there usual meaning)

Now we can establish the correspondence between the tuples of both the machines, i.e.

- Both machines operate on same set of states so $Q_o = Q_e$ (let it be Q),
- Both machines operate on same set of input symbols so $\Sigma_o = \Sigma_e$ (let it be Σ),
- Both machines operate on same set of output symbols so $\Delta_o = \Delta_e$ (let it be Δ),
- Both machines start on same starting state $\{r_0\}$.
- Transitions between states over input alphabets must be same in both machines so $\delta = \delta_e$ (let it be δ).
- The relation between the output function λ_e (Melay) to λ_o (Moore) will be defined as,

$$\lambda_e(r, a) = \lambda_o(\delta(r, a)) \quad [\text{for } \forall\, r \in Q \text{ and } \forall\, a \in \Sigma]$$

Alternatively, the return of output function λ_e from any state over the input symbol is same to the value of output function λ_e at the state obtain from the transition of that state over that input symbol.

For example consider again a Moore machine shown in Fig. 9.34, i.e.,

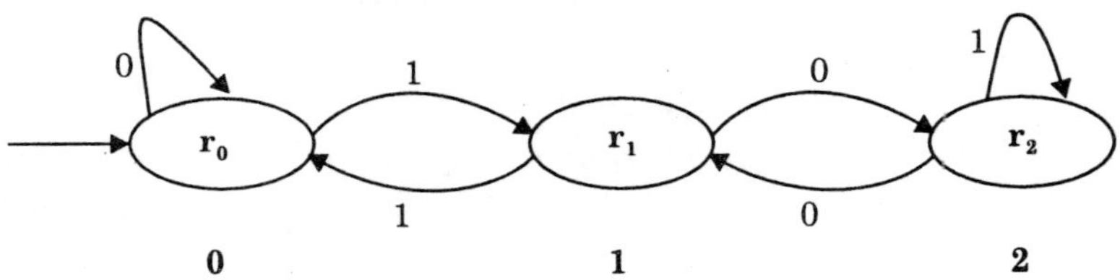

M_o

where the set of states $Q = \{r_0, r_1, r_2\}$, state $\{r_0\}$ is the starting state, set of input symbols $\Sigma = \{0, 1\}$, set of output symbols $\Delta = \{0, 1, 2\}$, transition function δ's are defined as,

$$\delta(r_0, 0) = r_0; \qquad \delta(r_0, 1) = r_1;$$
$$\delta(r_1, 0) = r_2; \qquad \delta(r_1, 1) = r_0;$$
$$\delta(r_2, 0) = r_1; \qquad \delta(r_2, 1) = r_2;$$

and output function λ are defined as,

$$\lambda(r_0) = 0; \quad \lambda(r_1) = 1; \quad \text{and} \quad \lambda(r_2) = 2;$$

(from the transition diagram shown)

Now determine the output function for Melay machine (λ_e) from the known output function for Moore machine (λ_o) i.e.,

$$\lambda_e(r_0, 0) = \lambda_o(\delta(r_0, 0)) = \lambda_o(r_0) = \mathbf{0}; \qquad \lambda_e(r_0, 1) = \lambda_o(\delta(r_0, 1)) = \lambda_o(r_1) = \mathbf{1};$$
$$\lambda_e(r_1, 0) = \lambda_o(\delta(r_1, 0)) = \lambda_o(r_2) = \mathbf{2}; \qquad \lambda_e(r_1, 1) = \lambda_o(\delta(r_1, 1)) = \lambda_o(r_0) = \mathbf{0};$$
$$\lambda_e(r_2, 0) = \lambda_o(\delta(r_2, 0)) = \lambda_o(r_1) = \mathbf{1}; \qquad \lambda_e(r_2, 1) = \lambda_o(\delta(r_2, 1)) = \lambda_o(r_2) = \mathbf{2};$$

Hence, the state diagram of equivalent Melay machine is constructed and which is shown below in Fig. 9.36, where transition arcs are labeled with compound symbols i.e., input and corresponding output symbol.

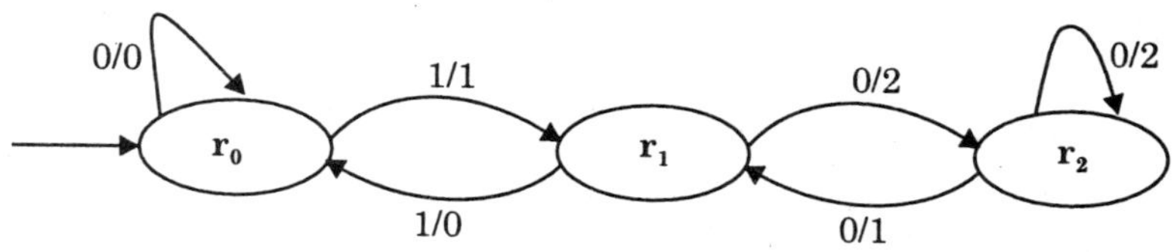

Fig. 9.36 M_e.

Note. *We observe from the state diagram of Melay machine that all incoming arcs to a state must be labeled the output symbol which is equivalent to that state itself. Conversely, the role of state for its outgoing arcs is nothing in the output generation. For example, consider a snapshot of machine M_e (Fig. 9.37) where state r_0 has two incoming arcs labeled with input symbol 0 and 1. So the output symbol would corresponds to state r_0 only, which is 0, so both arcs are labeled with output symbol 0.*

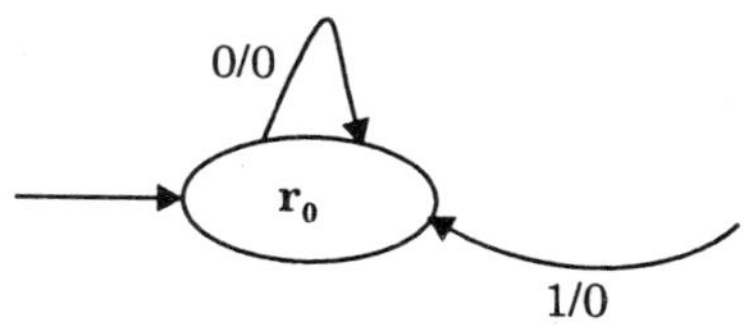

Fig. 9.37

Similarly, with state r_1, incoming arcs labeled with input and there corresponding output symbol are shown below.

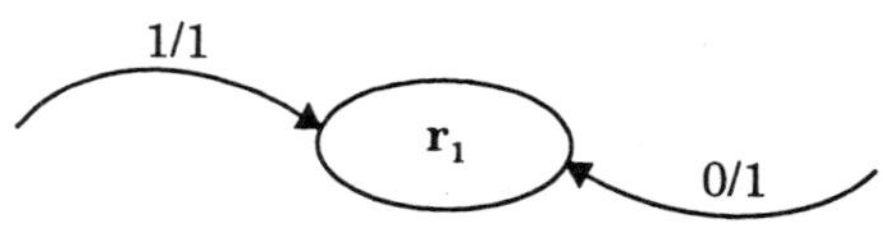

Fig. 9.38

Similarly output for other states can be determined.

9.7.2 Melay Machine-to-Moore Machine

Now we shall discuss the method how an equivalent Moore machine is constructed form a given Melay machine. Assume, M_e be a Melay machine which is defined by following set of tuples,

$$M_e = (Q_e, \Sigma, \Delta, \delta_e, \lambda_e, r_0)$$

then an equivalent Moore machine M_o can be constructed from M_e where,

$$M_o = (Q_o, \Sigma, \Delta, \delta_o, \lambda_o, [r_0, b])$$

(where all tuples as there usual meaning)

Now we can establish the relation between corresponding tuples of both the machines, i.e.,

- Both machines operate on same set of input symbols Σ and same set of output symbols Δ.
- $Q_o = Q_e \times \Delta$, i.e., states of the Moore machine is represented by an pair whose first element is the state ($\in Q_e$) and the second element is the output symbol ($\in \Delta$). For example, state $[r, a] \in Q_o$, where state $r \in Q_e$ and $a \in \Delta$.

- Start state of Moore machine is defined as $[r_0, b]$, where r_0 is the starting state of Melay machine and b is any arbitrary symbol $\in \Delta$.
- The return of output function λ_o when operated on the state like $[r, a] \in Q_o$, will be the output symbol that exist as the second element of the pair i.e.,

$$\lambda_o([r, a]) = a$$

- Transition function δ_o relates to δ_e like as,

$$\delta_o([r, a], b) = [\delta_e(r, b), \lambda_e(r, b)] = [p, d]$$

where, $\delta_e(r, b) = p$ ($\in Q_e$) and $\lambda_e(r, b) = d \in \Delta$.

Example 9.12. *Now we discuss some simple conversions from Melay machine to Moore machine.*
(*i*) Consider a snapshot of Melay machine is shown in Fig. 9.39 (*a*) then its equivalent Moore machine will be shown in Fig. 9.39 (*b*). (In the Moore machine second symbol of the state is the output produced by the machine at that state)

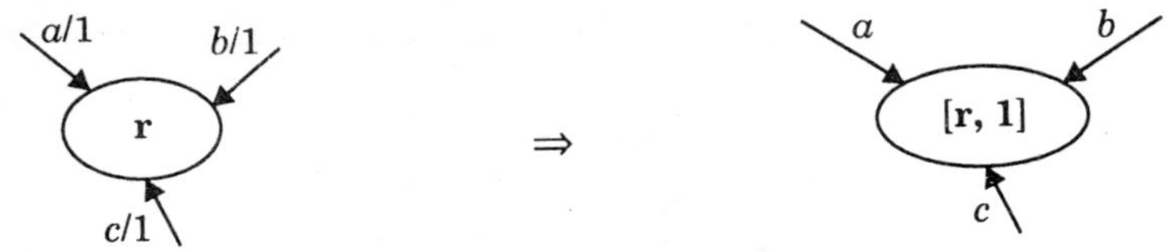

(*a*) Melay Machine (*b*) Moore Machine

Fig. 9.39

(*ii*) since, output symbols are {0, 1} so the states of Moore machines are $[r, 0]$ and $[r, 1]$ and there equivalence are shown in Fig. 9.40.

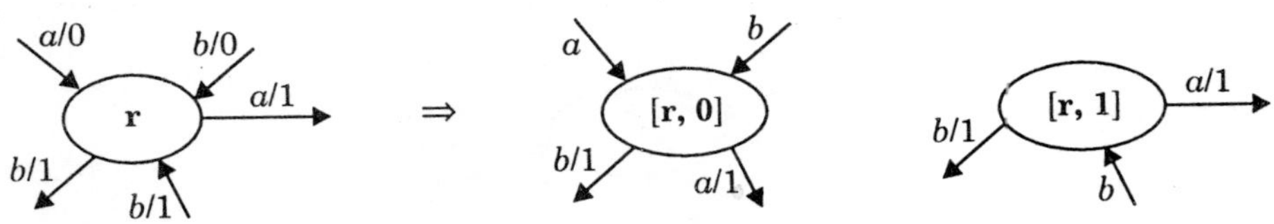

(*a*) Melay machine (*b*) Moore machine

Fig. 9.40

Example 9.13. *Construct the Moore machine from the Melay machine M_e shown in Fig. 9.41*

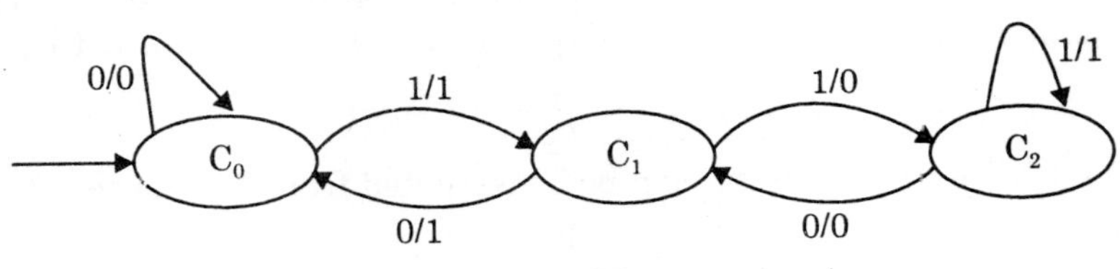

Fig. 9.41

Sol. The given Melay machine M_e can be defined as,

$$M_e = (\{C_0, C_1, C_2\}, \{0, 1\}, \{0, 1\}, \delta_e, \lambda_e, C_0) \text{ and}$$

Where the output function (λ_e) is shown in table I.

Table I

State	Input symbol	
	0	1
→ C_0	0	1
C_1	1	0
C_2	0	1

And the transition function (δ_e) is shown in table II.

Table II

State	Input symbol	
	0	1
→ C_0	C_0	C_1
C_1	C_0	C_2
C_2	C_1	C_2

Let M_o be the Moore machine which is constructed from given M_e then M_o is defined as, $M_o = (Q_o, \Sigma, \Delta, \delta_o, \lambda_o, [C_0, b])$, where $\Sigma = \{0, 1\}$, $b \in \Delta = \{0, 1\}$.

- Set $Q_o = Q_e \times \Delta = \{C_0, C_1, C_2\} \times \{0, 1\}$
  $= \{[C_0, 0], [C_0, 1]\ [C_1, 0]\ [C_1, 1]\ [C_2, 0]\ [C_2, 1]\}$
- Output function (λ_o) will be determine as,
  $\lambda_o\ [q, a] = a, \quad \text{for } \forall q \in Q_e \text{ and } \forall a \in \Sigma$
- Determine transition function δ_o (using table I & II) i.e.,

$$\delta_o([C_0, 0], 0) = [\delta_e(C_0, 0), \lambda_e(C_0, 0)] = [C_0, 0]$$
$$\delta_o([C_0, 0], 1) = [\delta_e(C_0, 1), \lambda_e(C_0, 1)] = [C_1, 1]$$
$$\delta_o([C_0, 1], 0) = [\delta_e(C_0, 0), \lambda_e(C_0, 0)] = [C_0, 0]$$
$$\delta_o([C_0, 1], 1) = [\delta_e(C_0, 1), \lambda_e(C_0, 1)] = [C_1, 1]$$
$$\delta_o([C_1, 0], 0) = [\delta_e(C_1, 0), \lambda_e(C_1, 0)] = [C_0, 1]$$
$$\delta_o([C_1, 0], 1) = [\delta_e(C_1, 1), \lambda_e(C_1, 1)] = [C_2, 0]$$
$$\delta_o([C_1, 1], 0) = [\delta_e(C_1, 0), \lambda_e(C_1, 0)] = [C_0, 1]$$
$$\delta_o([C_1, 1], 1) = [\delta_e(C_1, 1), \lambda_e(C_1, 1)] = [C_2, 0]$$
$$\delta_o([C_2, 0], 0) = [\delta_e(C_2, 0), \lambda_e(C_2, 0)] = [C_1, 0]$$
$$\delta_o([C_2, 0], 1) = [\delta_e(C_2, 1), \lambda_e(C_2, 1)] = [C_2, 1]$$
$$\delta_o([C_2, 1], 0) = [\delta_e(C_2, 0), \lambda_e(C_2, 0)] = [C_1, 0]$$
$$\delta_o([C_2, 1], 1) = [\delta_e(C_2, 1), \lambda_e(C_2, 1)] = [C_2, 1]$$

Hence, we prepare a table III that shows all δ_o's for Moore machine.

Table III

State	Input symbol	
	0	1
→ $[C_0, 0]$	$[C_0, 0]$	$[C_1, 1]$
$[C_0, 1]$	$[C_0, 0]$	$[C_1, 1]$
$[C_1, 0]$	$[C_0, 1]$	$[C_2, 0]$
$[C_1, 1]$	$[C_0, 1]$	$[C_2, 0]$
$[C_2, 0]$	$[C_1, 0]$	$[C_2, 1]$
$[C_2, 1]$	$[C_1, 0]$	$[C_2, 1]$

Since C_0 is the start state of the Melay machine corresponds to that we obtain two states of Moore, from them any one is selected as starting state which is marked by an arrow. Let we select $[C_0, 0]$ is the starting state then we construct the state diagram of the Moore machine shown in Fig. 9.42.

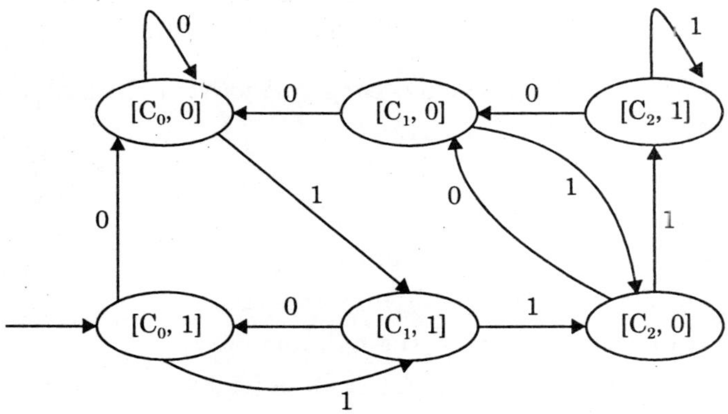

Fig. 9.42 Moore machine.

Example 9.15. *Construct the equivalent Moore machine from Melay machine shown in Fig. 9.43.*

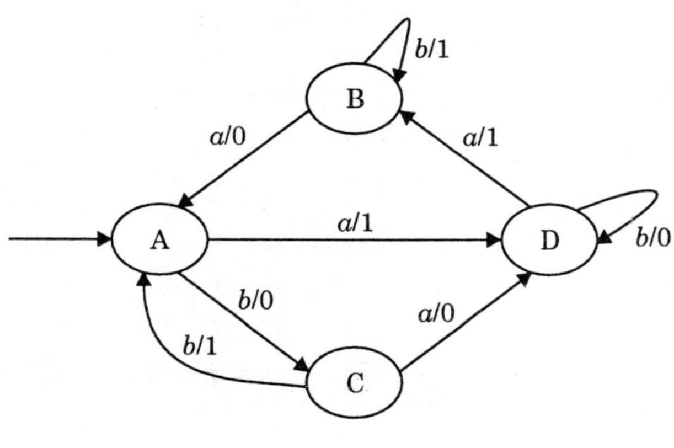

Fig. 9.43

Sol. Construct the output function (λ_e) table I for the given Moore machine.

Table I

State	Input symbol	
	0	**1**
→ A	1	0
B	0	1
C	0	1
D	1	0

Similarly construct the transition function (δ_e) table II.

Table II

State	Input symbol	
	a	**b**
→ A	D	C
B	A	B
C	D	A
D	B	D

Let we define the equivalent Moore machine (Mo) which is constructed from given Melay machine i.e.,

$$M_o = (Q_o, \Sigma, \Delta, \delta_o, \lambda_o, [A, 0]), \text{ where } \Sigma = \{a, b\}, \text{ and } 0 \in \Delta.$$

- Now set of state $Q_o = \{A, B, C, D\} \times \{0, 1\}$
$$= \{[A, 0], [A, 1]\ [B, 0]\ [B, 1]\ [C, 0]\ [C, 1], [D, 0], [D, 1]\}$$
- Determine transition functions δ_o (using table I & II) i.e.,

$$\delta_o([A, 0], a) = [\delta_e(A, a), \lambda_e(A, a)] = [D, 1]$$
$$\delta_o([A, 0], b) = [\delta_e(A, b), \lambda_e(A, b)] = [C, 0]$$
$$\delta_o([A, 1], a) = [\delta_e(A, a), \lambda_e(A, a)] = [D, 1]$$
$$\delta_o([A, 1], b) = [\delta_e(A, b), \lambda_e(A, b)] = [C, 0]$$
$$\delta_o([B, 0], a) = [\delta_e(B, a), \lambda_e(B, a)] = [A, 0]$$
$$\delta_o([B, 0], b) = [\delta_e(B, b), \lambda_e(B, b)] = [B, 1]$$
$$\delta_o([B, 1], a) = [\delta_e(B, a), \lambda_e(B, a)] = [A, 0]$$
$$\delta_o([B, 1], b) = [\delta_e(B, b), \lambda_e(B, b)] = [B, 1]$$
$$\delta_o([C, 0], a) = [\delta_e(C, a), \lambda_e(C, a)] = [D, 0]$$
$$\delta_o([C, 0], b) = [\delta_e(C, b), \lambda_e(C, b)] = [A, 1]$$
$$\delta_o([C, 1], a) = [\delta_e(C, a), \lambda_e(C, a)] = [D, 0]$$
$$\delta_o([C, 1], b) = [\delta_e(C, b), \lambda_e(C, b)] = [A, 1]$$
$$\delta_o([D, 0], a) = [\delta_e(D, a), \lambda_e(D, a)] = [B, 1]$$
$$\delta_o([D, 0], b) = [\delta_e(D, b), \lambda_e(D, b)] = [D, 0]$$
$$\delta_o([D, 1], a) = [\delta_e(D, a), \lambda_e(D, a)] = [B, 1]$$
$$\delta_o([D, 1], b) = [\delta_e(D, b), \lambda_e(D, b)] = [D, 0]$$

Hence, we prepare a transition function table III for Moore machine.

Table III

State	Input symbol	
	a	b
→ [A, 0]	[D, 1]	[C, 0]
[A, 1]	[D, 1]	[C, 0]
[B, 0]	[A, 0]	[B, 1]
[B, 1]	[A, 0]	[B, 1]
[C, 0]	[D, 0]	[A, 1]
[C, 1]	[D, 0]	[A, 1]
[D, 0]	[B, 1]	[D, 0]
[D, 1]	[B, 1]	[D, 0]

Since we assume that [A, 0] is the start state of the Melay machine so it is marked by an arrow in the transition table. The state diagram of the Moore machine shown in Fig. 9.44.

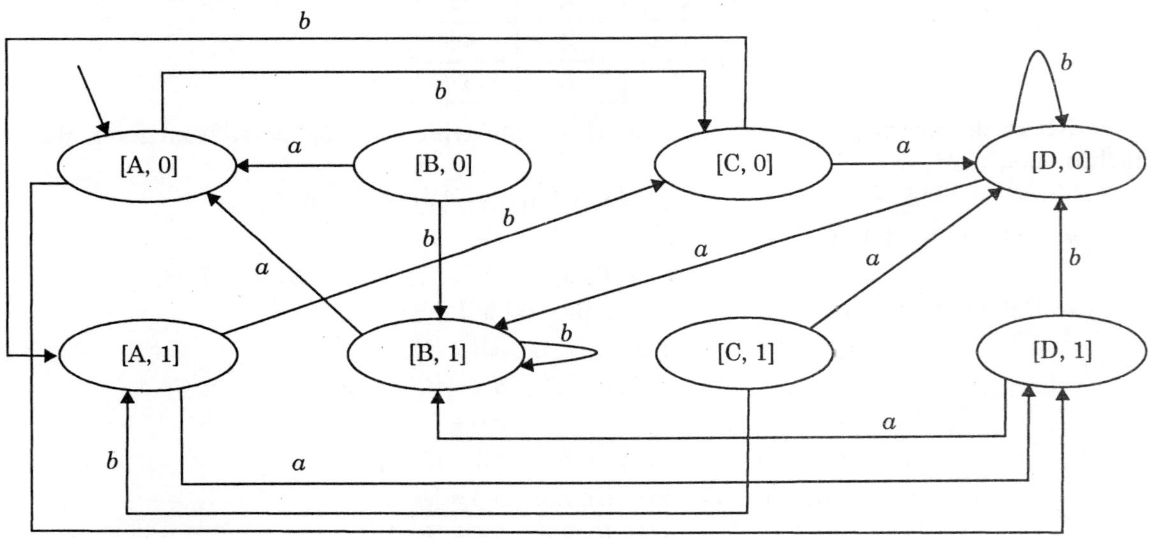

Fig. 9.44 Moore machine.

EXERCISES

9.1 Write regular expressions for each of the following languages over the alphabet {0, 1}.

(*i*) The set of all strings containing at least of two 0's.

(*ii*) The set of all strings not containing 001 as a substring.

(*iii*) The set of all strings with an equal number of 0's and 1's.

(*iv*) The set of all strings of odd length.

(*v*) The set of all strings containing of both 100 and 011 as substrings.

9.2 Write regular expressions for each of the following languages over the alphabet {a, b}.

(*i*) All strings that don't have substring ba.

(*ii*) All strings that don't have substring aab and baa.

(*iii*) All strings that have even number of a's and odd number of b's.

(*iv*) All strings in which a's or b's is doubled but not both.

(*v*) All strings in which symbol b is never tripled.

(*vi*) All strings in which number of a's are divisible by 5.

9.3 Construct the FA for the following regular expressions.

(*i*) **(11 + 0)* 0* (00 + 1)***

(*ii*) **01((10* + 11) + 0)***

(*iii*) **((0 + 1) (0 + 1))* + 11 + 0(1 + 0)* + ∈**

9.4 Construct the regular expression for the following DFA, shown in Fig. 9.45.

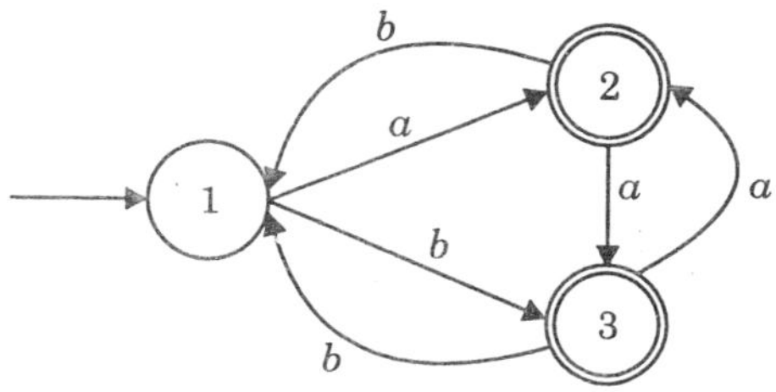

Fig. 9.45

9.5 Describe the language denoted by the following regular expressions

(*i*) **((b + aa)*)***

(*ii*) **(b (a + bb)*)***

(*iii*) **(b (abb)* a (baa)*)***

(*iv*) **(a + b) a (ab)***

(*v*) **(a*b*)***

9.6 Prove are disprove the following for regular expressions

(*i*) **(a*b*)* = (a + b)***

(*ii*) **(a + b)* = a* + b***

(*iii*) **(a + b)* a (a + b)* b (a + b)* = (a + b)* ab (a + b)***

(*iv*) **(a + b)* ab (a + b)* + b*a* = (a + b)***

(*v*) **(aa*1)*1 = 1 + a (a + 1a)*11**

9.7 Construct the regular expression corresponding to the followng FAs shown in Fig. 9.46.

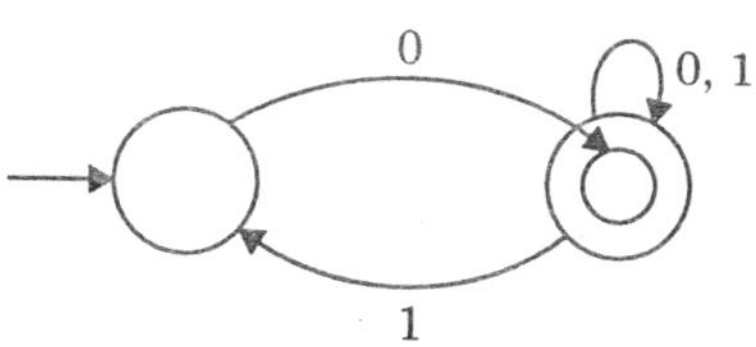

(*a*)

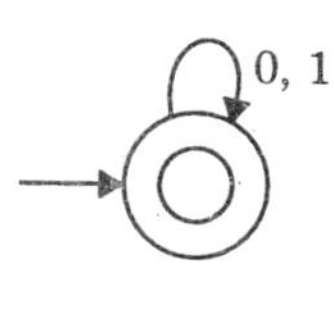

(*b*)

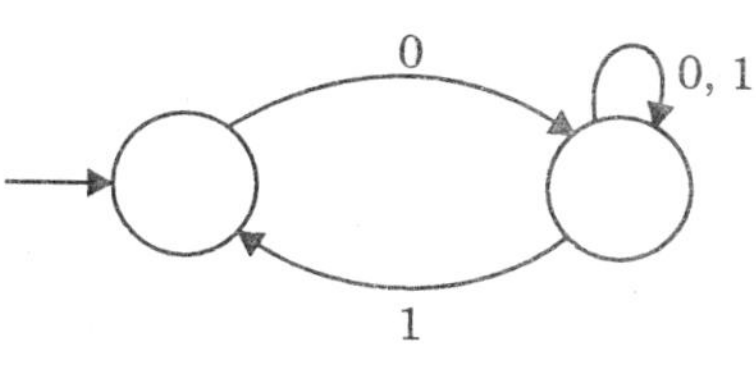

(*c*)

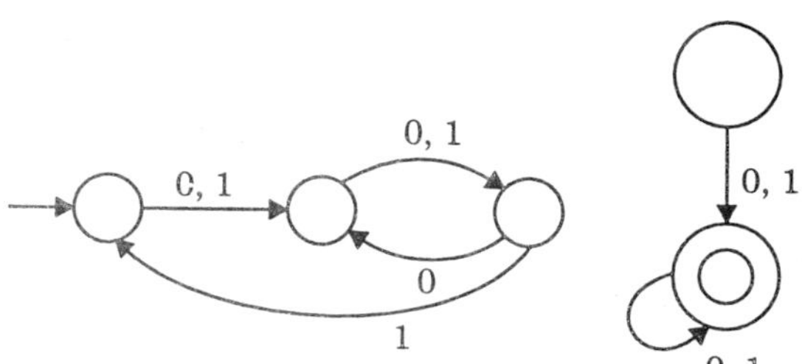

(*d*)

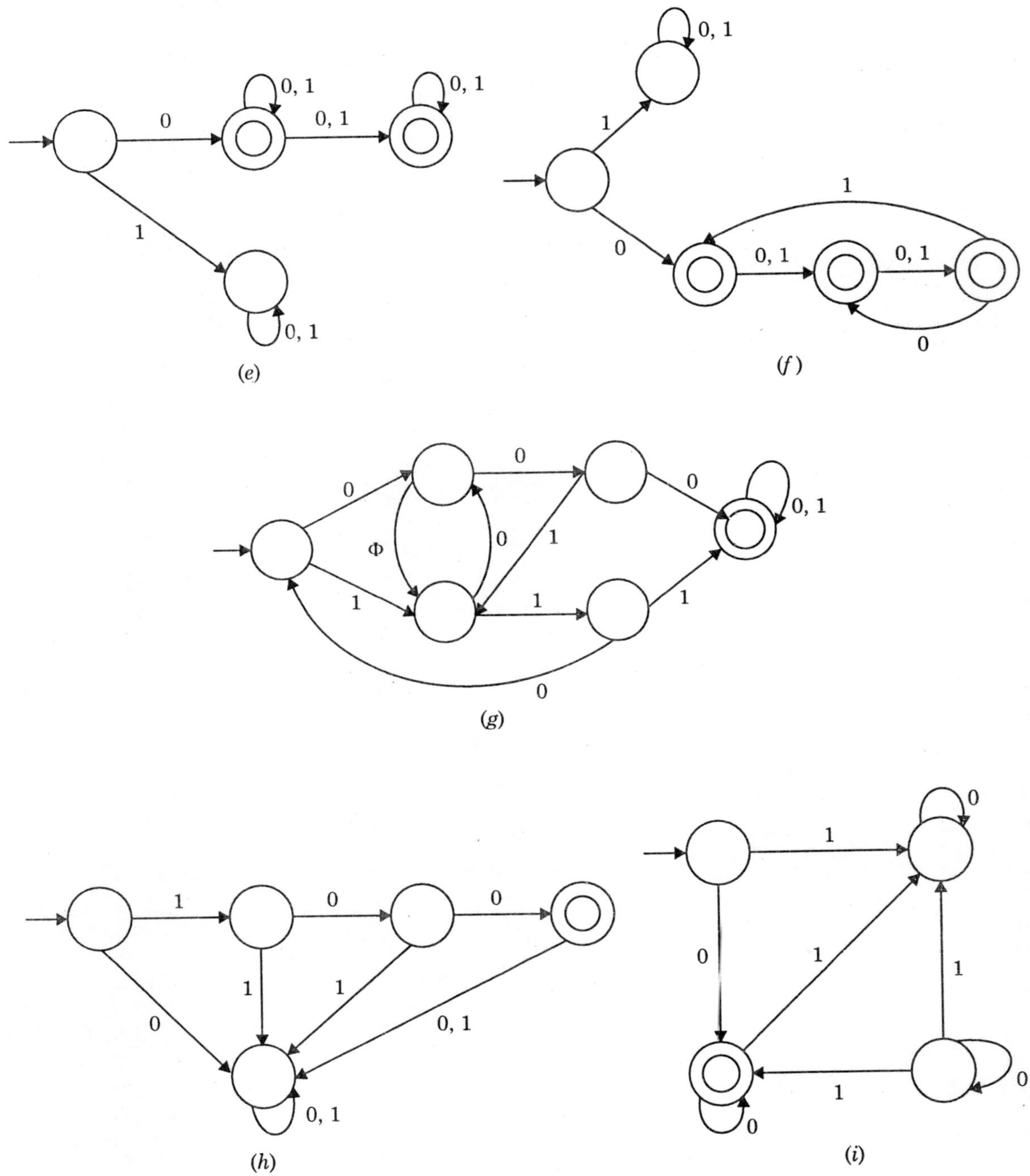
0, 1
0, 1
0
0, 1
1
0, 1
(e)
0, 1
1
1
0
0, 1
0, 1
0
(f)
0
0
0
Φ
0
1
0, 1
1
1
1
0
(g)
1
0
0
1
1
0
0, 1
0, 1
(h)
0
1
0
1
1
1
0
0
(i)

Fig. 9.46

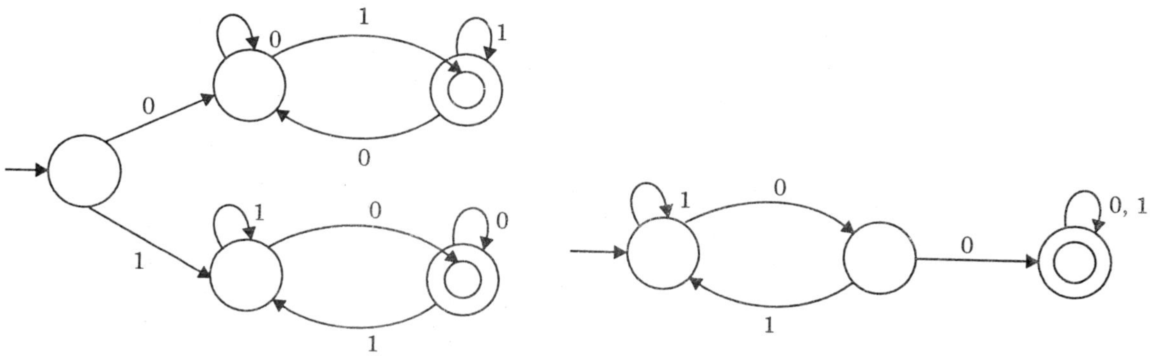

(j) (k)

Fig. 9.46

9.8 Comment on the property of the given Melay machine shown in Fig. 9.47 (*a*) & (*b*)

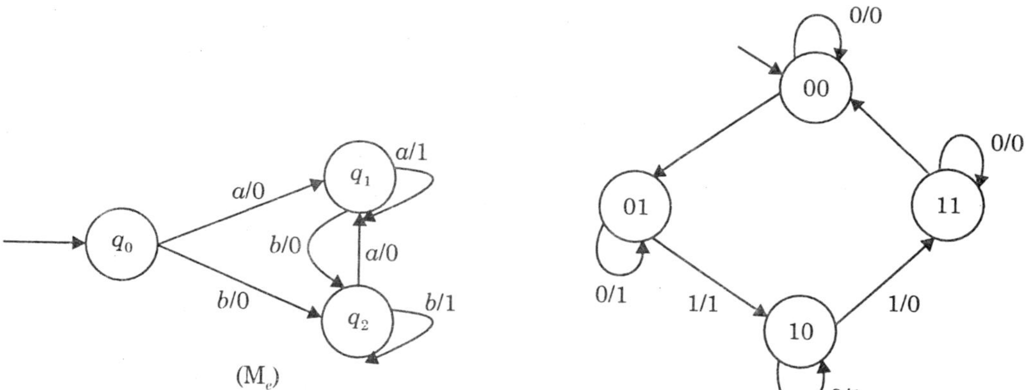

(*a*) (*b*)

Fig. 9.47

9.9 Design a Melay Machine to perform the addition of 2 binary numbers.

REGULAR AND NONREGULAR LANGUAGES

10 Regular and Nonregular Languages

10.1 INTRODUCTION

From exploring the knowledge of the previous chapters, for checking the regularity of any language, we might say that, a language is said to be regular language if there exist a Finite Automaton (FA) that accept it. In other words, a machine with finite number of states (DFA/ NFA/NFA with ε-moves) including definite halting state and no other means of storage, recognizes the language that language is a regular language; otherwise language is not regular.

To prove any language is regular or not we discuss a theorem called pumping lemma for regular language in the next section. Through pumping lemma we necessarily check the regularity of any language. Section 10.2 and 10.3 discuses more about regularity and nonregularity of any languages.

There are some inherent characterizations, if the language recognize as the regular language. Closure characterization is one of them. Closure characteristics tell about the nature of regular languages over operators. In section 10.4 we will see the nature of regular languages over operations like union, concatenation, intersection and kleeny closure that also return a regular language.

The problem of equivalence of regular languages can be a general one. Whether two regular languages are equivalent, alternatively we have two DFAs corresponding to two different regular languages, then whether these DFAs are equivalent. The solution of above problem is finding out by the construction of a minimum state DFA that recognizes both the languages. We discuss the problem of minimization of DFA with some other problems of regularity under topic "Decision problems" in section 10.5 in details.

10.2 PUMPING LEMMA FOR REGULAR LANGUAGE

Lemma 10.1. If L is a regular language then there exist a constant n such that if a string Z ∈ L and

$|Z| = n$, then Z can be written as,

$$Z = u.v.w$$

where, 1. $|v| \geq 1$

2. $|u.v| \leq n$

3. $\forall i \geq 0,\ u.v^i.w \in L$

(where n depends only on language)

The statement of the pumping lemma says if we select any string Z from the set of regular language L, such that string Z can be break into substrings u followed by substring v followed by substring w then we always locate a middle substring v (in between of length n) that contains at least a symbol (or nonempty) can be 'pump' zero/more (finite) times causes the resulting string returns in language L.

Proof. For proving above lemma we assume that there is a DFA of n distinct states that accept the regular language L. Let string Z is of k symbols where $k \geq n$ then string Z can be written as,

$$Z = a_1 \cdot a_2 \cdot a_3 \cdot a_4 \cdots\cdots a_k.$$

i.e., $| Z | = k$ so $| z | \geq n$.

Since we assume that $k = n$ so a DFA accepting the string Z must have following possibilities,

- Either, it is a n state DFA *i.e.*, if one symbol corresponds to one transition arc and if string contains k symbols where $k = n$ (take one such case), then the string Z = u.v.w where $| Z | = n$, is accepted.

Or

- For accepting the string of length $\geq n$, an n state DFA must has one/more repetitive transition arcs on few intermediate states.

Let DFA operates over states set Q where Q contains start state q_0 and other states q_1, $q_2, q_3, \ldots\ldots, q_m$ where $q_m \in F$. Then after consuming string $a_1 . a_2 . a_3 . a_4 \ldots a_k$, the path taken by DFA is as follows,

$$q_0 \xrightarrow{a_1} q_1 \xrightarrow{a_2} q_2 \xrightarrow{a_3} \ldots\ldots q_i \xrightarrow{a_{i+1}} q_{i+1} \ldots\ldots q_{j-1} \xrightarrow{a_j} q_j \ldots\ldots q_{m-1} \xrightarrow{a_m} q_m$$

Since, $| Z | \geq n$, or number of symbols in string Z is more than m (number of states) so there must be at least one duplication of states. In other words at least two states must be same (Fig. 10.1). Assume states q_i and q_j are same thus there exists at least one symbol in between a_i and a_j *i.e.*, $| v | \geq 1$. The discussed situation is shown below.

$$\underbrace{(a_1 . a_2 . a_3 \ldots\ldots a_i)}_{u} \cdot \underbrace{(a_{i+1} \ldots\ldots a_j)}_{v\,(\neq \in)} \cdot \underbrace{(a_{j+1} \ldots a_k)}_{w}$$

because of same states of q_i and q_j

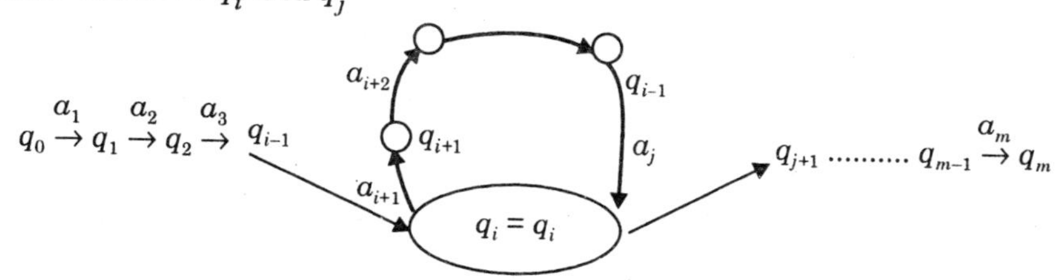

Fig. 10.1

The states diagram of DFA M is shown in Fig. 10.2.

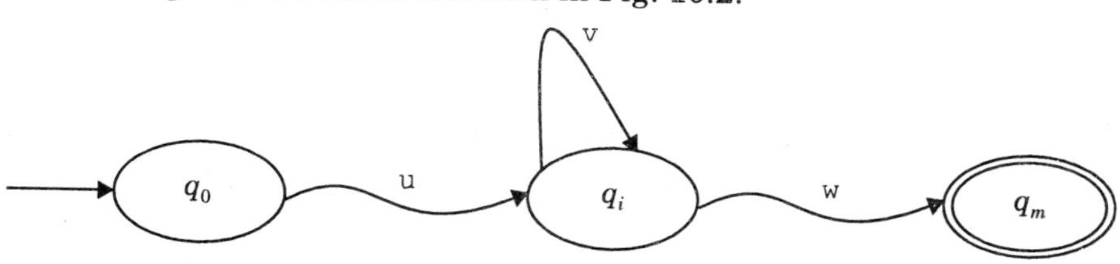

M

Fig. 10.2

Therefore string v can be pumped as many as you can such that the resulting string $\{u.v^i.w/\forall i \geq 0\}$ will be accepted by DFA M. Hence language is a regular language.

Remember, above lemma checks the regularity of any language whose length is greater then or equal to the number of states of its DFA. So, initially break the string into three substrings and then test the effects of finite repetition of middle string on any of the intermediate state (not the final state) if it causes final string is in language then language is regular otherwise language is nonregular.

10.3 REGULAR AND NONREGULAR LANGUAGES SOLVED EXAMPLES

Now we test the regularity of any language using pumping lemma discussed above. This section gives the idea that how to proceed to testify the language is a regular language using pumping lemma. The examples discussed below presented the approach to reach the conclusion to the problems.

Example 10.1. *Let $\Sigma = \{0, 1\}$, then check the regularity of language $L = \{0^k 1^k \mid k \geq 0\}$.*

Sol. The language L consists of following set of string {∈, 01, 0011, 000111, ...}. We shall prove the regularity of L by method of contradiction. Thus, assume L is regular and n is any constant then string Z can be written as,

$$Z = 0^n . 1^n \quad i.e., \quad |Z| = 2n \text{ so } |Z| > n$$

Now break the string Z into substrings u , v and w (Fig. 10.3) i.e.,

$$Z = 0^n . 1^n = u . v . w$$

where substrings fulfill the condition such that

(000............0 0......000) . (111..................1111)

← u → ← v → ← w →

Fig. 10.3

We observe that string u.v consist only of 0's so $|u . v| \leq n$ and $|v| \geq 1$. For the verification of the base case of pumping lemma i.e., string $Z = u.v^i.w \Rightarrow u.w$ (for $i = 0$). Lemma says if L is regular then u.w ∈ L. Since substring u contains 0's that are fewer than n (because of few 0's are part of substring v) and substring w contains exactly n, 1's. So, string u.w doesn't have equal numbers of 0's followed by equal number of 1's. Hence, we obtain a contradiction therefore L is not regular.

Example 10.2. *If $\Sigma = \{0\}$ and language defined over Σ is $L = \{0^{i^2} \mid i \geq 0\}$ then L is not regular.*

Sol. Now, the strings in the set L = {∈, 0, 0000, 00000000, ...}.

Assume L is regular, then there exist a constant n s.t.

String $Z = 0^{n^2}$ ($|Z| = n^2 \geq n$) and it can be broken into substrings u, v and w s.t.

$Z = u . v . w$ and these substrings are:

(0........0 0........00) . (0...........00)..............................(0..................00)

← u → ← v → ← w →

(In the string Z there are n sets that contains n number of 0's, so total n^2 0's)

Since, $v \neq \in$ and $|u . v| \leq n$; means that sub string uv should be in first set that contains n, 0's. Substring u has less than n 0's because some of 0's are in v.

Remaining $(n - 1)$ set of n number of 0's are in w.

For the base case of pumping lemma, if $u.w$ is in L then L is regular.

The strings u.w contains fewer than n 0's , followed by $(n - 1)$ set of n number of 0's. So, total numbers of 0's in $u.v$ are, where we assume u has k 0's s.t. $k < n$.

So, $0^{k+(n-1).n}$ is not a perfect square $\Rightarrow u.w \notin$ L

So, there is a contradiction. Hence language L is not regular.

Or, Assume $Z = 0^{n^2} \equiv u \,.\, v \,.\, w \in$ L.

Check the string $u.v^2.w$ if this is in L then number are 0's should be perfect square.

i.e. $| u \,.\, v^2 \,.\, w | = | u \,.\, v \,.\, w | + | v |$

$= n^2 + | v |$

since $| v |$ is least 1,

Hence, $n^2 + | v | > n^2$

Max length of substring $| v | = n$

So, $n^2 < | u \,.\, v^2 \,.\, w | < n^2 + n \rightarrow$ to make perfect square add constant $(n + 1)$

$\Rightarrow$ $n^2 < | u \,.\, v^2 \,.\, w | < n^2 + n + (n + 1)$

$\Rightarrow$ $n^2 < | u \,.\, v^2 \,.\, w | < (n + 1)^2$

i.e. the length of string $\neq (n + 1)^2$ a perfect square $\Rightarrow u \,.\, v^2 \,.\, w \notin$ L.

Hence, Language is not regular.

Example 10.3. *If language L = {0^i 1^j 2^i | i and j are arbitrary Integers} then L is not regular.*

Sol. Language L contains the strings that have equal number of 0's and 2's, and in between 0's and 2's it has any number of 1's.

Assume a constant n (and a constant m where $n > m$), so that string Z = $0^n\, 1^m\, 2^n$;

If L is regular then, Z can be break into substring u , v and w s.t.

$Z = 0^n\, 1^m\, 2^n = u \,.\, v \,.\, w$ where u, v and w are given as follows:

(0............0 0..................0) (1......................1) (2.......................2)

$\longleftarrow u \longrightarrow$ $\longleftarrow v \longrightarrow$ $\longleftarrow w \longrightarrow$

substring $v \neq \in$ $\Rightarrow$ $| v | \geq 1$ and $| u \,.\, v | \leq n$

Proof by contradiction:

Assume L is regular so $\forall\, i \geq 0$, $u \,.\, v^i \,.\, w \in$ L.

For base case ($i = 0$) of pumping lemma, $u \,.\, w \in$ L if L is regular.

Since, $u \,.\, w$ has fewer than n 0's (because some of 0's are part of v) followed by m 1's and n 0's.

From the nature of language L we find that only those strings are in L that have equal number of 0's (followed by any number of 1's) and 2's.

However, $u \,.\, w$ doesn't fulfill above condition. So, a contradiction,

Hence, $u \,.\, w \notin$ L.

For $i = 2$, string Z $= u \,.\, v^i \,.\, w \Rightarrow u \,.\, v^2 \,.\, w$

So, $| u \,.\, v^2 \,.\, w | = | u \,.\, v \,.\, w | + | v |$

$\Rightarrow$ $= (2n + m) + | v |$ where $1 \leq | v | \leq n$

$\Rightarrow$ $(2n + m) + | v | > (2n + m)$

i.e., $(2n + m) < | u \,.\, v^2 \,.\, w | < (2n + m) + n$

$\Rightarrow$ $(2n + m) < | u . v^2 . w | < (2n + m) + n$;

[to make equal, number of 0's and 2's add more n 2's on right side of equality]

$\Rightarrow$ $(2n + m) < | u . v^2 . w | < (2n + m) + n + n$; [for $2n$ 0's and $2n$ 2's]

$\Rightarrow$ $(2n + m) < | u . v^2 . w | < [2(2n) + m]$

That we see from the right side of equality, string $| u . v^2 . w | \neq 4n + m$

$\Rightarrow$ $u . v^2 . w \notin L$

Hence language is not regular.

10.4 PROPERTIES OF REGULAR LANGUAGES

As we said earlier there are some inherent characterizations of a language if it is regular. These inherent characterizations we summarize here as the properties of regular languages, equally says the properties of regular expressions.

Among these properties:

- Regular expressions are closed under $\cup$ operation
- Regular expressions are closed under concatenation operation
- Regular expressions are closed under Complementation
- Regular expressions are closed under $\cap$ operation
- Regular expressions are closed under Subtraction operation
- Regular expressions are closed under $\star$ operation (Kleeny Closure)

Regular expression are closed under $\cup$ operation

This property says that the union of regular expressions is a regular expression. If $\mathbf{r}_1$ and $\mathbf{r}_2$ are two regular expressions and there languages are $L(\mathbf{r}_1)$ and $L(\mathbf{r}_2)$ then, union of $\mathbf{r}_1$ and $\mathbf{r}_2$ is given as $(\mathbf{r}_1 + \mathbf{r}_2)$ means either $\mathbf{r}_1$ or $\mathbf{r}_2$, that is a regular expression.

It denotes the language $L(\mathbf{r}_1 + \mathbf{r}_2)$; which is the language denoted by $L(\mathbf{r}_1)$ or language denoted by $L(\mathbf{r}_2)$. This is a regular language in either case.

Or we say,

$$L(\mathbf{r}_1 + \mathbf{r}_2) = L(\mathbf{r}_1) \cup L(\mathbf{r}_2)$$

Hence, Regular languages are closed under union.

Regular expressions are closed under concatenation operation

Concatenation of regular expressions are a regular expression. If $\mathbf{r}_1$ and $\mathbf{r}_2$ are two regular expressions and there languages are $L(\mathbf{r}_1)$ and $L(\mathbf{r}_2)$ then concatenation of $\mathbf{r}_1$ and $\mathbf{r}_2$ is given as, $(\mathbf{r}_1 . \mathbf{r}_2)$ means regular expression $\mathbf{r}_1$ followed by regular expression $\mathbf{r}_2$. That results a regular expression.

Now, the language of composite of regular expression $(\mathbf{r}_1 . \mathbf{r}_2)$ is $L(\mathbf{r}_1 . \mathbf{r}_2)$, that must be language of $\mathbf{r}_1$ followed by the language of $\mathbf{r}_2$, which is again a regular language.

i.e., $$L(\mathbf{r}_1 . \mathbf{r}_2) = L(\mathbf{r}_1) . L(\mathbf{r}_2)$$

Hence Regular languages are closed under concatenation.

Regular expression is closed under complementation operation

The property says that complement of the regular expression is a regular expression. Let **r** is a regular expression and it denotes the regular language L (i.e. $L = L(r)$)

Let regular language is defined over set of symbols Σ, then complement of L returns all possible strings formed over Σ excluded the strings of the set L.

i.e. $\overline{L} = \Sigma^* - L$;

Now we see that how $\overline{L}$ is also a regular language.

We know that a language is regular if it is accepted by some DFA. If we construct a DFA that accept complement of language L, then we say it is also regular.

Let M be a DFA accepting L define as,

$$M = (Q, \Sigma, \delta, q_0, F) \text{ and } L = L(M)$$

Now if we construct a new DFA M′ by using the information of DFA M such that, the set of final states in M′ is F′ which is given as,

$$F' = Q - F$$

Then DFA $M' = (Q, \Sigma, \delta, q_0, Q - F)$ accepts complement of the language L.

Example 10.4. *A DFA M is shown in Fig. 10.4, that accepts that language given by the regular expression*

$$(1 + 0 \,.\, 1^* \,.\, 0)\,(0 + 1)^*$$

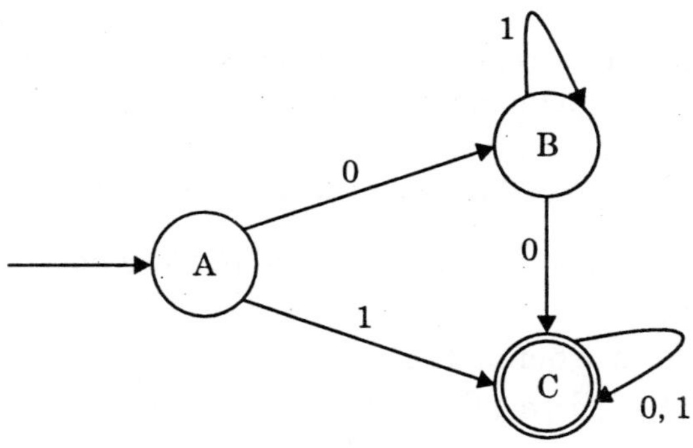

Fig. 10.4. (M)

Now we construct the DFA M′ that accepts the complement of language L.

Sol. In the complemented DFA M′ all non final states will be final states and final state will be nonfinal state, i.e. we obtain the DFA M′ show in Fig. 10.5.

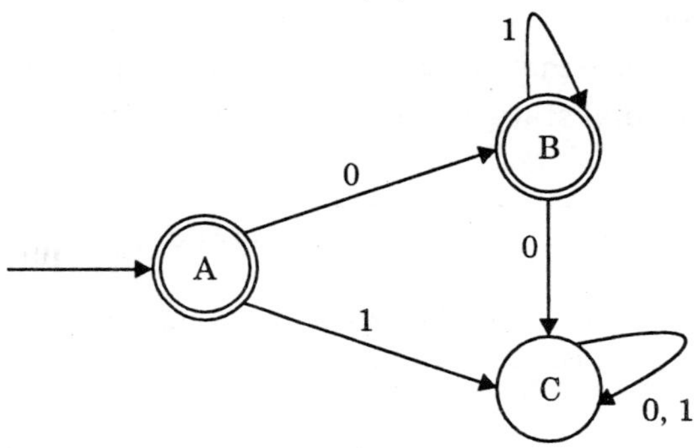

M′

Fig. 10.5. (M′)

Thus, M′ accepts the language of the regular expression $(\epsilon + 0 \,.\, 1^*)$ which is the complement of L.

$$L(M') = L(\in + \mathbf{0}\,.\,\mathbf{1}^*) = \{\in, 0, 01, 011, \ldots\}$$

and, $L(M) = L\,[(\mathbf{1} + \mathbf{0.1}^*.\,\mathbf{0})\,(\mathbf{0} + \mathbf{1})^*] = \{(1, 00, 010, 0110, \ldots), (1, 00, 010, 0110, \ldots)\,0, (1, 00, 010, 0110, \ldots)1, (1, 00, 010, 0110, \ldots)\,00, \ldots\}$

we see L(M′) excluded all the strings of the set of L(M) formed over {0,1}.

So, $L(M') = \Sigma^* - L(M) = \bar{L}$

Regular expressions are closed under ∩ operation

This property says that if intersection operation is performed over regular expressions we again get the regular expression, in other words, intersection of two regular languages is a regular language.

Assume $\mathbf{r_1}$ and $\mathbf{r_2}$ are regular expressions and there languages are L_1 and L_2. Then there intersection will be, $L_1 \cap L_2$.

Applying the De Morgan Law that complement of complement is effectless. So,

$$L_1 \cap L_2 = \overline{\overline{[(L_1 \cap L_2)]}}$$

$$= \overline{[\bar{L}_1 \cup \bar{L}_2]} \qquad \text{[using De Morgan Law]}$$

⇒ a Regular language

Because, complement of a regular language is regular; union of regular languages is regular and subsequently complement of a regular language is regular. So, $L_1 \cap L_2$ returns regular.

Hence, Regular expressions (languages) are closed under intersection.

Theorem 10.1. *If M_1, M_2 are two DFAs that accept the language L_1 and L_2 then there exist a DFA M that accept $L_1 \cap L_2$.*

Proof. Let DFA M_1 and M_2 are defined as,

$$M_1 = (Q_1, \Sigma, \delta_1, q_1, F_1) \text{ and } L_1 = L(M_1); \text{ and}$$

$$M_2 = (Q_2, \Sigma, \delta_2, q_2, F_2) \text{ and } L_2 = L(M_2)$$

Assume DFA $M = (Q, \Sigma, \delta, q_0, F)$ accepts the language $L(M) = L_1 \cup L_2$, where M has following characteristics:

- $Q = Q_1 \times Q_2$; Set Q contains all possible set of states formed over Q_1 with Q_2.
- Same set of input symbols Σ
- Transition function δ†
- Starting state is a state that contains pair of starting states i.e., $q_0 = (q_1, q_2)$.
- $F = F_1 \times F_2$; Set of Final state F contains all pairs of final states formed over F_1 with F_2.

---

† Transition function δ is the mapping of a pair of states (∈ Q) with input symbol (∈ Σ) and return a pair of states.

Let pair of states is (p, q) and $\Sigma = \{a\}$ then transition function δ will be:

$$\delta((p, q), a) = (\delta_1(p, a), \delta_2(q, a))$$

$$\downarrow \qquad \downarrow$$

$= (\,r \quad , \quad s\,)$ [where r and s are there respective next states of M_1 and M_2.]

If a is the language of DFA M, certainly state $r \in F_1$ as well as state $s \in F_2$.

So, finally we get the machine $M = (Q_1 \times Q_2, \Sigma, \delta, (q_1, q_2), F_1 \times F_2)$.

Example 10.5. *Two DFAs M_1 and M_2 are shown in Fig 10.6. Construct the machine that*

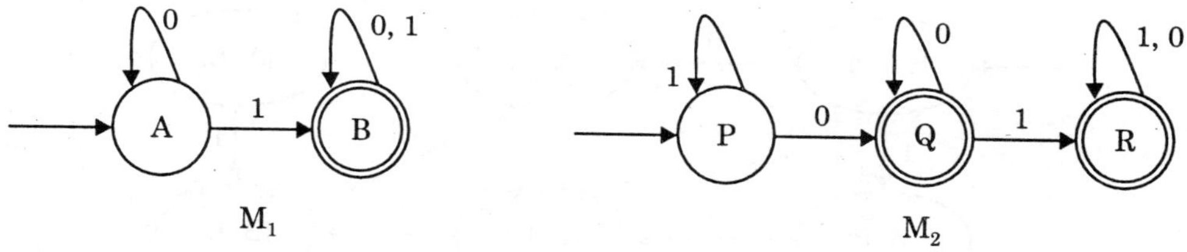

Fig. 10.6

accepts intersection of Language of M_1 and language of M_2.

Sol. Machine M_1 accepts the language expressed by the regular expression **0* . 1 . (0 + 1)*** and machine M_2 accepts the language expressed by the regular expression **1* . 0 . (0* + 0* . 1 . (1 + 0)*)**. Now we construct the machine M that accepts intersection of language of M_1 as well M_2.

Let M = (Q, Σ, δ, {A, P}, $F_1 \times F_2$), where

- Q = (A, B) × (P, Q, R)
  ⇒ ({A, P}, {A, Q}, {A, R}, {B, P}, (B, Q), {B, R});
- Σ = { 0, 1}
- Starting state is the pair of starting state of M_1 as well M_2, so {A, P}
- F = {B} × {Q, R}
  ⇒ ({B, Q}, {B, R})
- Transition functions δ are given in the table shown in Fig. 10.7.

δ({A, P}, 0) = [δ(A, 0), δ(P, 0)] = {A, Q} and similarly we compute other transition functions.

State	Input symbol	
	0	**1**
→ {A, P}	{A, Q}	{B, P}
{A, Q}	{A, Q}	{B, R}
{A, R}	{A, R}	{B, R}
{B, P}	{B, Q}	{B, P}
● {B, Q}	{B, Q}	{B, R}
● {B, R}	{B, R}	{B, R}

Fig. 10.7

Hence, the transition diagram of DFA M is shown in Fig. 10.8

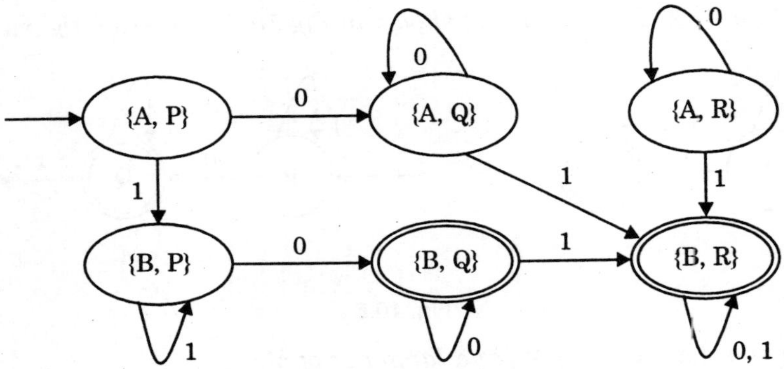

Fig. 10.8

Regular languages are closed under Subtraction

Subtraction (Difference) of two regular languages is a regular language ‡.

Let $\mathbf{r_1}$ and $\mathbf{r_2}$ are regular expressions and there languages are L_1 and L_2 then there difference is $\mathbf{r_1} - \mathbf{r_2}$, which denotes the language $L(r_1 - r_2)$,

$$\Rightarrow \qquad L(r_1) - L(r_2) \quad \text{or} \quad L_1 - L_2 = L$$

It contains set of strings that are in L_1 but not in L_2. If it is L then L is called difference set of L_1 with L_2.

So, language is closed under difference.

For example assume regular expressions $\mathbf{r_1} = \mathbf{(0 + 1)^*}$ and $\mathbf{r_2} = \mathbf{1^*}$ then difference of regular expressions is $\mathbf{r_1} - \mathbf{r_2} = \mathbf{(0 + 1)^* - 1^*}$, that can be simplify after knowing the language expressed by both regular expressions.

Since, language expressed by $\mathbf{r_1}$ is $L(\mathbf{r_1})$ = {all strings formed over 0'and 1's} and
Language expressed by $\mathbf{r_2}$ is $L(\mathbf{r_2})$ = {∈, all strings formed over 1's}

If difference of languages $L(\mathbf{r_1})$ and $L(\mathbf{r_2})$ is L then L contains all the those strings that doesn't have all 1's. So L contains all those strings that have at least a, 0.

Hence, regular expression of such language is $\mathbf{0^* . (1 + 0)^* . 0^*}$ (which also generate ∈, but in L ∈ will not be there). So, to exclude symbol ∈ from the language of regular expression, the new regular expression is constructed without affecting the nature of language it generates i.e.,

$$[\mathbf{0 . 0^* . (1 + 0)^* . 0^* + 0^* . (1 + 0)^* . 0^* . 0}].$$

Hence language L is

$$L([\mathbf{0 . 0^* . (1 + 0)^* . 0^* + 0^* . (1 + 0)^* . 0^* . 0}]) = \{0, 00, 01, 10, 100, \ldots\}$$

That contains all strings formed over 0's and 1's that have at least a, 0.

Reversal of regular language is regular

Let w is any string abcd......xyz then reverse of w is a string zyx......$dcba$. If w is regular then reverse of w is also regular. Now we discuss a lemma so the things are more clearer.

‡ We can't say directly that difference of regular expression is regular expression, because subtraction operation is not a part of the definition of regular expression. After few steps of simplification we may get the difference of regular expression.

Lemma 10.2.

*Let **r** is a regular expression and it generates the language L. Assume regular expression **r** can be formed by concatenation of regular expressions $r_1, r_2, r_3, \ldots\ldots\ldots r_n$, where r_i, ($\forall\, i \geq 1$) may be formed by addition of regular expressions or kleeny closure of it.*

$\mathbf{r} = \mathbf{r_1 . r_2 . r_3 ...... r_n}$. (because concatenations of regular expressions are regular expression)

If we concatenate the above regular expressions in reverse order we get again a regular expression.

$$\mathbf{r^{REV} = r_n . r_{n-1} ...... r_3 . r_2 . r_1}$$

Regular expression $\mathbf{r^{REV}}$ generates the language that certainly contains the strings that are reverse of the strings of L.

For example $\mathbf{r = a_1 . a_2 . a_3 ...... a_n}$ and it expresses the language L = $a_1a_2a_3......a_n$ then reverse of L is $a_n......a_3a_2a_1$. That is generated from the concatenation of the regular expressions in reverse order

i.e., $$\mathbf{r^{REV} = a_n ...... a_3 . a_2 . a_1}$$

Since, $\mathbf{r^{REV}}$ is a regular expression. Hence its language is also regular.

FACT

If L is the language accepted by some DFA then we can construct the DFA (one/more) that accepts reverse of all the strings of L.

Proof. Let DFA M = (Q, Σ, δ, q_0, F) is represented by equivalent regular expression **r** where L = L(**r**). Let reverse of L is L^R where $L^R = (L)^R = (L(\mathbf{r}))^R = L(\mathbf{r}^R)$ says reverse of L is expressed by a regular expression $\mathbf{r}^R$. Hence, there exist some DFA equivalent to regular expression $\mathbf{r}^R$.

Now, we construct the DFA M_R with following consideratons, i.e.,

- Starting state of M becomes the final state of M_R.
- Final state of M will be the starting state of M_R.
- If M has more than one final state then number of DFA M_R are more (number of M_R will be depend upon the number of final states)
  1. Select any one final state (of M) that will be the starting state of M_{R1}, remaining final states becomes non final states of M_{R1}.
  2. Pick next final state (of M) that will be the starting state of M_{R2} and remaining final states becomes non final states of M_{R2}.
  3. Repeat step 2 until all final states becomes starting state of M_{R1}, M_{R2},......M_{Rk} where *k* is the number of final states in M. So there are K possible DFA (M_R) that accept reverse of language L.
- Reverse direction of all the transition arcs.

For example Fig. 10.9 shows a DFA M accepts language L, where L is the language denoted by regular expression **0*. 1 . 1* + 0* . 1 . 1* . 0 . (1 + 0)***

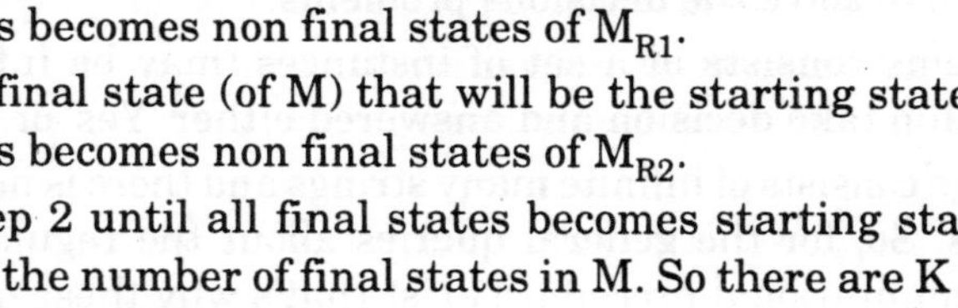

Fig. 10.9

For accepting the reverse of the strings of Language L, we can construct the M_R using above disumed points, i.e.,

- State A will be the starting state.
- Firstly choose final state B that will be the starting state. (Fig. 10.10(*a*))
- Next state C will be the starting state. (Fig. 10.10(*b*))
- Reverse the direction of transition arcs,

Thus, we get two DFA M_{R1} and M_{R2} that are shown in Fig. 10.10.

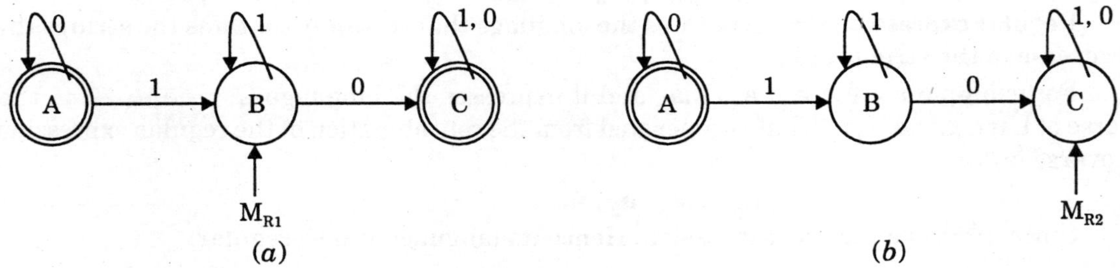

Fig. 10.10

For automaton M_{R1} equivalent regular expression is **1* . 1 . 0*** which is the reverse of the first part of previous regular expression.

Similarly M_{R2} has equivalent regular expression **(0 + 1)* . 0 . 1* . 1 . 0*** which is the reverse of the second part of previous regular expression.

Hence, we see that reverse of language L are accepted by DFA M_{R1} or M_{R2}.

Therefore, reverse of a regular language is also regular.

10.5 DECISION PROBLEMS (DP) OF REGULAR LANGUAGES

Decision problems of regular languages are computational problems. We know the fact that regular languages are the languages of the finite automatons. So, Finite automaton provides computational procedure to solve the decisions problems.

A decision problems consists of a set of instances (may be infinite). On these set of instances finite automaton take decision and answered either 'Yes' or 'No'.

A regular language consists of infinite many strings and there is no finite way to represent the complete languages. So, for the general queries about the regular languages those are discussed below, the computational procedure exist that's why these queries are the decision problems of regular languages.

Following are the decision problems:

1. Emptiness problem
2. Finiteness problem
3. Membership problem
4. Equivalence problem and problem of Minimization

10.5.1 (DP1)-Emptiness Problem

If L is a regular language then the question arises; Is L empty?

To answer the question let M = (Q, Σ δ, q_0, F) be a DFA accepts language L, i.e. L = L(M), then above problem may be stated as,

Is Empty (M) → Yes, if L(M) is Empty or L(M) = Ø;
Is Empty (M) → No, if L(M) is Nonempty or L(M) ≠ Ø;

if L(M) = Ø ⇒ Finite automata has no path between starting state and final state/s or there is no way to reach to accepting state/s. Hence language is empty.

if L (M) ≠ Ø ⇒ There are one/more transition/s so that we can reach from starting state to final state/s. hence language is nonempty.

FACT. *If M be a DFA of n states, then L(M) is nonempty if and only if M accepts a string x where* $| x | \le n$.

To test the emptiness nature of the regular expressions, always remember following points:

- Let **r** be a regular expression then if **r** = **Ø** or L(**r**) = **Ø** then it is empty.
- If $\mathbf{r} = \mathbf{r_1} . \mathbf{Ø}$ ⇒ **r** = **Ø** or L(**r**) = **Ø** then it is empty (whatever regular expression $\mathbf{r_1}$ is).
- If **r** = **Ø** + **Ø** ⇒ **r** = **Ø** or L(**r**) = **Ø** then it is empty.
- If $\mathbf{r} = \mathbf{r_1}^*$ ⇒ L(**r**) contains at least a symbol that is ∈ (whatever the regular expression $\mathbf{r_1}$) so it is never empty.

10.5.2 (DP2)-Finiteness Problem

Let L is a regular language accepted by some finite automaton M then the question arises; Is L(M) finite ?

FACT. If M be a *n* states DFA then language L(M) is infinite if and only if M accepts a string *x* s.t. $n \le | x | < 2n$.

From the pumping lemma of regular languages we see that if the language L (M) accepts any string of length ≥ Y n then L (M) is infinite because string can be written as `u.v.w` where, $| v | \ge 1$ and $|u.v| \le n$ and $\forall i \ge 0,\ u.v^i.w \in L$ (infinite many strings).

Prove the fact by contradiction:

Since L(M) is infinite, let a string $x \in L$ of length at least $2n$($| x | \ge 2n$). Apply the pumping lemma on *x*. So, *x* can be written as $u . v . w$ s.t. $| u . v | \le n$ and $| v | \ge 1$.

Since $| u . v . w | \ge 2n$ and $| v | \le n \Rightarrow | u . w | \ge n$.

Further, $| u . w | < | u . v . w |$, because $| v | \ge 1$.

Hence,

$\Rightarrow | u . w | \ge n$ and $| u . w | < | u . v . w |$

$\Rightarrow n \le | u . w | < 2n$ [or $2n \le | u . w | < | x |$]

Under this range there is no $x \in$ L(M) or $n \le | x | < 2n$. So, it contradicts the assumption of the string of length ≥ 2*n* is in L.

Hence, if no strings of length less than 2*n* are accepted, then L(M) is finite, otherwise it is infinite.

10.5.3 (DP3)-Membership Problem

Another important decision problem is, for any given string x and regular language L the question arises; Is x is in L? or whether string x is the member of set of strings of L?

Since, we know that, if L is a regular language then there exists a finite automaton (DFA) M that accepts L. Now above membership problem can be formulated as, given a DFA M and a string x, is x is accepted by M?

The solution of above decision problem is determined by the acceptance nature of DFA M over the string x; i.e.,

- *if automata reaches to its final state / s after processing string x then* $x \in L$; *(yes) so it is the member of the set of regular language L, or*
- *if automata is not react to its final state / s after processing string x then* $x \notin L$; *(no) so it is not the member of L.*

To reach on to the solution, above computational procedure ends within finite number of steps; this fact is because of the deterministic nature of automata M.

Assume M is a n states DFA then if length of the string x is at most n then to reach on to the final decision it takes $O(n)$ times or in linear time (by assuming that each transition requires constant time).

If L has other representation like NFA or NFA with $\in$-moves, then we first convert it to a DFA and then apply the procedure diseumed earlier.

10.5.4 DP4-Equivalence Problem

Given two sets of regular languages, then the question arises; whether these sets are equivalent or they define same set of regular language? Or,

Given two finite automatons M_1 and M_2; are they accept the same language? i.e.;

$$L_1 = L_2. \qquad [\therefore \; L_1 = L(M_1) \;\&\; L_2 = L(M_2)]$$

The solution of above decision problem is fairly simple. If deference of two regular languages is empty then both are equivalent.

We say that if deference is L where L is given as:

$$L = (L_1 - L_2) \cup (L_2 - L_1) \text{ or}$$

$\Rightarrow$ $L = (L_1 \cap L_2') \cup (L_2 \cap L_1')$ where L_2' and L_1' are the complement of L_2 and L_1.

If $L = \varnothing \Rightarrow$ only when nothing is common in between one language and complement of other then both are equivalent.

Else if $L \neq \varnothing \Rightarrow$ regular languages are not equivalent.

Another consequence of equivalence problem is, two regular languages are equivalent if and only if they are the languages of some common DFA.

Let L_1 is the language of DFA M_1 and L_2 is the language of DFA M_2 and both languages are equivalent then both DFA M_1 and M_2 certainly converge to a common DFA. In fact, this DFA is the minimum states DFA constructed from above DFA's.

So, in this journey of finding solution of equivalence problem we reach to another problem that is minimization problem that is discussed in the next section.

10.5.5 Minimization Problem and Myhill Nerode Theorem (Optimizing DFA)

The Minimization problem suggest the way that how we will find a minimum state DFA equivalent to given DFA. *Since there is essentially an unique minimum state DFA for every regular expression Myhill Nerode theorem.*

Recall the discussion of equivalence relations and equivalence classes from section 1.4. Assume L be an arbitrary language and R_L be an equivalence relation i.e., $x\ R_L y$ if and only if for each a, either both xa and $ya \in$ L or neither is in L. Alternatively the number of equivalence classes is always finite if L is a regular language. Associated with the finite automaton there exists also a natural equivalence relation on its language set i.e., for any $x, y \in \Sigma^*$, $x\ R_L y$ if and only if $\delta(q_0, x) = \delta(q_0, y)$. The relation R_L divides the set Σ^* into equivalence classes which is finite. In addition, if $x\ R_I y$, then $xa\ R_L\ ya$ for all a $\in \Sigma^*$. An equivalence relation R_L such that $xR_L y = xa\ R_L$ ya is said to be *right invariant* with respect to concatenation. Later we will see that every FAs make a right invariant equivalence relation on its language set.

(Myhill Nerode theorem)

If L be a regular language then the set of equivalence classes of R_L *is finite.*

Alternatively the set L $\in Z^*$ *is accepted by some* FA, *and let* E_L *be the set of equivalence classes of the relation* R_L *on* Σ^*. *If* E_L *is a finite set then a* FA *accepts* L *provided that this* FA *has the fewest states then any* FA *accepting* L. *Besides other consequences of this theorem, its implication is that there exists always a unique minimum state* DFA *for any regular language.*

This suggests that from a given DFA some/more of the states might be equivalent or they are not distinguishable. All such states are form a group and placed in a class. So, the partitions of states are grouped into two different classes. One is the equivalence class of states and other is the class of distinguishable states. The transition nature of the class is similar to the transition of individual states in the group. So, these classes are equivalent to the different states of the DFA and we get minimum states DFA. (number of states would be less than the number of states of given DFA).

Finding equivalence of states

Assume DFA M = $(Q, \Sigma, \delta, q_0, F)$ and let r and s are the states $\in$ Q then, States r and s are said to be *equivalent* if for all strings x of L have:

- $\hat{\delta}(r, x) \in F$ and $\hat{\delta}(s, x) \in F$ (for $\forall x \in L$).

States r and s are said to be *distinguishable* if for at least a string $x \in$ L have:

- $\hat{\delta}(r, x) \in F$ and $\hat{\delta}(s, x) \notin F$; or
- $\hat{\delta}(r, x) \notin F$ and $\hat{\delta}(s, x) \in F$; or
- $\hat{\delta}(r, x) \notin F$ and $\hat{\delta}(s, x) \notin F$; (where F is the set of accepting state/s).

The equivalence of states have been categorized into various classes which is depend upon up to what extents of symbols of string x they behaves in similar nature (returns on the set F). These equivalence classes are 0-equivalence class, 1-equivalence class, 2-equivalence class,......k-equivalence class.

***k*-equivalence class**

Let states r and $s \in$ Q then r and s are k-equivalent states if and only if no string of length $\leq k$ can distinguish them. It says that, for all strings of length k or smaller up to zero (because symbol $\in$ has length 0) transition of states r and s reaches to final state.

We say that equivalence relation R_K exists between states r and s (pR_Kq). So, to distinguish the states on these bases and make partition, this partition of states is called *k*-equivalence classes.

Similarly we can define other equivalence classes.

0-equivalence class

Test the equivalence relation such as rR_0s for the string of length 0(Ignore the meaningless case of length less than 0). It means we are talking about the string containing symbol $\in$ ($|\in| = 0$) only. If both $\delta(r, \in) \in F$ and $\delta(s, \in) \in F$, then states *r* and *s* are said to be 0-equivalent states, and partition of states is 0-equivalent classes.

1-equivalence class

Similarly test the equivalence relation rR_1s for the string of length one or zero (i.e. length ≤ 1). Assume language L is define over Σ, where $\Sigma = \{0, 1\}$ then test the relation rR_1s over symbols 0, 1 and $\in$ only and make partition of states.

Example 10.6. *Let the Language L = {x ∈ {0, 1}* / the second symbol from the right is a 1} then the corresponding regular expression is* ***(0 + 1)* . 1 . (0 + 1)*** *and the possible DFA that accepts above regular expression is shown in Fig. 10.11.*

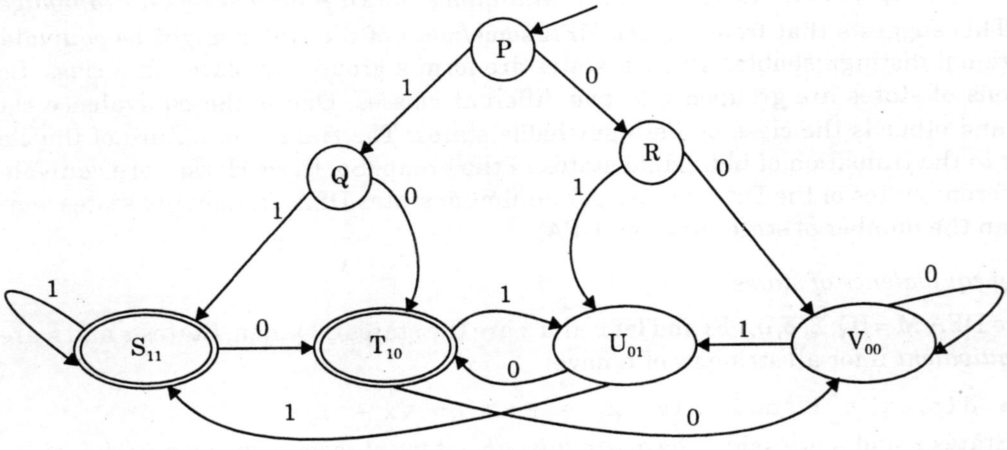

Fig. 10.11. (M)

Now, Is this is a minimum states DFA M? If not, then construct the minimum states DFA.

Where, M = ({P, Q, R, S, T, U, V}, {0, 1}, δ, {P}, {S, T})

Sol. ***Find equivalence classes***

0-equivalence classes

Test the transition of states over the symbol ∈ and make groups of the states which are equivalent and which are distinguishable.

Since, $PR_0Q \Rightarrow \delta(P, \in) = P(\notin F)$ and $\delta(Q, \in) = Q(\notin F)$ so they are Distinguishable.

And, $PR_0R \Rightarrow \delta(P, \in) = P(\notin F)$ and $\delta(R, \in) = R(\notin F)$ so they are Distinguishable.

And, $PR_0S \Rightarrow \delta(P, \in) = P(\notin F)$ and $\delta(S, \in) = S(\notin F)$ so they are Distinguishable.

Similarly test all other states with each other we find states P, Q, R, U and V are distinguishable so, they form a group:

{P, Q, R, U, V}

Only states S and T are equivalence, because

$SR_0T \Rightarrow \delta(S, \in) = S(\in F)$ and $\delta(T, \in) = T(\in F)$ so they are Equivalence and form another group {S, T}

Hence, 0-equivalence classes are,

{P, Q, R, U, V} and {S, T}

1-equivalence classes

Test the equivalence relation between states of groups for the strings of length less then or equal to one (i.e. for the symbols $\in$, 0 and 1).

First take up the group of states {P, Q, R, U, V} and test for equivalence,

Symbol $\in$ is not able to distinguish between states of above group so, test equivalence with respect to another symbols 0 and 1.

$PR_1Q \Rightarrow \delta(P, 0/1) = R/Q(\notin F)$ and $\delta(Q, 0/1) = T/S(\in F)$ so they are Distinguishable.

And, $PR_1R \Rightarrow \delta(P, 0/1) \notin F$ and $\delta(R, 0/1) \notin F$; so they are distinguishable.

And, $PR_1S \Rightarrow \delta(P, 0/1) \notin F$ and $\delta(S, 0/1) \in F$; so they are distinguishable.

And, $PR_1U \Rightarrow \delta(P, 0/1) \notin F$ and $\delta(U, 0/1) \in F$; so they are distinguishable.

And, $PR_1V \Rightarrow \delta(P, 0/1) \notin F$ and $\delta(V, 0/1) \notin F$; so they are distinguishable.

Similarly test for other pairs of states in this group, we find states Q and U are equivalent because,

$QR_1U \Rightarrow \delta(Q, 0/1) \in F$ and $\delta(U, 0/1) \in F$; so they places in other group.

Test equivalence relation for other group of states {S, T}, we see that

$SR_1T \Rightarrow \delta(S, 0/1) \in F$ and $\delta(T, 0/1) \notin F$; since they are distinguishable so they will not be in the same group.

Hence 1-equivalence classes are,

{P, R, V}, {Q, U}, {S} and {T}

(this is a refinement of 0-equivalence class)

2-equivalence classes

Now test the equivalence relation for the strings ε, 0,1,00,01,10,11 (all strings of length ≤ 2). Since we form the groups of states w.r.t. strings ε, 0, and 1 so further it can not be distinguish. Now test the equivalence relation between states of the groups only the over remaining strings. We say it *xy*, where *x* and *y* are either 0 or 1.

Since,

$PR_2R \Rightarrow \delta(P, 00/01) \notin F$ and $\delta(R, 00/01) \notin F$; so they are distinguishable.

And, $PR_1V \Rightarrow \delta(P, 00/01) \notin F$ and $\delta(V, 00/01) \notin F$; so they are distinguishable.

And, $RR_1V \Rightarrow \delta(R, 00/01) \notin F$ and $\delta(V, 00/01) \notin F$; so they are distinguishable.

Since, we couldn't find any equivalent of states in this group so there is no split in the group.

Next, test for equivalence in other group {Q, U}.

$QR_1U \Rightarrow \delta(Q, 00/01) \notin F$ and $\delta(U, 00/01) \notin F$; so they are distinguishable.

So there is no split in this group also.

Since, group {S} and {T} contains single state so further there is no split in these groups.

Hence, 2-equivalence classes are,

{P, R, V}, {Q, U}, {S} and **{T}**

That is similar to 1-equivalence classes and since there is no further refinement. So, process to find equivalence classes terminate.

Hence, equivalent states are $\Rightarrow$ **{P, R, V}, {Q, U}, {S} & {T}**

Therefore, minimum state DFA has just above 4-states.

Remember transition nature of groups is given by the transitions of all the states in the group that return on the same group or some other group. Thus we obtain the transition table shown in Fig. 10.12.

State	Input Symbol	
	0	**1**
→ {P, R, V}	Return on same group {P, R, V}	Return on group {Q, U}
{Q, U}	Return on group {T}	Return on group {S}
● {T}	Return on group {V}	Return on group {U}
● {S}	Return on group {T}	Return on group {S}

Fig. 10.12

And the minimum states DFA is shown in Fig. 10.13 :

[whose language is also the language expressed by the regular expression

(0 + 1)* . 1 . (0 + 1)]

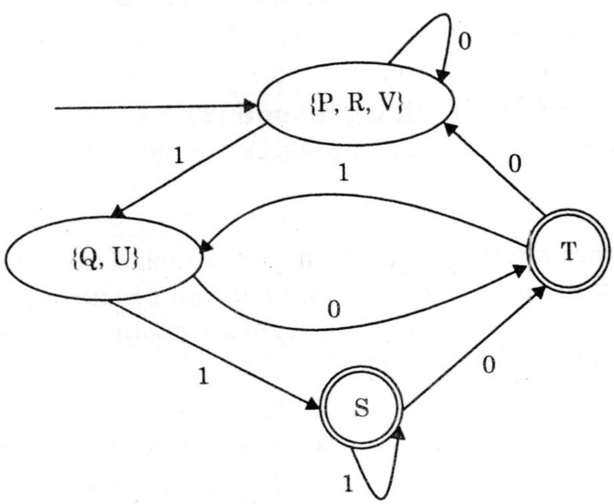

Fig. 10.13

Example 10.7. *Find a minimum states DFA of the finite automata shown in Fig. 10.14 which recognizes the same language.*

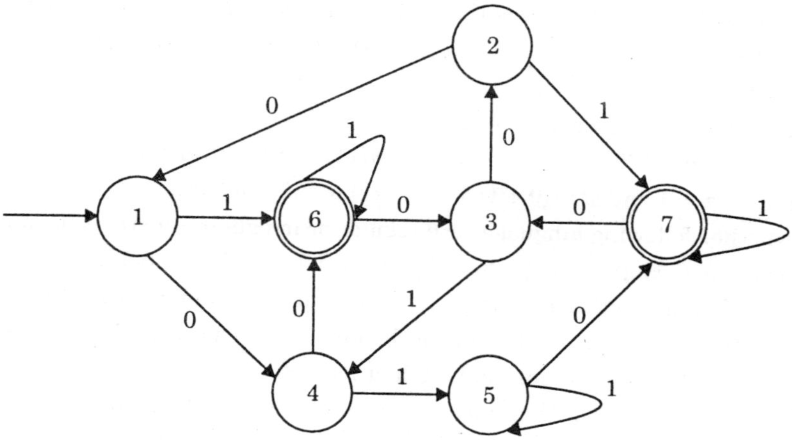

Fig. 10.14

Sol. Find equivalence classes,

0-equivalence classes. Here we test the equivalence over the symbol ∈ and we obtain that states 6 & 7 are equivalence so they place in the same group and all other states are distinguishable so they place in other group, i.e., **{1, 2, 3, 4, 5}** and **{6, 7}**.

1-equivalence classes. Now we test the equivalence over the symbols ∈, 0 and 1 and we find that there is no equivalence of states found in the first group while states 6 and 7 are distinguishable so they are not placed in the same group, i.e., **{1, 2, 3, 4, 5}**, **{6}** and **{7}**.

2- equivalence classes. Test the equivalence over the symbols 00, 01, 10, 11 including the symbols ∈, 0, and 1. Since there is no equivalence of states find in the groups further so the minimum state DFA has 3-states and after considering of the transitions of all the states over the alphabets we obtain the transition diagram which is shown in Fig. 10.15.

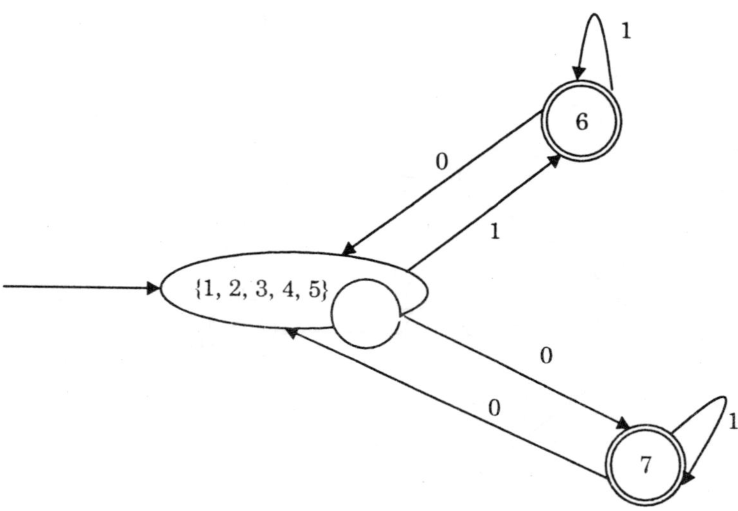

Fig. 10.15

EXERCISES

10.1 Prove or disprove the regularity of the following languages. (Justify your answer).

(i) $\{0^{2n} \mid n \geq 1\}$ (ii) $\{1^n 0^m 1^n \mid m \text{ and } n \geq 1\}$

(iii) $\{0^n 1^{2n} \mid n \geq 1\}$ (iv) $\{0^n 1^m \mid n \geq m\}\}$

(v) $\{0^n 1^n 0^m 1^m \mid m \text{ and } n \text{ are arbitrary integers}\}$

(vi) $\{w\,w \mid w \in (\mathbf{0} + \mathbf{1})^{\mathbf{0}}\}$ (vii) $\{w\,w^{R} \mid w \in (\mathbf{0} + \mathbf{1})^{+}\}$

(viii) $\{w\,1^n\,w^{R} \mid n \geq 1 \text{ and } w \in (\mathbf{0} + \mathbf{1})^{+}\}$ (ix) $\{0^n 1^m \mid n \geq m\}$.

10.2 Decide whether following languages are regular or irregular, (Justify your answer).

(i) The set of odd length strings over {0, 1} in which middle symbol is 0.

(ii) The set of even length strings over {0, 1} in which two middle symbol are same.

(iii) The set of strings over {0, 1} in which the number of 1's are perfect square.

(iv) The set of palindrome strings of length at least 3.

(v) The set of strings in which number of 0's and number of 1's both are divisible by 5.

10.3 Construct minimum state DFA from given FAs shown in Fig. 10.16.

(i)

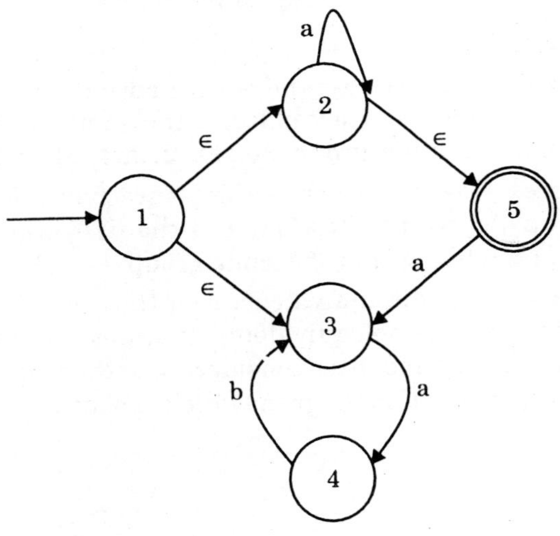

(ii)

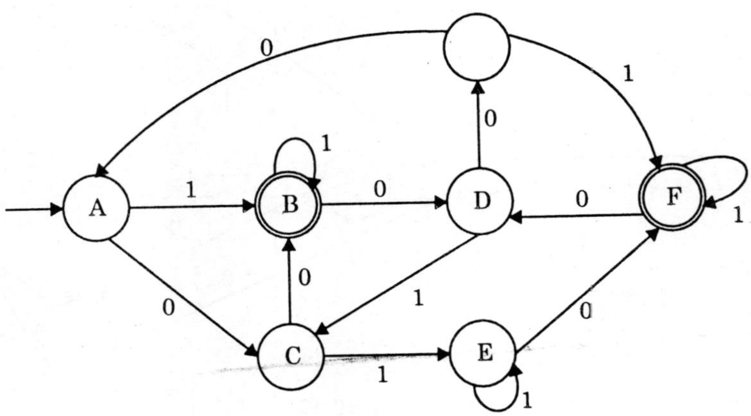

(*iii*)

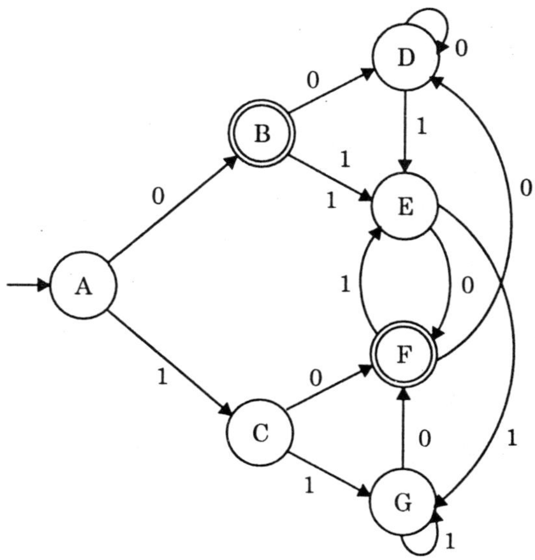

(*iv*)

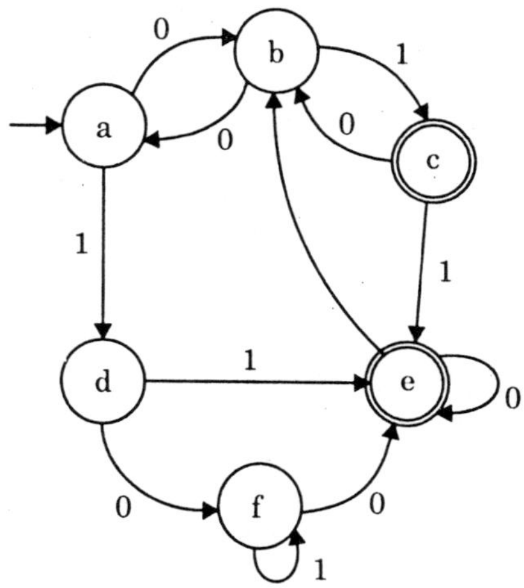

(*v*)

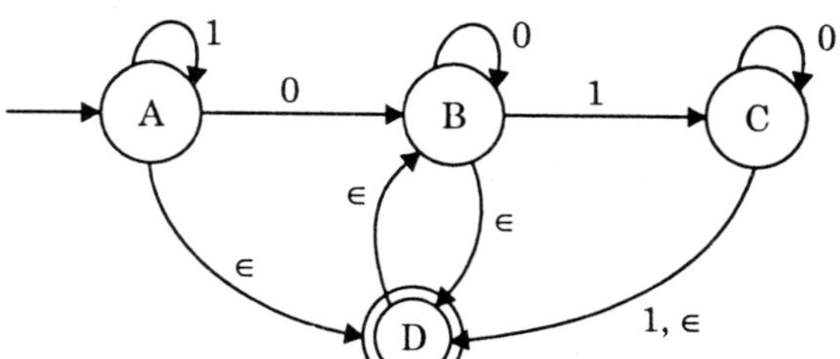

Fig. 10.16

10.4 Let L be a regular language then prove that ½(L) is also regular, where

$$\tfrac{1}{2}(L) = \{x \in \Sigma^*/x.y \in L \text{ for some } y \in \Sigma^* \text{ and } |x| = |y|\}$$

[**Hint :** Assume L = {0010, 01, 001110, 00, ...} then ½(L) = {00, 0, 001, 0, ...}. Let M be a DFA which accepts L i.e., $M = (Q, \Sigma, \delta, q_0, F)$ and the language ½(L) is accepted by the DFA $M' = (Q \times Q \times Q \cup \{q_0'\}, \Sigma, \delta', q_0', F')$. Further, assume

$$x.y = a_1 \quad a_2 \;\ldots\ldots\ldots\ldots\; a_n \;.\; b_1 \;.\; b_2 \;\ldots\ldots\ldots\ldots\; b_n$$
$$q_0 \quad q_1 \quad q_2 \qquad q_{n-1} \quad q_n \quad q_{n+1} \quad q_{n+2} \quad q_{2n-1} \quad q_{2n}$$

(where $q_{2n} \in F$)
So a state is the group of states p, q, and r i.e., $\{p, q, r\}$ where state p is concern with the first part of the string (i.e., x), state q is concern with the second part of the string (i.e., y), and state r is concern to the nondeterministic guess i.e. state q_n. Therefore $\delta'(\{p_1, p_2, p_3\}, a) = \{\delta(p_1, a), r, p_3\}$ if and only if $\delta(p_2, b) = r$ for some $b \in \Sigma$; $\delta(q_0', \in) = \{q_0, q, q\}$ s.t. for all $q \in Q$ and $F' = \{q, q_f, q\}$ s.t. for all $q \in Q$ and $q_f \in F$.
Let $\Sigma = \{0\}$ and $L = \{00\}^* = \{\in, 00, 0000, \ldots\ldots\ldots\}$ then $\frac{1}{2}(L) = \{\in, 0, 00, \ldots\ldots\}= \{0\}^*$. Thus there transitions diagram are shown in Fig. 10.17 (*a*) and (*b*) which are the FA's hence $\frac{1}{2}(L)$ is also regular].

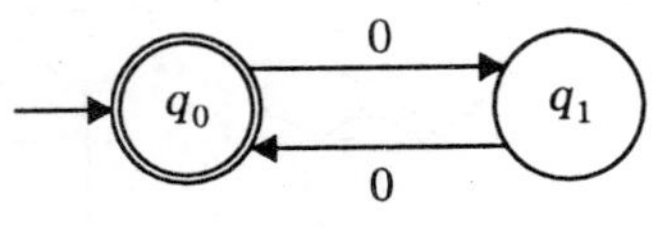

(*a*) M

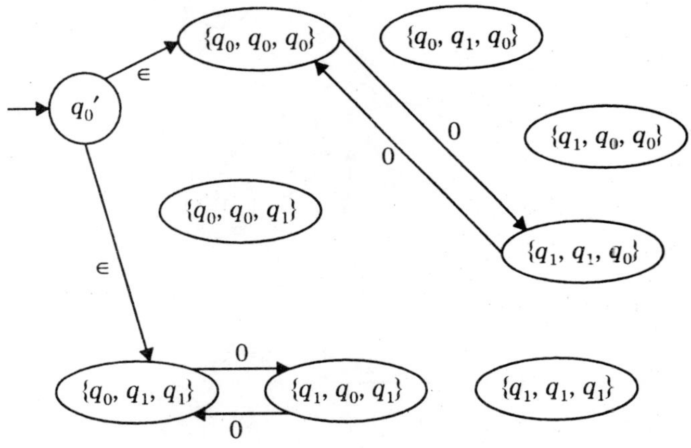

(*b*) M′

Fig. 10.17

10.5 Prove that $L = \{0^m 1^n / gcd(m, n) = 1\}$ is not regular.
[**Hint :** Assume $Z = 0^r 1^k = u.v.w$ where $r + k \geq n$ and $gcd(r, k) = 1$.
Let $r = p_1 . n!$ and $k = r! + 1$ where $r \geq n$ $(1 \leq |v| = n)$ and k is prime. Hence, test $u.v^{i+1}.w \in L$. Since $u.v^{i+1}$ is the string of full of 0's, i.e. number of 0's are

$$r + i\,|v| = r + n!\,(k - p_1)\,|v|/|v| \qquad \text{[because } i = n!\,(k - p_1)/|v|\text{]}$$
$$= r + n!\,(k - p_1)$$
$$= n!\,p_1 + n!\,k - n!\,p_1$$
$$= n!\,k \qquad \text{[number of 0's]}$$

Since number of 1's are k hence $gcd(r, k) \neq 1$.Hence, pumping lemma violated.
[Therefore L is not regular.]

10.6 Find an example of a nonregular language $L \in \{0, 1\}^*$ such that L^2 is regular.

10.7 Find an example of a language $L \in \{0, 1\}^*$ such that L^* is not regular.

10.8 Let L_1 and L_2 are two languages over Σ then we define quotient of L_1 and L_2 to be the language i.e.,

$$L_1/L_2 = \{x / \text{for some } y \in L_2, x\,y \in L_1\}$$

Show that if L_1 is regular then L_1/L_2 is also regular for any arbitrary language L_2.

NON-REGULAR GRAMMARS

11 Non-Regular Grammars

11.1 INTRODUCTION

We know that finite automata gives the abstract view of computation and the regular languages tell about the power of the finite automata. Non-regular grammar such as context free grammar is the grammar defined over simple recursive rules. And the set of strings generated using these recursive rules is called context free languages. So, Context free grammar contains infinite many strings. We say that context free grammar consists of finite set of recursive rules provides a way to represent infinite many strings.

Like regular languages that are accepted by the finite automaton, an automaton that accepts context free languages is called 'Pushdown Automata'.

Before begin to the study of context free grammar we will start our discussion with the meaning of a grammar.

11.2 GRAMMAR

A grammar consists of a finite nonempty set of rules which specify the syntax of the language. Grammar imposes structure on the sentences of the language.

In the context of an automaton a grammar is defined by possible set of tuples, *i.e.* let G be a grammar then G can be defined as,

$$G = (V_T, V_N, S, P)$$

where tuples are defined as follows,

- V_T is a finite set of *terminal symbols (token symbols)*,
- V_N is a finite set of *nonterminal symbols (variables)*,
- S is a *start symbol* ($S \in V_N$/S is a nonterminal symbol in the set of V_N), and
- P is a finite set of *productions / rules* over which grammar G is bounded.

Terminal symbols are those symbols over which language is formulated. For example, assume L is the language *i.e.*,

- L = {all strings formed over 0's and 1's}; so 0 and 1 are terminal symbols.
- If L = {*ab*, *aaab*, *abab*, *abbab*...}; here L is based on symbols *a* and *b* hence these are terminal symbols.

Nonterminal symbols or variables are used to establish the relationship (may be recursive) between itself and with other nonterminals and it must terminate to terminal symbol. For example, let E be an expression (defined over symbol a) and using operators +, / and * it returns an expression s.t. E + E, E/E, E * E and a itself. Hence, E is a nonterminal symbol.

Each grammar must start with a symbol which is called start symbol; all other symbols (terminals/nonterminals) are linked next to start symbol. Throughout the context we denote S as a start symbol and since it doesn't part of the language so $S \in V_N$. Hence,

- $V_N \neq \emptyset$ {set of nonterminal symbols must has at least a symbol that is a starting symbol S}
- $V_T \cap V_N = \emptyset$ {nothing is common between terminal symbols and variables}

In the grammar G productions are defined as,

$$\alpha \rightarrow \beta$$

It can be read as 'α derives β' or 'left symbol(*s*) derives right symbol(*s*)', where $\alpha, \beta \in (V_N \cup V_T)^*$

11.3 CLASSIFICATION OF GRAMMAR - CHOMESKY'S HEIRARCHY

Since productions or rules provides the basis to the grammar. A rule may be represented by $\alpha \rightarrow \beta$. There are several possibilities of the selection of the term α and β in the rule. On the basis of these selections of α and β we classify the productions. Therefore, there are several restrictions in the production $\alpha \rightarrow \beta$ on which grammars are classified.

I. Restriction 1

α must contain at least one nonterminal

i.e. $\alpha \in (V_N \cup V_T)^* . V_N . (V_N \cup V_T)^*$ and $\beta \in (V_N \cap V_T)^*$

Let $V_T = \{a, b, c\}$ and $V_N = \{S, A, B, C\}$ then applying this restriction following are only valid productions,

- $aABac \rightarrow abBC$

  (Here α (left side of production) is $aABac$, which contains two nonterminals A and B and β (right side of production) is $abBC$ and both α and $\beta \in (V_N \cap V_T)^*$.
- But $ab \rightarrow ABab$ is not a valid production, because on its left side there is not a single nonterminal symbol.
- If $\varepsilon \in V_T$ then, $Aab \rightarrow \varepsilon$ is a valid rule. [where ∈ is a null string]
- But $\varepsilon \rightarrow ab$ is not a valid production because $\varepsilon \in V_N$. Therefore, $\alpha \neq \varepsilon$.

The grammar defined under above restriction is called 'Phase Structured Grammar' or '***Type-0 Grammar***' or 'Recursive Enumerable Grammar' and the language generated by this grammar is called 'Phase Structured Language' or '***Type-0 Language***' or 'Recursive Enumerable Language'. The automata accept such language is Turing machine.

II. Restriction 2 (followed by restriction 1)

For the grammar G, if $\alpha \rightarrow \beta$ is a rule then along with the restriction I such that α contains at least a nonterminal it follows another restriction, $| \beta | \geq | \alpha |$ **; or length of right side derived symbols is not less than the length of left side derivatives symbols.**

i.e. $\alpha \in (V_N \cup V_T)^* . V_N . (V_N \cup V_T)^*$ and $\beta \in (V_N \cup V_T)^*$ and also $| \alpha | \leq | \beta |$ and $\beta \neq \varepsilon$.

- From the previous example of production *i.e.*, $aABac \rightarrow abBC$ is not a valid production here, because $| abBC | \not\geq | aABac |$, on left side there should at least five symbols (terminals/nonterminals) but it fulfill restriction 1.

- A production of type *b*ABc → *babbc* is certainly a valid production. On left side it contains 2 non terminals and the length of derived symbols (5) is greater than length of derivatives symbols (4).
- A*ab* → ε is not a valid production. Because, $|\, Aab \,| \not\leq |\, \varepsilon \,|$ or length of derived symbol (0) is not greater than or equal to the length of derivatives symbols (3).

The grammars follow restriction 2 along with restrictions 1 is called 'Context Sensitive Grammar' or '***Type-1 Grammar***' or 'Length Increasing Grammar' and its language is called 'Context Sensitive Language' or '***Type-1 Language***' or 'Length Increasing Language'.

III. Restriction 3 (followed Restriction 2 + Restriction 1)

If the grammar G has the production α → β then besides, restriction 1 & restriction 2, there is another restriction *i.e.*,

α ***must be a single non terminal symbol***

Examples of the valid productions are,

- A → *ab*; there is only a single derivative symbol that is A, and restriction 1 and 2 also fulfill.
- B → *a*ABc
- A → ε is also a valid production.

So the grammar that is bounded under these restrictions (1, 2 and 3) is '***Context Free Grammar***' or '***Type-2 Grammar***' and so the language is '***Context Free Language***' or '***Type-2 Language***'.

The automaton accepts such type of language is Push down Automata.

IV. Restriction 4 (followed Restriction 3 + Restriction 2 + Restriction 1)

In the grammar G, if α → β is a production then, besides above restrictions (1, 2, 3) restriction 4 says, β ***must be a single terminal symbol or a terminal followed by a nonterminal symbol.***

Such as, followings are the valid type productions:

- A → *b*; where $b \in V_T$.
- A → *b*C; a terminal symbol *b* is followed by symbol $C \in V_N$.

The grammar fulfill above restrictions (1,2,3,4) is **'Regular Grammar'** or **'Type-3 Grammar'** and the language generated by G is **'Regular Language'** or **'Type-3 Language'.**

As we say earlier if grammar $G = (V_T, V_N, S, P)$ then language generated by grammar G is L (G) where,

$$\mathbf{L\,(G) = \{x \in V_T{}^*/S \overset{*}{\Rightarrow} x\}}$$

From starting symbol S and by using the production/s (∈ P) we reaches to the string *x* (that is formed over set of terminal symbol/s) in finite steps.

Note. At any stage of productions propagation if, $\alpha_1 A \alpha_2 \Rightarrow \alpha_1 \gamma \alpha_2$ then surely, $A \rightarrow \gamma$ is a production where α_1 and $\alpha_2 \in (V_T \cup V_N)^*$

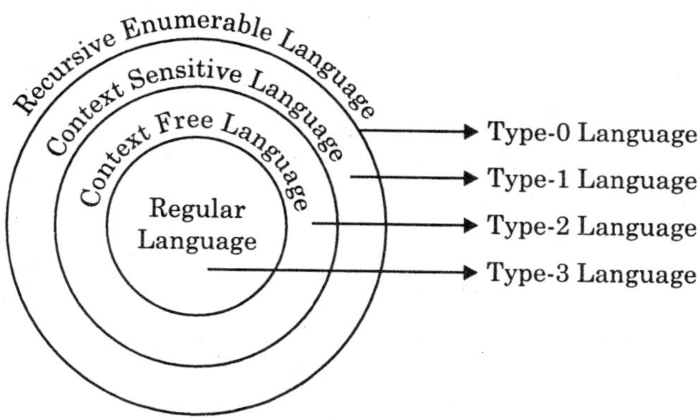

Fig. 11.0

So the classification of grammars canbe heirarchly arranged, which is shown in Fig. 11.0. This arrangement is known as Chomesky's heirarchy. Alternatively we say that

- A type-3 language has the property of , type-2 language, type-1 language & type-0 language.
- A type-2 language has the property of type-1 language & type-0 language.
- A type-1 language has the property of type-0 language.

Example 10.1. *A grammar (G) is defined as, $G = (V_T, V_N, S, P)$ where $V_T = \{a, b\}$; $V_N = \{S, A, B\}$ and the set of productions $P = \{S \to aB, S \to bA, A \to a, A \to aS, A \to bAA, B \to b, B \to bS, B \to aBB\}$ then at any stage of productions propagation if,*

$$\underset{\alpha_1}{aa}\ \underset{\alpha_2}{B\,BAb} \Rightarrow \underset{\alpha_1}{aa}\ \underset{\alpha_2}{aBB\,BAb}$$

then, $B \to aBB$ is a production ($\in P$)

(example of Type-2 grammar)

The language of the grammar G is given by L(G) where L(G) contains following set of string/s:

$$\begin{aligned}
S &\Rightarrow aB \\
&\Rightarrow aaBB && [\because\ B \to aBB] \text{ now we expand against rightmost nonterminal symbol (B) first} \\
&\Rightarrow aaBaBB && [\because\ B \to aBB] \\
&\Rightarrow aabSaBB && [\because\ B \to bS] \\
&\Rightarrow aabSabB && [\because\ B \to b] \\
&\Rightarrow aabbAabB && [\because\ S \to bA] \\
&\Rightarrow aabbAabb && [\because\ B \to b] \\
&\Rightarrow aabbaabb && [\because\ A \to a]
\end{aligned}$$

or $S \overset{*}{\Rightarrow} aabbaabb$

Hence, $aabbaabb \in L(G)$. Similarly many strings can be generated using the productions that are the in language of G.

$\overset{*}{\Rightarrow}$ The relation (deriving in zero or finite number of steps) is reflexive and transitive i.e. If $X \overset{*}{\Rightarrow} X$ then it concluded that $X \Rightarrow X$ in zero step, hence reflexive, and if $X \overset{*}{\Rightarrow} Y$ and $Y \Rightarrow Z$ in one step then certainly $X \overset{*}{\Rightarrow} Y$ on some finite step/s.

Hence we say that if,

$$\alpha_1 \Rightarrow \alpha_2 \Rightarrow \alpha_3 \Rightarrow \ldots\ldots\ldots\alpha_{n-1} \Rightarrow \alpha_n$$

then, $\alpha_1 \overset{*}{\Rightarrow} \alpha_n$ or α_1 derives α_2 in some finite steps.

Example 11.2. *A grammar G is defined over V_N = {S, A}, V_T = {0, 1}, start symbol is S and following productions are in set P:*

$$P = \{S \to 0S, \quad A \to 1S,$$
$$S \to 0A, \quad A \to 0,$$
$$A \to 0A, \quad S \to 1\};$$

Sol. These productions can also be written as:

$$S \to 0S/1A/1$$
$$A \to 0A/1S/0$$

Above grammar is a Type-3 grammar/regular grammar hence there exist a finite automaton (shown in Fig. 11.1) that accepts the L(G).

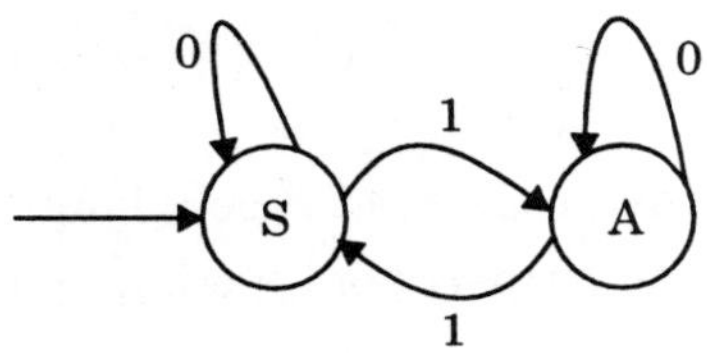

Fig. 11.1

Construction of Finite Automata is very easy. All nonterminals in the grammar are corresponding to the states of finite automata. From starting state S an arc labeled 0 returns itself because S derives 0S. Similarly an arc labeled 1 goes to state A due to production S derives 1A and so on.

Now at what state automata stop. We see the production S → 1A and S → 1 are only possible if A is a stopping state. (Fig. 11.2)

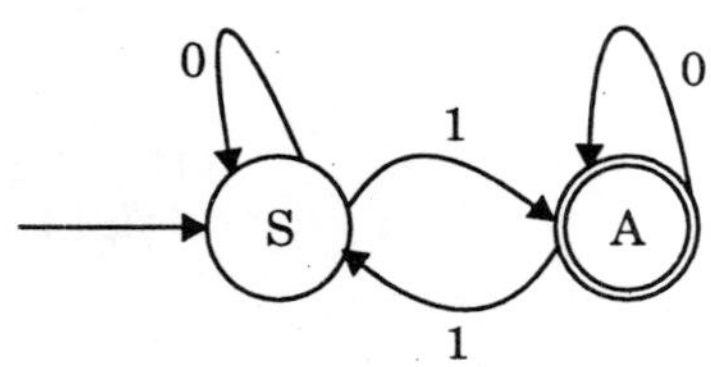

Fig. 11.2

The strings that are in L(G) are constructed as follows:

S ⇒ 1;

S ⇒ 0S ⇒ 01;

S ⇒ 0S ⇒ 00S ⇒ 001;

S ⇒ 0S ⇒ 00S ⇒ 001A ⇒ 0010/0010A/0011S and similarly derived other strings.

Example 11.3. *A grammar G is defined over V_N = {a}, V_T = {S}, S is the starting symbol and productions are:*

$$S \to aaaa\,/\,aaaaS$$

Then L (G) contains following strings:

$$S \Rightarrow aaaa;$$
$$S \Rightarrow aaaaS \Rightarrow \text{aaaa aaaa};$$
$$S \Rightarrow aaaaS \Rightarrow aaaa\ aaaaS \Rightarrow aaaa\ aaaa\ aaaa;\ \text{and so on.}$$

Hence L(G) = {multiple of 4a's}

11.4 SENTENTIAL FORM

For any grammar all derivation starts from S, where S is the starting symbol. If S drive $x(\in V_T)$ in finite steps i.e.,

$S \overset{*}{\Rightarrow} x$ and if $\alpha_1, \alpha_2, \alpha_3, \ldots\ldots$are some intermediate derivatives that are in $(V_N \cup V_T)^*$ then,

$$S \Rightarrow \alpha_1 \Rightarrow \alpha_2 \Rightarrow \alpha_3 \Rightarrow \ldots\ldots \Rightarrow \alpha_n \Rightarrow x$$

This sequence of derivations is called sentential form.

Left sentential form

If $S \overset{*}{\Rightarrow} x$ by means of means of deriving leftmost nonterminal symbol first then the sequence of derivations is called left sentential form.

Right sentential form

If $S \overset{*}{\Rightarrow} x$ by means of deriving rightmost nonterminal symbol first then the sequence of derivation is called right sentential form.

Lemma 11.1

($\in$) *is not in the language of Type-1 grammar.*

Proof. Since we know that if grammar is type-1 then its productions $\alpha \rightarrow \beta$ fulfill the restrictions:

- α must have at least single nonterminal, and
- $|\beta| \geq |\alpha|$

Now if $A \rightarrow \varepsilon$ is any production of this grammar then it's fulfill previous restriction but, because ε says zero occurrences of symbols so, $|\varepsilon| = 0$. Hence it does it, fulfill the next restriction.

Hence we conclude the proof.

Theorem 11.1. *If L is a regular language then there exists a type-3 grammar G, i.e.,*

$$L = L(G).$$

Proof. Since L is regular, hence there exists a DFA that accepts it. ......

Let DFA M is defined as,

$M = (Q, \Sigma, \delta, q_0, F)$ where all tuples has their usual meaning.

Now the theorem says, from the DFA we can construct a type-3 grammar G i.e.,

$L = L(G)$.

Assume that grammar G is defined as,

$G = (V_N, V_T, S, P)$ where tuples have been related with the tuples of M like as,

- All states ($\in$ Q) will be in the set of non terminals, s.t. $V_N = Q$.
- All input symbols ($\in \Sigma$) will be the variables, s.t. $V_T = \Sigma$.

- Starting state (q_0) will corresponds to the starting symbol S, and
- Set of productions (P) takes the meaning from the transition function (δ).

For example,

- If δ(A, a) = B is one of the transition function then its state diagram will be shown in Fig. 11.3, i.e.,

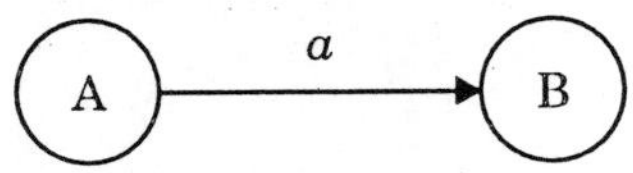

Fig. 11.3

from state A, automata consumes symbol a and reach to state B. Hence, the production will A → aB, means that from non terminal symbol A, generate the variable symbol a and reach to another non terminal symbol B.

- If δ(A, a) = B and state B is the final state then, state diagram will be as in Fig. 11.4 the productions are A → a, because automata terminates as soon as it reaches to state B and A → a B, because machine reaches to state B after consuming symbol a from state A.

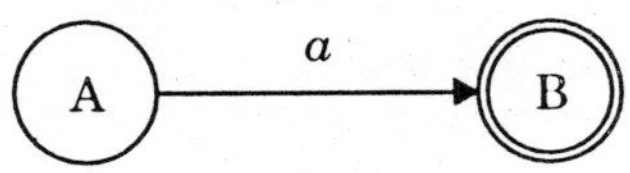

Fig. 11.4

- If starting state is the final state or δ(S, ε) = S then, state diagram will be as Fig. 11.5

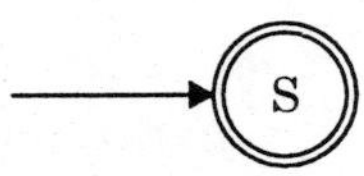

Fig. 11.5

Hence, S → ε will be the production.

Since, all above constructed productions must obey the restrictions 1, 2, 3 and 4. Therefore, grammar is a Type-3 grammar.

Example 11.4. *Let Σ = {a} and the language L = {ε} ∪ {a, aaa, aaaaa,......}. Since L is regular hence there exists a DFA M shown in Fig. 11.6 that accepts the language L.*

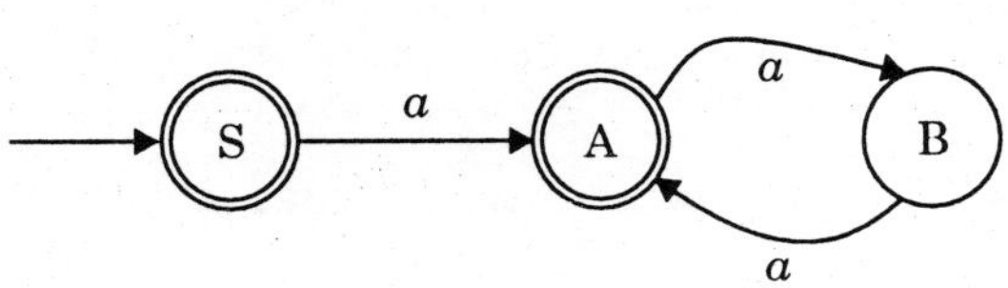

Fig. 11.6. (M)

Following transition functions can be translated into productions as follows,

- δ(S, a) = A ⇒ S → a A(S generates a and reaches to A)
- δ(A, a) = B ⇒ A → a B(A generates a and reaches to B)
- δ(B, a) = A ⇒ B → a A(B generates a and reaches to A)

Since S and A are the final states hence, following are some more productions:

- Start state is the final state, means that machine M halts in real no consumption of any input symbol. So, for transition function $\delta(S, \in) = S \Rightarrow S \Rightarrow \in$ is a production.
- For those strings that are terminated on state A, the productions are,

  $S \rightarrow a$ (stop) and $B \rightarrow a$ (stop)

Hence the set P contains following productions:

$$S \rightarrow \in/a/aA$$
$$A \rightarrow aB$$
$$B \rightarrow aA/a$$

Since, above productions obey the required restrictions (1, 2, 3 and 4) hence these productions are from type-3 grammar.

We can also see that the language generated by grammar G is L(G) is same as the language of DFA M or L(G) = L(M).

$S \Rightarrow \in \equiv S \Rightarrow a,$

$S \Rightarrow aA \Rightarrow aaB \Rightarrow aaa,$

$S \Rightarrow aA \Rightarrow aaB \Rightarrow aaaA \Rightarrow aaaaB \Rightarrow aaaaa$

So, $L(G) = \{\in, a, aaa, aaaaa, ...\} = L(M)$

Theorem 11.2. *If L is generated from a Type-3 grammar G then L is regular.*

Proof. Above theorem suggest the way how to construct the DFA from given grammar.

Let grammar $G = (V_N, V_T, S, P)$ then the tuples of DFA $M = (Q, \Sigma, \delta, q_o, F)$ relates the tuples of G in following manner,

- $Q = V_N \cup \{q_f\}$ where q_f is the new final state added in this set.
- $\Sigma = V_T$
- $q_0 = S$
- $F = \{q_f\} \cup \{S\}$ if $\in \in L$, or $\{q_f\}$ if $\in \notin L$.
- From given definition of productions, transition functions are to be determin, i.e.

For example, ...

If productions of G are:

$$S \rightarrow aA/a/\in \qquad A \rightarrow aB \qquad \text{and} \qquad B \rightarrow a\,A/a$$

Then following will be the FA, (Fig. 11.7)

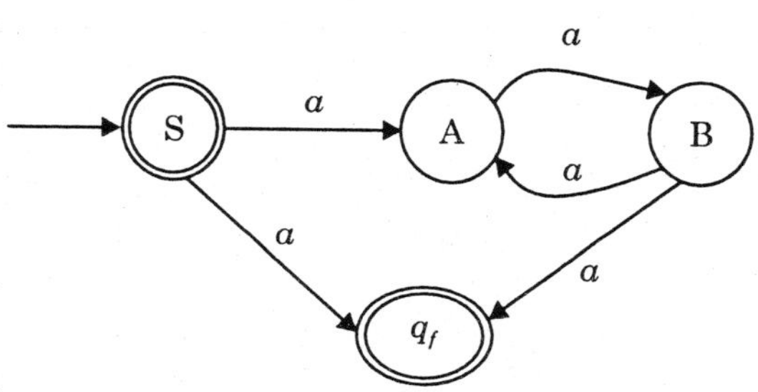

Fig. 11.7

Note *that machine might be a NFA at this level. So convert it Fig. 11.7 to the DFA. i.e. the minimum state* DFA will be shown in Fig. 11.8.

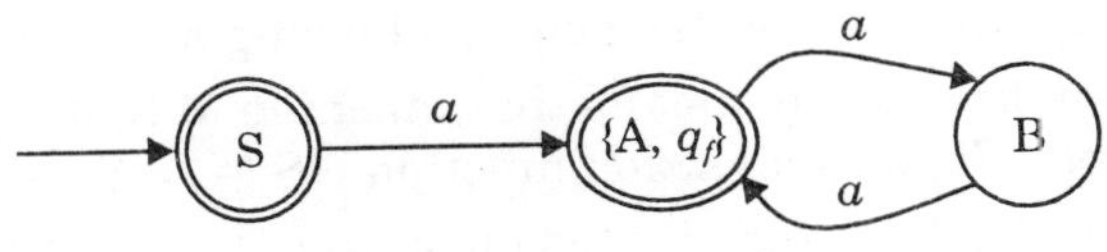

Fig. 11.8

11.5 CONTEXT FREE GRAMMARS (CFG)/(TYPE-2 GRAMMAR) AND CONTEXT FREE LANGUAGES (CFL)

As we see earlier, that a grammar $G = (V_N, V_T, S, P)$ is said to be context free grammar if P contains the production of type $\alpha \to \beta$, i.e.,

- α must be a single non terminal, and
- $|\beta| \geq |\alpha|$.

For the case that if ε be in the language of the grammar G then $S \to \varepsilon$ is also a production is in set P exceptionally.

And the language generated by context free grammar G is context free language that is L(G) where,

$$L(G) = \{x \in V_T^*/S \overset{*}{\Rightarrow} x\}$$

Solve the examples of CFGs and CFLs

Example 11.5. *If a language $L = \{a^k\ b^k / k \geq 1\}$ then L is CFL. Prove it.*

Sol. Since L is CFL if and only if it generates from CFG. So, try to find the Grammar G i.e. L = L (G).

where L = {*ab*, *aabb*, *aaabbb*, ...}

Let the grammar $G = (V_N, V_T, S, P)$ where,

$V_T = \{a, b\}$, V_N = {S, A ....select arbitrary symbols as per the requirements}, S is the starting symbol and set of productions are determined as follows:

- Since L contains string '*ab*' hence productin will be,

  $S \to ab$

- For the next strings there is a recursive iterations of string '*a* S *b*' so production will be,

  $S \to a\,S\,b$

Using productions $S \to ab \mid a\,S\,b$ we can derive all the strings of L such as,

$S \Rightarrow ab$,

$S \Rightarrow a\,S\,b \quad \Rightarrow a\,a\,b\,b$.

$S \Rightarrow a\,S\,b \quad \Rightarrow a\,a\,S\,b\,b \Rightarrow a\,a\,a\,b\,b\,b$ and so on.

Hence L(G) = L and since there is no further need of the non terminal symbols hence V_N contains only symbol S.

So, $G = (\{S\}, \{a, b\}, S, \{S \to a\,b \mid a\,S\,b\})$ is the required grammar.

Since, both productions fulfill the restrictions. Hence G is a CFG and language L is CFL.

Example 11.6. *Prove that Language $L = \{a^k\ b^k\ c^l / k \geq 1 \text{ and } l \geq 1\}$ is a CFL.*

Proof. We will Construct the grammar G for the language L i.e. L = L(G)

Now, we see that in the language L,

1. All strings formed by two different substrings
2. One substring starting with a's followed by equal number of b's *i.e.* '*ab*, *aabb*,.'
3. Followed by other substring that generates c's only *i.e.* '*c*, *cc*, *ccc*......'

Let S is the starting symbol and A and C are other non terminal symbols, then following are the productions (P)

$$S \rightarrow AC \quad \text{(corresponding to 1)}$$
$$A \rightarrow a\,b \mid a\,A\,b \quad \text{(corresponding to 2)} \quad \text{and}$$
$$C \rightarrow c \mid c\,C \quad \text{(corresponding to 3)}$$

Thus the grammar G = ({S, A, C}, {a, b}, S, P)

We can also see that,

$$S \Rightarrow A\,C \Rightarrow a\,b\,C \Rightarrow a\,b\,c,$$

$$S \Rightarrow A\,C \Rightarrow a\,A\,b\,C \Rightarrow a\,a\,b\,b\,C \begin{cases} \rightarrow a\,a\,b\,b\,c, \text{ or} \\ \rightarrow a\,a\,b\,b\,c\,C \longrightarrow a\,a\,b\,b\,c\,c \text{ and so on.} \end{cases}$$

Example 11.7. *Prove that Language L = {$a^k\, b^l\, c^l$ / k ≥ 1 and l ≥ 1} is a CFL.*

Sol. We observe that L contains strings of following nature, i.e.

1. all strings formed by two substrings,
2. first substring formed over symbol a's *viz.* '*a*, *aa*, *aaa*.........'
3. followed by other substring that contains the symbol b's followed by a equal number of c's *viz.* '*bc*, *bbcc*, *bbbccc*.........'

Let S is the starting symbol and A and B are the other non terminals.

So, under above observations the following are the productions (P)

$$S \rightarrow A\,B \quad \text{(corresponds to 1)}$$
$$A \rightarrow a \mid a\,A \quad \text{(corresponds to 2) and}$$
$$B \rightarrow b\,c \mid b\,B\,c \quad \text{(corresponds to 3)}$$

These productions fulfill the restrictions that all are derived from a single non terminal (S or A or B) and length of derived symbol/s is greater than or equal to the length of its derivative symbol (| AB | = | S |; | a | = | A |; | aA | = | A |; | bc | = | B |; | b B c| = | B |).

Hence, the Grammar

({S, A, B}, {a, b, c}, S, P} is a CFG and the language is a CFL.

Example 11.8. *A language L is defined over Σ = {a, b} such that it contains equal number of a's and b's. Construct the grammar for above grammar and checks its ambiguity.*

Sol. We see that the L contains following possible set of strings, i.e.,

1. strings starting with symbol a's s.t. it has equal number of a's and b's
2. strings starting with symbol b's s.t. it has equal number of b's and a's

Let S be the starting symbol and A and B are other non terminals then following are the productions:

Corresponds to 1:	Corresponds to 2:
$S \rightarrow a\,B$	$S \rightarrow b\,A$
$B \rightarrow b \mid b\,S \mid a\,B\,B$	$A \rightarrow a \mid a\,S \mid b\,A\,A$

Now derive the arbitrary string '*abbaabab*' (that has equal number of a's and b's) from above set of productions, i.e.,

$S \Rightarrow a\,B \Rightarrow a\,b\,S \Rightarrow a\,b\,b\,A \Rightarrow a\,b\,b\,a\,S \Rightarrow a\,b\,b\,a\,a\,B$
$\Rightarrow a\,b\,b\,a\,a\,b\,S \Rightarrow a\,b\,b\,a\,a\,b\,a\,B \Rightarrow a\,b\,b\,a\,a\,b\,a\,b$

Assume the string '*aabbabab*', and then following will be the derivation sequences.

- $S \Rightarrow a\,B \Rightarrow a\,a\,B\,B \Rightarrow a\,a\,b\,b\,S \Rightarrow a\,a\,b\,b\,a\,B \Rightarrow a\,a\,b\,b\,a\,b\,S$
  $\Rightarrow a\,a\,b\,b\,a\,b\,a\,B \Rightarrow a\,a\,b\,b\,a\,b\,a\,b$, (using *lm* derivatin sequence)
- $S \Rightarrow a\,B \Rightarrow a\,a\,B\,B \Rightarrow a\,a\,b\,S\,B \Rightarrow a\,a\,b\,b\,A\,B \Rightarrow a\,a\,b\,b\,a\,B$
  $\Rightarrow a\,a\,b\,b\,a\,b\,S \Rightarrow a\,a\,b\,b\,a\,b\,a\,B \Rightarrow a\,a\,b\,b\,a\,b\,a\,b$
  (using *lm* derivation sequence)

Both derivation sequences are different and their derivation trees are shown in Fig. 11.9

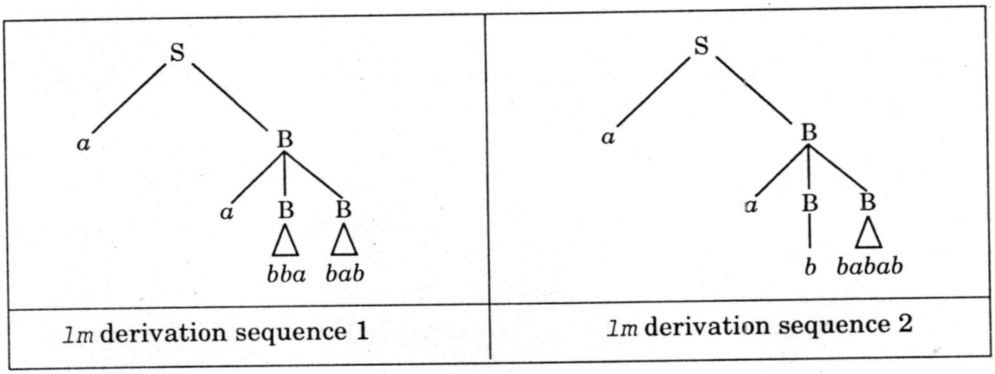

Fig. 11.9

Since the string has two derivation trees so grammar is ambiguous and the language it generates is an ambiguous language.

Example 11.9. *Construct the CFG for the language* $L = \{a^k\, b^l\, c^k \,/\, k \geq 0,\ l \geq 0\}$.

Sol. Since the language L = {∈, *b*, *bb*......, *ac*, *aacc*......, *abc*,......}, where,

- ε is in language and it derives from start symbol S hence ......

  $S \rightarrow \in$ is a production
- strings '*b*, *bb*, *bbb*,......' are derived from the productions

  $S \rightarrow b$ or $S \rightarrow b\,S$
- strings '*ac*, *aacc*, ...' are derived from productions

  $S \rightarrow a\,c$ or $S \rightarrow a\,S\,c$

Remaining strings can be derived using above productions, i.e.,

For example,

$S \Rightarrow \in$; $S \Rightarrow b$; $S \Rightarrow b\,S \Rightarrow b\,b$; $S \Rightarrow b\,S \Rightarrow b\,b\,S \Rightarrow b\,b\,b$ and so on

$S \Rightarrow a\,c$; $S \Rightarrow a\,S\,c \Rightarrow a\,a\,S\,c\,c \Rightarrow a\,a\,\varepsilon\,c\,c \Rightarrow a\,a\,c\,c$; and so on.

$S \Rightarrow a\,S\,c \Rightarrow a\,b\,c$; $S \Rightarrow a\,S\,c \Rightarrow a\,b\,S\,c \Rightarrow a\,b\,b\,c$; and so on.

So, the responsible grammar for language L has the productions

$$S \rightarrow \in \mid b \mid b\,S \mid a \mid a\,S\,c$$

Since, the productions fulfill the restrictions required for CFG, so the grammar is CFG.

Alternatively, if the language $L = \{a^k\, b^l\, c^k / k \geq 1, l \geq 1\}$ then the production

$S \rightarrow a\,S\,c$

for the strings that have equal number of a's and c's and in between there are multiple of b's so $S \rightarrow a\ A\ c$ and $A \rightarrow b \mid b\ A$ are the additional productions.

Hence, grammar has the productions

$$S \rightarrow a\,S\,c \mid a\,A\,c$$
$$A \rightarrow b \mid b\,A$$

That is also a context free grammar (CFG).

11.6 DERIVATION TREE (PARSE TREE)

When we constructed the language (strings) from the grammar, we will go through a sequence of derivations. The tree representation of the derivations are called derivation tree/parse tree. Parse tree shows how the terminal symbol/s are generated and grouped into strings. The recursive inferences of the productions are also visualize in the parse tree.

The ambiguity characteristic of the grammars and languages is an important application of parse trees. In the compiler theory parse tree provide the way how the source program is translated into the machine level program.

11.6.1 Parse Tree Construction

Let the grammar $G = (V_N, V_T, S, P)$ then, the derivation tree of G has following characteristics,

- The nodes of this tree have labeled from $V_N \cup V_T \cup \{\varepsilon\}$,
- The root of the tree has labeled S (start symbol),
- All internal nodes in the tree have labeled from V_N,
- If a node has label X and $X_1, X_2, X_3, \ldots\ldots\ldots X_K$ are the labels of its children (from left-to-right) then $X \rightarrow X_1\,X_2\,X_3 \ldots\ldots\ldots X_K$ must be the production,
- If a node has label ε then it must be a leaf node and also it must be the only son of its parent.

On bases of these characteristics we can construct the parse tree.

Example 11.10. *Let $V_N = \{S\}$, $V_T = \{+, \star, (,), a\}$ and the productions are $S \rightarrow S + S \,/\, S \star S \,/\, (S) \,/\, a$. Then construct the derivation tree for the terminal string $(a + (a \star a))$.*

Sol. First we go through the derivation sequence for the given terminal string, i.e.,

$S \Rightarrow (S)$ [we start from this production because the first terminal string is '(']

$S \Rightarrow (S + S)$ $\quad [\therefore\ S \rightarrow S + S]$

$S \Rightarrow (a + S)$ $\quad [\therefore\ S \rightarrow a]$

$S \Rightarrow (a + (S))$ $\quad [\therefore\ S \rightarrow (S)]$

$S \Rightarrow (a + (S \star S))$ $\quad [\therefore\ S \rightarrow S \star S]$

$S \Rightarrow (a + (a \star S))$ $\quad [\therefore\ S \rightarrow a]$

$S \Rightarrow (a + (a \star a))$ $\quad [\therefore\ S \rightarrow a]$

So, from starting symbol S we reaches to the terminal string $(a + (a \star a))$, and its derivation tree is shown in Fig. 11.10.

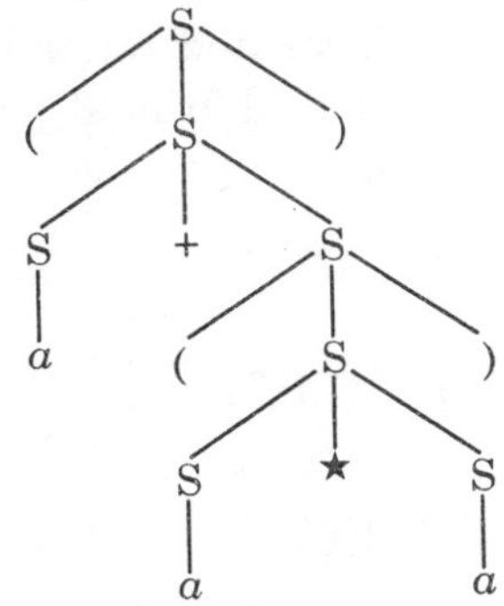

Fig. 11.10

Hence, $S \overset{*}{\Rightarrow} (a + (a \star a))$ is the *yield of the derivation tree* which is the concatenation of all terminal symbols (leaves) of the tree from left-to-right.

Since, in the derivation sequence we derive the left most non terminal first. Hence, the derivation is called '*left-most-derivation* (*lm*) and the derivation tree is left-most-derivation-tree.

So, $$S \underset{lm}{\overset{*}{\Rightarrow}} (a + (a \star a))$$

For *right-most-derivation* (*rm*) sequence derive right most non terminal first. Hence, we get the right-most-derivation-tree.

Like in this example when we derive right most derivation first we go through a different derivation sequence for the same terminal string '$(a + (a \star a))$' *viz.*

S ⇒ (S) [we start from this production because the first terminal string is '(']

$S \Rightarrow (S + S)$ [∴ $S \to S + S$]

$S \Rightarrow (S + (S))$ [∴ $S \to (S)$]

$S \Rightarrow (S + (S \star S))$ [∴ $S \to S \star S$]

$S \Rightarrow (S + (S \star a))$ [∴ $S \to a$]

$S \Rightarrow (S + (a \star a))$ [∴ $S \to a$]

$S \Rightarrow (a + (a \star a))$ [∴ $S \to a$]

Hence, $S \underset{rm}{\overset{*}{\Rightarrow}} (a + (a \star a))$

And its right most derivation tree is shown in Fig. 11.11

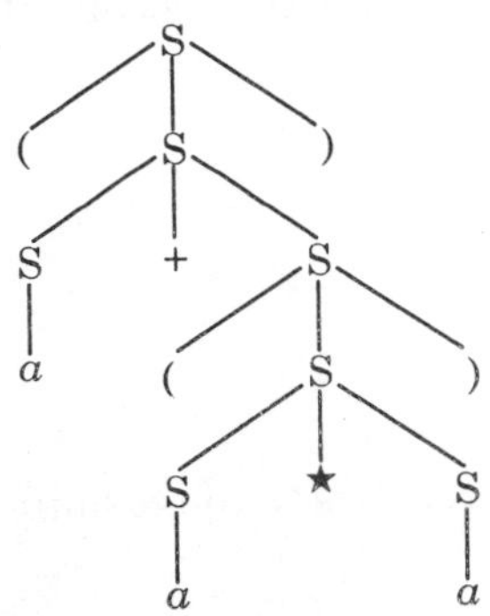

Fig. 11.11

Thus, we may find more derivation sequences and consequently more derivation trees for a single terminal string.

Every tree has exactly one left derivation sequence and exactly one right derivation sequence and also possible that both derivation sequences may be the same. Hence, a string may have more than one derivation trees.

Example 11.11. *Fig. 11.12 shows a left-most-derivation tree for the string 'a + a ⋆ a' using the previous grammar G, i.e. {S, {+, *, (,), a}, S, {S → S + S / S * S / (S) / a}.*

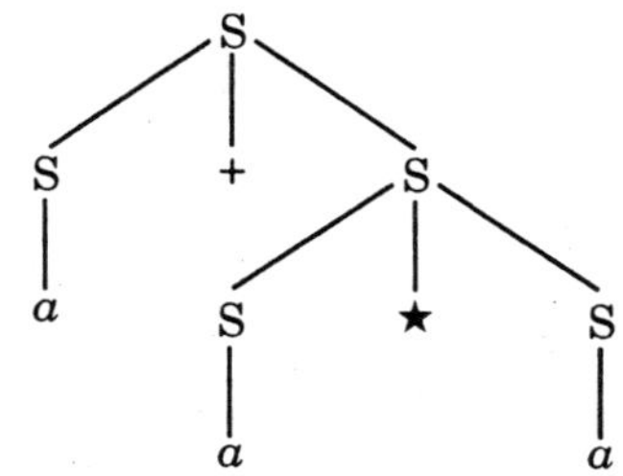

Fig. 11.12

For the following derivation sequence:

$S \Rightarrow S + S \Rightarrow a + S \Rightarrow a + S \Rightarrow S \Rightarrow a + a \star S \Rightarrow a + a \star a$

There exists another *lm* derivation sequence for the same string, i.e.,

$S \Rightarrow S \star S \Rightarrow S + S \star S \Rightarrow a + S \star S \Rightarrow a + a \star S \Rightarrow a + a \star a$

So, there exists another *lm* derivation tree shown in Fig. 11.13.

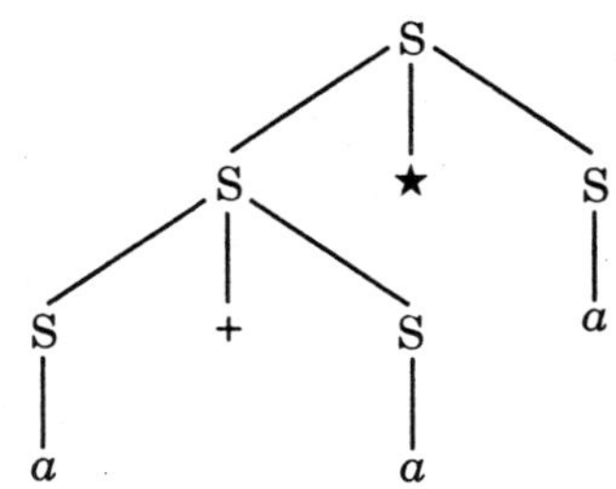

Fig. 11.13

Next, we see the right-most-derivation sequences for the same string, i.e.,

$S \Rightarrow S \star S \Rightarrow S * a \Rightarrow S + S \star a \Rightarrow S + a \star a \Rightarrow a + a \star a$

or $S \underset{rm}{\overset{\star}{\Rightarrow}} a + a \star a$

Fig. 11.14 shows its *rm* derivation tree.

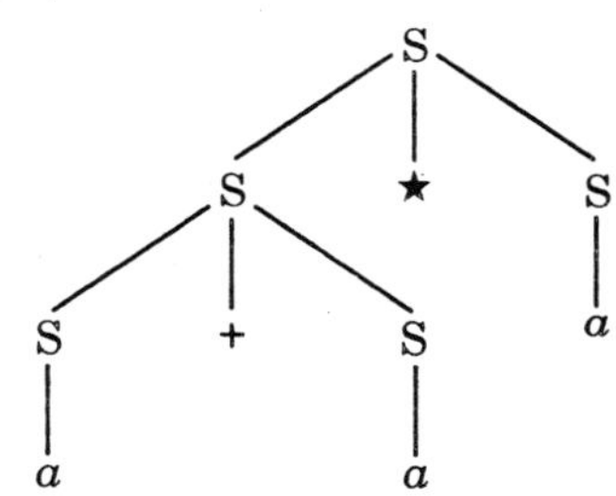

Fig. 11.14

There exists another right most derivation sequence for the string '$a + a \star a$', i.e.,

$S \Rightarrow S+S \Rightarrow S+S\star S \Rightarrow S+S\star a \Rightarrow S+a\star a \Rightarrow a+a\star a.$

For above *rm* derivation sequence the *rm* derivation tree is shown in Fig. 11.15.

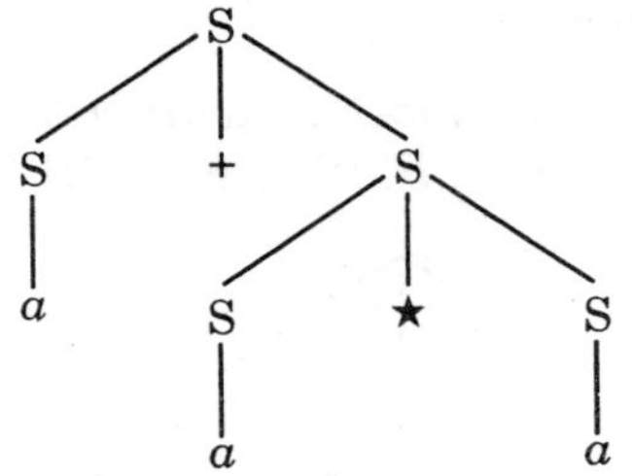

Fig. 11.15

Hence, the string '$a + a * a$' has two *lm* & two *rm* derivation trees.

11.7 AMBIGUOUS GRAMMAR

As we have seen that the derivation tree provides the structure of construction for the strings in its language. This structure is unique for each string that is in the language. Although, few grammars fails to provide a unique structures for all the strings that are in its language. We mean to say that, such grammar's language contains at least one string that has two or more essentially different derivations. Those grammars are known as 'ambiguous grammars'.

11.7.1 Definition

A grammar is said to be ambiguous if, for its any one string, produce at least two distinct derivation tree either two distinct *rm* derivation tree or two distinct *lm* derivation tree.

So, a context free grammar G is said to be *ambiguous* if we can find two or more different parse tree for at least a string $\in$ L (G).

If each string has one and only one derivation tree (derived either by *lm* derivation sequences or *rm* derivation sequences) then the grammar is *an unambiguous* grammar.

11.7.2 Ambiguous Context Free Language

A context free language L is said to be ambiguous if and only if, every CFG generating L is ambiguous.

Above definition says that the CFG grammars that are responsible for generating the language L must be *all* ambiguous CFGs.

That is, if context free language L can be generated from CFG $G_1, G_2, G_3 \ldots G_K$ then L is ambiguous context free language (CFL) iff $\forall G_i (i = 1 \text{ to } k)$ are ambiguous CFGs.

Example 11.12. *Let G be the CFG with the productions*

$$S \to T + S / T$$
$$T \to F \star T / F$$
$$F \to a / (S)$$

Test the ambiguity of G.

Sol. We take the string '$a + a \star a$' that is in L(G) and construct its most possible derivation sequences, i.e.,

I. *lm* derivation sequence

$S \Rightarrow T + S \Rightarrow F + S \Rightarrow a + S \Rightarrow a + T \Rightarrow a + F \star T \Rightarrow a + a \star T$
$\Rightarrow a + a \star F \Rightarrow a + a \star a$

(Fig. 11.16 shows its *lm* derivation tree)

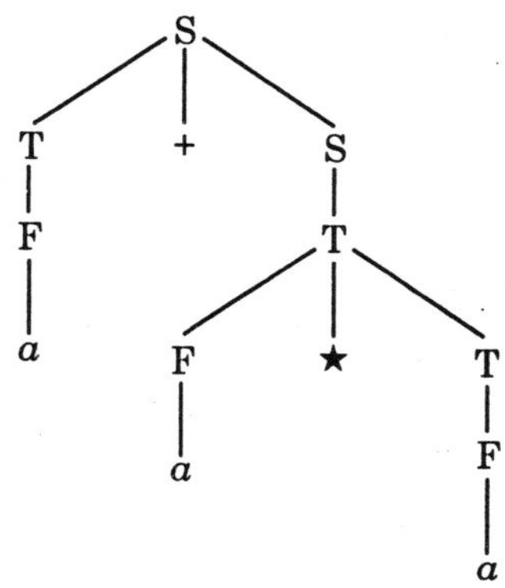

Fig. 11.16

II. *rm* derivation sequence

$S \Rightarrow T + S \Rightarrow T + T \Rightarrow T + F \star T \Rightarrow T + F \star F \Rightarrow T + F \star a$
$\Rightarrow T + a \star a \Rightarrow F + a \star a \Rightarrow a + a \star a$

(Fig. 11.17 shows its *rm* derivation tree)

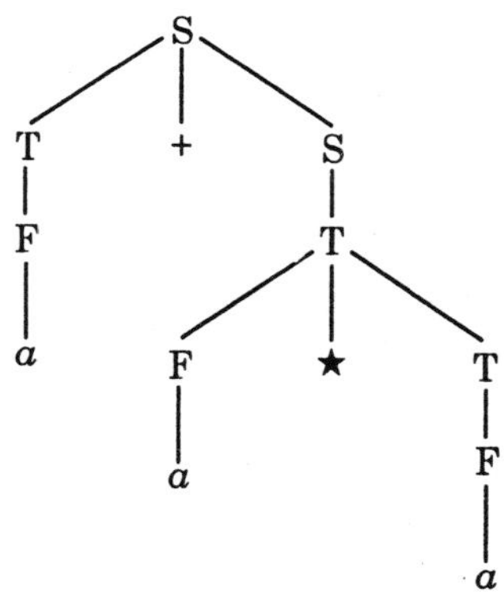

Fig. 11.17

After compare the derivation tree structures we find that both are similar. So the string has a unique derivation tree hence G is an *unambiguous* grammar.

Example 11.13. *Show that CFG G with productions*

$$S \to a \mid Sa \mid bSS \mid SSb \mid SbS$$

is ambiguous.

Sol. If G is ambiguous then it must has two or more derivation trees for at least a strings of L(G). Since L(G) = {*a*, *aa*, *aaa*, ..., *baa*, *baaaa*,....., *aab*,......, *aba*,......, *baab*,......}

- Test the ambiguity of G on string '*baa*'. For that following are the derivation sequences, i.e.,
  - $S \Rightarrow bSS \Rightarrow baS \Rightarrow baa$ (using *lm* derivation sequence)
  - $S \Rightarrow bSS \Rightarrow bSa \Rightarrow baa$ (using *rm* derivation sequence)

Both shows unique derivation tree. Hence G may be unambiguous.

- Test with the string '*baaab*'.

  We construct most possible derivation sequences for this string, i.e.,

  - $S \Rightarrow SSb \Rightarrow bSSSb \Rightarrow baSSb \Rightarrow baaSb \Rightarrow baaab$ (using *lm* derivation sequences).
  - $S \Rightarrow bSS \Rightarrow baS \Rightarrow baSSb \Rightarrow baaSb \Rightarrow baaab$ (using *lm* derivation sequences).
  - $S \Rightarrow bSS \Rightarrow bSSSb \Rightarrow bSSab \Rightarrow bSaab \Rightarrow baaab$ (using *rm* derivation sequences)

There derivation trees are shown in Fig. 11.18(*a*) (*b*) (*c*) respectively.

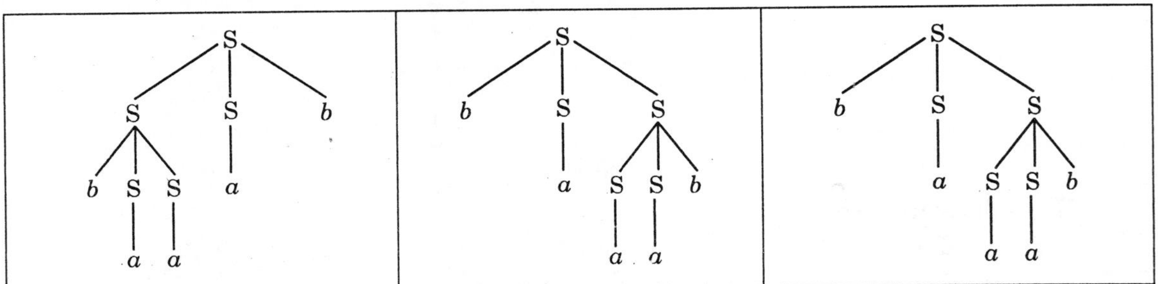

lm derivation tree 1	*lm* derivation tree 2	*rm* derivation tree *Similar* to *lm* derivation tree 2
(*a*)	(*b*)	(*c*)

Fig. 11.18

Thus, for this string we have two different derivation trees that are shown above. So, grammar G fails to provide unique derivation tree, hence G is *an ambiguous* CFG.

Example 11.14. *Show that CFG G with productions*

$$S \Rightarrow S(S) \mid \in$$

is unambiguous.

Sol. Construct the context free language (CFL) i.e., (G) = {∈, ∈(∈), ∈(∈)(∈), ∈(∈(∈)),......}

Now test the ambiguity of CFG G and show that there is a unique derivation tree for all of its strings ∈ L(G).

- For string ∈ there is one and only one possible derivation sequence $S \Rightarrow \varepsilon$.
- For string ∈(∈):

  $$S \Rightarrow S(S) \Rightarrow \in(S) \Rightarrow \in(\in)$$

  We get a unique derivation tree either derive *lm* or *rm* derivation sequence.
- For string ∈(∈)(∈):

  $$S \Rightarrow S(S) \Rightarrow S(S)(S) \Rightarrow \in(S)(S) \Rightarrow \in(\in)(S) \Rightarrow \in(\in)(\in)$$

  There is no other derivation sequence possible for this string. Hence, we again reach to unique derivation tree.

- For string $\in(\in(\in))$:

$$S \Rightarrow S(S) \Rightarrow S(S(S)) \Rightarrow S(S(\in)) \Rightarrow S(\in(\in)) \Rightarrow \in(\in(\in))$$

Here we again reach to a unique derivation tree.

And similarly test for other strings of L(G). We find that the above case is true for all of its strings. Hence, CFG G is an *unambiguous* grammar.

Note → By careful observation of above examples we find that in a grammar, from starting symbol S if two are more intermediate productions reaches on the same string then grammar may be an ambiguous grammar.

Let G has productions $S \to A1 \mid A2 \ldots\ldots \mid Ak$

where $A1 \overset{*}{\Rightarrow} x (\in V_T^*)$

and $A2 \overset{*}{\Rightarrow} x (\in V_T^*)$

then G is ambiguous.

11.8 PUSHDOWN AUTOMATON

Pushdown automaton (PDA) is an extended finite state automaton model of computation such that it recognizes the context free languages (CFLs). The abstract machine model of the PDA is shown in Fig. 11.19 essentially has an *input tape*, a *finite control*, and additionally a *stack* (FILO) of infinite length whose bottom boundary is known but no top boundary.

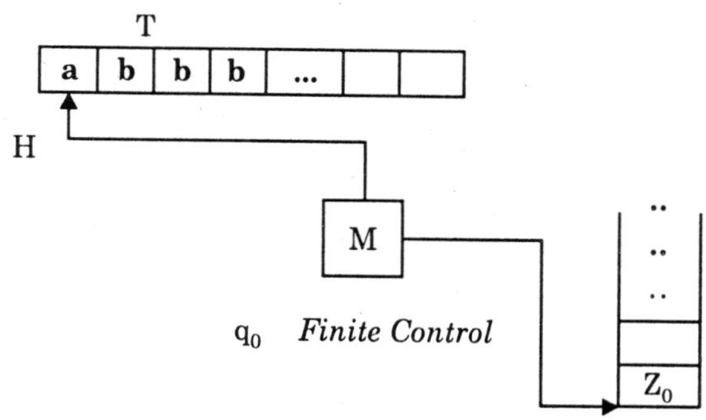

Fig. 11.19

The stack contains a string of symbols from some alphabets. The leftmost symbol of the stack is considered to be at the top of the stack. Assume Γ is the finite set of stack symbols whose first element is Z_0. The automaton will be deterministic, having some finite number of possible transitions in each situation. Let Q be the set of states. Tape T consists of input alphabets from the set of input alphabets Σ. Initially ($t = 0$) assume that automaton is in state q_0 and the stack pointer points to the stack start symbol Z_0. Tape cells are scanned by the read only tape head H which move right on each scan of the cell and never returns back.

PDA follows two types of moves. In the first type of move, an input symbol is used. Depending upon the input symbol, the top stack symbol, and the state of the automaton, several transitions are possible. These transitions consist of a next state from the set Q and a possible string of symbols (possibly empty) to replace (push/pop) the top stack symbol then tape head move one cell right. The second type of move is similar to the first, except that the input symbol is not used, and the tape head is not advanced after the move. This type of move allows the PDA to manipulate the stack without reading the input alphabets.

Thus the transition function δ will be a partial mapping i.e.,

$$\delta : Q \times (\Sigma \cup \in) \times \Gamma \rightarrow \text{A finite subsets of } (Q \times \Gamma^*)$$

For example, let automaton is in state p ($\in$ Q) and ready to scan the input alphabet $a \in (\Sigma \cup \in)$ from the tape cell and the stack pointer points the symbol A ($\in \Gamma^*$) then choices of transitions are as follows,

$$\delta(p, a, A) \rightarrow \{(q_1, \gamma_1), (q_2, \gamma_2), (q_3, \gamma_3), \ldots\ldots\ldots\ldots, (q_k, \gamma_k)\}$$

where state $q_i \in Q$, stack symbol $\gamma_i \in \Gamma^*$ for all $1 \le i \le k$.

Therefore, we can define a PDA using following tuples,

$$M = (Q, \Sigma, \Gamma, \delta, q_0, Z_0, F)$$

where the symbol $F \subseteq Q$ is the set of final states.

Note. Unless stated otherwise, we use lower case letters to denote input alphabets and upper case letters to denote stack symbols.

If a PDA satisfies following conditions then the PDA will be a deterministic PDA or DPDA, i.e.,

- For any transition $\delta(p, a, A)$, it must have only a single empty ($\forall p \in Q, \forall a \in \Sigma, \forall A \in \Gamma^*$)
- Whenever $\delta(p, \in, A)$ is nonempty then $\delta(p, a, A)$ must be empty ($\forall p \in Q, \forall a \in \Sigma, \forall A \in \Gamma^*$)

(Remember that acceptance power of both model PDA and DPDA will be different)

Instantaneous Descriptions (ID)

ID describes the configuration of the PDA at a given instant with the record of the state and the stack contents. For example,

$$(q, ax, \gamma) \underset{M}{\vdash} (p, x, A\gamma) \qquad [\therefore \delta(q, a, \gamma) = (p, A)]$$

This situation is shown in fig. 11.20 (a) and (b).

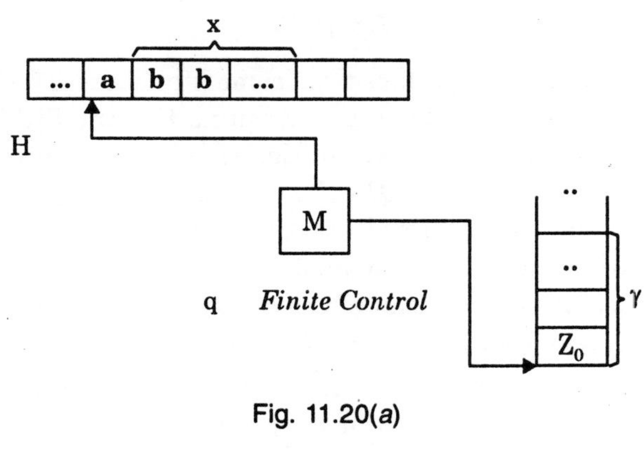

Fig. 11.20(a)

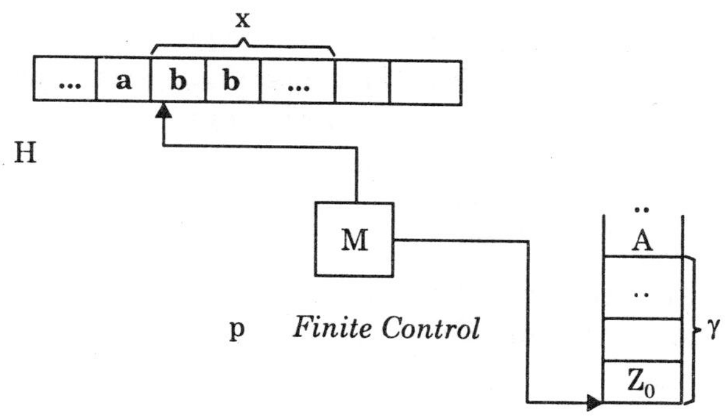

Fig. 11.20(*b*)

Language of a PDA

Finally, we define the language of a PDA. There are two natural ways to define the language accepted by a PDA. The first will be the acceptance by the empty stack mechanism and second will be the acceptance by the final state mechanism.

Acceptance by Empty Stack Mechanism

As we have seen that language accepted by the PDA is the set of all input alphabets for which some sequence of moves causes the PDA to *empty the stack* no matter in what state PDA is in that instant. Assume M be a PDA and its language be N(M) then

$$N(M) = \{x \in \Sigma^* / (q_0, x, Z_0) \overset{*}{\underset{M}{\vdash}} (q, \in, \in)\}$$

Acceptance by Final State Mechanism

In this way we define the language accepted by the PDA similar to the way a FA accepts the inputs. Such that we designate some states as final states and define the language as the set of all input alphabets for which some choice of moves causes the PDA to reach to the *final state* no matter what stack pointer points to. Assume M be a PDA and its language be L(M) then

$$L(M) = \{x \in \Sigma^* / (q_0, x, Z_0) \overset{*}{\underset{M}{\vdash}} (p, \in, \gamma)\}$$

Note for a particular PDA M both definitions of acceptance i.e., N(M) and L(M) are not always equivalent but of course they are both context free languages (CFLs).

Although the acceptance by final state mechanism is the more common notation, but the acceptance by the empty stack mechanism provides an easier way to prove the basic theorems of PDA. In the latter examples we will construct the PDA by assuming that the given language is the language accepted by empty stack.

Example 11.15. *Construct a PDA for the language* $L = \{a^i b^i \mid i \geq 1\}$.

Sol. Since language L is a context free language whose grammar will be $S \rightarrow ab \mid aSb$ so an equivalent PDA can be constructed. Also assume L = N(M), where PDA M will be

$$M = (\{q_1, q_2\}, \{a, b\}, \{Z_0, X\}, \delta, q_1, Z_0, \varnothing)$$

The moves are as follows,

- $\delta(q_1, a, Z_0) \rightarrow \{(q_1, XZ_0)\}$ [Corresponding to the first input alphabet a, stack symbol X will be pushed]
- $\delta(q_1, a, X) \rightarrow \{(q_1, XX)\}$ [For the consecutive occurrences of a's, same stack symbol X will be pushed again]

- $\delta(q_1, b, X) \to \{(q_2, \in)\}$ [If next input alphabet is b then pop the stack symbol]
- $\delta(q_2, b, X) \to \{(q_2, \in)\}$ [For the consecutive occurrences of b's, stack symbol will be poped again]
- $\delta(q_2, \in, Z_0) \to \{(q_2, \in)\}$ [If there is no input symbol left and stack also left with start symbol Z_0 only then this symbol is also poped]

And the machine stops.

Here we show only the accepted moves of the PDA and other moves like, $\delta(q_2, a, Z_0) \to \emptyset$ and $\delta(q_2, b, Z_0) \to \emptyset$ where state $\emptyset$ signifies that automaton crashes if it reaches to this state.

Hence we define L as,

$$L = L(N) = \{x \mid (q_1, x, Z_0) \vdash^* (q_2, \in, \in)\}$$

To verify that above moves are correct we assume a string $x = a\,a\,a\,b\,b\,b \in L$, then trace the transitions over x, i.e.,

$$(q_1, a\,a\,a\,b\,b\,b, Z_0) \vdash (q_1, a\,a\,b\,b\,b, XZ_0) \vdash (q1, a\,b\,b\,b, XXZ_0) \vdash (q_1, b\,b\,b, XXXZ_0) \vdash$$
$$(q_2, b\,b, XXZ_0) \vdash (q_2, b, XZ_0) \vdash (q_2, \in, Z_0) \vdash (q_2, \in, \in) \text{ [Accepted]}$$

Example 11.16. *Construct a PDA for the language $L = \{w\,c\,w^R \mid w \in \{a, b\}^*\}$.*

Sol. Since language L is a context free language so an equivalent PDA can be constructed. Also assume L = N(M), where assume PDA M will be,

$$M = (\{q_1, q_2\}, \{a, b, c\}, \{Z_0, A, B\}, \delta, q_1, Z_0, \emptyset)$$

Where δ are as follows,

- $\delta(q_1, a, Z_0) \to \{(q_1, AZ_0)\}$ [If the first input alphabet is a, then symbol A will be pushed into the stack];

  $\delta(q_1, b, Z_0) \to \{(q_1, BZ_0)\}$ [If the first input alphabet is b, then symbol B will be pushed into the stack];

  $\delta(q_1, c, Z_0) \to \{(q_2, Z_0)\}$ [If input alphabet is *c* then stack remains unchanged];
- $\delta(q_1, a, A) \to \{(q_1, AA)\}$ [For the next occurrence of *a*'s, stack symbols A's will be pumped];

  $\delta(q_1, b, A) \to \{(q_1, BA)\}$ [For the next occurrence of *b*'s, stack symbols B's will be pumped];

  $\delta(q_1, c, A) \to \{(q_2, A)\}$ [For the next occurrence of *c*, stack remains unchanged];

Similarly,

- $\delta(q_1, a, B) \to \{(q_1, AB)\}$;

  $\delta(q_1, b, B) \to \{(q_1, BB)\}$;

  $\delta(q_1, c, B) \to \{(q_2, B)\}$;

For the matching of substring lies left side of symbol c with the substring lies right side of *c*, following are the moves

- $\delta(q_2, a, A) \to \{(q_2, \in)\}$
- $\delta(q_2, b, B) \to \{(q_2, \in)\}$

Finally,

- $\delta(q_2, \in, Z_0) \to \{(q_2, \in)\}$ ***Accepted***

[While other moves like $\delta(q_2, a, Z_0) \to \emptyset$ and $\delta(q_2, b, Z_0) \to \emptyset$ where state $\emptyset$ signifies that automaton crashes if it reaches to this state]

Hence PDA will be an deterministic PDA.

To verify that above moves are correct we assume a string $w = a\ b\ a\ c\ a\ b\ a$, then trace the transitions over w, i.e.,

$(q_1, a\ b\ a\ c\ a\ b\ a, Z_0) \vdash (q_1, b\ a\ c\ a\ b\ a, AZ_0) \vdash (q_1, a\ c\ a\ b\ a, BAZ_0) \vdash (q_1, c\ a\ b\ a, ABAZ_0) \vdash (q_2, a\ b\ a, ABAZ_0) \vdash (q_2, b\ a, BAZ_0) \vdash (q_2, a, AZ_0) \vdash (q_2, \epsilon, Z_0) \vdash (q_2, \epsilon, \epsilon)$ **[Accepted]**

Example 11.17. *Construct a PDA for the language $L = \{w \in \{a, b\}^* \ / \ w\ w^R\}$.*

Sol. From the exercise 11.11 we found that language L is a context free language so an equivalent PDA can be constructed for it. Since we assume that language L is the language accepted by the PDA having empty stack mechanism i.e., L = N(M), where M be a PDA where,

$$M = (\{q_1, q_2\}, \{a, b\}, \{Z_0, A, B), \delta, q_1, Z_0, \emptyset)$$

where δ's are constructed as follows,

- Since ϵ is in the language L so, $\delta(q_1, \epsilon, Z_0) \to \{(q_1, \epsilon)\}$
- For the first occurrence of input symbol a or b corresponding stack symbol A or B will be pumped, i.e.

$$\delta(q_1, a, Z_0) \to \{(q_1, AZ_0)\}$$
$$\delta(q_1, b, Z_0) \to \{(q_1, BZ_0)\}$$

- For the next occurrences of consecutive a's or consecutive b's, there are two possible moves such that either stack symbol will be popped or corresponding symbol A or B will be pushed, i.e.

$$\delta(q_1, a, A) \to \{(q_2, \epsilon), (q_1, AA)\}$$
$$\delta(q_1, b, B) \to \{(q_2, \epsilon), (q_1, BB)\}$$

- For alternate occurrences of symbols a and b corresponding stack symbol A or B will be pumped, i.e.

$$\delta(q_1, a, B) \to \{(q_1, AB)\}$$
$$\delta(q_1, b, A) \to \{(q_1, BA)\}$$

- During cross checking of occurrences of input symbols (from state q_2) corresponding stack symbols will be popped, i.e.

$$\delta(q_2, a, A) \to \{(q_2, \epsilon)\}$$
$$\delta(q_2, b, B) \to \{(q_2, \epsilon)\}$$

- Finally, $\delta(q_2, \epsilon, Z_0) \to \{(q_2, \epsilon)\}$ ***Accepted***

To verify above moves consider an string $w = a\ a\ b\ b\ a\ a$ ($\in$ L), and then trace the moves, *i.e.*,

$$(q_1, a\ a\ b\ b\ a\ a, Z_0) \vdash (q_1, a\ b\ b\ a\ a, AZ_0) \vdash \{\underset{\textbf{I}}{(q_2, b\ b\ a\ a, Z_0)}, \underset{\textbf{II}}{(q_1, b\ b\ a\ a, AAZ_0)}\}$$

Trace the moves from ID **I** and from ID **II** separately, i.e.

I. $(q_2, b\ b\ a\ a, Z_0) \vdash (q_2, b\ a\ a, \epsilon)$ ×

Since stack becomes empty without reading of complete input string so automaton crashes through this path.

II. $(q_1, b\,b\,a\,a, AAZ_0) \vdash (q_1, b\,a\,a, BAAZ_0) \vdash \{(q_1, a\,a, BBAAZ_0), (q_2, a\,a, AAZ_0)\}$

II′ II″

From ID **II′** following are the moves,

$(q_1, a\,a, BBAAZ_0) \vdash (q_1, a, ABBAAZ_0)$

$\vdash \{(q_1, \in, AABBAAZ_0), (q_2, \in, BBAAZ_0)$

× ×

Since both these moves don't empty the stack hence by this path string w is not accepted. From ID **II″** following are the moves,

$(q_2, a\,a, AAZ_0) \vdash (q_2, a, AZ_0) \vdash (q_2, \in, Z_0) \vdash (q_2, \in, \in)$ ***Accepted***

11.9 SIMPLIFICATION OF GRAMMARS

In the previous section we have studied Context free grammars, derivation trees and the generation of languages from CFG the context free languages. In this section we will study the simplification of the grammars including simplification of CFGs.

The simplification of grammar means to perform certain operations over its set of production/s so that it may reach to some standard form (normal form) of the grammar. So before going to study the normal form of a grammar first we discuss the preliminary means of simplification of the grammar. In the chapter we generally restrict our self and discuss the simplification of context free grammars. In fact, the means of simplification that are discussed below are equally useful for the simplification of are other type of grammars.

The means of simplification are as follows,

1. Remove all null production/s
2. Remove all useless production/s
3. Remove all unit production/s
4. Remove all useless symbol/s

Now we will discuss each means of simplification in details.

1. Remove all null productions

A production is said to be null production if it derives a null string ($\in$). For example, production $A \to \varepsilon$ is a *null production* where, A is a non terminal and $\in$ is a variable/terminal.

All non terminals that derive the string $\in$ in one/more steps of derivation are called *nullable* non terminals of a grammar *viz*.

- If $X \stackrel{*}{\Rightarrow} \in$ then X is nullable.
- If $A \to \in$ is a production then $A \Rightarrow \in$, so A is nullable.
- If $A \to B$ and $B \to \in$ are the productions then $A \Rightarrow B \Rightarrow \in$ and $B \Rightarrow \in$, so A and B are nullable.
- If $A \to BC$ and $B \to \in$ and $C \to \in$ are the productions then all non terminals A, B and C are nullable.

By eliminating the null productions it is likely to increase the number of productions in the grammar. (The ambiguity characteristic of the grammar remain unaltered)

Lemma 11.1

Let G = (V_N, V_T, S, P) be a CFG that allows null production/s (A $\rightarrow \in$) then the language L(G) – {$\in$} can be generated from a equivalent grammar G′ = (V_N', V_T', S′, P′) such that G′ has no null production.

So, Grammar G′ has a new production

$S_{new} \rightarrow S \mid \in$ followed by all productions derive from S as usual.

Constructive proof

Assume a grammar G has the productions

$S \rightarrow a\,b \mid AB \mid A$

$A \rightarrow B \mid a$

$B \rightarrow S \mid b \mid \in$

Then remove all null productions from G.

Observe the null production / s of the grammar G. Remove all null productions such that resultant grammar generates the similar language excluding string $\in$.

- We find the production B $\rightarrow \in$ is a null production (nullable B) so remove it from G.

(–) $B \rightarrow \in$

(+) $S \rightarrow A$

(+) $A \rightarrow \in$

So, add two new productions in the grammar because, all the productions that derive including symbol B are manipulated according to following possibilities:

If we use the definition B $\rightarrow \varepsilon$ then S $\rightarrow$ A B becomes S $\rightarrow$ A and A $\rightarrow$ B becomes A $\rightarrow \in$.

Otherwise, production S $\rightarrow$ A B and A $\rightarrow$ B remains in the grammar for using next production definitions B $\rightarrow$ S and B $\rightarrow$ *b*.

The, new set of productions are

$S \rightarrow a\,b \mid A\,B \mid A \mid A$ remove duplicate productions i.e.

So, Grammar becomes

$S \rightarrow a\,b \mid A\,B \mid A$

$A \rightarrow B \mid a \mid \in$

$B \rightarrow S \mid b$

- Next null production is A $\rightarrow \in$ (A is nullable), remove it from the grammar i.e.,

(–) $A \rightarrow \rightarrow \in$

(+) $S \rightarrow \in$ (S $\rightarrow \in$ can be derive from S $\rightarrow$ A when A $\rightarrow \in$)

(+) $S \rightarrow B$ (S $\rightarrow$ B can be derive from S $\rightarrow$ A B when A $\rightarrow \in$)

Thus, new set of productions are.

$S \rightarrow a\,b \mid A\,B \mid A \mid B \mid \in$

$A \rightarrow B \mid a$

$B \rightarrow S \mid b$

- $S \rightarrow \in$ is a nullable production (S is nullable), remove it from G, i.e.,

$$(-)\ S \rightarrow \in$$
$$(+)\ B \rightarrow \in \qquad (B \rightarrow \in \text{ can be derive from } B \rightarrow S \text{ when } S \rightarrow \in)$$

Thus, new set of productions are,

$$S \rightarrow a\,b \mid A\,B \mid A \mid B$$
$$A \rightarrow B \mid a$$
$$B \rightarrow \in \mid b$$

Again symbol B becomes nullable so we find a cycle of occurrence of nullable symbols that never terminate. Hence the sequential removal of nullables might not free the grammar from null production. Therefore, we search for alternate method of elimination of null production/s.

Hence, we ask for another method of elimination of null production/s.

Algorithm

```
(For finding the nullable)
    //Assume a grammar G = (V_N, V_T, S, P)
    1 begin
    2    old V = Ø;       // old V is the set of nullable symbols
    3    new V = {A ∈ V_N | A → ∈ is in P};    // new V is the set of
                                                 nullable currently search
    4    while (Old V ≠ New V) do
    5         begin
    6         old V = new V;
    7         new V = new V ∪ {A ∈ V_N | A → α is in P and α ∈ (old V)*};
    8         end;
    9 end.
```

Fig. 11.19

Example 11.18. *Simplify the following grammar and find nullable symbols.*

$$S \rightarrow a\,b \mid A\,B \mid A$$
$$A \rightarrow B \mid a$$
$$B \rightarrow S \mid b \mid \in$$

Sol. Since we know that symbol N is nullable if N derives ε in one/more derivations, i.e.

$$N \stackrel{*}{\Rightarrow} \in$$

Thus G contains following {B, A, S} are the nullables.

Explanation

Using algorithm shown in Fig. 11.19, initially old V set contains no nullable (line 2). After line 3 we get symbol B is in set new V. while new V is not equal to old V repeat line 6 and 7.

- First iteration,
  old V = {B} and new V = {B} ∪ {A} or {B, A} because $A \rightarrow B$ and $B \in$ old V.
- Second iteration,
  old V = {B, A} and new V = {B, A} ∪ {S} or {B, A, S} because $S \rightarrow A\,B$ and $A\,B \in$ (old V)*.

- Third iteration,

  Old V = {B, A, S} and new V = {B, A, S} with non existence of other nullable.

  Now, old V equal to new V so while loop is terminated and program is terminated.

Hence, nullable symbols are {B, A, S}.

Remove all nullables. Simultaneously we add following productions (so that meaning of the grammar doesn't change).

(+) $S \to B$ [derive from $S \to A\,B$ when $A \to \in$]

(+) $S \to A$ [derive from $S \to A\,B$ when $B \to \in$]

Thus we obtain grammar G′ i.e.,

$S \to a\,b \mid A\,B \mid A \mid A$

$S \to a\,b \mid A\,B \mid A$

$A \to B \mid a$ and $B \to S \mid b$

and its language L (G′) = L(G) – {∈}. Alternatively we say that grammar G′ generates the similar set of strings as grammar G except the null string (∈).

To generate string ε by G′ add the production $S_{new} \to \in \mid S$, so the grammar G′ becomes

$S_{new} \to \in \mid S$

$S \to a\,b \mid A\,B \mid A$

$A \to B \mid a$

$B \to S \mid b$

Example 11.19. *A grammar G has the production*

$S \to a\,X\,Y\,Z \mid a\,b$

$X \to a\,A\,b \mid A \mid a$

$Y \to b\,B\,a \mid B \mid b$

$Z \to a \mid a\,A \mid X\,Y$

$A \to \in \mid a \mid a\,A$

$B \to \in \mid b \mid b\,B$

Simplify the grammar (by removing all null productions).

Sol. Find nullable symbols that are

- B [$\therefore$ $B \Rightarrow \in$]
- A [$\therefore$ $A \Rightarrow \in$]
- Y [$\therefore$ $Y \Rightarrow B \Rightarrow \in$]
- X [$\therefore$ $X \Rightarrow A \Rightarrow \in$]
- Z [$\therefore$ $Z \Rightarrow XY \Rightarrow \in\ Y \Rightarrow \in\in \Rightarrow \in$]

So, {B, A, Y, X, Z} are nullables.

After dropping the nullables add following productions i.e.

(+) $X \to a\,b$ [$X \to a\,A\,b$ when $A \to \in$ is removed]

(+) $Y \to b\,a$ [$Y \to b\,B\,a$ when $B \to \in$ is removed]

(+) $Z \to X$ [$Z \to X\,Y$ when $Y \to \in$ is removed]

(+) $Z \to Y$ [$Z \to X\,Y$ when $X \to \in$ is removed]

(+) $S \to a\,Y\,Z$ [$S \to a\,X\,Y\,Z$ when $X \to \in$ is removed]

(+) $S \to a\,X\,Z$ [$S \to a\,X\,Y\,Z$ when $Y \to \in$ is removed]

(+) $S \rightarrow a\,X\,Y$ [$S \rightarrow a\,X\,Y\,Z$ when $Z \rightarrow \in$ is removed]

also production

(+) $Z \rightarrow a$ [$Z \rightarrow a\,A$ when $A \rightarrow \in$] but this is a repeatatine production so there is no need to add further into the grammar.

Hence the new grammar G' has following productions

$S \rightarrow a\,X\,Y\,Z \mid a\,b \mid a\,Y\,Z \mid a\,X\,Z \mid a\,X\,Y$

$X \rightarrow a\,A\,b \mid A \mid a \mid a\,b$

$Y \rightarrow b\,B\,a \mid B \mid b \mid b\,a$

$Z \rightarrow a \mid a\,A \mid X\,Y$

$A \rightarrow a \mid a\,A$

$B \rightarrow b \mid b\,B$

Example 11.20. *A language L is expressed by the regular expression* ***r = (a + b)* . b . b . (a . b)*.***

Express the grammar G i.e. L = L (G) and simplify it.

Sol. Let Grammar G can be defined as

$G = (V_N, \{a, b\}, S, P)$

where, V_N = {S and some other symbols} and set of productions P contains:

- $S \rightarrow W\,Z$ [assume W is responsible for generating the strings for **(a + b)* . b** and Z is responsible for generating the strings for **b . (a . b)***]
- $W \rightarrow X\,b$ [symbol X generate the strings corresponds to **(a + b)***]
- $Z \rightarrow b\,Y$ [symbol Y generate the strings corresponds to **(a . b)***]
- $X \rightarrow \in$ [X also generates string ε]
- $X \rightarrow a\,X \mid b\,X$ [all strings formed over {a, b}either start with symbol a or b]
- $Y \rightarrow \in$ [Y also generates string ε]
- $Y \rightarrow a\,b\,Y$ [Y derives the strings containing multiple of 'ab']

Thus, grammar G consists of above set of rules. Now, for simplification remove all null productions from G. So, find the nullable symbols first, there are,

- X [because $X \Rightarrow \in$], and
- Y [because $Y \Rightarrow \in$].

hence [X, Y] are nullables.

So, after removing the nullable, from G we must add following productions,

(+) $X \rightarrow a$ [from $X \rightarrow a\,X$ when $X \rightarrow \in$ is removed]

(+) $X \rightarrow b$ [from $X \rightarrow b\,X$ when $X \rightarrow \in$ is removed]

(+) $W \rightarrow b$ [from $W \rightarrow X\,b$ when $X \rightarrow \in$ is removed]

(+) $Y \rightarrow a\,b$ [from $Y \rightarrow a\,b\,Y$ when $Y \rightarrow \in$ is removed]

(+) $Z \rightarrow b$ [from $Z \rightarrow b\,Y$ when $Y \rightarrow \in$ is removed]

Hence we obtain the new grammar G′ i.e.,

$S \rightarrow W\,Z$

$W \rightarrow X\,b \mid b$

$Z \rightarrow b\,Y \mid b$

$X \rightarrow a\,X \mid b\,X \mid a \mid b$

$Y \rightarrow a\,b\,Y \mid a\,b$

and its language s.t. $L(G') = L(G) - \{\in\}$.

Example 11.21. *Similar to previous example, let language L is expressed by the regular expression*

$$r = (a + b)^* . b . b . (a + b)^*$$

Express its grammar and simplify it.

Sol. Assume grammar G = (V_N, {a, b}, S, P) then it expresses the language s.t. L(G) = L (**r**), where we can consult following let of productions, i.e.

- $S \to W Z$ [assume W is responsible for generating the strings for **(a + b)* . b** and Z is responsible for generating the strings for **b . (a + b)***]
- $W \to X b$ [symbol X generate the strings corresponds to **(a + b)***]
- $Z \to b Y$ [symbol Y generate the strings corresponds to **(a + b)***]
- $X \to \epsilon$ [X also generates string ε]
- $X \to a X \mid b X$ [all strings formed over {a, b}either start with symbol a or b]
- $Y \to X$ [Y is similar to X]

So nullables are {X, Y}.

Now following productions are added in G after removing the nullables,

(+) $X \to a$ [from $X \to a X$ when $X \to \epsilon$ is removed]

(+) $X \to b$ [from $X \to b X$ when $X \to \epsilon$ is removed]

(+) $W \to b$ [from $W \to X b$ when $X \to \epsilon$ is removed]

(+) $Z \to b$ [from $Z \to b Y$ when $Y \to \epsilon$ is removed]

($Y \to X$ remains there in grammar for holding rest of the definition of X excluding deriving ϵ)

Thus we obtain a new grammar G′ i.e.,

$$S \to W Z$$
$$W \to X b \mid b$$
$$Z \to b Y \mid b$$
$$X \to a X \mid b X \mid a \mid b$$
$$Y \to X$$

That has the language s.t. L(G′) = L(G) – {∈}.

2. Remove all useless productions

A production is said to be *useless* if there is no way to reach to that production in the grammar. So, a production $\alpha \to \beta$ is useless if and only if the non terminal symbol α is non reachable from any deriving non terminal in the grammar s.t. for all productions

$$\gamma \to \lambda \text{ then } \lambda \neq \alpha$$

Then α is the *useless symbol* of the grammar. A symbol is again useless if it is *non terminative*, i.e. For example, $A \to a A \mid b A$. In this production there is no way to come out from the definition of A or there is no recovery derivation is defined from A. Since, A is non terminative so A is a useless symbol and simultaneously this production is a useless production for the grammar. So, during simplification of the grammar we remove all useless production/s and also useless symbol/s. For example a grammar is expressed using following productions

$$S \to A B \mid a$$
$$A \to a A \mid b A$$
$$B \to a \mid a B$$

- Since, definition of production A is non terminative so it is a useless production, simultaneously symbol A is a useless symbol. (mark by ×)

$$\not{A} \rightarrow a\, \not{A} \mid b\, \not{A}$$

- Because of the useless symbol A the production

  $S \rightarrow \not{A}\, B$ has no meaning so it is a useless production.

- And because of the useless production S → A B it is meaningless to include the production of B into the grammar.

Hence, $B \rightarrow a \mid a\, B$ becomes the useless production.

Finally, we find that S → a is the only meaningful production of the grammar.

Example 11.22. *Simplify the grammar*

$$S \rightarrow a \mid A\, B \mid D$$
$$A \rightarrow a \mid a\, A$$
$$B \rightarrow b\, B \mid a\, B$$
$$C \rightarrow d\, C \mid d$$

Sol. Let us find the reachable symbols of the grammar i.e.,

- *a*, A, B and D are reachable from S,
- *b* is also reachable because B is reachable,
- Nothing else is reachable.
  (There is no way to reach to symbol C from Starting symbol S)

So, {S, *a*, A, B, D, *b*} are reachable symbols.

Now, from the reachable symbols find the useful symbols

- S → *a* is useful production,
- B is not useful because of non terminative production of B,
- S ⇒ A B ⇒ *a* B ⇒ ... that never reach to terminal string because of non terminative production of B; B is useless symbol; so eliminate production S → AB.
- Because S → A B is a useless production hence it is useless to define the production of A or A → *a* | *a* A are the useless productions.
- The deriving symbol/s from D are undefined hence S → D is useless production.

Summarize the useful symbols we find that S → *a* is the only production of the grammar.

3. Eliminate the Unit Productions

A production of form X → Y (where X and Y ∈ V_N) is a unit production. These productions may be useful or may not be useful (useless). If derivation of unit productions terminated on terminals then it is useful like as, whenever, X → Y is a unit production and $Y \overset{*}{\Rightarrow} \alpha \in (V_T)^*$, then we can add the production X → α (after removing unit production X → Y) in the set P and whenever, X → Y and Y → Z are unit productions and $Z \overset{*}{\Rightarrow} \alpha \in (V_T)^*$, then we can add the production X → α (after removing unit productions X → Y and Y → Z) in the set P. A cycle of unit productions is the case of all useless unit productions. For example, A → B, B → C, C → A are useless productions.

Example 11.23. *Consider the grammar*

$$S \to S + T \mid T$$
$$T \to T \star F \mid F$$
$$F \to (S) \mid a$$

Remove unit productions from the grammar.

Sol. **1.** Remove the unit production S → T, thus we can add following productions i.e.,

- T ⇒ T ⇒ F, so add production **S → T ⋆ F**.
- T ⇒ F ⇒ *a*, so add production **S → a**.
- T ⇒ F ⇒ (S), so add production **S → (S)**.

2. Remove the unit production T → F, thus we can add following productions i.e.,

- F ⇒ (S), so add production **T → (S)**.
- F ⇒ *a*, so add production **T → a**.

3. No other production is the unit production.

Hence grammar left with following productions which are free form unit productions.

$$S \to S + T \mid T \star F \mid a \mid (S)$$
$$T \to T \star F \mid (S) \mid a$$
$$F \to (S) \mid a$$

Example 11.24. *Consider the grammar G has following productions*

$$S \to A \mid B \mid C$$
$$A \to a\,A\,a \mid B$$
$$B \to b\,B \mid b\,b$$
$$C \to a\,C\,a\,a\,a \mid D$$

Find the grammar G′, which has no unit productions, that generates the language L(G), i.e. L(G′) = L(G).

Sol. Since grammar G has 3 unit productions S → A, S → B and S → C so remove these productions from the grammar and add new productions so that new grammar generates same language.

1. Remove the unit production S → A, thus we can do following

- S ⇒ A ⇒ *a* A *a*; S generates *a* A *a*; so add production S → *a* A *a*.
- S ⇒ A ⇒ B; S generates B; so add production S → B.

2. Remove the unit production S → B, thus we can do following

- S ⇒ B ⇒ *b* B; S generates *b* B; so add production S → *b* B.
- S ⇒ B ⇒ *b b*; S generates *b b*; so add production S → *b b*.

3. Remove the unit production S → C, thus we can do following

- S ⇒ C ⇒ *a* C *a a a*; S generates *a* C *a a a*; so add production S → *a* C *a a a*.
- S ⇒ C ⇒ D; S generates D; so add production S → D.

Hence Grammar becomes

$$S \to aAa \mid B \mid bB \mid bb \mid aCaaa \mid D$$
$$A \to aAa \mid B$$
$$B \to bB \mid bb$$
$$C \to aCaaa \mid D$$

We see that, the new grammar still has some new unit productions. Unit productions S → D and C → D are the useless productions because grammar doesn't have any production derive from D that terminates on terminal string. So remove these productions.

It has another, unit production A → B. Thus can remove while adding the productions A → *b* B | *b b*.

Hence we get the grammar G′ (free from unit production)

$$S \to aAa \mid B \mid bB \mid bb \mid aCaaa$$
$$A \to aAa \mid bB \mid bb$$
$$B \to bB \mid bb$$
$$C \to aCaaa$$

where L(G′) = L(G) [Reader may verify it]

Example 11.25. *Consider the grammar*

$$S \to A \mid b\,b$$
$$A \to B \mid a$$
$$B \to S \mid b$$

Remove all unit productions from the grammar.

Sol. • First we remove the production A → B so, we must add two more productions i.e.,

$$(+)\ A \to S \quad [\because\ B \to S]$$
$$(+)\ A \to b \quad [\because\ B \to b]$$

Thus grammar becomes

$$S \to A \mid b\,b$$
$$A \to S \mid b \mid a$$
$$B \to S \mid b$$

• Next, remove the unit production B → S so we can add the following productions, i.e.

$$(+)\ B \to A \quad [\because\ S \to A]$$
$$(+)\ B \to b\,b \quad [\because\ S \to b\,b]$$

Now the grammar becomes

$$S \to A \mid b\,b$$
$$A \to S \mid b \mid a$$
$$B \to A \mid b\,b \mid b$$

• Next, remove the unit production B → A so we add the productions

$$(+)\ B \to S \quad [\because\ A \to S]$$
$$(+)\ B \to b \quad [\because\ A \to b]$$
$$(+)\ B \to a \quad [\because\ A \to a]$$

Hence the grammar becomes

$$S \to A \mid b\,b$$
$$A \to S \mid b \mid a$$
$$B \to S \mid b\,b \mid b \mid a$$

This grammar again has the unit production B → S, which is not terminative. So, there is the existence of a cycle of unit productions in ths grammar. Therefore, to simplify the grammar that contains cyclic case of unit productions an alternative approach is used, which is discussed below :

1. Remove unit production $S \rightarrow A$

- while, $\mathbf{S \Rightarrow A}$ and A derives terminal then we say that S generates that terminal. Or, $S \Rightarrow A \Rightarrow a$, so add production $S \rightarrow a$.
- while, $\mathbf{S \Rightarrow A \Rightarrow B}$ and B derives terminals then certainly S generates that terminal. Or, $S \Rightarrow A \Rightarrow B \Rightarrow b$, so add production $S \rightarrow b$.

2. Remove unit production $A \rightarrow B$

- while, $\mathbf{A \Rightarrow B}$ and B derives terminals then we say that A generates that terminal. Or, $A \Rightarrow B \Rightarrow b$, so add production $A \Rightarrow b$.
- while, $\mathbf{A \Rightarrow B \Rightarrow S}$ and S derives terminal then we say that A generate that terminal. Or, $A \Rightarrow B \Rightarrow S \Rightarrow b\,b$, so add production $A \rightarrow b\,b$.

3. Remove unit production $B \rightarrow S$

- while, $\mathbf{B \Rightarrow S}$ and S derives terminal then we say that B generates that that terminal. Or, $B \Rightarrow S \Rightarrow b\,b$, so add production $B \rightarrow b\,b$.
- while, $\mathbf{B \Rightarrow S \Rightarrow A}$ and A derives the terminal then we say that B generates that terminal.

  Or, $B \Rightarrow S \Rightarrow A \Rightarrow a$, so add production $B \rightarrow a$.

Hence the grammar becomes

$$S \rightarrow a \mid b \mid b\,b$$
$$A \rightarrow b \mid b\,b \mid a$$
$$B \rightarrow b\,b \mid a \mid b$$

We further find that symbols A and B are not reachable so they are useless symbols (all production derived from A and from B are useless productions) hence remove from the grammar.

Therefore, after simplification we obtain the new grammar which is free from all unit productions, i.e.,

$$\mathbf{S \rightarrow a \mid b \mid b\,b}$$

4. Remove all useless symbols

There is another approach to eliminate the useless symbols. We may start to search the useful symbols. The useful symbols are reachable symbols and active non terminals.

Useful Symbol

A symbol X is *useful* if it occurs in the derivation of terminals from starting symbol S, i.e.

$$S \overset{*}{\Rightarrow} \alpha X \beta \overset{*}{\Rightarrow} x\ (\in {V_T}^*) \quad \text{for some } \alpha \text{ and } \beta$$

[or, $S \overset{1}{\Rightarrow} x \in (V_T)^*$ then $S \rightarrow x$ is the useful production]

Active non terminal

Symbol A is active non terminal if it generates the terminal string i.e.

$$A \overset{*}{\Rightarrow} x(\in V_T)^*$$

Algorithm

Assume a grammar $G = (V_N, V_T, S, P)$ then we find active non terminals as follows:

```
    begin
    Old V = Ø;
    New V = {A ∈ V_N / A → α is in P and α ∈ V_T*)
    While (old V < > new V) do
          Begin
               Old V = new V
               New V = new V ∪ {A ∈ V_N /A generates α is in P,
                                              so α ∈ (V_T ∪ old V*}
          end;
end.
```

Fig. 11.21

Reachable Symbol

If there exist the derivation $S \overset{*}{\Rightarrow} \alpha X \beta$ (for some α and β) then symbol X is said to be *reachable* symbol. Start symbol is always consider as a reachable symbol. Now we discuss the *Algorithm* to find useful symbol:

Step 1. Find active non terminals and drop rest of the non active non terminals from the grammar.

Step 2. Find reachable symbols and remove non reachable symbols from the grammar.

Example 11.26. *A grammar G is given, find an equivalent grammar with no useless symbols.*

$$S \to a \mid AB$$
$$A \to a \mid aA$$
$$B \to bB \mid aB$$
$$C \to d \mid dC$$

Sol. • First,we will find active non terminals, these are {S, A, C} all these generated terminal strings.

(Symbol B is not active non terminal bêcause it's not generate the terminal string)

So, we have following grammar

$$S \to a \mid AB$$
$$A \to a \mid aA$$
$$C \to d \mid dC$$

• Now, we will find reachable symbols.

From S symbol '*a*' is generated so '*a*' is reachable. Symbols A and B are also reachable but fortunately, there is no production derive from B so it is a useless hence S derive AB is useless and drop both symbols. Clearly, C is non reachable symbol so drop C. Therefore, only reachable symbols are {S, *a*}.

Hence, the grammar G left with a single useful production

$$\mathbf{S \to a}$$

Example 11.27. *A grammar G is given, find an equivalent grammar with no useless symbols.*

$$S \to AB \mid AC$$
$$A \to aAb \mid bAa \mid a$$
$$B \to bbA \mid aaB \mid AB$$

$$C \to abCa \mid aDb$$
$$D \to bD \mid aC$$

Sol. Since grammar G uses the non terminals {S, A, B, C, D} and terminals $\{a, b\}$.

We test the non terminals; and find the active non terminals and drop non active ones i.e.

- D $\Rightarrow bD$ or D $\Rightarrow aC$ never terminates on terminals so non active;
- C $\Rightarrow abCa$ or C $\Rightarrow aDb \Rightarrow$ never terminates on terminals so non active;
- B $\Rightarrow bbA \Rightarrow bba$; so active non terminal.
- A $\Rightarrow a$; so active non terminal.
- S $\Rightarrow$ AB $\Rightarrow$ terminated on terminals because both A and B are active; so active one.

Since, {S, A, B} are only active non terminals so the productions defined and using these symbols are

$$S \to AB$$
$$A \to aAb \mid bAa \mid a$$
$$B \to bbA \mid aaB \mid AB$$

Now, we test the reachability of the symbols used in grammar G.

- Symbols A and B are reachable because S $\Rightarrow$ AB.
- Symbol a and b are also reachable because S $\Rightarrow$ AB $\Rightarrow aAbB$ and so on.

Hence, all symbols used in the previous simplified step of grammar$\{S, A, B, a, b\}$ are reachable symbols.

So, the simplified grammar with no useless symbols is

$$S \to AB$$
$$A \to aAb \mid bAa \mid a$$
$$B \to bbA \mid aaB \mid AB$$

11.10 CHOMSKY NORMAL FORM (CNF)

Let G be the context free grammar then we find another context free grammar G′ such that all productions in G′ are either of forms:

- A $\to a$, where A is non terminal and a is a terminal, or
- A $\to$ BD, where A, B and D are non terminals.

and $L(G') = L(G) - \{\varepsilon\}$ means grammar G′ is free from null productions then grammar G′ is said to be in *Chomsky Normal Form* (CNF).

To obtain the CFG in CNF we apply the means of simplification 1 to 4, such that grammar is free from null productions, useless productions, unit productions and useless symbols.

Now, the remaining productions of the context free grammar are of form $\alpha \to \beta$ that is either,

- where α is a non terminal ($\in V_N$) and β is a terminal ($\in V_T$) or, a allowed form of CNF
- $|\beta| \geq |\alpha|$ or β contains two or more symbols i.e.
    - if one is terminal and other is non terminal then replace the terminal symbol by a new non terminal viz.

$A \to aB$ [then replace a by X_a] s.t.

(+) $X_a \to a$

So, $A \to X_aB$, and

$X_a \to a$ are in CNF.

- If both symbols are non terminals then production is in CNF.
- If b has more than two non terminals then replace all non terminals except first by a new non terminal viz.

$A \to BCD$ [then replace CD by R (a new non terminal] s.t.

(+) $R \to CD$

Hence,.productions are

$A \to BR$

$R \to CD$ are in CNF

- Or, in general if

$A \to A_1A_2A_3......A_K$ [then replace $A_2\ A_3...A_K$ by B_1] s.t.

(+) $B_1 \to A_2A_3......A_K$

Hence, productions becomes

$A \to A_1B_1$ [is in CNF]

$B_1 \to A_2B_2$ [where B_2 is replacement of $A_3......A_K$] s.t.

(+) $B_2 \to A_3......A_K$

Hence, production becomes

$A \to A_1B_1$

$B_1 \to A_2B_2$ [where B_2 is replacement of $A_3......A_K$] s.t.

$B_2 \to A_3B_3$ [and so on]

....

....

$B_{K-2} \to A_{K-1}A_K$

In this way we can convert all productions into the CNF productions.

Example 11.28. *A CFG G is given, convert it to CNF.*

$S \to aB \mid bA$

$A \to aS \mid a \mid bAA$

$B \to bS \mid b \mid aBB$

Sol. • First, we simplify the grammar and find that grammar is in simplified form Next, we see that the productions $A \to a$ & $B \to b$ are in desired form of CNF. Now, replace a by X_a and b by X_b through adding the productions i.e.

$$X_a \to a \quad \text{and} \quad X_b \to b$$

Thus the grammar becomes

$S \to X_aB \mid X_bA$

$A \to X_aS \mid a \mid X_bAA$

$B \to X_bS \mid b \mid X_aBB$

Now we have the remaining non CNF form productions are

(*i*) $A \rightarrow X_bAA$ and

(*ii*) $B \rightarrow X_aBB$

In (*i*) we put X in place of AA s.t.

$(+)\ A \rightarrow X_bX$ and
$(+)\ X \rightarrow AA$ are in CNF $\quad (-)\ A \rightarrow X_bAA$

In (*ii*) put R in place of BB s.t.

$B \rightarrow X_aR$ and
$R \rightarrow BB$ are in CNF $\quad (-)\ B \rightarrow X_aBB$

Hence We obtain the final CNF grammar is

$$S \rightarrow X_aB \mid X_bA$$
$$A \rightarrow X_aS \mid a \mid X_bX$$
$$X \rightarrow AA$$
$$B \rightarrow X_bS \mid b \mid X_aR$$
$$R \rightarrow BB$$

11.11 GREIBACH NORMAL FORM (GNF)

If the grammar consists the productions of the form $A \rightarrow a\,\alpha$ where $\alpha \in (V_N)^*$ then grammar is said to be in greibach normal form. It means if the derived string consists of a terminal followed by one/more non-terminals then this form of production is a GNF production.

Immediate Left Recursion (ILR)

The production shown in the Fig. 11.22 where the derived string contains the same non terminal as it derived from on its left most position is an ILR production.

$$A \rightarrow A\,a$$

Fig. 11.22

[But $A \overset{*}{\Rightarrow} A\gamma$ where $\gamma \in (V_T \cup V_N)^*$ is not ILR]

Immediate Right Recursion (IRR)

If the derived string in the production contains the same non terminal as it derived from on its right most position then production is IRR, i.e.,

$A \rightarrow a\,A$ or $A \rightarrow a\,b\,B\,A$

(*a*) (*b*)

Fig. 11.23

IRR shown in Fig. 11.23(*a*) is a GNF production but production shown in Fig. 11.23(*b*) is not a GNF production.

So, our objective is to convert the ILR and rest of the IRR production to GNF productions.

- Productions of type ILR can be converted as follows,

  Assume $A \rightarrow A\ a$ is a given ILR production followed by another known production $A \rightarrow b$ in the grammar then remove both productions like as

(–) $A \to A\, a \mid b$
(+) $A \to b \mid b\, A'$
(+) $A' \to a \mid a\, A'$

Or, in general

(–) $A \to A\, a_1 \mid A\, a_2 \mid A\, a_3 \mid \ldots\ldots \mid A\, a_n \mid b_1 \mid b_2 \mid b_3 \mid \ldots\ldots \mid b_n$

then (+) $A \to b_1 \mid b_2 \mid b_3 \mid \ldots\ldots \mid$ bn | b1 A' | b2 A'| b3 A'| .... | b_n A'

and (+) $A' \to a_1 \mid a_2 \mid a_3 \mid \ldots\ldots \mid a_n \mid a_1\, A' \mid a_2\, A' \mid a_3\, A' \mid \ldots\ldots \mid a_n\, A'$

So, we get the productions free from ILR.

Algorithm to convert the given grammar to GNF

Step 1. Simplify and convert the grammar to CNF

Step 2. Order the non terminals in the productions through substitution so that it becomes ILR form

Step 3.
+ Convert ILR production into GNF production. (So we find that few productions derived from *ILR non terminal*† that are in GNF)
+ use the GNF productions such that its derived string/s (right side) is substituted in other production/s where ILR non terminal occurs in left most position on its right side.
+ By this substitution we modified non GNF productions to GNF productions.

Step 4. Repeat step 2 and 3 until we convert all productions into GNF productions.

We can remove left recursion both immediate left recursion (ILR) and non immediate left recursion begin using following procedure,

```
begin for i = 1 to n do// where n is the number of ILR non terminals
{    for j = 1 to (i - 1) do
     {    for every production of form Ai → Aj α  do
          {    for every production Aj → β do
               begin
                    Add Ai → β α in the grammar
                    Remove Ai → Aj α from the grammar
               end
               // remove ILR from Ai
          }
     }
}
end
```

Fig. 11.24

Example 11.29. *Convert the grammar into GNF*

$$S \to A\, A \mid a$$
$$A \to S\, S \mid b$$

† *ILR non terminal*

If 'A → A a' is ILR production then symbol A is called ILR non terminal.

Sol. Step 1. Since the grammar is in simplified form also in and CNF so directly switch to next step.

Step 2. We see that grammar contains none of the productions are of ILR so try to make ILR production/s i.e., in the production $S \rightarrow A\ A$ if A is replaced by S S [$\therefore$ $A \rightarrow S\ S$]

then $S \rightarrow S\ S\ A$ and

further substitute b in place of A [$\therefore$ $A \rightarrow b$) so

$$S \rightarrow b\ A$$

Now the productions are

$S \rightarrow S\ S\ A \mid b\ A \mid a$ [ILR productions]

$A \rightarrow S\ S \mid b$ [non ILR productions]

Following assumptions are made for ILR productions

$S \rightarrow S\ \alpha \mid \beta_1 \mid \beta_2$ [where α is S A; β_1 is b A; β_2 is a;]
(S is ILR non terminal)

Step 3. To, remove ILR productions

(+) $S \rightarrow \beta_1 \mid \beta_2 \mid \beta_1 R \mid \beta_2 R$ here we assume that R is a new non terminal

(+) $R \rightarrow \alpha \mid \alpha R$

Substitutes the values of α, β_1 and β_2 then we get

$S \rightarrow bA \mid a \mid bAR \mid aR$ are in GNF and

$R \rightarrow SA \mid SAR$

Thus, we get following productions are in GNF

$S \rightarrow bA \mid a \mid bAR \mid aR$

$A \rightarrow b$

and modify remaining non GNF productions i.e.

$A \rightarrow SS$ and $R \rightarrow SA \mid SAR$

In these productions ILR non terminal (S) position is leftmost (on right side), so substitute GNF derived symbols in place of S. Hence we get GNF productions.

$A \rightarrow bA\ S \mid a\ S \mid bAR\ S \mid aR\ S$

$R \rightarrow bA\ A \mid a\ A \mid bAR\ A \mid aR\ A$

$R \rightarrow bA\ AR \mid a\ AR \mid bAR\ AR \mid aR\ AR.$

Step 4. Since, the grammar has no more non GNF production so process stop.

Therefore, grammar has following GNF productions.

$S \rightarrow bA \mid a \mid bAR \mid aR$

$A \rightarrow bA\ S \mid a\ S \mid bAR\ S \mid aR\ S \mid b$

$R \rightarrow bA\ A \mid a\ A \mid bAR\ A \mid aR\ A$

$R \rightarrow bA\ AR \mid a\ AR \mid bAR\ AR \mid aR\ AR$

Example 11.30. *Convert the grammar into GNF,*

$A_1 \rightarrow A_2 A_3 \mid a$

$A_2 \rightarrow A_3 A_1 \mid b$

$A_3 \rightarrow A_2 A_3 A_2 \mid a\ A_2 \mid c$

Sol. Step 1. Given grammar is in simplified form and its productions are of CNF.

Step 2. Examine the productions and we find that if A_2 is replaced by A_3A_1 [$\therefore$ $A_2 \rightarrow A_3A_1$] in the production $A_3 \rightarrow A_2A_3A_2$ then this production becomes an ILR production i.e.

$$A_3 \rightarrow A_3A_1A_3A_2$$

and further A_2 is replaced through $b[\because \; A_2 \rightarrow b]$ so $A_3 \rightarrow A_2A_3A_2$ becomes

$$A_3 \rightarrow bA_3A_2$$

Since, (–) $A_3 \rightarrow A_2A_3A_2$

(+) $A_3 \rightarrow A_3A_1A_3A_2$ and

(+) $A_3 \rightarrow bA_3A_2$

thus grammar has following ILR productions

$$A_3 \rightarrow A_3A_1A_3A_2 \mid bA_3A_2 \mid aA_2 \mid c \qquad \text{[ILR non-terminal is } A_3]$$

with other productions

$$A_1 \rightarrow A_2A_3 \mid a$$
$$A_2 \rightarrow A_3A_1 \mid b$$

Step 3

- remove ILR productions i.e.

$$A_3 \rightarrow A_3A_1A_3A_2 \mid bA_3A_2 \mid aA_2 \mid c$$

[By assuming that $A_1A_3A_2$ is α; $bA_3\,A_2$ is β_1; aA_2 is β_2; c is β_3; so clear ILR production are

$$A_3 \rightarrow A_3\alpha \mid \beta_1 \mid \beta_2 \mid \beta_3$$

which are connected on $A_3 \rightarrow \beta_1 \mid \beta_2 \mid \beta_3 \mid \beta_1 C \mid \beta_2 C \mid \beta_3 C$ and $C \rightarrow \alpha \mid \alpha C$ where C is a new non terminal

Substitute the values we get

(–) $A_3 \rightarrow A_3A_1A_3A_2 \mid bA_3\,A_2 \mid aA_2 \mid c$

(+) $A_3 \rightarrow bA_3\,A_2 \mid aA_2 \mid c \mid bA_3\,A_2\,C \mid aA_2\,C \mid c\,C$

and (+) $C \rightarrow A_1A_3A_2 \mid A_1A_3A_2\,C$

(So, we find GNF productions derived from A_3)

Now the grammar has following GNF productions

$$A_3 \rightarrow bA_3\,A_2 \mid aA_2 \mid c \mid bA_3\,A_2\,C \mid aA_2\,C \mid c\,C \text{ and}$$

remaining non GNF productions

$$A_1 \rightarrow A_2\,A_3 \mid a$$
$$A_2 \rightarrow A_3\,A_1 \mid b$$

- Modify non GNF productions to GNF where A_3 (ILR non terminal) is left most on right side ($A_2 \rightarrow A_3\,A_1 \mid b$) by substituting GNF derived symbols

  $A_2 \rightarrow bA_3\,A_2\,A_1 \mid aA_2\,A_1 \mid c\,A_1 \mid bA_3\,A_2\,C\,A_1 \mid aA_2\,C\,A_1 \mid c\,C\,A_1 \mid b$

- Now A_2 derived GNF productions so non GNF production $A_1 \rightarrow A_2A_3 \mid a$ is modified to GNF through replacing A_2 by GNF derived symbols as

  $A_1 \rightarrow bA_3A_2A_1A_3 \mid aA_2A_1A_3 \mid c\,A_1A_3 \mid bA_3A_2C\,A_1A_3 \mid aA_2C\,A_1A_3$
  $\mid c\,C\,A_1A_3 \mid bA_3 \mid a$

- Since, A_1 derived GNF productions so remaining non GNF productions where A_1 is in the left most on right side ($C \rightarrow A_1A_3A_2 \mid A_1A_3A_2\,C$) are modified to GNF through replacing A_1 by GNF derived symbols as

  $C \rightarrow bA_3A_2A_1A_3A_3A_2 \mid aA_2A_1A_3A_3A_2 \mid cA_1A_3A_3A_2 \mid bA_3A_2CA_1A_3A_3A_2 \mid aA_2$
  $CA_1A_3A_3A_2 \mid cCA_1A_3A_3A_2 \mid bA_3A_3A_2 \mid aA_3A_2$

and $C \rightarrow bA_3A_2A_1A_3A_3A_2C \mid aA_2A_1A_3A_3A_2C \mid cA_1A_3A_3A_2C \mid bA_3A_2CA_1A_3A_3A_2$
$CA_3A_2C \mid aA_2CA_1A_3A_3A_2C \mid cCA_1A_3A_3A_2C \mid bA_3A_3A_2C \mid aA_3A_2C$

Step 4. Since, grammar has no more non GNF productions hence we reach to end and process stop.

(All GNF productions are shown by bold productions)

11.12 PUMPING LEMMA FOR CONTEXT FREE LANGUAGES

In chapter 10 we have studied the lemma for the testing certain language is regular or not, like that here we study a similar type of lemma which is called the lemma for context free languages. On the basis of this lemma we must insure that for a sufficiently long string of a CFL we can find small sub strings that can be pumped. That is, pumping as many copies of the substrings yields strings will be in the language.

So, before deriving the pumping lemma for CFL we will study the nature of its parse tree. One advantage of the conversion of CFG into CNF is to turn the parse tree into binary tree with following fact,

Fact

If a CFG is in CNF and the length of the largest path in a derivation tree is n then the terminal string derived in the tree have length $\leq 2^{n-1}$.

Proof

In CNF the possible forms of productions are

$$A \rightarrow a \quad \text{or} \quad A \rightarrow BC$$

and their derivation trees are shown in Fig. 11.25 (*a*) & (*b*)

(a root and one leaf node) 

Fig. 11.25(*a*)

Here length of the largest path is one ($n = 1$) so the derived string length is 1. Since $2^{1-1} = 1$ that is symbol '*a*' in this case, fact is true.

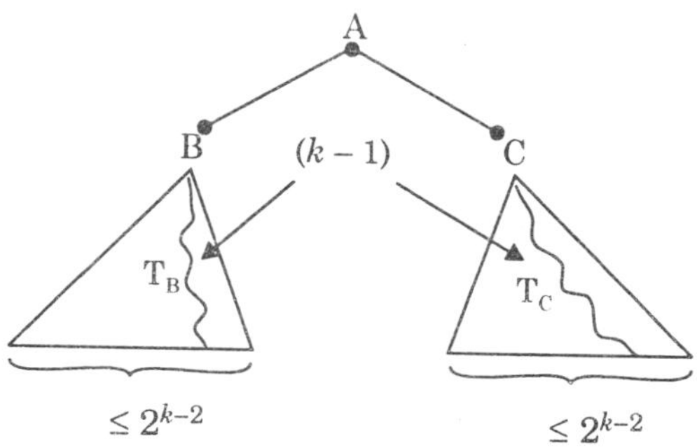

Fig. 11.25(*b*)

Assume length of largest path is $k(k > 1)$ then the sub trees T_B and T_C has the largest path is $\leq (k-1)$.

From the binary tree properties we know that tree extended up to level $(k-1)$ yields a string of length at most 2^{k-2}. So, the sub trees T_B and T_C each yields the substrings of at most 2^{k-2}. Because $A \Rightarrow BC \Rightarrow$ terminal string; whose yield is the concatenation of yields of tree T_B and yields of tree T_C. That is, at most of

$$2^{k-2} + 2^{k-2} = 2 \,.\, 2^{k-2}$$

$$= 2^{k-1} \qquad \text{(so the fact is true)}$$

Similarly using method of induction we can see that for any $k = n$ above fact is true.

Pumping lemma

If G be CFG then there exist a constant n such that if Z is any string s.t. Z ∈ L(G) and | Z | ≥ n then Z can be written as

```
G = u.v.w.x.y
```

where,

i. |v.x| ≥ 1

ii. |v.w.x| ≤ n

iii. $\forall$i ≥ 0, $u.v^i.w.x^i.y$ ∈ L(G)

Proof. We construct the proof for the CNF that of the CFG $G = (V_N, V_T, S, P)$. Assume the grammar has k non terminals i.e.,

$$| V_N | = k$$

Let the constant $n = 2^k$ and assume a string Z that is in L(G) with $| Z | \geq n$.

Now, consider the derivation tree for the string Z and apply the above fact. Since, G has k non terminals and a type of GNF so the length of the largest path in the derivation tree is at most k that yields the string of length at most $(2k - 1)$.

i.e., $$2^{k-1} = 2^k/2 = n/2$$

So, the grammar G generates the string of length at most of $n/2$.

Although we assume that the string $| Z | \geq n$ but the derivation tree yields the string of length $= n/2$ $(\neq n)$.

So, the derivation tree that yields the string Z where $| Z | \geq n$ has the path length more than k or at least $(k + 1)$.

Draw the derivation tree that has one of the path lengths at least $(k + 1)$. Hence the number of nodes (non terminals) in the path is at least $(k + 2)$.

Since, G has only k different non terminals thus this path has at least two duplicate non terminals so that total number of non terminals becomes at least $(k + 2)$.

Fig. 11.26 shows that X, Y, A .....are k non terminals and assume symbol A occurs at least twice in the path. Then it is possible to divide the tree as shown in Fig. 11.26.

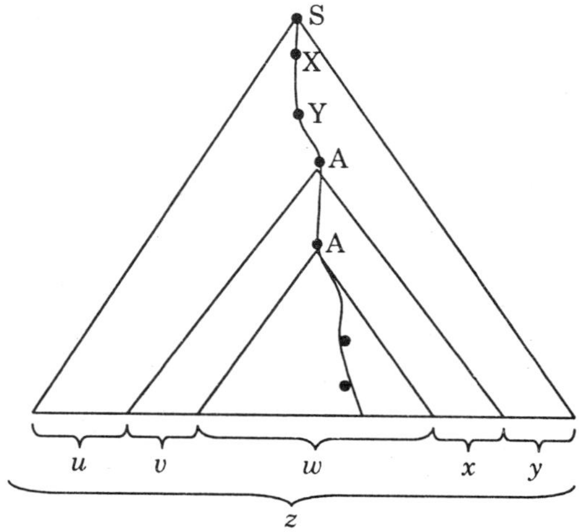

Fig. 11.26

String w is the yield of sub tree rooted at lower A. v and x are the left and right sub strings of w in the yield of the sub tree rooted at higher A and finally u and y are its left most and right most substrings.

Since, $A \stackrel{*}{\Rightarrow} w$ and A is reachable.

Hence, from Starting symbol S (active and reachable) we reach to A, or $S^* \Rightarrow \alpha A \beta$ where α and β are any arbitrary symbols.

Since, $S \stackrel{*}{\Rightarrow} u\,A\,y$ where u and y are terminal strings (Fig. 11.27(a))

And $A \stackrel{*}{\Rightarrow} v\,A\,x$ (Fig. 11.27(c)) and $A \stackrel{*}{\Rightarrow} w$ (Fig. 11.27(b))

Then,

either $S \stackrel{*}{\Rightarrow} u\,A\,y \stackrel{*}{\Rightarrow} u\,w\,y \in L$ (case for $i = 0$ shown in Fig. 11.27(d))

or $S \stackrel{*}{\Rightarrow} u\,A\,y \stackrel{*}{\Rightarrow} u\,v\,A\,x\,y$

$\stackrel{*}{\Rightarrow} u\,v\,v\,A\,x\,y$

$\stackrel{*}{\Rightarrow} u\,v^i\,w\,x^i\,y$ is also in L (Fig. 11.27(e))

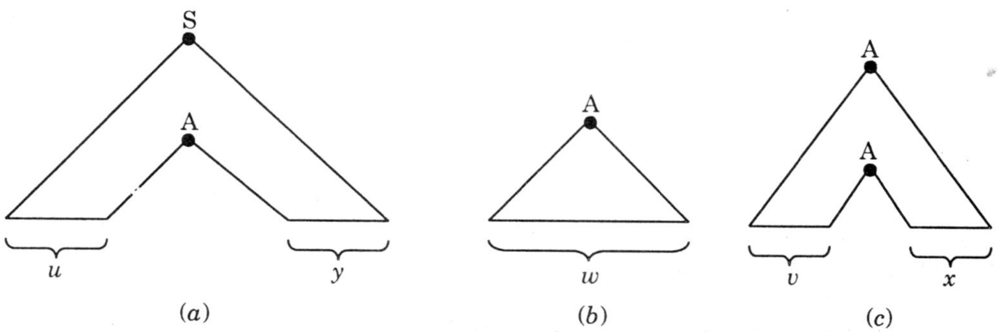

Fig. 11.27

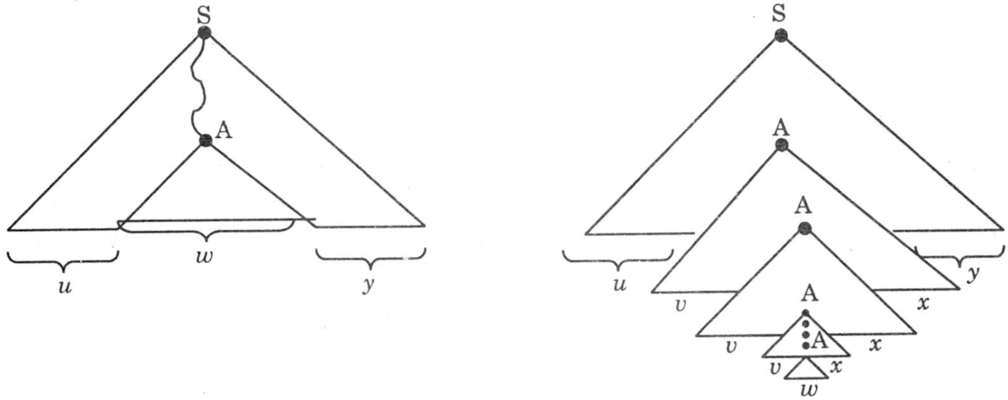

(d) (e)

Fig. 11.27 (Continued)

In the derivation trees we have seen that duplicates of A occur at the different node points (not at the same node point) hence sub strings v and x together not be empty so,

$$| v . x | \geq 1 \qquad \text{proved cond. } (i)$$

From the derivation tree it is also seen that non terminal A is chosen near or to the bottom of the tree. So the largest path in the sub tree rooted at A is at most $(k + 1)$. Hence, it yields the string of length at most $2^{(k+1)-1}$. That is at most $2k$ or n.

Thus, $$| v . w . x | \leq n \qquad \text{proved cond. } (ii)$$

Proved.

Now we solve some examples and see the application of pumping lemma to testify the language whether it is a CFL or not CFL.

Example 11.31. *A language L is defined over $\Sigma = \{a, b, c\}$ s.t. $L = \{a_i\, b_i\, c_i / i \geq 1\}$. Prove that L is not a CFL.*

Sol. We suppose L is a CFL. Let's take a constant n (for lemma) and assume a string $Z \in L$ i.e. $| Z | \geq n$ and $Z = a^n b^n c^n$, which can be break into sub strings u, v, w, x and y s.t.

$$Z = u . v . w . x . y$$

and satisfying the conditions (i), (ii) and (iii) of the pumping lemma.

Since $| v . w . x | \leq n$, the string vwx can contain at most two distinct type of symbols *viz.* (and since $| v . x | \geq 1$, v and x together contain at least one)

- If string $v . w . x \in a^n$ then string $u . w . y$ must have fewer than n a's besides possible n b's and n c's $\Rightarrow$ string doesn't contains equal numbers of all symbols.
- String $v . w . x \in a^n b^n$; then vx consists of only a's and b's with at least one of the symbols. So, uwy has n c's but fewer than n a's or fewer than n b's or both $\Rightarrow$ string doesn't contains equal numbers of all symbols.
- String $v . w . x \in b^n$; so string $\notin$ L
- String $v . w . x \in b^n c^n$; $\Rightarrow$ so string $\notin$ L
- String $v . w . x \in c^n$; $\Rightarrow$ so string $\notin$ L

Therefore, neither string is in the language L. Condition (ii) of lemma is violated, hence L is not a CFL.

11.13 PROPERTIES OF CONTEXT FREE LANGUAGES

In the previous chapter of regular expressions we have seen that certain operations are defined over regular expressions so that its base case definitions are unaltered these are called closure properties of regular expressions. Like that some operations are also defined over context free languages that are guaranteed to return context free language. We shall now study these operations as *closure properties* of context free languages.

Among these properties:

- Context free languages are closed under $\cup$ operation
- Context free languages are closed under concatenation operation
- Context free language is closed under kleeny closure operation

Context free languages are closed under $\cup$ operation

This property of context free language states that union operation between CFLs return the CFL. To prove this closure property assume that L_1 and L_2 are context free languages that are generated from CFG G_1 and G_2 respectively, where

$$G_1 = (V_{N1}, V_{T1}, S_1, P_1) \text{ and } G_2 = (V_{N2}, V_{T2}, S_2, P_2)$$

Now construct a new grammar G(to take in mind that it generates $L_1 \cup L_2$) that has following tuples,

- The set of non terminals $V_N = V_{N1} \cup V_{N2} \cup \{S\}$ where S is a new start symbol (Assume $V_{N1} \cap V_{N2} = \varnothing$)
- The set of terminals $V_T = V_{T1} \cup V_{T2}$
- A new start symbol S
- The set P of productions are $S \to S_1 \mid S_2 \cup P_1 \cup P_2$ where, S_1 and S_2 are reachable from S and so P_1 and P_2 which are defined for G_1 and G_2 respectively.

Since G_1 and G_2 are CFG so $G = (V_N, V_T, S, P)$ is a CFG.

The constructed CFG G generates the language $L_1 \cup L_2$. Hence, language is a CFL.

Further, we see that,

If $x \in L_1$ then it generates from grammar G as,

$$S \Rightarrow S_1 \overset{*}{\Rightarrow} x \text{ (all } G_1 \text{ productions are in G)}$$

If $y \in L_2$ then from grammar G it is generated with following derivation,

$$S \Rightarrow S_2 \overset{*}{\Rightarrow} y \text{ (all } G_2 \text{ productions are in G)}$$

Thus, $L_1 \cup L_2 \in L(G)$.

Context free languages are closed under concatenation operation

The second closure property says concatenations of context free languages are context free language. Assume L_1 and L_2 are CFLs that are generated from CFGs G_1 and G_2 respectively, where,

$$G_1 = (V_{N1}, V_{T1}, S_1, P_1) \text{ and } G_2 = (V_{N2}, V_{T2}, S_2, P_2)$$

Now we construct the grammar G that will generate $L_1 . L_2$ certainly has following tuples,

- The set of non terminals V_N contains all the non terminals of G_1 as well as of G_2 with a new start symbol S i.e.,

$$V_N = V_{N1} \cup V_{N2} \cup S$$

- The set of terminals contains all the terminals of G_1 as well as of G_2 i.e.,

$$V_T = V_{T1} \cup V_{T2}$$

- Assume a new start symbol S.
- The set P of productions contains all the productions of P_1, all the productions of P_2 and a new production $S \rightarrow S_1S_2$ that are responsible to generate the strings of G_1 concatenated with strings of G_2 so,

$$S \rightarrow S_1S_2 \cup P_1 \cup P_2$$

Since P_1 and P_2 are the productions of G_1 and G_2, that are CFG, hence grammar G is CFG.

So, we conclude that $L_1 . L_2$ is CFL.

Further assume that if string $x \in L_1$ and $y \in L_2$ then

$$S_1 \overset{*}{\Rightarrow} x \text{ and } S_2 \overset{*}{\Rightarrow} y$$

Thus, for the concatenation of these strings xy (Fig. 11.28 shows the derivation tree) following is the derivation sequence,

$$S \Rightarrow S_1S_2 \overset{*}{\Rightarrow} x\,S_2 \overset{*}{\Rightarrow} xy, \text{ that is } L_1 . L_2$$

Hence $L_1 . L_2 \in L(G)$.

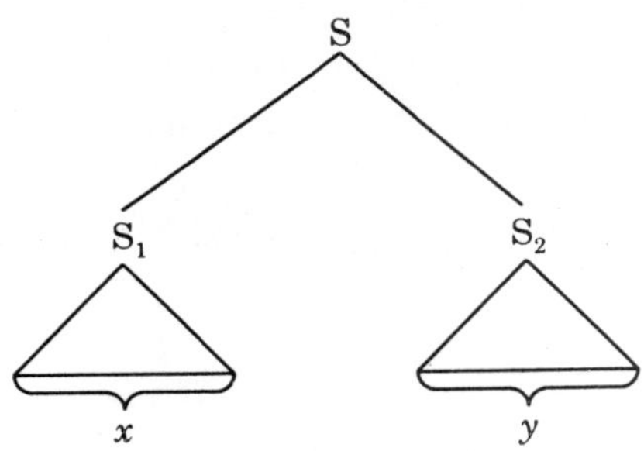

Fig. 11.28

Context free language is closed under kleeny closure operation

Kleeny closure of context free language is context free language. To prove this property we assume that L is a CFL and its grammar $G = (V_N, V_T, S, P)$. Now construct a new grammar G′ using the definition of G (without violating the properties of CFG) so that it generates kleeny closure of L, that is L*.

Before constructing the grammar G′ we recall following facts for L*,

- A new string ∈ be the part of its language so G′ has a null production. Because we can't alter the rules of set P so we introduce a new production for this cause, deriving from a new non terminal S' that is the start symbol for G′.

$$S' \rightarrow \in$$

- Since $L^* = \in \cup L . L \cup L . L . L \cup ....$

  From S we can generate the possible string of (single) L. For the generation of strings of multiple L's, G′ must have following production

$$S' \rightarrow S\,S'$$

Like as, $S' \Rightarrow SS' \Rightarrow S . \in \Rightarrow S$ (that generates the strings ∈ L)

$S' \Rightarrow SS' \Rightarrow SSS' \Rightarrow SS . \in \Rightarrow SS$ (that generates the strings ∈ L . L)

and $S' \overset{*}{\Rightarrow} SS......S$ (that generates the strings ∈ L . L . L......L)

So, G′ includes following tuples,

- Set of non terminals i.e., $V_N \cup S'$,
- Set of terminals i.e., $V_T \cup \{\varepsilon\}$,
- A new start symbol S′ and
- Set of productions i.e., $P \cup \{S' \to S\,S' \mid \varepsilon\}$

All the productions of G' fulfilling the properties of CFG hence its language L* is a CFL.

Besides above discussed closure properties for context free languages nothing is predicted for the operations like intersection and complementation.

Theorem 11.1. *If L_1 and L_2 are CFLs then $L_1 \cap L_2$ may or may not be a CFL.*

Proof. The proof of the above theorem is seen by solving of following example.

Assume languages $L_1 = \{a^I\, b^I\, c^J / I \geq 1, J \geq 1\}$ and $L_2 = \{a^J\, b^I\, c^I / I \geq 1, J \geq 1\}$ and there are generated from the grammars G_1 and G_2 respectively,

where G_1 is given as,

$$S \to AB$$
$$A \to ab \mid aAb$$
$$B \to c \mid cB$$

and G_2 is given as,

$$S \to AB$$
$$A \to a \mid aA$$
$$B \to bc \mid bBc$$

These are context free grammars (CFGs) so L_1 and L_2 are CFLs.

However we find that, language $L_1 \cap L_2$ contains all the strings of equal number of *a*'s, *b*'s and *c*'s or

$$L_1 \cap L_2 = \{a^I\, b^I\, c^I / I \geq 1\} = L \text{ (let)}$$

For language L it is not possible to construct the context free language hence, L is not CFL or $L_1 \cap L_2$ is not a CFL.

Theorem 11.2. *If L_1 is a CFL and L_2 is a regular language then $L_1 \cap L_2$ is a CFL.*

Proof. [**Hint :** Reader may prove this theorem with the help of Chamosky's hierarchy]

Theorem 11.3. *Let L be a CFL so its complement $\overline{L}$ may or may not be a CFL.*

Proof. Theorem says that for the complement of the language L i.e.

$$\overline{L} = \Sigma^* - L$$

nothing is predicted such that for the remaining strings which are not in L not necessarily the part of CFL. We can prove this by method of contradiction.

Assume that $\overline{L_1}$ and $\overline{L_2}$ are CFLs then

$$L_1 \cup L_2 = \overline{\overline{(L_1 \cap L_2)}} \qquad \text{[DeMorgan Law]}$$

$$= \overline{(\overline{L_1} \cup \overline{L_2})}$$

Since union of CFLs is CFL so the intersection is CFL that is a contradiction. Hence, complement of language $\overline{L}$ is not a CFL.

11.14 DECISION PROBLEMS (DP) OF CONTEXT FREE LANGUAGES

In the previous chapter of regular expression we study a number of its decision problems and simultaneously, we have discussed some computational tools to answer these problems. Analogous to these problems we formulate, some of the problems for context free languages. For some of the problems of CFLs like emptiness problem, finiteness problem and membership problem the computational procedure exists but a lot more problems have no algorithms such problems are known as undecidable problems of CFLs.

So, following are the decision problems:

1. Finiteness problem
2. Emptiness problem
3. Membership problem

DP1–Finiteness Problem

Given a CFG G and its language L (G), then the question arises Is L (G) finite?

To answer the question we perform following tasks,

- First, transform the grammar G to G′ that is in CNF and
- Then make a directed graph corresponding to grammar G′. Let G′ be,

$$G' = (V_N, V_T, S, P)$$

Since G′ is in CNF so it has following types of productions either A → BC or A → a whose directed graphs are shown in Fig. 11.29(a) & (b) respectively.

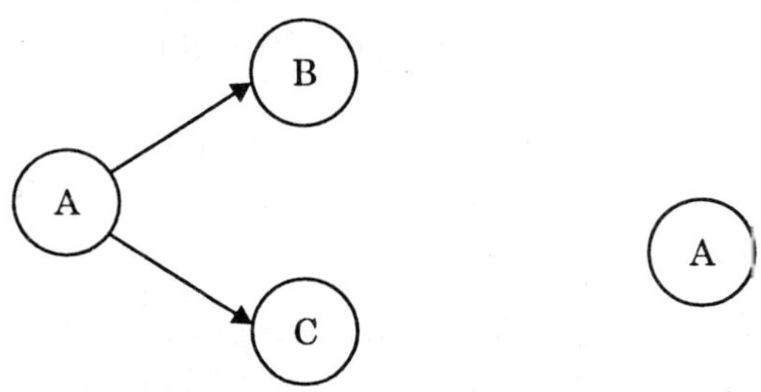

(a) (b)

Fig. 11.29

Directed graph is drawn from vertex (non terminal A) with an edge to each other vertices (derived non terminals B and C) if A → BC is a production. If derived symbol is terminal like, A → a then there is no edge shown in the directed graph corresponding to this production.

- Check for cycle/s. If the directed graph has at least a cycle then L(G) is infinite, otherwise, L(G) is finite, (if no cycle is there).

For example, consider a grammar G of following productions

$$S \rightarrow AB \mid a$$
$$A \rightarrow a \mid AB$$
$$B \rightarrow b$$

Since the grammar is in CNF and Fig. 11.30 shows the directed graph for it.

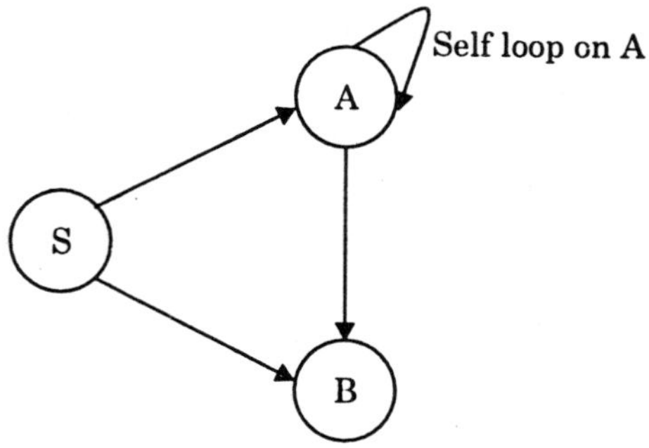

Fig. 11.30

The directed graph of $A \to AB$ has self loop on symbol A so there exist a cycle. Hence, L(G) is infinite.

Consider another example of grammar G

$$S \to AB \mid a$$
$$A \to a$$
$$B \to b$$

The directed graph of above grammar (Fig. 11.31) has no cycle. Hence L(G) is finite.

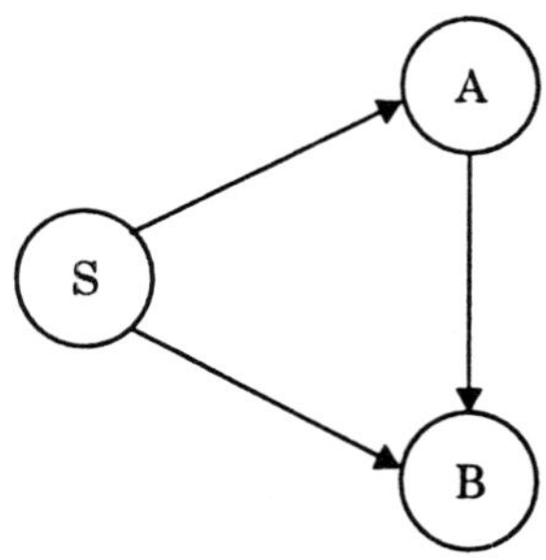

Fig. 11.31

Now we study above following general cases i.e.,

Case I

Suppose the graph has a cycle which causes due to following vertices arrangement in the directed graph,

$$X_0, X_1, X_2, \ldots\ldots\ldots\ldots\ldots\ldots X_n, X_0.$$

Since all vertices are connected through arcs. So there is an arc from X_0 to X_1 with possible production $X_0 \to X_1A$ or $X_0 \to BX_1$.

So, $X_0 \Rightarrow \alpha_1X_1\beta_1$ where α_1 and α_1 are $\in V_N$ and $|\alpha_1\beta_1| = 1$ and for next arc from X_1 to X_2 possible production $X_1 \to X_2A$ or $X_1 \to BX_2$.

So, $X_0 \Rightarrow \alpha_1X_1\beta_1 \Rightarrow \alpha_2X_2\beta_2$ where α_2 and $\alpha_2 \in V_N$ and $|\alpha_2\beta_2| = 2$, and so on.

[*where* $X_0 \Rightarrow a_1X_1b_1$ *means*

$\Rightarrow AX_1$

($\because$ $X_0 \Rightarrow AX_1$ *is the defined prodn. Here* α_1 *is A and* β_1 *is nothing so* $|\alpha_1\beta_1|$ *is 1)*

$\Rightarrow AX_2B$

($\because$ $X_1 \Rightarrow X_2B$ is the defined prodn. Here α_2 is A and β_2 is B so $|a_2b_2|$ is 2) and $|\alpha_i\beta_i| = i$ and so on.]

Hence, there exists a derivation sequence

$$X_0 \Rightarrow \alpha_1X_1\beta_1 \Rightarrow \alpha_2X_1\beta_2 \Rightarrow \ldots\ldots\ldots \Rightarrow \alpha_nX_n\beta_n \Rightarrow \alpha_{n+1}X_0\beta_{n+1}$$

Or, $X_0 \overset{*}{\Rightarrow} \alpha_{n+1}X_0\beta_{n+1}$ and since each non terminal of CNF is active so it must generate terminal string.

Let's assume,

$$\alpha_{n+1} \overset{*}{\Rightarrow} v \text{ and } \beta_{n+1} \overset{*}{\Rightarrow} x \text{ where } v \text{ and } x \in V_T^* \text{ and so the length } |v \,.\, x| = (n+1)$$

Thus,

$$X_0 \overset{*}{\Rightarrow} v \,.\, X_0 \,.\, x \qquad \text{and also } X_0 \overset{*}{\Rightarrow} w \in V_T^*$$

Since X_0 is useful so it is reachable from start state that is,

$S \overset{*}{\Rightarrow} \alpha X_0\beta$, we can find the terminal strings u and y s.t.

$$S \overset{*}{\Rightarrow} u \,.\, X_0 \,.\, y$$

Then,

$$S \overset{*}{\Rightarrow} u \,.\, X_0 \,.\, y \overset{*}{\Rightarrow} u \,.\, v \,.\, X_0 \,.\, x \,.\, y$$

$$\overset{*}{\Rightarrow} u \,.\, v \,.\, v \,.\, X_0 \,.\, x \,.\, x \,.\, y$$

(for any number $i \geq 0$) $\overset{*}{\Rightarrow} u \,.\, v^i \,.\, X_0 \,.\, x^i \,.\, y$

Therefore, it has infinite many strings.

Case II

Suppose graph has no cycle. Define a new term *rank* of a node in the graph that is the length of the longest path starting from node A.

Consider, $A \rightarrow BC$ and rank of B or rank (B) = r then,

$$\text{rank (A)} \geq r + 1$$

Because, A derived B (and C) and length from A is one more than length from B

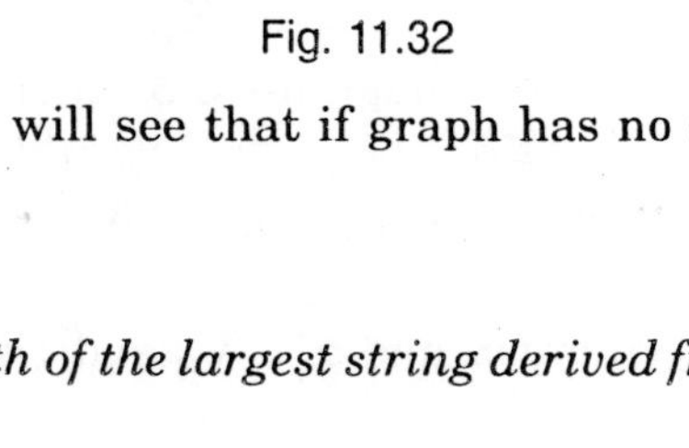

Fig. 11.32

From the Fig. 11.32 we will see that if graph has no cycle then rank of each node is finite.

FACT

If rank of a node is r, then length of the largest string derived from this node will have length $\leq 2^r$.

Proof. Let us assume rank (r) of any node is 0. So, there is no possible path away from this node. It means the production derived from this node is of the type $A \rightarrow a$ (assume grammar is in CNF). Where, the derived string is of length 1. (Fact is true for base case).

Induction Hypothesis

Assume that fact is true for all ranks $\leq r - 1$. Then examine, for node rank (A) = r. Since A derived B and C so rank (B) or rank (C) $\leq r - 1$. (Fig. 11.33).

From the derivation tree and by using the fact of CFL the length of the largest string derived from B or C is $\leq 2^{r-1}$.

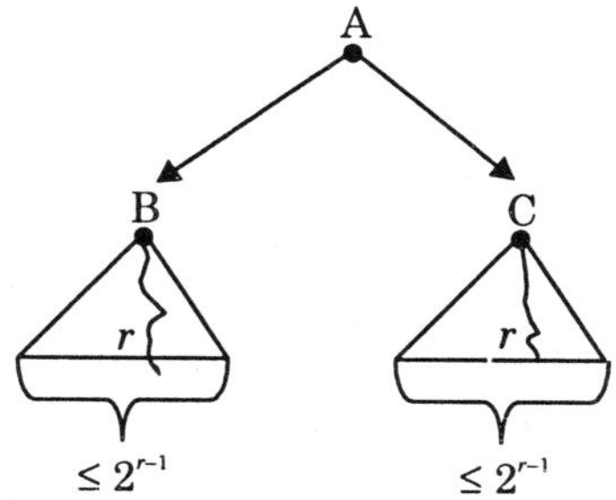

Fig. 11.33

Thus, A derived a string of length = $2r - 1 + 2r - 1$ or $\leq 2r$. So we reach the fact hence it is true for all ranks.

Since node rank (A) is finite and reachable (terminates to terminal string) so from starting symbol S, rank (S) = r' is a finite and the length of the largest string is no greater than $2^{r'}$ is also finite.

DP2–Emptiness Problem

Given a CFG G, then emptiness problem says: Is L (G) = ∅ (empty) ?

There is an inefficient way to examine the emptiness of the CFG G for the language L(G). As we studied earlier under the topic of simplification of the grammar that, if the grammar G has at least a nonterminal which is active and reachable, then it certainly derived a terminal string and because it is reachable so the start symbol S generates the terminal string. Then L(G) is non empty, i.e. L(G) ≠ ∅.

Conversely, L(G) is empty only if S generates no string of terminals. Or, G has none of its nonterminals are active and reachable.

Even if ∈ is in L(G) then L(G) ≠ ∅.

DP3–Membership Problem

Let G be a CFG and x be any terminal string then: Does string $x \in$ L(G)? or Is string x is the member of L(G) ?

There is an efficient way to solve membership problem through CYK algorithm that is based on dynamic programming. The algorithm operated over CNF grammar G for the language L(G).

There are few terms used in the algorithm such as,

$x_{i,j}$ = a substring of x starting from ith position in x and of length j.

$V_{i,j}$ = (set of nonterminals) or $\{A \in V_N \mid A \overset{*}{\Rightarrow} x_{i,j}\}$

For example, let string x = abba and the grammar G is,

$$S \rightarrow aB \mid bA$$
$$A \rightarrow a \mid aS \mid bAA$$
$$B \rightarrow b \mid bS \mid aBB$$

Then, $x_{i,j}$ and $V_{i,j}$ are as follows,

Case I. for the substring of length one ($x_{i,1}$ for $\forall i = 1$ to $|x|$)

- $x_{1,1}$ = a and $V_{1,1}$ = {A} [A $\Rightarrow$ *a* and A $\in V_N$.]
- $x_{2,1}$ = b and $V_{2,1}$ = {B} [B $\Rightarrow$ *b* and * B $\in V_N$.]
- $x_{3,1}$ = b and $V_{3,1}$ = {B} [B $\Rightarrow$ *b* and * B $\in V_N$.]
- $x_{4,1}$ = a and $V_{4,1}$ = {A} [A $\Rightarrow$ *a* and A $\in V_N$.]

Case II. for the substring of length two ($x_{i,2}$ for $\forall i = 1$ to $|x|-1$) determine $V_{i,2}$ for all substrings $x_{i,2}$. Since partition for length two ($j = 2$) are only 3 ($|x| - 1 = 4 - 1$) for string of length 4. Those are shown below,

$$\underbrace{a\ b}\ \ b\ \ a \qquad a\ \underbrace{b\ b}\ a \qquad a\ b\ \underbrace{b\ a}$$

Case III. Similarly make next partitions for the substring of length three ($x_{i,3}$ for $\forall i = 1$ to $|x|-2$) and determine $V_{i,3}$ for all the substrings $x_{i,3}$.

These partitions are,

$$\underbrace{a\ b\ b}\ a \qquad a\ \underbrace{b\ b\ a}$$

In this case two partitions are possible ($|x| - 2 = 4 - 2$) those are starting from position first and second.

Case *end*: This is the last case for the partitioning of the substring that is completely contains whole of the string x. for example the string of length 4 i.e. *abba*, $x_{i,4}$ for $\forall i = 1$ to $|x| - 3 = 4 - 3 = 1$ or $x_{1,4}$ only, so, determine $V_{1,4}$ that derive the string $x_{1,4}$.

$$\underbrace{a\ b\ b\ a}$$

The CYK algorithm stands on the way that how frequently we can determine the set of nonterminals $V_{i,j}$ for each case of $x_{i,j}$. The method uses dynamic programming approach to find $V_{i,j}$. This is a tabulation method and fact is that in $O(n^3)$ time the algorithm constructs the table for all $V_{i,j}$ to decide whether string x is in L(G).

The method constructs a triangular table shown in Fig. 11.34

$x_{i,j}$ \ $V_{i,j}$	$V_{i,1}$	$V_{i,2}$	$V_{i,3}$	$V_{i,4}$
a	$V_{1,1}$			
		$V_{1,2} = V_{1,1} * V_{2,1}$	$V_{1,3} = \begin{cases} V_{1,1} * V_{2,2} \text{ or} \\ V_{1,2} * V_{3,1} \end{cases}$	
b	$V_{2,1}$			
		$V_{2,2} = V_{2,1} * V_{3,1}$		$V_{1,4}$
b	$V_{3,1}$			
		$V_{3,2} = V_{3,1} * V_{4,1}$	$V_{2,3} = \begin{cases} V_{2,1} * V_{3,2} \text{ or} \\ V_{2,2} * V_{4,1} \end{cases}$	
a	$V_{4,1}$			
	$x_{i,1}$	$x_{i,2}$	$x_{i,3}$	$x_{i,4}$

Fig. 11.34

Now CYK algorithm starts with CNF grammar of G. So, convert the grammar G into CNF that is,

(+) X → a (+) R → AA

(+) Y → b (+) Q → BB

So the grammar becomes,

S → XB | YA ; X → a; R → AA;

A → a | XS | YR; Y → b; Q → BB;

B → b | YS | XQ;

Now Construct the table, i.e.,

On first column j = 1

That means only single length substrings of x is considered.

Now, $x_{i,j} \Rightarrow x_{1,1} \Rightarrow$ substring starting from Ist position and of length 1 is *a*, (*a bba*)

Similarly, $x_{2,1}$ = b (a b b a)

$X_{3,1}$ = b (a b b a)

$X_{4,1}$ = b (a b b a)

- So, $V_{1,1}$ corresponding to $x_{1,1}$ means $\alpha \stackrel{*}{\Rightarrow} x_{1,1}$ (where $\alpha \in V_N$ of G)

(∴ $x_{1,1}$ = a) so only productions are A → a and X → a.

Therefore, $V_{1,1}$ = **{A, X}.**

- Similarly, substring $x_{2,1} = b$ will be derived from productions B → *b* and Y → *b*

⇒ $V_{2,1}$ = **{B, Y}.**

- For substring $x_{3,1}$ = b ⇒ $V_{3,1}$ = **{B, Y}** and
- for substring $x_{4,1}$ = a ⇒ $V_{4,1}$ = **{A, X}**

These entries are shown in column 1 in the table (Fig. 11.35).

		$V_{i,1}$	$V_{i,2}$	$V_{i,3}$	$V_{i,4}$
i = 1	**a**	{A, X}	{S}	{B}	{S}
i = 2	**b**	{B, Y}	{Q}	{B}	
i = 3	**b**	{B, Y}	{S}		
i = 4	**a**	{A, X}			
		j = 1	**j = 2**	**j = 3**	**j = 4**

Fig. 11.35

On Second column j = 2

(substrings of length 2 is considered)

So, $x_{i,2}$ are:

- $x_{1,2} \Rightarrow$ ab (a b b a)

So, $V_{1,2} = V_{1,1} * V_{2,1}$ (take the values from column one that are earlier find)
$= \{A, X\} * \{B, Y\} = \{AB, XB, AY \text{ and } XY\}$ we get a set of derived ←

symbols. Now, from r.h.s. select those entries that are found in productions of G.

only XB is found in rule of G.

Therefore, $\mathbf{V_{1,2} = \{S\}}$ $(\therefore S \Rightarrow XB\}$

Similarly,

- For $x_{2,2} \Rightarrow$ bb (a b b a)

So, $V_{2,2} = V_{2,1} * V_{3,1} = \{B, Y\} * \{B, Y\} = \{BB, YB, YY \text{ and } BY\}$

Search for derived symbols that are in G which is BB.

Therefore, $\mathbf{V_{2,2} = \{Q\}}$ $(\therefore Q \Rightarrow BB\}$

- For $x_{3,2} \Rightarrow$ ba (a b b a)

So, $V_{3,2} = V_{3,1} * V_{4,1} = \{B, Y\} * \{A, X\} = \{BA, YA, BX \text{ and } YX\}$ ←

We find derived symbol YA that are in G.

Therefore, $\mathbf{V_{3,2} = \{S\}}$ $(\because S \Rightarrow YA\}$

See second column of the table shown in Fig. 11.35.

On Third column j = 3

(consider only substrings of length 3)

That are,

- $x_{1,3} \Rightarrow$ abb (a b b a)

So, $V_{1,3}$ can be determine either through $V_{1,2} * V_{3,1}$ or $V_{1,1} * V_{2,2}$

That are,

{S} * {B, Y} = {SB, SY} nothing is in G.

or $\{A, X\} * \{Q\} = \{AQ, XQ\}$. We find derived string XQ are in rules of G

Therefore, $\mathbf{V_{1,3} = \{B\}}$ $(\therefore B \Rightarrow XQ\}$

And next possible substring is

- $x_{2,3} \Rightarrow$ bba (a b b a)

So, $V_{2,3}$ can be determined either through $V_{2,1} * V_{3,2}$ or $V_{2,2} * V_{4,1}$

That are,

$\{B, Y\} * \{S\} = \{BS, YS\}$ we find YS is in G so no need to consider other way.

Therefore, $\mathbf{V_{2,3} = \{B\}}$ $(\therefore B \Rightarrow YS\}$

See third column of table shown in Fig. 11.35.

On last column j = 4

(complete string is considered as a whole)

- $x_{1,4} \Rightarrow$ abba (a b b a)

So, $V_{1,4}$ can be determined either through

$V_{1} * V_{2,3} = \{A, X\} * \{B\} = \{AB, XB\} \Rightarrow$ XB is in G that is derived from S.

or $V_{1,2} * V_{3,2}$ = {S} * {S} = {SS} we find nothing.

or $V_{1,3} * V_{4,1}$ = {B} * {A, X} and find nothing.

Therefore, $\mathbf{V_{1,4} = \{S\}}$ (∴ S ⇒ XB}

This entry is shown in Fourth column of table shown in Fig. 11.35.

Conclusion

From the table (Fig. 11.35) we see that its last column contains the nonterminal/s that derived the complete string x. If this column contains the start symbol S it means,

$$S \overset{*}{\Rightarrow} x$$

Then, string $x \in L(G)$.

Conversely, if start symbol $S \notin V_{1,n}$ (last column) then $x \notin L(G)$.

CYK Algorithm

Start with the CNF grammar $G = (V_N, V_T, S, P)$, and assume that string x is of length $n(|\ x\ | = n)$.

```
begin
    For i = 1 to n do    // for all substring of length 1
      Vi,1 = {α ∈ VN | A → xi,1 is a production in G}
    End for (i)
    For i = 2 to n do // for all substring of length 2
      For j = 1 to n-i+1 do
          Vj,i = ∅
          For k = 1 to i-1 do
          Vj,i = Vj,i ∪ {A ∈ VN A → BC is a production in G and B ∈ Vj,k
                      and C ∈ Vj+k, i-k}
      End for (k)
    End for (j)
  End for (i)
  If S ∈ Vi,1 then x ∈ L(G) otherwise x ∉ L(G)
end
```

So, the algorithm must terminate with in the time complexity $O(n^3)$ due to nested three for loops with variables *k*, *j* and *i*.

[In general the compiler of 'C' and 'PASCAL' languages are of linear time complexity i.e. $O(n)$.]

11.15 UNDECIDED PROBLEMS (UDP) OF CONTEXT FREE LANGUAGES

There are a lot more problems of the context free languages (CFLs) that have no known solution, such problems are called undecidable problems. For example, following problems for CFGs/CFLs have no algorithms, i.e.,

- ***Problem of equivalence***

Remember, problem of equivalence is decidable for regular languages that says that if L_1 and L_2 are two regular languages then they are equivalence if and only if,

$$(L_1 - L_2) \cup (L_2 - L_1) = \varnothing$$

But for the case of CFLs there is no answer of this question. Why? Because for the CFGs G_1 and G_2 this problem says,

Is $L(G_1) = L(G_2)$?

Or, to evaluate the function

$$\text{Equiv\_}cfg(G_1, G_2) \begin{cases} \rightarrow \text{Yes} \\ \rightarrow \text{No} \end{cases}$$

Algorithm never exists.

- ***Problem of Ambiguity***

Given a CFG G, Is G ambiguous? Or,

For a given CFL L, Is L ambiguous?

Algorithm never exists.

- ***Problem of Intersection***

Given two CFGs G_1 and G_2, Is there intersection $L(G_1) \cap L(G_2)$ is also CFL?

To decide whether there intersection returns a CFL, no algorithm exists.

- ***Problem of Complementation***

Given a CFG G, then what's about the complement of its language?

Is $\overline{L(G)}$ is CFL?

Algorithm never exists.

- ***Problem of equivalence of languages of ambiguous and unambiguous CFG***

Given an ambiguous CFG G, Does there exist an equivalent unambiguous CFG G′ s.t. L (G) = L(G′)?

No algorithm exists.

- ***Problem of regularity***

Given a CFL L, Is L regular?

There is no way to find that L is also a regular language.

EXERCISES

11.1 Classify the grammar and construct the language generated by them

(*i*) $S \rightarrow aSBC/abC$

$bB \rightarrow bb$

$bC \rightarrow bc$

$CB \rightarrow BC$

$cC \rightarrow cc$

(*ii*) $S \rightarrow 0A0$

$A \rightarrow 0A0/1$

(*iii*) $S \rightarrow 0S/0B$

$B \rightarrow 1C$

$C \rightarrow 0C/0$

11.2 Construct the grammar for the given language and identify the types of language.
(*i*) $L = \{a^n\ b\ a^n \mid n \geq 1\}$ (*ii*) $L = \{a^m\ b\ a^n \mid m, n \geq 1\}$
(*iii*) $L = \{a^{n2} \mid n \geq 1\}$

11.3 Construct the CFG which generates following languages.
(*i*) $L = \{0^i\ 1^j\ 2^k \mid i = j + k\}$ (*ii*) $L = \{0^i\ 1^j\ 2^k \mid i < j \text{ or } i > k\}$
(*iii*) $L = \{0^i\ 1^j\ 2^k \mid i \neq j + k\}$ (*iv*) $L = \{0^i\ 1^j \mid i \leq j \leq 1.5\ i\}$

11.4 Show that given grammars are regular grammars. Find the regular expressions for each grammar.
(*i*) $S \to aP/aS,\ P \to bQ,\ Q \to aQ/a$ (*ii*) $S \to aA/a,\ A \to aA/bB/a,\ B \to bB/c$
(*iii*) $S \to 0A,\ A \to 0A/0B,\ B \to 1C,\ C \to 0B/0$.

11.5 What language is generated by the following grammars.
(*i*) $S \to a\ S\ b/b\ S\ a/\epsilon$ (*ii*) $S \to a\ S\ b/b$
(*iii*) $S \to a\ B/b\ B/\epsilon,\ B \to a/b\ B$
(*iv*) $S \to 0A/1C/b,\ A \to 0S/1B,\ B \to 0C/1A/0,\ C \to 0B/1S$
(*v*) $S \to 1S/0A/\epsilon,\ A \to 0A/1B/1,\ B \to 1S$.

11.6 Construct the grammar for the number representations, viz.
(*i*) Integer numbers (*ii*) Real numbers
(*iii*) Floating Point numbers.

11.7 Shows following grammars are ambiguous grammar.
(*i*) $S \to 0S1S/1S0S/\epsilon$ (*ii*) $S \to SS/0/1$
(*iii*) $S \to P/Q,\ P \to 0P1/01,\ Q \to 01Q/\epsilon$ (*iv*) $S \to PQP,\ P \to 0P/\epsilon,\ Q \to 1Q/\epsilon$
(*v*) $S \to aS/aSbS/c$ (*vi*) $S \to AbB,\ A \to aA/\epsilon,\ B \to aB/bB/\epsilon$

11.8 Find the equivalent unambiguous grammar from the ambiguous grammars shown from previous exercises 11.7.

11.9 Show that following languages are not CFL.
(*i*) $L = \{0^n\ 1^n\ 2^n \mid n \geq 1\}$ (*ii*) $L = \{0^n\ 1^n\ 2^m \mid m > n\}$
(*iii*) $L = \{0^n\ 1^m\ 2^l \mid n \leq m \leq l\}$ (*iv*) $L = \{0^n\ 1^{2n}\ 2^n \mid n \geq 0\}$
(*v*) $L = \{0^n\ 1^m\ 2^l \mid n \neq m,\ m \neq l, \text{ and } l \neq n\}$ (*vi*) $L = \{0^n\ 1^m \mid m = n^2\}$
(*vii*) $L = \{s\ s/s \in \{a, b\}^*\}$.

11.10 Show that language $L = \{0^n\ 1^n \mid n \geq 1\}$ is derived from the grammar $S \to 0\ S\ 1,\ \ S \to 0\ 1$.

11.11 Show that language $L = \{w\ w^R \mid w \in \{0, 1\}^*\}$ is derived from the grammar $S \to 0\ S\ 0,\ S \to 1\ S\ 1,\ S \to \epsilon$.

11.12 Show that following languages are CFL.
(*i*) $L_1 = \{0^n\ 1^n\ 2^m \mid n \geq 1, m \geq 1\}$ (*ii*) $L_2 = \{0^n\ 1^m\ 2^m \mid n, m \geq l\}$

11.13 Let two grammars G_1 and G_2 are given below. Show that there languages be L_1 and L_2 shown in exercise 11.12.

(*i*) G_1
$S \to AB$
$A \to 0A1/01$
$B \to 2B/2$

(*ii*) G_2
$S \to CD$
$C \to 0C/0$
$D \to 1D2/12$

11.14 From the given CFG G, convert into CNF.
(*i*) $S \to SS/(S)/\epsilon$
(*ii*) $S \to bA/aB,\ A \to bAA/aS/a,\ B \to aBB/b$

(*iii*) S → 0S0/1S1/∈

A → 0B1/1B0

B → 0B/1B/∈

(*iv*) S → *ab*S*b*/*a*/*a*A*b*, A → *b*S/*a*AA*b*

11.15 Convert CFG into GNF.

(*i*) Convert the grammar to GNF

S → AA | 0

A → SS | 1

(*ii*) S → PQ | 0

P → QS | 1

Q → PQP | 0P | 2

11.16 Prove that the grammar for the language L = $\{0^n\ 1^n\ 2^n \mid n \geq 1\}$ is not a context free grammar.

[**Hint :** Let G is the grammar for L then G has following productions,

S → 0 1 2 | 0 S B 2

2 B → B 2

1 B → 1 1

which is a length increasing grammar]

11.17 Prove that the language L = $\{0^{n^2} \mid n \geq 1\}$ is neither a regular language nor a context free language.

[**Hint :** When we construct the grammar for the language L then its grammar must has following set of productions,

S → 0 | CD

C → ACB | AB

AB → 0BA

B0 → 0B

A0 → 0A

AD → D0

BD → E0

BE → E0

E → 0

Which are of type 1-grammar productions. Therefore the language is neither a regular language nor a context free language]

11.18 Construct the grammar for the language L = $\{0^{2^n} \mid n = 1\}$.

[**Hint :** Similar to exercise 1.17 we can construct the grammar for L that contains following set of productions,

S → AC0B

C0 → 00C

CB → DB | E

0D → D0

AD → AC

0E → E0

AE → ∈

which is a type 0 grammar]

INTRODUCTION TO TURNING MACHINE

12 Introduction to Turning Machine

12.1 INTRODUCTION

We have discussed so far comperatively small and simple classes of languages which are regular languages and context free languages and their corresponding automatons FA's and PDA's respectively. These automatons are not capable to stores no more than a fixed amount of information and simultaneously the information can be retrieved only in accordance of LIFO fashion during activation (live) of the machine. So in totality these modules provide a 'limited view of computation'.

Thus, the question arises, what class of language is defined by any computational model. In general we ask about the capability of the machine or automaton.

Now we extend the approach of computation and discuss a more general model of computation. An abstract machine called Turing Machine is an accepted form of 'general model of computation'. We may hypothetically assume that Turing Machine is flexible to store enormous amount of information and also has enormous computing power. So, particular this model can accommodate the idea of stored program machine like a computer and that is analogous to the working of human brain. This hypothetical model of computation provides the basis for the computers.

In 1936, Allan M. Turing proposed a machine known as Turing Machine as a 'general model of any possible computation'. To say that any possible algorithm procedure that can be imagined or immerged by humans can be carried out by some Turing machine. Conversely, Turing machine provides the way to implement all algorithmic procedures (theoretically). This hypothesis is known as *Church thesis* or *Church—Turing Thesis*.

12.2 BASIC FEATURES OF A TURING MACHINE(TM)

Allan Turing literally proposes a human like Computer. A human has a pen and paper and solve the problem in discrete and isolated computational steps like FA/PDA, it has finite set of states corresponding to possible 'states of mind'. In Turing Machine the paper is replaced by the linear tape of infinite length (whose left boundary is known but no right boundary). Tape is divided into cells that can hold one symbol at a time.

Tape cells contains symbols of two types,

- First, symbols those are from the list of the set of '*input symbols*'. (so it is a input device)
- Second, '*tape symbols*' are those symbols that are used for replacing the input symbols during computation. (it is a output device because the string of tape symbols left on the tape at the end of computation will be the output generated by TM)

A cell contains no input symbol and no tape symbol certainly contains the '*blank symbol*'. It is used to distinguish between the input symbols and tape symbols.

The tape is pointed by the tape head such that at any moment tape is head centered on one of the cell of the tape. The movement of the tape head may consists of following:

1. It moves one cell left (unless it is not on the left most cell)/right at a time.
2. It replaces the current symbol either by a tape symbol or through blank symbol.
3. And changing the state.

12.2.1 Abstract View of a TM

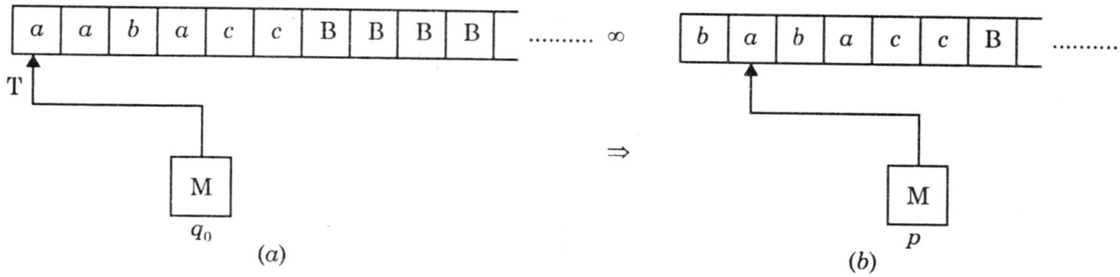

Fig. 12.1

Assume that at time $t = 0$ Machine M is in state q_0 (initial state) and its tape head pointing to its left most cell. Tape cells contain the string of input symbols (form over Σ) and the remaining cells hold the blank symbol/s that is shown by B's. Machine has a read/write tape head T that scans one cell at a time. Assume that after reading the symbol '*a*' machine reaches to state *p* and simultaneously tape head replaces the input symbol by another tape symbol let it be '*b*' and move to right. Now tape head pointed to the second cell containing the input symbol '*a*'. In this way M scans all cells that contain the input symbol and left the tape symbols that will be the possible form of output generated by the Turing Machine M. The abstract view of turing machine is shown in Fig. 12.1(*a*) & (*b*).

12.2.2 Definition of a TM

Once we know the characteristics of the Turing Machine, we can easily define it in the forms of set of following tuples,

- A finite set of states (Q)
- A finite set of input symbols (Σ)
- A finite set of tape symbols (Γ); where $\Sigma \subset \Gamma$
- Blank symbol (B); where B Σ Γ but $B \notin \Sigma$
- A starting state (q_0); where $q_0 \in Q$
- Transition function ∂, where ∂ is: (partial mapping of)

$$\delta : Q * \{\Gamma \cup \Sigma\} \rightarrow Q * \{\Gamma \cup \Sigma\} * (L, R)$$

That is the arguments of ∂ are a state q ($\in$ Q) and a tape/input symbol '*a*' ($\in \{\Gamma \cup \Sigma\}$) and returns to the next state p ($\in$ Q), replacing another symbol '*b*' ($\cup \{\Gamma \cup \Sigma\}$) and moves either left or right, i.e.

$$\delta (q, a) = (p, b, R);$$ here we assume tape head moves right.

- The set of final state/s (F); where $F \subseteq Q$

So, above 7-tuples describe the TM M as,

$$M = (Q, \Sigma, \Gamma, B, q_0, \delta, F)$$

Note: It is always remember that

1. ***Machine crashes*** *if δ is not define or tape head crosses left most boundary.*
   For example, $\delta(q_0, a) = (p, a, L)$ *(from Fig. 12.1(a)) is not possible.*
2. *Machine is deterministic and without ∈-transitions.*

12.2.3 Instantaneous Description (ID) of a Turing Machine

In this section we will describe instantaneous description of the Turing machine. Instantaneous Description (ID) shows the sequence of moves and its configuration from one instant to next.

As we see that the status of the Turing machine (at any moment) is given by the contents of the cell/s that already scanned, the present state, and the remaining nonblank cells entry including the current tape head entry.

Fig. 12.2 shows the configuration of Turing machine at any time t, where M is in state q and the tape cell entries are shown below,

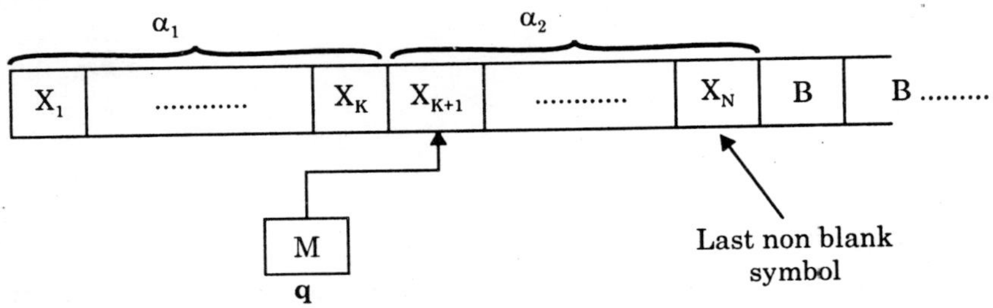

Fig. 12.2

So, ID is given as, $\alpha_1\, q\, \alpha_2$

where, α_1 and α_2 are the strings of nonblank symbols.

In general, ID is given by as, $\Gamma^*\, Q\, \Gamma^*$ (because $\alpha_1 \in \Gamma^*$, $q \in Q$ and $\alpha_2 \in \Gamma^*$)

We describe the moves of the Turing machine by $\vdash$ notation that is called move relation. And the meaning of $\vdash^*$ is as usual, zero/one/more (finite) moves of Turing Machine M.

Hence, the meaning of $I_1 \vdash I_2$ tells that Turing machine M reaches from one instant (1) to next (2) in exactly one step.

Further we see that the nature of $\vdash^*$ is reflexive† and transitive‡ closure of '$\vdash$'.

From Fig. 12.2 the ID of TM M is,

$$\alpha_1\, \mathbf{q}\, \alpha_2$$

where, string $\alpha_1 = X_1 X_2 X_3 \ldots\ldots\ldots X_K$ and $\alpha_2 = X_{K+1} X_{K+2} \ldots\ldots\ldots X_n$ (by assuming that $X_1 X_2 X_3 \ldots\ldots\ldots X_n$ is the portion of tape between left most and right most non blanks, i.e.

$$X_1 X_2 \ldots\ldots X_K\, \mathbf{q}\, X_{K+1} X_{K+2} \ldots\ldots\ldots X_n \;\vdash\; X_1 X_2 \ldots\ldots\ldots X_K\, Y\, \mathbf{p}\, X_{K+2} \ldots\ldots\ldots X_n,$$

if and only if $\partial\, (\mathbf{q}, \mathbf{X_{K+1}}) = (\mathbf{p}, \mathbf{Y}, \mathbf{R})$ i.e. tape head move rightward.

---

† Suppose Turing machine presently in ID – I and it remains to ID – I in no move i.e. $ID_I \vdash_0 ID_I$; hence '$\vdash$' is reflexive.

‡ Let TM M reaches from ID – I to J in one step and from J to K in some finite steps i.e. $ID_I \vdash^1 ID_J$ and $ID_J \vdash^* ID_K$ then M reaches ID – I to K in some fine steps. i.e. $ID_I \vdash^* ID_K$; hence '$\vdash$' is transitive.

This situation is shown in Fig. 12.3.

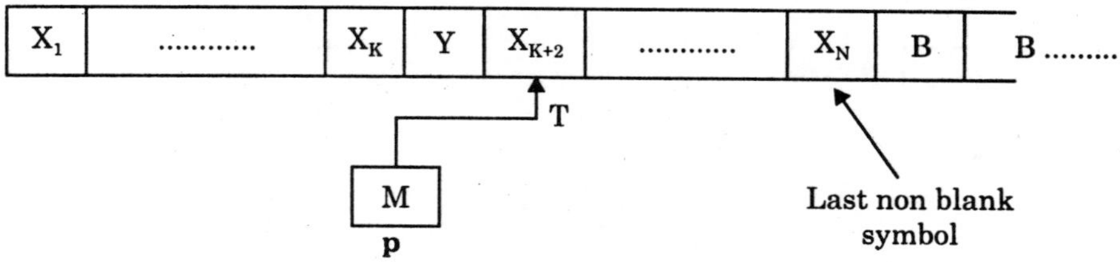

Fig. 12.3

The limitations of this move are:

- If tape head points to the rightmost nonblank cell that is $X_K = X_N$ then next to its right is blank. Thus,

$$X_1 X_2 \ldots\ldots X_{n-1}\, \mathbf{q}\, X_n \vdash X_1 X_2 \ldots\ldots X_{n-1}\, Y\, \mathbf{p}\, B \qquad \text{and no more ID.}$$

- If tape head point to the Ist cell and Y = B, that is symbol X_1 is replaced by B. That causes infinite sequence of leading blanks and not appears in the next ID. So,

$$\mathbf{q}\, X_1 X_2 \ldots\ldots X_n \vdash \mathbf{p}\, X_2 \ldots\ldots X_n$$

Suppose $\partial\, (\mathbf{q}, X_{K+1}) = (\mathbf{p}, Y, L)$ i.e. tape head move leftward then,

$$X_1 X_2 \ldots\ldots X_K\, \mathbf{q}\, X_{K+1} X_{K+2} \ldots\ldots X_n \vdash X_1 X_2 \ldots\ldots X_{K-1}\, \mathbf{p}\, X_K\, Y\, X_{K+2} \ldots X_n,$$

This situation is shown in Fig. 12.4.

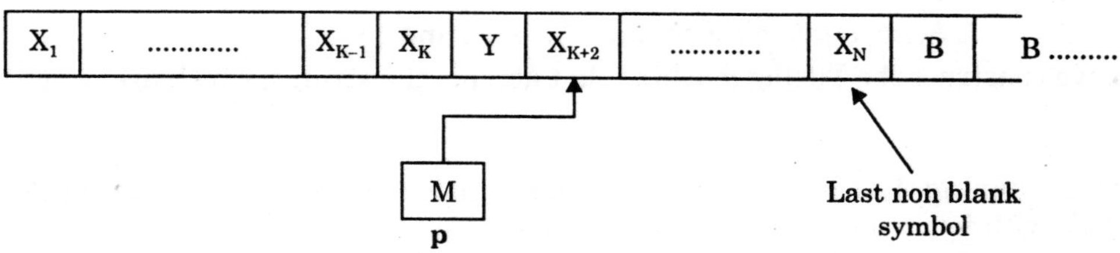

Fig. 12.4

12.2.4 Representation of a Turing Machine

We can represent the moves of the Turing machine by *state diagram* or *by transition table.* For example the move

$$\partial(q, a) = (p, X, R)$$

is represented by the state diagram shown in Fig. 12.5

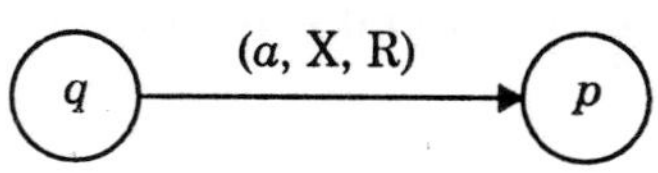

Fig. 12.5

It tells that machine is in state q reading the input symbol a and it perform the operation to replace the symbol a by X and the head moves right of the current cell and ready to read the next symbol, these situation are clearly smalised in Fig. 12.6(a) & (b).

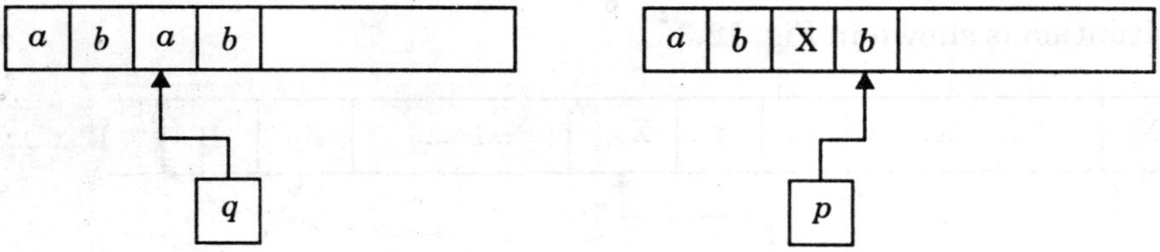

(a) (b)

Fig. 12.6

As usual a state is represented by a circle, A start state is represented by a circle marked with an arrow, and the final state (halting state) is represented by the double circle.

Alternatively state diagram of Fig. 12.7

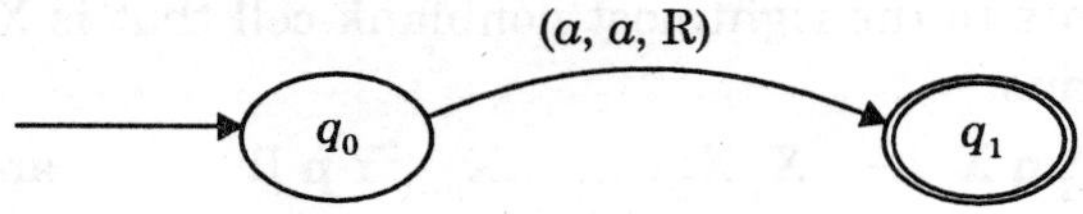

Fig. 12.7

shows that from the starting state q_0 machine reads the symbol a and left the same symbol a (over write a by a) and move to right and reaches to state q_1 and halted (shown by double circled).

Let us consider an example and ***construct the Turing machine for the language*** $L = \{a^i\ b^i \mid i \geq 0\}$. We see that language L contains all the strings of equal number of a's followed by equal number of b's like,

L = {ab, $aabb$, $aaabbb$, ... and ∈}

So, we construct the Turing machine that accepts the strings, which are in set L.

Logic

The logic for scanning the accepted nature strings is depend upon the counting of the number of a's and b's with followings steps: (assume string is '$aaabbb$')

- Read the first symbol a, converted to X, move right and find the equivalent b at the end of the string (before the blank symbol B) and converted to B.

  a *a a b b b* B B ⇒ **X** *a a b b* **B** B B

- Move back and reach to the next starting symbol a and repeat the previous step like as,

  X **a** *a b b* B B B ⇒ X **X** *a b* **B** B B B

  and X X **a** *b* B B B B ⇒ X X **<u>X B</u>** B B B B (*a* string of only X and blanks B)

- The string of equal number of a's followed by b's certainly returns the string shown above that is last X followed by B and this may be taken as the halting condition of the machine.

Transition functions (δ)

Let machine M = (Q, Σ, Γ, B, q_0, δ, F) where q_0 is the starting state, set Q = {q_0, q_1, q_2, q_3, q_4}, Σ = {a, b}, Γ = {a, b, X, B} (because Σ ⊂ Γ) and δ are defined as follows:

- $\delta(q_0, a) = (q_1, X, R)$ // first a is replaced by X
- $\delta(q_1, a) = (q_1, a, R)$ and $\delta(q_1, b) = (q_1, b, R)$ // skip all a's and b's and move right so it reaches to symbol B

- $\delta(q_1, B) = (q_2, B, L)$ // find the last b
- $\delta(q_2, b) = (q_3, B, L)$ // last b is replaced by B and move left
- $\delta(q_3, b) = (q_3, b, L)$ and $\delta(q_3, a) = (q_3, a, L)$ // skip all a's and b's and move left and reaches to X
- $\delta(q_3, X) = (q_0, X, R)$ // X remains X and move right
- $\delta(q_0, B) = (q_4, B, R)$ // B remains B and halt.

So, F = $\{q_4\}$ or halting state

State Diagram

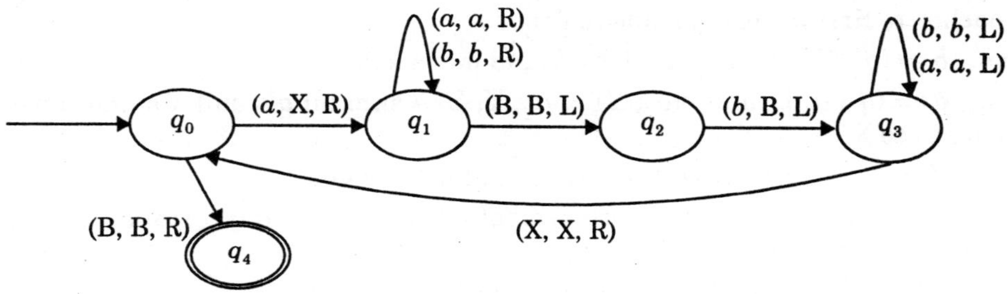

Fig. 12.8

Note, the definitions of δ defined above are the only possibilities for the acceptance of the strings of L. For rest of the moves (not defined above) machine will crashes or disappear.

ID's View

(Start) q_0 **a** $a\,b\,b \vdash$ X q_1 **a** $b\,b \vdash$ X $a\,q_1$ $b\,b \vdash$ X $a\,q_1$ **b** $b \vdash$ X $a\,b\,q_1$ **b** $\vdash$ X $a\,b\,b\,q_1$ **B** $\vdash$ X $a\,b\,q_2$ **b** $\vdash$ X $a\,q_3$ **b** $\vdash$ X q_3 **a** $b \vdash q_3$ **X** $a\,b \vdash$ X q_0 **a** $b \vdash$ X X q_1 **b** $\vdash$ X X $b\,q_1$ **B** $\vdash$ X X q_2 **b** $\vdash$ X q_3 **X** $\vdash$ X X q_0 **B** $\vdash$ X X B q_4 B **(Halt)**

12.3 LANGUAGE OF A TURING MACHINE

Let M be a Turing machine defined as, M = (Q, Σ, Γ, B, q_0, δ, F) then language of M be L(M), where

$$L(M) = \{x \in \Sigma^* \mid q_0\, x \vdash^* \alpha_1\, p\, \alpha_2 \text{ and } p \in F\} \text{ where } \alpha_1, \alpha_2 \in \Gamma^*$$

It means that the string x is in the language of machine if from starting state q_0 machine M reaches to the state p (final state) after scanning the complete string x (whatever the tape symbols it left α_1 and α_2)

The language of the Turing machine is the recursive enumerable language. The acceptance that is commonly used for turing machines is the acceptance by halting. It means turing machine halts if there is no move define further in that instance of problem state. Alternatively we can always assume that a turing machine always halts when it is in an accepting state.

In fact a class of languages whose turing machine halts, regardless of whether or not it reaches an accepting state are called recursive languages. The other class of languages consists of there recursive enumerable languages that are not accepted by any turing machine with the guarantee of halting. These languages are accepted in an in convenient way.

Example 12.1. *Construct the TM for the language* $L = \{a^i\, b^i \mid i \geq 1\}$.

Sol. We can construct the TM for L by applying different logic used in the previous example, i.e., for counting equal number of a's followed by b's we go through following steps:

- replace starting symbol a by X, then reaches to the first b and replace by Y
- move back and find next starting symbol a and repeat the previous step
- until found X followed by Y

Lets input string is '$aabb$'. Then applying above steps it will converted on 'XXYY'

The machine will terminate certainly with the condition that last X is followed by Y.

Let q_0 be the starting state, $Q = \{q_0, q_1, q_2, q_3, q_4\}$, $\Sigma = \{a, b\}$, $\Gamma = \{a, b, X, Y, B\}$ and halting state $F = \{q_4\}$ then ***Transition function*** (∂) are follows:

- $\delta(q_0, a) = (q_1, X, R)$
- $\delta(q_1, a) = (q_1, a, R)$ and $\delta(q_1, Y) = (q_1, Y, R)$ // skip all a's and Y's and move right and reaches to first b (corresponds to first a)
- $\delta(q_1, b) = (q_2, Y, L)$ // replace b by Y and move left
- $\delta(q_2, a) = (q_2, a, L)$ and $\delta(q_2, Y) = (q_2, Y, L)$ // skip all a's and Y's and move left and reaches to X
- $\delta(q_2, X) = (q_0, X, R)$ // X will remain X and move right
- $\delta(q_0, Y) = (q_3, Y, R)$ // if no more symbol left then machine certainly reaches to Y It remains Y and move to right
- $\delta(q_3, Y) = (q_3, Y, R)$ // skip all Y's and reaches to blank
- $\delta(q_3, B) = (q_4, B, R)$ // blank remains blank and halt

State Diagram

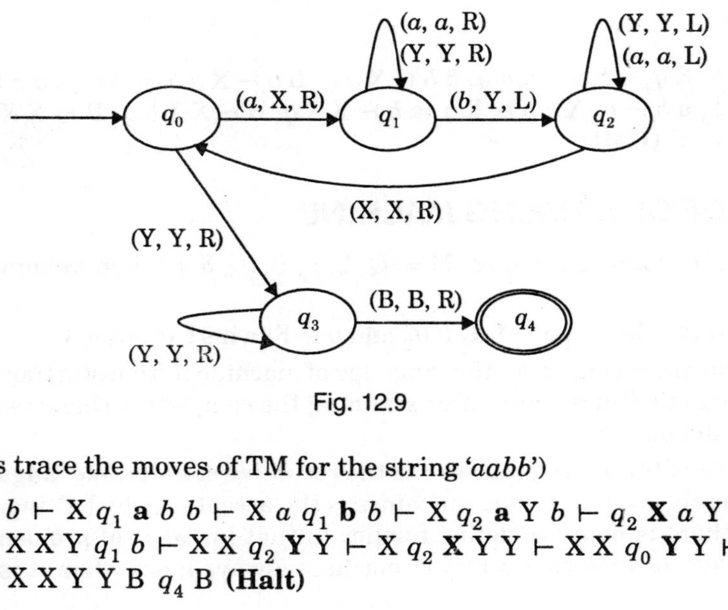

Fig. 12.9

ID View's (Let's trace the moves of TM for the string '$aabb$')

(Start) q_0 **a** $a\ b\ b \vdash$ X q_1 **a** $b\ b \vdash$ X a q_1 **b** $b \vdash$ X q_2 **a** Y $b \vdash$ q_2 **X** a Y $b \vdash$ X q_0 **a** Y b $\vdash$ X X q_1 **Y** $b \vdash$ X X Y q_1 $b \vdash$ X X q_2 **Y** Y $\vdash$ X q_2 **X** Y Y $\vdash$ X X q_0 **Y** Y $\vdash$ X X Y q_3 **Y** $\vdash$ X X Y Y q_3 **B** $\vdash$ X X Y Y B q_4 B **(Halt)**

Example 12.2. *Construct the Turing machine for the Context Sensitive Language*

$$L = \{a^i\ b^i\ a^i \mid i \geq 0\}.$$

Sol. Here the language L consist of strings of equal number of a's followed by equal number of b's followed by equal number of a's resembling {aba, $aabbaa$, $aaabbbaaa$....}. So to check up this condition we apply following logic:

- The first symbol a is replaced by X (we count one a); skip all a's and reaches to last b; replace it by a (now we have counted 2a's); Corresponding to it last 2a's converted to blank,

$a\ a\ a\ b\ b\ b\ a\ a\ a$

$X\ a\ a\ b\ b\ a\ a\ B\ B$

- Repeat the previous step for next starting symbol a and so on we get

$X\ a\ a\ b\ b\ a\ a\ B\ B$ and similarly $X\ X\ a\ b\ a\ B\ B\ B\ B$

$X\ X\ a\ b\ a\ B\ B\ B\ B \Rightarrow X\ X\ X\ a\ a\ B\ B\ B\ B$

$\Rightarrow X\ X\ X\ B\ B\ B\ B\ B\ B$

- Therefore, the string is accepted (counted successfully) if and only if the machine returns the string of tape symbols X's followed by B's (blank).

Transition function (∂)

Assume Turing machine $M = (\{q_1, q_2, q_3, q_4, q_5, q_6, q_7, q_8\}, \{a, b\}, \{a, b, X, B\}, B, q_0, \partial, \{q_8\})$ where δ's are follows,

- $\delta(q_0, a) = (q_1, X, R)$
- $\delta(q_1, a) = (q_1, a, R)$ // skip all a's and reaches to first symbol b
- $\delta(q_1, b) = (q_2, b, R)$ // b remain b and move right
- $\delta(q_2, b) = (q_2, b, R)$ // skip all b's and reaches to first a
- $\delta(q_2, a) = (q_3, a, L)$ // reaches to last b
- $\delta(q_3, b) = (q_4, a, R)$ // replace last b by a
- $\delta(q_4, a) = (q_4, a, R)$ // skip all a's and move right so it reaches to blank
- $\delta(q_4, B) = (q_5, B, L)$ // reaches to last a
- $\delta(q_5, a) = (q_6, B, L)$ // replace it by Blank and move left
- $\delta(q_6, a) = (q_7, B, L)$ // replace one more a by Blank and move left
- $\delta(q_7, a) = (q_7, a, L)$ and $\delta(q_7, b) = (q_7, b, L)$ // skip all a's and b's and reaches to X
- $\delta(q_7, X) = (q_0, X, R)$ // X remain X and ready for next iteration and so on it reaches to symbol blank
- $\delta(q_0, B) = (q_8, B, R)$ // if no more input symbol left so machine halts or terminates successfully.

State Diagram

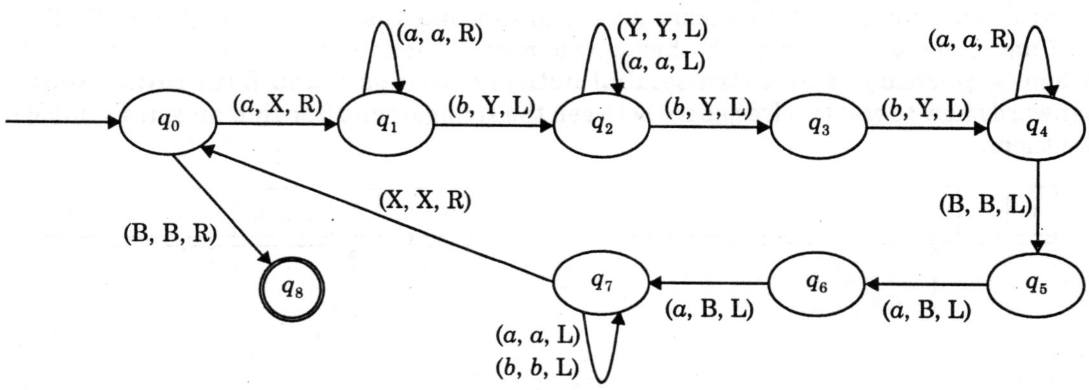

Fig. 12.10

Example 12.3. *Construct the Turing machine for the language L = {$a^i b^i c^i$ | $i \geq 0$}.*

Sol. The construction of Turing machine M is similar to the previous example. Here the machine count the equal number of *a*'s followed by same number of *b*'s followed by same number of *c*'s. By applying the similar logic we proceed as,

- Replace first a by X (count one *a*); reaches to last *b*; replace last *b* by c(counted symbols are 2); replaces last 2 *c*'s to B (blank) corresponding to the 2 symbols that are first *a* and last *b*.
- Repeat the previous step until the string of tape symbol X's followed by B's will found.

~~a~~ a a b b ~~b~~ c ¢ ¢

⇒ X ~~a~~ a b ~~b~~ ¢ ¢ B B

⇒ X X ~~a~~ ~~b~~ c B B B B

⇒ X X X ¢ ¢ B B B B ⇒ X X X B B B B B B

In the similar fashion we define the transition functions and thus we obtain the state diagram of the Turing machine which is shown in Fig. 12.11.

State Diagram

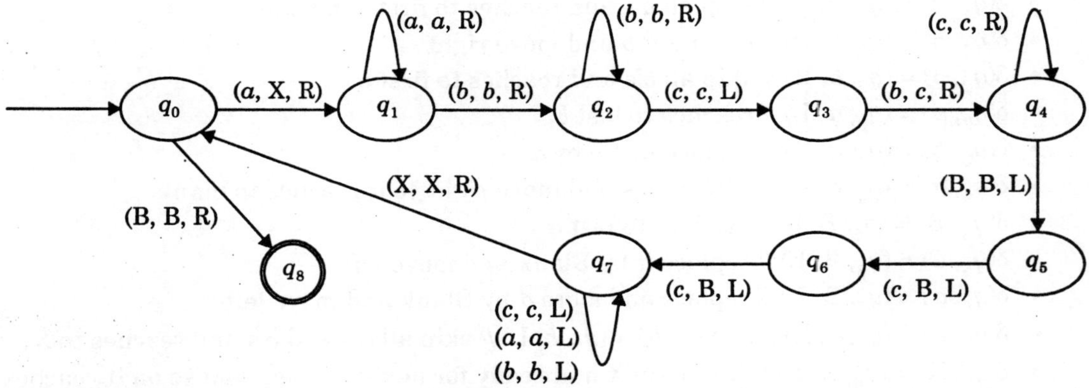

Fig. 12.11

12.4 GENERAL PROBLEMS OF A TURING MACHINE

Now we discuss the general problems of a turing machine that is if, $\alpha q \beta \vdash^* \alpha p \xi \beta$ where $\alpha, \beta \in \Gamma^*$ and q and $p \in Q$ and $\xi \in \Sigma$; then how a machine handle this situation. The fact of the problem is, **pushing of an extra symbol between strings α and β (in finite steps)**. In other words how to create a free space between the strings α and β so that an extra symbol will place them.

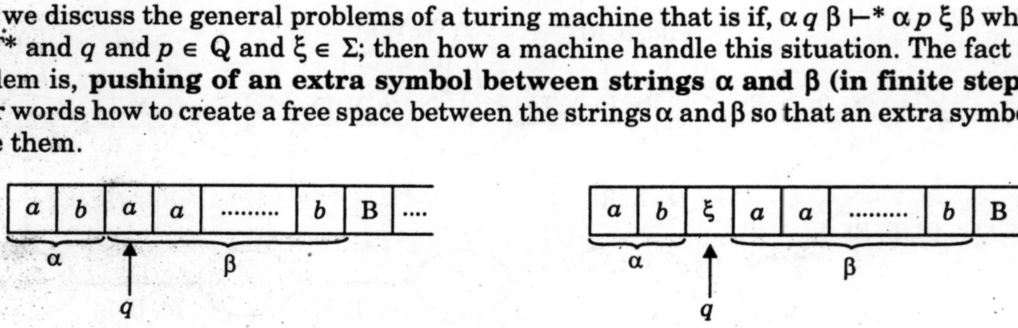

(*a*) (*b*)

Fig. 12.12

That is, to shift the complete string β *one cell right* and to push a symbol ξ before β.

Here we assume that set of input string $\Sigma = \{a, b\}$.

Fig. 12.13 shows the transition diagram of the Turing machine M from state q which reaches to state p in finite steps and creates a blank space before string b that is replaced by an extra symbol ξ and tape head move forward.

State Diagram

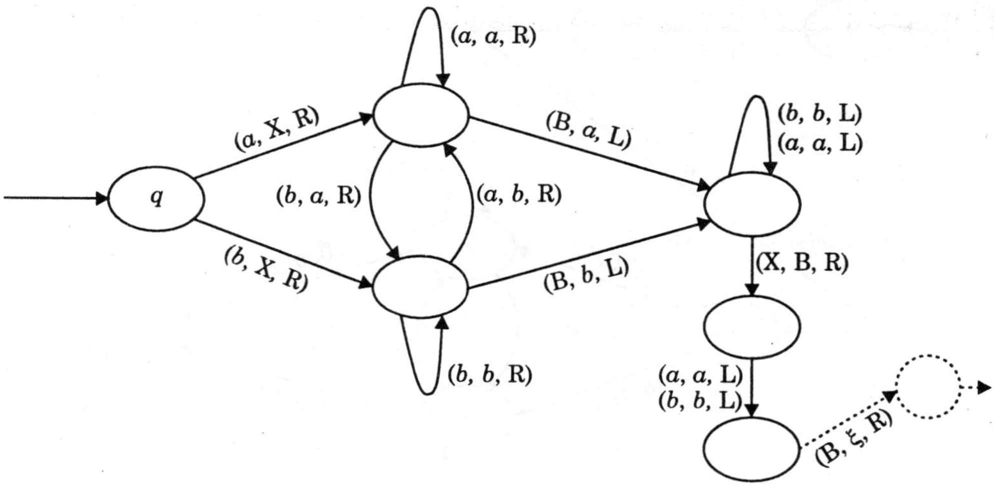

Fig. 12.13

A similar problem is occasionally facing, **how to shift one cell left of the loaded string** on the tape i.e.

$\alpha\, q\, \xi\, \beta \vdash^* \alpha\, p\, \beta$ where $\alpha, \beta \in \Gamma^*$ and p & $q \in Q$ and $\xi \in \{a, b\}$.

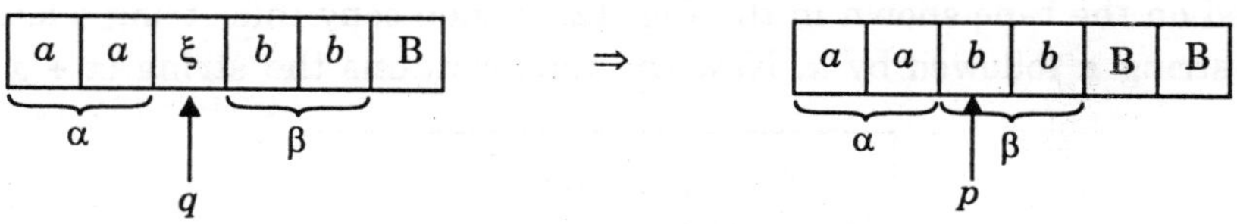

Fig. 12.14

Here machine is in state q and ready to read the string β′ where $\beta' = \xi\, b$ (*a* symbol ξ and substring β) and in finite steps it reaches to state p and ready to read the remaining string β.

Fig. 12.15 shows the state diagram of the Turing machine.

Following are the steps:

- Machine reads the first symbol ξ that is either symbol a or b. This cell should be blank. So create a blank space at this cell by replacing symbol a or b to B and move right.
- Skip all a's and b's so as reaches to blank.
- Replace the last symbol either a or b to blank and follow the move:
- r to p through s if β is a string of all a's,

- *r* to *p* through *t* if β is a string of all *b*'s,
- *r* to *p* through *s* and *t* as required for mix strings.

State Diagram

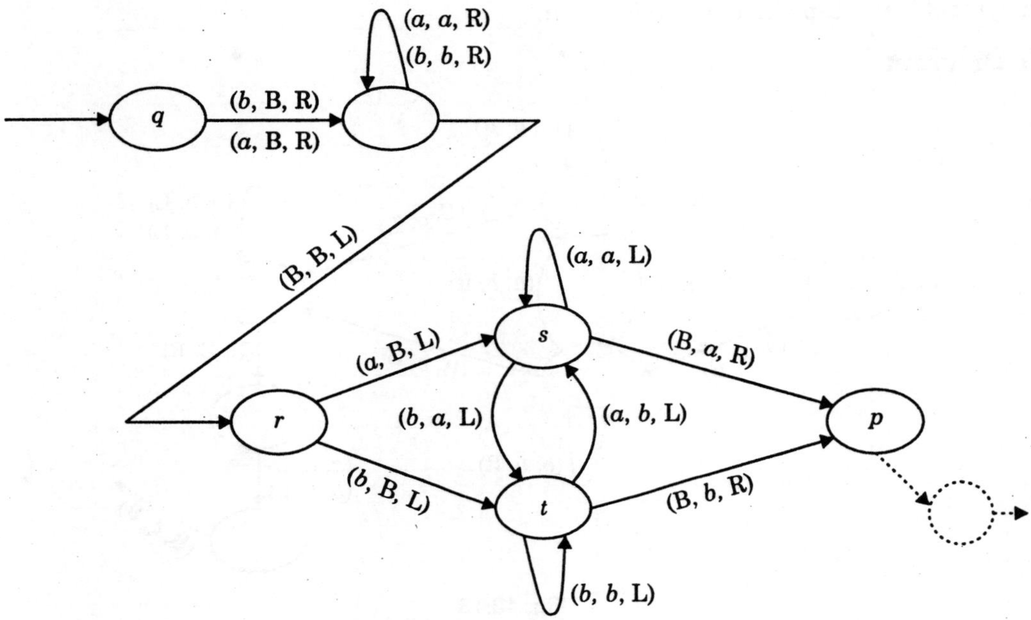

Fig. 12.15

Let us solve another problem of Turing machine. This problem states how to ***copying the block*** (that is loaded the tape symbol string) i.e. if x is the string formed over symbols $\{a, b\}$ is loaded on the tape shown in the Fig. 12.14 then copy this string x s.t. the resulting string is the string x followed by x. Now the tape contains the string $(x + x)$.

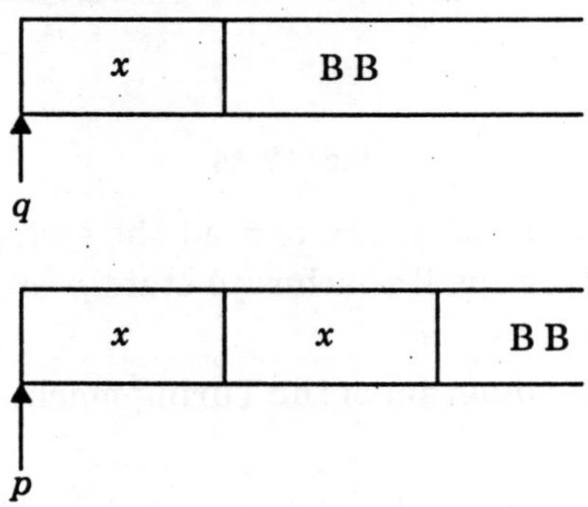

Fig. 12.16

A simple way to construct the Turing machine for copying the string by assuming that a cell is blank before the string x so ID of the machine would be $q \text{ B } x \vdash^* p \text{ B } x \text{ B } x$

The state diagram of the Turing machine is shown in Fig. 12.17

State Diagram

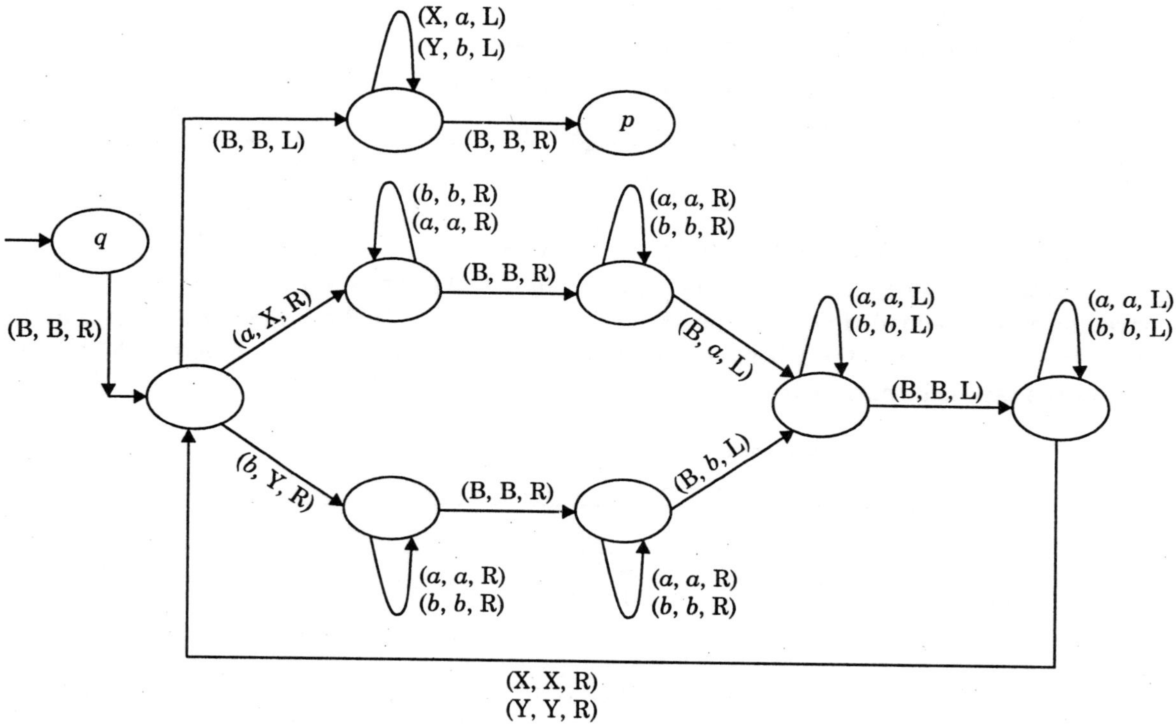

Fig. 12.17

12.5 TURING MACHINE IS THE COMPUTER OF NATURAL FUNCTIONS

Let f be a function defined on natural numbers N such that

$$f : N^k = N \qquad \text{(for arbitrary } k)$$

Alternatively, we can represent the function $f(x_1, x_2, \ldots\ldots x_k) = y$. Reader must remind that functions can be classified into total functions and partial functions. Total functions are those functions which are defined for all input parameters. Conversely, if the functions are not defined for all input parameters then those functions are called partial functions. For example, the function

$$f(x_1, x_2, \ldots\ldots x_k) = x_1/x_2\,; \quad \text{if } x_2 \neq 0$$

is an partial function. Natural functions can be evaluated by the Turing machine. For, total functions we always construct a recursive Turing machine while for the partial functions we can construct a Turing machine which never stop.

Procedure for Computation of Natural functions

Consider an natural function $f(u, v) = w$, i.e., u, v and $w \in$ N, where u and v are two inputs and w is the output of the function these are all decimal numbers. We make assumption that decimal numbers are represented by a stream of zeros, for example,

Number 0 is represented by	0
Number 1 is represented by	00
Number 2 is represented by	000
Number 3 is represented by	0000
... .	...
... .	...
... .	...
Number k is represented by	$(k + 1)$ 0's

Thus number u and v are represented by $(u + 1)$ 0's and $(v + 1)$ 0's respectively. These streams of 0's are loaded on the tape of the Turing machine. To distinguish numbers u and v we introduced a separator 1 between them. This number 1 is called the *breaker*. Fig. 12.18 shows the tape cells entries before the start of the machine.

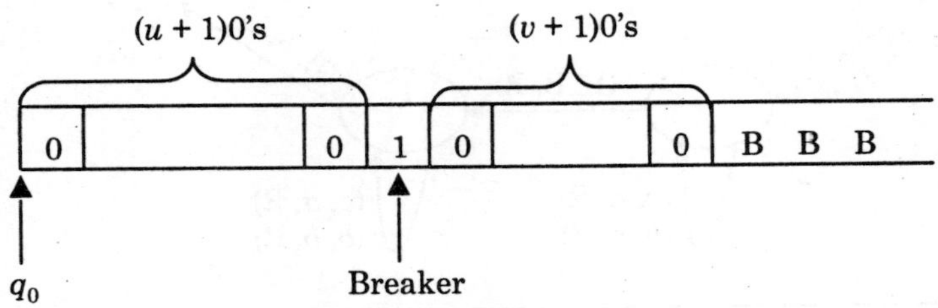

Fig. 12.18

Fig. 12.19 shows the situation of the Turing machine computation for the function f which is outputted w i.e., a stream of $(w + 1)$ 0's in finite steps, where X's are the tape symbols that comes after the replacement of input symbol 0's.

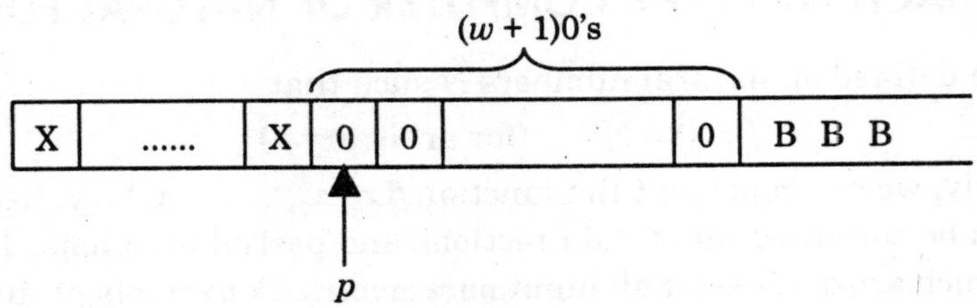

Fig 12.19

Consider an example to construct a Turing machine for the function f which evaluate the addition of two numbers x_1 and x_2, i.e.,

$$f(x_1, x_2) = x_1 + x_2$$

Since, f is the natural function so we can construct an equivalent Turing machine for the addition of two numbers x_1, x_2. As per the requirement we can assume that numbers x_1 and x_2 are represented by $(x_1 + 1)$ 0's and $(x_2 + 1)$ 0's and these streams of 0's are to be placed on the tape cells of the machine with the breaker 1. Fig 12.20 pictured the above situation.

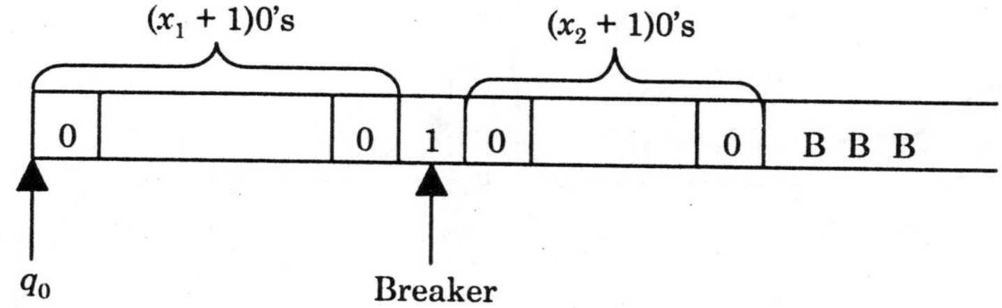

Fig. 12.20

Turing machine starts the computation over input strings and at instance of state $\{q_2\}$ it counts number of 0's are $(x_1 + 1 + x_2 + 1)$. Since it has an extra 0 so this extra 0 will be replaced by symbol blank (B). Thus, at state $\{q_4\}$ numbers of 0's counted are $(x_1 + x_2 + 1)$. Finally, machine stops at the state $\{q_5\}$ which is the left most end of the tape cells. Fig. 20.21 shows the state diagram of the Turing machine for the function *f*.

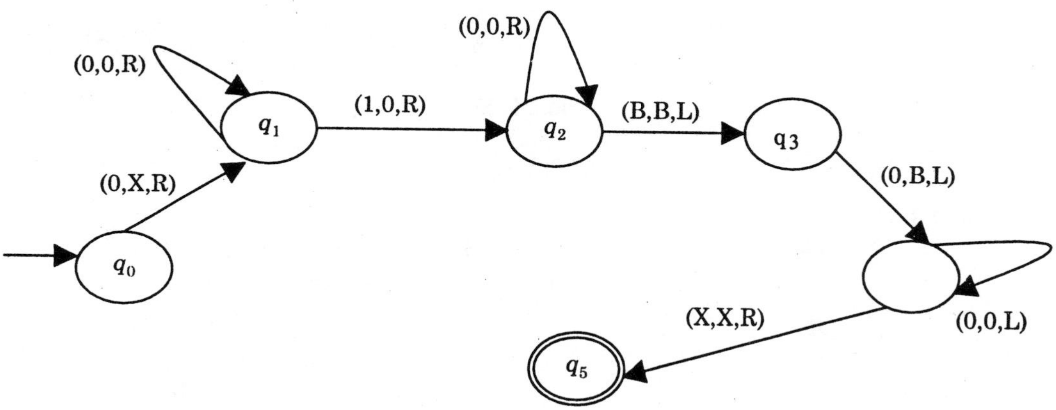

Fig. 12.21

Example 12.4 *Construct the Turing machine for the natural function ($f : N^k \rightarrow N$) which evaluates the proper subtraction, i.e., if x and y are two numbers then $f(x, y) = x - y$ if $x \geq y$, and $f(x, y) = 0$, otherwise.*

Sol. Assume Turing machine starts the computation from the starting state q_0. Since tape cells contain a total of $(x + 1)$ 0's followed by $(y + 1)$ 0's and between them a breaker of symbol 1. The machine computes the subtraction between numbers x and y using the following computation logic i.e.,

- For the case if $x \geq y$ then $(y + 1)$ 0's must be crossed and they are all converted to blanks with the corresponding 0's of the string x which are converted to symbols X's. Fig. 12.22 shows the snapshots (from state q_0 to q_4 and returned to q_0) of the state diagram for the discussed situation. Thus we have remaining 0's of the string x including a symbol 1. Symbol 1 is converted to 0 and since we have a lack of 0 so one symbol X is also converted to 0. Thus machine will return a total of $(x - y + 1)$ 0's hence it will stop at state q_6. The state diagram of the machine is shown in Fig. 12.22.
- For the case if $x < y$ then result should be 0. To implement this case, we will found that in between the computation of crossing of 0's of the string y corresponding to 0's of string x if there is no more 0's left in the string x for the remaining 0's of string y then machine will search a new path. The state diagram of the Fig. 12.23 shows that there is a new path from the state q_0 to q_8 and then halting state q_6 for this situation.

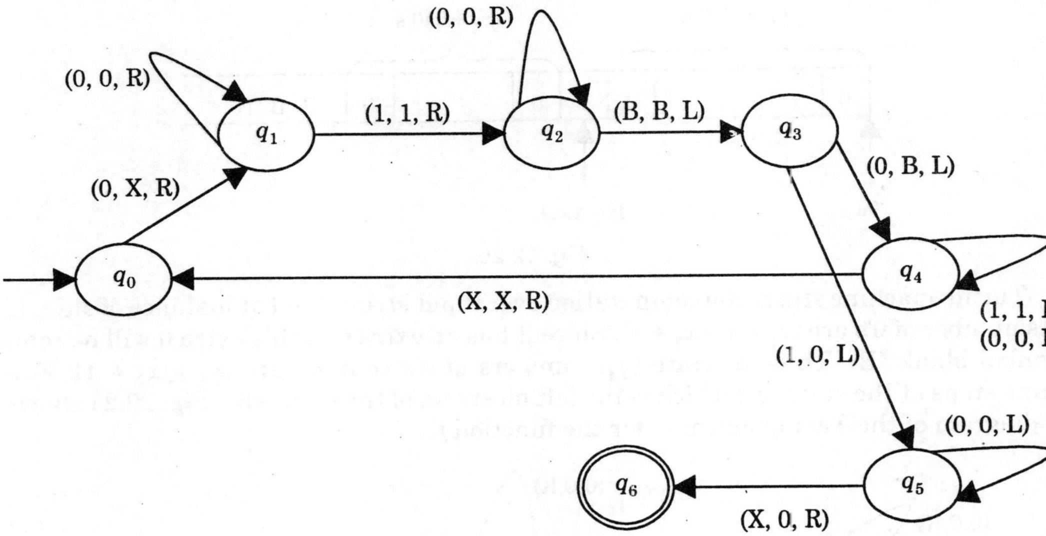

Fig. 12.22

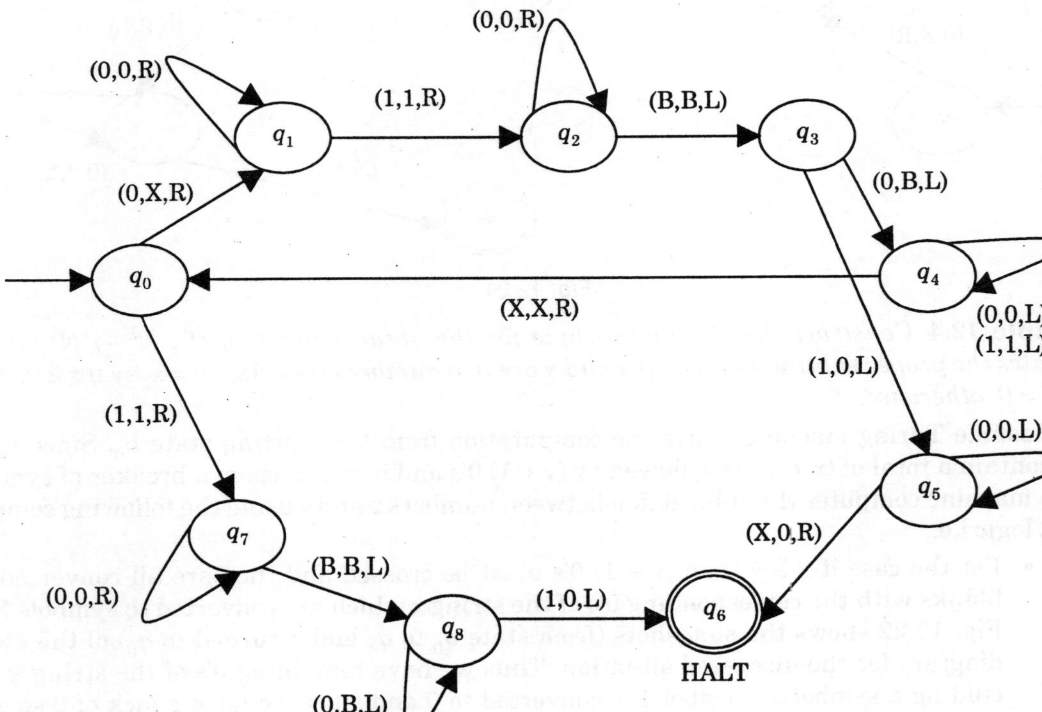

Fig. 12.23

Example 12.5 ***Construct the Turing machine for the natural function ($f : N^k \to N$) which evaluates the multiplication of two numbers, i.e., for numbers x and y, $f(x, y) = x * y$.***

Sol. Since the meaning of multiplication of $x * y$ is the successive addition of x, y times. This is one of the computation logic which to determine the multiplication of two numbers. Initially tape cells contains $(x + 1)$ 0's corresponding to string x followed by a symbol 1 (breaker) and next to it symbol blanks. Now our task is to copy this block of $(x + 1)$ 0's, y times.

Thus, Turing machine starts the computation over the string x and it copy the block according to the state diagram shown in Fig. 12.24.

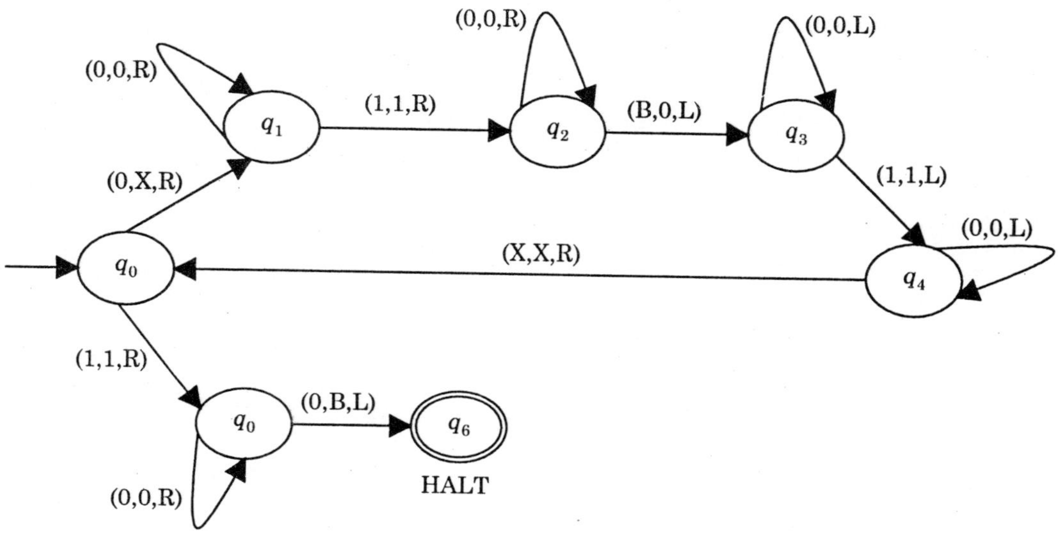

Fig. 12.24

This state diagram will copy the string x once hence, repetition of this sequence y times will compute the required result i.e., $x * y$.

EXERCISES

12.1 Construct the TM for the following languages over {0, 1}.

(*i*) L = {x/x contains the substring 000} (*ii*) L = {x/x is palindrome}

(*iii*) L = {$w\ w/w \in \{0, 1\}^*$} (*iv*) L = {$w\ w^{Rev}/w \in \{0, 1\}^*$}

(*v*) L = {$w\ c\ w^{Rev}/w \in \{0, 1\}^*$} (*vi*) L = {$w\ w\ w/w \in \{0, 1\}^*$}

12.2 Construct the TM for languages L_1 and L_2.

(*i*) $L_1 = \{0^n\ 1^n\ 2^n/n \geq 1\}$ (*ii*) $L_2 = \{0^n\ 1^n\ 2^n/n \geq 0\}$

12.3 Construct the TM that computes the indicated functions ($f : N^k \to N$), where $x, y, z \in N$.

(*i*) $f(x) = x + 7$ (*ii*) $f(x) = x^3$

(*iii*) $f(x) = x$ ***mod*** 7 (*iv*) $f(x, y) = x^2 + xy$

(*v*) $f(x, y, z) = x + 2y + 3z$ (*vi*) $f(x, y, z) = 2x + 3y + z^2$

(*vii*) $f(x)$ = smallest integer greater then or equal to $\log_2 (x + 1)$, i.e.,

$f(0) = 0, f(1) = 1, f(2) = f(3) = 2, f(4) = \ldots = f(7) = 3$, and so on.

12.4 Consider f_1 and f_2 are two natural functions that are computed by TMs M_1 and M_2 respectively. Construct a TM that computes each of the following functions,

(*i*) $f_1 + f_2$ (*ii*) $f_1 - f_2$

(*iii*) mod (f_1, f_2) (*iv*) max (f_1, f_2)

(*v*) min (f_1, f_2).

Boolean Algebra

Appendix

A Boolean Algebra

A.1 INTRODUCTION

Like any other mathematical system, *Boolean algebra,* is defined by a set of elements X, a set of operators Y, and a set of postulates (axioms) that defines the properties of X and Y. A *set* is a collection of objects sharing a common property. Set of *operators* Y = {**AND, OR, NOT**}, where **AND** and **OR** are binary operators represented by ' . ' and '+' respectively, and **NOT** is a unary operator represented by '''. The *postulates* are the basic assumptions of the algebraic structures on which it is possible to construe the rules and theorems of the system. The postulates need no proof. It provides the basis to the theorems. Here we summarize some of the common postulates used by various algebraic structures:

I. *Closure.* The operators ' . ' and '+' are closed, which means that if x and $y \in$ X, then $x + y$ and $x \,.\, y$ are also $\in$ X and unique.

II. *Commutative.* Binary operators ' . ' and '+' are commutative on a set X such that if x and $y \in$ X, then we have,

$$x + y = y + x \quad \text{and} \quad x \,.\, y = y \,.\, x$$

III. *Associative.* Binary operators ' . ' and '+' are associative on a set X such that if x, y and $z \in$ X, then we have,

$$x + (y + z) = (x + y) + z \quad \text{and} \quad x \,.\, (y \,.\, z) = (x \,.\, y) \,.\, z$$

IV. *Existence of an Identity Element.* There exists an identity element ę for $\forall x \in$ X with respect to binary operators ' . ' and '+' i.e.

$$x + ę = ę + x = x \quad \text{and} \quad x \,.\, ę = ę \,.\, x = x$$

For example, 0 is the identity element for algebraic structure (I, +), where I is the set of integers and '+' is the binary addition operation of integers i.e., $x + 0 = 0 + x = x$, for $\forall x \in$ I. Therefore, element 0 is called additive identity. (Reader self verify that element 1 will be a multiplicative identity).

V. *Existence of an Inverse Element.* There exists an inverse element $y \in$ X for $\forall x \in$ X with respect to binary operators ' . ' and '+' i.e.,

$$x + y = ę \quad \text{and} \quad x \,.\, y = ę$$

For example, the additive inverse define the subtraction s.t. $x + (-x) = ę$. Similarly, the multiplication inverse defines division s.t. $x \,.\, (1/x) = ę$.

VI. *Distributive Property.* Since ' . ' and '+' are two binary operators on set X, and if x, y and $z \in$ X then operator ' . ' is said to be distributive over operator '+' whenever,

$$x \,.\, (y + z) = x \,.\, y + x \,.\, z$$

and also operator '+' is distributive over operator ' . ' whenever,

$$x + (y \,.\, z) = (x + y) \,.\, (x + z)$$

One of the example of an algebraic system is a *field.* A field is defined by a set of elements, binary operations ' . ' and '+', a set of postulates 1 to 5, and combination of both operations fulfilling postulates 6. A field of real numbers is a common example consists of set of real numbers, with binary operations ' . ' and '+' which is the basis for ordinary algebra.

A.2 DEFINITION OF BOOLEAN ALGEBRA

A Boolean algebra is an algebraic structure denoted as (X, +, . , ′, 0, 1) in which (X, +, .) is a lattice, where X is a set of elements and binary operations + and . are called GLB and LUB respectively. 0 and 1 are least and greatest element of the poset (X, ≤). Fig. A.1 shows the postulates that are satisfied by Boolean algebra.

No.	Name of the postulates	Statement of the postulates	
		These pairs of laws are dual to each other	
1	***Closure***	Closure w.r.t. operator '+'	Closure w.r.t. operator ' . '
2	***Existence of an Identity Element***	There exist elements 0, 1 ∈ X such that for all $x \in$ X	
		$x + 0 = 0 + x = x$	$x \,.\, 1 = 1 \,.\, x = x$
3	***Commutative Law***	$x + y = y + x$	$x \,.\, y = y \,.\, x$
4	***Distributive Law***	$x \,.\, (y + z) = (x \,.\, y) + (x \,.\, z)$	$x + (y \,.\, z) = (x + y) \,.\, (x + z)$
5	***Complement***	$\forall x \in$ X there exist an element x' (known as complement of x) such that	
		$x + x' = 1$	$x \,.\, x' = 0$
6	***Uniqueness***	There exists at least two elements $x, y \in$ X i.e., $x \neq y$	

(Postulates 1–6 are called Huntington postulates)

Fig. A.1

We can formulate many Boolean algebra, depending upon the choice of the set X and the rules of operations. For example, a *two-value Boolean algebra* is defined on a set of two elements X = {0, 1}. The operations (+, . , ′) are shown in Fig. A.2 (*a*), (*b*) and (*c*) respectively. The two-value Boolean algebra is denoted by a Boolean structure ({0, 1}, +, . , ′ , 0, 1) and it satisfies all the postulates 1-6. It is the only Boolean structure whose representation is a chain.

x	y	$x + y$
0	0	0
0	1	1
1	0	1
1	1	1

(*a*) operations same as OR

x	y	$x \,.\, y$
0	0	0
0	1	0
1	0	0
1	1	1

(*b*) operations same as AND

x	x'
0	1
1	0

(*c*) operations same as NOT

Fig. A.2

We can also verify that Huntington postulates 1–6 are satisfied by a two-value Boolean algebra ({0, 1}, +, ., ′, 0, 1), i.e.,

- Closure is obvious, because from the operations tables shown in Fig. A.2 we saw that result of each operation is either 0 or 1 that is in set X.

- Since, 0 + 0 = 0 and 0 + 1 = 0 + 1 = 1 (existence of an identity 0 for operation '+') and 1 . 1 = 1 and 0 . 1 = 1 . 0 = 0 (existence of an identity 1 for operation ' . ').
- Commutative law is obvious from the symmetry of the binary operations '+' and ' . ' shown in tables.
- Distribution law such that distribution of operation '.' over operation '+' such that $x . (y + z) = (x . y) + (x . z)$ hold valid. That can be verified from the same truth values shown in the column 5 and 8 of the table Fig. A.3.

x	y	z	y + z	x . (y + z)	x . y	x . z	(x . y) + (x . z)
0	0	0	0	***0***	0	0	***0***
0	0	1	1	***0***	0	0	***0***
0	1	0	1	***0***	0	0	***0***
0	1	1	1	***0***	0	0	***0***
1	0	0	0	***0***	0	0	***0***
1	0	1	1	***1***	0	1	***1***
1	1	0	1	***1***	1	0	***1***
1	1	1	1	***1***	1	1	***1***
1	2	3	4	***5***	6	7	***8***

← Column number

Fig. A.3

Similarly we can verify the distribution of the operation '+' over operation '.' using truth table.

- For the verification of **x** + x' = **1** (and $x . x' = 0$) the complement of the elements 0 and 1, since, **0** + 0′ = 0 + 1 = **1** and **1** + 1′ = 1 + 0 = **1** (and also 0 . 0′ = 0 . 1 = 0 and 1 . 1′ = 1 . 0 = 0).
- Since, set X = {0, 1} or the set contains unique elements i.e., 0 ≠ 1.

A.3 THEOREMS OF BOOLEAN ALGEBRA

Now we can discuss the basic theorems of Boolean algebra and its most common postulates. The postulates shown in the in the table (Fig. A.4) is abbreviated by P1 – P4 and the theorems by T1 – T6.

Abbreviation	Statement of Rules		Name
P1	$x + 0 = x$	$x . 1 = x$	
P2	$x + x' = 1$	$x . x' = 0$	
P3	$x + y = y + x$	$x . y = y . x$	Commutative
P4	$x . (y + z) = x . y + x . z$	$x + y . z = (x + y) . (x + z)$	Distributive
T1	$x + x = x$	$x . x = x$	
T2	$x + 1 = 1$	$x . 0 = 0$	
T3	$(x')' = x$		Involution
T4	$x + (y + z) = (x + y) + z$	$x . (y . z) = (x . y) . z$	Associative
T5	$(x + y)' = x' . y'$	$(x . y)' = x' + y'$	De Morgan's
T6	$x + x . y = x$	$x . (x + y) = x$	Absorption

Fig. A.4

Since, postulates are the basic axioms of algebraic structures and so they required no proof. We can prove the listed theorems from the given postulates.

(T1) *LHS*

$x + x = (x + x) . 1$	$\therefore x . 1 = x$	**P1**
$= (x + x) . (x + x')$	$\therefore x + x' = 1$	**P2**
$= x + x . x'$	$\therefore (x + y)(x + z) = x + y . z$	**P4**
$= x + 0$	$\therefore x . x' = 0$	**P2**
$= x$	$\therefore x + 0 = x$	**P1**

RHS *Hence proved.*

Dual part of Theorem T1 can be proved similarly such as,

(T1′) *LHS*

$x . x = x . x + 0$	$\therefore x + 0 = x$	**P1**
$= x . x + x . x'$	$\therefore x . x' = 0$	**P2**
$= x . (x + x')$	$\therefore x . y + x . z = x . (y + z)$	**P4**
$= x . 1$	$\therefore x + x' = 1$	**P2**
$= x$	$\therefore x . 1 = x$	**P1**

RHS *Hence, proved.*

(T2) *LHS*

$x + 1 = (x + 1) . 1$	$\therefore x .1 = x$	**P1**
$= (x + 1) . (x + x')$	$\therefore x + x' = 1$	**P2**
$= x + 1 . x'$	$\therefore (x + y) . (x + z) = x + y . z$	**P4**
$= x + x'$	$\therefore 1 . x' = x'$	**P1**
$= 1$	$\therefore x + x' = x$	**P2**

RHS *Hence, proved.*

(T2′) *LHS*

$x . 0 = (x . 0) + 0$	$\therefore x + 0 = x$	**P1**
$= (x . 0) + (x . x')$	$\therefore x . x' = 0$	**P2**
$= x . (x' + 0)$	$\therefore x . y + x . z = x . (y + z)$	**P4**
$= x . x'$	$\therefore x' + 0 = x'$	**P1**
$= 0$	$\therefore x . x' = 0$	**P2**

RHS *Hence, proved*

(T3) Since, $x + x' = 1$ and $x . x' = 0$ (*i*) **P2**

Define the complement of x i.e. x'. So to determine the complement of x' we have,

$(x')' + x' = 1$ and $(x')' . x' = 0$ (*ii*) **P2**

On comparing (*i*) and (*ii*) we obtain,

$$(x')' = x$$

Hence, proved.

Theorem involving 2/3 variables can be proved algebraically by using the postulates and the theorems proved above. Validity of the theorems T4 and T5 can be seen using truth table similar to the table shown in Fig. A.3. Next we shall discuss the proof of the theorem T6.

(T6) *LHS*

$x + x \,.\, y = x \,.\, 1 + x \,.\, y$	$\therefore x \,.\, 1 = x$	**P1**
$= x \,.\, (1 + y)$	$\therefore x \,.\, y + x \,.\, z = x \,.\, (y + z)$	**P4**
$= x \,.\, (y + 1)$	$\therefore x + y = y + x$	**P3**
$= x \,.\, 1$	$\therefore y + 1 = 1$	**T2**
$= x$	$\therefore x \,.\, 1 = x$	**P1**

RHS *Hence, proved.*

(T6′) *LHS*

$x \,.\, (x + y) = (x + 0) \,.\, (x + y)$	$\therefore x + 0 = x$	**P1**
$= x + 0 \,.\, y$	$\therefore x + y \,.\, z = (x + y) \,.\, (x + z)$	**P4**
$= x + 0$	$\therefore 0 \,.\, x = 0$	**T3**
$= x$	$\therefore x + 0 = x$	**P1**

RHS *Hence, proved.*

Duality Theorem

Every algebraic expression is construe from the postulates of the Boolean algebra remains valid if the both operators and identity elements are interchanged.

Principle of duality states that any Boolean expression remains true if AND, OR, 1, 0 are replaced by OR, AND, 0, 1 respectively. This principle reflects the obvious symmetry existing among the operators and the Boolean variables that allows many concepts to exist in dual form. For example, the pairs of the postulates listed in the table (Fig. A.4) are dual to each other, one may be obtained from other if operator '+' is interchange to ' . ' and replaces the identity element from 1 to 0 and vice versa.

A.4 BOOLEAN FUNCTIONS

A Boolean function is a Boolean expression consisting of one/more variables, binary operators (OR, AND) that are denoted by (+, .) respectively, unary operator (NOT) denoted by (′) and parenthesis. Since, Boolean variables can take value either 0 or 1, so truth value of the function is either 0 or 1 on each possible interpretation. The truth values of the Boolean function on various combinations of truth values of Boolean variables are obtained using truth table. For example, the truth values of following Boolean functions are shown in truth table in Fig. A.5.

(*i*) $F_1 = x\,y\,z$

(*ii*) $F_2 = x \,.\, y + y' \,.\, z$

(*iii*) $F_3 = (x + y) \,.\, (y + z')$

(*iv*) $F_4 = x + y \,.\, z$

x	y	z	F_1	F_2	F_3	F_4
0	0	0	1	0	0	0
0	0	1	0	1	0	0
0	1	0	0	0	1	0
0	1	1	0	0	0	1
1	0	0	0	0	1	1
1	0	1	0	1	0	1
1	1	0	0	1	1	1
1	1	1	0	1	0	1

Fig. A.5. Truth table for F_1, F_2, F_3, and F_4.

We can represent any Boolean function by using truth table. An n variable Boolean function must contain 2^n rows in the truth table starting from 0 to $2^n - 1$. It is also possible that two Boolean expressions can be instigating from same Boolean function because, by applying theorems and axioms of Boolean algebra, we can simplify the expression that return to some common function. Alternatively, two Boolean functions are said to be similar to each other if the truth values of both functions are same for all possible interpretations.

While, evaluating the Boolean function the precedence of the parenthesis is the highest, next precedence is of the complement, then the operator AND and finally the operator OR. Alternatively, the expression written inside the parenthesis will be evaluated first, follows the complement, then follows the ' . ' and finally follows the '+' operations.

A.5 SIMPLIFICATION OF BOOLEAN FUNCTIONS

The objective of the simplification of a Boolean function is to minimize the number of literals. Since, each term of Boolean function is implemented with a logic gate, and then each literal in the function designates an input to a gate. To, minimize the number of literals and the number of terms certainly trim down the circuit and equipments. Although it is not always possible to minimize both factors simultaneously.

We can simplify the Boolean function by using most common postulates and basic theorems of Boolean algebra through *trail & chance*. Of course, there is no specific procedure of deduction that yields the minimized expression. In the following example we can see that, by way of trail & chance we can simplify the Boolean function.

Example A.1 *Simplify the following Boolean functions to a minimum number of literals.*

1. $\mathbf{f = x\,y + x\,y'}$

$= x\,(y + y')$ **P4**

$= x\,.\,1$ **P2**

$= \mathbf{x}$ **P1**

2. $\mathbf{f = y\,(w\,z' + w\,z) + x\,y}$

$= y\,.\,w\,(z' + z) + x\,y$ **P2**

$= y\,.\,w\,.\,1 + x\,y$ **P1**

$= y\,w + x\,y$ **P1**

$= y\,w + y\,x$ **P3**

$= \mathbf{y\,(w + x)}$ **P4**

3. f = (x + y)′ . (x′ + y′)′

Simplification of such Boolean function can be easily done by using involution law (**T3**) which states that the complement of the complement is effectless i.e., if we take complement of complement of Boolean function f then we have,

$$(f')' = f$$

Thus $f' = ((x + y)' \,.\, (x' + y')')'$

$= ((x + y)')' + ((x' + y')')'$ **T5 (De Morgan's)**

$= (x + y) + (x' + y')$ **T3 (Involution)**

$= (x + x') + (y + y')$ **T4 (Associativity)**

$= 1 + 1$ **P2**

so $f' = 1$ **T2**

Further, if we take the complement of f' i.e.,

$(f')' = (1)' = 0$; then **f = 0.**

The complement of Boolean function can be obtained through straight forward way by interchanging the values 0's for 1's and 1's for 0's.

De Morgan's law (**T5**) using two binary variables x and y states that, $(x + y)' = x' \,.\, y'$ and also $(x \,.\, y)' = x' + y'$ that can be generalized for any number of binary variables i.e.,

$$(x_1 + x_2 + x_3 + \ldots\ldots\ldots\ldots + x_k)' = x_1' \,.\, x_2' \,.\, x_3' \ldots\ldots\ldots\ldots\ldots\ldots\ldots\ldots\ldots x_k'$$

and, $$(x_1 \,.\, x_2 \,.\, x_3 \,.\, \ldots\ldots\ldots\ldots\ldots\ldots\ldots \,.\, x_k)' = x_1' + x_2' + x_3' + \ldots\ldots + x_k'$$

The generalized form of De Morgan's law states that complement of an expression will interchange the binary operators '+' into ' . ' and vise versa and complement each literal.

Example A.2. *Find the complement and simplify the following Boolean functions.*

1. f = p q′ + r′ s′

Then complement of f is obtain as,

$f' = (p\,q' + r'\,s')' = (p\,q')' \,.\, (r'\,s')'$ **T5 (De Morgan's)**

= (p′ + q) . (r + s) **T5 & T3**

2. f = (q r′ + p′ s) . (p q′ + r s′)

Then complement of f is given as,

$f' = [(q\,r' + p'\,s) \,.\, (p\,q' + r\,s')]'$

$= (q\,r' + p'\,s)' + (p\,q' + r\,s')'$ **T5**

$= \text{X} + \text{Y}$

where, we assume, $(q\,r' + p'\,s)' = \text{X}$ and $(p\,q' + r\,s')' = \text{Y}$ and solve separately,

So we have,

$\text{X} = (q\,r' + p'\,s)' = (q\,r')' \,.\, (p'\,s)'$ **T5**

$= (q' + r) \,.\, (p + s')$ **T5 & T3**

$= (q' + r) \,.\, p + (q' + r) \,.\, s'$ **P4**

$= q'\,p + r\,p + q'\,s' + r\,s'$

Similarly,

$\text{Y} = (p\,q' + r\,s')' = (p\,q')' \,.\, (r\,s')'$ **T5**

$= (p' + q) \,.\, (r' + s)$ **T5 & T3**

$= (p' + q) \,.\, r' + (p' + q) \,.\, s$ **P4**

$= p'\,r' + q\,r' + p'\,s + q\,s$

Then, $f' = X + Y = q'p + rp + q's' + rs' + p'r' + qr' + p's + qs$

$= \mathbf{1}$ (reader may solve the remaining part of the expression to verify the result).

3. $\mathbf{f = [(p\,q')\,p] \times [(p\,q)'\,q]}$

Then complement of f will be obtain as,

$$f' = \{[(p\,q')\,p]\ .\ [(p\,q)'\,q]\}'$$

$= [(p\,q')\,p]' + [(p\,q)'\,q]'$	**T5**
$= [(p\,q')' + p'] + [(p\,q) + q']$	**T5 & T3**
$= [p' + q + p'] + [p\,q + q']$	**T5 & T3**
$= [p' + q] + [p\,q + q']$	**T1**
$= [p' + p\,q] + [q + q']$	**T4**
$= [p' + p\,q] + 1$	**P2**
$= [p' + p\,q] + 1$	**P2**
$= 1$	**T2**

Hence, $\mathbf{f' = 1}$.

A.6 FORMS OF BOOLEAN FUNCTIONS

A Boolean function can be expressed in any of the two forms, (1) Canonical form, or (2) Standard form. The class of canonical form further slices into (1.1) sum of minterms, or (1.2) product of maxterms. In the *sum of minterms* form, by 'sum' meant **OR**ing of minterms, where each minterm is obtained from an **AND** term of the n variables that are either prime (*true*) or unprimed (*false*). Similarly, in the product of maxterms form, by 'product' meant **AND**ing of maxterms, where each maxterm is obtained from an **OR** term of n variables that are being prime or unprimed.

So in general, n variables can be combined to form 2^n minterms and 2^n maxterms. The 2^n different minterms and maxterms can be determined by the method similar to one shown in Fig. A.6 for three variables that has 8 (= 2^3) minterms and 8 (= 2^3) maxterms.

x	y	z	Minterms		Maxterms	
			Term	**Symbol**	**Term**	**Symbol**
0	0	0	m_0	$x'.y'.z'$	M_0	$x+y+z$
0	0	1	m_1	$x'.y'.z$	M_1	$x+y+z'$
0	1	0	m_2	$x'.y.z'$	M_0	$x+y'+z$
0	1	1	m_3	$x'.y.z$	M_0	$x+y'+z'$
1	0	0	m_4	$x.y'.z'$	M_0	$x'+y+z$
1	0	1	m_5	$x.y'.z$	M_0	$x'+y+z'$
1	1	0	m_6	$x.y.z'$	M_0	$x'+y'+z$
1	1	1	m_7	$x.y.z$	M_0	$x'+y'+z'$

Fig. A.6

Thus we can express the Boolean function f containing n variables $(x_1, x_2, \ldots\ldots\ldots\ldots x_n)$ in sum of minterms or product of maxterms respectively as,

$$f(x_1, x_2, \ldots\ldots\ldots\ldots x_n) = \Sigma\, m_k \qquad \ldots(I)$$

and $$f(x_1, x_2, \ldots\ldots\ldots\ldots x_n) = \Pi\, m_k \qquad \ldots(II)$$

Where, we take those k's $(0 \le k \le 2^n - 1)$ for which combination of variables results truth value 1. The symbols Σ and Π denotes the logical sum (**OR**) and product (**AND**) operations. It is also observed from the truth table that each maxterm is the complement of its corresponding minterms, and vice-versa. A Boolean function expressed as a sum of minterms or product of maxterms is said to be in canonical form.

Example A.3. *Express the Boolean function f_1 and f_2 shown in Fig. A.7 in sum of minterms and product of maxterms forms.*

x	y	z	f_1	f_2
0	0	0	1	0
0	0	1	1	0
0	1	0	1	0
0	1	1	0	1
1	0	0	0	1
1	0	1	0	1
1	1	0	0	1
1	1	1	0	1

Fig. A.7

Sol. Functions f_1 is of three variables x, y, and z. Since the combinations of terms $x'y'z'$, $x'y'z$, and $x'yz'$ of corresponding minterms m_0, m_1, and m_2 respectively yields the truth value of $f_1 = 1$. Thus we have,

$$f_1(x, y, z) = x'y'z' + x'y'z + x'yz'$$
$$= m_0 + m_1 + m_2;$$

or, equivalently it can be expressed as,

$$f_1(x, y, z) = \Sigma\,(0, 1, 2);$$

Now to express the complement of function f_1, we consider those minterms for which combination of variables results truth value 0 in the f_1 such that $m_3, \ldots m_7$.

So, we have $$f_1'(x, y, z) = m_3 + m_4 + m_5 + m_6 + m_7 = \Sigma\,(3, 4, 5, 6, 7);$$
$$= x'yz + xy'z' + xy'z + xyz' + xyz$$

Since, $(f_1')' = f$ **T3 (Involution)**

Thus we obtain,

$$(f_1'(x, y, z))' = (x'yz + xy'z' + xy'z + xyz' + xyz)'$$
$$f_1(x, y, z) = (x'yz)' \,.\, (xy'z')' \,.\, (xy'z)' \,.\, (xyz')' \,.\, (xyz)' \qquad \textbf{T5 (De Morgan's)}$$
$$= (x + y' + z') \,.\, (x' + y + z) \,.\, (x' + y + z') \,.\, (x' + y' + z) \,.\, (x' + y' + z')$$

T5 (DeM)

$$= M_3 \;.\; M_4 \;.\; M_5 \;.\; M_6 \;.\; M_7$$

(Product of maxterms)

so, $$f_1(x, y, z) = \pi\,(3, 4, 5, 6, 7);$$

Similarly we can obtain,

$$f_2(x, y, z) = x'yz + xy'z' + xy'z + xyz' + xyz$$

$$= m_3 + m_4 + m_5 + m_6 + m_7;$$

or, $$= \Sigma\,(3, 4, 5, 6, 7);$$

and $$(f_2'(x, y, z))' = f_2(x, y, z) = \pi\,(0, 1, 2);$$

Therefore we can say that, $\mathbf{m_k}' = \mathbf{M_k}$; that is, maxterm with subscript k is a complement of the minterms with the same subscript k or conversely, minterms with subscript k is a complement of the maxterms of same subscript k. Therefore, Boolean function can be converted from one canonical form to other by simply interchanging the symbols Σ and Π and add the missing numbers that was not in the original form. One thing must be insured before finding of the missing terms that, sum of minterms and sum of maxterms should be 2^n for an n variables Boolean function.

Besides the canonical form representation of Boolean functions, there is another form to express the Boolean functions called ***standard form***, where each term may contain any number of literals. Standard form is of two types:

- Sum of Product (**SoP**)
- Product of Sum (**PoS**)

SoP (PoS) is similar to sum of minterms (product of maxterms) except that in SoP (PoS) each term of Boolean function may have any number of literals. For example,

$$f_1(x, y, z) = x + y\,z + x'\,y\,z \qquad \text{SoP}$$

$$f_2(x, y, z) = (x + y) \times z \times (x + y' + z) \qquad \text{PoS}$$

Any Boolean function expressed in SoP (PoS) where, product terms (sum terms) contains less literals than minterms (maxterms) could be expressed in sum of minterms (product of maxterms) by applying following procedure,

*Inspect the Boolean function and see, if it is in SoP (PoS) form, and if each term contains all the literals, then do nothing; Otherwise, missed one or more literals is/are **ANDed (ORed)** with an expression such as x + x' (x . x') where x is one of the missing literal.*

In the context of the statement calculus (discuss in next chapter 6) we may say that any statement formula can be expressed in either of any form (SoP/PoS). Therefore, it is convenient if we replace the word product by 'conjunction' and sum by 'disjunction'. While, SoP is also called ***disjunctive normal form*** (**DNF**) and PoS is also called as ***conjunctive normal form*** (**CNF**). Alternately, the sum of minterms is called ***'principle disjunctive normal form'*** (**PDNF**) and product of maxterms is called ***'principle conjunctive normal form'*** (**PCNF**).

Example A.4 *(i) Consider the Boolean function* $\boldsymbol{f_1(x, y, z) = x + y\,z + x'\,y\,z}$*; which is in standard form (SoP). Express f in a sum of minterms.*

Sol. Since, function contains three variables x, y, and z and the first term is missing of variables y and z so ***ANDed*** $(y + y')$ and $(z + z')$ in the first term. Similarly, ***ANDed*** $(x + x')$ in the second term and nothing ***ANDed*** in the third term. Thus, way obtain,

$$f_1(x, y, z) = x\,(y + y')\,(z + z') + (x + x')\,y\,z + x'\,y\,z$$

$$= xyz + xy'z + xyz' + xy'z' + xyz + x'yz + x'yz$$

Simplifying and removing those minterms that appears more than once and rearranging the minterms thus we obtain,

$$f_1(x, y, z) = x'yz + xy'z' + xy'z + xyz' + xyz$$

$$\boldsymbol{f_1(x, y, z) = \Sigma\,(3, 4, 5, 6, 7);} \quad \textbf{PDNF}$$

(*ii*) Consider the next Boolean function $\mathbf{f_2(x, y, z) = (x + y) . z . (x + y' + z)}$; that is in standard form (PoS). Express f in a product of maxterms. Since, function contains three variables x, y, and z and the first term is missing of variable z so ***ORed*** $(z\,z')$ in the first term. Similarly, ***ORed*** $(x\,x')$ and $(y\,y')$ in the second term and nothing ***ORed*** in the third term. Therefore, we obtain,

$$f_2(x, y, z) = (x + y + z\,z') \,.\, (x\,x' + y\,y' + z) \,.\, (x + y' + z)$$

Since,

$$(x + y + z\,z') = (x + y + z)\,(x + y + z'); \qquad \textbf{P4 [Distribution]}$$

and, $$(x\,x' + y\,y' + z) = (x + y\,y' + z)\,(x' + y\,y' + z) \qquad \textbf{P4 [Distribution]}$$
$$= (x + y + z)\,(x + y' + z)\,(x' + y + z)\,(x' + y' + z);$$

Combining all the maxterms and removing those maxterms that appear more than once, thus we obtain,

$$f_2(x, y, z) = (x + y + z)\,(x + y + z')\,(x + y' + z)\,(x' + y + z)\,(x' + y' + z);$$
$$= M_0 \,.\, M_1 \,.\, M_2 \,.\, M_4 \,.\, M_6$$

$\mathbf{f_2(x, y, z) = \Pi\ (0, 1, 2, 4, 6)}$; **PCNF**

Example A.5. *Express the following functions in a sum of minterms and a product of maxterms.*

(*i*) $\mathbf{f(r, s, t) = (r' + s)\,(s' + t)}$

Since, the Boolean function f is not in standard form (SoP/PoS) so use distributive law to remove parenthesis thus, we get the function is in standard form i.e.

$$f(r, s, t) = (r' + s)\,(s' + t)$$
$$= r'\,s' + s\,s' + r'\,t + s\,t \qquad \textbf{P4}$$
$$= r'\,s' + 0 + r'\,t + s\,t \qquad \therefore s, s' = 0 \quad \textbf{P2}$$
$$= r'\,s' + r'\,t + s\,t \qquad \therefore x + 0 = x \quad \textbf{P1}$$

(SoP form)

To express the function f in sum of minterms, we find that the missing variables in the first, second, and in the third terms are t, s, and r; therefore ***ANDed*** expressions are $(t + t')$, $(s + s')$, and $(r + r')$ respectively. Thus we have,

$$= r'\,s'\,(t + t') + r'(s + s')\,t + (r + r')\,s\,t$$
$$= r's't + r's't' + r's\,t + r's'\,t + r\,s\,t + r'\,s\,t \qquad \textbf{P4}$$

Simplifying and rearrange the minterms thus we obtain

$$= r's't' + r's't + r's\,t + r\,s\,t$$
$$(\therefore r's't + r's't = r's't \text{ and } r's\,t + r's\,t = r's\,t)\,\textbf{T1}$$

so, $$f(r, s, t) = r's't' + r's't + r's\,t + r\,s\,t$$

$\mathbf{f(r, s, t) = \Sigma\ (0, 1, 3, 7)}$; **PDNF**

Hence, $\mathbf{f(r, s, t) = \Pi\ (2, 4, 5, 6)}$; **PCNF**

(*ii*) $\mathbf{f(r, s, t) = 1}$

Since we know that sum of all minterms of a Boolean function of n variable is 1. Here function has three variables thus we have,

$$f(r, s, t) = r's'\,t' + r's't + r's\,t' + r'\,s\,t + r\,s'\,t' + r\,s'\,t + r\,s\,t' + r\,s\,t$$

Conversely, we can prove above fact also i.e.

$$f(r, s, t) = r's'\,t' + r's't + r's\,t' + r'\,s\,t + r\,s'\,t' + r\,s'\,t + r\,s\,t' + r\,s\,t$$
$$= r's'\,(t' + t) + r's\,(t' + t) + r\,s'\,(t' + t) + r\,s\,(t' + t)$$

$= r's' + r's + r s' + r s$ $\quad (\because t' + t = 1)$ **P2**

$= r' (s + s') + r (s' + s)$ **P4**

$= r' \times 1 + r \times 1$ **P2**

$= r' + r$ **P1**

$= 1$ **P2**

Therefore, **f(r, s, t) = 1 = Σ (0, 1, 2, 3, 4, 5, 6, 7); PDNF**

f(r, s, t) = 1; then no maxterms; PCNF

(*iii*) **p q + p′ q r**

We first express the equivalent PDNF formula from the given formula. Since the formula contains three variables and in the first term variable r is missing so ANDed the expression $(r + r')$ in this term. Thus we have,

$= p\, q\, .\, 1 + p'\, q\, r$ **P1**

$= p\, q\, (r + r') + p'\, q\, r$ **P2**

$= p\, q\, r + p\, q\, r' + p'\, q\, r$ **P4**

which, is an equivalent PDNF formula.

To obtain the equivalent PCNF formula we write the formula as,

$= p\, q + p'\, q\, r = (p\, q + p')\, (p\, q + q\, r)$ $\quad [\therefore x + y\, z = (x + y)\, (x + z)]$ **P4**

$= (p' + p\, q)\, (p\, q + q\, r)$ $\quad [\therefore x + y = y + x]$ **P3**

$= (p' + p)\, (p' + q)\, (p\, q + q\, r)$ **P4**

$= 1\, .\, (p' + q)\, (p\, q + q\, r)$ **P2**

$= (p' + q)\, (p\, q + q\, r)$ **P1**

$= (p' + q)\, (p\, q + q)\, (p\, q + r)$ **P4**

$= (p' + q)\, (q + p\, q)\, (p\, q + r)$ **P3**

$= (p' + q)\, (q + p)\, (q + q)\, (p\, q + r)$ **P4**

$= (p' + q)\, (q + p)\, q\, (p\, q + r)$ **T1**

$= (p' + q)\, (q + p)\, q\, (r + p\, q)$ **P3**

$= (p' + q)\, (q + p)\, q\, (r + p)\, (r + q)$ **P4**

Above formula is in CNF; to obtain the PCNF we find the missing variables in each terms. The missing variables from left to right terms are r, r, p and r, q, and p so, **ORed** the expressions $r\, r'$, $r\, r'$, $p\, p'$ and $r\, r'$, $q\, q'$, and $p\, p'$ respectively. Thus we have,

$= (p' + q + r\, r')\, (p + q + r\, r')\, (p\, p' + q + r\, r')\, (p + q\, q' + r)\, (p\, p' + q + r)$ **P3**

$= (p' + q + r)\, (p' + q + r')\, (p + q + r\, r')\, (p\, p' + q + r\, r')\, (p + q\, q' + r)\, (p\, p' + q + r)$ **P4**

$= (p' + q + r)(p' + q + r')(p + q + r)(p + q + r')(p\, p' + q + r\, r')(p + q\, q' + r)(p\, p' + q + r)$ **P4**

$= (p' + q + r)(p' + q + r')(p + q + r)(p + q + r')(p\, p' + q + r)(p\, p' + q + r')$
$(p + q\, q' + r)(p\, p' + q + r)$ **P4**

$= (p' + q + r)(p' + q + r')(p + q + r)(p + q + r')(p + q + r)(p' + q + r)$
$(p\, p' + q + r')(p + q\, q' + r)(p\, p' + q + r)$ **P4**

$= (p' + q + r)(p' + q + r')(p + q + r)(p + q + r')(p + q + r)(p' + q + r)(p + q + r')(p' + q + r)$
$(p + q\, q' + r)(p\, p' + q + r)$ **P4**

$= (p' + q + r)(p' + q + r')(p + q + r)(p + q + r')(p + q + r)(p' + q + r)(p + q + r')(p' + q + r)$
$(p + q + r)(p + q' + r)(p\, p' + q + r)$ **P4**

$$= (p' + q + r)(p' + q + r')(p + q + r)(p + q + r')(p + q + r)(p' + q + r)(p + q + r')(p' + q + r)$$
$$(p + q + r)(p + q' + r)(p + q + r)\,(p' + q + r) \quad \textbf{P4}$$

Rearrange the maxterms and remove those that are appears more than once, so we get the required PCNF,

$$= \mathbf{(p + q + r)\,(p + q + r')\,(p + q' + r)\,(p' + q + r)\,(p' + q + r')}$$

(*iv*) Express the function **f(x, y, z) = x** in PCNF.

Since, function contains three variables x, y, and z and the first term is missing of the variables y and z, so ORed the expression $y\,y'$ and $z\,z'$ in this term.

Thus we obtain,

$$f(x, y, z) = x + y\,y' + z\,z' \qquad [\because y\,y' = z\,z' = 0]\ \textbf{P2} \text{ and } [\because x + 0 = x]\ \textbf{P1}$$
$$= (x + y\,y' + z)\,(x + y\,y' + z') \qquad [\because x + y\,z = (x + y)(x + z)]\ \textbf{P4}$$
$$= (x + y + z)\,(x + y' + z)\,(x + y\,y' + z') \qquad \textbf{P4}$$
$$= (x + y + z)\,(x + y' + z)\,(x + y + z')\,(x + y' + z') \qquad \textbf{P4}$$
$$\mathbf{f(x, y, z) = (x + y + z)\,(x + y + z')\,(x + y' + z)\,(x + y' + z')} \qquad \textbf{P3}$$

PCNF

(*v*) Express function **f(x, y, z) = (x + y)′** in PCNF.

$$F(x, y, z) = (x + y)'$$
$$= (x')\,(y') \qquad \textbf{T5 [DeM]}$$
$$= (x' + 0)\,(y' + 0) \qquad \textbf{P1}$$
$$= (x' + y\,y')\,(y' + z\,z') \qquad \textbf{P2}$$
$$= (x' + y)\,(x' + y')\,(y' + z)\,(y' + z') \qquad \textbf{P4}$$
$$= (x' + y + 0)\,(x' + y' + 0)\,(0 + y' + z)\,(0 + y' + z') \qquad \textbf{P1}$$
$$= (x' + y + z\,z')\,(x' + y' + z\,z')\,(x\,x' + y' + z)\,(x\,x' + y' + z') \qquad \textbf{P2}$$
$$= (x' + y + z)(x' + y + z')\,(x' + y' + z)\,(x' + y' + z')\,(x + y' + z)$$
$$(x' + y' + z')(x + y' + z')\,(x' + y' + z') \qquad \textbf{P4}$$

Rearranging the maxterms and remove those maxterms that appears in the expression more than once so we obtain,

$$\mathbf{f(x, y, z) = (x + y' + z)(x + y' + z')(x' + y + z)(x' + y + z')(x' + y' + z)\,(x' + y' + z')}$$

PCNF

Example A.6 *Obtain the PCNF and PDNF of following formulas.*

(1) $(y \rightarrow x)\,(x'\,y)$

(2) $x \rightarrow (x\,.\,(y \rightarrow x))$

(3) $x + (x' \rightarrow (y + (y' \rightarrow z)))$

(4) $(x' \rightarrow z)\,(y \leftrightarrow x)$

Sol. Since we know that any formula can be expressed in either PDNF or PCNF that are using only operations +, . , and ′. The other operators (connectives) like → or ↔ can be converted into +, . , and ′ operators by following equivalence formulas,

(*i*) $\mathbf{(A \rightarrow B) = (A' + B)}$

(*ii*) $\mathbf{(A \leftrightarrow B) = (A \rightarrow B)\,.\,(B \rightarrow A)}$

First, we obtain the **PCNF** of the formula,

(1) $$(y \rightarrow x)\,(x'\,y) = (y' + x)\,(x'\,y) \qquad \textbf{Equiv. (i)}$$
$$= (x + y')\,(x')\,(y) \qquad \textbf{P3}$$

$= (x + y')\,(x' + 0)\,(0 + y)$ **P1**

$= (x + y')\,(x' + y\,y')\,(x\,x' + y)$ **P2**

$= (x + y')\,(x' + y)\,(x' + y')\,(x + y)\,(x' + y)$ **P4**

After simplifying we obtain,

$= (x + y)\,(x + y')\,(x' + y)\,(x' + y')$

To obtain the **PDNF**, we proceed like as,

$= (y' + x)\,(x'\,y)$

$= y'\,x'\,y + x\,x'\,y$ **P4**

$= x'\,y'\,y + x\,x'\,y$ **P3**

$= x' \,.\, 0 + 0 \,.\, y$ **P2**

$= 0 + 0$ **T3**

$= \mathbf{0}$ **P1**

(2) $x \to (x \,.\, (y \to x)) = x \to (x \,.\, (y' + x))$ **Equiv. (i)**

$= x \to (x \,.\, y' + x \,.\, x)$ **P4**

$= x \to (x \,.\, y' + x)$ **T1**

$= x' + (x \,.\, y' + x)$ **Equiv. (i)**

$= x' + x + x\,y'$ **P3**

$= 1 + x\,y'$ **P2**

$= 1$ **T2**

So a PCNF expression is, $(x + x')\,(y + y')$ **P2**

To obtain PDNF we proceed as,

$= (x + x')\,(y + y')$ **P2**

$= x\,y + x'\,y + x\,y' + x'\,y'$ **P4**

$= x'\,y' + x'\,y + x\,y' + x\,y$ **P3**

$= x'\,y'(z + z') + x'\,y\,(z + z') + x\,y'(z + z') + x\,y\,(z + z')$

$= x'\,y'\,z + x'\,y'\,z' + x'\,y\,z + x'\,y\,z' + x\,y'\,z + x\,y'\,z' + x\,y\,z + x\,y\,z'$ **P4**

PDNF

(3) exercise to readers.

(4) Let $f(x, y, z) = (x' \to z)\,(y \leftrightarrow x)$

$= ((x')' + z)\,(y \to x)\,(x \to y)$ **Equiv. (i) & (ii)**

$= (x + z)\,(y \to x)\,(x \to y)$ **T3**

$= (x + z)\,(y' + x)\,(x' + y)$ **Equiv. (i)**

$= (x + z)\,(x + y')\,(x' + y)$ **P3**

$= (x + 0 + z)\,(x + y' + 0)\,(x' + y + 0)$ **P1**

$= (x + y\,y' + z)\,(x + y' + z\,z')\,(x' + y + z\,z')$ **P2**

$= (x + y + z)\,(x + y' + z)\,(x + y' + z)\,(x + y' + z')\,(x' + y + z)\,(x' + y + z')$ **P4**

$= (x + y + z)\,(x + y' + z)\,(x + y' + z')\,(x' + y + z)\,(x' + y + z')$ **Simp.**

PCNF

Find the PDNF,

$= (x' \to z)\,(y \leftrightarrow x)$

$= (x + z)\,(x + y')\,(x' + y)$

$= (x\,x + z\,x + x\,y' + z\,y')\,(x' + y)$ **P4**

$= (x + x\,z + x\,y' + y'\,z)\,(x' + y)$ **T1 & P3**

$= x\,(x' + y) + x\,z\,(x' + y) + x\,y'\,(x' + y) + y'\,z\,(x' + y)$ **P4**

$= x\,x' + x\,y + x\,z\,x' + x\,z\,y + x\,y'x' + x\,y'\,y + y'\,z\,x' + y'\,z\,y$ **P4**

$= 0 + x\,y + 0 + x\,y\,z + 0 + 0 + x'\,y'\,z + 0$ **P2 & P3**

$= x\,y + x\,y\,z + x'\,y'\,z$ **P1**

$= x\,y\,(z + z') + x\,y\,z + x'\,y'\,z$ **P1**

After Simplifying and rearranging we get the expression,

$= x'\,y'\,z + x\,y\,z' + x\,y\,z$

PDNF

A.7 SIMPLIFICATION OF BOOLEAN FUNCTION USING K-MAP

Instead of squabble that simplification of Boolean function lacks specific deduction procedure (Sec 5.4) in this section we will discuss a well known graphical method of minimization of the Boolean functions for small values of n, where n is the number of Boolean variables. This method developed in 1950s at AT and T lab known as Karnaugh Map or K-map method simplifying the Boolean functions that are expressed in standard forms only.

A K-map of n variables function is a two dimensional array consisting of 2^n cells that are lying on a surface. It means, top and bottom boundaries and left and right boundaries of the array touching each other to form adjacent cells. Each cell represents one minterms. Since, SoP expression of any Boolean function consists of a sum of minterms; so entries of the cells in the K-map will be 1 (0) with respect to presence (absence) of the corresponding minterms in the Boolean function. The cells in the map are arranged according to the reflected-code sequence (Gray-Code) such that logically adjacent minterms are almost adjacent to each other. The presence of minterms in the function is all marked by 1 on the K-map, and the objective is to frame the groups from the marked cells, so a minimal set is selected.

K-map for 2 variables

K-map for two variable Boolean function is shown in Fig. A.8. It has 4 (= 22) cells and the cells are recognized by the minterms m_0, m_1, m_2, m_3. Assume variables are x and y.

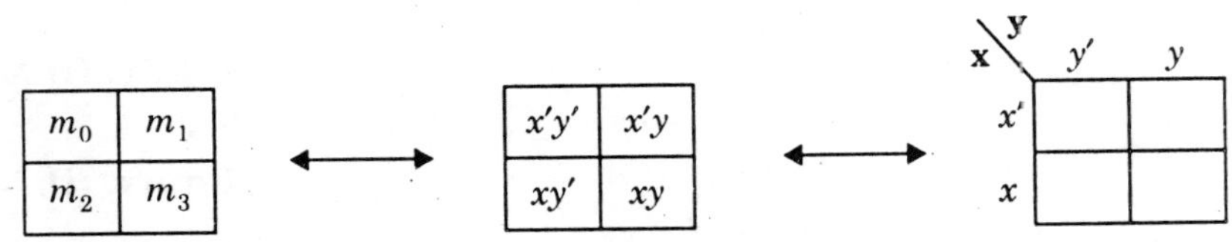

(a) (b) (c)

Fig. A.8 K- map for 2 variables.

In the Fig. A.8 (b) minterms are shown. The presence of minterms in the function for that cells entries are 1's often called implicants. In the next figure prime implicants are shown s.t. x' and x are prime implicants corresponding to Ist and IInd row and similarly y' and y are the prime implicants corresponding to Ist and IInd column of the K-map.

Let the function $f_1(x, y) = x\,y'\,(m_3)$; so place 1 on the cell represented by m_3 that shows the presence of that minterms only. (see Fig. A.9 (a))

	y'	y
x'		
x		1

(*a*)

	y'	y
x'		1
x	1	1

(*b*)

Fig. A.9

Consider another example, $f_2(x, y) = x + y + xy$; here first and second term of the function are prime implicants so all the cells corresponding to IInd row (for x) and IInd column (for y) are filled by 1's. Also place 1 corresponding to the third term of the function in the cell m_3. Therefore, K-map of f_2 could be seen in the Fig. A.9 (*b*).

Alternatively, $f(x, y) = x + y + x\,y$

$= x\,.\,1 + 1\,.\,y + x\,y$ **P1**

$= x\,(y + y') + (x + x')\,y + x\,y$ (ANDed the missing term) **P2**

$= x\,y + x\,y' + x'y$ (Simplification)

which, is represented by K-map shown in Fig. A.9 (*b*).

K - map for 3 variables

K-map for three variables shall consists of $8(= 2^3)$ cells corresponds to the minterms $m_0, \ldots\ldots m_7$ shown in Fig. A.10. Here we assume the variables x, y, and z.

m_0	m_1	m_3	m_2
m_4	m_5	m_7	m_6

(*a*)

↔

$x'y'z'$	$x'y'z$	$x'yz$	$x'yz'$
$xy'z'$	$xy'z$	xyz	xyz'

(*b*)

↕

x \ yz	$y'z'$	yz'	yz	yz'
x'				
x				

(*c*)

Fig. A.10

Fig. A.10 (*c*) shows the prime implicants corresponding to rows and columns.

For example, let Boolean function $f(x, y, z) = x\,y\,z' + x\,y\,z + x'\,y'\,z' = m_0 + m_6 + m_7$; Boolean function f can be represented by the K-map shown in Fig. A.11.

	$y'z'$	yz'	yz	yz'
x'	1			
x	1	1		1

Fig. A.11

Similarly **K-map of 4 variables** consists of 16 (= 2^4) cells for the minterms $m_0, \ldots\ldots m_{15}$. The arrangement of different cells is shown in the Fig. A.12.

m_0	m_1	m_3	m_2
m_4	m_5	m_7	m_6
m_8	m_9	m_{11}	m_{10}
m_{12}	m_{13}	m_{15}	m_{14}

(*a*)

↔

wx \ yz	$y'z'$	$y'z$	yz	yz'
$w'x'$				
$w'x$				
wx				
wx'				

(*b*)

Fig. A.12

Since, Fig. A.12 (*b*) shows the prime implicants for rows and columns. The minterms of each cell can be determined by the concatenation of the corresponding row label with column label where rows and columns are labeled by the prime implicants.

For example, consider the function $f(w, x, y, z) = w\, x\, y'\, z' + x\, y$; the Ist term of the function corresponds to minterm m_{12}. In the second term there is missing of variables w and z. So, IInd term will be obtain from the summation of minterms *i.e.*

$$x\,y = (w + w')\,x\,y$$

$$= w\,x\,y + w'\,x\,y$$

$$= w\,x\,y\,(z + z') + w'\,x\,y\,(z + z')$$

$$= w\,x\,y\,z + w\,x\,y\,z' + w'\,x\,y\,z + w'\,x\,y\,z'$$

$$f(w, x, y, z) = w\,x\,y'\,z' + w\,x\,y\,z + w\,x\,y\,z' + w'\,x\,y\,z + w'\,x\,y\,z'$$

After rearranging the terms we get,

$$= m_6 + m_7 + m_{12} + m_{14} + m_{15}$$

So, places 1's in the K-map for cells m_6, m_7, m_{12}, m_{14}, and m_{15}; that is shown in Fig. A.13.

	$y'z'$	$y'z$	yz	yz'
$w'x'$				
$w'x$			1	1
wx				
wx'	1		1	1

Fig. A.13

It is also noted that each row or column has labeled by the expressions (prime implicants) corresponding to the sequence of numbers generated using Gray code number system.

In general we assume that a minimized function Boolean function is that where sum of products (product of sums) have minimal number of literals. Through K-map representation of any Boolean function we may obtain the minimized Boolean function. (? How). Since, the cells in the K-map are so arranged that the adjacent cells are differs only by a single variable. This variable must be prime (presence) in one cell and unprimed (absence) in other cell. Remaining variables are same in both adjacent cells. Therefore, the summation (**ORed**) of two adjacent cells (minterms) can be simplified to a single **ANDed** term consisting of one variable less.

For example, in a three variables K-map consider the summation of two adjacent cells recognized by minterms m_4 and m_5 will be,

$$= x\,y'\,z' + x\,y'\,z$$

$$= x\,y'\,(z' + z) = x\,y'\,.\,1 = x\,y' \qquad \text{(free from one variable)}$$

and is shown in Fig. A.14.

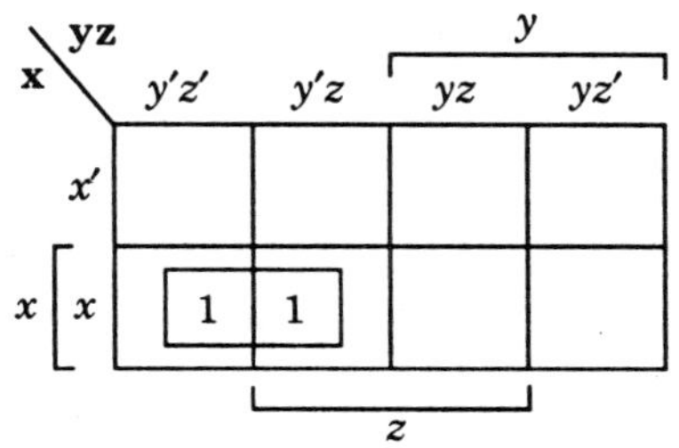

Fig. A.14

Similarly summation of four adjacent cells can be simplified to a single term that will be free from two variables, for example consider the summation of adjacent cells m_1, m_3, m_5, and m_7 in a three variables K-map is shown in Fig. A.15.

That will be,

$$= m_1 + m_3 + m_5 + m_7$$

$$= x'\,y'\,z + x'\,y\,z + x\,y'\,z + x\,y\,z$$

$$= x'\,(y' + y)\,z + x\,(y' + y)\,z$$

$$= x'\,z + x\,z$$

$$= (x' + x)\,z = 1\,.\,z = z \qquad \text{(free from two variables)}$$

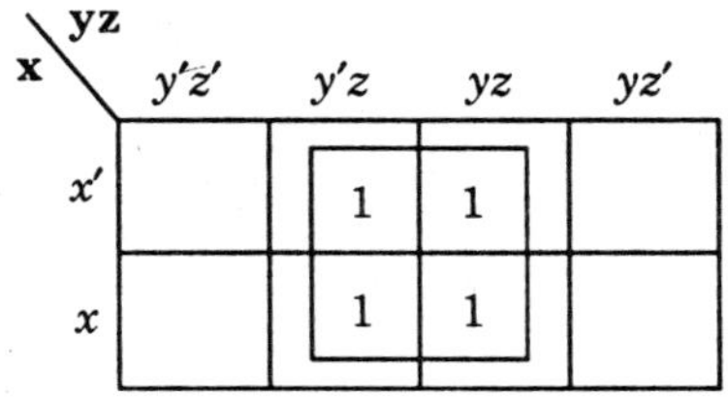

Fig. A.15

As we mentioned earlier that K-map is lies on the surface such that top and bottom edges as well as left and right edges are touching each other to form adjacent cells. For example in a three variables K-map cells recognized by m_0, m_1, m_3, m_2, are adjacent to cells m_4, m_5, m_7, m_6 respectively; similarly cells m_0, m_4 are adjacent to cells m_2, m_6 respectively. In the similar sense we can acknowledge the adjacent cells for four or more variables K-map.

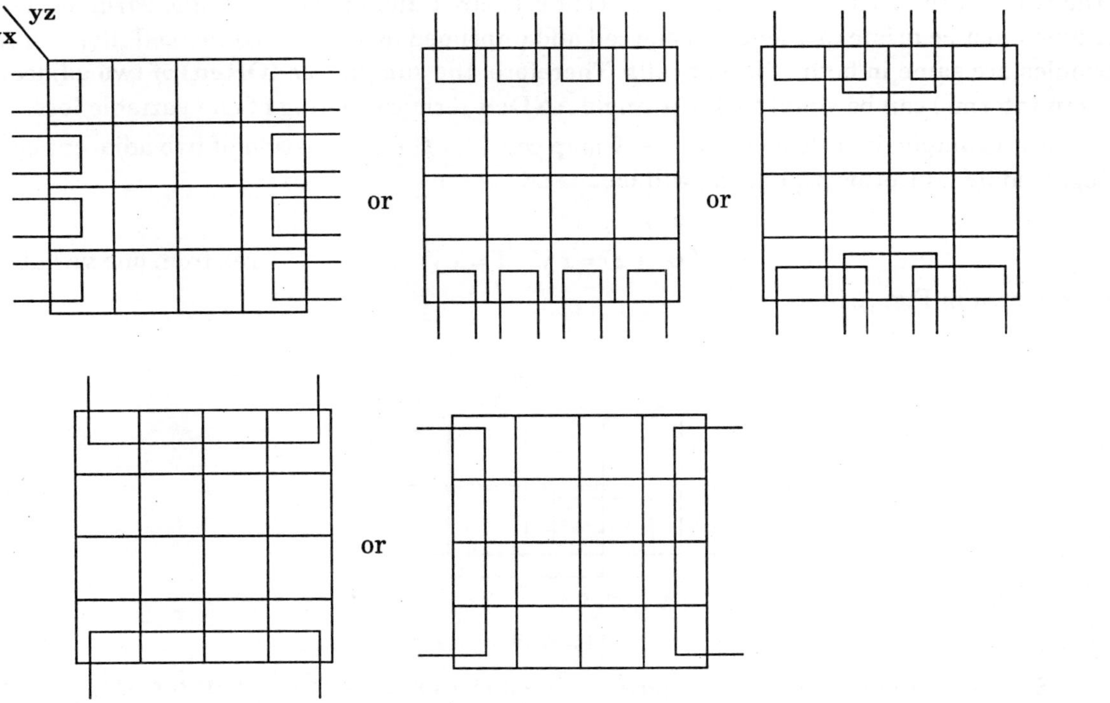

Fig. A.16

Example 5.7. *Simplify the K-map shown in Fig. A.17.*

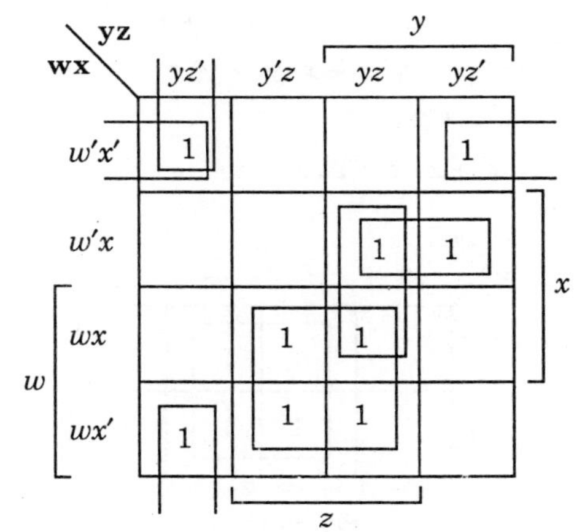

Fig. A.17

$$f(x, y, z) = w'\,x' + w'\,xy + x\,y\,z + w\,z + y'\,z' \quad \text{(5 minterms)}$$

Solution: Since, we know that maxterms is dual to the minterms; so in the K-map representation of any Boolean function if we groups the 0's instead of 1's we obtain the minimized Boolean function that is in products of maxterms. In the previous example grouping of 0's instead 1's are shown below in Fig. A.18.

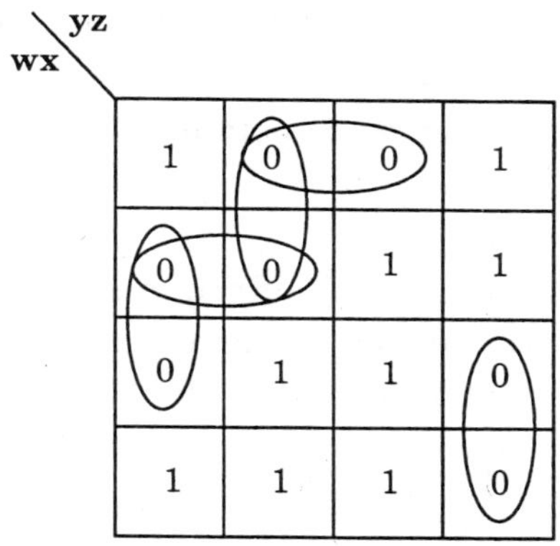

Fig. A.18

$$f(x, y, z) = (w + x + y')\,(w + x' + y)(x' + y + z)\,(w' + y'\,z)\,(w + y + z') \quad \text{(5 minterms)}$$

Example A.8. *Simplify the Boolean function f(x, y, z) = Σ (0, 2, 4, 6).*

Solution: Here, summation of minterms are given by their equivalent decimal numbers. Since, function f has three variables so K-map of three variables must be used to represent *f*. The minterms of the function are marked by 1's in the K-map shown in Fig. A.19.

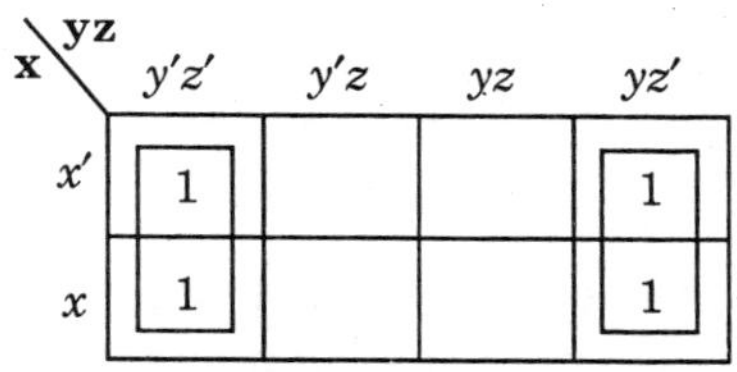

Fig. A.19

The adjacent cells marked by 1's can be combined to form the term free from one variable such as,

$$x'\,y'\,z' + x\,y'\,z' = (x' + x)\,y'\,z' = 1\,.\,y'\,z' = y'\,z'\,;$$

and,
$$x'\,y\,z' + x\,y\,z' = (x' + x)\,y\,z' = 1\,.\,y\,z' = y\,z'\,;$$

Further, these expression lies on the adjacent edges so it can be simplified as,

$$= y'\,z' + y\,z' = (y' + y)\,z' = 1\,.\,z' = z' \qquad \text{....(1)}$$

Cells holding 1's can also be combined as, (see Fig. A.20)

$$x'\,y'\,z' + x'\,y\,z' = x'\,(y' + y)\,z' = x'\,.\,1\,.\,z' = x'\,z';$$

and,
$$x\,y'\,z' + x\,y\,z' = x\,(y' + y)\,z' = x\,.\,1\,.\,z' = x\,z'\,;$$

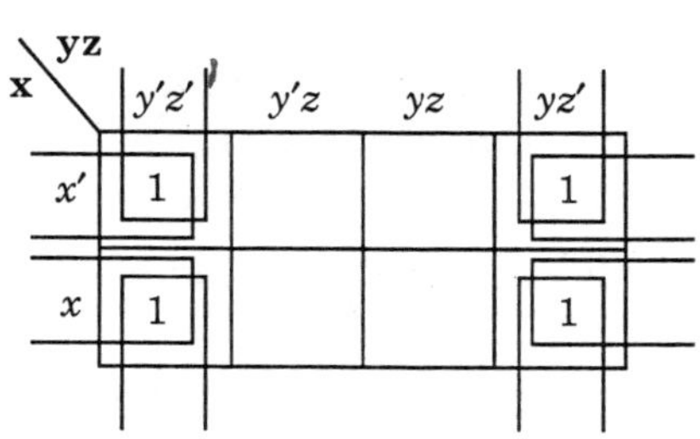

Fig. A.20

Further, these expression lies on the adjacent edges so it can be simplified as,

$$= x' z' + x z' = (x' + x) z' = 1 . z' = z' \qquad ...(2)$$

Combining expressions (1) and (2) we obtain,

$$f(x, y, z) = z' + z'$$
$$= z'$$

Example A.9. *Simplify the Boolean function f(p, q, r, s) = Σ (0, 1, 2, 4, 5, 6, 8, 9, 12, 13, 14).*

Sol. K-map representation of the function using four variables are is shown in Fig. A.21 and the presence of minterms in the function are shown by placing 1's in the corresponding cells.

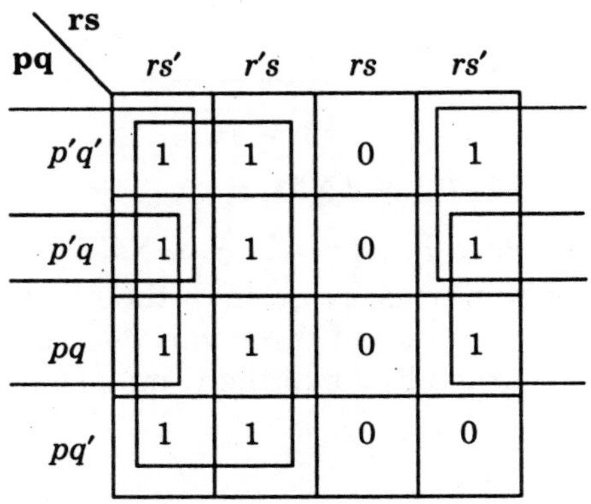

Fig. A.21

We see from the figure that eight cells are adjacent so they can group as to give the expression r'. Remaining 1's (three) near the right edge are adjacent to the similar number of 1's of left edge but grouping of these adjacent cells can't return the minimized expression. Therefore, we group these 1's as,

$p'r's' + p'r s' = p'(r' + r) s' = p' . 1 . s' = p' s'$ (top two left 1's are grouped with top two right 1's), and

$q r's' + q r s' = q (r' + r) s' = q . 1 . s' = q s'$ (grouping of 1's that lies middle rows and two end columns)

Hence, the simplified Boolean function is,

$$F(p, q, r, s) = r' + p' s' + q s'$$

The simplification approach using K-map is convenient for Boolean function of variables not more than five or six. Because, when number of variables increases then it is difficult to visualize the logical adjacency between cells. Therefore K-map is unfeasible for the simplification of Boolean functions of large variables. Of course, using similar approach with algebraic manipulations known as Quine McCluskey method can be used for the minimizing the Boolean function of variables up to ten. Functions of large variables can be simplified using approximation techniques or heuristics approaches based on trial - and - chance.

Example A.10 *Obtain the simplify the Boolean function F(p, q, r, s) = Σ(0, 1, 2, 5, 8, 9, 10) in sum of products (SoP) and product of sums (PoS).*

Sol. Since function *f* is given in the sum of minterms form such as,

$$F (p, q, r, s) = m_0 + m_1 + m_2 + m_5 + m_8 + m_9 + m_{10};$$

That can be represented by the K-map shown in Fig. A.22.

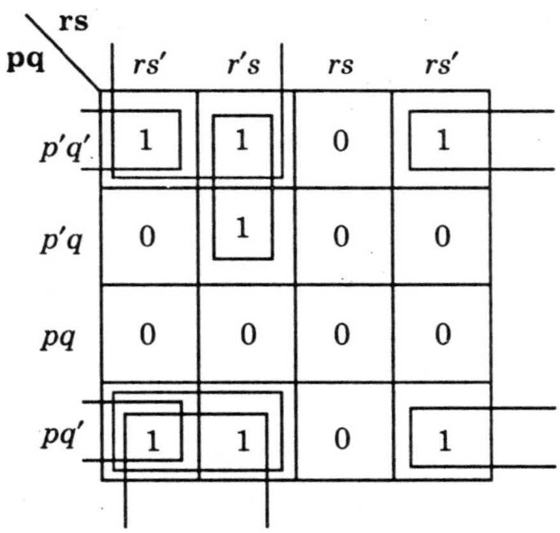

Fig. A.22

We can group the cells recognized by 1's as,

- Top two cells of 1's can grouped to the lowest two cells of 1's; return the expression
$$p'q' r' + p\, q' r' = (p' + p)\, q' r' = 1 \,.\, q' r' = q' r';$$
- Combing four 1's at corner gives the simplified expression, $q' s'$
- Grouping of top two 1's at second column gives the expression, $p' r' s$

Therefore simplified Boolean function is,
$$F\,(p, q, r, s) = q' r' + q' s' + p' r' s \qquad \textbf{(SoP)}$$

To obtain the product of sum expression we shall combine the cells marked with 0's. Since, combining the cells of 0's represent the minterms not included in the function, hence it denotes the complement of F that gives the simplified function in **PoS**.

- Combing 0's that lies middle rows and two end columns gives the expression,
$$q\, r' s' + q\, r\, s' = q\, s'$$
- Combing all 0's of third row gives the expression, $p\, q$
- Combining all 0's of third column gives the expression, $r\, s$ (Fig. A.23)

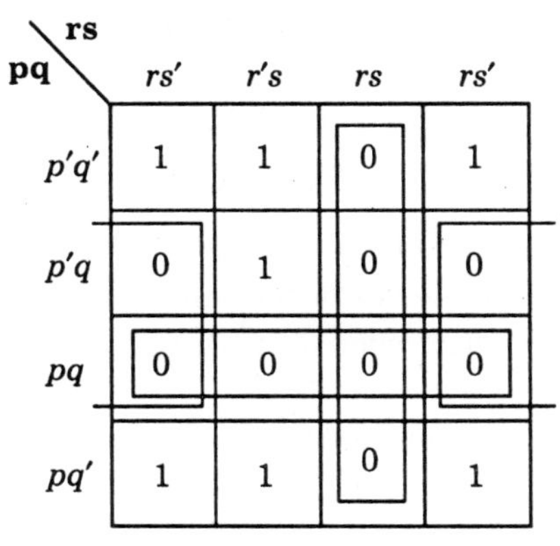

Fig. A.23

Since, no more 0 left in the K-map for consideration, therefore we get the simplified complemented function,

$$F' = q\,s' + p\,q + r\,s;$$

Take complement, thus

$$(F')' = (q\,s' + p\,q + r\,s)'$$

$$F = (q' + s)\,(p' + q')\,(r' + s') \quad \text{(Using DeMorgan and involution law)}$$

(PoS)

Example A.11 *Given truth table (Fig. A.24) that defines the functions X_1 and X_2, obtain the simplified functions in SoP and PoS.*

Sol. From the table shown in Fig. A.24 we obtain the given function X_1 and X_2 are in sum of minterms forms as,

$$X_1 = \Sigma\,(1, 3, 4, 5) = m_1 + m_3 + m_4 + m_5;$$

and,

$$X_2 = \Sigma\,(0, 1, 2, 5, 7) = m_0 + m_1 + m_2 + m_5 + m_7;$$

x	y	z	X_1	X_2
0	0	0	0	1
0	0	1	1	1
0	1	0	0	1
0	1	1	1	0
1	0	0	1	1
1	0	1	0	0
1	1	0	0	0
1	1	1	0	1

Fig. A.24

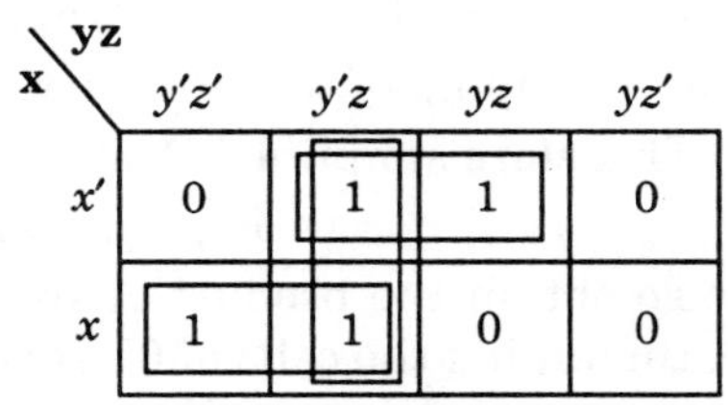

Fig. A.24 (a)

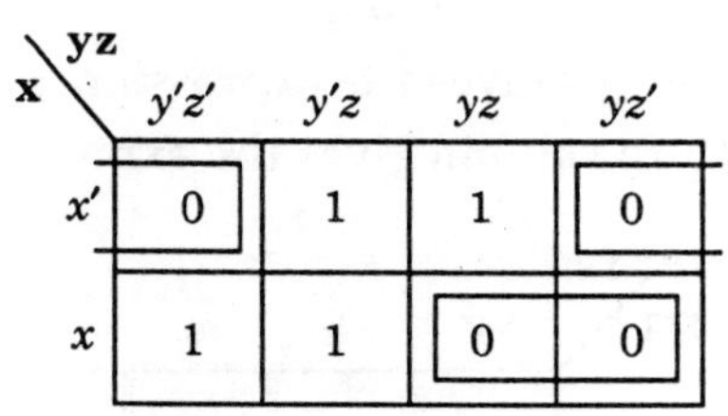

Fig. A.24 (*b*)

Functions X_1 and X_2 can be represented using K-map (Fig. A.24 (*a*) and (*b*)) where 1's placed in cells represent all the minterms of the functions X_1 and X_2 and the cells marked with 0's represents the absence of the minterms in the functions hence it denotes the complement of the functions X_1 and X_2.

Combining 1's we get the simplified expressions of functions X_1 & X_2 in **SoP** as,

$$X_1 = x\,y' + y\,z' + x'\,z$$

and

$$X_2 = x'\,y' + z'$$

To obtain X_1 and X_2 in PoS, combing 0's so we get the complement of the function that are expressed in sum of minterms as,

$$X_1' = (x\,y' + y\,z' + x'\,z)$$

and

$$X_2' = (x'\,y' + z')$$

Applying DeMorgan and involution theorem we get the simplified expressions,

$$(X_1')' = (x\,y' + y\,z' + x'\,z)'$$

$$X_1 = (x' + y)\,(y' + z)\,(x + z'); \quad \textbf{(SoP)}$$

Similarly,

$$(X_2')' = (x'\,y' + z')'$$

$$X_2 = (x + y)\,z; \ \textbf{(SoP)}$$

Example A.12 *Simplify the Boolean expression*

$$f(x, y, z) = \Sigma\,(0, 2, 4, 5, 6)$$

Sol. The K-map of function f is shown in Fig. A.25.

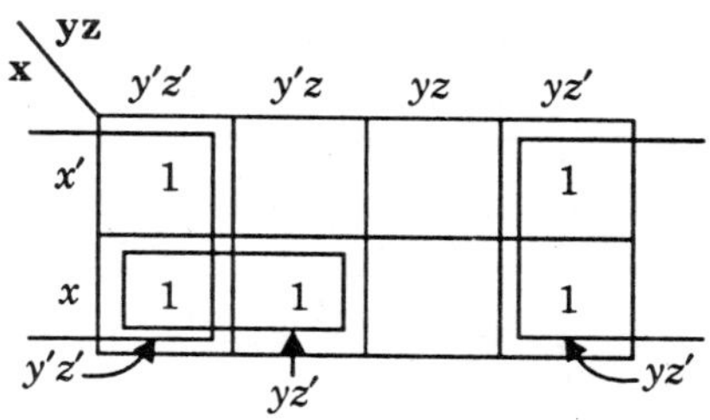

Fig. A.25

Since, $y'z'$ and yz' are adjacent to each other so their simplification yields z'.

So, $f(x, y, z) = z' + xy'$.

EXERCISES

A.1 Obtain the truth table of the following expressions:

(*i*) $xy + xy'$ (*ii*) $xy + xy' + y'z$

(*iii*) $xy + x'y' + y'z$ (*iv*) $(x' + y + z')\,(y' + z)\,x'$

(*v*) $w' + y(x' + z')$ (*vi*) $x'y'z + x'yz' + xyz'$

(*vii*) $xy' + [(x' + z)\,y]$

Also show its K-map representation.

A.2 Express the following functions into PDNF and PCNF:

(*i*) $F(x, y, z) = (xy + z)\,(y + xz)$ (*ii*) $F(x, y, z) = xy + yz'$

(*iii*) $F(p, q, r) = (p' + q)\,(q' + r)$ (*iv*) $F(w, x, y, z) = y'z + wxy' + wxz' + w'x'z$

A.3 Expand the following functions into their canonical SoP forms (DNF):

(*i*) $f(x, y, z) = xy + yz'$ (*ii*) $f(A, B, C, D) = BC + CA'D$

(*iii*) $f(A, B, C, D) = A + C'D + B'C$ (*iv*) $f(A, B, C, D) = 1$.

A.4 Using K-map representation find the minimal DNF expression for each of the following functions:

(*i*) $f(x, y, z) = \Sigma\,(0, 1, 4, 6)$ (*ii*) $f(x, y, z) = \Sigma\,(1, 3, 7)$

(*iii*) $f(x, y, z) = \Sigma\,(0, 2, 3, 7)$ (*iv*) $f(w, x, y, z) = \Sigma\,(0, 1, 2, 3, 13, 15)$

(*v*) $f(w, x, y, z) = \Sigma\,(0, 2, 6, 7, 8, 9, 13, 15)$.

A.5 Using K-map representation find the minimal CNF expression for each of the following functions:

(*i*) $f(x, y, z, w) = \Pi\ (0, 1, 2, 3, 4, 10, 11)$ (*ii*) $f(x, y, z) = \Pi\ (0, 1, 4, 5)$

(*iii*) $f(w, x, y, z) = \Pi\ (0, 1, 2, 3, 4, 6, 12)$ (*iv*) $f(w, x, y, z) = \Pi\ (0, 2, 6, 7, 8, 9, 13, 15)$.

A.6 Consider X = 01001001, Y = 01111000, and Z = 10000111 then find

(*i*) X + Y′ + Z (*ii*) (X′ + Z) Y (*iii*) X Y Z.

A.7 Let $f(A, B, C) = AB' + ABC' + A'BC'$, then show that

(*i*) $f(A, B, C) + AC' = f(A, B, C)$ (*ii*) $f(A, B, C) + A \neq f(A, B, C)$

(*iii*) $f(A, B, C) + C' \neq f(A, B, C)$.

A.8 Write the dual of each Boolean equation,

(*i*) $x + xy = x + y$ (*ii*) $(x \cdot 1)(0 + x') = 0$.

A.9 Show that the dual of $f(x, y) = xy + x'y'$ is equal to its complement.

A.10 In the truth table shown in Fig. A.26 that defines the functions f_1 and f_2, obtain the simplified functions in SoP and PoS.

x	y	z	f_1	f_2
0	0	0	1	1
0	0	1	1	0
0	1	0	1	1
0	1	1	0	1
1	0	0	0	1
1	0	1	1	1
1	1	0	0	0
1	1	1	1	0

Fig. A.26